THE PROSECUTION OF INTERNATIONAL CRIMES

THE PROSECUTION OF INTERNATIONAL CRIMES

EDITED BY
ROGER S. CLARK
AND
MADELEINE SANN

Taylor & Francis Group

LONDON AND NEW YORK

Originally published as vol. 5, nos. 2-3 (1994) of *Criminal Law Forum: An International Journal* by Rutgers University School of Law, Camden, New Jersey.

Published 1996 by Transaction Publishers

Published 2017 by Routledge
2 Park Square, Milton Park, Abingdon, Oxon OX14 4RN
711 Third Avenue, New York, NY 10017, USA

Routledge is an imprint of the Taylor & Francis Group, an informa business

Copyright © 1996 by Taylor & Francis

All rights reserved. No part of this book may be reprinted or reproduced or utilised in any form or by any electronic, mechanical, or other means, now known or hereafter invented, including photocopying and recording, or in any information storage or retrieval system, without permission in writing from the publishers.

Notice:
Product or corporate names may be trademarks or registered trademarks, and are used only for identification and explanation without intent to infringe.

Library of Congress Catalog Number: 96-3549

Library of Congress Cataloging-in-Publication Data

The prosecution of international crimes : a critical study of the International Tribunal for the Former Yugoslavia / edited by Roger S. Clark and Madeleine Sann.
    p. cm.
    Originally published as vol. 5, nos. 2-3 (1994), special issue of Criminal law forum: an international journal.
    Includes bibliographical references.
    ISBN 0-7658-0527-8 (alk. paper)
    1. International criminal courts. 2. International Tribunal for the Prosecution of Persons Responsible for Serious Violations of International Humanitarian Law Committed in the Territory of the Former Yugoslavia since 1991. 3. Yugoslav War, 1991—Atrocities. I. Clark, Roger Stenson. II. Sann, Madeleine. III. Criminal law forum. Special issue.

JX5428.P76 1996
341.6' 9' 09497—dc20
                                                      96-3549
                                                        CIP

ISBN 13: 978-0-7658-0527-0 (pbk)
ISBN 13: 978-1-56000-269-7 (hbk)

Contents

Editors' Preface — vii

PART I: INTRODUCTORY REMARKS

Introduction — 3
Dušan Cotič

1. International Criminal Prosecution: The Precedent of Nuremberg Confirmed — 17
Christian Tomuschat

2. Toward International Criminal Justice — 29
Jules Deschênes

PART II: FACT-FINDING

3. The Commission of Experts Established pursuant to Security Council Resolution 780: Investigating Violations of International Humanitarian Law in the Former Yugoslavia — 61
M. Cherif Bassiouni

PART III: ESTABLISHMENT OF THE TRIBUNAL

4. An International Criminal Tribunal: The Difficult Union of Principle and Politics — 125
Peter Burns

5. An Ad Hoc International Tribunal for the Prosecution of Serious Violations of International Humanitarian Law in the Former Yugoslavia — 165
Roman A. Kolodkin

6. Politics and the International Tribunal for the Former Yugoslavia — 185
David P. Forsythe

Contents

7. Legal and Practical Implications, from the Perspective of the Host Country, Relating to the Establishment of the International Tribunal for the Former Yugoslavia ... 207
Julian J.E. Schutte

PART IV: SUBSTANTIVE AND PROCEDURAL ISSUES

8. A Slovenian Perspective on the Statute and Rules of the International Tribunal for the Former Yugoslavia ... 237
Pavel Dolenc

9. Rape and Other Forms of Sexual Assault in the Armed Conflict in the Former Yugoslavia: Legal, Procedural, and Evidentiary Issues ... 257
C.P.M. Cleiren and M.E.M. Tijssen

10. Rules of Procedure and Evidence of the International Tribunal for the Former Yugoslavia ... 293
Daniel D. Ntanda Nsereko

11. Securing the Presence of Defendants before the International Tribunal for the Former Yugoslavia: Breaking with Extradition ... 343
Kenneth S. Gallant

PART V: APPENDIXES

Appendix A: Security Council Resolutions 780, 808, and 827 ... 377

Appendix B: *Report of the Secretary-General pursuant to Paragraph 2 of Security Council Resolution 808* (including the Statute of the International Tribunal for the Former Yugoslavia) ... 385

Appendix C: Rules of Procedure and Evidence of the International Tribunal for the Former Yugoslavia ... 439

Appendix D: Security Council Resolutions 935 and 955 (including the Statute of the International Tribunal for Rwanda) ... 483

Editors' Preface

The essays in this collection were originally published as a special issue of *Criminal Law Forum: An International Journal.*[1] We conceived this study as a comprehensive account, by experts from a variety of backgrounds, of an unprecedented effort by the United Nations community to bring international law to bear on an ongoing armed conflict. On May 25, 1993, the Security Council, through Resolution 827, voted unanimously to set up an international criminal court for the "prosecution of persons responsible for serious violations of international humanitarian law" committed in the territory of the former Yugoslavia since 1991, the year war broke out. The objectives behind the creation of the International Tribunal for the Former Yugoslavia were to restore peace to the region, to put an end to such crimes, and to bring the perpetrators to justice.

Unfortunately, the conflict is still ongoing and many of the concerns raised by the contributors to this volume remain unresolved. In the early fall of 1995, the United States brokered a cease-fire but there have been significant breaches on all sides and reports of mass executions of Muslim civilians in northwestern Bosnia. In a few key areas, however, the passage of time has begun to provide answers. Four issues in particular require comment: the legality of the creation of the Tribunal, legal proceedings to date, funding, and political support in the international community for the prosecution of war criminals. This brief survey brings the story forward through October 1995.

Legality. The effectiveness of the Tribunal depends, as an initial matter, on whether the Security Council had authority under the United

---

[1] Vol. 5, Nos. 2–3 (1994). Hence the cross-references in the notes to "this issue of *Criminal Law Forum.*"

Nations Charter to create an ad hoc judicial organ. The first defendant to come before the court argued against this proposition in a pretrial motion decided August 10, 1995 (The Prosecutor v. Dusko Tadic, Case No. IT-94-I-T). The Trial Chamber asserted that it lacked authority to pass judgment on the legality of the Tribunal's creation because the Statute of the Tribunal expressly limits its competence to deciding criminal cases brought under the substantive provisions of that instrument. Moreover, the Tribunal was set up under Chapter VII of the UN Charter. This and other chapters confer primary responsibility on the Security Council for maintaining international peace and security. The judges could find no basis in the Charter, its drafting history, or the jurisprudence of the International Court of Justice for conducting a judicial review of any decisions taken by the Security Council in the exercise of its peacekeeping functions.

Without deciding this question, the judges were nonetheless unanimously of the opinion that the Tribunal had been lawfully established. Chapter VII provides that the Security Council shall "determine the existence of any threat to the peace" and shall "decide what measures shall be taken." Tracing the series of actions by the Security Council that led up to the adoption of Resolution 827, the Trial Chamber concluded that the Council had duly determined the existence of a threat to international peace and security from the war in the former Yugoslavia. Examining the scope of discretion afforded under the Charter where the Security Council makes such a determination, the Trial Chamber concluded that the Council had authority to set up an international criminal court as an enforcement measure to help "maintain or restore peace" in the region. The judges further found no violation of the right to a fair trial, as protected under international law, in the creation of the Tribunal.

The defense appealed, and on October 2, 1995, the Appeals Chamber delivered its judgment. The Appeals Chamber took a broader approach to the meaning of "competence," holding four to one that as a judicial organ it had inherent power to assess the lawfulness of the Security Council's actions for the sole purpose of ascertaining whether the Tribunal might properly entertain the defendant's challenge to its jurisdiction. The Appeals Chamber then went on to hold that the Security Council's decision to establish the Tribunal was a legitimate measure aimed at the restoration of peace that conforms both to the UN

Charter and to the rule of law. This decision would appear to foreclose similar challenges to the Tribunal's competence in the future.

Proceedings. Much skepticism has been voiced as to whether the Tribunal will vigorously and impartially carry out its mandate to investigate and prosecute persons suspected of serious violations of international humanitarian law in the region of the former Yugoslavia. The signs are encouraging. As of early October 1995, 43 individuals had been indicted.

In July 1995, the Tribunal confirmed indictments against Radovan Karadzic, president of the self-proclaimed Bosnian Serb Republic, and Ratko Mladic, the Bosnian Serb military commander, despite considerable political pressure not to do so. Karadzic and Mladic are charged with genocide, crimes against humanity, war crimes, and grave breaches of the Geneva Conventions of 1949 on the basis of events that occurred from April 1992 through mid-June 1995. The Tribunal has indicated that ongoing investigations into the apparent massacre by Bosnian Serb forces of thousands of Muslim men and boys from Srebrenica in July 1995 may result in additional charges against Karadzic and Mladic. There is mounting evidence as well that Bosnian Serb forces killed thousands of Muslim males in the Banja Luka area in the fall of 1995 around the time the cease-fire was to go into effect. While it is impossible to predict whether Karadzic and Mladic will be apprehended, they are vulnerable to arrest if they travel outside friendly (essentially, Serb or Bosnian Serb) territory, and sanctions may be imposed by the Security Council on states that refuse to cooperate with the Tribunal in their surrender.

Another important development is the indictment in September 1995 of the first non-Serb, Ivica Rajic. Rajic, who is in the custody of Bosnian Croat authorities on unrelated charges, commanded a Croat militia that allegedly murdered Muslim civilians in a village in central Bosnia in October 1993. He is expected to be surrendered to the Tribunal and will join Dusko Tadic as the second accused in custody. The Tribunal is pursuing investigations of other serious humanitarian law violations alleged to have been committed by non-Serbs—both Muslims and Croats. However, investigations into crimes against Serb victims have been frustrated by lack of cooperation from Belgrade and Pale (the Bosnian Serb headquarters).

Most recently, on October 9, 1995, proceedings were begun

against the first person indicted by the Tribunal, Dragan Nikolic, the commander of the "Susica" death camp in Bosnia. Like most of the accused, Nikolic is not in custody, but the Tribunal's rules of procedure provide in such circumstances for the Trial Chamber to hear the evidence in open court and create a public record. Under Rule 61, if the judges find reasonable grounds for believing that the accused is guilty of any of the crimes charged, the Tribunal will issue an international arrest warrant and take other steps toward enforcement. Such a warrant was issued against Nikolic on October 20. More Rule 61 proceedings are likely to follow. Chief Prosecutor Richard Goldstone believes that publishing the truth is a critical function of the Tribunal.

The Tadic trial was expected to begin in November 1995. In the United States, Court-TV has heavily advertised gavel-to-gavel coverage of what it is billing as "a real trial of the century." However, lack of funds for preparation of the defense has delayed the trial, tentatively until early May 1996.

Funding. Before creating the Tribunal in May 1993, the Security Council set up a Commission of Experts (October 1992) to investigate violations of international humanitarian law in the former Yugoslavia. The task of financing the Commission, and later the Tribunal, fell to the General Assembly under its Charter responsibility for the UN budget. Institutional tensions and political jockeying by UN member states resulted in virtually no funding for the Commission's 18-month effort to carry out investigations and analyze data, and in such severe underfunding of the Tribunal that initial plans for staff and premises had to be cut by about two-thirds. Wrangling over financing continued long after the Tribunal got under way, with disagreement not only over the size of its budget but also over whether to allocate funds from peacekeeping operations or from the UN's "regular account." In the spring of 1995, the Tribunal's budget for the current year was approved, but it was not until July 20 that the General Assembly finally worked out a compromise arrangement to split funding equally between peacekeeping and the regular account. Despite these developments, a spending freeze that the United Nations was forced to institute in the fall of 1995 threatens the Tribunal's ability to carry out investigations and hold legal proceedings through the end of the year. Moreover, it is estimated that for 1996–1997 the Tribunal will need to double its budget and it remains to be seen whether the General Assembly will approve this level of funding.

Political Support. The attack on the Sarajevo market in August 1995 appeared to mark a turning point in the conflict in Bosnia. In September 1995 the world witnessed a novel mix of events: large-scale, sustained NATO air attacks against Bosnian Serb targets, a long-awaited agreement from President Slobodan Milosevic of Yugoslavia to negotiate on behalf of the Bosnian Serbs, and a U.S.-brokered peace plan that has support from the governments of Bosnia and Herzegovina, Yugoslavia, and Croatia. It is noteworthy that amnesty for suspected war criminals does not figure in the proposed settlement, and indeed Karadzic and Mladic have been unable to participate in negotiations abroad—most notably, the peace conference scheduled to open in Ohio on November 1, 1995—due to their indictment by the Tribunal. The United States, in particular, remains outspoken in its support for war crimes trials and the Bosnian government continues to insist that the indicted leaders of the Bosnian Serbs face prosecution. There is, then, room to believe that the political will is there to see at least some trials through to a conclusion.

I
Introductory Remarks

Introduction*

*Dušan Cotič***

I

Over the past decades, various international initiatives undertaken under the auspices of the United Nations, other international organizations (such as the Organization of American States and the Council of Europe), and nongovernmental organizations (such as the Association Internationale de Droit Pénal) have addressed the question of creating effective international mechanisms for stopping aggression, genocide, crimes against humanity, and violations of internationally established rules of warfare.[1] Despite recently completed texts of a Draft

---

*   *Editor's note:* research for this article was updated through February 14, 1995.

**   Member, former United Nations Committee on Crime Prevention and Control, 1978–1992, and Chairman, 1990–1992; Professor of Criminal Law, University of Belgrade, Belgrade, Yugoslavia, 1977–1984; Deputy Secretary of Justice, Socialist Federal Republic of Yugoslavia, 1972–1978; Justice of the Supreme Court, Socialist Federal Republic of Yugoslavia, 1978–1986; LL.B., M.A., LL.D., Ph.D. For many years, the author was President of the Yugoslav Association for Criminal Law and Criminology and Chief Editor of the Yugoslav *Review of Criminology and Criminal Law* and of the *Collected Court Decisions* of Yugoslavia.

[1]   Some of these efforts are discussed in M. Cherif Bassiouni, *Draft Statute — International Tribunal* (Association Internationale de Droit Pénal, Nouvelles Études Penales No. 10, 2d ed. 1993); *Commentaries on the International Law Commission's 1991 Draft Code of Crimes against the Peace and Security of Mankind* (Association Internationale de Droit Pénal, Nouvelles Études Penales No. 11, M. Cherif Bassiouni ed., 1993); Peter

Code of Crimes against the Peace and Security of Mankind[2] and a Draft Statute for an International Criminal Court,[3] we nevertheless do not

---

Burns, *An International Criminal Tribunal: The Difficult Union of Principle and Politics*, in this issue of *Criminal Law Forum;* Jules Deschênes, *Toward International Criminal Justice*, in this issue of *Criminal Law Forum*.

See, in particular, Affirmation of the Principles of International Law Recognized by the Charter of the Nuremberg Tribunal, G.A. Res. 95 (I), U.N. Doc. A/64/Add.1, at 188 (1946); Universal Declaration of Human Rights, G.A. Res. 217A (III), U.N. Doc. A/810, at 71 (1948); Convention on the Prevention and Punishment of the Crime of Genocide, *adopted* Dec. 9, 1948, 78 U.N.T.S. 277; European Convention for the Protection of Human Rights and Fundamental Freedoms, *opened for signature* Nov. 4, 1950, Europ. T.S. 5; Protocol Amending the Slavery Convention of September 25, 1926, *opened for signature* Dec. 7, 1953, 212 U.N.T.S. 17; Supplementary Convention on the Abolition of Slavery, the Slave Trade, and Institutions and Practices Similar to Slavery, *adopted* Sept. 7, 1956, 266 U.N.T.S. 3; ILO Convention (No. 105) Concerning the Abolition of Forced Labour, *adopted* June 25, 1956, 320 U.N.T.S. 291; International Covenant on Civil and Political Rights, *adopted* Dec. 19, 1966, 999 U.N.T.S. 171; Protocol Additional to the Geneva Conventions of 12 August 1949, and Relating to the Protection of Victims of International Armed Conflicts (Additional Protocol I), *adopted* June 8, 1977, 1125 U.N.T.S. 3 (entered into force Dec. 7, 1978); Protocol Additional to the Geneva Conventions of 12 August 1949, and Relating to the Protection of Victims of Non-international Armed Conflicts (Additional Protocol II), *adopted* June 8, 1977, 1125 U.N.T.S. 609 (entered into force Dec. 7, 1978); Convention against Torture and Other Cruel, Inhuman, or Degrading Treatment or Punishment, G.A. Res. 39/46, U.N. GAOR, 39th Sess., Supp. No. 51, at 197, U.N. Doc. A/39/51 (1984); Inter-American Convention to Prevent and Punish Torture, Dec. 9, 1985, O.A.S. T.S. 67, *reprinted in* 25 I.L.M. 519; European Convention for the Prevention of Torture and Inhuman or Degrading Treatment or Punishment, *done* Nov. 26, 1987, Europ. T.S. 126; *see also* sources cited *infra* notes 2–3. Many of these instruments are collected in Albert P. Blaustein et al., *Human Rights Sourcebook* (1987).

[2] Draft Code of Crimes against the Peace and Security of Mankind, in *Report of the International Law Commission on Its Forty-third Session*, U.N. GAOR, 46th Sess., Supp. No. 10, at 238, U.N. Doc. A/46/10 (1991); for a discussion, see Timothy L.H. McCormack & Gerry J. Simpson, *The International Law Commission's Draft Code of Crimes against the Peace and Security of Mankind: An Appraisal of the Substantive Provisions*, 5 Crim. L.F. 1 (1994); for more recent developments, see *Report of the International Law Commission on Its Forty-sixth Session*, U.N. GAOR, 49th Sess., Supp. No. 10, at 161, U.N. Doc. A/49/10 (1994).

[3] Draft Statute for an International Criminal Court, in *Report of the International Law Commission on Its Forty-sixth Session*, U.N. GAOR, 49th Sess., Supp. No. 10, at 43,

expect to see a permanent international criminal court for some time. The principle of sovereignty and states' assertion of exclusive competence over criminal matters still dominate the international scene.[4] Despite the fact that the post–World War II period has witnessed numerous armed conflicts characterized by extreme examples of violations of relevant obligatory international norms, the community of nations is not likely soon to agree to a binding convention ceding jurisdiction to an international criminal regime. Thus, the establishment of an ad hoc international tribunal[5] "for the sole purpose of prosecuting persons responsible for serious violations of international humanitarian law committed in the territory of the former Yugoslavia between 1 January 1991 and a date to be determined by the Security Council upon the restoration of peace," under Security Council Resolution 827,[6] represents a precedent deserving special attention from a historical, sociological, political, and especially an international law point of view.

II

Yugoslavia was founded in 1918, following World War I, as the Kingdom of Serbs, Croats, and Slovenians. The name "Yugoslavia" was adopted in 1930. After the second world war, Yugoslavia became a republic and, through minor modifications introduced in the 1974 Constitution, it became the Socialist Federal Republic of Yugoslavia. It is beyond the scope of my introduction to this study of the International

---

U.N. Doc. A/49/10 (1994); in this regard, see G.A. Res. 49/53, U.N. GAOR, 49th Sess., 84th plen. mtg., U.N. Doc. A/49/53 (1994).

[4]   *See generally* Roman A. Kolodkin, *An Ad Hoc International Tribunal for the Prosecution of Serious Violations of International Humanitarian Law in the Former Yugoslavia*, in this issue of *Criminal Law Forum*.

[5]   On the establishment of the Tribunal and for references to the submissions by various states on this question, see Burns, *supra* note 1; Kolodkin, *supra* note 4.

[6]   S.C. Res. 827, U.N. SCOR, 48th Year, 3217th mtg. at 1, ¶ 2, U.N. Doc. S/RES/827 (1993), *reprinted in* appendix A of this issue of *Criminal Law Forum* and *in* 32 I.L.M. 1203.

Tribunal for the Former Yugoslavia to examine in detail the historical and contemporary factors behind the current crisis and the disintegration of Yugoslavia—a state that had existed for seventy years as a union of Southern Slavs and that had, despite its problems, held a respected position in the international community. Suffice it to say that a complex mix of internal and external factors have contributed to the most atrocious bloodshed in contemporary Europe since World War II. These include cultural differences among the nations of the Balkans dating back to the division of the region between the eastern and the western Roman Empire, the schism in the Catholic and Orthodox churches, and the centuries' long rule and domination by the Turkish and Austro-Hungarian empires (which bordered this region), coupled with often violent confrontations among the Slav peoples under foreign flags. One historical event that may be singled out for its consequences in the current conflict is that a considerable number of Slavs converted to Islam under the pressure of five centuries of rule, and persecution of Christians, by the Turks. Bosnia in particular—occupied partly by the Turks and partly by the Austro-Hungarians, and later annexed by Austria—was in a sense predestined to become a battlefield of mutual conflicts between groups distinguishable primarily by their religious convictions and the cultural legacy of the various influences noted above.

An important division along nationalistic lines also emerged between Orthodox Christian Serbs and Catholic Croats—the East and the West. This conflict plagued the Kingdom of Serbs, Croats, and Slovenians and, later, Yugoslavia. In this struggle, Serb extremists assassinated two deputies of the National Assembly who belonged to the Croatian Rural Party, and Croatian extremists of fascist sympathies (Ustashi) assassinated King Alexander I of Yugoslavia some years later. The conflict reached a peak during World War II, when the Axis powers proclaimed the Independent State of Croatia, a puppet Ustashi–fascist entity. This period saw the terrible genocide of hundreds of thousands of Serbs, Jews, and Gypsies in the region. This is not to forget that many Croats participated in the struggle against fascism. Josip Broz Tito, commander-in-chief of the Partisans, was himself a Croat.[7]

---

[7]   Angus Deming, *Yugoslavia: The Man Who Bent Marxism*, Newsweek, May 12, 1980, *available in* LEXIS, World Library, Allnws File. It is worth noting that an

Introduction 7

However, despite an official policy of "fraternity and unity" aimed at national unification and reconciliation in Yugoslavia, intolerance and mistrust ran deep at the local level, especially in the areas currently engaged in armed conflict (such as the Serbian enclave of Krajina in Croatia), only to erupt into armed resistance on the part of Serbs when the new Republic of Croatia declared its independence from Yugoslavia in 1991.[8] The situation was aggravated because the original Constitution of the new republic declared itself to be a state only of Croats,[9] and the new government adopted symbols of state that disturbed the Serbs due to their similarity, if not identity, to the flag and other state symbols of the wartime Axis puppet government. The Croatian authorities took the position that local Serbs were rebels, terrorists, and aggressors against the newly declared Croatian republic, which further complicated efforts to find a peaceful settlement of the conflict.

From the outset of the breakup of the union, Serbs throughout the territory of the former Yugoslavia have maintained that the dismantling of the federal republic has affected their interests most adversely since they, unlike the other constitutional peoples of the old federation, did not achieve unification into an ethnically homogeneous state. They argue that they should have the same right to self-determination that Croats, Slovenians, and Macedonians exercised in forming their own states and in securing international recognition.[10]

---

important factor in the disintegration of the Socialist Federal Republic of Yugoslavia was the death of its longtime leader, Josip Broz Tito, in 1980. Tito, a skilled statesman and political leader, was instrumental in preserving unity.

[8] The armed conflict can be traced back to the decision by the Serbian National Council in February 1991 to separate the Serbian Autonomous Region from Croatia. Later that year, this region declared itself to be the Serb Republic of Krajina and set up a capital at Knin. The other regions in Croatia controlled by Serbs (Slavonia, Baranja, and Western Srem) united with the Serb Republic of Krajina in December 1991. Armed conflict with the Croatians followed.

[9] In light of later events, the new Croatian government offered the Serbs limited local self-rule, cultural autonomy, and participation in state governance, but these concessions were not satisfactory to the Serbs.

[10] A detailed history of the establishment of the republics of Slovenia, Croatia, and Macedonia and their admission to membership in the United Nations is beyond the

Bosnia–Herzegovina, a republic under the Constitution of the former Yugoslavia, was a community comprising three separate nations—Muslims, 43.7 percent; Serbs, 31.4 percent; and Croats, 17.3

---

scope of this introduction. In brief, each held popular referenda that endorsed independence. International recognition of Slovenia and Croatia was forthcoming in late 1991 and early 1992, with recognition of Macedonia delayed because of Greek opposition to the naming of the new state. Slovenia, S.C. Res. 754, U.N. SCOR, 47th Year, 1992 Res. & Dec. at 115, U.N. Doc. S/INF/48 (1992); G.A. Res. 46/236, U.N. GAOR, 46th Sess., Supp. No. 49A (vol. II), at 5, U.N. Doc. A/46/49/Add.1 (1992), and Croatia, S.C. Res. 753, U.N. SCOR, 47th Year, 1992 Res. & Dec. at 115, U.N. Doc. S/INF/48 (1992); G.A. Res. 46/238, U.N. GAOR, 46th Sess., Supp. No. 49A (vol. II), at 5, U.N. Doc. A/46/49/Add.1 (1992), became UN members in May 1992. Macedonia (Former Yugoslav Republic of Macedonia) was admitted in April 1993. S.C. Res. 817, U.N. SCOR, 48th Year, 1993 Res. & Dec. at 132, U.N. Doc. S/INF/49 (1993); G.A. Res. 47/225, U.N. GAOR, 47th Sess., Supp. No. 49A (vol. II), at 6, U.N. Doc. A/47/49 (1993). On Bosnia, see *infra* notes 11–12 and accompanying text.

In September 1992, the Security Council adopted a resolution on the UN membership of the Federal Republic of Yugoslavia, S.C. Res. 777, U.N. SCOR, 47th Year, 1992 Res. & Dec. at 34, U.N. Doc. S/INF/48 (1992), providing in relevant part:

Considering that the State formerly known as the Socialist Federal Republic of Yugoslavia has ceased to exist,

Recalling in particular [Security Council] resolution 757 . . . in which [the Council] noted that "the claim by the Federal Republic of Yugoslavia (Serbia and Montenegro) to continue automatically the membership of the former Socialist Federal Republic of Yugoslavia in the United Nations has not been generally accepted",

1. *Considers* that the Federal Republic of Yugoslavia . . . cannot continue automatically the membership of the former Socialist Federal Republic . . . in the United Nations, and therefore recommends to the General Assembly that it decide that the Federal Republic . . . should apply for membership in the United Nations and that it shall not participate in the work of the General Assembly.

The General Assembly then adopted G.A. Res. 47/1, U.N. GAOR, 47th Sess., Supp. No. 49, at 12, U.N. Doc. A/47/49 (1993), providing that the Federal Republic of Yugoslavia "cannot continue automatically the membership of the former Socialist Federal Republic of Yugoslavia in the United Nations; and therefore [the Assembly] decides that the Federal Republic of Yugoslavia . . . should apply for membership in the United Nations and . . . shall not participate in the work of the General Assembly."

percent—while 5.5 percent of the population identified themselves as Yugoslavian, and 2.1 percent of the population belonged to other ethnic groups. Thus, Bosnia–Herzegovina presented a special case and, unlike the other new republics, kept its historical name for the very reason that it does not have an overwhelming majority of one ethnic group.[11] The Bosnian Serbs, asserting their constitutional right that all major political decisions can be implemented only by consensus of all three national groups, rejected the referendum to separate Bosnia from Yugoslavia. They seized by force, and at least at the beginning with the help of the Yugoslav National Army and volunteers from Serbia, nearly 70 percent of the territory of Bosnia, especially areas they considered traditionally to belong to them.[12] The Bosnian Croats had a similar interest in forming their own Herzeg-Bosna community. Their aim was to preclude political domination on the part of the Bosnian Muslims and eventually to form close links with the Croatian republic. It seemed clear to people living in the area that the Muslims, with a demographic advantage, had a strong interest, and still have, in becoming politically dominant in Bosnia. This three-way conflict has been limited somewhat by the formation, under foreign pressure, of a federation between Muslims and Croats, a shaky alliance that has faltered at times (such as the heavy fighting around Mostar in the late fall of 1992, with participation from the Croatian Army). At the same time, there have been confrontations among the Muslims themselves in western Bosnia, due primarily to conflicting views over the character and organization of the Bosnian state.

Armed clashes in the Balkans have always been brutal. The historical record—its political, cultural, and social dimensions—goes far toward explaining the present crisis in which countless grave violations of international humanitarian law have occurred and continue to occur.

---

[11] Bosnia–Herzegovina was admitted to the United Nations in May 1992. S.C. Res. 755, U.N. SCOR, 47th Year, 1992 Res. & Dec. at 116, U.N. Doc. S/INF/48 (1992); G.A. Res. 46/237, U.N. GAOR, 46th Sess., Supp. No. 49A (vol. II), at 5, U.N. Doc. A/46/49/Add.1 (1992).

[12] The decision to separate from the Republic of Bosnia–Herzegovina was taken by the Serbs, following earlier initiatives to form their own republic, by a referendum held February 29–March 1, 1992. On April 7, 1992, the independence and the Constitution of the Bosnian Serb Republic were proclaimed.

Hundreds of thousands of persons have been victimized,[13] and media coverage has brought their plight to the public's attention. This in turn has put pressure on national and world leaders to "do something." Without in any way attempting to condone the crimes that we have witnessed, it is also clear that there has been manipulation of even the most influential world media, as well as biased reporting. There is evidence, for example, that partisans of all sides have attacked their own people in an attempt to sway public opinion against the supposed attackers and to prompt an international military response.[14] Moreover, while we can appreciate the difficulties and the personal dangers that journalists have experienced in covering an ongoing war, some correspondents have deliberately falsified reports either because of partisan feeling or because of pressure to do so. Early in the war, in particular, the public in the territory of the former Yugoslavia relied heavily for information on nationally controlled television, which consistently showed its own partisans as victims and placed the blame for the brutal crimes being committed on enemy forces. Even with greater coverage by foreign media and independent domestic media, objectivity has not necessarily been the rule.[15]

---

[13] *See* Letter from the Secretary-General to the President of the Security Council, May 24, 1994, U.N. Doc. S/1994/674 (1994), transmitting *Final Report of the Commission of Experts Established pursuant to Security Council Resolution 780 (1992), available in* U.N. Gopher\Current Information\Secretary-General's Reports; Letter from the Secretary-General to the President of the Security Council, Oct. 5, 1993, U.N. Doc. S/26545 (1993), transmitting *Second Interim Report of the Commission of Experts Established pursuant to Security Council Resolution 780 (1992);* Letter from the Secretary-General to the President of the Security Council, Feb. 9, 1993, U.N. Doc. S/25274 (1993), transmitting *Interim Report of the Commission of Experts Established pursuant to Security Council Resolution 780 (1992).* Tadeusz Mazowiecki, UN Commission on Human Rights — Special Rapporteur for the Former Yugoslavia, has issued a series of reports, two of which are cited *infra* notes 16–17.

[14] Joel Brand, *U.N. Implies Muslims Deliberately Shelled Own Civilians,* The Times (London), Nov. 11, 1994, *available in* LEXIS, World Library, Allnws File; Leonard Doyle, *Muslims "Slaughter Their Own People,"* The Independent, Aug. 22, 1992, *available in* LEXIS, World Library, Allnws File (citing reports that all sides have staged attacks on their own people).

[15] Mark Thompson, Article 19 — International Centre against Censorship, *Forging War: The Media in Serbia, Croatia, and Bosnia* (1994); Peter Brock, *Bias in Bosnia: Are*

This "media war" has had a crucial influence on the international community in taking certain emergency measures, such as the imposition of political and economic sanctions on Serbia and Montenegro and an arms embargo on the republics of the former Yugoslavia; the organization of humanitarian assistance to the wounded, refugees, and others affected by the war; the deployment of international peacekeeping forces; and finally the establishment of the Commission of Experts for the investigation, and of the International Tribunal for the prosecution, of serious violations of international humanitarian law. Regardless of whether one approves or condemns these efforts, the world community is to be faulted for not intervening in the early stages of the disintegration of Yugoslavia, when it might have been possible to avert the war and the ensuing bloodbath. As a result, when it finally did act, the United Nations (and other intergovernmental organizations) made some hasty decisions of vital importance to a country that had been a conscientious member of the United Nations and to all the peoples living in the region.

III

The establishment of the International Tribunal for the Former Yugoslavia attracted special attention not only among political and academic circles throughout the territory of the former Yugoslavia but also among the public in general. This was particularly true in Yugoslavia (Serbia and Montenegro) because the discussions surrounding the creation of such a court were focused almost entirely on crimes allegedly committed by Serbs (the Federal Army, Serbs from Krajina and the Bosnian Serb Republic, and Serbian volunteers) and their leadership.[16]

We Getting the Whole Story, Montreal Gazette, Feb. 19, 1994, *available in* LEXIS, World Library, Allnws File; Andrew Culf, *Press Accused by Ex-minister of Biased Coverage of Bosnia*, The Guardian (Manchester), Sept. 18, 1993, *available in* LEXIS, World Library, Allnws File (reporting comments by British Foreign Secretary Douglas Hurd and ex-Minister of Defense Archie Hamilton).

[16] *E.g.*, Valery Shashkov, *Sanctions against Belgrade Approved*, Tass, May 12, 1992, *available in* LEXIS, World Library, Allnws File (Council of Ministers of the European

This presumption, and the bias in media coverage noted earlier, undoubtedly rallied Serbian public opinion against the proposed court and other international initiatives. Later this one-sided picture began to change somewhat. Thus, in May 1993, UN Special Rapporteur for Human Rights in the Former Yugoslavia, Tadeusz Mazowiecki, issued an official statement condemning crimes perpetrated by Muslims against Serbs;[17] shortly thereafter, the European Parliament adopted a resolution condemning both Serb and Croat attacks.[18] Nonetheless, the initial direction of world public opinion was such that it persuaded Croats and

---

Community adopts declaration laying the "main blame for continuing hostilities in Bosnia and Herzegovina on the Federal Army and the Serbian leadership controlling it"); Fredrik Dahl, *CSCE Restricts Yugoslav Role in Bosnia Decisions,* Reuters, May 12, 1992, *available in* LEXIS, World Library, Allnws File (Conference on Security and Cooperation in Europe meeting of senior officials reaches a similar conclusion); U.N. SCOR, 47th Year, 3146th mtg., U.N. Doc. S/PV.3146 (1992) (requesting new measures against Bosnian Serbs and "those supporting them"); *Put Serbs on Trial as War Criminals, Eagleburger Urges,* Montreal Gazette, Dec. 15, 1992, *available in* LEXIS, World Library, Allnws File (U.S. Secretary of State Lawrence Eagleburger addressing a meeting of foreign ministers in Geneva convened to consider the situation in the former Yugoslavia); Note transmitting *Report on the Situation of Human Rights in the Territory of the Former Yugoslavia,* prepared by Tadeusz Mazowiecki, UN Commission on Human Rights—Special Rapporteur for the Former Yugoslavia, U.N. Doc. S/25341 (1993) (reporting that Serbs had "primary responsibility" for ethnic cleansing and other war crimes); *"One-sided Accusations" against Serbs in Human Rights Commission,* BBC Summary of World Broadcasts (Yugo. Telegraph Serv.), Feb. 15, 1993, *available in* LEXIS, World Library, Allnws File (discussing Mazowiecki's report); *U.N. Condemns Serbian Forces for War Crimes,* The Guardian (Manchester), Feb. 24, 1993, *available in* LEXIS, World Library, Allnws File (discussing Mazowiecki's report).

[17]   Note transmitting *Periodic Report on the Situation of Human Rights in the Territory of the Former Yugoslavia,* prepared by Tadeusz Mazowiecki, UN Commission on Human Rights—Special Rapporteur for the Former Yugoslavia, U.N. Doc. S/25792 (1993) (reporting allegations of human rights violations on the part of both Croats and Muslims); Michael Binyon, *Vance–Owen Plan Blamed for "Ethnic Cleansing,"* The Times (London), May 20, 1993, *available in* LEXIS, World Library, Allnws File; *U.N. Human Rights Envoy Presents Report on Croat and Muslim "War Crimes,"* BBC Summary of World Broadcasts (Yugo. Telegraph Serv.), May 22, 1993, *available in* LEXIS, World Library, Allnws File.

[18]   *EC: Europe Documents No. 1788 — Resolution on Relations between the European Community and the Republics of the Former Yugoslavia (adopted* June 12, 1992), Reuters Agence Europe, June 24, 1992, *available in* LEXIS, World Library, Allnws File.

Bosnians, and their governments, to give their support to the swift establishment of the International Tribunal.[19]

Experts in international criminal law also took up their positions. Among legal experts in Serbia, the prevailing opinion is that "the Security Council has no mandate to set up such a tribunal" under chapter VII of the UN Charter, that the invocation of article 29 of the Charter is legally unfounded and arbitrary, and that "such a tribunal is not a subsidiary organ of the Security Council. No independent tribunal, particularly an International Tribunal, can be a subsidiary organ of any body."[20] The establishment of the Tribunal is viewed as an assertion of political supremacy over small nations that would not be attempted in relation to big powers. Imposing an international criminal jurisdiction without the consent of the states directly affected is considered to be an infringement of their sovereignty and independence, particularly given the binding obligations of cooperation and assistance set out in Security Council Resolution 827,[21] the Statute of the

---

[19] CSCE Rapporteurs (Corell–Turk–Thune), Moscow Human Dimension Mechanism to Bosnia, Herzegovina, and Croatia, *Proposal for an International War Crimes Tribunal for the Former Yugoslavia* 23, 97 (1993); *Tudjman Demands U.N. Security Council Implement Vance Plan by Force If Necessary*, BBC Summary of World Broadcasts (Croatian Radio), Dec. 14, 1992, *available in* LEXIS, World Library, Allnws File (noting Croatia's support for a war crimes tribunal); *War Crimes Tribunal Could Start in 1994*, Reuters, Feb. 19, 1993, *available in* LEXIS, World Library, Allnws File (Hans Corell, Rapporteur on the Former Yugoslavia for the Conference on Security and Cooperation in Europe, noting promises of support for an international war crimes tribunal from Bosnia–Herzegovina, Croatia, and Slovenia).

[20] Letter from the Permanent Mission of Yugoslavia to the Secretary-General, May 19, 1993, U.N. Doc. S/25801 (1993), transmitting Letter of May 17 from the Deputy Prime Minister and Minister for Foreign Affairs of the Federal Republic of Yugoslavia on the establishment of an international tribunal for the former Yugoslavia under S.C. Res. 808. See Letter of May 17, *supra*, at 3. For a critical discussion of the legal basis for establishing the Tribunal, see Kolodkin, *supra* note 4.

[21] In S.C. Res. 827, *supra* note 6, ¶ 4, the Security Council *"decide[d]"* that all States shall cooperate fully with the International Tribunal and its organs in accordance with the present resolution and the Statute of the International Tribunal and that consequently all States shall take any measures necessary under their domestic law to implement the provisions of the present resolution and the Statute."

Tribunal,[22] and the Tribunal's Rules of Procedure and Evidence,[23] which extend to making necessary amendments to national constitutions and laws.[24] In light of the current political situation, such changes are unlikely in the Federal Republic of Yugoslavia, as well as in the self-proclaimed Serb Republic of Krajina and the Bosnian Serb Republic. For all these reasons, most legal experts in Serbia take the position that national courts should have primacy, if not exclusive competence, with respect to the prosecution of the crimes over which the International Tribunal has competence—genocide, crimes against humanity, grave breaches of the 1949 Geneva Conventions, and violations of the laws or customs of war.[25]

At present, the government of Yugoslavia has agreed to limited

---

[22] *Report of the Secretary-General pursuant to Paragraph 2 of Security Council Resolution 808 (1993)*, ¶ 125, U.N. Doc. S/25704 & Add.1 (1993), *reprinted in* appendix B of this issue of *Criminal Law Forum* and *in* 32 I.L.M. 1163 ("the establishment of the International Tribunal on the basis of a Chapter VII decision creates a binding obligation on all States to take whatever steps are required to implement the decision"). The Statute of the International Tribunal is set out as an annex to *Secretary-General's Report, supra*, and is *reprinted in* appendix B of this issue of *Criminal Law Forum* and *in* 32 I.L.M. 1192. *Id.* art. 29 mandates cooperation and judicial assistance.

[23] International Tribunal for the Prosecution of Persons Responsible for Serious Violations of International Humanitarian Law Committed in the Territory of the Former Yugoslavia since 1991, Rules of Procedure and Evidence RR. 8, 40, 56, 58, 61(E), U.N. Doc. IT/32 (1994), *amended by* U.N. Doc. IT/32/Rev.1 (1994), U.N. Doc. IT/32/Rev.2 (1994), U.N. Doc. IT/32/Rev.3 (1995), *reprinted in* appendix C of this issue of *Criminal Law Forum*.

[24] Pavel Dolenc, *A Slovenian Perspective on the Statute and Rules of the International Tribunal for the Former Yugoslavia*, in this issue of *Criminal Law Forum*, explores the constitutional and legal implications for Slovenia of the obligation on states to cooperate with the Tribunal.

[25] Round Table, Faculty of Law, University of Belgrade, Belgrade, Federal Republic of Yugoslavia, Apr. 13, 1993; Milan Bulajic, *Alternative Yugoslav Tribunal* 210 (1995); similar views are expressed in Alfred P. Rubin, *An International Criminal Tribunal for Former Yugoslavia?*, 6(1) Pace Int'l L. Rev. 7 (1994); *see also* Letter from the Secretary-General to the Minister for Foreign Affairs of the Federal Republic of Yugoslavia, Apr. 27, 1994 (encouraging national trials of war crimes but reaffirming the primacy of the International Tribunal and the mandatory character of the obligation on states to cooperate with the Tribunal).

cooperation with the International Tribunal.²⁶ For example, where a domestic prosecution is not possible, the government has indicated that it will provide all available documentation pertinent to the case to the International Tribunal. Where the Tribunal presents evidence of crimes by persons at large in Yugoslavia, the domestic courts will initiate prosecutions if possible. The government has also agreed that certain judicial officers will serve as intermediaries between representatives of the Tribunal and alleged perpetrators, relaying questions and responses. At the same time, the government of Yugoslavia takes the position that as no war was fought in its territory, the Tribunal should focus its efforts on those areas where armed conflict has taken place.²⁷ Moreover, the leadership of the Bosnian Serb Republic has declared that it will not extradite the Serbs recently indicted by the Tribunal for their alleged participation in criminal acts at the "Omarska" concentration camp,²⁸ and this may well reflect the general attitude of the Bosnian Serbs toward the Tribunal. It is uncertain how Croatia and Bosnia will respond if their citizens are sought by the Tribunal, although on record these governments have expressed their intention to cooperate fully.²⁹

---

²⁶ *See* Mark Fuller, *Yugoslavia: Croatia, Bosnia Set to Surrender War Crimes Suspects*, Inter Press Serv., Oct. 11, 1994, *available in* LEXIS, World Library, Allnws File; Branko Milinkovic, *Yugoslavia: Mixed Reaction to War Crimes Tribunal Visit*, Inter Press Serv., Oct. 11, 1994, *available in* LEXIS, World Library, Allnws File; *Federal Affairs: War Crimes Prosecutor Holds Talks with Federal Officials*, BBC Summary of World Broadcasts (Yugo. Telegraph Serv.), Oct. 10, 1994, *available in* LEXIS, World Library, Allnws File.

²⁷ Letter from Uros Klikovac, Vice-President and Minister of Justice of the Federal Republic of Yugoslavia, to the Hon. Richard Goldstone, Prosecutor of the International Tribunal for the Former Yugoslavia, Dec. 20, 1994.

²⁸ Prosecutor of the International Tribunal for the Former Yugoslavia v. Dusan Tadic and Twenty Named Co-defendants, Attachment to Tribunal Press Release, Feb. 13, 1995, U.N. Doc. CC/PIO/004-E (1995). Tadic had been arrested earlier in Germany and will be transferred to the jurisdiction of the Tribunal. *Bonn Changes Law to Hand Over War Criminals*, Reuters, Dec. 16, 1994, *available in* LEXIS, World Library, Allnws File. The remaining defendants are thought to be in Bosnia. Jon Henley, *Serb Jailers Charged with Murder, Rape, and Torture*, The Guardian (Manchester), Feb. 14, 1995, *available in* LEXIS, World Library, Allnws File.

²⁹ Fuller, *supra* note 26; *supra* note 19 and accompanying text.

This review suggests that the International Tribunal will encounter significant obstacles. Nevertheless, the very creation of the Tribunal, the work already done by the Commission of Experts and the Special Rapporteur for Human Rights in the Former Yugoslavia, and the publicity surrounding these efforts have themselves to some extent made the responsible parties and participants in the conflict more mindful of their obligations under international humanitarian law. If the Tribunal shows itself to be unbiased and effective, it will help achieve a measure of justice in the region and further the development of international law as a vigorous protector of human rights.

1
International Criminal Prosecution: The Precedent of Nuremberg Confirmed*

Christian Tomuschat**

One may call it truly amazing that the international community, acting through the Security Council, has been able to set up two international criminal jurisdictions in the recent past. The International Tribunal for the Prosecution of Persons Responsible for Serious Violations of International Humanitarian Law Committed in the Territory of the Former Yugoslavia since 1991 was established by Security Council Resolution 827 of May 25, 1993.[1] The International Tribunal for the Prosecution of Persons Responsible for Genocide and Other Serious Violations of International Humanitarian Law Committed in the Territory of Rwanda and Rwandan Citizens Responsible for Genocide and Other Such Violations Committed in the Territory of Neighbouring States, between 1 January 1994 and 31 December 1994, came into being by virtue of Security Council Resolution 955 of November 8, 1994.[2]

---

* *Editor's note:* research for this article was updated through February 13, 1995.

** Member, International Law Commission Working Group on a Draft Statute for an International Criminal Court; Professor of Law, University of Bonn, Bonn, Germany.

[1] S.C. Res. 827, U.N. SCOR, 48th Year, 3217th mtg. at 1, U.N. Doc. S/RES/827 (1993), *reprinted in* appendix A of this issue of *Criminal Law Forum* and *in* 32 I.L.M. 1203.

[2] S.C. Res. 955, U.N. SCOR, 49th Year, 3453d mtg. at 1, U.N. Doc. S/RES/955 (1994), *reprinted in* appendix D of this issue of *Criminal Law Forum* and *available in* U.N. Gopher\Documents\Security Council Resolutions.

Since the trials of Nuremberg and Tokyo,[3] this is the first attempt by the international community to prosecute the authors of atrocious crimes that shock the conscience of humankind and seem to roll back to square one the concept of international protection of human rights. Indeed, the Nuremberg and Tokyo trials represented a great leap forward after the horrors of World War II; namely, that no one should be left totally abandoned to the vagaries of his or her government and that, at least in situations where basic rights are infringed systematically and on a vast scale by power wielders, the international community will not stand idly by, restrained by the traditional rule of nonintervention from taking remedial action.

Over the years, the United Nations has gradually put in place machinery for the protection of human rights that has achieved a high degree of sophistication. In terms of actual effectiveness, however, this elaborate system is fairly weak. It is based on admonition and reprobation, presupposing that the government concerned is eager to keep its good international reputation and will thus do its best to refrain from actions that may provoke massive international criticism. However, when irrationality erupts and all considerations of humanity are brushed aside in power struggles, which may be nurtured by age-old hatreds, internationally recognized moral values may be not only forgotten but

---

[3] The International Military Tribunal at Nuremberg was established pursuant to Agreement for the Prosecution and Punishment of the Major War Criminals of the European Axis, Aug. 8, 1945, 82 U.N.T.S. 279. The Charter of the International Military Tribunal at Nuremberg is set out in *id.* at 284. The proceedings are reported in *Trial of the Major War Criminals before the International Military Tribunal, Nuremberg, 14 October 1945–1 October 1946* (1947–1949).

The International Military Tribunal for the Far East was established in Tokyo pursuant to Special Proclamation by the Supreme Commander for the Allied Powers, Establishment of an International Tribunal for the Far East, Jan. 19, 1946, 4 Bevans 20, *reprinted in* 1 Benjamin Ferencz, *Defining International Aggression* 522 (1975). It operated pursuant to Charter of the International Military Tribunal for the Far East, Jan. 19, 1946 *(as amended* Apr. 26, 1946), 4 Bevans 21, *reprinted in* 1 Ferencz, *supra,* at 523. The proceedings are available on microfilm. *Record of the Proceedings of the International Military Tribunal for the Far East, Tokyo, Japan* (1946–1948). Majority and dissenting opinions have been collected in *The Tokyo Judgment: The International Military Tribunal for the Far East, 29 April 1946–12 November 1948* (Bert V.A. Röling & Christiaan Frederik Rüter eds., 1977).

even deliberately ignored. In such cases, the international community, in order to remain credible, should have recourse to other means besides censure.

Of course, prevention is always the best course. From an international law perspective, the precedents set in Somalia[4] and Haiti[5] under the authority of chapter VII of the UN Charter have cleared the way for UN intervention in civil wars. Yet, in practice, as the developments of 1994 have made abundantly clear, it is tremendously difficult to get agreement on such actions. There are too many trouble spots in the world, and it would always be the same powers shouldering the largest part of the response. Now that the cold war is (momentarily?) over, the role of international policeman has become much less attractive than it appeared to be in the past. Thus, Somalia will be left to its own devices after March 31, 1995,[6] and in Bosnia the victims of aggression are denied military assistance. Not even the openly declared war against the civilian population there meets with any response from the international community, with the most brutal violations of the rules of warfare occurring on a daily basis.

There is no escaping the conclusion that establishing an international criminal tribunal mandated to try persons responsible for violations of international humanitarian law is the second-best solution. Given the current political context, it seems clear that, at least in the case of the former Yugoslavia, there exists neither the might nor the intention to catch the "big fish," those whose inflammatory propaganda set in motion the abhorrent process of "ethnic cleansing." Indeed, since the interna-

---

[4] The Security Council determined in S.C. Res. 794 that the "magnitude of the human tragedy" unfolding in Somalia constituted a threat to international peace and security in the sense contemplated by U.N. Charter ch. VII. S.C. Res. 794, U.N. SCOR, 47th Year, 1992 S.C. Res. & Dec. at 63, U.N. Doc. S/INF/48 (1992).

[5] In the case of Haiti, intervention to restore democracy was based also on U.N. Charter ch. VII. S.C. Res. 940, U.N. SCOR, 49th Year, 3413 mtg. at 1, U.N. Doc. S/RES/940 (1994), *available in* U.N. Gopher\Documents\Security Council Resolutions.

[6] S.C. Res. 954, U.N. SCOR, 49th Year, 3451th mtg. at 1, U.N. Doc. S/RES/954 (1994); *Security Council Extends UNOSOM II for Final Period until 31 March 1995, Demands Somali Parties Refrain from Intimidation or Violence*, Fed. News Serv., Nov. 7, 1994, *available in* LEXIS, World Library, Allnws File.

tional community continuously repeats its standard refrain that a peace settlement can be reached only by negotiation, it needs those in power at the conference table. Even if Richard Goldstone, chief prosecutor of both tribunals, wishes in the case of the former Yugoslavia to try the key figures in planning and organizing one of the most glaring attacks on human rights standards and rules of humanitarian law since the second world war, his hands will be tied. He can hope no more than to get hold of some criminal individuals of a lower command level arrested fortuitously in neighboring states, who as asylum seekers had hoped not to be identified. This is not to say that these individuals are not to be blamed: the actions with which some of them are being charged constitute, more often than not, horrendous stories of human debasement.[7] But the overall picture stands in stark contrast to what happened at Nuremberg and Tokyo. Before those two tribunals, the major war criminals—the intellectual authors of untold suffering—were held accountable for their deeds. In all probability, as David Forsythe points out in his contribution to this issue of *Criminal Law Forum*, the International Tribunal for the Former Yugoslavia will try only persons arrested at random, who are not among the group that planned the territorial restructuring of Bosnia and Croatia by means of murder, torture, rape, and plunder.

One should not lose sight of this whole political context in trying to assess the International Tribunal for the Former Yugoslavia, as well as

---

[7] The first person indicted by the International Tribunal for the Former Yugoslavia (Dragan Nikolic) is alleged to have been the commander of a concentration camp operated by the Bosnian Serbs. Roger Cohen, *Tribunal Charges Serbian Camp Commander with War Crimes*, N.Y. Times, Nov. 8, 1994, at A5, *available in* LEXIS, World Library, Allnws File; *see also* Melinda Crane-Engel, *Germany vs. Genocide*, N.Y. Times, Oct. 30, 1994, § 6, at 56, *available in* LEXIS, World Library, Allnws File (discussing a suspect held in Germany, Dusan Tadic, who is sought by the International Tribunal); *Serb War Crimes Trial Referred to Supreme Court*, Agence France Presse, Dec. 12, 1994, *available in* LEXIS, World Library, Allnws File (discussing a prosecution in Austria); *War Crimes Panel Convicts Bosnian*, Chi. Tribune, Nov. 23, 1994, at 3, *available in* LEXIS, World Library, Allnws File (discussing a prosecution in Denmark). *See generally* Letter from the Secretary-General to the President of the Security Council, May 24, 1994, U.N. Doc. S/1994/674 (1994), transmitting *Final Report of the Commission of Experts Established pursuant to Security Council Resolution 780 (1992)*, *available in* U.N. Gopher\Current Information\Secretary-General's Reports. *See infra* note 11.

the International Tribunal for Rwanda, for which the prospects are even dimmer. As a lawyer, one may—and should—hail the establishment of these two international tribunals as a decisive step forward in the slow process of building institutions for the maintenance of a minimum level of world order that one may rightly call "civilized." However, even a lawyer is entitled to ask searching questions and should attempt to determine whether the international community does in fact support the institutions it has brought into being by taking the requisite next steps. From this perspective, financing is the most delicate and revealing issue. In his article, Julian Schutte provides a telling account of past difficulties in this regard. It has been reported that the Fifth Committee of the General Assembly has been extremely reluctant in appropriating the necessary funds for investigative purposes.[8] This is a devastating signal. Inadequate funding may condemn the two tribunals to a standstill. Indeed, it is no more than a truism to say that prevention would be infinitely less expensive than cost-intensive trials, which may become a playground for prominent lawyers versed in the latest refinements of U.S. criminal procedure.

The contributors to this collection rightly agree that chapter VII of the Charter provides a sufficient legal basis for the establishment of the two tribunals. To maintain and restore international peace and security means not only meeting the direct challenge of aggression but also taking measures for the definitive settlement of an armed conflict. There is no denying that somewhere a line must be drawn. The Security Council obviously cannot, under chapter VII, address the root causes of

---

[8] Thomas S. Warrick, *U.N. Foot-dragging Could Make a Sham of the War Crimes Tribunal*, Dec. 21, 1994, at 4, *available in* LEXIS, World Library, Allnws File (citing $562,300 of $32.6 million for investigations); Editorial, *Prosecute Bosnia's War Criminals*, N.Y. Times, Jan. 4, 1995, at A18 (citing less than 2 percent of $28 million). Prosecutor Goldstone unofficially threatened to resign his post if the Tribunal were not adequately financed for 1995, Christoph Driessen, *War Crimes Tribunal Slowly Prepares for Proceedings*, Deutsche Presse-Agentur, Nov. 6, 1994, *available in* LEXIS, World Library, Allnws File, and for the first quarter of 1995 the Fifth Committee proposed a budget of $7 million, *Fifth Committee Approves $352.5 Million for UNDOF, UNIFIL, UNOSOM II, International Criminal Tribunal and Human Rights Programmes*, U.N. Press Release, U.N. Doc. GA/AB/2981 (Dec. 21, 1994), *available in* U.N. Gopher\Current Information\Press Releases.

internal strife like poverty, lack of education, and unjust distribution of land. But this organ must be able to deal with the direct consequences of events that qualify as a threat to, or a breach of, the peace under article 39 of the UN Charter. This conclusion appears all the more justified since the establishment of the two tribunals is intended not only to punish the responsible authors of crimes but also to deter future violations—an effect, unfortunately, that this undertaking may fail to have.

One specific feature of the two tribunals' statutes is sometimes misunderstood.[9] In articles 2–5 of the Statute of the International Tribunal for the Former Yugoslavia, and similarly in articles 2–4 of the Statute of the International Tribunal for Rwanda, the Security Council has not set forth substantive law. The purpose of these provisions is simply to determine and circumscribe the jurisdiction of each court. Any attempt at creating new substantive penal rules would have run counter to the basic principle of *nullum crimen, nulla poena sine lege*. I fully agree with Kenneth Gallant and Roman Kolodkin in this respect. One has to admit, however, that a formulation in writing of rules that supposedly preexist as customary norms may cross the thin line between codification and creation of new law. This difficulty may affect in particular article 5 of the Statute of the International Tribunal for the Former Yugoslavia and article 3 of the Statute of the International Tribunal for Rwanda. It is by no means certain that before 1993 crimes against humanity had acquired the status of customary law with as large a scope as is attributed to them by those articles. It will be one of the main tasks of the two tribunals to verify whether all the offenses over which they have competence qualify as offenses under customary law. It should be noted, in this connection, that the International Law Commission's Draft Code of Crimes against the Peace and Security of Mankind offers a widely divergent categorization of crimes against

---

[9] The Statute of the International Tribunal for the Former Yugoslavia is set out as an annex to *Report of the Secretary-General pursuant to Paragraph 2 of Security Council Resolution 808 (1993)*, U.N. Doc. S/25704 & Add.1 (1993) [hereinafter *Secretary-General's Report*], and is *reprinted in* appendix B of this issue of *Criminal Law Forum* and *in* 32 I.L.M. 1192 [hereinafter Statute]. The Statute of the International Tribunal for Rwanda is set out as an annex to S.C. Res. 955, *supra* note 2, and is *reprinted in* appendix D of this issue of *Criminal Law Forum*.

humanity, labeling them "systematic or mass violations of human rights."[10] Given this substantial difference in treatment, it might be argued that in some borderline cases the international and customary law character of the relevant offense has not been sufficiently established.

However, the observation just made must be refined in one important respect. While the statutes do not set out to create new criminal offenses but instead purport to reference a set of crimes already prohibited under customary international law, both instruments contain rules that one normally encounters in the general part of a domestic penal code. In particular, article 7 of the Statute of the International Tribunal for the Former Yugoslavia and article 6 of the Statute of the International Tribunal for Rwanda define who may be individually criminally responsible as author or accomplice of any crimes under the jurisdiction of the two tribunals. This determination, however, has the character of an auxiliary legal rule and does not infringe the basic requirement of *nullum crimen, nulla poena sine lege.*

It will not be easy to prove the commission of crimes falling within the competence of the International Tribunal for the Former Yugoslavia. Even more difficult will be the task of the International Tribunal for Rwanda. Back in 1945, ample factual evidence was available. The victorious Allied powers had access to all the archives of Germany and Japan, where much of the illegal activities of the two regimes had been carefully documented. The International Tribunal for the Former Yugoslavia, in contrast, is constrained to act from outside the territory of the former Yugoslavia. Its main source of evidence will therefore be testimony by witnesses. Thus, over and beyond the problem of arresting any intellectual authors, there is a tremendous risk that acts of planning, organizing, and incitement may not be capable of being proven at the level of proof required for conviction. In any event, testimonial evidence is the most expensive and time-consuming category of evidence. In a given case, it may be necessary to hear dozens of witnesses. If the scarcity of funding of the International Tribunal for the Former Yugoslavia does not allow witnesses to be brought to the Hague

---

[10] Draft Code of Crimes against the Peace and Security of Mankind art. 21, in *Report of the International Law Commission on Its Forty-third Session,* U.N. GAOR, 46th Sess., Supp. No. 10, at 238, U.N. Doc. A/46/10 (1991).

or on-site investigations to be carried out, as indicated by Cherif Bassiouni, the work of this court may collapse. The current record of the court seems to confirm these apprehensions. As of the end of 1994 only one indictment had been issued. In view of the large number of the crimes committed, this single case would seem to be almost irrelevant.[11]

Apart from the concept of international crimes, which connotes individual penal responsibility directly by virtue of rules of international law and irrespective of the rules of a territorially competent legislature, a striking legal feature of this initiative is the legal precedence attributed to the International Tribunal for the Former Yugoslavia under Security Council Resolution 827.

On the face of it, the Tribunal has been endowed with powers akin to those of the Security Council itself, powers susceptible of producing binding legal effects for states. The most conspicuous expression of this precedence is found in articles 9 and 29 of the Tribunal's Statute. Under article 9(2), the International Tribunal for the Former Yugoslavia may at any stage of the procedure "request" a national court to defer to its competence. It emerges from the relevant report by the UN Secretary-General that this is not a simple request that a state would be free either to grant or to deny, but rather a binding order with which every state is duty-bound to comply.[12] The report unequivocally asserts the "primacy" of the Tribunal, leaving only details of implementation to the Rules of Procedure and Evidence.[13] Under article 29(2),

---

[11] *Editor's note:* as this issue went to press, the Tribunal indicted 21 Bosnian Serbs, including Dusan Tadic, see *supra* note 7, for crimes committed at the Omarska concentration camp in northwestern Bosnia in 1992. Andrew Kelly, *U.N. Tribunal Charges 21 Serbs with Atrocities,* Reuters, Feb. 13, 1995, *available in* LEXIS, World Library, Allnws File. Except for Tadic, all are at large. Both the Bosnian Serb leader, Radovan Karadzic, and the government of Yugoslavia have asserted they will not hand over any of the accused. *Bosnia Serb Leader Rejects Handover of Suspects,* Reuters, Feb. 13, 1995, *available in* LEXIS, World Library, Allnws File.

[12] *Secretary-General's Report, supra* note 9, ¶ 65.

[13] *Id.;* International Tribunal for the Prosecution of Persons Responsible for Serious Violations of International Humanitarian Law Committed in the Territory of the Former Yugoslavia since 1991, Rules of Procedure and Evidence RR. 8–11, U.N. Doc. IT/32 (1994), *amended by* U.N. Doc. IT/32/Rev.1 (1994), U.N. Doc. IT/32/Rev.2

states "shall," in particular, "comply without undue delay with any request for assistance or an order issued by a Trial Chamber." Here, the wording is crystal clear. National agencies are placed under the authority of the International Tribunal for the Former Yugoslavia, which may, not unlike the Security Council, issue orders or injunctions that must be heeded fully, leaving no discretion to governments.

Yet, the Tribunal's powers transcend even the traditional pattern of linkage between the UN Security Council and member states. To date, the Security Council has mostly addressed its orders to states as such. A typical example of the technique ordinarily followed is provided by the numerous embargo resolutions, which enjoin "all states" to interrupt trade and other commercial intercourse with a targeted state. These resolutions do not directly affect the legal position of private individuals but require measures of national implementation to become applicable to the enterprises whose commercial activities they are designed to bring to a halt. In the case of the International Tribunal for the Former Yugoslavia, this two-stage process cannot be implemented. Once a case is pending, the Tribunal deals directly with the individual concerned. This relationship is not deferred until the last stage of a proceeding, when the accused has been transferred to the Hague. A direct legal relationship between the International Tribunal and a person under investigation comes into being as soon as an indictment has been confirmed by the competent trial chamber under article 19 of the Statute. Upon confirmation, a judge of the Tribunal may issue a warrant of arrest. Such a warrant constitutes, according to the perception upon which the Statute is predicated, a legal act that is directly enforceable vis-à-vis the accused. Under rule 55 of the Rules of Procedure and Evidence, the international warrant shall be executed as it stands; it does not require further action by a national authority to transform it into a legally binding decision. Thus, the international warrant itself constitutes a valid mandate to effect an arrest, which is supposed to satisfy all requirements of correct legal procedure in conformity with the applicable rules of habeas corpus.

Such a direct legal effect on private citizens is a feature that until

---

(1994), U.N. Doc. IT/32/Rev.3 (1995), *reprinted in* appendix C of this issue of *Criminal Law Forum* [hereinafter I.T. R. Proc. & Evid.].

now was encountered only in European Community law. Under the Statute and the Rules of Procedure and Evidence, this device has been made to apply within a UN context. For many states it will not be easy to adapt their legal thinking to this new situation. Legal assistance and extradition are both age-old institutions based on mutual cooperation between states. Notwithstanding the legal obligations deriving from the many treaties in this field, states still make sovereign determinations on whether to grant an extradition request. Now, not only has political discretion disappeared, but, equally novel, an international institution—the International Tribunal for the Former Yugoslavia—has been empowered to issue orders that have a direct effect on persons. In this scenario, states are confined to translating such orders into factual reality as agents of execution, without having any additional role of review in which they might exercise discretion. Since all domestic legislation is based on the old concepts, a lot will have to be done by way of adjusting to the new legal position, as Pavel Dolenc notes in relation to Slovenia. One thing is clear, however. States are not entitled to object to a surrender sought by the Tribunal by claiming that their national rules do not address or permit the "surrender" or "transfer" of a person to an international tribunal and that, therefore, they are unable to heed such a request.[14] Of course, what is true for a small state is true also for a big power like Russia or the United States, at least in terms of the express language of the Statute and the Rules of Procedure and Evidence.

The fate of the International Tribunal for the Former Yugoslavia is still open. Should it founder, without being able to conclude proceedings in even a single case, a most unfortunate precedent may be set. In particular, it would become almost impossible, and in any event useless, to pursue further the efforts completed in 1994 by the International Law Commission toward creating a treaty-based international criminal court.[15] Failure of the international community to make the

---

[14] *Secretary-General's Report, supra* note 9, ¶¶ 125–126; Statute, *supra* note 9, art. 29; I.T. R. Proc. & Evid., *supra* note 13, R. 58.

[15] Draft Statute for an International Criminal Court, in *Report of the International Law Commission on Its Forty-sixth Session,* U.N. GAOR, 49th Sess., Supp. No. 10, at 43, U.N. Doc. A/49/10 (1994). The deliberations in the Sixth Committee in the fall of 1994 suggest that the international community may be unwilling to act on the proposals

International Tribunal for the Former Yugoslavia a workable international institution would also retroactively shed a grey light of doubt on the Nuremberg and Tokyo trials. A disservice to the cause of law and justice would also be done if it were decided to accept a general amnesty—an idea that obviously is most attractive to those who see themselves already as the winners of the war in Bosnia–Herzegovina. The Inter-American Commission on Human Rights has stated that with regard to grave violations of human rights an amnesty cannot be validly declared.[16] It is to be hoped that this pronouncement will at all times be remembered at the United Nations.

---

of the International Law Commission. *Report of the Sixth Committee*, U.N. GAOR, 49th Sess., Agenda Item 137, U.N. Doc. A/49/738, at 17 (1994); G.A. Res. 49/53, U.N. GAOR, 49th Sess., 84th plen. mtg., U.N. Doc. A/49/53 (1994).

[16] Report No. 28/92 (Oct. 2, 1992) (consolidating 6 cases from Arg.), Inter-Am. C.H.R. 41 (1993); Report No. 29/92 (Oct. 2, 1992) (consolidating 8 cases from Uru.), Inter-Am. C.H.R. 154 (1993).

2
Toward International Criminal Justice*

*Jules Deschênes***

I—LANGUAGE AND RIGHTS

The Tower of Babel has not stopped causing us problems yet, and the conflicts that it sets off cast their shadow over Canada, and in particular, French-speaking Canada. Thus, when my English-speaking friends talk about the rights to which the René Cassin Lectureship is dedicated, they use the neutral expression "human rights." It is the same with Spanish speakers when they refer to "derechos humanos." But in French, the phrase "droits humains" does not sound quite right, and tradition dictates that we speak of "droits de l'homme." Accordingly, it was only natural that the United Nations would, in 1948, adopt the Déclaration universelle des *droits de l'homme* (Universal Declaration of Human Rights). But this French expression is not neutral, and of late it has prompted such sharp controversy among us that both national legislation in Canada and provincial legislation in Quebec have opted in

---

* This is a revised and updated version of the René Cassin Lectureship in Human Rights, which was presented under the auspices of InterAmicus, Faculty of Law, McGill University, Montréal, Québec, Canada, March 17, 1994. The original address included both French and English passages. The French has been translated by Madeleine Sann, Director of Publication, *Criminal Law Forum*, and Rosanne Loesch, Esq.

Editor's note: research for this article was updated through December 31, 1994.

** Judge, International Tribunal for the Prosecution of Persons Responsible for Serious Violations of International Humanitarian Law Committed in the Territory of the Former Yugoslavia since 1991, the Hague, Netherlands; C.C., Q.C., LL.D., F.R.S.C.

their French texts for the phrase "droits de la personne."

About a decade ago, in the course of deliberations in a United Nations commission in Geneva, I took advantage of a chance opening in the debate to raise this question of terminology. My intervention provoked a passionate reply from the French delegate in the name of tradition, grammar, and the most sacrosanct of dictionaries—all obviously French!

I do not wish this evening to launch a crusade to replace "droits de l'homme" with "droits de la personne" in the French-speaking world. It is nonetheless interesting to note that even in the very way we name them, varying with national philosophies and cultures, these rights demand thought, when they are not actually provoking controversy.

There is, then, no shortage of avenues that feed into this lecture. I would like, this evening, to talk to you about certain efforts on the international level to suppress violations of human rights ("droits de la personne") in the name of, and by means of, international criminal law.

Of course, this is not an invention of our time. History books are full of examples of cruel episodes in which war crimes and crimes against humanity have been committed with impunity. One example of the latter kind: the killing of all male infants less than two years old ordered, around year one of our era, by King Herod, to prevent the raising of a pretender to his throne.[1]

II—1474: AN EXPERIMENT IN INTERNATIONAL CRIMINAL JUSTICE

This does not mean that consciences were not awakened from time to time to the necessity of curbing those criminal abuses of power. Yet one had to wait until the fifteenth century to see a real attempt at international criminal justice. This shows that the Secretary-General of the United Nations was right when, on January 21, 1994, he addressed the second plenary meeting of the eleven judges of the International

---

[1] *Matthew* 2:16.

Criminal Tribunal for the Former Yugoslavia in the Hague. Mr. Boutros Boutros-Ghali said:

> [T]he building of an international society governed by law is a slow, modest, chaotic and uncertain business. It gives satisfaction neither to sensation-mongers nor to short-term adventurers. Nevertheless, it is just such patient progress in setting international standards that most effectively shapes each stage in the development of a universal moral code.[2]

The events at issue occurred in the Year of Our Lord 1474. Relations had soured between Charles, Duke of Burgundy, and his neighbors Austria, France, and Switzerland. For financial reasons, the Archduke of Austria had pledged to Charles of Burgundy his town of Breisach. Charles installed Peter von Hagenbach as his governor. Von Hagenbach, no doubt carrying out his master's instructions to reduce Breisach into submission, acted together with his henchmen with extreme brutality: murder, rape, pillage, wanton confiscation, "no conceivable evil," wrote a chronicler of the time, "was beyond him."[3]

A revolt occurred in Breisach; von Hagenbach was seized and put on trial. The court which tried Von Hagenbach was composed of twenty-eight judges nominated by each of the allied towns from the Alsace, Upper Rhine, and Swiss Confederation and was presided over by a judge appointed by the Archduke of Austria, in whose territory von Hagenbach had been captured. The prosecutor charged that the accused had "trampled under foot the laws of God and man." Von Hagenbach's spokesman relied on the defense of superior orders.

The court found the accused guilty, deprived him of his knighthood, and condemned him to death. The sentence was carried

---

[2] *Secretary-General Believes Tribunal for Crimes in Former Yugoslavia Opens New Prospects for Punishment of War Crimes,* U.N. Doc. SG/SM/5207 (Jan. 25, 1994), *available in* U.N. Gopher\Current Information\Press Releases (English translation of statement delivered in French).

[3] John Knebel Capellani, *Basel Diary 1473–1476,* quoted in 2 Georg Schwarzenberger, *International Law as Applied by International Courts and Tribunals* 465 n.10 (1968).

out.

This is the first recorded instance in the Western world of an international criminal trial. It is worth noting that, if it did not arise out of war crimes strictly speaking, it was surely based on what we would now call crimes against humanity.

III — FIVE CENTURIES OF INACTION

Nevertheless, the next five centuries were distinguished by a clear lack of political will to tackle this problem effectively. Following the Napoleonic wars, the victorious states, still under the sway, it seems, of the imperial era, elected to deal with the fallen emperor by executive act; hence exile, a political decision, rather than death, a judicial sanction.

At the end of the first world war, the Treaty of Versailles contemplated the prosecution of Kaiser Wilhelm II, along with twenty-one thousand individuals suspected of war crimes. We have all witnessed, for example, those appalling scenes of airplanes strafing columns of refugees fleeing before advancing enemy forces. But the Kaiser took refuge in the Netherlands, and the Allies abandoned the idea of an international tribunal.

In the same period, the Treaty of Sèvres of 1920 was supposed to have served as the legal basis for prosecuting Turkish officials deemed responsible for the first episode of genocide in this century: the massacre of some 600,000 Armenians. But the treaty was never ratified. It was, in fact, superseded by the Treaty of Lausanne of 1923, which did not even mention the question, and this crime against humanity continued to go unpunished.

Then, in 1937, the League of Nations adopted a convention against terrorism, which set out a statute for an international criminal tribunal. One country alone, India, ratified this convention and the statute never entered into force.[4]

---

[4] Convention for the Prevention and Punishment of Terrorism, *opened for signature* Nov. 16, 1937, *reprinted in* 7 *International Legislation* 862 (Manley O. Hudson ed., 1941) (which received a single ratification from India); Convention for the Creation

Since that time, a number of international conventions have been adopted to suppress dangerous criminal activities that transcend national boundaries. But none of these has contemplated the creation of an institutional mechanism with competence to enforce its provisions through penal sanctions.

It is true that ad hoc tribunals were established at the end of the second world war at Nuremberg and Tokyo. The bombing of civilian targets, intended to terrorize the resident population and destroy whole cities — London, Dresden, Coventry, Hiroshima — was not forgotten. Nor the spectacle of forced laborers reduced to virtual slavery in munitions factories. Nor the deliberate annihilation of millions in the death camps. But even here the international community proved itself incapable of putting into place a permanent judicial mechanism, so that to this day crimes of immeasurable seriousness continue to be committed with impunity. One has only to think of Biafra, Burundi, Bangladesh, Cambodia, South Africa, Vietnam, Central America, Colombia, and, closer to us, Haiti.

Thus, due to lack of international consensus and, it must be noted, fear on the part of some heads of state that with an international criminal court they run the risk of being called to account for their own illegal actions taken under the convenient cloak of national security, nothing has changed until recently in the traditional paradigm in which each government exercises its sovereign right to decide whether to prosecute these international criminals in its national tribunals.

Besides, a government must have information that will allow it to initiate prosecutions in full knowledge of the facts. It was, without doubt, this concern which hovered in the air here in Canada on Friday, February 7, 1985.

IV — INQUIRY ON WAR CRIMINALS IN CANADA

Christmas had now jingled into the polar night and a dull winter week was coming to an end. My office telephone rang: "How would you

---

of an International Criminal Court, *opened for signature* Nov. 16, 1937, *reprinted in* 7 *International Legislation, supra,* at 878 (which received no ratifications).

like," asked a familiar voice, "to chair a Commission of Inquiry into Nazi war criminals in Canada?" A rough translation of this unexpected call might have been: "How would you like to board the next NASA flight to the moon?"

During World War II hundreds of members of the Canadian Armed Forces had fallen victims of criminal action by the enemy. One hundred and seventy-one cases were actually investigated. At the outset, the Canadian forces launched their own prosecutions and held their own public trials in Aurich, Germany. Ten trials took place, involving some thirty-five accused.

By 1947, however, Canadian troops had been repatriated and no Canadian personnel remained overseas for the conduct of further trials. But an agreement was reached with the British authorities, who held, on behalf of Canada, six other trials involving twenty-eight accused.

Yet the year 1948 was dawning and the British had turned their thoughts to the political future of Europe. On July 13, 1948, the British Commonwealth Relations Office sent a secret telegram to the seven Dominions (as they were then called); it suggested essentially that no fresh trials of war criminals should be started after August 31, 1948.

The British government had asked for comments. On July 22, 1948, Canada answered by an equally secret cable that it had "no comment to make." The six other Dominions either expressly or tacitly also agreed. So the matter of war criminals quietly disappeared from the scene. It would remain generally dormant for a full third of a century. Indeed, on February 16, 1982, when a member of the House of Commons asked whether attempts were being made to track down former Nazis suspected of living in Canada, the government of the day answered a flat no.

But the matter then took a dramatic turn.

On June 17, 1982, a former Nazi, Albert Helmut Rauca, was arrested in Toronto on charges of war crimes, at the request of West Germany. It was reliably established during the extradition hearing in Toronto that in a single day he had sent thirteen thousand Jews to their deaths in a concentration camp.[5] He was extradited and died abroad in

---

[5] Federal Republic of Germany v. Rauca, 141 D.L.R.3d 412 (Ont. High Ct. 1982), *aff'd*, 145 D.L.R.3d 638 (Can. Ont. Ct. App. 1983).

prison while awaiting trial. Rauca's was the first war crimes case on Canadian soil.

Then a public outcry was spurred around the end of January 1985 by the publication in the *New York Times* of an article dealing with Dr. Josef Mengele, the infamous "Angel of Death." The third paragraph read:

> Other records indicate that Mengele applied to the Canadian Embassy in Buenos Aires for a Canadian visa in 1962 under a pseudonym and that the Canadians informed American intelligence officials of the attempt.[6]

A. The Inquiry Is Launched

On February 7, 1985, the government of Canada, on the recommendation of the Prime Minister, decided to launch an inquiry into the Mengele affair and, more generally, into the matter of Nazi war criminals: were there any in Canada, how did they gain entry, and how should they be dealt with?

I think I can safely state that the matter had never stood at the forefront of popular interest in Canada. But it obviously presented a challenge and the questions that it raised would be eminently suitable for someone trained in the judicial process.

These thoughts, and others, were flashing through my mind as I was discussing the offer with my caller: I gave him an affirmative answer.

The wheels had to be set in motion. I realized at a glance that I would need a first-rate legal team, investigation team, research team, and secretariat.

The choice of legal counsel was critical. I was lucky enough to prevail upon my first two contacts to accept the brief.

One was Mr. Yves Fortier, C.C., Q.C., of Montréal, a former president of the Canadian Bar Association who was destined to become Canadian Ambassador to the United Nations; the other was Mr. Michael

---

[6] Ralph Blumenthal, *Papers Indicate Mengele May Have Been Held and Freed after War*, N.Y. Times, Jan. 23, 1985, at A4, *available in* LEXIS, World Library, Allnws File.

Meighen, Q.C., of Toronto, a former president of the Progressive Conservative party of Canada who was destined to become a member of the Senate. Equally brilliant and polished, they were fully independent from the various ethnic groups which were already showing an interest in the work of the Commission of Inquiry. At the same time, they assured the balance required in Canadian affairs: from Montréal and Toronto, of French and English extraction, Roman Catholic and Anglican, liberal and conservative, both fully bilingual and highly competent; they rendered to my inquiry the most eminent services.

We soon discovered, however, that the load would far exceed the capabilities of the original group: six other full-time lawyers were hired at the head office in Ottawa and seven legal consultants were retained across the country.

Add to the group five vastly experienced investigators, three researchers, and a competent personnel under the direction of an Oxford graduate in military history: we were in business.

My first task consisted, of course, in finding out whether there were residing in Canada any people suspected of war crimes. A surprisingly large number of sources, public and private, Canadian and foreign, volunteered information. The Commission thus built a master list of 883 suspects. It already appeared, however, that some allegations were obviously spurious. A single example will suffice: the denunciation as war criminals of a couple, based on the fact that they bore a German name, lived in a secluded place under the protection of two black dogs, and offered old European furniture for sale.

In due course the Commission established that 86 of its suspects had died in Canada, 341 had never entered Canada, 21 had crossed our borders but later left for other countries, 4 could not be traced, and there was not a shadow of evidence against 154 others. Six hundred and six files were thus closed.

B. *Sittings: Public and Private*

Some general questions had, however, to be addressed and a certain number of individual files needed deeper screening. The Commission therefore held both public and closed sittings in Montréal, Hull, Ottawa, Toronto, Windsor, Winnipeg, Calgary, and Vancouver. We sat 28 days in public and 38 days in private; we received 23 briefs and heard 85 witnesses, including a number of suspects themselves.

Let me explain at once why the Commission held a relatively high number of sittings behind closed doors. Different from a common law court, the Commission had the power to summon the suspects and order them to testify. Imagine for a moment such a hearing taking place in public with a former Nazi suspected of war crimes and a host of witnesses offered as a daily diet to the media. Experience of similar hearings had shown that the suspect would have been crucified and could only with great difficulty have subsequently had a fair trial before a jury. Since I did not want the inquiry to be transformed into a media show and I expected, should credible evidence come forward, that the suspects would be charged and brought to trial, I had no alternative but to hear those cases in camera, for the protection of the elementary rights of the suspects and the vindication of the rule of law.

The public sittings had enhanced my knowledge of the matter and permitted me better to grasp the role played by the various agencies of the Canadian government in the postwar immigration process. But it was the private sittings that put me in closer touch with the matter of war criminals. I had isolated some thirty cases which warranted detailed study. All those suspects were summoned before the Commission, together with a number of relevant witnesses. Two of the suspects challenged the right of the Commission to force them to testify. I dismissed their submissions on the basis of detailed reasons which have been published. The suspects did not persist and they gave their testimony. I thus learnt that there are living in Canada people who have suffered terrible stress during World War II, others who have been involved in untold misdeeds, and still others who have found themselves at the center of important political events.

Those hearings were not devoid of incidents.

On one occasion, a few minutes before a closed sitting, a witness from Los Angeles suffered a heart attack just outside the hearing room. He was hospitalized, then returned to California. Fortunately, he recovered and came back to give lengthy evidence three months later.

Another day a witness states that, over forty years ago, he was bashed on the head by a police officer who stood behind him and whom he had never actually seen face to face. The suspect, who had been summoned on the strength of independent evidence, swears in turn that he never worked at the place identified by the witness. At the end of the suspect's testimony, the two men shake hands, turn their back to me, and launch into a lively conversation as though they were standing at Peel and Ste-Catherine in downtown Montréal. I had to call them severely to order so that the hearing could continue.

It is also known that members of the S.S. wore under their left arm a tattoo of their blood type. A suspect, living in a remote countryside village, had been said to bear such a mark. I had sent a doctor to examine him, but the examination was prevented by unforeseen circumstances. I summon the suspect, who is requested, at the hearing, to undress; he does so, comes next to me, raises his arm, and I discover the quite visible tattoo. The man gave an exculpatory explanation which the courts, I suppose, will consider if he is ever prosecuted.

Some suspects readily acknowledged their presence in given locations but denied their participation in alleged crimes. Others denied even their presence and, who knows, maybe they were telling the truth. The difficulty is easy to imagine: we have before us, on the one hand, the photograph of a man in his early thirties, wearing a cap and a military uniform; on the other hand, a man in his seventies, in civilian clothes and hatless. Forty-five years stand between an image and a reality, and the witnesses have never seen the suspect in the meantime.

In some cases identification is borne out by the reference to certain peculiarities which cannot lie. But in other cases identification was far from positive. Take the case of a European photograph showing a dozen men in uniform, in two rows, making the Nazi salute. A witness identifies the suspect in the upper row, the next witness recognizes the suspect in the lower row, and the suspect himself states unequivocally that he appears nowhere in the picture: which statement should be believed?

C. Collecting Evidence Abroad

But a more general problem was arising and needed to be solved before I would make my recommendations on individual cases. By chance, certain witnesses had settled in Canada and the United States, but the majority were still living abroad: some in western Europe, the larger number behind the Iron Curtain—to use a phrase popular at the time. The question was open: was it legal and advisable for the Commission to go and collect that evidence?

It had been done by the Office of Special Investigations, in the United States. I had seen films of those interrogatories. It had also been done in an action in damages which was then pending in Toronto and which involved charges of war crimes preferred by a television network. I knew, however, that the question was stirring deeply held passions. So I gave to the parties which had standing before the Commission the opportunity of urging their respective points of view.

On November 14, 1985, I decided the question in the affirmative.[7] I examined in detail all the submissions made on either side. Over and above the relevant legal provisions, the Canadian Constitution and the Charter of Rights and Freedoms, I studied a judgment rendered in the United Kingdom, another one in Canada, two in the Federal Republic of Germany, and the numerous judgments in eighteen cases which had been submitted to the courts of the United States. I concluded:

> So there is no reason in fact why evidence should not be sought and heard, even in Eastern bloc countries. There is no reason of policy why this evidence should be automatically excluded. There is no support in jurisprudence why this effort should be stopped a priori. Thus the law, the facts and the jurisprudence point to the advisability of the Commission pursuing its efforts, even on foreign soil.[8]

As soon as my decision had been rendered, I began discussions through diplomatic channels with a view to organizing examinations of witnesses in the U.S.S.R. and other Eastern bloc countries. For instance, in the cases of two particular suspects, we knew of thirty-four witnesses who, according to the U.S.S.R., were still available. We had received similar information from Poland. But it took seven months to arrive at a first agreement with the U.S.S.R. I was rather proud of the achievement. Indeed, in his book *Quiet Neighbors*, Allan A. Ryan, Jr., had described the agreement between Soviet and American lawyers concern-

---

[7] Commission of Inquiry on War Criminals, Can., *Report of the Commission of Inquiry on War Criminals—Part I (Public)* 869 (1986) [hereinafter Can. Comm'n].

[8] *Id.* at 890.

ing the examination of war crimes witnesses in the U.S.S.R.[9] In my respectful view, our agreement was of superior quality and offered better guarantees of objectivity and authenticity. We were, however, betrayed by the time factor.

D. *Reporting*

I had been requested to report by the end of 1985. I had obtained two extensions, to June 30, then September 30, 1986. The government was legitimately interested in receiving my recommendations without further delay. Now, the work at home was not yet finished. Embarking upon examinations of witnesses abroad would have meant another extension of one, and conceivably two, years. In the context of the times, such a delay, however otherwise justified, was unthinkable. I must therefore conclude and report on the basis of the oral and written evidence at hand.

I filed my report on December 30, 1986. The first part, a printed volume of a thousand pages, was destined for publication.[10] The second part, a five-hundred-page typewritten volume, was confidential; it contains the lists of suspects and twenty-nine detailed opinions on as many particular cases.

The public report contains eighty-two findings and recommendations. On the legal side, the report was aiming at the following results:

>   1. to facilitate the extradition process;
>   2. to allow the prosecution of war criminals in Canada;
>   3. to streamline the process of revocation of citizenship and deportation;
>   4. to prevent the immigration of, or the granting of citizenship to, suspected war criminals.

On the factual side, the report indicated the practical steps which should be taken in order to secure a positive follow-up to the Commis-

---

[9] Allan A. Ryan, Jr., *The Moscow Agreement: Old Allies, New Realities*, in *Quiet Neighbors: Prosecuting Nazi War Criminals in America* 64 (1984).

[10] Can. Comm'n, *supra* note 7.

sion's work in the litigious cases.

In Parliament the report received unanimous approval from the three national parties.

In the country, the Jewish and Ukrainian communities, which had been so often at odds during the inquiry, gave the report an equal mark of satisfaction.

From east to west, public opinion in Canada generally gave the report the warmest praise.

In the United States, Mr. Martin Mendelsohn, the Washington attorney who acted as legal counsel to the Wiesenthal Center in Los Angeles, wrote that the report was "better than anything produced in any country or by any government on the subject of War Criminals."

E. Government Answer

Upon rendering my report public on March 12, 1987, the Minister of Justice, the Honorable Ray Hnatyshyn (until recently Governor-General of Canada), laid before Parliament the government's response to my recommendations. It may be summarized as follows:

> 1. the government agreed with the recommendations dealing with prosecution of suspected war criminals in Canada and would move to amend the laws accordingly;
> 2. the government agreed with the recommendations dealing with immigration and citizenship and would also introduce the required amendments;
> 3. the government did not intend, however, to act on the recommendations dealing with extradition or revocation of citizenship and deportation;
> 4. the government would take the necessary steps to make sure that the investigations would be completed abroad and that, if warranted, prosecutions would be started.

On June 23, 1987, a bill was laid before the House to amend the Criminal Code, the Citizenship Act, and the Immigration Act of

1976 (Bill C-71). It became law on September 16, 1987.[11]

Subsequently, agreements on procedure were concluded between Canada and no less than fourteen countries. But the interesting part is, of course, what has developed since then in practical terms.

F. *Foreign Cases*

Let me first say a word about commissions of inquiry that, along the Canadian model, though with slight differences of approach, were set up in Australia and in the United Kingdom. The Australian Commission submitted its report in November 1986.[12] The Commission had identified some seventy suspects, but its mandate had not permitted it to make an on-site inquiry. Nonetheless, Parliament amended the law in order to permit trials in Australia and three prosecutions were undertaken.

In the *Berezowsky* case, eyewitnesses living in the Ukraine were unable to come to Australia. The complaint was dismissed at the preliminary hearing for lack of evidence.

In the *Polyukhovich* case, the accused faced charges of having taken part in the murder of 850 Jews in the Ukraine when it was under German occupation. The accused first challenged the constitutionality of the new law under which he was being prosecuted. The High Court of Australia, in a four-to-three decision, upheld the challenged legislation.[13] At trial, however, the defense successfully raised objections alleging lack of reliability on the part of witnesses coming from Eastern countries and the jury ultimately acquitted the defendant.

In the *Wagner* case, the accused suffered a heart attack shortly before trial. The defense introduced expert medical opinion that the stress of trial would probably prove fatal to the accused. The prosecu-

---

[11] 1987 S.C., ch. 37 (Can.).

[12] A.C. Menzies, *Review of Material Relating to the Entry of Suspected War Criminals into Australia* (1986).

[13] Polyukhovich v. Australia, 95 A.L.R. 502 (Austl. 1990) (granting stay of criminal proceedings pending decision on defendant's constitutional challenge); Polyukhovich v. Australia, 172 C.L.R. 501 (Austl. 1991) (upholding War Crimes (Amendment) Act, 1988).

tion was then definitely stayed.

The Australian special investigations unit was disbanded in February 1994 after what must be recognized as the utter failure of this effort in Australia to convict Nazis suspected of war crimes.[14]

In the United Kingdom, the Commission made its report in June 1989.[15] It studied 301 cases. The Commission recommended a special inquest in three cases and additional investigation in seventy-five others. The Commission also suggested amending the law to permit prosecutions in the United Kingdom. A bill to this effect was defeated twice in the House of Lords, but the House of Commons persisted and the bill finally passed.[16] There has nevertheless not yet been a single prosecution for war crimes in the United Kingdom, although further evidence has been gathered. At the end of 1994, instructions were expected from the relevant government authority.

In Israel, the *Demjanjuk* case monopolized public attention since the suspect was extradited from the United States. Demjanjuk had held steadfastly that he was the victim of a wrong identification. He was tried by the High Court of Israel, convicted of war crimes, and sentenced to death. Following an automatic appeal to the Supreme Court, both the prosecution and the defense obtained leave to reopen the case and both adduced new evidence. Demjanjuk was given the benefit of the doubt and acquitted by the Supreme Court. He was then returned to the United States.[17]

Strangely enough, after Demjanjuk's return, the United States Court of Appeal for the Sixth Circuit took an extraordinary step: on November 17, 1993, it vacated the original extradition order under

---

[14] For background on the Australian investigations and prosecutions, see Martin Daly, *Australia: Cry for Nazi Justice Ends in a Bitter Whimper*, The Age (Melbourne), Jan. 7, 1994, *available in* LEXIS, Aust Library, Auspub File; Maryann Stenberg, *Australia: End to War Crimes Trials*, Dec. 11, 1993, The Age (Melbourne), *available in* LEXIS, Aust Library, Auspub File.

[15] War Crimes Inquiry, U.K., *War Crimes: Report of the War Crimes Inquiry* (1989).

[16] War Crimes Act, 1991 (U.K.).

[17] Demjanjuk v. Israel (Isr. July 29, 1993) (translation of case unreported as yet but on file with Israeli Embassy, Washington, D.C., U.S.A.).

which Demjanjuk had been sent to Israel.[18] The final dispositive paragraph of the judgment reads as follows:

> For the reasons set out herein we vacate the judgment of the district court and the judgment of this court in the extradition proceedings on the ground that the judgments were wrongly procured as a result of prosecutorial misconduct that constituted fraud on the court.[19]

On that basis, Demjanjuk should never have been extradited and could never have been tried by Israeli courts. He is lucky indeed that the death sentence passed on him had not been executed in the intervening period.

In the United States, several cases are moving through the court system. The practice of the United States is to seek revocation of citizenship, then to deport the alien suspect, usually to his country of origin.

G. *Canadian Results*

In our country, large teams have been summoned together by the Department of Justice and by the R.C.M.P. (Royal Canadian Mounted Police) to carry on the task.

There lingers, however, a feeling of uneasy irony when one stops to think that the inquiry had been triggered to a large extent by the outraged allegations concerning Dr. Josef Mengele's attempt at entering Canada. After a thorough investigation, the Commission had concluded:

> (6) [O]n the basis of the weight of the available evidence, it is established beyond a reasonable doubt that Dr. Joseph (Josef) Mengele has never entered Canada.

---

[18] Demjanjuk v. Petrovsky, 10 F.3d 338 (6th Cir. 1993), *cert. denied sub nom.* Rison v. Demjanjuk, 115 S. Ct. 295 (1994); Steven Lubet, *Disturbing Echoes in U.S. Court Opinion*, Nat'l L.J., Jan. 10, 1994, at 17.

[19] *Demjanjuk*, 10 F.3d at 356.

. . . .

(8) Dr. Joseph (Josef) Mengele did not apply in Buenos Aires in 1962 for a visa to enter Canada, either under his own name or under any of his several known aliases.[20]

Now let us turn to the practical panorama in our country. Five cases have been initiated.

In *Reistetter*, witnesses had died and the Crown was forced to declare, at the opening of the trial, that it had no more evidence to offer. The case was dismissed.

In *Pawlowski*, charged with some five hundred murders in Poland, two Crown motions for leave to collect evidence abroad have been dismissed.[21] The Supreme Court of Canada denied the Crown leave to appeal on February 6, 1992.[22] The case has now been definitely stayed.

In *Finta*, charged essentially with the kidnapping and manslaughter of some eight thousand Jews in Hungary, the accused, who had testified in my inquiry but chose not to take the stand at his trial, was acquitted by the jury.[23] The Court of Appeal of Ontario dismissed the Crown's appeal by a decision of three to two.[24] Leave to appeal was granted to the Crown by the Supreme Court of Canada. The Court, however, also gave Finta leave to raise the question of the constitutionality of the enabling legislation. On March 24, 1994, the Supreme Court dismissed the Crown's appeal by a majority of four to three and the defendant's appeal unanimously, thus finally confirming Finta's

---

[20] Can. Comm'n, *supra* note 7, at 4, 67–85.

[21] On May 4, 1990, and June 21, 1991. Regarding these motions, and the history of this case, see subsequent litigation concerning costs. R. v. Pawlowski, 13 C.R.4th 228 (Ont. Ct. Gen'l Div. 1992) (awarding costs to defendant), *aff'd*, 101 D.L.R.4th 267 (Ont. Ct. App. 1993), *leave to appeal denied*, [1993] 3 S.C.R. viii (Can.).

[22] R. v. Pawlowski, [1992] 1 S.C.R. x (Can.).

[23] R. v. Finta, 61 D.L.R.4th 85 (Can. Ont. High Ct. 1989).

[24] R. v. Finta, 92 D.L.R.4th 1 (Can. Ont. Ct. App. 1992).

acquittal.[25]

The fourth instance is the one case which has been positively concluded insofar as Canada is concerned: the matter of *Jacob Luitjens*. A Dutch citizen, Luitjens had been sentenced at the end of the war to life imprisonment for war crimes. He escaped to South America, where he married and from where he later immigrated to Canada through Vancouver. He acquired Canadian citizenship and became a full professor at the University of British Columbia. His past, however, then came to the surface on the occasion of my inquiry and, in October 1991, the Federal Court of Canada recommended the revocation of his Canadian citizenship.[26]

His appeal was quashed for lack of jurisdiction[27] and he was denied leave to appeal by the Supreme Court of Canada.[28] The federal government then sought an order of deportation and Luitjens was finally returned to the Netherlands on November 27, 1992.

He was jailed upon arrival and his efforts at regaining his

---

[25] R. v. Finta, [1994] 1 S.C.R. 701. This decision has prompted a great deal of controversy. David Vienneau, *Finta Ruling Belittles Holocaust, Says Jewish Congress*, Ottawa Citizen, Apr. 3, 1994, at A10, *available in* LEXIS, Canada Library, Canpub File; David Vienneau, *Supreme Court Asked to Clarify War Crimes Ruling: Government Backs Jewish Groups over Finta Acquittal*, Ottawa Citizen, May 12, 1994, at A1, *available in* LEXIS, Canada Library, Canpub File (noting that Justice Minister Allan Rock had asked lawyers in the federal war crimes unit to support an application to have the case reopened to clarify the law for the benefit of future prosecutions). An application for rehearing from the federal government and private Jewish groups was dismissed. *R. v. Finta*, Nos. 23023 & 23097 (Can. June 23, 1994). A coalition of Montréal synagogues then tried to get the Supreme Court to rehear the case or issue supplementary reasons. Stephen Bindman, *Jews Ask Court to Reconsider Ruling of War-Crimes Law*, Vancouver Sun, Aug. 30, 1994, at A7, *available in* LEXIS, Canada Library, Canpub File. This application was dismissed in December 1994. Stephen Bindman, *Ruling Feared to Favor War Criminals Not Reviewed*, Vancouver Sun, Dec. 27, 1994, at A4, *available in* LEXIS, Canada Library, Canpub File.

[26] Canada (Secretary of State) v. Luitjens, 15 Immigr. L.R.2d 40 (Can. Fed. Ct. Trial Div. 1991).

[27] Canada (Secretary of State) v. Luitjens, 142 N.R. 173 (Can. Fed. Ct. App. 1992).

[28] Canada (Secretary of State) v. Luitjens, [1992] 2 S.C.R. viii (Can.).

freedom were fruitless. He then moved the Queen for a pardon, and in March 1994 his request was granted in part. Due to a change of approach to these cases over the years, the Dutch Minister of Justice said, as well as previous decisions in similar cases, the blameless life of Luitjens since his escape, and his current age—he is now seventy-four—his penalty has been reduced to six years less acquired credits and he will be released at the end of March 1995.

Finally, a fifth case was started in 1993, when charges were preferred against one *Grujicic,* alias *Jankovic,* in Windsor, Ontario. Trial was scheduled for April 1994, where use would probably have been made of evidence collected in Budapest in the previous weeks. The Crown, however, dropped the prosecution, apparently due to the illness and advanced age of the accused.

Whether other prosecutions will be launched is a well-guarded secret within the Department of Justice. Time will tell. But for sure an immense effort has been brought to bear since 1982 on the matter of Nazi war criminals in Canada. One may feel, after twelve years, that the results have not been up to the expectation. But we must remember that the main actors had already been brought to justice in the several trials that were held in Europe and in Asia in the years immediately following the second world war. Furthermore, the forty-five years since then had taken their toll, so that eighty-six of the suspects in Canada had died between 1953 and 1986.

Still, this effort has produced some rather unexpected results in the field of immigration and has made it possible to prevent certain undesirable persons from taking refuge in Canada in the past few years. A few examples, which are far from exhaustive, should allow us to sketch the situation briefly.

Arthur Rudolph, a German scientist, had forced prisoners of war to work under inhumane conditions. The Federal Court of Appeal held that his conduct constituted a crime against humanity.[29] He left Canada before a deportation order could be executed.

In late 1993, the Federal Court of Appeal affirmed the denial of refugee status to a citizen of Sri Lanka because of his participation in

---

[29] Rudolph v. Canada (Minister of Employment and Immigration), [1992] 2 F.C. 653 (Can. Fed. Ct. App.).

crimes against humanity in the context of the Tamil conflict.[30]

Thus, the legislative initiatives undertaken in the wake of the 1986 Commission of Inquiry report have begun to bear fruit. It must be hoped that this jurisprudence will deepen and mature, all the more so because the cases involved have their roots not only in Germany but also, more recently, in Asia.

V — INTERNATIONAL CRIMINAL JUSTICE

May we still hope that the international community will finally take the necessary measures and establish the appropriate institutions to protect the great principles that it has enshrined in the landmark international instruments in this field?

Again, the world community must first muster the political will for this purpose.

Now, there appears to be flowing a majority current of thought favorable as never before to the setting up of a permanent international mechanism to deal with international crimes and their authors.

A. *International Criminal Tribunal for the Former Yugoslavia*

What may be considered a first step has been the creation by the Security Council, last year, of the International Criminal Tribunal for the Former Yugoslavia, le Tribunal pénal international pour l'ex-Yougoslavie.[31] Founded under chapter VII of the Charter of the United

---

[30] Sivakumar v. Canada (Minister of Employment and Immigration), 44 A.C.W.S.3d 563 (Can. Fed. Ct. App. 1993). For further discussion of this topic, see Joseph Rikhof, *War Crimes, Crimes against Humanity, and Immigration Law*, 19 Immigr. L.R.2d 18 (Can. 1993); Alain Joffe, *Les crimes contre l'humanité dans le code criminel: contribution canadienne au droit international [Crimes against Humanity in the Criminal Code: The Canadian Contribution to International Law]* 76–77 nn.221–222 (1993).

[31] S.C. Res. 808, U.N. SCOR, 48th Year, 3175th mtg. at 1, U.N. Doc. S/RES/808 (1993), *reprinted in* appendix A of this issue of *Criminal Law Forum* and *available in* U.N. Gopher\Documents\Security Council Resolutions; S.C. Res. 827, U.N. SCOR, 48th Year, 3217th mtg. at 1, U.N. Doc. S/RES/827 (1993), *reprinted in* appendix A of this issue of *Criminal Law Forum* and *in* 32 I.L.M. 1203.

Nations ("Action with respect to threats to the peace, breaches of the peace, and acts of aggression"), the Tribunal, which has its seat in the Hague, comprises eleven judges coming from the five continents. It is the first time in history that such an independent judicial body has been set up to deal with international criminal conduct.

Strikingly enough, only nine months had elapsed since the decision in principle by the Security Council to set up the Tribunal[32] through the approval of the *Secretary-General's Report* and of the Statute of the Tribunal,[33] the election of the eleven judges by the General Assembly,[34] and the official inauguration of the Tribunal in the Hague.[35]

Starting from scratch and navigating uncharted waters, the judges have been busy drafting their Rules of Procedure and Evidence and trying to strike a satisfactory balance between their acute realization of the necessity of achieving early results and their no less vivid perception of the need for adopting the best possible rules for the conduct of business before this new tribunal. They were faced with a host of questions, for instance:

o how to assure the primacy of the Tribunal over national courts?

o how to assure the smooth functioning of two three-judge trial chambers and one five-judge appeals chamber, with a full

---

[32] S.C. Res. 808, *supra* note 31.

[33] S.C. Res. 827, *supra* note 31; *Report of the Secretary-General pursuant to Paragraph 2 of Security Council Resolution 808 (1993)*, U.N. Doc. S/25704 & Add.1 (1993), *reprinted in* appendix B of this issue of *Criminal Law Forum* and *in* 32 I.L.M. 1163. The Statute of the International Tribunal is set out as an annex to *Secretary-General's Report, supra,* and is *reprinted in* appendix B of this issue of *Criminal Law Forum* and *in* 32 I.L.M. 1192.

[34] G.A. Dec. 47/328, U.N. GAOR, 47th Sess., Supp. No. 49 (vol. II), at 45, U.N. Doc. A/47/49 (1993).

[35] *Report on First Session of International Tribunal for War Crimes in Former Yugoslavia,* U.N. Press Release, U.N. Doc. SC/5767 (Dec. 23, 1993), *available in* U.N. Gopher\Current Information\Press Releases; *International War Crimes Tribunal for Former Yugoslavia Elects Its President, Members of Appeals and Trial Chambers,* Fed. News Serv., Nov. 19, 1993, *available in* LEXIS, World Library, Allnws File.

complement of exactly eleven judges?
- how to guide the prosecutor's investigations?
- how to regulate the judicial approval of indictments?
- how to protect the rights of suspects and accused persons?
- how to organize legal assistance for the indigent?
- how to organize the registry?
- how to obtain the necessary cooperation of states?
- how to determine the parameters of the legality of evidence?
- how to deal with prosecutions involving sexual offenses?
- how to obtain evidence under the perilous conditions of the Yugoslav conflict?
- how to protect victims and witnesses?
- how to organize detention of accused and restitution of property?
- how to regulate the powers of appeal, review, and pardon?

These fourteen questions offer only a sample of the mass of contentious issues which confronted us during our often passionate, but always civilized, debates, when Malaysia and the United States, or Pakistan and France, or Nigeria and Canada had to reconcile their conflicting legal approaches. But as we are wont in Québec, it belonged to the Canadian judge to find himself with the obligation to raise the language issue.

French and English are the two working languages of the Tribunal. But the first draft of the Rules of Procedure and Evidence ended with the following article:

> These rules are done in English and French, the English text being authoritative.

As luck would have it, there was no judge from France present at our deliberations that day: the French judge had just resigned following our first two weeks of work and his successor had not yet taken up his responsibilities. I nonetheless managed to open up the debate with this final article of the draft, declaring myself "adamantly opposed" to it. After having explained my reasons, I suggested replacing this provision with a version inspired by the Canadian Official Languages Act.[36]

The reaction was immediate, and the ten judges present agreed by consensus to replace the disputed article set out in the draft rules with the one just proposed. Canada had insured respect for the French-speaking world within the very heart of the Tribunal. The final text of the rule reads as follows:

> The English and French texts of the Rules shall be equally authentic. In case of discrepancy, the version which is more consonant with the spirit of the Statute and the Rules shall prevail.[37]

To top things off, the Tribunal has just finalized the drafting of the Rules of Procedure and Evidence; it has resolved a series of administrative problems and fervently hopes that with the help of the prosecutor and the cooperation of the states concerned, it can hold its first judicial hearings in the fall of 1994.[38] In the meantime, the momentum toward international criminal justice has again been felt through the setting up

---

[36] 1985 R.S.C., ch. O-3 (Can.).

[37] International Tribunal for the Prosecution of Persons Responsible for Serious Violations of International Humanitarian Law Committed in the Territory of the Former Yugoslavia since 1991, Rules of Procedure and Evidence R. 7, U.N. Doc. IT/32 (1994), *amended by* U.N. Doc. IT/32/Rev.1 (1994), U.N. Doc. IT/32/Rev.2 (1994), U.N. Doc. IT/32/Rev.3 (1995), *reprinted in* appendix C of this issue of *Criminal Law Forum*.

[38] In early November 1994, the Tribunal requested Germany to transfer to its jurisdiction a Bosnian Serb in custody. Peter S. Canellos, *U.N. Tribunal Seeks a Serb: Ethnic Cleansing Alleged as Trial Begins in the Hague,* Boston Globe, Nov. 9, 1994, at 26, *available in* LEXIS, World Library, Allnws File; *Yugo War Crimes Court Asks Germany to Extradite Bosnian Serb,* Agence France Presse, Nov. 8, 1994, *available in* LEXIS, World Library, Allnws File. The first indictment was also handed down at that time. Sara Henley, *U.N. War Crimes Tribunal Charges First Suspect,* Reuters, Nov. 8, 1994, *available in* LEXIS, World Library, Allnws File. Germany amended its law late in 1994 to permit the extradition of foreign residents to the Tribunal and expects to amend the Constitution to permit the extradition of citizens as well. *Bonn Changes Law to Hand Over War Criminals,* Reuters, Dec. 16, 1994, *available in* LEXIS, World Library, Allnws File.

of the International Tribunal for Rwanda,[39] of which I am also a member in the appeals chamber.

B. Permanent International Criminal Court

But there is more to come, namely, a permanent and universal criminal court.

We all know that the General Assembly of the United Nations first devoted its attention to this question in 1948,[40] that a draft statute was produced in the early fifties,[41] and that the matter was then tabled until 1989, when it was revived in the context of illicit drug trafficking.[42]

---

[39] S.C. Res. 955, U.N. SCOR, 49th Year, 3453d mtg. at 1, U.N. Doc. S/RES/955 (1994), *reprinted in* appendix D of this issue of *Criminal Law Forum* and *available in* U.N. Gopher\Documents\Security Council Resolutions.

[40] G.A. Res. 174 (II), U.N. Doc. A/519, at 105 (1947) (establishing the International Law Commission (ILC)); G.A. Res. 177 (II), U.N. Doc. A/519, at 111 (1947) (requesting the ILC to "formulate the principles of international law" embodied in the Nuremberg Charter and judgment and to prepare a "draft code of offences against the peace and security of mankind"); G.A. Res. 260B (III), U.N. Doc. A/810, at 177 (1948) (requesting the ILC to consider also the question of creating an international criminal tribunal, possibly as a chamber of the International Court of Justice).

[41] G.A. Res. 489 (V), U.N. GAOR, 5th Sess., Supp. No. 20, at 77, U.N. Doc. A/1775 (1950) (implementing a suggestion from the ILC to create a separate Committee on International Criminal Jurisdiction to examine the possibility of establishing a permanent international criminal court); *Report of the Committee on International Criminal Jurisdiction on Its Session Held from 1 to 31 August 1951*, U.N. GAOR, 7th Sess., Supp. No. 11, at 21, U.N. Doc. A/2136 (1952) (including a draft statute), *reprinted in* 2 Benjamin Ferencz, *An International Criminal Court: A Step toward World Peace* 337 (1980); *Report of the 1953 Committee on International Criminal Jurisdiction, 27 July–20 August 1953*, U.N. GAOR, 9th Sess., Supp. No. 12, at 23, U.N. Doc. A/2645 (1954) (including a revised statute), *reprinted in* 2 Ferencz, *supra*, at 429.

[42] Remarks by Ms. Thorpe, Representative of Trinidad and Tobago, *International Criminal Responsibility of Individuals and Entities Engaged in Illicit Trafficking in Narcotic Drugs across National Frontiers and Other Transnational Crimes: Establishment of an International Criminal Court with Jurisdiction over Such Crimes*, U.N. GAOR 6th Comm., 44th Sess., 38th mtg. at 8–11, U.N. Doc. A/C.6/44/SR.38 (1989); G.A. Res. 44/39, U.N. GAOR, 44th Sess., Supp. No. 49, at 311, ¶ 1, U.N. Doc. A/44/49 (1989) (requesting the ILC, in its work on the Draft Code of Crimes against the Peace and Security of Mankind, to "address the question of establishing an international criminal

But at the request of the General Assembly,[43] the International Law Commission has, of late, devoted much attention to this question,[44] as has, in parallel fashion, the UN Crime Prevention and Criminal Justice Branch in Vienna.[45]

In September 1990, the Eighth United Nations Congress on the Prevention of Crime and the Treatment of Offenders, held in Havana, Cuba, resolved (in part):

> [T]he possibility might be considered of establishing an international criminal court or appropriate mechanism with each and all

---

court or other international criminal trial mechanism with jurisdiction over persons alleged to have committed crimes which may be covered under such a code of crimes, including persons engaged in illicit trafficking in narcotic drugs across national frontiers").

[43]   G.A. Res. 45/41, U.N. GAOR, 45th Sess., Supp. No. 49A, at 363, ¶ 3, U.N. Doc. A/45/49 (1990) (requesting the ILC, in its work on the Draft Code of Crimes, to consider further the possibility of establishing an international criminal court or other international criminal trial mechanism); G.A. Res. 46/54, U.N. GAOR, 46th Sess., Supp. No. 49, at 286, ¶ 3, U.N. Doc. A/46/49 (1991) (reiterating this request); G.A. Res. 47/33, U.N. GAOR, 47th Sess., Supp. No. 49, at 287, ¶ 6, U.N. Doc. A/47/49 (1992) (requesting the ILC to "continue its work on the question [of an international criminal jurisdiction] by undertaking the project for the elaboration of a draft statute for an international criminal court as a matter of priority"); G.A. Res. 48/31, U.N. GAOR, 48th Sess., Supp. No. 49, at 328, ¶ 6, U.N. Doc. A/48/49 (1993) (requesting the ILC "to continue its work as a matter of priority on this question with a view to elaborating a draft statute, if possible at its forty-sixth session in 1994").

[44]   *Report of the Working Group on the Question of an International Criminal Jurisdiction*, in *Report of the International Law Commission on Its Forty-fourth Session*, U.N. GAOR, 47th Sess., Supp. No. 10, at 143, U.N. Doc. A/47/10 (1992) [hereinafter *ILC 44th Session Report*]; *Report of the Working Group on a Draft Statute for an International Criminal Court*, in *Report of the International Law Commission on Its Forty-fifth Session*, U.N. GAOR, 48th Sess., Supp. No. 10, at 255, U.N. Doc. A/48/10 (1993) [hereinafter *ILC 45th Session Report*]; Draft Statute for an International Criminal Court, in *Report of the International Law Commission on Its Forty-sixth Session*, U.N. GAOR, 49th Sess., Supp. No. 10, at 43, U.N. Doc. A/49/10 (1994) [hereinafter *ILC 46th Session Report*].

[45]   *E.g.*, Report on the International Meeting of Experts on the Establishment of an International Criminal Tribunal (International Centre for Criminal Law Reform and Criminal Justice Policy, Vancouver, British Columbia, Canada, Mar. 22–26, 1993), presented to UN Commission on Crime Prevention and Criminal Justice, 2d sess., Vienna, Apr. 13–23, 1993, U.N. Doc. No. E/CN.15/1993/CRP.8 (1993).

of the procedural and substantive arrangements that might guarantee both its effective operation and absolute respect for the sovereignty and the territorial and political integrity of States and the self-determination of peoples.[46]

The end of the resolution was evidently designed to assuage the objections of those states for which sovereignty is an absolute and intangible dogma. They are, however, fighting a losing battle in a world where interdependence is now the keyword; and the demonstration has been made that a mechanism can be devised which would be both legally efficient and politically respectful of state entities.

Indeed, in its report of July 1992, the International Law Commission took the position that it had "completed the task of analysis" and requested from the General Assembly a clear mandate to draft a statute for an international criminal court.[47] In her speech in September 1992 to the General Assembly, the then Secretary of State for External Affairs, the Honorable Barbara McDougall, stated that Canada strongly supported such a mandate.[48]

This already involved a few clear choices, though some basic questions remained unresolved. But given political goodwill, none of those obstacles appeared insurmountable. In October 1992 I could therefore state, in placing before the Sixth Committee of the General Assembly the position of Canada:

> Such a body [an international criminal court] would, we believe, strengthen the principle of universal jurisdiction over individuals who have committed international criminal acts, objectively and uniformly implementing criminal liability provisions found in

---

[46] Resolution on Terrorist Criminal Activities, in *Eighth United Nations Congress on the Prevention of Crime and the Treatment of Offenders, Havana, 27 August–7 September 1990: Report Prepared by the Secretariat* 181, 187, U.N. Doc. A/CONF.144/28/Rev.1, U.N. Sales No. E.91.IV.2 (1991).

[47] *ILC 44th Session Report, supra* note 44, at 146.

[48] Ian Waddell, Editorial, *A Force to Reckon With: How and Why an International Court Would Help Keep Peace*, Vancouver Sun, Oct. 10, 1992, at A17, *available in* LEXIS, Canada Library, Canpub File.

existing treaty law. This would, we hope, have a significant deterrent value.

> ... [W]e can now confidently call upon the International Law Commission to move as quickly as possible in its work on a draft statute.

Several voices echoed this view. I could quote at random the European Community through its British representative, Japan, the Nordic countries through their Norwegian representative, France, and Nigeria.

The United States did not share this general enthusiasm and pleaded for another year's delay. But the plea went unheeded and, on November 25, 1992, the General Assembly, having expressed its satisfaction with the work of the International Law Commission, requested it to "undertak[e] the project for the elaboration of a draft statute for an international criminal court as a matter of priority as from its next session ... with a view to drafting a statute on the basis of the report of the Working Group."[49]

Setting down to work with remarkable dispatch, the International Law Commission (ILC) devoted to the task its session of May, June, and July 1993 and produced, on July 19, 1993, an all-encompassing draft statute of sixty-seven articles with accompanying commentary.[50] This statute aims at establishing an international criminal tribunal of eighteen judges elected for a single term of twelve years. The court would sit in chambers of five judges. Appeals would be lodged before an appeals chamber of seven judges. At the beginning, at least, this court would not be a full-time body. The judges would receive no annual salary, but a daily allowance plus expenses. The court would have jurisdiction over a large number of offenses defined by treaties, such as genocide, grave breaches of the 1949 Geneva Conventions, apartheid, seizure of aircraft, hostage-taking, and acts against the safety of maritime navigation.

But states would have to confer jurisdiction upon the court over such crimes as they chose. States, or the Security Council, would have the capacity to lay a complaint. Upon a finding of guilt, the court could

---

[49] G.A. Res. 47/33, *supra* note 43, ¶ 6.
[50] See generally *ILC 45th Session Report*, *supra* note 44, at 258–335.

pass a sentence of fine, jail, or return of property, but not the death sentence.

An interesting aspect of the proposal is the discussion of whether separate or dissenting opinions should be allowed in parallel with the judgment of the court. Strong views were expressed in favor of both theses, but the negative opinion finally carried the day.[51]

In its comments of October 25, 1993, Canada, while fully supporting the project, said:

> To assist the Appeals Chamber in its work, Canada believes that provision should be made in Article 51 to enable dissenting judges to express their opinion.[52]

This opinion did not prevail and the ILC stood by its original view of a single judgment when it issued its final report on July 14, 1994.[53] This report proposed a draft statute for an international criminal court and recommended the adoption of a convention to that end.[54] This proposal, while drawing wide support, ran into strong opposition, in particular from the United States. On November 23, 1994, the Sixth Committee decided, in substance,

> (1) to establish an ad hoc committee open to all UN member states and members of specialized agencies to review the "major substantive and administrative issues arising out of the draft statute" and consider the "convening of an international conference of plenipotentiaries";
> (2) to instruct the ad hoc committee to report to the next General Assembly;

---

[51] *Id.* at 315–16.

[52] Remarks by Barry Mawhinney, Representative of Canada, U.N. GAOR 6th Comm., 48th Sess., 18th mtg. at 7, U.N. Doc. A/C.6/48/SR.18 (1993).

[53] Draft Statute for an International Criminal Court art. 45(5), in *ILC 46th Session Report, supra* note 44, at 122 ("The judgment shall be in writing and shall contain a full and reasoned statement of the findings and conclusions. It shall be the sole judgement issued . . . .").

[54] *Id.* at 43.

(3) to invite written comments from member states and the relevant international organs on the ILC's draft statute;

(4) to ask the Secretary-General to prepare estimates for the establishment and operation of an international criminal court;

(5) to study during the next session of the General Assembly the report of the ad hoc committee and the written comments by states and to "decide on the convening of an international conference of plenipotentiaries to conclude a convention on the establishment of an international criminal court."[55]

VI—THE FUTURE

Thus we may see, during the very next few years, a universal criminal court taking its place side by side with the present International Court of Justice. Criminal and civil justice would take their equal place in the world, and humankind's dream of many years would become a reality.

That day will be the greatest day for the defenders of human rights since the adoption of the Universal Declaration of Human Rights. Our friends Professors John P. Humphrey[56] and Irwin Cotler[57] will be

---

[55] *Report of the Sixth Committee*, U.N. GAOR, 49th Sess., Agenda Item 137, U.N. Doc. A/49/738, at 17-18 (1994). The General Assembly adopted the Sixth Committee's resolution without a vote. G.A. Res. 49/53, U.N. GAOR, 49th Sess., 84th plen. mtg., U.N. Doc. A/49/53 (1994).

[56] Professor Humphrey, Faculty of Law, McGill University, was the first Director of the UN Division of Human Rights (as it was then called), a position he held for 20 years. He was instrumental in putting together the original draft of the Universal Declaration of Human Rights. For his memoirs, see John P. Humphrey, *Human Rights and the United Nations: A Great Adventure* (1984).

[57] Professor Cotler, Faculty of Law, McGill University, a widely known human rights activist, is the founding President of InterAmicus, under whose auspices this lecture was given. He was instrumental in obtaining the release from a Soviet prison of the well-known dissenter Natan Sharansky. In this connection, see Irwin Cotler, *Inside the Gulag*, Jerusalem Post, Nov. 2, 1990, *available in* LEXIS, World Library, Allnws File. He also appeared as counsel before the Israeli Supreme Court in the *Demjanjuk* case. For his

able to see in this, with genuine pride, the culmination of a lifetime of effort, in a direct line from the precedent set by René Cassin.

---

reflections on this decision, see Irwin Cotler, *Unreasonable in the Extreme*, Jerusalem Post, Aug. 17, 1993, *available in* LEXIS, World Library, Allnws File.

II
Fact-Finding

3

The Commission of Experts Established pursuant to Security Council Resolution 780: Investigating Violations of International Humanitarian Law in the Former Yugoslavia*

M. Cherif Bassiouni**

THE COMMISSION'S ESTABLISHMENT

On October 6, 1992, the Security Council adopted Resolution 780, establishing a Commission of Experts to investigate and collect evidence on "grave breaches of the Geneva Conventions and other violations of international humanitarian law" in the conflict in the

---

*   *Editor's note:* research for this article was updated through February 14, 1995.

**   Former Chairman and Rapporteur on the Gathering and Analysis of Facts, Commission of Experts Established pursuant to Security Council Resolution 780 (1992); Professor of Law and President, International Human Rights Law Institute, DePaul University, Chicago, Illinois, United States; President, International Association of Penal Law, Paris, France; President, International Institute of Higher Studies in Criminal Sciences, Siracusa, Italy; J.D., Indiana University 1964; LL.M., John Marshall School of Law 1966; S.J.D., George Washington University 1973; Dottore in Guirisprudenza Honoris Causa, University of Torino 1979; Docteur en Droit (d'Etat) Honoris Causa, University of Pau 1988.

The views expressed herein are those of the author and do not represent the views of the Commission of Experts or the United Nations. The assistance of Carolyn Durnik, Assistant Project Director of the IHRLI Database Project, and David Gualtieri, IHRLI Staff Attorney, is gratefully acknowledged.

former Yugoslavia.[1] Not since the International Military Tribunal at Nuremberg (1945)[2] had the world community taken collective action to provide for an international body to investigate violations of international humanitarian law with a view to prosecuting its perpetrators before an ad hoc international tribunal.[3]

On February 22, 1993, following the submission of the Commission's *First Interim Report*, which stated that the establishment of an ad hoc international criminal tribunal would be "consistent with the direction of its work,"[4] the Security Council provided for such a

---

[1] S.C. Res. 780, U.N. SCOR, 47th Year, 1992 S.C. Res. & Dec. at 36, ¶ 2, U.N. Doc. S/INF/48 (1992), *reprinted in* appendix A of this issue of *Criminal Law Forum*. *See generally* M. Cherif Bassiouni, Current Developments, *The United Nations Commission of Experts Established Pursuant to Security Council Resolution 780 (1992)*, 88 Am. J. Int'l L. 784 (1994).

[2] Agreement for the Prosecution and Punishment of the Major War Criminals of the European Axis, Aug. 8, 1945, 82 U.N.T.S. 279 (London Agreement). The Charter of the International Military Tribunal at Nuremberg is set out in *id.* at 284.

[3] On the basis of the precedent of the former Yugoslavia, the Security Council established a similar Commission of Experts to investigate violations in the Rwandan civil war. S.C. Res. 935, U.N. SCOR, 49th Year, 3400th mtg. at 1, U.N. Doc. S/RES/935 (1994), *reprinted in* appendix D of this issue of *Criminal Law Forum* and *available in* U.N. Gopher\Documents\Security Council Resolutions. This Commission submitted a preliminary report in the early fall of 1994. Letter from the Secretary-General to the President of the Security Council, Oct. 1, 1994, U.N. Doc. S/1994/1125 (1994), transmitting *Preliminary Report of the Independent Commission of Experts Established in Accordance with Security Council Resolution 935 (1994), available in* U.N. Gopher\Current Information\Secretary-General's Reports. The Security Council set up a judicial mechanism about a month later, with institutional ties to the International Tribunal for the Former Yugoslavia. The relevant resolution adopts and annexes the Tribunal's Statute. S.C. Res. 955, U.N. SCOR, 49th Year, 3453d mtg. at 1, U.N. Doc. S/RES/955 (1994), *reprinted in* appendix D of this issue of *Criminal Law Forum* and *available in* U.N. Gopher\Documents\Security Council Resolutions. The Commission subsequently submitted its final report. Letter from the Secretary-General to the President of the Security Council, Dec. 9, 1994, U.N. Doc. S/1994/1405 (1994), transmitting *Final Report of the Commission of Experts Established pursuant to Security Council Resolution 935 (1994), available in* U.N. Gopher\Current Information\Secretary-General Reports.

[4] Letter from the Secretary-General to the President of the Security Council, Feb. 9, 1993, U.N. Doc. S/25274 (1993), transmitting *Interim Report of the Commission of Experts Established pursuant to Security Council Resolution 780 (1992)*, ¶ 74 [hereinafter *First Interim Report*].

tribunal.⁵ Through Resolution 808, the Security Council

> *[d]ecide[d]* that an international criminal tribunal shall be established for the prosecution of persons responsible for serious violations of international humanitarian law committed in the territory of the former Yugoslavia since 1991[.]⁶

In its deliberations on this matter, the Security Council had considered three initial proposals for the establishment of a tribunal for the former Yugoslavia, presented by France, by Italy, and by Sweden on behalf of the Conference on Security and Cooperation in Europe (CSCE).⁷

---

⁵ S.C. Res. 808, U.N. SCOR, 48th Year, 3175th mtg. at 1, U.N. Doc. S/RES/808 (1993), *reprinted in* appendix A of this issue of *Criminal Law Forum* and *available in* U.N. Gopher\Documents\Security Council Resolutions.

⁶ *Id.* ¶ 1.

⁷ Letter from the Permanent Representative of France to the Secretary-General, Feb. 10, 1993, U.N. Doc. S/25266 (1993), transmitting a report on the establishment of an international criminal tribunal for the former Yugoslavia prepared by a national Committee of Jurists; Letter from the Permanent Representative of Italy to the Secretary-General, Feb. 16, 1993, U.N. Doc. S/25300 (1993), transmitting a draft statute for an international criminal tribunal for the former Yugoslavia prepared by a national Commission of Jurists; Letter from the Permanent Representative of Sweden to the Secretary-General, Feb. 18, 1993, U.N. Doc. S/25307 (1993), annexing a summary of CSCE Rapporteurs (Corell–Turk–Thune), Moscow Human Dimension Mechanism to Bosnia, Herzegovina, and Croatia, *Proposal for an International War Crimes Tribunal for the Former Yugoslavia* (1993), and the text of a decision by CSCE participating states on this proposal. All three submissions were inspired by M. Cherif Bassiouni, *Draft Statute for the Establishment of an International Criminal Tribunal* (Association Internationale de Droit Pénal, Nouvelles Études Penales No. 9, 1992); *see also* M. Cherif Bassiouni, *A Draft International Criminal Code and Draft Statute for an International Criminal Tribunal* (2d rev. ed. 1987). Following the French, Italian, and CSCE submissions, a number of other governments and organizations forwarded comments or proposals, including Russia, Letter from the Permanent Representative of the Russian Federation to the Secretary-General, Apr. 5, 1993, U.N. Doc. S/25537 (1993); the United States, Letter from the Permanent Representative of the United States of America to the Secretary-General, Apr. 5, 1993, U.N. Doc. S/25575 (1993); and the Organization of the Islamic Conference, Letter from the Permanent Representatives of Egypt, Iran, Malaysia, Pakistan, Saudi Arabia, Senegal, and Turkey, on behalf of the Organization of the Islamic Conference, to the Secretary-General, Mar. 31, 1993, U.N. Doc. S/25512 (1993).

Pursuant to Resolution 808, the Secretary-General submitted a report to the Security Council on May 3, 1993.[8] The *Secretary-General's Report* includes the Statute of the International Tribunal for the Prosecution of Persons Responsible for Serious Violations of International Humanitarian Law Committed in the Territory of the Former Yugoslavia since 1991.[9] On May 25, 1993, the Security Council unanimously approved Resolution 827, establishing an International Tribunal "for the sole purpose of prosecuting persons responsible for serious violations of international humanitarian law committed in the territory of the former Yugoslavia," and it adopted the proposed statute without change.[10] The Security Council stated further that

> pending the appointment of the Prosecutor of the International Tribunal, the Commission of Experts established pursuant to resolution 780 (1992) should continue on an urgent basis the collection of information relating to evidence of grave breaches of the Geneva Conventions and other violations of international humanitarian law as proposed in its interim report.[11]

---

[8] *Report of the Secretary-General pursuant to Paragraph 2 of Security Council Resolution 808 (1993)*, U.N. Doc. S/25704 & Add.1 (1993), *reprinted in* appendix B of this issue of *Criminal Law Forum* and *in* 32 I.L.M. 1163 [hereinafter *Secretary-General's Report*].

[9] The Statute of the International Tribunal is set out as an annex to *Secretary-General's Report, supra* note 8, and is *reprinted in* appendix B of this issue of *Criminal Law Forum* and *in* 32 I.L.M. 1192 [hereinafter *Statute*].

[10] S.C. Res. 827, U.N. SCOR, 48th Year, 3217th mtg. at 1, ¶ 2, U.N. Doc. S/RES/827 (1993), *reprinted in* appendix A of this issue of *Criminal Law Forum* and *in* 32 I.L.M. 1203.

[11] *Id.* preambular ¶ 10. The Commission's work was ended on April 30, 1994, even though there was no prosecutor in office at that time. The Secretary-General had formally nominated me for this post in August 1993. The Security Council decided to act on the nomination by "consensus," instead of by vote, and consensus was not reached on my candidacy. *See* Paul Lewis, *Disputes Hamper U.N. Drive for a War Crimes Tribunal,* N.Y. Times, Sept. 9, 1993, at A10, *available in* LEXIS, World Library, Allnws File; Stanley Meisler, *U.N. Is Deadlocked on War-Crimes Prosecutor,* Montreal Gazette, Sept. 12, 1993, at B1, *available in* LEXIS, World Library, Allnws File. The Security Council later reached a consensus on Ramón Escovar-Salom, from Venezuela. S.C. Res.

The Commission of Experts was, therefore, the first stage in the establishment of the Tribunal. This article discusses the history of the Commission, the methods used to gather evidence, and the Commission's findings, which form the basis for the Tribunal's prosecutions.

THE COMMISSION'S MANDATE AND COMPOSITION

Security Council Resolution 780 established the Commission's mandate as follows, requesting the Secretary-General

> to establish, as a matter of urgency, an impartial Commission of Experts to examine and analyse the information submitted pursuant to resolution 771 (1992) and the present resolution, together with such further information as the Commission of Experts may obtain through its own investigations or efforts, of other persons or bodies pursuant to resolution 771 (1992), with a view to providing the Secretary-General with its conclusions on the evidence of grave breaches of the Geneva Conventions and other violations of international humanitarian law committed in the territory of the former Yugoslavia[.][12]

877, U.N. SCOR, 48th Sess., 3296th mtg. at 1, U.N. Doc. S/RES/877 (1993), *available in* U.N. Gopher\Documents\Security Council Resolutions. Escovar-Salom soon resigned, without taking office, in order to assume the position of Minister of the Interior of Venezuela. *Bosnia — Venezuela: Boutros-Ghali Accepts Prosecutor's Resignation,* Inter Press Serv., Feb. 8, 1994, *available in* LEXIS, World Library, Allnws File; *Secretary-General Appoints Graham Blewitt as Acting Deputy Prosecutor, War Crimes Tribunal, for Humanitarian Law Violations in Former Yugoslavia,* U.N. Press Release, U.N. Doc. SG/SM/5221 (Feb. 8, 1994), *available in* U.N. Gopher\Current Information\Press Releases. Nearly half a year later, the Secretary-General recommended Judge Richard J. Goldstone of South Africa to fill the vacancy, the Security Council agreed, and Judge Goldstone took office on August 15, 1994. S.C. Res. 936, U.N. SCOR, 49th Year, 3401st mtg. at 1, U.N. Doc. S/RES/936 (1994), *available in* U.N. Gopher\Documents\Security Council Resolutions; Paul Lewis, *South African Is to Prosecute Balkan War Crimes,* N.Y. Times, July 9, 1994, at A2, *available in* LEXIS, World Library, Allnws File; *Yugoslav War Crimes Prosecutor Delays Mission,* Reuters, Aug. 26, 1994, *available in* LEXIS, World Library, Allnws File.

[12] S.C. Res. 780, *supra* note 1, ¶ 2.

The Commission interpreted its mandate as requiring the collection of all possibly relevant information and evidence concerning violations of international humanitarian law that it could secure given its resources and capabilities.[13]

Resolution 780 reiterated the Council's previous request in Resolution 771 that governments and organizations submit reports to the Security Council containing information relating to violations of international humanitarian law, including grave breaches of the Geneva Conventions of 1949.[14] The later resolution, however, called upon governments, UN bodies, intergovernmental organizations (IGOs), and nongovernmental organizations (NGOs) to make such information available specifically to the Commission of Experts.[15] Subsequently, in Resolution 787, the Security Council welcomed the establishment of the Commission and requested it "to pursue actively its investigations" of "grave breaches . . . and other violations of international humanitarian law."[16] Resolution 787 also reasserted the UN's condemnation of all violations of international humanitarian law, including the practice of "ethnic cleansing" and the deliberate obstruction of the delivery of food

---

[13] There were suggestions at the first session of the Commission by then Under-Secretary-General for Legal Affairs and UN Legal Counsel Carl-August Fleischhauer that the term "evidence" was not to be construed in its technical sense as understood in criminal law. This issue was of concern to the Commission, as was the question of the resources needed to secure legally relevant and admissible evidence. Thus, the information and evidence that the Commission gathered, as well as the reports that it prepared, were not compiled with a view that they would be used exclusively by the prosecutor as evidence but also would have a more general purpose of describing the policies, patterns, and outcomes of violations.

[14] S.C. Res. 771, U.N. SCOR, 47th Year, 1992 S.C. Res. & Dec. at 25, ¶ 5, U.N. Doc. S/INF/48 (1992).

[15] S.C. Res. 780, *supra* note 1, ¶ 1. At the time, very few reports were submitted by governments. Additionally, some reports, such as those of the United States, contained mostly NGO- and media-generated information, which was in the public domain. None of the information and evidence available to governments with intelligence-gathering capabilities was submitted. See *infra* sections entitled "Critical Assessment of the Information Received" and "Reports from Governments."

[16] S.C. Res. 787, U.N. SCOR, 47th Year, 1992 S.C. Res. & Dec. at 29, ¶ 8, U.N. Doc. S/INF/48 (1992).

and medical supplies to the civilian population of Bosnia–Herzegovina.[17] It also reaffirmed that those who committed or ordered the commission of such acts would be held individually responsible.[18]

Although Resolution 780 did not specify the size of the Commission, Secretary-General Boutros Boutros-Ghali appointed five persons in their individual capacity on the basis of their expertise and integrity.[19] The Commission members did not represent their governments, ensuring the political independence and impartiality of this fact-finding body. The original five Commission members appointed by the Secretary-General included Professor Frits Kalshoven, Emeritus Professor of International Humanitarian Law at the University of Leiden (the Netherlands), as Chairman of the Commission of Experts; Commander William Fenrick, Director of Law for Operations and Training in the Department of Defence (Canada); the Hon. Keba M'Baye, former President of the Supreme Court of Senegal, former President of the Constitutional Council of Senegal, and former President of the International Court of Justice (Senegal); Professor Torkel Opsahl, Professor of Human Rights Law at Oslo University, President of the Norwegian Institute of Human Rights, and former member of the UN Committee on Human Rights and the European Commission on Human Rights (Norway); and myself, Professor of Law at DePaul University College of Law and President of DePaul University's International Human Rights Law Institute (Egypt).[20]

---

[17] *Id.* ¶ 7.

Editor's note: While we condemn the policy and practice of "ethnic cleansing" in the strongest terms, this term is so widely understood and used by the public and the media to refer to a policy and acts of genocide that quotations marks appear redundant and are used only to introduce the term.

[18] *Id.*

[19] *Report of the Secretary-General on the Establishment of the Commission of Experts pursuant to Paragraph 2 of Security Council Resolution 780 (1992)*, U.N. Doc. S/24657 (1992). This report to the Security Council left open the possibility that the Commission might be enlarged, but this did not occur.

[20] Though a naturalized U.S. citizen, I was appointed on the basis of my citizenship of origin, as it had been decided not to have experts from the permanent members of the Security Council.

In August 1993, Professor Kalshoven took an indefinite medical leave and subsequently resigned his chairmanship. Professor Opsahl served as acting chairman from then until his sudden death on September 16, 1993.[21] As a consequence of the resignation of Kalshoven and the death of Opsahl, the Secretary-General reconstituted the Commission. On October 19, 1993, he announced my appointment as Chairman of the Commission of Experts and the appointments of Professor Christine Cleiren, Professor of Criminal Law, Erasmus University of Rotterdam (the Netherlands); and the Hon. Hanne Sophie Greve, Judge of the Court of Appeals of Bergen (Norway), to fill the vacancies on the Commission.[22]

THE COMMISSION'S FINANCES

The Commission did not have an independent budget, nor did the United Nations provide resources for investigation and data collection.[23] The UN Office of Legal Affairs (OLA) provided limited support for the work of the Commission in the form of personnel and some of the

---

[21] In a letter to the Security Council, the Secretary-General noted Professor Opsahl's important contribution to the work of the Commission and described his untimely death as a great loss to the Commission, the United Nations, and the international legal community. Letter from the Secretary-General to the President of the Security Council ¶ 4, Oct. 5, 1993, U.N. Doc. S/26545 (1993), transmitting *Second Interim Report of the Commission of Experts Established pursuant to Security Council Resolution 780 (1992)* [hereinafter *Second Interim Report*].

[22] *Id.; Women Legal Experts Named to U.N. War Crimes Panel*, Reuters, Oct. 21, 1993, *available in* LEXIS, World Library, Allnws File.

[23] The United Nations funds its bodies through the regular budget, which is first approved by the Advisory Committee on Administrative and Budgetary Questions (ACABQ) and then by the Fifth Committee of the General Assembly. The Security Council funds peacekeeping activities through a special budget. Neither organ funded the Commission, and its ability to fulfill its mandate was seriously hampered as a result. The lesson here is that when the Security Council establishes a body like the Commission of Experts, it should probably fund it through its peacekeeping budget and set the budget of the new entity at the time it is created.

Commission members' travel and per diem expenses. In addition, the Secretary-General established a voluntary trust fund on March 26, 1993, although the Secretariat did not act on this matter until May 24, 1993, when letters were sent to UN member states inviting contributions.[24]

For a period of nine months (December 1, 1992–August 31, 1993), the United Nations funded the cost of travel and honoraria of the Commission members; the salary of the chairman (the only full-time Commission member); and the salary of two (later three) OLA-seconded professional staff members, two secretaries, and (later) an administrative clerk. From August 1993 to April 1994, no budget existed for the Commission, although the OLA continued to contribute the personnel mentioned above. Since no other UN resources were forthcoming, the Commission used the monies from the voluntary trust fund to cover its operating costs, as well as to fund its investigations. It is unclear why the OLA, which serviced the Commission, failed to present a budget request to the ACABQ and the General Assembly's Fifth Committee to fund the Commission, even though the budget request for January 1–July 31, 1994, had been prepared by the Commission and forwarded to the OLA in due time.[25]

---

[24] Because of this delay (for which no explanation was given), funds were not available to the Commission until July–August 1993. The following countries contributed a total of $1,320,631: Austria, $20,000; Canada, $237,869; Czech Republic, $1,000; Denmark, $15,201; Germany, $16,000; Hungary, $3,000; Iceland, $500; Liechtenstein, $3,184; Micronesia, $300; Morocco, $5,000; the Netherlands, $260,152; New Zealand, $53,492; Norway, $49,978; Sweden, $94,955; Switzerland, $50,000; Turkey, $10,000; the United States, $500,000. Letter from the Secretary-General to the President of the Security Council, May 24, 1994, U.N. Doc. S/1994/674 (1994), transmitting *Final Report of the Commission of Experts Established pursuant to Security Council Resolution 780 (1992),* ¶¶ 12–17 & n.4, *available in* U.N. Gopher\Current Information\Secretary-General's Reports [hereinafter *Final Report*].

[25] Deputy UN Legal Counsel Ralph Zacklin told Iain Guest, a journalist who wrote a report for the Open Society Institute (unpublished manuscript, on file with Cherif Bassiouni) on the prosecution of war criminals, that he "forgot" to present the Commission's budget to the ACABQ in November because of other pressing business. As a result, the ACABQ did not fund the Commission's 1994 budget. The Secretary-General reportedly agreed with Mr. Fleischhauer on terminating the Commission prematurely, even though the Commission still had over $230,000 in the voluntary trust fund on April 30, 1994. Since the Commission's monthly costs at that time were

Because of these financial constraints, the Commission turned to governments for contributed personnel and volunteers. Certain governments did indeed provide personnel to the Commission, as did Physicians for Human Rights, and an ad hoc group of legal and mental health experts volunteered their services as well.[26] In addition, the Commission's database project, discussed below, was funded by the DePaul University International Human Rights Law Institute (IHRLI) through private grants it obtained.[27]

Considering the Commission's mandate and the extent and range of the violations reported,[28] it is incomprehensible that no resources were

---

approximately $50,000, it could easily have continued until July 31 and completed its work.

[26] Personnel were made available as follows: Canada, military lawyers and investigators seconded to participate in investigations in Sarajevo, Dobrinja, Dubrovnik, Medak, and United Nations Protected Area (UNPA) Sector West, Croatia; the Netherlands, combat engineers, including radiological experts to perform mass grave and radiological investigations, and experts in finding unmarked graves—whose contribution was vital to the success of the mass graves investigation in UNPA Sector West, Croatia; Norway, military lawyers who worked on the Dubrovnik investigation. Governments also contributed personnel to the Commission's secretariat in Geneva: France, the Hon. Jean-Paul Laborde; the Netherlands, Lieutenant-Colonel Anton Kempenaars; Norway, Morten Bergsmo.

Physicians for Human Rights contributed three different teams to investigate the mass grave at Ovcara/Vukovar and to conduct the exhumations in UNPA Sector West, Croatia, totaling 24 experts whose services were funded by the United States and private sources. These teams were led by world-renowned forensic experts Dr. Clyde Snow, Dr. Robert Kirschner, and Dr. Eric Stover (Executive Director of Physicians for Human Rights).

An international team of female attorneys and mental health experts and male mental health specialists volunteered to conduct the rape and sexual assault investigation. See *infra* note 79.

On these various projects, see *infra* section entitled "The Commission's On-site Investigations."

[27] IHRLI received grants from the Soros Foundation, the Open Society Fund, and the John D. and Catherine T. MacArthur Foundation.

[28] The scale of victimization in the former Yugoslavia is staggering. The Commission reported that of a population of 6 million, 1.5–2 million are now refugees abroad after being deported or forced to flee their homes. *Final Report, supra* note 24, ¶ 310 n.87. In addition, civilian and military casualties reportedly exceeded 200,000 at

made available through the regular UN budget process for either the investigations or the operating expenses of the Commission. Even the voluntary trust fund, which had been informally requested by the Commission at its first meeting (November 1992) and formally in its *First Interim Report* (February 1993) was not communicated to member states until the end of May 1993, delaying the collection of funds. The exceptional results achieved by the Commission were due to the contribution of personnel referred to above, to monies donated to the voluntary trust fund, and to foundation and university support of the IHRLI database project. But these resources were extremely limited.

THE COMMISSION'S WORKING METHODS

From November 1992 to April 1994, the Commission held twelve sessions, at which the members discussed a number of substantive, methodological, and organizational problems related to the Commission's mandate.[29] At the third session (January 25–26, 1993), the Commission

---

the time the Commission's *Final Report* was published. *Id.* The high estimated number of casualties is supported by the reported discovery of 187 mass graves. *Id.* ¶¶ 254–264. In addition, over 700 prison camps were reported, where violations such as rape and torture occurred. *Id.* ¶¶ 216–231. Further study of the documents received by the Commission indicated that there were reportedly 960 places of detention. *Final Report of the Commission of Experts Established pursuant to Security Council Resolution 780 (1992),* Annex VIII: *Prison Camps* ¶ 9, U.N. Doc. S/1994/674/Add.2 (Vol. IV) (1994). Some 3,000 rape cases were reported. *Final Report, supra* note 24, ¶¶ 232–253. From the high number of these incident reports, the Commission surmised that earlier projections by various sources of 20,000 cases of rape were not completely unreasonable. *Id.* ¶ 310 n.87.

[29] Sessions were held on the following dates: first session, November 4–5, 1992; second session, December 14–16, 1992; third session, January 25–26, 1993; fourth session, March 1–3, 1993; fifth session, May 24–25, 1993; sixth session, July 13–14, 1993; seventh session, August 30–31, 1993; eighth session, October 27, 1993; ninth session, December 14–15, 1993; tenth session, January 11–12, 1994; eleventh session, February 15–16, 1994; twelfth session, April 11–15, 1994. All of the sessions, except the first, which was convened in New York, were held in Geneva. *Final Report, supra* note 24, ¶ 9 n.1.

formally adopted Rules of Procedure, which defined its working methods.[30] The Commission also at this time formally appointed rapporteurs for several general and specific issues. Commander William Fenrick was appointed Rapporteur for On-site Investigations and Rapporteur on Issues of Law, and I was appointed Rapporteur for the Gathering and Analysis of Facts. In November 1993, the Hon. Hanne Sophie Greve and the Hon. Keba M'Baye were appointed, respectively, Rapporteur for the Prijedor Project and Rapporteur on the Destruction of Cultural Property. Professor Christine Cleiren was asked to prepare a report on the legal aspects of rape and sexual assault.

The Commission relied on three methods in its work: (1) collection and analysis of data sent to, or requested by, the Commission; (2) on-site investigative missions in the former Yugoslavia or in other countries to interview witnesses, collect additional information, and verify facts; and (3) collection of information by governments on the Commission's behalf.[31] The materials available to the Commission included reports from governments, UN bodies, NGOs, and IGOs; victim and witness statements; and reports by the media and other public sources. This information was forwarded to IHRLI for entry into the database and for analysis, as discussed below.

DATA GATHERING BY THE COMMISSION SECRETARIAT AND THE RAPPORTEUR FOR THE GATHERING AND ANALYSIS OF FACTS

Both the Commission Secretariat and I in my role as Rapporteur for the Gathering and Analysis of Facts actively pursued many avenues of information gathering and developed links with a variety of sources, including the state War Crimes Commissions of Bosnia–Herzegovina,

---

[30] Commission of Experts Established pursuant to Security Council Resolution 780 (1992), Rules of Procedure [hereinafter Comm'n Rules], in *First Interim Report, supra* note 4, at 21–23. These rules were informally adopted at the December 1992 meeting after having been generally agreed upon at the November 1992 meeting.

[31] *Final Report, supra* note 24, ¶ 19.

Croatia, and the Federal Republic of Yugoslavia (Yugoslavia). These bodies were given copies of the IHRLI database to help make their data input uniform. Close contacts were also developed with other national organizations, NGOs, the media, and individuals in more than forty countries.

Video Archive

My staff and I gathered valuable information from print,[32] broadcast, and electronic media, including LEXIS/NEXIS and the Foreign Broadcast Information Service (FBIS). In addition to a survey of international print media, a video library was assembled, containing media-generated and other sources of footage depicting violations of international humanitarian law. Footage was obtained from the major U.S. and European television networks—such as ABC, NBC, CBS, and CNN in the United States; the BBC and ITN in the United Kingdom; and various French, Italian, Austrian, and German television stations. In addition, footage from within the former Yugoslavia was gathered from FRY-RTV Belgrade, Studio One Belgrade, Croatian TV in Zagreb, Bosnian TV in Sarajevo, and other local stations. Footage was also obtained from local citizens who taped both personal accounts and unfolding events with home recorders. Altogether, an archive of more than three hundred videotapes was compiled.[33]

---

[32] Several organizations and individuals assisted in a volunteer capacity in the collection of print media. Chief among them were Minnesota Advocates for Human Rights and Thomas Warrick from the Washington, D.C., law firm of Pierson, Semmes & Bemis.

[33] Video documentation was done by Linden Productions (Los Angeles, California) on a largely volunteer basis. Linden Productions received a grant from IHRLI of $80,000, funded by the Soros Foundation, but the bulk of this enormously costly project was funded by Linden, thanks to the generosity of its president, Pippa Scott.
  Linden created a unique computerized videotape archive, classifying the tapes into such subject-matter categories as violence against persons (civilian and military); killing, torture, and mistreatment in camps; violence against women — rape; use of special paramilitary groups; forced deportation; and destruction of religious and cultural property. Each videotape was broken down, shot by shot, and every screen image was fully described in the videotape database and time-coded according to incidents, locations, dates,

A video documentarian catalogued all videotapes received by IHRLI.[34] The testimonies of individuals on tape concern treatment in detention centers, rape, torture, and ethnic cleansing. Many of these testimonies identify alleged perpetrators. The footage also provides graphic, visual evidence of the destruction of property, such as civilian homes, schools, hospitals, cultural landmarks, and places of worship. In addition to its intrinsic informational value, this material is very useful for the identification of persons and places by witnesses.

IHRLI Database

At the Commission's first session, I proposed establishing a documentation center and database. However, the Commission had neither the space nor the resources to do so at its secretariat in Geneva. IHRLI offered its facilities and resources and pledged to obtain the additional necessary funds. At first, the suggestion met with resistance from the OLA, which insisted that the project be carried out on UN premises. I believed, however, that my mandate did not state where the work

---

victims, witnesses, perpetrators, and other important characteristics that could be seen on the screen. Complete transcripts were made of all videotapes as the final step in the archiving process. The videotapes were placed in humidity and dust-free vaults, which were protected by security systems and available only to authorized personnel. The entire computerized system and the videotapes have been made available to the Tribunal's prosecutor. The system developed by Linden Productions is particularly useful as it permits computerized selection of tapes, events, places, and persons. The computer program can also be linked to the IHRLI database and to FBIS to merge all sources of information. To date, however, the prosecutor's office has not pursued the possibility of merging the databases and is instead in the process of developing a new system for organizing information, funded by the United States. *See Annual Report of the International Tribunal for the Prosecution of Persons Responsible for Serious Violations of International Humanitarian Law Committed in the Territory of the Former Yugoslavia since 1991*, ¶ 158, U.N. SCOR, 49th Year, Agenda Item 152, U.N. Doc. S/1994/1007 (1994) [hereinafter *Tribunal Annual Report*].

[34] The video documentarian labeled each videotape with the following information: date received, submitter, title, and sequential identification number for easy retrieval. The video documentarian screened all of the videotapes and prepared a summary for the video master index, indicating the videotape's contents, running time, source, and broadcast date, if any.

should be conducted and, indeed, most rapporteurs of UN bodies work elsewhere than at UN facilities. On this basis, I proceeded with the creation of a database in Chicago at IHRLI to organize the mass of information so as to facilitate its retrieval and analysis.[35] It was not until several months later that then Chairman Kalshoven acknowledged the existence of the database and requested what was already in place: security measures to protect the data and to insure confidentiality on the part of the database staff.[36] Eventually, the work I carried out as rapporteur met with the approval of the Commission, the Secretary-General, and the Security Council.[37]

---

[35] The Commission and IHRLI agreed that data gathering, establishment of the database, and data analysis would be done by IHRLI under my direction as rapporteur. IHRLI agreed to provide the Commission with copies of the database software and to forward database information on a regular basis. When the Commission ended its work in April 1994, IHRLI forwarded a complete set of documents and a copy of the database to the office of the prosecutor. *See Tribunal Annual Report, supra* note 33, ¶ 157. IHRLI has continued to assist the prosecutor's staff in connection with the technical aspects of the database and the transfer of documents.

[36] Several security measures were implemented to prevent leaks of information or tampering with the documents. First, the space provided by DePaul University for the database project was protected by an electronic security system. University Security, which is linked to the Chicago Police Department, monitored the security system. Second, each person working on the project at IHRLI signed a confidentiality agreement. Lastly, original and photocopied documents were stored in locked file cabinets in the offices protected by the electronic security system. In addition, copies of all documents were stored in a secure off-site facility.

[37] The Commission endorsed the efforts of the Rapporteur in its *First Interim Report* to the Security Council, stating that it wished "to place on record its deep appreciation to the Rapporteur on the Gathering and Analysis of Facts for his invaluable contribution to this undertaking." *First Interim Report, supra* note 4, ¶ 25. The Secretary-General also urged the continuation of the database work in his letter transmitting this report to the Security Council. *Id.* at 2; *see also infra* text accompanying note 158. When the Security Council established the Tribunal, it also urged the continuation of the Commission's work, including its data gathering, stating that "the Commission of Experts . . . should continue on an urgent basis the collection of information . . . as proposed in its interim report." S.C. Res. 827, *supra* note 10, preambular ¶ 10. By letter dated May 27, 1993, to Cherif Bassiouni, Chairman Kalshoven formally expressed his gratitude to the rapporteur and his staff for the work that had been done. The Commission stated in October 1993 that "the database has

The cost of the database operation from December 1992 through December 1994 was approximately $1.4 million.[38] As noted earlier, neither the United Nations nor the Commission covered any of this sum.

As Rapporteur for the Gathering and Analysis of Facts, I had a staff, over a two-year period, of an average of forty people.[39] In addition, a number of attorneys in Chicago, New York, Minnesota, and Washington, D.C., contributed their services pro bono.[40] They were particularly skilled in the fields of criminal prosecution generally, and sexual assault specifically, multiparty litigation, and computer-assisted document management. Their efforts were especially beneficial in the development of the documentation system, the assessment of the data, the preparation of reports, and the formulation of an investigation strategy.

As of the middle of 1993, an average of 3,500 documents were being received each month; by April 30, 1994, IHRLI had over 65,000 pages of documents. The documentation system was developed with the

---

already proved to be of great assistance to the Commission as a basis of support for its specific missions and investigations." *Second Interim Report, supra* note 21, ¶ 105.

[38] This sum took the form of contributions from DePaul University (office space) and the foundations cited *supra* note 27. I also wish to make note of the invaluable contribution of thousands of hours of volunteer work by lawyers, law students, data analysts, and others. In this regard, see *infra* notes 39–40.

[39] Despite some turnover, staff regularly included 20–25 salaried and volunteer attorneys, 10–15 paid and volunteer law students, 5–10 data analysts, 2 computer programmers, 1 documentarian, and 1 video documentarian. Three salaried attorneys administered the day-to-day operations, oversaw the substantive work, and analyzed the database results with the assistance of other attorneys.

[40] Among those providing exceptional pro bono services to IHRLI and the Commission were a number of attorneys volunteering their services through Minnesota Advocates for Human Rights; Edwin E. Brooks, Ami de Chapeaurouge, Paul A. Duffy, Helen L. Hackett, Amy A. Hijjawi, Alan E. Molotsky, Nancy K. Tordai, and Richard W. Waller from the Chicago law firm of Katten, Muchin & Zavis; Joan Marsh from the Chicago law firm of Kirkland & Ellis; Susan A. McColgan and Ann C. Taylor from the Chicago law firm of Lord, Bissell & Brook; Alexander S. Vesselinovitch from the Chicago law firm of Seyfarth, Shaw, Fairweather & Geraldson; Duane Layton from the Washington, D.C., law firm of Thompson & Mitchell; Thomas Warrick from the Washington, D.C., law firm of Pierson, Semmes & Bemis; and Penny Venetis from the New York law firm of O'Melveny & Myers.

following goals in mind: (1) preserving the integrity of the documents submitted to the Commission; (2) verifying that documents containing allegations of grave breaches were analyzed and correlated; (3) facilitating the retrieval of documents; and (4) insuring that the information retrieval method was useful to research and analysis.

The IHRLI project was organized as follows. First, the documentarian sequentially numbered all original "source documents" pertinent to the work of the Commission and then stored them according to number in a pristine master file. Once source documents were filed in the master file, they could not be removed without the permission of the documentarian. A source document might, for example, be a report from a local or an international human rights group or a government submission. A single source document might describe one incident or several incidents, and any given incident might involve multiple victims and/or multiple violations of international humanitarian law.

Next, an attorney analyzed all documents in the master file in order to determine whether they were relevant to the war crimes database. Relevant documents were photocopied for future entry into the system according to guidelines established by the legal staff.[41] These guidelines covered every category of information in the database and were necessary because of the wide variability in the quality and format of information coming in from a multitude of sources. A staff attorney distributed assignments for database entry and monitored the progress of documents through the data-entry phase.

Data entry was carried out by data analysts with legal and/or human rights experience. Data entry proceeded on a small, independent computer network consisting of five workstations linked by a file server. Data were simultaneously entered from each computer workstation.

Before data entry began, the data analysts reviewed the documents they had been assigned and identified information pertinent to the database. They then entered this information into the appropriate categories of the database, according to the guidelines established by the legal staff. All allegations of possible grave breaches or other violations of international humanitarian law were entered. Distinctions relating to

---

[41] *Data Entry Procedures for the Staff of the Rapporteur on Data Gathering and Analysis* (IHRLI Internal Document, Apr. 6, 1993).

credibility, accuracy, or bias in source documents were not made until the analytical stage of this project, nor was any attempt made at this point to eliminate duplication of information.

The documentarian also entered source information about each document into a separate documentarian's database. Data analysts were able to access the documentarian's database during the entry of data into the war crimes database so that source information recorded there would be consistent and accurate. A narrative description of each incident, capturing every important item of information relating to it (names, locations, dates, alleged violations, and so forth), was also entered into the war crimes database.

The computerized database provided a comprehensive, systematic, and manageable record of alleged violations. Nearly six thousand "cases" were entered into the database. The cases often concerned multiple events that may have constituted several independent violations of international humanitarian law. In the interests of time and efficiency, it was not feasible to create a separate data file for each event or possible violation. If a source document contained roughly the same set of facts regarding location, time frame, victims, witnesses, and perpetrators, then the facts were combined into a single incident report, or "case." For example, a source document detailing the rapes of a series of women at a particular camp by the same guards over a period of several months would likely be processed as a single case.

Several quality control measures ensured the consistency and accuracy of the database. Once all information relating to a given incident had been entered into the system, the data analyst generated, printed, and edited an "incident report." The data analyst then gave the incident report and the source document to a supervising attorney for quality control analysis. The attorney either approved the incident report or returned it so that corrections could be made. If the report was approved, the source document went back to the documentarian to be filed.

Apart from storing information in an organized, retrievable fashion, the database performed the following functions that proved particularly useful to the Commission's work: (1) generating reports by information category and (2) making possible "context-sensitive" searches. The category-specific reports were either statistical (calculating the number of times a particular violation occurred) or thematic (assembling significant amounts of information relating to a particular category). For example, a "location report" would identify for a particular location the names of perpetrators and witnesses, the dates of incidents, and the source document(s). The context-sensitive searches were similar to a LEXIS or WESTLAW search, relying on keywords. When a search term (or "query") was entered, the computer searched certain categories of every file and produced a list of all case numbers where that term appeared. Search terms could be the name of a particular perpetrator, the name of a victim, a location, and so on.

Despite certain difficulties, such as the unverified nature of much of the information, the database provides strong indication of the types and quantity of violations that an ad hoc tribunal might encounter. The "cases" reveal that massive and brutal victimization, affecting thousands of individuals, has taken place in the territory of the former Yugoslavia. The majority of alleged violations involve murder, torture, kidnapping/hostage taking, forced eviction, and imprisonment. Large numbers of rapes and sexual assaults also have been reported.[42] As noted earlier, although approximately six thousand cases were entered into the database, the number of alleged violations and victims runs to tens of thousands. This is attributable to several factors. First, a single incident often concerned multiple victims, though the number of victims was also often rough and possibly inflated. Second, the same incident was sometimes reported by different sources. For example, the Vukovar mass grave, discussed below, was reported by several sources, each with estimates varying from two to three hundred victims. Some of these sources reported that the victims were missing, while others concluded that they had been killed. Data analysts were instructed to enter the information exactly as it had been reported, irrespective of inconsistencies or possible inaccuracies, since these problems could more properly be addressed during the analytical stage.

While multiple reports of the same incident led to inflated figures within the database, they tended to corroborate each other and therefore have some probative value. Once the data were analyzed and

---

[42] All parties to the conflict appear to have committed such violations of international humanitarian law. However, the database contains substantially more allegations of violations committed by Serbian and Bosnian Serb forces against Bosnian Muslim civilians than by or against any other ethnic or religious group.

case files assembled, these reports were filed together and any duplication was eliminated. Further analysis was done to clarify ambiguities and correct inaccuracies to the extent the data permitted.

Appraisal of Data-gathering Efforts

The Commission and I experienced mixed results in our efforts to gather data on, and evidence of, alleged violations of international humanitarian law. Reports prepared by governments, UN bodies, IGOs, and NGOs contain numerous allegations but most of them do not provide legally relevant or admissible evidence of violations. In some cases, more detailed information could have been obtained if the Commission had had the financial means to help willing sources that could not themselves afford the costs of duplicating documents, photographs, and videotapes or recording witness testimony. For example, the Yugoslavian War Crimes Commission and the Bosnian War Crimes Commission had neither the resources nor the capability to assemble and reproduce the information in their possession.[43]

It was also difficult to collect official documents, conduct on-site investigations, and interview victims, witnesses, and unbiased observers while the conflict in the former Yugoslavia was ongoing. Certain UN bodies, such as the United Nations Protection Force (UNPROFOR) and the United Nations High Commissioner for Refugees (UNHCR), as well as the International Committee of the Red Cross (ICRC), construed their mandates as excluding the transmission of such information. Thus, highly knowledgeable sources having firsthand information could not share it with the Commission, except through published reports or reports available for limited circulation but not containing evidence. Furthermore, the European Community Monitoring Mission for Yugoslavia (ECMM), which was potentially a very useful source of firsthand information, stored its reports in boxes piled up in a room at UNPROFOR headquarters in Zagreb. There was thus no easy way to

---

[43] Providing funds and other forms of support to bodies such as these could have helped to level the playing field. For example, the Croatian War Crimes Commission and some Croatian human rights organizations were comparatively well funded and equipped and thus better able to distribute their information than other such groups.

retrieve relevant information, and since the ECMM did not have a uniform system for monitors to follow, the reports varied in quality and content. Lastly, it appeared that some governments, including the United Kingdom, when chairing the ECMM, had removed some of the records.[44]

It should be noted as well that the Commission launched its data-gathering activities before the Tribunal was established and thus before the Tribunal's Rules of Procedure and Evidence were adopted.[45] Consequently, the Commission had no way of knowing what types of evidence would be considered admissible by the Tribunal,[46] and this further complicated its task.

Critical Assessment of Information Received

The Commission's data gathering and analysis would have benefited from greater input on the part of governments, UN bodies, IGOs, and NGOs. From the time that the Commission began compiling data in November 1992 until approximately a year later, the character and quality of the information submitted by the various sources did not change substantially. The material was generally limited and incomplete, lacking documents, records of interviews, videotapes of interviews,

---

[44] This was the case with field files for the second half of 1992, which was the worst period of ethnic cleansing in northern, central, and then eastern Bosnia–Herzegovina.

[45] International Tribunal for the Prosecution of Persons Responsible for Serious Violations of International Humanitarian Law Committed in the Territory of the Former Yugoslavia since 1991, Rules of Procedure and Evidence, U.N. Doc. IT/32 (1994), *amended by* U.N. Doc. IT/32/Rev.1 (1994), *reprinted in* appendix C of this issue of *Criminal Law Forum* [hereinafter I.T. R. Proc. & Evid.]; *see also supra* note 13 and accompanying text.

Editor's note: the Rules of Procedure and Evidence were amended Oct. 4, 1994, U.N. Doc. IT/32/Rev.2 (1994), and Jan. 30, 1995, U.N. Doc. IT/32/Rev.3 (1995). This article is based on U.N. Doc. IT/Rev.1. Appendix C prints the most recent text of the rules, U.N. Doc. IT/Rev.3, indicating all deletions from, and additions to, U.N. Doc. IT/32/Rev.1, so that the reader can reconstruct the full text of this earlier document.

[46] See in this regard *id.* RR. 89–98 (evidence), 71 (depositions).

photos, and other supporting evidence.[47]

While the reports adequately established the occurrence of large-scale victimization in the former Yugoslavia, they did not, for the most part, contain evidence in the legal sense, which is necessary to bring criminal charges under international criminal law or the domestic criminal law of states in whose territory these acts were committed. Several explanations are offered: NGOs wanted to protect their sources; some IGOs, like UNHCR and ICRC, thought that they were precluded by their mandates from giving evidence or even information; UNPROFOR (until October 1993) similarly interpreted its mandate as precluding it from furnishing evidence; some governments were uncertain about the fate of the Commission, and others probably had no political interest in turning over evidence. The parties to the conflict did their best to cooperate, but their resources were limited and they lacked trained personnel. They also faced the objective difficulty of gathering evidence during a war.

Several problems were common to the reports that the Commission received. The information varied widely in terms of form and substance, complicating data entry and analysis, as discussed below. Many of the reports also failed to provide sufficient detail about the events described (such as information relating to the identity of victims, perpetrators, and witnesses). Particularly troublesome was the consistent failure to identify the military units involved in alleged incidents, to provide information about "order of battle,"[48] and to give details about the location of military units at a given time. Each of these related factors is critical to establishing "command responsibility." All of these details had to be discovered, whenever possible, through other sources.

Governments did not provide any intelligence information in their possession—such as satellite and aerial photographs; intercepted telephone, radio, and cable communications; and other materials that

---

[47] There were exceptions, in particular the government of Croatia, Human Rights Watch, and, after October 1993, the governments of the United States, the United Kingdom, Sweden, and Austria, which provided detailed evidence, including witness statements. These materials proved highly valuable.

[48] This refers to a military organizational chart that gives details on type of units, strength, equipment, and command structure.

could have revealed the disposition and movement of troops and supplies, particularly important where national borders were crossed. Such information would help to establish the role of different governments in these multiple conflicts, the international character of the conflict, the chain of command, and the apex of command and control. It would also help to establish the role of the "warring factions" (Bosnian Serb, Bosnian Croat, and Bosnian government forces) in certain operations that were planned with a view to concealing that role, especially where serious violations of international humanitarian law were presumably contemplated. Such information leads not only to legal conclusions but also to political consequences, which may explain why it was not made available to the Commission. Furthermore, to my knowledge, such intelligence has not yet been made available to the prosecutor of the Tribunal, the Hon. Richard Goldstone.

Finally, the sources of information upon which reports were based were either not verified or not verifiable. Many reports did not disclose original sources, nor did they state whether any original evidence might be available (such as affidavits of victims, witnesses, or perpetrators; photographs; or medical reports or autopsy reports).[49] Without access to certain documents and sources, it was difficult to weigh the validity of allegations; assess the sufficiency and credibility of the evidence; decide whether further investigation in a given case was needed; ascertain the potential responsibility of alleged perpetrators; and determine the legal nature of a violation and the potential criminal charge.[50] Nevertheless, the cumulative effect of this information, much of which was corroborative, was to help establish patterns of violations from which certain policies could be identified, particularly the policy underlying the consistent failure of military and political leaders to act to prevent grave human rights violations and to punish their perpetrators.

As noted above, there were data-entry and analysis problems because sources varied significantly in terms of quality and content, in

---

[49] Some reports may have relied on diplomatic correspondence that cannot be publicly revealed. Other reports may have been based on media sources. These reports would not be useful unless the original source could be verified.

[50] These difficulties are exacerbated by the fact that most evidence of violations consists of oral testimony, affidavits, and statements made by victims and witnesses.

part reflecting their different data-gathering methodologies and goals. More specifically, spellings of names and locations were inconsistent due to transliteration or translation into the reporting language. Locations were, at first, difficult to pinpoint due to a lack of specific geographical information. Reports of the same incident sometimes varied in the numbers of persons involved and in the outcome described. Property damage reports rarely indicated more than the type of property affected; the location and value of property were rarely included. Numbers of victims, properties, and other variables were often reported in numerical ranges (for instance, 100–1,000). Names of victims, perpetrators, and witnesses were often altered or omitted from the reports. Finally, important details that may have seemed irrelevant to the reporting source but that were important in the data-gathering process were left out.

In order to correct for these deficiencies and errors, IHRLI secured the services of linguists familiar with the Bosnian, Croatian, and Serbian variants of Serbo-Croatian, as well as a professional cartographer; obtained detailed maps of the region, including digitalized maps on a 1:10,000 scale; installed a computer program to make the spelling of place-names uniform; and consulted older listings of towns and counties in Bosnia–Herzegovina and Croatia since the names of many places had been changed after their occupation. IHRLI also developed a training and data manual for the staff and working maps on which the locations, for example, of prison camps and mass graves were plotted.

Reports from Governments[51]

Some of the government reports relied heavily on hearsay and media sources, which could not be readily verified. In other instances, government reports were quite detailed and appeared to be based on

---

[51] The following governments submitted materials pertaining to war crimes and mass victimization: Albania, Australia, Austria, Belgium, Bosnia–Herzegovina, Burkina Faso, Canada, Colombia, Croatia, Denmark, France, Germany, Iran, Italy, Kenya, the Netherlands, Norway, Russia, Saudi Arabia, Slovenia, Spain, Sweden, Switzerland, Turkey, Ukraine, the United Arab Emirates, the United Kingdom, the United States, Venezuela, and Yugoslavia. In particular, Austria, Canada, France, Sweden, Switzerland, the United Kingdom, the United States, and the parties to the conflict provided valuable information of an evidentiary nature.

credible and verifiable eyewitness accounts. But, possibly for security or confidentiality reasons, the reports omitted important details relating to names of victims, perpetrators, and witnesses, as well as dates and specific locations. While these reports generally failed to state facts sufficient to make out a prima facie case, they clearly set out facts that, if substantiated, would constitute evidence of grave breaches and other violations of international humanitarian law.

The inadequacy of most government reports was particularly disappointing since these materials were intended to be the Commission's primary source of information.[52] Moreover, most governments did not turn over information already in their possession—interviews with refugees; "soft intelligence" and unclassified information; and data on order of battle, names of commanders, and troop movements. At least twenty countries outside the Balkans have large refugee populations from this region. Some of these refugees could have been interviewed and the interviews released in an edited form to ensure confidentiality or protect sensitive information. Some governments could have declassified relevant intelligence and released it to the Commission in a sanitized manner to protect original sources and methods by which such information is obtained. But this was not the case.

The governments that provided the most valuable information were Bosnia–Herzegovina, Croatia, and, as of the fall of 1993, Austria, Sweden, Switzerland, the United States, and the United Kingdom. In late 1993 and early 1994, the Federal Republic of Yugoslavia provided some valuable information but did not make sources and witnesses available. The authorities of the self-proclaimed Bosnian Serb Republic and Serb Republic of Krajina did not provide information, except for the latter's communications to Commissioner Fenrick and myself on purported mass graves in UNPA Sector West, Croatia, discussed below.

As the Commission's work progressed and gained credibility, more information and evidence was forthcoming, particularly from Yugoslavia. Indeed, had the Commission not been prematurely terminated, as discussed below, it would have obtained significantly more

---

[52] As noted earlier, the Security Council contemplated that reports from governments would be the best source of information. S.C. Res. 771, *supra* note 14, ¶ 5; S.C. Res. 780, *supra* note 1, ¶ 1.

valuable evidence from this source. In fact, Yugoslavia submitted a report to the United Nations in May 1994,[53] but the Commission had by that time submitted its *Final Report.*

REPORTS FROM UN BODIES AND INTERGOVERNMENTAL ORGANIZATIONS

The UN bodies that provided reports to the Commission of Experts included UN Commission on Human Rights—Special Rapporteur for the Former Yugoslavia Tadeusz Mazowiecki;[54] UNHCR; UNPROFOR; and UN Commission on Human Rights—Special Rapporteur on Extrajudicial, Summary, or Arbitrary Executions Bacre Waly Ndiaye. The IGOs that provided reports included the ECMM and the Conference on Security and Cooperation in Europe (CSCE). These reports gave clear indications of the types of massive and systematic violations of international humanitarian law and human rights taking place in the former Yugoslavia. They also contained examples and descriptions of particular instances.

As noted above, the Commission Secretariat made efforts to obtain UNHCR reports of alleged violations but was unsuccessful due to UNHCR's interpretation of its mandate. These materials could have included field reports, notes of field interviews, or copies of refugee interviews establishing, for example, allegations of murder, rape, and torture, which were contained in UNHCR's confidential internal reports.

The Commission Secretariat also tried to obtain documentation from UNPROFOR and its Civil Police unit (CIVPOL), but most of

---

[53] Letter from the Permanent Mission of Yugoslavia to the Secretary-General, May 6, 1994, U.N. Doc. S/1994/548 (1994), transmitting *Third Report Submitted to the Commission of Experts Established pursuant to Security Council Resolution 780 (1992)* [hereinafter *Yugoslavian Report*]. Moreover, in March 1994, I had met in Geneva with Yugoslavia's Minister of Justice, who is also chairman of the state War Crimes Commission, and expected to receive evidence from that source and to be able to conduct interviews of rape victims in Serbia. This was prevented by the premature termination of the Commission of Experts in April 1994. See *Yugoslavia to Continue Cooperation with U.N. War Crimes Commission,* BBC Summary of World Broadcasts, Mar. 19, 1994, *available in* LEXIS, World Library, Allnws File. See *infra* text accompanying note 164.

[54] The Commission of Experts established close cooperation with the Special Rapporteur and his staffs in both Geneva and Zagreb.

these reports were classified and not available for dissemination by UNPROFOR in light of its interpretation of its mandate. CIVPOL had firsthand knowledge of many events, as well as access to information and evidence of criminality, but apparently did not collect such evidence as a matter of policy. For example, when field officers reported certain facts, they were either not recorded in detailed CIVPOL reports or the information was not given to the Commission. CIVPOL, at least until the fall of 1993, was particularly concerned about jeopardizing its relations with the warring factions, especially the Serbs since they were not only the militarily dominant party but also the most intractable. Both UNPROFOR and CIVPOL, however, cooperated fully with the Commission in many other respects, most notably in providing logistical support that proved invaluable.[55]

The Commission Secretariat did not receive information from ICRC, also due to apprehension over exceeding its mandate. This material concerned the dates when camps opened and closed, the numbers and ethnicity of prisoners, and the conditions of detention.

Like the government reports, the published or unclassified reports from UN bodies and IGOs lacked the specificity needed to make out criminal responsibility but were useful in identifying patterns of conduct from which policies could be deduced. Additionally, information from these sources substantiated and corroborated other information the Commission received. For example, the UNPROFOR daily shelling activity report on Sarajevo proved invaluable in preparing Annex VI to the *Final Report*, on the battle and siege of Sarajevo, although most of the information used in this annex came from media sources.

REPORTS FROM NGOS

The reports received from a number of NGOs, particularly those in the region of the former Yugoslavia, proved very helpful in enabling the

---

[55] Sometime in October 1993, UNPROFOR investigated the Medak Pocket incident, which involved Croats against Serbs in Croatia, see *infra* section entitled "Investigation of the Medak Pocket," and the Stupni Do incident, which involved Croatian Defense Council forces against Muslim villagers in Bosnia–Herzegovina. The Commission was given access to these reports and they were turned over to the prosecutor of the Tribunal.

Commission to gather pertinent, substantiated data. Though NGOs are not in essence investigatory bodies, the extent of the investigations underlying these reports and the level of analysis they achieved indicated a true effort and genuine commitment by many such organizations to produce verifiable facts. The published reports of Helsinki Watch, for example, set out detailed information that came closest to the type of data the Commission required in attributing responsibility for violations of international humanitarian law. Witness interviews, in particular, were very useful not only for learning about the incidents they described but also for corroborating other events and reports.

However, as with the other reports submitted to the Commission, further data were required in order to construct effective cases against those groups or individuals responsible for alleged violations. Although many international and local NGOs were a better overall source of information, some did not provide the Commission with the supporting documentation it needed. Thus, the contributions from Helsinki Watch, which were the most useful, did not include original supporting documentation. Amnesty International, despite its initial cooperation and willingness to provide information, also failed to provide supporting documentation. Both maintained that doing so would breach express or implied promises of confidentiality or endanger informants. However, such concerns were addressed in some cases by excising names and other identifying information to protect confidentiality,[56] and a general practice along these lines could have been very worthwhile.

Nothing of what has just been said should be construed as criticism, because NGOs should not be regarded as a substitute for the criminal investigatory role of UN-created commissions. The service to humanity that NGOs provide is highly laudable.

MEDIA SOURCES

The media (print, electronic, and broadcast) proved to be an invaluable source of leads, significant facts, and corroboration. Many incident

---

[56] This procedure was followed in many cases involving governments, NGOs, and other organizations that provided information of a confidential nature. The Commission was particularly attentive to these concerns, and its procedures, as well as IHRLI's, proved to be entirely secure.

reports contained in the IHRLI database are based on media accounts of violations. Media reports also corroborated much of the information received by the Commission from other sources. Indeed, the service to the world that the media have performed in this conflict should not go unrecorded. Journalists were the first to discover some of the prison camps and the horrid conditions under which the detainees lived. Journalists provided the world with photographic and videotaped evidence of many violations of international humanitarian law, particularly in the prison camps. It is fair to say that the media brought the conflict to the attention of the world.[57]

THE COMMISSION'S ON-SITE INVESTIGATIONS

In addition to gathering information from the sources described in the preceding sections, the Commission conducted several on-site investigations, which it deemed necessary to the fulfillment of its mandate to secure evidence of violations of international humanitarian law and to verify allegations of the existence of certain patterns and policies of criminality.[58] Given the volume of the available information and the Commission's limited resources, such investigations could be carried out only on a selective basis. The Commission used the following objective criteria to decide which investigations to pursue: "the source of the information, the strength of the evidence, the number of victims, the identity and rank of the persons allegedly responsible, and the gravity of the alleged violations."[59] The Commission stated that an important factor in identifying the categories of crime in specific cases to be investigated in depth would be patterns of behavior sufficiently consistent to reveal a policy or system in such violations as genocide, ethnic

---

[57]   *See, e.g.,* Roy Gutman, *A Witness to Genocide* (1993).

[58]   S.C. Res. 780, *supra* note 1, ¶ 2. It must nevertheless be reiterated that the Commission's work was not viewed as part of the prosecutor's task of gathering evidence needed to prosecute under the Tribunal's rules. See *supra* notes 13, 45–46 and accompanying text.

[59]   *First Interim Report, supra* note 4, ¶ 31.

cleansing, or large-scale sexual assaults.[60]

Notwithstanding the best intentions and the ingenuity of the commissioners, practical and financial difficulties posed a severe obstacle. Nevertheless, from July 1993 until March 1994, the Commission undertook an extraordinary thirty-four field missions and conducted several major investigations. Discussed in more detail below, the most extensive efforts included the following: (1) an attempted mass grave exhumation in Ovcara/Vukovar, United Nations Protected Area (UNPA) Sector East, Croatia; (2) a mass grave exhumation in Pakracka Poljana, UNPA Sector West, Croatia; (3) an investigation, carried out in and outside the territory of the former Yugoslavia, of rape and sexual assault; (4) a radiological investigation in UNPA Sector West, Croatia (self-proclaimed Serb Republic of Krajina); (5) an investigation of the battle of Dubrovnik, Croatia, and the resulting destruction of cultural property; (6) an investigation into the 1993 attack in the Medak Pocket, UNPA Sector South, Croatia (self-proclaimed Serb Republic of Krajina); and (7) an investigation of ethnic cleansing in Prijedor, northwestern Bosnia–Herzegovina.

Mass Grave Exhumation in Ovcara/Vukovar

The Commission received reports of a mass grave in Ovcara, an agricultural cooperative a few kilometers from the city of Vukovar, which had been the site of a three-month siege by the Yugoslav National Army (JNA), with the support of Serb paramilitary groups and local militias. The grave was alleged to contain over two hundred bodies of wounded and sick Croats who were at the Vukovar hospital in November 1991, when the JNA and Krajina Serb militias took over the city.[61] The Commission visited the site to ascertain the existence of the shallow mass grave. Once the mass grave was identified, the Commission asked UNPROFOR to secure the location and then proceeded to plan for the investigation. Commissioner Fenrick visited officials in Vukovar, Belgrade, Zagreb, and Knin on several occasions in an effort to obtain

---

60   *Id.*

61   *Final Report, supra* note 24, ¶ 265.

the necessary cooperation to conduct an exhumation.[62] The Commission's objectives were to exhume the bodies, collect physical evidence, send the bodies to a morgue facility to conduct autopsies to establish identity and cause of death, and collect testimony.[63]

After considerable delay, officials of the Serb Republic of Krajina met with Commissioner Fenrick in Knin on September 5, 1993, and conveyed in writing their full cooperation with the exhumation. At the same time as the Ovcara dig was being planned, the Commission secured the cooperation of the Croatian government and of the Serb Republic of Krajina to conduct an exhumation of a mass grave in Pakracka Poljana/Marina Selo, which reportedly contained the bodies of Serbs killed by Croats.[64] The officials of the Serb Republic of Krajina provided additional written assurances in October 1993 after another meeting with the Commission, during which the Commission agreed that medical observers from Croatia and the Serb Republic of Krajina were welcome to be present during the exhumation and the postmortem examinations.[65] The postmortem examinations were to be conducted outside Croatia due to the lack of facilities locally to deal with such a large number of bodies.[66]

Thereafter, the Commission deployed its team of sixty-five investigators, led by Commander Fenrick, the Rapporteur for On-site Investigations. The team conducted preliminary site surveys but was unable to start the exhumation because a local commander informed them that the Parliament of the Serb Republic of Krajina had decided to postpone the exhumation until the conflict was resolved.[67] Then, in

---

[62] *See id.* ¶ 268.

[63] *Id.* ¶ 265.

[64] *See id.* ¶ 269.

[65] *See id.* ¶ 270. In connection with getting permission from the Knin authorities, see *infra* note 114.

[66] *Id.* ¶¶ 270, 283. Hospitals in the area could cope with 20–30 bodies at any one time. Capacity to accommodate 200 bodies is available only at the Chicago Medical Examiner's Office and the U.S. Air Force hospital and morgue in Wiesbaden, Germany.

[67] *Id.* ¶¶ 271–272.

November, the Krajina Serb authorities agreed again to cooperate fully.[68] Unfortunately, the Commission was forced to postpone the mission until the spring due to the winter weather conditions. The planned date for the exhumation was April 10, 1994, but the Commission was terminated as of the thirtieth of that month and thus the exhumation never took place.[69] All information regarding the mass grave was given to the office of the prosecutor of the Tribunal.[70] Although it is hoped that the prosecutor will conduct the exhumation, this is doubtful since Yugoslavia, the Serb Republic of Krajina, and the Bosnian Serb Republic refuse to recognize the competence of the Tribunal. Moreover, as time passes, not only does the forensic analysis become more difficult but also it becomes more difficult to obtain antemortem data, against which the postmortem evidence is compared for identification. These problems were foreseeable when the Commission was terminated prematurely.

Mass Grave Exhumation in Pakracka Poljana

The Commission confirmed the possibility of mass graves in this area during a reconnaissance mission in March 1993.[71] There were allegedly 1,700 bodies in what appeared to be seventeen trenches, each about ten meters long and two meters wide.[72] Local Serbs reported a large number of missing persons from the area. In October 1993, the Commission deployed the investigative team that had previously prepared the Ovcara site to conduct a site survey here. The seventeen trenches were dug out with a backhoe but nothing was found. The trenches were probably dug during the war for military purposes. Altogether seventy-one potential sites were excavated in the vicinity, but no mass grave was discovered.[73]

The Commission was concerned, however, that an undiscovered

---

[68] *Id.* ¶ 275.

[69] *Id.* ¶ 276.

[70] *Id.*

[71] *Id.* ¶ 277.

[72] *See id.* ¶ 282.

[73] *Id.*

mass grave existed in the area because of the large number of alleged missing persons. A team of Dutch specialists then conducted more searches and discovered nineteen bodies, which were exhumed. The forensic team concluded that the nineteen persons, who were buried in nine separate graves located in an open field, had been executed, as evidenced by expended cartridges surrounding the area and wounds visible on some of the bodies.[74] Furthermore, the graves appeared to be clandestine burial sites that had not been disturbed since the interment of the bodies.[75]

Krajina Serb officials would not allow the bodies to be moved to Croatia for postmortem examinations, and proper facilities did not exist in Pakracka Poljana. By then, winter had arrived and fieldwork could no longer be conducted. Therefore, the team eventually placed the bodies in body bags and properly reburied them at an identified place under UNPROFOR security.[76] Since it was terminated early the following spring, the Commission was unable to conduct a full criminal investigation. However, as in the case of Ovcara, all information regarding the mass grave was given to the office of the prosecutor of the Tribunal with the hope that the prosecutor will complete the investigation.[77]

Rape and Sexual Assault Investigation

The Commission conducted an unprecedented on-site investigation into rape and sexual assault in early 1994.[78] This investigation supplemented efforts to document the incident reports contained in the database of mass and systematic rape and other forms of sexual abuse. The cumulative nature of the information received reveals the tragic and barbarous resort to rape as an instrument of war and as part of the policy

---

[74] *Id.* ¶ 281.

[75] *Id.*

[76] *Id.* ¶ 283.

[77] *Id.* ¶ 284.

[78] *Id.* ¶¶ 241–253.

of ethnic cleansing conducted essentially, though not exclusively, by Serbs against Bosnian Muslims and Croats. Rapes were also reported to have been committed by Croats and Bosnians against Serbs.

The investigation was unprecedented because of its scope and method. About forty people participated—including female attorneys, female mental health specialists, male mental health specialists, female interpreters, and administrative support personnel.[79] All of the attorneys and mental health experts volunteered their time in support of the investigation, which resulted in interviews of 223 refugees—146 from Bosnia-Herzegovina and 77 from Croatia—in seven cities.[80] Both

---

[79] The investigation took place under my direction with assistance from Commissioner Cleiren and Commission staff Bruna Molina-Abrams, Deputy Secretary; Julio Baez, Assistant Secretary; and Lieutenant-Colonel Anton Kempenaars, Military Assistant to the Chairman of the Commission of Experts.

To implement the project, Karen Kenny, Interview Coordinator, was put in charge of the field work and performed exceptionally well under difficult circumstances. She worked closely with Maja Drazenovic, Chief Interpreter; Thomas Osorio, Field Officer; and Nancy Paterson, Coordinator of the Legal Team. Elenor Richter-Lyonett and Sabrina Negotovic served briefly as NGO Coordinators. Ms. Drazenovic recruited and selected the interpreters not only for their language skills but also for their ability to empathize with the interviewees.

The attorneys who conducted the interviews were from Bangladesh, Canada, Finland, Ireland, and the United States. All were prosecutors with the exception of one criminal defense lawyer. Interviewing teams usually consisted of three women: an attorney, an interpreter, and in most cases a mental health expert.

The legal team included Lena Andersson, Susan Axelrod, Francine Borsanyi, Linda S. Crawford, Sharon Janelle Crooks, Kenna Dalrymple, Feryal Gharahi, Sara Hossain, Nancy Paterson, Tanja Petrovar, Laura D. Silver, and Merja Pentikainen. The mental health experts, who did not conduct interviews but served as facilitators and support for the process, included Dr. Abigail Benton Sivan, Dr. Stephanie Cavanaugh, Dr. Wanda Fremont, Alice Geis (R.N.), Dr. Stephanie Gregory, Dr. Daniel Hardy, and Dr. Richard Rahe. Lisa Capitanini was part of the administrative staff serving in Split to organize interviews.

I am deeply grateful to the legal and mental health experts who volunteered their time to conduct this investigation, as well as the NGOs upon which the Commission relied. All of those who participated should be commended for their dedication and concern. I also wish to express my appreciation to Professor Catharine MacKinnon of the University of Michigan Law School, who gave generously of her time and help in contacting victims and witnesses whom she represented or otherwise knew.

[80] *Final Report, supra* note 24, ¶¶ 241–243.

women and men were the victims of sexual assault.

This investigation relied on the support of European and local NGOs, which secured about four hundred prospective witnesses. The Commission's efforts overcame significant initial resistance based on multiple grounds: distrust of the United Nations; fear of reprisals; protection of the witnesses' confidentiality; fear of retraumatizing the victims; and fear that information might fall into the wrong hands or be used for the wrong purposes. Overcoming these objections and other obstacles, including certain bureaucratic difficulties that caused the delay and almost the cancellation of the investigation, was in itself an accomplishment. The dedication of the people who planned and carried out the investigation was exemplary and quickly became known among the refugee community. The investigation turned into a healing process for the survivors and conveyed to them and their community that the world had not abandoned them.[81]

This effort produced significant goodwill for the United Nations, considering that so many victims blamed the United Nations for not protecting them. Toward the end of this project, the Commission's office at UNPROFOR was receiving ten to fifteen calls a day from victims and witnesses who wanted to be interviewed. It was an extraordinary manifestation of confidence that had emerged in the refugee community. Unfortunately, as with other on-site investigations, the investigation of rape and sexual assault was cut short (March 31) because the Commission was closed down ahead of schedule. To this writer and so many others, it was a tragic loss: the investigators knew of the horrible experiences that the interviewed victims had endured and how important it was to give them the cathartic and healing opportunity to tell their stories. The victims wanted the world to know what had happened to them and the perpetrators to be prosecuted.

The Commission compared the information obtained through the interviews with the information contained in the IHRLI database, which covered over 1,600 reported rape cases and over 4,500 insufficiently documented reports. The information, analyzed as a whole, established five patterns of rape:

---

[81] *Id.* ¶ 241 n.65.

1.   Individuals or small groups often committed sexual assaults in connection with intimidation and looting of a target ethnic group before fighting began in the area. Men would break into a house, steal, beat the inhabitants, and rape the women, usually in front of family members.[82]

2.   Individuals or small groups committed sexual assaults in connection with fighting in an area. Either women were raped in their homes or rounded up and selected from a group to be raped publicly after the town was secured.[83]

3.   Individuals or groups sexually assaulted women in detention. Soldiers, camp guards, paramilitaries, and civilians were allowed to choose women held in detention and remove them from the camp to rape them. Afterward, the men either killed the women or returned them to the camp. Women frequently reported gang rape and beatings or torture accompanying rape.[84]

4.   Individuals or groups committed sexual assaults as part of a policy of ethnic cleansing. Women were detained to be raped. The rapes usually occurred in front of other detainees, and victims were often beaten or tortured at the time. Women were held for the purpose of impregnation and not released until it was too late to obtain an abortion.[85]

5.   Women were also detained in hotels or homes for the sole purpose of sexually entertaining soldiers who came off the front line.[86]

---

[82]   *Id.* ¶ 245.

[83]   *Id.* ¶ 246.

[84]   *Id.* ¶ 247.

[85]   *Id.* ¶ 248.

[86]   *Id.* ¶ 249.

It is important to note that men were also the victims of sexual assault, including castration and genital mutilation.[87] Additionally, rape and sexual assault frequently occurred with the permission of camp commanders and/or in their presence.[88]

The Commission also conducted interviews in Slovenia and Austria.[89] The Turkish government extended an invitation to interview refugees in Turkey, but this could not be done because of the Commission's premature termination. The Commission also failed to get permission from the government of the Federal Republic of Yugoslavia to interview victims and witnesses in Serbia.[90] Although the government promised to conduct interviews and send the information to the Commission before its termination, none was received. It is believed, however, that given more time, Yugoslavia could have provided such information.

Radiological Investigation in UNPA Sector West

The Commission received reports from the Krajina Serbs regarding the dumping by Croatia of nuclear waste in areas throughout UNPA West Sector. In response, the Commission deployed to the sector an investigative team consisting of two specialists from the Royal Netherlands Army Nuclear, Biological, and Chemical School, seconded by the government of the Netherlands, under the direction of Commissioner Fenrick.[91] They took extensive soil samples in multiple areas that could have been used as dump sites, but the level of radioactivity of the samples was normal.[92] In March and April 1994, the administration of the Serb Republic of Krajina submitted new information with respect to other possible dump sites. However, the Commission was not able to conduct

---

[87] *Id.* ¶¶ 247, 250.

[88] *Id.* ¶¶ 247, 252.

[89] *Id.* ¶ 241 n.65.

[90] *See id.*

[91] *Id.* ¶ 302.

[92] *Id.* ¶ 303.

another investigation because of its premature termination, and the information was sent to the office of the prosecutor of the Tribunal.[93]

Battle of Dubrovnik Investigation

The Commission sent a team of military lawyers from Canada and Norway, along with a French art historian, to investigate the destruction of cultural property and attacks against civilians during the battle of Dubrovnik. The team had three objectives:

> 1. To determine whether and when indiscriminate attacks or deliberate attacks on civilian persons or civilian objects had occurred.
>
> 2. To quantify the loss of civilian life, injury to civilian persons, and damage to civilian property, including cultural property.
>
> 3. To attribute responsibility for apparent violations of the law of armed conflict.[94]

From the team's investigation, the Commission concluded that between eighty-two and eighty-eight civilians were killed during a one-year period due to the activity of the JNA.[95] In particular, the St. Nicholas Day bombardment of December 6, 1991, resulted in the death of thirteen civilians and the destruction of a significant amount of cultural and personal property in the town.[96] The Commission concluded that this was a deliberate attack on civilians and cultural property and that a prima facie case could be made against the JNA's commanding officers who were responsible for the bombardment.[97]

---

[93] *Id.* ¶ 305.
[94] *Id.* ¶ 298.
[95] *Id.* ¶ 299.
[96] *Id.*
[97] *Id.* ¶¶ 300–301.

Investigation of Ethnic Cleansing in Prijedor

Commissioner Greve conducted an in-depth investigation into the attack against non-Serbs and the ethnic cleansing of the county of Prijedor. She studied the situation from the time the Serbs took power on April 30, 1992, including military operations, opening of detention facilities, mass destruction of property, and forcible expulsion of persons. A comparison of 1991 census figures and the population count in June 1993 showed that 52,811 people had been killed or were missing—all non-Serbs.[98] From the data that Commissioner Greve collected and some four hundred interviews of witnesses to the destruction, she prepared a lengthy report describing not only the violations of international humanitarian law but also the pattern of conduct evidencing a deliberate policy that produced a significantly high level of victimization.[99] The Commission concluded that these practices, particularly in Prijedor, constituted crimes against humanity and possibly genocide.[100] This study, which was largely testimony driven, documents the policy and practice of ethnic cleansing in this region and suggests how it has been carried out elsewhere. Other reports and studies contained in the annexes to the *Final Report* reinforce these findings.

Investigation of the Medak Pocket

The Medak Pocket is a small territory located 150 kilometers southwest of Zagreb (partly in Croatia), in UNPA Sector South. Croatian forces attacked this cluster of rural villages in September 1993, when the area was under Serb control. After securing the area, the Croats agreed to retreat to their previous position. However, before relinquishing the territory, the Croatian forces burned or blew up all homes in the area and allegedly killed or took all livestock and looted personal property.[101] In addition, there was evidence that civilians had been injured or killed

---

[98] *Id.* ¶ 153.
[99] *Id.* ¶¶ 151–181.
[100] *Id.* ¶ 182. See *infra* note 143.
[101] *Id.* ¶ 210.

during the attack.[102] The Commission chose to conduct an investigation of the incident for two reasons. First, at the time, the incident was relatively recent; therefore, witnesses were still available and other evidence was still fresh. Second, UNPROFOR forces had arrived right at the end of the destructive retreat and were able to obtain much evidence. The Commission deployed a team of investigators to interview witnesses and procure the UNPROFOR report of the incident. They concluded that while "there was no strong unambiguous pattern of criminal killing sufficient at the time to affix responsibility upon the Croat commanders for deliberate killing of civilians," there was a "clear, obvious and overwhelming pattern of wanton destruction" of property for which named senior Croatian officials could be prosecuted.[103]

INVESTIGATIONS CONDUCTED BY GOVERNMENTS ON BEHALF OF THE COMMISSION

The Commission also relied on various governments to conduct interviews of refugees and to undertake investigations. Several governments were particularly helpful in this respect. The cumulative number of such interviews exceeded one thousand. However, details of this process, including the governments that participated, cannot be disclosed for reasons of security, confidentiality, and so forth.

THE COMMISSION'S REPORTS

Pursuant to its Rules of Procedure,[104] the Commission submitted two interim reports to the Secretary-General. The reports were approved, respectively, at the Commission's third (January 25–26, 1993) and seventh (August 30–31, 1993) sessions. The Secretary-General, in turn,

---

[102] *Id.* ¶ 212.

[103] *Id.* ¶¶ 212–214.

[104] Comm'n Rules, *supra* note 30, R. 10(2).

submitted these reports to the Security Council.[105] At the Commission's final and twelfth session (April 11–15, 1994), it unanimously adopted the *Final Report*, which was submitted to the Secretary-General on May 5, 1994. The Secretary-General forwarded the *Final Report* to the Security Council on May 24, 1994.[106] The 84-page *Final Report* refers to twelve annexes, running about 3,200 pages. Because the Commission considers the annexes to be an integral part of the report, for reasons discussed below, the Secretary-General agreed to their subsequent publication.[107]

First Interim Report

The *First Interim Report* provides a description of the Commission's activities from November 1992 to January 1993. The report contains an introductory section describing the Commission's mandate and composition and the information submitted to the Commission by various governments and other bodies. The introduction is followed by sections describing or discussing (1) the Commission's efforts to coordinate its work with other bodies, such as the CSCE; (2) the tasks carried out by the Commission to fulfill its mandate, such as the examination, verification, and analysis of information, identification of cases warranting in-depth investigation, and consideration of issues of law; (3) alleged mass grave sites; (4) the Commission's projected plan of work; and (5) the Commission's resources and budget requirements.

In this report, the Commission disclosed its decision to establish the IHRLI database in order to keep a comprehensive record of alleged violations. The commissioners felt that in order to fulfill the Commission's mandate objectively, they had to analyze the information systematically and the database permitted them to do so.[108] The

---

[105] *First Interim Report*, supra note 4; *Second Interim Report*, supra note 21.

[106] *Final Report*, supra note 24.

[107] The annexes were not attached to the report but are nevertheless part of it. *See generally* section *infra* entitled "Annexes to the Final Report." The annexes will be released as U.N. Doc. S/1994/674/Add.2 (vols. I–V) (1994).

[108] *First Interim Report*, supra note 4, ¶¶ 22–23.

Commission also stressed that the database could be only "as effective as the evidence received."[109] According to the Commission, many of the reports that it had received were not complete, lacking necessary information, such as names and locations. Additionally, reports seemed to rely on secondhand information, such as media sources. Therefore, the Commission requested that governments submit the files on which their reports had been based.[110] The Commission also discussed the necessity of obtaining tangible evidence, such as statements and forensic reports, on its own.[111]

The *First Interim Report* also contains a lengthy and important discussion of issues of law in relation to the conflict in the former Yugoslavia. The Commission determined that the character and complexity of the armed conflict in the region, considered in conjunction with agreements the parties had made, such as declaring themselves bound by the Geneva Conventions and the 1977 Protocols thereto, justified categorizing the situation as an international armed conflict subject to the international law of armed conflict and international humanitarian law.[112]

Second Interim Report

The *Second Interim Report* covers the period February 1993–August 1993 and discusses the following: (1) implementation of the Commission's projected plan of work set forth in the *First Interim Report*; (2) future projects to be undertaken; and (3) resources and budget requirements. This report describes plans to conduct on-site investigations of mass graves and detention facilities.[113] Knowing that the cooperation of local authorities was necessary to this undertaking, the Commission held talks

---

[109] *Id.* ¶ 28.

[110] *Id.*

[111] *Id.* ¶ 32.

[112] *See id.* ¶ 45.

[113] *Second Interim Report, supra* note 21, ¶¶ 76–80, 84–86.

with a series of officials.[114] In addition, the Commission stated its intention to use seconded personnel from various countries for the purpose of conducting these investigations.[115]

Final Report

The *Final Report* is a comprehensive account of the Commission's work and findings, addressing (1) its mandate, structure, and methods of work; (2) applicable law; (3) general studies on the military structure of the warring factions and on ethnic cleansing; (4) substantive findings on ethnic cleansing that relate to the county of Prijedor, the battle and siege of Sarajevo, a field investigation conducted in Sarajevo, a field investigation of the Medak Pocket, detention facilities, rape and other forms of sexual assault, mass graves in general and mass grave investigations conducted in Ovcara and Pakracka Poljana, the destruction of cultural property, the battle of Dubrovnik, and the radiological investigation conducted in UNPA Sector West; and (5) conclusions and recommendations.

The *Final Report* deals with a number of questions of law that the Commission thought needed clarification. Questions of command responsibility and superior orders are well established in customary international law.[116] However, because of certain claims by members of the warring factions, the Commission decided to affirm the inviolability

---

[114] *Id.* ¶ 12. During April 18–29, 1993, the Commission sent a delegation to the region of the former Yugoslavia. *Id.* ¶ 13. Chairman Kalshoven, Commissioner Fenrick, and I traveled to Zagreb and Belgrade. *Id.* ¶ 13 n.7. Then, Chairman Kalshoven went on to Ljubljana, while Commissioner Fenrick and I went to Sarajevo. *Id.* Commissioner Fenrick went to Knin May 17–19 to meet with the Prime Minister of Knin to request permission to conduct the mass grave exhumation at Ovcara. *Id.* ¶ 17.

[115] *Id.* ¶¶ 97–101.

[116] *See, e.g.,* United States v. Yamashita (1945), in 4 UN War Crimes Comm'n, *Law Reports of Trials of War Criminals* 1 (1947), *aff'd,* 327 U.S. 1 (1946); United States v. Ohlendorf (Einsatzgruppen Case), in 4 *Trials of War Criminals before the Nuernberg Military Tribunals under Control Council Law No. 10, Nuernberg, October 1946–April 1949,* Case No. 9 (1949–1953); William H. Parks, *Command Responsibility for War Crimes,* 62 Mil. L. Rev. 1 (1973); Richard L. Lael, *The Yamashita Precedent: War Crimes and Command Responsibility* (1982).

of the international humanitarian law applicable to the conflict.[117] It is also important to note that the Geneva Conventions were incorporated into the Criminal Code of the former Socialist Federal Republic of Yugoslavia. Moreover, the same acts that constitute grave breaches, such as murder, rape, and wanton destruction of property, are common crimes in the criminal codes of all the new republics that have emerged in the region. Claims by some of the warring factions with respect to reprisals also made it necessary to explain the limits of this concept under international humanitarian law.[118] Additionally, the Commission thought that it was important to affirm that both Protocols I and II of the Geneva Conventions apply to this conflict even though neither instrument is mentioned in the Statute of the Tribunal.[119]

The *Final Report* also addresses the scope of crimes within the competence of the International Tribunal,[120] particularly under articles 4 and 5 of the Statute. Thus, the report sought to clarify certain aspects of the category of crimes against humanity, particularly with respect to the element of intent and the selection of groups as part of a policy of persecution.[121] In order to be convicted of crimes against humanity, one must have had the intent to engage in specific conduct against a given

---

[117] *Final Report, supra* note 24, ¶¶ 41–109.

[118] *Id.* ¶¶ 63–66.

[119] *Id.* ¶ 51; Statute, *supra* note 9, art. 2 (jurisdiction over grave breaches of the Geneva Conventions of 1949); Protocol Additional to the Geneva Conventions of 12 August 1949, and Relating to the Protection of Victims of International Armed Conflicts (Additional Protocol I), *adopted* June 8, 1977, 1125 U.N.T.S. 3 (entered into force Dec. 7, 1978); Protocol Additional to the Geneva Conventions of 12 August 1949, and Relating to the Protection of Victims of Non-international Armed Conflicts (Additional Protocol II), *adopted* June 8, 1977, 1125 U.N.T.S. 609 (entered into force Dec. 7, 1978).

[120] *Final Report, supra* note 24, ¶¶ 41–109. For a discussion of rape and other sexual offenses, see C.P.M. Cleiren & M.E.M. Tijssen, *Rape and Other Forms of Sexual Assault in the Armed Conflict in the Former Yugoslavia: Legal, Procedural, and Evidentiary Issues*, in this issue of *Criminal Law Forum*.

[121] *Final Report, supra* note 24, ¶¶ 83–86; Statute, *supra* note 9, art. 5. See generally M. Cherif Bassiouni, *Crimes against Humanity: The Need for a Specialized Convention*, 31 Colum. J. Transnat'l L. 457 (1994).

group. The acts must be done as part of a systematic policy of persecution against this group. The intent to persecute or the intent to develop a policy of persecution is demonstrated objectively by the conduct that took place.

With respect to the crime of genocide, the Commission took the position that the definition of this crime in the Genocide Convention of 1948 is not static.[122] Rather, the definition is sufficiently pliable to encompass not only the targeting of an entire group, as stated in the convention, but also the targeting of certain segments of a given group, such as the Muslim elite or Muslim women. Furthermore, a given group can be defined on the basis of its regional existence, as opposed to a broader and all-inclusive concept encompassing all the members of that group who may be in different regions or areas. For example, all Muslims in Bosnia–Herzegovina could be considered a protected group. One could also define the group as all Muslims in a given area of Bosnia–Herzegovina, such as Prijedor, if the intent of the perpetrator is the elimination of that narrower group. In the context of the conflict in the former Yugoslavia, Albanians, Croats, Gypsies, Hungarians, Muslims, Serbs, and others constitute ethnic groups and "may, at least in part, be characterized by religion, ethnicity and nationality."[123] That is, it may be possible to consider the inhabitants of a given area irrespective of their religion as part of the entire group, as well as an identifiable group on its own, protected in either case by the Genocide

---

[122] *Final Report, supra* note 24, ¶ 96; Statute, *supra* note 9, art. 4; Convention on the Prevention and Punishment of the Crime of Genocide, *adopted* Dec. 9, 1948, art. 2, 78 U.N.T.S. 277. The Statute incorporates the convention's definition verbatim:

> Genocide means any of the following acts committed with intent to destroy, in whole or in part, a national, ethnical, racial or religious group, as such:
>
> (a) killing members of the group;
> (b) causing serious bodily or mental harm to members of the group;
> (c) deliberately inflicting on the group conditions of life calculated to bring about its physical destruction in whole or in part;
> (d) imposing measures intended to prevent births within the group;
> (e) forcibly transferring children of the group to another group.

[123] *Final Report, supra* note 24, ¶ 95.

Convention as incorporated into article 4 of the Statute.[124] For example, all Bosnians in Sarajevo, irrespective of ethnicity or religion, could constitute a protected group.

One of the major differences between genocide and crimes against humanity is that in order to establish genocide, the prosecution must show an intent to destroy the group in whole or in part, whereas in regard to crimes against humanity there is no requirement of destruction of the group. To establish the latter type of crime, the prosecution must show only an intent to persecute through a policy of systematic conduct, which can be proven by either a pattern of behavior or individual acts.

Since the *Final Report* was much longer than the UN standard of 30 pages, a waiver was needed in order to publish it. The report was completed in a relatively short period of time during the month of April 1994. It took into account all of the data and tentative conclusions contained in the annexes, which were still being completed. In effect, the report synthesizes the roughly 3,200 pages of material set out in the annexes. Regrettably, after April, the so-called warring factions, and several governments—in particular, note the Federal Republic of Yugoslavia submission in May 1994—indicated that additional information was available. Given the number of violations that occurred prior to the preparation of the *Final Report* and annexes and given that the conflict continues, it is certain that more crimes within the jurisdiction of the Tribunal have occurred. The termination of the Commission also means that there is no investigatory body to monitor continuing violations and to persist in gathering evidence related to policies and patterns of violence, such as ethnic cleansing and systematic rape. Whatever the Commission did on these and other subjects discussed in the *Final Report* and its annexes will remain as the only historic record available to document this tragic conflict.

Annexes to the Final Report

The *Final Report* incorporates by reference twelve annexes, which include a series of subannexes that bring the total number to twenty-three.

---

[124] *See id.* ¶ 96.

These twenty-three discrete reports run to about 3,200 pages of detailed information and analysis. The *Final Report* of the Commission states that the annexes are an integral part of the report and must therefore be published.[125] According to the letter by which the Secretary-General transmitted the *Final Report* to the Security Council:

> The final report includes several annexes containing reports of investigations and studies, which as a whole constitute an integral part of the report. In his letter to me of 6 May 1994, the Chairman of the Commission requested that the annexes be published, although for cost purposes and given their volume (approximately 3,000 pages) it was suggested that they be published in English only and funded from the remaining surplus in the Trust Fund of the Commission of Experts.[126]

Because the Commission was terminated before it could complete its program of work, the trust fund held over $230,000 as of May 1994. The Commission allocated this entire sum to the publication of the annexes, and the Secretary-General agreed to this proposal.

After the appointment of Judge Richard Goldstone of South Africa as prosecutor,[127] the OLA decided that he should have a chance to review the annexes to prevent the disclosure of sensitive information. Even though the Commission's findings are independent and not subject to anyone's veto, as chairman I considered this step to be reasonable and judicious. The process, however, took some time. The United Nations received the final text of the annexes on December 22, 1994, for distribution to the Security Council and for publication.

Annexes I–I.C are relatively short administrative or descriptive accounts prepared by the Commission's secretariat[128] or by IHRLI staff

---

[125] *Id.* ¶¶ 39–40.

[126] *Id.* at 2.

[127] See *supra* note 11.

[128] At the time, the Commission's secretariat included Vladimir Kotliar, Secretary; Bruna Molina-Abrams, Deputy Secretary; and Julio Baez, Assistant Secretary. The Commission's first Secretary was Jacqueline Dauchy.

under my supervision.[129] Annex I contains the Commission's Rules of Procedure, which were appended also to the *First Interim Report*.[130] Annex I.A includes an extensive explanation of the IHRLI database and documentation center and a description of the documents received by the Commission and catalogued by the IHRLI documentarian.[131] Annex I.B lists the thirty-four missions undertaken by the Commission.[132] Annex I.C lists and acknowledges the many organizations that assisted or supported the work of the Commission.[133]

Commissioner Cleiren prepared Annex II, which is an 18-page report on the criteria for applying international humanitarian law to the crime of rape and other sexual assaults.[134] In her analysis, she addresses sexual assaults not only on women but also on men and children.[135]

---

[129] Overall responsibility for editing the annexes was given to Carolyn Durnik and Marcia McCormick. The following staff attorneys assisted in the preparation of reports: Patsy Campbell, Carolyn Durnik, Georgann Grabiec, Marcia McCormick, Suzan Ozturk, Peter Spies, and Carson Wetzel. The following staff analysts assisted in the preparation of reports: Daniel Bronson, Richard Danis, Mirande Dupuy, Sebastien Mancel, Christine Matthews, Azra Mehdi, James Rogan, Diane Silverman, John Stomper, John Tomasic, Stacey White, Monica Witczak, and Mario Zadro.

[130] See *supra* note 30.

[131] Carson Wetzel, IHRLI Staff Attorney, was the principal analyst for Annex I.A.

[132] The Commission's secretariat prepared Annex I.B. Some missions were for reconnaissance purposes in order to decide whether an investigation should be conducted or in order to prepare for an investigation.

[133] The Commission's secretariat prepared Annex I.C.

[134] Commissioner Cleiren was assisted in the preparation of Annex II by Melanie E.M. Tijssen, Attorney and Assistant to Professor Menno Kamminga, Professor of Public International Law, Erasmus University of Rotterdam, the Netherlands.

[135] Although international humanitarian law does not specifically address violent sexual crimes against men, to exclude them would amount to impermissible discrimination on the basis of sex under international law. *E.g.*, Universal Declaration of Human Rights arts. 1–2, G.A. Res. 217A (III), U.N. Doc. A/810, at 71 (1948); International Covenant on Civil and Political Rights, *adopted* Dec. 19, 1966, art. 3, 999 U.N.T.S. 171.

Children are specifically protected by several international conventions. *E.g.*, Convention on the Rights of the Child, G.A. Res. 44/25, U.N. GAOR, 44th Sess., Supp. No. 49, at 166, U.N. Doc. A/44/49 (1989) (entered into force Sept. 2, 1990).

Annex III describes the basic military structure of the warring factions and the structure, strategy, and tactics of the military forces engaged in the conflict.[136] This 37-page annex looks specifically at the Yugoslav Army and its predecessor, the JNA; the Bosnian Serb Army; the Croatian Army; the Croatian Defense Council; and the Bosnian Army. Because the various forces were organized only recently, put together for the most part from the JNA or local territorial defense forces, the annex also sets out a history of the Yugoslav military and the territorial defense forces from World War II to the present.

Annex III.A details the activities of the "special forces" and paramilitary groups that have engaged in fighting during the conflict, acting either on their own or in conjunction with the regular military forces.[137] The report identifies not only the paramilitary groups but also the party to the conflict for which they have been fighting.[138] Sources consulted in preparing this report included documents and audio- and videotapes collected by the Commission or by IHRLI, as well as media reports. All information relating to the activities of paramilitary groups was analyzed, but general references, such as "Serbian paramilitaries," were not included in the statistical data. Only reports containing specific names of paramilitary organizations or names of leaders were used to prepare the annex. Based upon the documents, information sheets were generated for each identified paramilitary group and were used to make comparisons among the groups. The information sheets included the name of the unit, ethnicity, uniform, number of troops, place of origin, area(s) of operation, political affiliation, leader(s), alleged members,

---

[136] Annex III was prepared by me with the assistance of Richard Janney, IHRLI Staff Attorney; Peter M. Manikas, IHRLI Staff Attorney; and Edmund A. McAlister, Assistant to M. Cherif Bassiouni.

[137] Annex III.A was prepared under my direction. Mark W. Bennett, IHRLI Staff Attorney, was the principal legal analyst.

[138] Due to the uneven quality (with much of the information not verified) and the paucity of documents received by the Commission, the report should not be considered comprehensive. More groups may be discovered or their identity clarified upon further investigation. The documents received indicated 83 paramilitary groups as follows: 56 in support of Yugoslavia or the self-proclaimed Serb republics in Bosnia and Croatia; 13 in support of Croatia; and 14 in support of Bosnia–Herzegovina.

source(s) of information, and alleged activity. The annex comprises about 300 pages of material.

Annex IV pertains to the policy of ethnic cleansing.[139] This 90-page report contains three sections: first, a history of conflicts in the former Yugoslavia dating back to the first century A.D.; second, an analysis of the policy of ethnic cleansing; and, third, a study of the town of Zvornik, which was prepared by the Ludwig Boltzman Institute of Human Rights (Vienna, Austria). Since the ethnic rivalries in the territory of the former Yugoslavia are historically rooted, the first section describes the origins of the rivalries and the region's turbulent past in the hope of providing an understanding of the perspective of the parties involved in the current conflict. The second section examines the policy and practice of ethnic cleansing in the region, with an emphasis on the case of Serbian forces attempting to create a "Greater Serbia" by seizing territory in Bosnia–Herzegovina and Croatia.[140] The third section focuses on the town of Zvornik and the expulsion of almost its entire Muslim population.[141] The Boltzman Institute relied on information that it gathered from an evaluation of five hundred interviews of Bosnian refugees from the Zvornik area, which were conducted as part of a larger interview study involving nine hundred Bosnian refugees from the area. The institute also conducted thirty-one interviews itself, using experienced, bilingual interviewers who were specifically trained for this mission. The institute developed a complex questionnaire for the interviews. Among other things, refugees were asked to reconstruct in chronological order the events surrounding their expulsion and to identify perpetrators.

Commissioner Greve prepared Annex V, an extensive report on

---

[139] Annex IV was prepared by me with the assistance of Peter M. Manikas and Jan Brakel, IHRLI Staff Attorneys.

[140] *Id.* ¶ 2 defines "ethnic cleansing" as "the rendering of an area ethnically homogenous by using force or intimidation to remove persons of a given ethnic group from the area."

[141] Zvornik is situated on the Drina River, which marks the border between Bosnia–Herzegovina and Yugoslavia. The town is strategically important because it links these areas by both a road bridge and a railroad bridge. The bridges are significant in terms of troop movements from Serbia to Tuzla and Sarajevo. Of course, the bridges are important to Bosnian forces for the same reason.

the genocide and ethnic cleansing that occurred in the county of Prijedor, in northwestern Bosnia–Herzegovina.[142] Commissioner Greve based the approximately 140-page report on more than four hundred statements given by surviving victims and witnesses. In addition, she relied on local Serbian media reports of the events and her own research. Her investigation resulted in an in-depth and comprehensive report on the purge of Muslims and Croats from the county of Prijedor and the alleged violations of international humanitarian law that they suffered. However, the report is not likely to be published at this time because of the sensitive material it contains and because of impending indictments.[143]

Annex VI is a lengthy chronology and analysis of the battle and siege of Sarajevo.[144] The 1,300-page report covers the period April 5, 1992–February 28, 1994. The analysts relied on incident reports from the IHRLI database; source documents received by the Commission, particularly daily, weekly, and monthly UNPROFOR reports recording the number of shells entering the city; and media accounts of attacks on Sarajevo. The annex contains information on daily combat and shelling

---

[142] Because of the confidential nature of the material contained in Commissioner Greve's report, the complete annex will not be published until sometime in the future. Morten Bergsmo, whose services were contributed by Norway, assisted in the preparation of this report.

[143] However, the study on Prijedor and other information submitted by the Commission to the office of the prosecutor were relied upon in the application by Prosecutor Goldstone to Germany on November 8, 1994, to defer to the Tribunal in the prosecution of Dusko Tadic. For background, see Melinda Crane-Engel, *Germany vs. Genocide*, N.Y. Times, Oct. 30, 1994, § 6, at 56, *available in* LEXIS, World Library, Allnws File; *Yugo War Crimes Court Asks Germany to Extradite Bosnian Serb*, Agence France Presse, Nov. 8, 1994, *available in* LEXIS, World Library, Allnws File.
    On February 13, 1995, Prosecutor Goldstone returned 21 indictments for war crimes and crimes against humanity allegedly committed in the Prijedor area. Prosecutor of the International Tribunal for the Former Yugoslavia v. Dusan Tadic and Twenty Named Co-defendants, Attachment to Tribunal Press Release, Feb. 13, 1995, U.N. Doc. CC/PIO/004-E (1995); Jon Henley, *Serb Jailers Charged with Murder, Rape, and Torture*, The Guardian (Manchester), Feb. 14, 1995, *available in* LEXIS, World Library, Allnws File.

[144] Annex VI was prepared under my direction. William B. Schiller, IHRLI Staff Attorney, was the principal legal analyst.

activity; specific targets hit; known damage to targets; sniping activity; and total casualties reported. The annex also contains an account of daily military activities and international events, such as peace negotiations, related to the battle and siege. The purpose of the chronology is to record the events and effects of the battle and siege and to evaluate patterns of violations, as well as to determine command responsibility.

Annex VI.A also concerns Sarajevo.[145] The Commission decided to investigate a specific incident in the siege of Sarajevo to determine the feasibility of identifying and prosecuting alleged perpetrators. The Commission sent Commander Fenrick and a team of Canadian military lawyers to conduct the investigation. They chose to investigate the mortar shelling of a soccer game in Dobrinja, a suburb of Sarajevo, which occurred on June 1, 1993.[146] The investigation team interviewed many Bosnian witnesses but was unable to interview Serbian witnesses. Additionally, the team reviewed an UNPROFOR analysis of the mortar craters resulting from the shells. From the information gathered, the team wrote a six-page report.

Annex VI.B is a 37-page study of the battle and siege of Sarajevo and the law of armed conflict. The study was prepared by Commander Fenrick and Major A.J. van Veen, a military lawyer from the war crimes investigation team seconded by Canada, who visited Sarajevo in mid-1993, meeting with Bosnian officials and military personnel and visiting several areas that were shelled during the siege. The objective of the study was to impute command responsibility for violations of the laws of war. For this purpose, the authors prepared an analytical survey of the battle and all violations committed.

Annex VII is a 16-page report on the Medak Pocket operation, which occurred in early September 1993.[147] As discussed earlier,

---

[145] Annex VI.A was prepared by Sergeant J.L. Lamothe and Warrant Officer S. Murray-Ford, members of the Canadian war crimes investigation team, see *supra* note 26, under the direction of Commissioner Fenrick.

[146] The team did not choose the incident prior to arriving in Sarajevo. Criteria such as number of casualties and sources of information were used to determine which incident to investigate.

[147] Annex VII was prepared under the direction of Commissioner Fenrick. Major J.C. Holland, Canadian Armed Forces, was the principal legal analyst.

Croatian forces entered and attacked an area of small, rural villages known as the Medak Pocket. After agreeing to relinquish the territory, the forces allegedly destroyed and burned everything before they left. UNPROFOR troops arrived at the end of the retreat and were able to collect a significant amount of evidence. The investigation team produced the annex from several witness interviews that it conducted, as well as the UNPROFOR report.[148]

Annex VIII concerns prison camps and detention facilities within the territory of the former Yugoslavia.[149] The report spans 880 pages divided into two sections. The first section is a summary analysis that contains a discussion of methodology; the total number of detention facilities; the total number of detention facilities broken down by ethnic group in control; the total number of detention facilities by geographic region; and a discussion of patterns and commonalities identified from various reports. The second section divides the facilities by main regions (Bosnia–Herzegovina, Croatia, Yugoslavia, and Slovenia) and then by counties within those regions. Organized and analyzed by location, the documents relating to detention facilities yielded the following information: (1) the name, location, dates of operation, and physical description of the facilities; (2) the identity and ethnicity of camp commanders, guards, and anyone else involved in the operation of a given camp; (3) the ethnicity of prisoners and whether they were civilians or military personnel; (4) the transfer of prisoners from one camp to another; (5) the total reported prisoner population of a given camp; and (6) the treatment of prisoners and camp conditions, such as the availability of food, bathroom facilities, sleeping accommodations, and medical care, as well as the number of prisoners in one room.

Three annexes concern the issue of rape and sexual assault. The first, Annex IX, is an analysis based upon documents collected by the Commission and incident reports in the IHRLI database that include allegations of rape and sexual assault.[150] From these materials, summary

---

[148] See *supra* note 55.

[149] Annex VIII was prepared under my direction. Eric S. Krauss and William B. Schiller, IHRLI Staff Attorneys, were the principal legal analysts.

[150] Annex IX was prepared under my direction. Marcia McCormick, IHRLI Staff Attorney, was the principal legal analyst.

sheets were created for each allegation, setting out information such as the identity of victims, witnesses, and perpetrators; the date and location of the incident; the source of the report; and the method used to record the information. The sheets also summarize the incident itself. As with Annex III.A, the summary sheets were used as an analytical tool to compare information in a standardized format. The summaries were organized geographically, divided by the setting in which the rape occurred (custodial or noncustodial), and then arranged chronologically within the categories of custodial and noncustodial setting. The analytical portion of Annex IX is divided by geographical location as well. The 123-page report identifies specific individual cases of rape, as well as patterns or policies of rape, providing a foundation in fact for the allegation that rape has been used as an instrument of war.

Annex IX.A is a 62-page report on the sexual assault investigation conducted by the Commission in March 1994.[151] The annex contains two parts. Part one is a report by the interview coordinator, which contains the following: (1) a discussion of the methodology used both to choose the victims and witnesses to be interviewed and to conduct the interviews; (2) comments regarding the substance of allegations; (3) recommendations for further investigation; and (4) the plan of action for the interview process. Part two is a report by the mental health team, which discusses the activities and role of these experts, as well as the psychological effects of giving testimony and the psychological and physical status of those interviewed.

Annex IX.B is an eight-page report on a pilot rape study conducted in Sarajevo.[152] The investigation team consisted of two Canadian military police investigators and a Canadian military lawyer. Sarajevo was the chosen site because the Bosnian War Crimes Commis-

---

[151] Annex IX.A was prepared under my direction. Karen Kenny, Consultant to the Commission of Experts and Interview Coordinator for the investigation, was the principal legal analyst. Dr. Stephanie Cavanaugh, Consultant to the Commission, was the principal psychiatric analyst.

[152] Annex IX.B was prepared under the direction of Commissioner Fenrick. Lieutenant-Colonel Kim S. Carter, Canadian Armed Forces and Consultant to the Commission of Experts, was the principal legal analyst. Petty Officer J. Ross and Master Corporal T. McCombe, Canadian Armed Forces, served as the investigators.

sion and the League for the Help of Victims of Genocide are located in Sarajevo. Both organizations previously indicated that they had collected extensive information regarding rape. The objective of the study was to assess the feasibility of prosecuting alleged perpetrators and their superiors in certain cases of rape.

Three annexes were produced regarding the issue of mass graves. Annex X is a study based on 10,000 pages of documents received by the Commission and on database incident reports related to mass graves.[153] This 106-page report contains two sections. The first is a summary analysis of the information that discusses the methodology of the report and indicates the total number of graves, the number of graves in each geographic region, the number of graves by ethnicity of victims and perpetrators, the number of graves near detention facilities, and other information. This section also discusses patterns, trends, and commonalities identified from the various sources of information. The second section is an analysis by geographical location and describes grave sites by county, including information, when available, on the military activity in the county at the time the grave was created.

To compile and organize information for this report, IHRLI staff created a separate mass grave database within the main database. When an incident report of a mass grave was entered into the database, it was cross-checked against any information already entered to avoid duplication. Thus, if a file regarding a specific grave site already existed, any additional information was entered into the existing file; if a report concerned a new grave, a new file was opened for the site and the information was entered. The files allowed the analysts to organize a great deal of information and to corroborate accounts of mass graves.

Annex X.A is a report on the mass grave investigation conducted in Ovcara, in UNPA Sector East, Croatia.[154] This 14-page annex contains a report by the Canadian war crimes investigation team and a report by the forensic team. The Canadian team describes their efforts

---

[153] Annex X was prepared under my direction. Georgann Grabiec, IHRLI Staff Attorney, was the principal legal analyst.

[154] Commissioner Fenrick prepared Annex X.A with the assistance of members of the Canadian war crimes investigation team, members of the Royal Netherlands Army, and Dr. Eric Stover of Physicians for Human Rights.

to obtain the necessary permission from local Serbian authorities to conduct the investigation and all events leading up to UNPROFOR's securing the area. The forensic team, Physicians for Human Rights, discusses the technical equipment and procedures that were used during the preliminary site preparation, such as electronic mapping procedures, and that were to be employed during the mass grave exhumation.

Annex X.B concerns the mass grave exhumation at Pakracka Poljana, UNPA Sector West, Croatia.[155] It is substantially similar to Annex X.A but lengthier and more detailed because this exhumation was completed. The 47-page report comprises two parts: an interim report and an investigation report prepared by the Canadian team; and a forensic report by Physicians for Human Rights, which describes the methods employed to exhume the bodies and catalogue physical evidence, as well as the findings on how the victims were killed.

Annex XI is a 12-page study of the destruction of cultural property prepared by Commissioner M'Baye. The study does not attempt to cite every violation of the laws of war concerning the destruction of cultural property in the region. Rather, Commissioner M'Baye focused on two incidents: the battle of Dubrovnik (October–December 1991) and the destruction of the Mostar Bridge (November 9, 1993). The analysis of the incidents and the application of the laws of war are to serve as examples for the prosecutor to follow in investigating the deliberate destruction of cultural property.

Annex XI.A is a 33-page study of the battle of Dubrovnik and the law of armed conflict.[156] A team of experts on the law of armed

---

[155] Commissioner Fenrick prepared Annex X.B with the assistance of Major J.C. Holland and Major P. Olson, of the Canadian war crimes investigation team, members of the Royal Netherlands Army, and Dr. Eric Stover of Physicians for Human Rights.

[156] In 1979, UNESCO placed Dubrovnik on the World Heritage List. In 1991, the JNA attacked the town and caused extensive damage to historical, cultural, and religious property. The damage was allegedly out of proportion to what was reasonably necessary in light of valid military objectives. Therefore, the battle of Dubrovnik was chosen for a study of the laws of war as applied to the destruction of cultural property. Annex XI.A was prepared under the direction of Commissioner Fenrick by Major Oyvind Hoel, Norwegian Armed Forces; Dr. Colin Kaiser, Consultant to the Commission of Experts; Major Terje Lund, Norwegian Armed Forces; and Lieutenant-Colonel Dominic McAlea, Canadian Armed Forces.

conflict and an art historian were sent to Dubrovnik to investigate alleged damage to cultural property and civilians. The study attempted to determine when attacks on civilians and cultural property occurred and to ascertain the number of civilian deaths and injuries, as well as the extent of damage to civilian property and particularly cultural property. The study also attempted to attribute responsibility for violations of the law of armed conflict that occurred in the area. In the preparation of the annex, the team relied on the following evidence: oral and written statements of eyewitnesses; hearsay statements; photographs and videotapes; unexploded ordnance; reports from investigations conducted by national bodies, such as the civilian police, or other UN bodies, such as UNESCO; and a local criminal court judgment. In addition, the team sought out secondary sources of information to supplement its evidence.

Annex XII is a seven-page report on the radiological investigation of alleged nuclear waste dumping in UNPA Sector West, Croatia.[157] The allegations were not supported by the empirical results of this study, and there was no time to follow up subsequent claims by the Krajina Serbs about other sites.

The Secretary-General acknowledged in a letter to me the receipt of the annexes and their distribution to the Security Council:

> I take this opportunity to reiterate my gratitude and appreciation for the work done by the Commission of Experts, as well as the skill, time and effort invested in the preparation of its Final Report and voluminous Annexes. I wish, in this connection, to single out the International Human Rights Law Institute . . . which, under your direction, established the data-base as the core project of the Commission.
>
> The material and information collected and recorded in the data-base, now transferred to the Tribunal, will not only assist in the prosecution of persons responsible for serious violations of international humanitarian law, but will constitute

---

[157] Annex XII was prepared under the direction of Commissioner Fenrick by Captain J.J.H.M. Limbourg and Sergeant Major C.C.L. Daelman of the Royal Netherlands Army Nuclear, Biological, and Chemical School.

a permanent documentary record of the crimes committed in the former Yugoslavia, and thus remain the memorial for the hundreds of thousands of its innocent victims.[158]

THE COMMISSION'S TERMINATION

On April 30, 1994, the Commission indicated in writing to the Secretary-General that in the event of its discharge, the date should be July 31 of that year, in light of the Commission's proposed action plan. Some six months earlier, in its *Second Interim Report* (October 1993) to the Security Council, the Commission had outlined a plan of work based on a termination date of July 31, 1994. Thus, the Commission believed that the Security Council and the Secretary-General were in agreement on the appropriateness of this date. Also in October 1993, the Commission prepared its 1994 budget and submitted it to the OLA.[159] The budget closing date was likewise July 31, 1994. As late as November 2, 1994, I visited in New York with Mr. Fleischhauer and Mr. Zacklin, former and current OLA officials, respectively, and discussed the proposed budget. I also met with the Secretary-General at that time to brief him on the Commission's work and plan of action. No question was ever raised about the termination date of July 31, 1994.

Nonetheless, on December 13, 1993, then Under-Secretary-General for Legal Affairs and UN Legal Counsel Carl-August Fleischhauer had requested by letter that the Commission terminate its activities by April 30, 1994. No Security Council resolution ordered the termination of the Commission. Indeed, as noted earlier, Security Council Resolution 827, which established the Tribunal, stated that "pending the appointment of the Prosecutor of the International Tribunal," the Commission "should continue on an urgent basis the collection of information relating to evidence of grave breaches of the Geneva

---

[158] Letter from Boutros Boutros-Ghali, Secretary-General of the United Nations, to M. Cherif Bassiouni, President, International Human Rights Law Institute, DePaul University, Jan. 4, 1995.

[159] See *supra* note 25 and accompanying text.

Conventions and other violations of international humanitarian law as proposed in its interim report."[160] Between the time of Fleischhauer's request and the Commission's termination, there was no prosecutor in office, only an acting deputy prosecutor without any legal or investigatory staff.[161] Thus, the Secretariat's decision of December 13 violated the spirit, if not the letter, of Resolution 827. Ironically, only a few days after the OLA's notice of termination, the General Assembly commended the Commission for its work and supported its continuation.[162]

The untimely termination had damaging results. The Commission cut short several of its investigations. For example, as previously mentioned, the Commission could not continue its exhumation of the mass graves in Ovcara and Pakracka Poljana. Additionally, the rape investigation needed to continue for at least two more months in order to be sufficiently comprehensive. Because this investigation had to end on March 31, 1994, over two hundred interviews throughout the former Yugoslavia alone could not be conducted.[163] Lastly, the premature termination did not give Yugoslavia the opportunity to present information and evidence that the government had indicated it would provide, nor was there time for Yugoslavia's report, submitted in May 1994 to the United Nations,[164] to be taken into account in the Commission's *Final Report*.

By letter dated March 2, 1994, the Deputy Legal Counsel in charge of the OLA, Ralph Zacklin, requested that the Commission transfer all of its documents and the contents of the database to the

---

[160] S.C. Res. 827, *supra* note 10, preambular ¶ 10 (citation omitted).

[161] See *supra* note 11.

[162] *The Situation in Bosnia and Herzegovina*, U.N. GAOR, 48th Sess., U.N. Doc. A/48/L.50 (1993).

[163] There were approximately 200 more victims from Croatia and Bosnia–Herzegovina to be interviewed in Croatia, 7 Serbian victims to be interviewed in Belgrade, and an unspecified number of victims to be interviewed in Turkey at the request of the Turkish government. The Commission was left with having to ask the respective governments to conduct the interviews themselves and send the information to the prosecutor. Whether the governments did so is not known.

[164] *Yugoslavian Report*, *supra* note 53.

prosecutor's office. The Commission fully complied with this request and the transfer was complete by the time the Commission submitted its *Final Report* to the Secretary-General. As a result of the quick and unexpected transition, there was little opportunity for the Commission to review its work with the office of the prosecutor, which then consisted only of Acting Deputy Prosecutor Graham Blewitt and some secretarial staff.[165] Fortunately, since the appointment of Judge Goldstone, excellent collaborative relations have been established; members of the IHRLI staff and I have met with members of the prosecutor's staff in the Hague to discuss some of the Commission's findings and the database. This collaborative relationship was acknowledged by the Tribunal in its first annual report.[166] Furthermore, I worked closely with Prosecutor Goldstone and his staff in reviewing the annexes to make sure that they did not contain material that would be prejudicial to the prosecution. During this process, the prosecutor and his staff gave me their fullest cooperation, which I gratefully acknowledge.

CONCLUSION AND ASSESSMENT

The creation of the Commission of Experts by the UN Security Council was unprecedented. This step set the stage, and served as a model, for the Rwanda Commission, which was established in July 1994,[167] as it will for similar undertakings in the future. A new, action-oriented body of this sort required a great deal of support from the UN structure, which the latter was not prepared to give. There were, of course, understandable administrative reasons for some of the Commission's start-up difficulties. To this, one must add the problems of a cumbersome UN bureaucracy and the fact that the OLA, which serviced the

---

[165] Since the summer of 1994, Morten Bergsmo (Norway), William Fenrick (Canada), and Lieutenant-Colonel Anton Kempenaars (Norway) have joined the prosecutor's staff. Their presence ensures some continuity.

[166] The relationship between the Commission and the office of the prosecutor is acknowledged in *Tribunal Annual Report*, supra note 33, ¶¶ 157–158.

[167] See *supra* note 3.

Commission, was saddled with too much to do and had too few people to do it. Beyond that, however, it is hard to explain certain bureaucratic hurdles and delays that the Commission experienced. Above all, it is difficult to understand why no resources were made available by the General Assembly and why so few voluntary contributions were obtained from governments. If the Iran–*contra* investigation in the United States cost over $40 million, how could a $1.3 million trust fund be sufficient in the context of such large-scale victimization as has occurred in the former Yugoslavia? Perhaps in the future, the Security Council should allocate from its peacekeeping budget a sum for such commissions when it establishes them.

The premature termination of the Commission cannot be explained. Could it have been a purposeful political action to prevent the further discovery of the truth? Or was it simply an unwise administrative decision. Or perhaps it is the nature of the UN beast—part political, part bureaucratic—that accounts for what I believe to be an unconscionable outcome, no matter what the reason. It should be stated, however, that since the appointment of Hans Corell as Under-Secretary-General for Legal Affairs and Legal Counsel in February 1994, relations between the OLA and the Commission were excellent. Mr. Corell's support is gratefully acknowledged.

Despite the difficulties surveyed in this article, the Commission produced some extraordinary results. Without the foundation laid by the Commission, Prosecutor Goldstone would have had nothing to start with in the pursuit of his prosecutorial endeavors, even though many specific investigations will need to be conducted to convert the Commission's findings into indictable cases. The high visibility of the Commission and its work gave it credibility, which in turn gave the United Nations credibility. It also gave impetus to the Tribunal. Above all, the Commission established a significant, public record of violations that no one can ignore. Now justice is in the hands of the Tribunal. As stated in the *Final Report:*

> It is particularly striking to note the victims' high expectations that this Commission will establish the truth and that the International Tribunal will provide justice. All sides expect this. Thus, the conclusion is inescapable that peace in the future

requires justice, and that justice starts with establishing the truth. The Commission would be remiss if it did not emphasize the high expectation of justice conveyed by the parties to the conflict, as well as by victims, intergovernmental organizations, non-governmental organizations, the media and world public opinion. Consequently, the International Tribunal must be given the necessary resources and support to meet these expectations and accomplish its task. Furthermore, popular expectations of a new world order based on the international rule of law require no less than effective and permanent institutions of international justice. The International Tribunal for the Prosecution of Persons Responsible for Serious Violation of International Humanitarian Law Committed in the Territory of the Former Yugoslavia since 1991 must, therefore, be given the opportunity to produce the momentum for this future evolution.[168]

---

[168] *Final Report*, *supra* note 24, ¶ 320 (citation omitted).

III
Establishment of the Tribunal

4
An International Criminal Tribunal: The Difficult Union of Principle and Politics*

*Peter Burns*****

When the war criminal Adolf Eichmann was kidnapped from Argentina by agents of the state of Israel and forced to stand trial before an Israeli tribunal, world opinion was mixed. Almost everyone rejoiced that one of the most callous mass murderers of the twentieth century was finally being forced to take responsibility in public for his crimes. However, it was also recognized that the Israeli government's action compromised another state's sovereignty and was itself probably unlawful.[1]

---

*   This article is a revised and updated version of a paper delivered at the Eleventh International Congress of Criminology, Budapest, Hungary, August 26, 1993. I would like to thank Madeleine Sann, Director of Publication, *Criminal Law Forum*, for her work on this article.
       Editor's note: research for this article was updated through January 4, 1995.

**   Member, United Nations Committee against Torture and Cruel and Inhuman Treatment or Punishment; Professor of Law, University of British Columbia, Vancouver; Chairman, International Centre for Criminal Law Reform and Criminal Justice Policy, Vancouver, British Columbia, Canada; LL.B., Otago University 1962; LL.M. (first-class hons.), Otago University 1963; appointed Queen's Counsel 1984.

[1]   Attorney-General of Israel v. Eichmann, 36 I.L.R. 5 (Jerusalem Dist. Ct. 1961), *aff'd,* 36 I.L.R. 277 (Isr. 1962). For background and references, see Geoff Gilbert, *Aspects of Extradition Law* 184–85 (1991); Kenneth C. Randall, *Universal Jurisdiction under International Law,* 66 Tex. L. Rev. 785, 810–15 (1988); Helen Silving, *In re Eichmann: A Dilemma of Law and Morality,* 55 Am. J. Int'l L. 307 (1961); Ralph G. Steinhardt, *Statement before the Subcommittee on Civil and Constitutional Rights of the Committee on the Judiciary, U.S. House of Representatives,* 4 Crim. L.F. 135, 144–45 &

The *Eichmann* case is a modern illustration of a political and legal dilemma that has frustrated the mature development of international criminal law as a discrete discipline. Over the centuries, by custom and by treaty, rules governing the behavior of states and individuals in times of armed conflict have emerged as part of public international law. But one element essential to situating that body of rules firmly within the international legal system has been lacking: a means of enforcement.

Heads of state and government policymakers, whether ruling as princes by divine right or as democratically elected representatives of the people, have with few exceptions been able to avoid responsibility for their conduct by wrapping themselves up in the blanket of state sovereignty, secure in the knowledge that no international mechanism existed to call them to account. Until the twentieth century, the international community paid scant attention to the lack of an international forum to prosecute perpetrators of crimes against the international order, whether they be national leaders, field commanders, or soldiers acting on instructions from above. After the first world war, the international community made some tentative attempts to deal with this problem, but no such effort was pursued vigorously and none was successful.[2]

After the second world war, however, the victorious Allies took the decisive step of bringing key war criminals to trial in Nuremberg and Tokyo.[3] The jurisdiction of these tribunals extended to senior officials

---

nn.12–13 (1993) (testifying on United States v. Alvarez-Machain, 504 U.S. 655 (1992)); Julius Stone, The Eichmann Trial and the Rule of Law, Address to the Australian Section of the International Commission of Jurists (July 10, 1961) (transcript on file with the *Boston University Law Review*).

[2] For background, see 1 Benjamin Ferencz, *Defining International Aggression* (1975); M. Cherif Bassiouni, *The Time Has Come for an International Criminal Court*, 1 Ind. Int'l & Comp. L. Rev. 1, 2–4 (1991); Jules Deschênes, *Toward International Criminal Justice*, in this issue of *Criminal Law Forum;* Report on the International Meeting of Experts on the Establishment of an International Criminal Tribunal (International Centre for Criminal Law Reform and Criminal Justice Policy, Vancouver, British Columbia, Canada, Mar. 22–26, 1993) [hereinafter *Expert Report*]; *see also* sources cited *infra* note 9.

[3] The International Military Tribunal at Nuremberg was established pursuant to Agreement for the Prosecution and Punishment of the Major War Criminals of the

in the German and Japanese governments and went beyond traditional war crimes[4] to include crimes against the peace and crimes against humanity.[5] Although the Nuremberg and Tokyo trials accorded, for the

---

European Axis, Aug. 8, 1945, 82 U.N.T.S. 279. The Charter of the International Military Tribunal at Nuremberg is set out in *id.* at 284 [hereinafter Nuremberg Charter].

The International Military Tribunal for the Far East was established in Tokyo pursuant to Special Proclamation by the Supreme Commander for the Allied Powers, Establishment of an International Tribunal for the Far East, Jan. 19, 1946, 4 Bevans 20, *reprinted in* 1 Ferencz, *supra* note 2, at 522, and it operated pursuant to Charter of the International Military Tribunal for the Far East, Jan. 19, 1946 *(as amended* Apr. 26, 1946), 4 Bevans 21, *reprinted in* 1 Ferencz, *supra,* at 523.

[4]   For references and a discussion of the Hague and Geneva conventions, see Albert P. Blaustein et al., *Human Rights Sourcebook* 661–88 (1987).

[5]   The Nuremberg Charter, *supra* note 3, art. 6, provides:

The following acts, or any of them, are crimes coming within the jurisdiction of the Tribunal for which there shall be individual responsibility: —

(a)   *Crimes against peace:* namely, planning, preparation, initiation or waging a war of aggression, or a war in violation of international treaties, agreements or assurances, or participation in a common plan or conspiracy for the accomplishment of any of the foregoing.

(b)   *War crimes:* namely, violations of the laws or customs of war . . . [including] murder, ill-treatment or deportation to slave labour or for any other purpose of civilian population . . . , murder or ill-treatment of prisoners of war . . . killing of hostages, plunder of public or private property, wanton destruction of cities, towns or villages, or devastation not justified by military necessity.

(c)   *Crimes against humanity:* namely, murder, extermination, enslavement, deportation, and other inhumane acts committed against any civilian population, before or during the war, or persecutions on political, racial or religious grounds in execution of or in connection with any crime within the jurisdiction of the Tribunal, whether or not in violation of the domestic law of the country where perpetrated.

Leaders, organisers, instigators and accomplices participating in the formulation or execution of a common plan or conspiracy to commit any of the foregoing crimes are responsible for all acts performed by any persons in execution of such plan.

most part, with accepted standards of procedural justice, they were clearly tainted by the way in which they had been created: they were set up by the victors and were widely perceived, by the vanquished at least, as the imposition of victors' law.[6]

The need to establish an independent international criminal tribunal with relatively broad jurisdiction was recognized by the United Nations early on.[7] The goal of setting up such a court, which would have jurisdiction over individuals alleged to have committed a number of international crimes, has been championed down the years by various intergovernmental and nongovernmental organizations, diplomats, and international law experts, most notable among the latter being Professor M. Cherif Bassiouni.[8] Unfortunately, efforts in this direction have repeatedly foundered,[9] with the issue resurfacing in an immediate way only in response to the ghastly events being played out in the former Yugoslavia.[10] Although there seems to be growing support for a

---

[6] For background, see Richard H. Minear, *Victors' Justice: The Tokyo War Crimes Trial* (1971); William B. Simons, *The Jurisdictional Bases of the International Military Tribunal at Nuremberg*, in *The Nuremberg Trial and International Law* 39 (George Ginsburgs & V.N. Kudriavtsev eds., 1990); *see also* Theodor Meron, Editorial Comment, *War Crimes in Yugoslavia and the Development of International Law*, 88 Am. J. Int'l L. 78, 83–87 (1994) (comparing the Statute of the Tribunal and the Nuremberg Charter).

[7] *See* M. Cherif Bassiouni, *Draft Statute—International Tribunal* 3–32 (Association Internationale de Droit Pénal, Nouvelles Études Penales No. 10, 2d ed. 1993); Bassiouni, *supra* note 2, at 7–11.

[8] *E.g., Commentaries on the International Law Commission's 1991 Draft Code of Crimes against the Peace and Security of Mankind* (M. Cherif Bassiouni ed., Association Internationale de Droit Pénal, Nouvelles Études Penales No. 11, 1993); M. Cherif Bassiouni, *Crimes against Humanity in International Criminal Law* (1992); Bassiouni, *supra* note 2; *see also* works by Bassiouni cited *infra* note 9.

[9] *See generally* M. Cherif Bassiouni, *A Draft International Criminal Code and Draft Statute for an International Criminal Tribunal* (2d rev. ed. 1987); Benjamin Ferencz, *An International Criminal Court* (1980); M. Cherif Bassiouni & Christopher L. Blakesley, *The Need for an International Criminal Court in the New International World Order*, 25 Vand. J. Transnat'l L. 151 (1992). For further discussion and additional references, see *infra* notes 28–43 and accompanying text.

[10] The principal documents include S.C. Res. 780, U.N. SCOR, 47th Year, 1992 S.C. Res. & Dec. at 36, U.N. Doc. S/INF/48 (1992), *reprinted in* appendix A of this

permanent international criminal tribunal, the community of nations has not yet reached consensus even on the range of offenses that would fall within its jurisdiction.[11] Perhaps a permanent court will emerge in the near future, prompted finally by the tragedy of Yugoslavia and Rwanda.

THE COMMISSION AND THE TRIBUNAL

Although UN peacekeeping forces are deployed today in many trouble spots around the world, the events that moved the United Nations to

---

issue of *Criminal Law Forum;* S.C. Res. 808, U.N. SCOR, 48th Year, 3175th mtg. at 1, U.N. Doc. S/RES/808 (1993), *reprinted in* appendix A of this issue of *Criminal Law Forum* and *available in* U.N. Gopher\Documents\Security Council Resolutions; S.C. Res. 827, U.N. SCOR, 48th Year, 3217th mtg. at 1, U.N. Doc. S/RES/827 (1993), *reprinted in* appendix A of this issue of *Criminal Law Forum* and *in* 32 I.L.M. 1203; *Report of the Secretary-General pursuant to Paragraph 2 of Security Council Resolution 808 (1993)*, U.N. Doc. S/25704 & Add.1 (1993), *reprinted in* appendix B of this issue of *Criminal Law Forum* and *in* 32 I.L.M. 1163 [hereinafter *Secretary-General's Report*].

[11] See references in Bassiouni, *supra* note 9, at 1 n.1. *See generally* Timothy L.H. McCormack & Gerry J. Simpson, *The International Law Commission's Draft Code of Crimes against the Peace and Security of Mankind: An Appraisal of the Substantive Provisions*, 5 Crim. L.F. 1 (1994). This initiative has been largely the province of the International Law Commission (ILC) for over four decades. Draft Code of Offences against the Peace and Security of Mankind (submitted in July 1951), in *Report of the International Law Commission on Its Third Session*, U.N. GAOR, 6th Sess., Supp. No. 9, at 11, U.N. Doc. A/1858 (1951); Draft Code of Offences (submitted in July 1954), in *Report of the International Law Commission on Its Sixth Session*, U.N. GAOR, 9th Sess., Supp. No. 9, at 9, U.N. Doc. A/2693 (1954); Draft Code of Crimes against the Peace and Security of Mankind [hereinafter 1991 Draft Code], in *Report of the International Law Commission on Its Forty-third Session*, U.N. GAOR, 46th Sess., Supp. No. 10, at 238, U.N. Doc. A/46/10 (1991) [hereinafter *ILC 43d Session Report*]; *Report of the Working Group on the Question of an International Criminal Jurisdiction* [hereinafter *ILC International Criminal Jurisdiction Report*], in *Report of the International Law Commission on Its Forty-fourth Session*, U.N. GAOR, 47th Sess., Supp. No. 10, at 143, U.N. Doc. A/47/10 (1992) [hereinafter *ILC 44th Session Report*]; *Report of the Working Group on a Draft Statute for an International Criminal Court* [hereinafter *ILC Draft Statute Report*], in *Report of the International Law Commission on Its Forty-fifth Session*, U.N. GAOR, 48th Sess., Supp. No. 10, at 255, U.N. Doc. A/48/10 (1993) [hereinafter *ILC 45th Session Report*]. On the most recent ILC efforts in this area, see *infra* notes 34, 43.

intervene in the former Yugoslavia appear to have stirred world opinion most profoundly—at least until civil war broke out in Rwanda.[12] Postwar society had not seen rape used as a weapon of state psychological terror, nor genocide—masquerading as "ethnic cleansing"—as an overt strategy of domination. The news media, and particularly television, have brought these horrors into our homes. The public's call for bringing to account the rapists, torturers, and murderers, and especially those responsible for formulating the policies that support, if not expressly authorize, these crimes, led to unprecedented action by the Security Council.

In October 1992, the Security Council, by Resolution 780,

---

[12] By S.C. Res. 935, U.N. SCOR, 49th Year, 3400th mtg. at 1, ¶ 2, U.N. Doc. S/RES/935 (1994), *reprinted in* appendix D of this issue of *Criminal Law Forum* and *available in* U.N. Gopher\Documents\Security Council Resolutions, the Security Council requested the Secretary-General to establish an impartial Commission of Experts to investigate reports of "grave violations of international humanitarian law committed in the territory of Rwanda." After the Commission issued a preliminary report, Letter from the Secretary-General to the President of the Security Council, Oct. 1, 1994, U.N. Doc. S/1994/1125 (1994), transmitting *Preliminary Report of the Independent Commission of Experts Established in Accordance with Security Council Resolution 935 (1994)*, *available in* U.N. Gopher\Current Information\Secretary-General Reports, the Security Council voted (in November 1994) to create the International Tribunal for Rwanda, which shares the appeals chamber and the chief prosecutor with the International Tribunal for the Former Yugoslavia, S.C. Res. 955, U.N. SCOR, 49th Year, 3453d mtg. at 1, U.N. Doc. S/RES/955 (1994), *reprinted in* appendix D of this issue of *Criminal Law Forum* and *available in* U.N. Gopher\Documents\Security Council Resolutions. The Commission later issued its final report. Letter from the Secretary-General to the President of the Security Council, Dec. 9, 1994, U.N. Doc. S/1994/1405 (1994), transmitting *Final Report of the Commission of Experts Established pursuant to Security Council Resolution 935 (1994)*, *available in* U.N. Gopher\Current Information\Secretary-General Reports.

For background, see Anthony Goodman, *Spain Urges Rwanda War Crimes Commission*, Reuters, June 14, 1994, *available in* LEXIS, World Library, Allnws File; *Plan for Rwanda War Crimes Trial Gains Backing*, Agence France Presse, July 1, 1994, *available in* LEXIS, World Library, Allnws File; Sue Pleming, *Rwandan Government Gears Up for War Tribunal*, Reuters, July 23, 1994, *available in* LEXIS, World Library, Allnws File (discussing the request by the new government of President Pasteur Bizimungu for help from the international community in setting up an international tribunal); *U.N. Should Extend Mandate of Crimes Tribunal to Rwanda*, Agence France Presse, July 2, 1994, *available in* LEXIS, World Library, Allnws File (discussing recommendation from the International Commission of Jurists).

requested the Secretary-General to establish a Commission of Experts to conduct such investigations as might be necessary to determine whether or not grave breaches of the Geneva Conventions and other violations of international humanitarian law had been, and were being, committed in the territory of the former Yugoslavia.[13] The five-member Commission was appointed toward the end of October[14] and it forwarded a preliminary report to the Secretary-General in early 1993.[15]

---

[13] S.C. Res. 780, *supra* note 10, ¶ 2 (requesting the Secretary-General to appoint an investigatory commission "with a view to providing the Secretary-General with its conclusions on the evidence of grave breaches of the Geneva Conventions and other violations of international humanitarian law").

[14] *See generally* M. Cherif Bassiouni, Current Developments, *The United Nations Commission of Experts Established pursuant to Security Council Resolution 780 (1992)*, 88 Am. J. Int'l L. 784 (1994); Hilaire McCoubrey, *The Armed Conflict in Bosnia and Proposed War Crimes Trials*, 11 Int'l Rel. 411 (1993); James C. O'Brien, *The International Tribunal for Violations of International Humanitarian Law in the Former Yugoslavia*, 87 Am. J. Int'l L. 639 (1993); Elizabeth L. Pearl, *Punishing Balkan War Criminals: Could the End of Yugoslavia Provide an End to Victors' Justice?*, 30 Am. Crim. L. Rev. 1373 (1993).

[15] The Commission carried out a series of investigations and issued three reports. Letter from the Secretary-General to the President of the Security Council, Feb. 9, 1993, U.N. Doc. S/25274 (1993), transmitting *Interim Report of the Commission of Experts Established pursuant to Security Council Resolution 780 (1992)* [hereinafter *First Interim Report*]; Letter from the Secretary-General to the President of the Security Council, Oct. 5, 1993, U.N. Doc. S/26545 (1993), transmitting *Second Interim Report of the Commission of Experts Established pursuant to Security Council Resolution 780 (1992);* Letter from the Secretary-General to the President of the Security Council, May 24, 1994, U.N. Doc. S/1994/674 (1994), transmitting *Final Report of the Commission of Experts Established pursuant to Security Council Resolution 780 (1992), available in* U.N. Gopher\Current Information\Secretary-General's Reports [hereinafter *Final Report*].

Over its lifetime, the Commission was not without its share of difficulties. For a detailed discussion, see M. Cherif Bassiouni, *The Commission of Experts Established pursuant to Security Council Resolution 780: Investigating Violations of International Humanitarian Law in the Former Yugoslavia*, in this issue of *Criminal Law Forum*. Most obvious were inadequate funding, personnel problems, and lack of cooperation from officials in the region. Frits Kalshoven, the original chairman, resigned in September 1993, "citing health concerns and frustration over lukewarm U.N. support." Carol J. Williams, *Serbian Authorities Thwart U.N. War Crimes Investigation in Balkans*, L.A. Times, Nov. 21, 1993, at A8, *available in* LEXIS, World Library, Allnws File; Andrew Kelly, *Head of U.N. War Crimes Panel Resigns*, Reuters, Oct. 1, 1993, *available in* LEXIS, World

In the view of the Secretary-General, this report demonstrated that violations of international humanitarian law had been committed, including wilful killing, ethnic cleansing and mass killings, torture, rape, pillage and destruction of civilian property, destruction of cultural and religious property, and arbitrary arrests. He noted, however, that the information that the Commission had received was of "uneven value" and would require verification. The Commission's report was forwarded by the Secretary-General to the President of the Security Council in early February 1993.[16]

On February 22, 1993, the Security Council adopted Resolution 808, asserting "that an international tribunal shall be established for the prosecution of persons responsible for serious violations of international humanitarian law committed in the territory of former Yugoslavia since 1991."[17] The Secretary-General proceeded to form a Committee of Experts to draft a statute for such a tribunal.[18] Resolution 808 also requested the Secretary-General to submit to the Security Council "a report on all aspects of this matter, including specific proposals and where appropriate options for the effective and expeditious implementation of the decision [to establish a tribunal], taking into account suggestions put forward in this regard by Member States."[19] The Secretary-General reported back in early May, and on May 25, 1993, the

---

Library, Allnws File. On lack of support from the United Nations and opposition from local authorities to gathering evidence, see George Rodrigue, *Doubts Surround Opening of Balkan War-Crimes Court*, Dallas Morning News, Nov. 15, 1993, at 14A, *available in* LEXIS, World Library, Allnws File; Williams, *supra*. New appointments to the Commission were announced in October 1993, *Women Legal Experts Named to U.N. War Crimes Panel*, Reuters, Oct. 21, 1993, *available in* LEXIS, World Library, Allnws File (Professor Christine Cleiren and the Hon. Hanne Sophie Greve), and Cherif Bassiouni was named chairman, *Security Council Appoints Prosecutor for Balkans War Crimes*, UPI, Oct. 21, 1993, *available in* LEXIS, World Library, Allnws File. On the controversial closing down of the Commission, see Bassiouni, *supra; see also infra* note 143 and accompanying text.

[16] *First Interim Report, supra* note 15; *Secretary-General's Report, supra* note 10, ¶ 9.

[17] S.C. Res. 808, *supra* note 10, ¶ 1.

[18] *Secretary-General's Report, supra* note 10, ¶ 8.

[19] S.C. Res. 808, *supra* note 10, ¶ 2.

Security Council voted unanimously to set up an ad hoc war crimes tribunal upon the terms of the draft statute appended to Mr. Boutros-Ghali's report.[20] As discussed below, the Security Council created the tribunal pursuant to chapter VII of the Charter of the United Nations, which confers on this organ authority to maintain or restore international peace or security. The judges of the Tribunal were elected in September 1993 and the court held its inaugural session in the Hague in mid-November of that year.[21]

The Security Council's establishment of the International Tribunal for the Former Yugoslavia was a momentous step forward because it put in place an impartial international mechanism to bring the architects and perpetrators of grave international crimes to justice. Moreover, although limited in terms of geographical and subject matter

---

[20] S.C. Res. 827, *supra* note 10. The Statute of the International Tribunal is set out as an annex to *Secretary-General's Report*, *supra* note 10, and is *reprinted in* appendix B of this issue of *Criminal Law Forum* and *in* 32 I.L.M. 1192 [hereinafter Statute].

[21] G.A. Dec. 47/328, U.N. GAOR, 47th Sess., Supp. No. 49 (vol. II), at 45, U.N. Doc. A/47/49 (1993). The International Tribunal originally comprised the following judges: Georges Michel Abi-Saab (Egypt), Antonio Cassese (Italy), Jules Deschênes (Canada), Adolphus Godwin Karibi-Whyte (Nigeria), Germain Le Foyer de Costil (France), Li Haopei (China), Gabrielle Kirk McDonald (United States), Elizabeth Odio Benito (Costa Rica), Rustam S. Sidhwa (Pakistan), Sir Ninian Stephen (Australia), and Lal Chand Vohrah (Malaysia). *Judge Antonio Cassese of Italy Elected President of International Tribunal for Crimes in Former Yugoslavia*, Fed. News Serv., Dec. 2, 1993, *available in* LEXIS, World Library, Allnws File; *U.N. Names 11 to War Crimes Panel: Serbian Leader Says Peace Plan Is Near*, Hous. Chronicle, Sept. 18, 1993, at A24, *available in* LEXIS, World Library, Allnws File.

Since the selection of the Tribunal's eleven judges in September 1993, the French candidate resigned for reasons of health and was replaced by another Frenchman, Claude Jorda, under the terms of Statute, *supra* note 20, art. 13(3). *See Yougoslavie: Un nouveau juge français au Tribunal international sur les crimes de guerre*, Le Monde, Jan. 24, 1994, *available in* LEXIS, France Library, Presse File.

At the court's first session, Judge Cassese was elected president of the Tribunal; Judge Odio Benito, vice-president. *International War Crimes Tribunal for Former Yugoslavia Elects Its President, Members of Appeals and Trial Chambers*, Fed. News Serv., Nov. 19, 1993, *available in* LEXIS, World Library, Allnws File. *See generally Report on First Session of International Tribunal for War Crimes in Former Yugoslavia*, U.N. Press Release, U.N. Doc. SC/5767 (Dec. 23, 1993), *available in* U.N. Gopher\Current Information\Press Releases.

jurisdiction, the Tribunal can provide a paradigm for a permanent international criminal court if the international community can be persuaded to take that final logical step toward this goal:

> Whatever the practical achievements of the [Tribunal], the United Nations Security Council has established the first truly international criminal tribunal for the prosecution of persons responsible for serious violations of international humanitarian law. . . .
> . . . [T]he establishment of the tribunal as an enforcement measure under the binding authority of chapter VII [of the UN Charter], rather than through a treaty . . . may foreshadow more effective international responses to violations of humanitarian law.[22]

Before turning to the organization and jurisdiction of the Tribunal, it is useful to outline some of the events and ideas that led to its establishment and in many respects gave this court its final form.

INFLUENCES BEHIND THE CREATION OF THE TRIBUNAL

Cherif Bassiouni

Professor Bassiouni, both in his academic capacity and in his role as president of the International Association of Penal Law, has been enormously influential in shaping the intellectual climate needed for setting up an international criminal tribunal. Particularly noteworthy in this regard has been his role over the past decade and a half in drafting a statute for an international criminal court. Originally prepared in 1979–1980 at the request of the UN Commission on Human Rights, his draft has been revised and refined over the years, most recently in a 1993

---

[22] Meron, *supra* note 6, at 78–79 (citations omitted).

monograph entitled *Draft Statute — International Tribunal*.[23] Although his writings have focused principally on the establishment of a permanent judicial institution,[24] many of Professor Bassiouni's ideas have clearly had an impact on the structure of the International Tribunal for the Former Yugoslavia, as noted later in this article.[25]

Professor Bassiouni has also been directly involved with laying the groundwork for the Tribunal. Originally appointed to the Commission of Experts as Rapporteur for the Gathering and Analysis of Facts, he was, in the fall of 1993, named chairman of this Commission.[26] He was, moreover, a leading candidate for the office of prosecutor.[27]

International Law Commission

The early 1990s also saw the International Law Commission (ILC) make significant progress toward establishing a permanent international criminal court. The ILC was created by the General Assembly in 1947 and its first specific tasks were to "formulate the principles of international law" embodied in the Charter and judgment of the Nuremberg Tribunal and to prepare a Draft Code of Offences against the Peace and Security of Mankind.[28] Shortly afterward, the Assembly asked the ILC

---

[23] Bassiouni, *supra* note 7. Professor Bassiouni has taken an active part in the past four UN Congresses on the Prevention of Crime and the Treatment of Offenders, in particular with regard to the preparation of a draft international criminal code and a draft statute for an international criminal court. *Id.* at 3–19.

[24] See sources cited *supra* notes 2, 7–9.

[25] See *infra* notes 52, 55, 58 and accompanying text.

[26] *Security Council Appoints Prosecutor for Balkans War Crimes, supra* note 15. See generally *supra* note 15 on the Commission of Experts.

[27] See sources cited *infra* note 103.

[28] G.A. Res. 174 (II), U.N. Doc. A/519, at 105 (1947) (establishing the ILC); G.A. Res. 177 (II), U.N. Doc. A/519, at 111 (1947) (conferring these responsibilities). For background, see *Report of the International Law Commission on Its Forty-second Session*, U.N. GAOR, 45th Sess., Supp. No. 10, at 10–70, U.N. Doc. A/45/10 (1990) [hereinafter *ILC 42d Session Report*]; *Report of the International Law Commission on Its Thirty-fifth Session*, U.N. GAOR, 38th Sess., Supp. No. 10, ¶¶ 26–41, U.N. Doc. A/38/10 (1983).

also to consider the related question of creating an international criminal tribunal, possibly as a chamber of the International Court of Justice; in late 1950, this mandate was transferred to a special committee charged with "preparing . . . draft conventions and proposals relating to the establishment and the statute of an international criminal court."[29] Although the ILC and the new Committee on International Criminal Jurisdiction, respectively, elaborated and revised texts of such a draft code and a draft statute in the early 1950s, political considerations dictated that these projects were to be put on hold for the next several decades.[30]

As the cold war began to show signs of coming to an end, the possibility of an international criminal court took on new life. In a series of resolutions beginning in 1981, the General Assembly requested the ILC initially to resume work on its Draft Code of Crimes (previously, "Offences") and later, within the context of that effort, to study the question of setting up an international criminal court or other type of international trial mechanism.[31] In 1982, the ILC appointed Doudou

---

[29]   G.A. Res. 260B (III), U.N. Doc. A/810, at 177 (1948) (requesting the ILC to consider the question of creating an international criminal tribunal); G.A. Res. 489 (V), U.N. GAOR, 5th Sess., Supp. No. 20, at 77, U.N. Doc. A/1775 (1950) (establishing the Committee on International Criminal Jurisdiction to consider this question); 2 Ferencz, *supra* note 9, at 5–48 (discussing the history within and outside the United Nations of preparing a code of international crimes and a statute for an international criminal court); James Crawford, *The ILC's Draft Statute for an International Criminal Court*, 88 Am. J. Int'l L. 140, 141 (1994).

[30]   *Report of the Committee on International Criminal Jurisdiction on Its Session Held from 1 to 31 August 1951*, U.N. GAOR, 7th Sess., Supp. No. 11, at 21, U.N. Doc. A/2136 (1952) (including a draft statute), *reprinted in* 2 Ferencz, *supra* note 9, at 337; *Report of the 1953 Committee on International Criminal Jurisdiction, 27 July–20 August 1953*, U.N. GAOR, 9th Sess., Supp. No. 12, at 23, U.N. Doc. A/2645 (1954) (including a revised statute), *reprinted in* 2 Ferencz, *supra*, at 429.

[31]   Particularly relevant in this regard are G.A. Res. 36/106, U.N. GAOR, 36th Sess., Supp. No. 51, at 239, ¶ 1, U.N. Doc. A/36/51 (1981) (requesting the ILC to resume work on the Draft Code); G.A. Res. 43/164, U.N. GAOR, 43d Sess., Supp. No. 49, at 280, ¶¶ 1–2, U.N. Doc. A/43/49 (1988) (inviting the ILC to continue its work on the Draft Code and its examination of the question of a judicial mechanism to enforce it); G.A. Res. 44/39, U.N. GAOR, 44th Sess., Supp. No. 49, at 311, ¶ 1, U.N. Doc. A/44/49 (1989) (requesting the ILC, in continuing its work on the Draft Code, to "address the question of establishing an international criminal court . . . with jurisdiction

Thiam Special Rapporteur for the Draft Code of Crimes.[32] In the intervening years, he has produced a dozen reports that set out draft articles for such a code, as well as draft articles for a statute for an international criminal court.[33] The Draft Code is expected to be finalized in 1995.[34]

In May 1992 the ILC appointed a Working Group on the

---

over persons alleged to have committed crimes which may be covered under such a code of crimes"); G.A. Res. 45/41, U.N. GAOR, 45th Sess., Supp. No. 49A, at 363, ¶ 3, U.N. Doc. A/45/49 (1990) (requesting the ILC, in its work on the Draft Code, to consider further the possibility of establishing an international criminal court or other international criminal trial mechanism); G.A. Res. 46/54, U.N. GAOR, 46th Sess., Supp. No. 49, at 286, ¶ 3, U.N. Doc. A/46/49 (1991) (reiterating this request). For some background, see *ILC 42d Session Report, supra* note 28, at 36–54. For the latest developments, see *infra* notes 34, 43.

[32] See *ILC 44th Session Report, supra* note 11, ¶¶ 20–21.

[33] For references to the first nine reports, see *id.* at 10 n.17; for a reference to and summary of the tenth report, see *id.* ¶¶ 11, 24–97; for a reference to and summary of the eleventh report, see *ILC 45th Session Report, supra* note 11, ¶¶ 13–14, 33–95; the most recent is Doudou Thiam, *Twelfth Report on the Draft Code of Crimes against the Peace and Security of Mankind,* U.N. Doc. A/CN.4/460 (1994), submitted to the International Law Commission at its forty-sixth session in May–July 1994. On the ILC's forty-sixth session, see *infra* notes 42–43 and accompanying text.

[34] At its forty-third session in 1991, the ILC provisionally adopted on a first reading a Draft Code based in large part on the extensive work of the special rapporteur. See *ILC 43d Session Report, supra* note 11, at 198, 238. At its forty-sixth session in 1994, the ILC considered the twelfth report of the special rapporteur, dealing with the general part of the Draft Code (as adopted on its first reading in 1991), in conjunction with the comments from governments on the general part. *Report of the International Law Commission on Its Forty-sixth Session,* U.N. GAOR, 49th Sess., Supp. No. 10, at 161, U.N. Doc. A/49/10 (1994) [hereinafter *ILC 46th Session Report*]. The Commission decided to refer articles 1–15 of the Draft Code to the drafting committee, "with the understanding that the work on the draft Code and on the draft statute for an international criminal court should be coordinated by the Special Rapporteur on the draft Code and by the Chairman and members of the Drafting Committee and of the Working Group on a Draft Statute for an International Criminal Court." *Id.* ¶¶ 92–96. The special part of the Draft Code will be the topic of Mr. Thiam's thirteenth report and is to be taken up by the ILC in 1995 at its forty-seventh session. Thiam, *supra* note 33, ¶¶ 1–4.

Question of an International Criminal Jurisdiction.[35] The Working Group proposed the creation of a treaty-based court with personal jurisdiction over individuals, not states,[36] and with subject matter jurisdiction over international crimes as defined by conventional international law, including (but not limited to) the Draft Code of Crimes in the form in which it will finally be adopted and enter into force.[37] These recommendations, while distinct in their focus on a permanent court, accord in many, but not all, respects with the provisions adopted by the Security Council in the Statute for the International Tribunal, as discussed below. Subsequently, the ILC went on, again at the request of the General Assembly,[38] to prepare a more formal Draft Statute for an International Criminal Court.[39] In carrying out this task, the Working Group[40] had before it, among other documents, the *Report of the Secretary-General pursuant to Paragraph 2 of Security Council Resolution 808 (1993)*,[41] demonstrating the close interplay between the creation of the ad hoc International Tribunal and the evolution of international criminal law toward a permanent court. The Draft Statute was finalized at the forty-sixth session of the ILC in the summer of 1994.[42] Although

---

[35] *ILC 44th Session Report*, supra note 11, ¶¶ 6, 393–395. *See generally* Crawford, supra note 29.

[36] *ILC International Criminal Jurisdiction Report*, supra note 11, ¶¶ 396, 432, 437, 444–448, 452–458. As noted in *id.* at 144 n.84, individual, rather than state, responsibility conforms to the approach in the 1991 Draft Code, supra note 11, art. 3.

[37] *ILC International Criminal Jurisdiction Report*, supra note 11, ¶¶ 449–451.

[38] G.A. Res. 47/33, U.N. GAOR, 47th Sess., Supp. No. 49, at 287, ¶ 6, U.N. Doc. A/47/49 (1992) (requesting the ILC to "continue its work on the question [of an international criminal jurisdiction] by undertaking the project for the elaboration of a draft statute for an international criminal court as a matter of priority").

[39] *ILC Draft Statute Report*, supra note 11.

[40] At the ILC's forty-fifth session, the working group was reconvened, with mostly the same members, as the Working Group on a Draft Statute for an International Criminal Court. *ILC 45th Session Report*, supra note 11, ¶¶ 9, 13–14, 96–97.

[41] *Id.* ¶ 473; *Secretary-General's Report*, supra note 10.

[42] Draft Statute for an International Criminal Court, in *ILC 46th Session Report*, supra note 34, at 43.

the General Assembly had seemed to regard this project as a matter of high priority, the Sixth Committee failed during the General Assembly's forty-ninth session to take the next step toward establishing a permanent international criminal court along the lines suggested by the ILC.[43]

European and Other Voices

Whereas Europe appeared to be suffering from paralysis in the first year or so following the breakup of the former Yugoslavia, the situation began to change toward the end of 1992. The first significant step in the direction of creating an impartial international criminal tribunal was the *Moscow Human Dimension Mechanism Report*, prepared under the auspices of the Conference on Security and Cooperation in Europe (CSCE).[44] Although the authors of this report did not visit the region, they cited a variety of accounts of atrocities committed by all the protagonists in the war and set out a proposal for an international war crimes tribunal to be put in place by treaty once hostilities ceased. The CSCE report was among the documents cited by the Secretary-General as having been consulted in the preparation of his report to the Security

---

[43] G.A. Res. 48/31, U.N. GAOR, 48th Sess., Supp. No. 49, at 328, ¶ 6, U.N. Doc. A/48/49 (1993) (requesting the ILC "to continue its work as a matter of priority on this question with a view to elaborating a draft statute, if possible at its forty-sixth session in 1994" and to resume consideration of the Draft Code of Crimes); G.A. Res. 47/33, *supra* note 38, ¶ 6; Virginia Morris & M.-Christiane Bourloyannis-Vrailas, Current Developments, *The Work of the Sixth Committee at the Forty-eighth Session of the U.N. General Assembly*, 88 Am. J. Int'l L. 343, 349–53 (1994).

With strong opposition from the United States, plans to create the international criminal court are now basically on hold. *See* G.A. Res. 49/53, 84th plen. mtg., U.N. Doc. A/49/53 (1994); Thalif Deen, *United Nations: U.N. Split over International Criminal Court*, Inter Press Serv., Dec. 21, 1994, *available in* LEXIS, World Library, Allnws File.

[44] CSCE Rapporteurs (Corell–Turk–Thune), Moscow Human Dimension Mechanism to Bosnia, Herzegovina, and Croatia, *Proposal for an International War Crimes Tribunal for the Former Yugoslavia* (1993) [hereinafter CSCE Proposal]; Letter from the Permanent Representative of Sweden to the Secretary-General, Feb. 18, 1993, U.N. Doc. S/25307 (1993), annexing a summary of CSCE Proposal, *supra*, and the text of a decision by CSCE participating states on this proposal. The rapporteurs set out a draft convention for an international war crimes tribunal for the former Yugoslavia.

Council.⁴⁵

At about the same time that the CSCE report was released, a committee of French jurists, which was appointed for the specific purpose of making recommendations on creating an international tribunal for the former Yugoslavia, submitted a comprehensive proposal on this question.⁴⁶ Shortly thereafter, a similar Italian commission put forth a set of recommendations.⁴⁷ In addition, the Secretary-General had the benefit, in preparing his report to the Security Council, of the views of a great many other states both inside and outside Europe,⁴⁸ the *Report on the International Meeting of Experts on the Establishment of an International Criminal Tribunal*,⁴⁹ and comments from a number of nongovernmental organizations.⁵⁰

Bringing Order out of Diversity

Given such a collection of expert views, it should come as no surprise that opinions differed on a number of matters. Some differences were relatively trivial, but others were quite substantial. There is little practical distinction, for example, among the French proposal for a commission that would be responsible for investigating complaints, gathering evidence, and determining whether or not complaints should

---

[45]   *Secretary-General's Report, supra* note 10, ¶ 13.

[46]   Letter from the Permanent Representative of France to the Secretary-General, Feb. 10, 1993, U.N. Doc. S/25266 (1993), transmitting a report on the establishment of an international criminal tribunal for the former Yugoslavia prepared by a national Committee of Jurists [hereinafter French Proposal].

[47]   Letter from the Permanent Representative of Italy to the Secretary-General, Feb. 16, 1993, U.N. Doc. S/25300 (1993), transmitting a draft statute for an international criminal tribunal for the former Yugoslavia prepared by a national Commission of Jurists [hereinafter Italian Proposal].

[48]   *Secretary-General's Report, supra* note 10, ¶ 13.

[49]   *Expert Report, supra* note 2.

[50]   *Secretary-General's Report, supra* note 10, ¶ 14.

proceed by indictment before the Tribunal,[51] Professor Bassiouni's recommendation for a procuracy to carry out these functions (on behalf of a permanent court),[52] and the Italian suggestion for a "prosecutor's office,"[53] which was also put forward by the ILC Working Group on the Question of an International Criminal Jurisdiction.[54] Nomenclature is of little significance where in each case the same broad functions are to be carried out.

There were sharper differences on the question of trial procedure and the rights of the accused. Some, including Professor Bassiouni, favored a preliminary hearing by the trial court before defendants could be required to stand trial,[55] but the French[56] and Italian[57] proposals recommended direct transfer to a trial court from the decision of the prosecutor's office to proceed. As we shall see, Professor Bassiouni's

---

[51] French Proposal, *supra* note 46, at 27–29. In the French proposal, the existing Commission of Experts would fulfill this function. *See* Alfred de Zayas, *The Kalshoven Commission*, 6 Leiden J. Int'l L. 131 (1993).

[52] Bassiouni, *supra* note 7, at 35, 50–51 (discussing a permanent, rather than an ad hoc, tribunal).

[53] Italian Proposal, *supra* note 47, art. 9.

[54] *ILC International Criminal Jurisdiction Report, supra* note 11, ¶¶ 504–517.

[55] Bassiouni, *supra* note 7, at 75–76; *see also* Letter from the Permanent Representative of the United States of America to the Secretary-General, Apr. 5, 1993, U.N. Doc. S/25575 (1993), transmitting views and proposals on establishing an international criminal tribunal for the former Yugoslavia. According to *id.* art. 17:

> (a) Without delay after an accused person comes into the custody of the Tribunal, there shall be a preliminary hearing at which an Indictment shall be presented to the Trial Court and to the accused person.
>
> (b) The accused person shall have the right to give an explanation relevant to the charges made against him or her and to enter a plea.
>
> (c) After this hearing, the Trial Court shall decide whether there is reasonable cause to hold the accused person over for trial.

[56] French Proposal, *supra* note 46, at 32–33.

[57] Italian Proposal, *supra* note 47, art. 11.

position was the one adopted by the Security Council.[58]

All the reports and communications to the Secretary-General emphasized the need for rules of procedure that would be efficient and fair and reflect the standards expected of the international community. From this common starting point, however, France favored trial in absentia in some circumstances,[59] whereas Italy did not.[60] The Italian position ultimately was adopted by the Security Council.[61]

The French report also took the position that sentences should be executed by states that volunteered to do so, with the Tribunal selecting the appropriate state and the international community bearing the cost.[62] This is, broadly speaking, the view of the CSCE report[63] as well and the one enacted.[64]

In short, the drafting committee had a wealth of expert views available in preparing the Statute for the International Tribunal. These reflected the nuances of the various legal cultures throughout the world and, although details may have differed, the same general conclusion prevailed: an international tribunal was an essential feature in reintroducing the rule of law in the region of the former Yugoslavia.

THE STATUTE OF THE TRIBUNAL

Resolution 808 in effect expressed the Security Council's view that the establishment of the Tribunal not only would assist in ending the

---

[58] Statute, *supra* note 20, arts. 18–19.

[59] French Proposal, *supra* note 46, at 30.

[60] Italian Proposal, *supra* note 47, art. 11(d). This is also the position advocated in *ILC International Criminal Jurisdiction Report, supra* note 11, ¶ 504 (citing International Covenant on Civil and Political Rights, *adopted* Dec. 19, 1966, art. 14(3)(d), 999 U.N.T.S. 171).

[61] Statute, *supra* note 20, art. 21(4)(d).

[62] French Proposal, *supra* note 46, at 41.

[63] CSCE Proposal, *supra* note 44, at 200–03.

[64] Statute, *supra* note 20, art. 27.

commission of such crimes as fell within the court's jurisdiction but also, by holding those responsible for these crimes legally accountable, would contribute to the restoration and maintenance of peace. In the words of the Secretary-General:

> [T]he Security Council would be establishing, as an enforcement measure under Chapter VII, a subsidiary organ within the terms of Article 29 of the Charter, but one of a judicial nature. This organ would, of course, have to perform its functions independently of political considerations; it would not be subject to the authority or control of the Security Council with regard to the performance of its judicial functions. As an enforcement measure under Chapter VII, however, the life span of the international tribunal would be linked to the restoration and maintenance of international peace and security in the territory of the former Yugoslavia, and Security Council decisions related thereto.[65]

Article 1 of the Statute gives the Tribunal

> the power to prosecute persons responsible for serious violations of international humanitarian law committed in the territory of the former Yugoslavia since 1991 in accordance with the provisions of the present Statute.[66]

This article limits the Tribunal's jurisdiction both geographically and temporally. It also significantly limits subject matter jurisdiction, giving the Tribunal competence to apply international humanitarian law as it is presently understood. Since this is an area not without ambiguity,[67]

---

[65] *Secretary-General's Report, supra* note 10, ¶ 28; *see also* S.C. Res. 827, *supra* note 10, ¶ 2.

[66] Statute, *supra* note 20, art. 1.

[67] *E.g.*, Theodor Meron, *The Geneva Conventions as Customary Law*, 81 Am. J. Int'l L. 348, 363 (1987) (noting the possibility of deliberate ambiguity in humanitarian instruments); Diane F. Orentlicher, *Settling Accounts: The Duty to Prosecute Human Rights Violations of a Prior Regime*, 100 Yale L.J. 2537 (1991) (noting ambiguities

and since the Tribunal's jurisdiction is further restricted to "serious violations," considerable uncertainty is injected into the Tribunal's competence *ratione materiae*. This concern noted, these limitations were intended to ensure that the principle *nullum crimen sine lege* is observed:

> [T]he application of the principle *nullum crimen sine lege* requires that the international tribunal should apply rules of international humanitarian law which are beyond any doubt part of customary law so that the problem of adherence of some but not all States to specific conventions does not arise. . . .[68]

In conformity with this principle, the Statute confers jurisdiction on the Tribunal over

> [t]he part of conventional international humanitarian law which has beyond doubt become part of international customary law [namely,] the law applicable in armed conflict as embodied in: the Geneva Conventions of 12 August 1949 for the Protection of War Victims; the Hague Convention (IV) Respecting the Laws and Customs of War on Land and the Regulations annexed thereto of 18 October 1907; the Convention on the Prevention and Punishment of the Crime of Genocide of 9 December 1948; and the Charter of the International Military Tribunal of 8 August 1945.[69]

Article 2 proceeds to give the International Tribunal

> the power to prosecute persons committing or ordering to be committed grave breaches of the Geneva Conventions of 12

---

associated with crimes against humanity); John Embry Parkerson, Jr., *United States Compliance with Humanitarian Law respecting Civilians during Operation Just Cause*, 133 Mil. L. Rev. 31 (1991) (noting various ambiguities in the Hague and Geneva conventions and the difficulties these created in the context of the invasion of Panama). *See generally* McCormack & Simpson, *supra* note 11.

[68] *Secretary-General's Report, supra* note 10, ¶ 34.

[69] *Id.* ¶ 35 (citations omitted); for the corresponding provisions, see Statute, *supra* note 20, arts. 2–5.

August 1949, namely the following acts against persons or property protected under the provisions of the relevant Geneva Convention:

>(a)   wilful killing;
>(b)   torture or inhuman treatment, including biological experiments;
>(c)   wilfully causing great suffering or serious injury to body or health;
>(d)   extensive destruction and appropriation of property, not justified by military necessity and carried out unlawfully and wantonly;
>(e)   compelling a prisoner of war or a civilian to serve in the forces of a hostile power;
>(f)   wilfully depriving a prisoner of war or a civilian of the rights of fair and regular trial;
>(g)   unlawful deportation or transfer or unlawful confinement of a civilian;
>(h)   taking civilians as hostages.[70]

Article 3 identifies the various violations of the laws or customs of war that fall within the jurisdiction of the Tribunal. These include such acts as use of poisonous weapons; wanton destruction of cities, towns, or villages; attacks on undefended settlements or buildings; destruction of, or wilful damage to, "institutions dedicated to religion, charity and education, the arts and sciences, historic monuments and works of art and science"; and plunder of public or private property.[71]

Article 4 defines the crime of genocide as any one of a set of enumerated acts "committed with intent to destroy, in whole or in part, a national, ethnical, racial or religious group."[72] This category of offense is broadly drafted to include conspiracy to commit genocide; direct and public incitement to commit genocide; attempt to commit genocide; and

---

[70] Statute, *supra* note 20, art. 2.

[71] *Id.* art. 3(a)–(e).

[72] *Id.* art. 4(2).

complicity in genocide.[73]

Crimes against humanity also fall under the jurisdiction of the International Tribunal:

> Crimes against humanity refer to inhumane acts of a very serious nature, such as wilful killing, torture or rape, committed as part of a widespread or systematic attack against any civilian population on national, political, ethnic, racial or religious grounds. . . .[74]

Accordingly, article 5 of the Statute gives the International Tribunal

> the power to prosecute persons responsible for the following crimes when committed in armed conflict, whether international or internal in character, and directed against any civilian population:
>
> (a) murder;
> (b) extermination;
> (c) enslavement;
> (d) deportation;
> (e) imprisonment;
> (f) torture;
> (g) rape;
> (h) persecutions on political, racial and religious grounds;
> (i) other inhumane acts.[75]

While article 6 limits the International Tribunal's jurisdiction to "natural persons,"[76] to the exclusion of "juridical persons,"[77] within these

---

[73] *Id.* art. 4(3).

[74] *Secretary-General's Report, supra* note 10, ¶ 48.

[75] Statute, *supra* note 20, art. 5.

[76] *Id.* art. 6.

[77] *Secretary-General's Report, supra* note 10, ¶¶ 50–51.

constraints the court has broad competence *ratione personae*. This extends to "person[s] who planned, instigated, ordered, committed or otherwise aided and abetted in the planning, preparation or execution of a crime referred to in articles 2 to 5 of the present Statute."[78] Moreover, in deference to "[v]irtually all of the written comments received by the Secretary-General," the Statute "contain[s] provisions which specify that a plea of head of State immunity or that an act was committed in the official capacity of the accused will not constitute a defence, nor will it mitigate punishment."[79] In practical terms, this means that

> [a] person in a position of superior authority should . . . be held individually responsible for giving the unlawful order to commit a crime under the present statute. But he should also be held responsible for failure to prevent a crime or to deter the unlawful behaviour of his subordinates. This imputed responsibility or criminal negligence is engaged if the person in superior authority knew or had reason to know that his subordinates were about to commit or had committed crimes and yet failed to take the necessary and reasonable steps to prevent or repress the commission of such crimes or to punish those who had committed them.[80]

The Statute embodies these principles in article 7(2) and 7(3).[81] Article 7 further specifies that "[t]he fact that an accused person acted pursuant to an order of a Government or of a superior," while not sufficient to "relieve him of criminal responsibility . . . may be considered in

---

[78] Statute, *supra* note 20, art. 7(1).

[79] *Secretary-General's Report, supra* note 10, ¶ 55.

[80] *Id.* ¶ 56.

[81] Statute, *supra* note 20, art. 7(2), provides that the "official position of any accused person, whether as Head of State or Government or as a responsible Government official, shall not relieve such person of criminal responsibility nor mitigate punishment." *Id.* art. 7(3) attributes criminal liability for acts committed by a subordinate to a superior who "knew or had reason to know that the subordinate was about to commit such acts or had done so and the superior failed to take the necessary and reasonable measures to prevent such acts or to punish the perpetrators thereof."

mitigation of punishment if the International Tribunal determines that justice so requires."[82]

Article 8 elaborates upon the geographical and temporal limits that are introduced in article 1. The International Tribunal's jurisdiction is restricted to the territory of the former Socialist Federal Republic of Yugoslavia from the starting date of January 1, 1991.[83]

Article 9 makes the Tribunal's jurisdiction concurrent with that of national courts.[84] However,

> [t]he International Tribunal shall have primacy over national courts. At any stage of the procedure, the International Tribunal may formally request national courts to defer to the competence of the International Tribunal in accordance with the present Statute and the Rules of Procedure and Evidence of the International Tribunal.[85]

Article 10 incorporates the rule of *non bis in idem*, which protects persons from being tried twice for the same crime.[86] To accommodate the primacy of the International Tribunal over national courts, as articulated in article 9, the Statute precludes subsequent trial before a national court for "acts constituting serious violations of international humanitarian law under the present Statute, for which [the accused] has already been tried by the International Tribunal."[87] Article 10 further specifies, however, that

> [a] person who has been tried by a national court for acts constituting serious violations of international humanitarian law may be subsequently tried by the International Tribunal . . . if:

---

[82] *Id.* art. 7(4).

[83] *Id.* art. 8.

[84] *Id.* art. 9(1).

[85] *Id.* art. 9(2).

[86] See *Secretary-General's Report, supra* note 10, ¶ 66.

[87] Statute, *supra* note 20, art. 10(1).

>   (a) the act for which he or she was tried was characterized as an ordinary crime; or
>
>   (b) the national court proceedings were not impartial or independent, were designed to shield the accused from international criminal responsibility, or the case was not diligently prosecuted.[88]

Pursuant to article 11, the International Tribunal comprises a prosecutor, a judicial organ consisting of two trial chambers and an appeals chamber, and a registry, with responsibility shared as follows:[89]

> It would be the function of the prosecutorial organ to investigate cases, prepare indictments and prosecute persons responsible for committing the violations [set out in the Statute]. The judicial organ would hear the cases presented to its Trial Chambers, and consider appeals from the Trial Chambers in its Appeals Chamber. A secretariat or Registry would be required to service both the prosecutorial and judicial organs.[90]

Article 12 calls for the judicial complement of the Tribunal to include eleven judges, no two of whom may be nationals of the same state. Three judges shall serve in each of the two trial chambers; five shall serve in the appeals chamber.[91] The term of office is four years.[92] Article 13 sets out the qualifications of judges:

> [J]udges shall be persons of high moral character, impartiality and integrity who possess the qualifications required in their

---

[88] *Id.* art. 10(2).

[89] *Id.* art. 11; *see Secretary-General's Report, supra* note 10, ¶¶ 69–70.

[90] *Secretary-General's Report, supra* note 10, ¶ 69.

[91] Statute, *supra* note 20, art. 12. Assignments to chambers are for a period of one year, after which judges will rotate. The presidency is a two-year term, renewable for an additional two years. On the initial assignments, see *Judge Antonio Cassese of Italy Elected President of International Tribunal for Crimes in Former Yugoslavia, supra* note 21.

[92] Statute, *supra* note 20, art. 13(4).

respective countries for appointment to the highest judicial offices. In the overall composition of the Chambers due account shall be taken of the experience of the judges in criminal law, international law, including international humanitarian law and human rights law.[93]

Under article 13's provisions on the election of judges, member states and nonmember states with permanent observer missions at the United Nations were invited by the Secretary-General to nominate up to two judicial candidates. The Secretary-General forwarded over forty nominations from the General Assembly to the Security Council, which then submitted a short list of twenty-three candidates back to the General Assembly; the General Assembly selected eleven judges from this list.[94]

Organizational matters, such as the election of a president of the Tribunal and the assignment of judges to the various chambers, are the subject of article 14.[95] The following article empowers the judges to "adopt rules of procedure and evidence for the conduct of the pre-trial phase of the proceedings, trials and appeals, the admission of evidence, the protection of victims and witnesses and other appropriate matters."[96] Rules of Procedure and Evidence were adopted February 11, 1994.[97]

---

[93]   *Id.* art. 13(1).

[94]   *Id.* art. 13(2); Anthony Goodman, *23 Candidates Picked for 11-Judge War Crimes Court,* Reuters, Aug. 20, 1993, *available in* LEXIS, World Library, Allnws File. See *supra* note 21 and accompanying text.

[95]   Statute, *supra* note 20, art. 14.

[96]   *Id.* art. 15.

[97]   International Tribunal for the Prosecution of Persons Responsible for Serious Violations of International Humanitarian Law Committed in the Territory of the Former Yugoslavia since 1991, Rules of Procedure and Evidence, U.N. Doc. IT/32 (1994), *amended by* U.N. Doc. IT/32/Rev.1 (1994), *reprinted in* appendix C of this issue of *Criminal Law Forum* [hereinafter I.T. R. Proc. & Evid.]. The rules regarding sexual assault were amended in May 1994. For a discussion of the rules, see Daniel D. Ntanda Nsereko, *Rules of Procedure and Evidence of the International Tribunal for the Former Yugoslavia,* in this issue of *Criminal Law Forum.*

Editor's note: the Rules of Procedure and Evidence were amended Oct. 4, 1994, U.N. Doc. IT/32/Rev.2 (1994), and Jan. 30, 1995, U.N. Doc. IT/32/Rev.3 (1995).

Rules of Detention were adopted in early May 1994.[98]

The selection and the mandate of the prosecutor are outlined in article 16.[99] The prosecutor is charged with "the investigation and prosecution of persons responsible for serious violations of international humanitarian law committed in the territory of the former Yugoslavia since 1 January 1991."[100] The prosecutor is enjoined to "act independently as a separate organ of the International Tribunal. He or she shall not seek or receive instructions from any Government or from any other source."[101] As it turned out, the Security Council's selection of a prosecutor[102] proved to be a highly contentious process.[103] Moreover, the successful candidate, Ramón Escovar-Salom, resigned to join the newly formed government of Venezuela without taking up his official duties

---

This article is based on U.N. Doc. IT/Rev.1. Appendix C prints the most recent text of the rules, U.N. Doc. IT/Rev.3, indicating all deletions from, and additions to, U.N. Doc. IT/32/Rev.1, so that the reader can reconstruct the full text of this earlier version.

[98] International Tribunal for the Prosecution of Persons Responsible for Serious Violations of International Humanitarian Law Committed in the Territory of the Former Yugoslavia since 1991, Rules Governing the Detention of Persons Awaiting Trial or Appeal before the Tribunal or Otherwise Detained on the Authority of the Tribunal, U.N. Doc. IT/38/Rev.3 (1994); *International Criminal Tribunal for Former Yugoslavia Adopts Rules of Detention*, Fed. News Serv., May 9, 1994, *available in* LEXIS, World Library, Allnws File; *War Crimes Tribunal Says Trials May Begin by Year End*, Reuters, May 6, 1994, *available in* LEXIS, World Library, Allnws File.

[99] Statute, *supra* note 20, art. 16.

[100] *Id.* art. 16(1).

[101] *Id.* art. 16(2).

[102] *Id.* art. 16(4).

[103] *E.g., Balkans War Crimes Tribunal Blocked by Strains within Security Council*, Agence France Presse, Aug. 20, 1993, *available in* LEXIS, World Library, Allnws File; Paul Lewis, *Disputes Hamper U.N. Drive for a War Crimes Tribunal*, N.Y. Times, Sept. 9, 1993, at A10, *available in* LEXIS, World Library, Allnws File; Stanley Meisler, *U.N. Is Deadlocked on War-Crimes Prosecutor*, Montreal Gazette, Sept. 12, 1993, at B1, *available in* LEXIS, World Library, Allnws File; *Venezuelan on War Crimes Panel: Tribunal Will Probe Atrocities in Former Yugoslavia*, Chi. Tribune, Oct. 22, 1993, at 10, *available in* LEXIS, World Library, Allnws File.

with the Tribunal.[104] Finding a replacement was just as divisive politically,[105] with Russia blocking all NATO candidates.[106] In July 1994, a judge of the appellate division of the South African Supreme Court, Richard J. Goldstone, was named to this post[107] some five months after Escovar-Salom's resignation.

Article 17 provides for administrative support to the judicial and prosecutorial arms of the Tribunal in the form of a registry.[108]

Pursuant to article 18, the prosecutor "shall initiate investigations *ex officio* or on the basis of information obtained from any source, particularly from Governments, United Nations organs, intergovernmen-

---

[104] On the prosecutor's appointment, see S.C. Res. 877, U.N. SCOR, 48th Sess., 3296th mtg. at 1, U.N. Doc. S/RES/877 (1993), *available in* U.N. Gopher\Documents\Security Council Resolutions. On his resignation, see *Bosnia–Venezuela: Boutros-Ghali Accepts Prosecutor's Resignation,* Inter Press Serv., Feb. 8, 1994, *available in* LEXIS, World Library, Allnws File; *Secretary-General Appoints Graham Blewitt as Acting Deputy Prosecutor, War Crimes Tribunal, for Humanitarian Law Violations in Former Yugoslavia,* U.N. Press Release, U.N. Doc. SG/SM/5221 (Feb. 8, 1994), *available in* U.N. Gopher\Current Information\Press Releases.

[105] Anthony Lewis, *At Home Abroad: The Civilized World,* N.Y. Times, July 1, 1994, at A25, *available in* LEXIS, World Library, Allnws File.

[106] Paul Lewis, *South African Is to Prosecute Balkan War Crimes,* N.Y. Times, July 9, 1994, at A2, *available in* LEXIS, World Library, Allnws File. For the atmosphere immediately preceding Goldstone's appointment, see Stephen Eagleburger, *Balkan War-Crimes Prosecution Bogs Down,* N.Y. Times, July 7, 1994, at A5, *available in* LEXIS, World Library, Allnws File; Lewis, *supra* note 105.

[107] S.C. Res. 936, U.N. SCOR, 49th Year, 3401st mtg. at 1, U.N. Doc. S/RES/936 (1994), *available in* U.N. Gopher\Documents\Security Council Resolutions; Lewis, *supra* note 106. Goldstone served as chairman of a commission constituted in 1991 to investigate political violence and human rights abuses in preparation for the April 1994 elections in South Africa. *Id.* Graham Blewitt, acting deputy prosecutor, will stay on as deputy, and because both Blewitt and Goldstone come from common law jurisdictions, Goldstone will appoint an additional deputy from a civil law jurisdiction. *Id.*

[108] Statute, *supra* note 20, art. 17. Theodoor Van Boven, a human rights expert, served as registrar throughout 1994. *Secretary-General Appoints Theodoor C. Van Boven as Acting Registrar for International Tribunal for Former Yugoslavia,* Fed. News Serv., Jan. 24, 1994, *available in* LEXIS, World Library, Allnws File. A permanent registrar, Dorothee de Sampayo, was appointed in early 1995. *Dutch Jurist Appointed to War Crimes Tribunal,* Jan. 4, 1995, Reuters, *available in* LEXIS, World Library, Allnws File.

tal and non-governmental organizations."[109] If the prosecutor determines that a prima facie case exists, an indictment will be prepared and transmitted to a judge of the Trial Chamber.[110] The judge has authority under article 19 to review the indictment and "[i]f satisfied that a *prima facie* case has been established by the Prosecutor, he shall confirm the indictment. If not so satisfied, the indictment shall be dismissed."[111] If the indictment is confirmed, "the judge may, at the request of the Prosecutor, issue such orders and warrants for the arrest, detention, surrender or transfer of persons, and any other orders as may be required for the conduct of the trial."[112]

Articles 20 and 21 govern the conduct of proceedings and provide "due process protections [that] exceed those in the Charters of the Nuremberg and Tokyo Tribunals. Articles 20 and 21 . . . are exemplary in this regard . . . ."[113] The defendant is "entitled to a fair and public hearing," subject to the protection in article 22 of victims and witnesses,[114] is "presumed innocent until proved guilty according to the provisions of the present Statute,"[115] and is "entitled to the following minimum guarantees, in full equality":

> (a) to be informed promptly and in detail in a language which he understands of the nature and cause of the charge against him;
> (b) to have adequate time and facilities for the preparation of his defence and to communicate with counsel of his own choosing;
> (c) to be tried without undue delay;
> (d) to be tried in his presence, and to defend himself in

---

[109] Statute, *supra* note 20, art. 18(1).

[110] *Id.* art. 18(4).

[111] *Id.* art. 19(1).

[112] *Id.* art. 19(2).

[113] Meron, *supra* note 6, at 83.

[114] Statute, *supra* note 20, art. 21(2).

[115] *Id.* art. 21(3).

person or through legal assistance of his own choosing; to be informed, if he does not have legal assistance, of this right; and to have legal assistance assigned to him, in any case where the interests of justice so require, and without payment by him in any such case if he does not have sufficient means to pay for it;
(e)   to examine, or have examined, the witnesses against him and to obtain the attendance and examination of witnesses on his behalf under the same conditions as witnesses against him;
(f)   to have the free assistance of an interpreter if he cannot understand or speak the language used in the International Tribunal;
(g)   not to be compelled to testify against himself or to confess guilt.[116]

As noted earlier, the Security Council declined to adopt France's recommendation for trials in absentia, a position vigorously opposed by many but in particular by common law jurists.[117] However, the Tribunal reached a procedural compromise whereby defendants who refuse to appear before the International Tribunal "will have charges, evidence and arrest warrants against them made public."[118] This solution seems to accord well with the objective of achieving a stable peace in the region.

Article 22 enjoins the Tribunal to include appropriate protections

---

[116]   *Id.* art. 21(4).

[117]   See *supra* notes 59–61 and accompanying text.

[118]   I.T. R. Proc. & Evid., *supra* note 97, RR. 52, 60, 61, 78; Sabine Gillot, *Tribunal Will Reveal War Crimes Evidence against Absent Defendants*, Agence France Presse, Feb. 11, 1994, *available in* LEXIS, World Library, Allnws File. Judge Claude Jorda, of the International Tribunal, quoted in *id.*, explained:

> We have taken the French concept [of trial in absentia] to its limits, which has allowed us to establish a procedure which, while not judging the accused in absentia, will allow us to make public the charge against him. . . . [International arrest warrants] would also be published, so that any accused refusing to attend would be unable to plead his innocence before any other body. . . . [E]vidence on charges against an absent defendant will be presented at public hearings, whose proceedings will be passed verbatim to the United Nations Security Council and the country believed to be sheltering the accused.

in its Rules of Procedure and Evidence for victims and witnesses.[119]

Articles 23 and 24, respectively, confer sentencing powers on the International Tribunal and provide for penalties. Judgment must be by majority and must be delivered in public.[120] The judgment must "be accompanied by a reasoned opinion in writing, to which separate or dissenting opinions may be appended."[121] Article 24 makes available both imprisonment[122] and "the return of any property and proceeds acquired by criminal conduct, including by means of duress, to their rightful owners."[123] Although the Statute itself does not provide for fines, which might have yielded a compensation fund, Security Council Resolution 827 makes it clear that judgments by the Tribunal "shall be carried out without prejudice to the right of the victims to seek, through appropriate means, compensation for damages incurred as a result of violations of international humanitarian law."[124]

Under article 25, both the defendant and the prosecutor have a right of appeal on the basis of "an error on a question of law invalidating the decision" or "an error of fact which has occasioned a miscarriage of justice."[125] The defendant's right of appeal is deemed "a fundamental element of individual civil and political rights and has, *inter alia*, been incorporated in the International Covenant on Civil and Political Rights."[126] The appeals chamber may affirm, reverse, or revise decisions

---

[119] Statute, *supra* note 20, art. 22.

[120] *Id.* art. 23(2).

[121] *Id.*

[122] *Id.* art. 24(1).

[123] *Id.* art. 24(3).

[124] S.C. Res. 827, *supra* note 10, ¶ 7; *see also* Remarks by Madeleine K. Albright, U.S. Ambassador, U.N. SCOR, 48th Year, 3217th mtg. at 17, U.N. Doc. S/PV.3217 (1993) ("[W]ith respect to Article 24, it is [the U.S.] understanding that compensation to victims by a convicted person may be an appropriate part of decisions on sentencing, reduction of sentences, parole or commutation.").

[125] Statute, *supra* note 20, art. 25(1).

[126] *Secretary-General's Report, supra* note 10, ¶ 116.

taken by the trial chambers.[127] Article 26 permits applications for review of both trial and appellate judgments:

> Where a new fact has been discovered which was not known at the time of the proceedings before the Trial Chambers or the Appeals Chamber and which could have been a decisive factor in reaching the decision, the convicted person or the Prosecutor may submit to the International Tribunal an application for review of the judgement.[128]

Article 27 provides that terms of imprisonment are to be served in states that have indicated their willingness to accept convicted persons and have then been designated by the International Tribunal to carry out particular sentences. The former Yugoslav republics are apparently not eligible to execute sentences of imprisonment "given the nature of the crimes in question and the international character of the tribunal."[129] "[I]mprisonment shall be in accordance with the applicable law of the State concerned, subject to the supervision of the International Tribunal."[130]

Pursuant to article 28, eligibility for pardon or commutation of sentence is to be determined by the domestic law of the state where the defendant is imprisoned. If either option is available, "the State concerned shall notify the International Tribunal accordingly. The President of the International Tribunal, in consultation with the judges, shall decide the matter on the basis of the interests of justice and the general principles of law."[131]

Because the Tribunal was created through the Security Council's exercise of its powers under chapter VII of the Charter, all states are under a binding obligation "to cooperate with the International Tribunal

---

[127] Statute, *supra* note 20, art. 25(2).

[128] *Id.* art. 26.

[129] *Secretary-General's Report, supra* note 10, ¶ 121.

[130] Statute, *supra* note 20, art. 27.

[131] *Id.* art. 28.

and to assist it in all stages of the proceedings"—such as ensuring "compliance with requests for assistance in the gathering of evidence, hearing of witnesses, suspects and experts, identification and location of persons and the service of documents" and with "orders issued by the Trial Chambers, such as warrants of arrest, search warrants, warrants for surrender or transfer of persons, and any other orders necessary for the conduct of the trial."[132] Article 29 sets out an illustrative, but not exhaustive, list of the obligations on states to cooperate with the Tribunal, along the lines sketched above.[133]

Article 30 renders applicable to the judges, the prosecutor, and the registrar the privileges and immunities of diplomatic envoys under international law;[134] and to their staff, the privileges and immunities of UN officials under the Convention on the Privileges and Immunities of the United Nations.[135] Article 30(4) provides, rather generally, that "[o]ther persons, including the accused, required at the seat of the International Tribunal shall be accorded such treatment as is necessary for the proper functioning of the International Tribunal."

Articles 31–34 address various administrative matters, including the location of the Tribunal, its working languages, and its financing.

PROSPECTS FOR THE FUTURE

Two major questions now confront us. The first is, how successful will the International Tribunal be? The second and perhaps more important

---

[132] *Secretary-General's Report,* supra note 10, ¶ 125.

[133] Statute, *supra* note 20, art. 29(2).

[134] *Id.* art. 30(1)–(2). For practical purposes, the most significant immunity is that accorded by Vienna Convention on Diplomatic Relations, *done* Apr. 18, 1961, art. 31, 500 U.N.T.S. 95 (immunity from the criminal and civil jurisdiction of the receiving state).

[135] Statute, *supra* note 20, art. 30(1), (3); Convention on the Privileges and Immunities of the United Nations, *adopted* Feb. 13, 1946, 1 U.N.T.S. 15. The most significant immunity is that under *id.* § 22 (immunity for covered persons from legal process of every kind in respect of words spoken or written and acts done in the course of the performance of their mission).

question is, to what extent will the creation of the International Tribunal assist in establishing a permanent international criminal court?

The first question depends both on the level of financial and political support that the Tribunal ultimately musters[136] and on the degree to which the prosecution of cases achieves the Security Council's stated goals of deterrence, justice, and peace—halting future, and redressing past, violations of international humanitarian law, and breaking the cycle of ethnic violence and retribution in the region.[137] The signs are not encouraging in this regard. The General Assembly has declined thus far to meet the Secretary-General's recommendations for funding the Tribunal,[138] although individual governments have made

---

[136] Lewis, *supra* note 105 ("In the end the success of this attempt to hold individuals responsible for the appalling brutalities in Bosnia will of course be a test of international political will. One early indication will be whether the U.N. General Assembly approves an adequate budget for the tribunal next fall [1994].").

[137] See S.C. Res. 827, *supra* note 10; S.C. Res. 808, *supra* note 10; *see also* Andrew Kelly, *Yugoslavia War Crimes Tribunal Starts Work*, Chi. Sun-Times, Nov. 18, 1993, at 52, *available in* LEXIS, World Library, Allnws File (quoting then UN Legal Counsel and Under-Secretary-General for Legal Affairs Carl-August Fleischhauer):

> [T]he tribunal was set up with three aims: ending war crimes, bringing the perpetrators to justice and breaking the cycle of ethnic violence and retribution.
> "These three important goals . . . are intertwined in the fundamental reason for the establishment of this tribunal, namely to bring the rule of law to bear upon the perpetrators of the atrocities in the territory of the former Yugoslavia and, hopefully, to bring an end to this long nightmare of human suffering and tragedy," [Fleischhauer] said.

[138] The Secretary-General ultimately requested approximately $33 million for the biennium 1994–1995. *Report of the Secretary-General as Requested by the General Assembly in Resolution 47/235: Revised Estimates—Financing of the International Tribunal for the Prosecution of Persons Responsible for Serious Violations of International Humanitarian Law Committed in the Territory of the Former Yugoslavia since 1991,* U.N. GAOR Fifth Comm., 48th Sess., Agenda Item 159, U.N. Doc. A/C.5/48/44/Add.1 (1994). About $11 million was allocated to the Tribunal for calendar year 1994. *General Assembly Authorizes $90 Million for UNPROFOR, MINURSO, International War Crimes Tribunal,* U.N. Press Release, U.N. Doc. GA/8661 (Apr. 14, 1994), *available in* U.N. Gopher\Current Information\Press Releases; *War Crimes Tribunal Says Trials May Begin by Year End, supra* note 98 (since the Security Council set up the Tribunal, "U.N. funding [has been] in doubt. Then on April 15 [1994] the General Assembly voted the body

pledges of financial and other forms of support.[139] At the same time, there have been complaints about the failure of Western nations to adhere to promises to second staff to the prosecution team.[140] Concerns have also been raised in many quarters about whether the Tribunal is only "a convenient way to quiet human rights activists and other supporters of the Bosnians. . . . a bargaining chip to win Serbian and Croatian agreement to a peace settlement."[141] An unnamed senior

---

$11.5 million to get it through 1994, rather than the $32 million it was seeking to take it through end-1995.").

The funding of the Tribunal is discussed at some length in Julian J.E. Schutte, *Legal and Practical Implications, from the Perspective of the Host Country, Relating to the Establishment of the International Tribunal for the Former Yugoslavia*, in this issue of *Criminal Law Forum*.

[139] Among them are the United States, Thomas W. Lippman, *U.S. Accuses the Serbs of More Atrocities*, Int'l Herald Tribune, Dec. 30, 1994, *available in* LEXIS, World Library, Allnws File (reporting contribution of $13 million in cash and services to the Tribunal); Carol J. Williams, *No Amnesty for Perpetrators of Balkans Atrocities, U.S. Says*, N.Y. Times, Jan. 7, 1994, at A6, *available in* LEXIS, World Library, Allnws File; Pakistan, *Pakistan Gives $1 Million to Bosnian War Crimes Tribunal*, UPI, Feb. 1, 1994, *available in* LEXIS, World Library, Allnws File; and the Netherlands, Schutte, *supra* note 138. For more information, see *Annual Report of the International Tribunal for the Prosecution of Persons Responsible for Serious Violations of International Humanitarian Law Committed in the Territory of the Former Yugoslavia since 1991*, ¶¶ 183–188, U.N. SCOR, 49th Year, Agenda Item 152, U.N. Doc. S/1994/1007 (1994) [hereinafter *Tribunal Annual Report*]; David P. Forsythe, *Politics and the International Tribunal for the Former Yugoslavia*, in this issue of *Criminal Law Forum*.

[140] Eagleburger, *supra* note 106 (speaking about promises of staff from Britain and Canada, then Acting Deputy Prosecutor Graham Blewitt said, "They're not materializing, and I have some doubts that they will materialize."). *But see* Maryann Stenberg, *United Nations: Australians Help in Bosnia War Crime Prosecution*, The Age (Melbourne), June 21, 1994, *available in* LEXIS, World Library, Allnws File (discussing Australian personnel working for the International Tribunal).

[141] Sadruddin Aga Khan, *War Crimes without Punishment*, N.Y. Times, Feb. 8, 1994, at A23, *available in* LEXIS, World Library, Allnws File. To similar effect is Eagleburger, *supra* note 106 ("The hopes of bringing such war criminals to international justice . . . have been dimmed by wrangles among United Nations member nations and lack of enthusiasm among key European allies, who fear that prosecution might interfere with the continuing search for a diplomatic settlement."); Rodrigue, *supra* note 15 (querying lack of personnel, funding, and other resources needed by the Commission of

Clinton administration official was quoted as saying that while "[a]cts of genocide and war crimes have been committed, orchestrated by leaders from on high," support for the Tribunal "drops off fast outside the United States."[142] The chairman of the Commission of Experts, Cherif Bassiouni, expressed deep dissatisfaction with what he termed the premature termination of the Commission in April 1994. He criticized this decision from a moral perspective because "[i]t would be the worst disservice to humanity to push it all under the rug"; from a practical perspective because the Commission's work could not be completed and because no prosecutor had yet been appointed; and from an institutional perspective because the announcement to close down the Commission came only from the UN Office of Legal Affairs, not the Security Council itself.[143] Nor has the creation of the Tribunal done much to deter the

---

Experts as either an "act of superb diplomatic hypocrisy" or an "act of superb diplomatic inattention").

[142] Eagleburger, *supra* note 106.

[143] Philippe Naughton, *Yugoslav War Crimes Investigator Assails U.N.*, Reuters, Mar. 18, 1994, *available in* LEXIS, World Library, Allnws File. The decision to close down the Commission in April 1994 was highly controversial. To quote a former UN High Commissioner for Refugees:

> [The] abrupt closing of the investigation before the tribunal is properly up and running is already having consequences on the ground. It has raised doubts about the tribunal's legal authority for completing the exhumation of a mass grave of Croatian victims . . . in Vukovar. Future investigations, and therefore prosecutions, are also likely to be undercut.
>
> . . . .
>
> For critics of the West's cowardly stance during this savage war . . . the tribunal mattered: it offered some prospect of accountability. Although it was never likely that the paper trail would exist to implicate top officials, the successful prosecution of field commanders and local extremists, who encouraged mass rape and murder, might have begun a healing process after the war.
>
> Now, though, the neutering of the international tribunal is under way. Only a facade will remain, it seems—one that can be counted on not to produce embarrassing prosecutions. . . .

Sadruddin Aga Khan, *supra* note 141.

perpetrators.[144]

On a more positive note, domestic legal measures to implement Security Council Resolution 827 have been taken or are being planned by various UN member states,[145] and investigations or prosecutions have begun in several European states against suspected war criminals from the former Yugoslavia.[146] The Security Council's arduous journey to select

---

[144] *See* Aga Khan, *supra* note 141 (decrying the attack of Feb. 5, 1994, on the Sarajevo market that killed some 70 civilians); *Human Rights: Civilian Massacres Are Crimes, Mazowiecki Says,* Inter Press Serv., Feb. 7, 1994, *available in* LEXIS, World Library, Allnws File (Tadeusz Mazowiecki, UN Special Rapporteur for Human Rights in the Former Yugoslavia, condemning the Sarajevo market attack and other murders of civilians in "safe zones" early in 1994). On the later siege of Gorazde, see Roger Cohen, *Conflict in the Balkans: Isolation as Tactic,* N.Y. Times, Apr. 19, 1994, at A10, *available in* LEXIS, World Library, Allnws File; Michael Specter, *Yeltsin Warns Bosnian Serbs to Stop Assault on Gorazde,* N.Y. Times, Apr. 20, 1994, at A12, *available in* LEXIS, World Library, Allnws File. The Security Council adopted a resolution condemning the attack on Gorazde. S.C. Res. 913, U.N. SCOR, 49th Year, 3367th mtg. at 1, U.N. Doc. S/RES/913 (1994), *available in* U.N. Gopher\Documents\Security Council Resolutions. Sarajevo again faced intense pressure from the Bosnian Serbs in September 1994. Roger Cohen, *NATO Jets Strike Serbs near Sarajevo,* N.Y. Times, Sept. 23, 1994, at A8, *available in* LEXIS, World Library, Allnws File. Gross and flagrant violations of international humanitarian law and defiance of the United Nations occurred in late 1994 in the Bihac area. *E.g.,* Roger Cohen, *Conflict in the Balkans: The Overview — Leader of Serbs Spurns a Meeting with Head of U.N.,* N.Y. Times, Dec. 1, 1994, at A1, *available in* LEXIS, World Library, Allnws File; Roger Cohen, *Serbs Close in On Bosnian Town: U.N. and NATO Unable to Act,* N.Y. Times, Nov. 29, 1994, at A1, *available in* LEXIS, World Library, Allnws File.

[145] *Tribunal Annual Report, supra* note 139, ¶¶ 172–182; Act on the Jurisdiction of the International Tribunal for the Prosecution of Persons Responsible for Crimes Committed in the Territory of the Former Yugoslavia and on Legal Assistance to the International Tribunal (Fin. Jan. 5, 1994); on Germany, see *infra* note 150; on the Netherlands, see Schutte, *supra* note 138; on Slovenia, see Pavel Dolenc, *A Slovenian Perspective on the Statute and Rules of the International Tribunal for the Former Yugoslavia,* in this issue of *Criminal Law Forum.*

[146] Lewis, *supra* note 105 ("Germany, Denmark, and Switzerland have already arrested suspects and are holding them for trial there or by the international tribunal."); *Austria's War Crime Trial of Serb Adjourned,* Reuters, Oct. 20, 1994, *available in* LEXIS, World Library, Allnws File (citing proceedings in Austria, Denmark, and Switzerland).

The Austrian case ended in a mistrial, and the Supreme Court must assign a

a prosecutor ended successfully.[147] The Commission of Experts submitted to the Tribunal a voluminous final report, and all its evidentiary record (some 65,000 pages of documents, 300 hours of videotape, and a computerized database), which should help prove allegations of serious violations of international humanitarian law.[148] Funding for 1995 promises to be more solid than in the past.[149] And the Tribunal's first indictment was handed down in late 1994.[150]

---

new panel of judges to rehear it. *Serb War Crimes Trial Referred to Supreme Court,* Agence France Presse, Dec. 12, 1994, *available in* LEXIS, World Library, Allnws File.

On Denmark, see *20 Cases Sent by Denmark to War Crimes Tribunal on ex-Yugoslavia,* Agence France Presse, Jan. 31, 1994, *available in* LEXIS, World Library, Allnws File; *Moslem Refugee Goes on Trial for War Crimes,* Agence France Presse, Nov. 7, 1994, *available in* LEXIS, World Library, Allnws File. The latter case resulted in a conviction, with the Danish court imposing an 8-year prison sentence on a Bosnian Muslim who had savagely beaten and in several cases killed fellow prisoners in a Croat-run camp in cooperation with the camp authorities. *War Crimes Panel Convicts Bosnian,* Chi. Tribune, Nov. 23, 1994, at 3, *available in* LEXIS, World Library, Allnws File.

On Germany, see Stephen Kinzer, *Germans Arrest Serb as Balkan War Criminal,* N.Y. Times, Feb. 16, 1994, at A6, *available in* LEXIS, World Library, Allnws File; *Germany Looks towards Yugoslav War Crimes Tribunal,* Reuters, Apr. 20, 1994, *available in* LEXIS, World Library, Allnws File (Germany anticipates handing over more than forty cases to the International Tribunal). On more recent developments, see *infra* note 150.

On Switzerland, see *Bosnia to Bring Cases of Suspected War Criminals before Swiss Court,* Agence France Presse, Apr. 18, 1994, *available in* LEXIS, World Library, Allnws File; *Swiss Military Court May Court-martial Ex-Yugoslav,* Reuters, Apr. 13, 1994, *available in* LEXIS, World Library, Allnws File.

[147] See *supra* notes 103–107.

[148] *Final Report, supra* note 15; Bassiouni, *supra* note 15; Paul Lewis, *U.N. Report Accuses Serbs of "Crimes against Humanity,"* N.Y. Times, June 3, 1994, at A3, *available in* LEXIS, World Library, Allnws File; Stephanie Nebehay, *U.N. Panel Links Bosnian Serbs to Genocide,* Reuters, Apr. 15, 1994, *available in* LEXIS, World Library, Allnws File.

[149] For the first quarter of 1995, the Fifth Committee of the General Assembly proposed a budget of $7 million. *Fifth Committee Approves $352.5 Million for UNDOF, UNIFIL, UNOSOM II, International Criminal Tribunal and Human Rights Programmes,* U.N. Press Release, U.N. Doc. GA/AB/2981 (Dec. 21, 1994), *available in* U.N. Gopher\Current Information\Press Releases, compared to about $11 million for all of 1994. See sources cited *supra* note 138.

[150] The first indictment (Dragan Nikolic) was handed down in November 1994. Sara Henley, *U.N. War Crimes Tribunal Charges First Suspect,* Reuters, Nov. 8, 1994,

The ultimate hope is that the Tribunal will succeed in calling vicious criminals to account and send a loud and resounding message to the international community that persons who order or commit the sorts of crimes under the Tribunal's jurisdiction run a very real risk of punishment. This assumes, of course, that similar ad hoc international tribunals will be created by the Security Council as the need arises, or that the International Tribunal's jurisdiction will be extended to other conflicts,[151] if no permanent judicial mechanism is put in place.[152] It assumes, as well, that effective measures of cooperation with the Tribunal will be incorporated into any negotiated settlement of the conflict in Bosnia–Herzegovina and that all governments in the region will comply with their obligations generally under the Statute and specifically under articles 9 and 29,[153] if not voluntarily than in response to pressure from the international community.[154]

---

available in LEXIS, World Library, Allnws File. At the same time, the Tribunal requested Germany to transfer to its jurisdiction a Bosnian Serb (Dusan Tadic) being held in custody. Peter S. Canellos, *U.N. Tribunal Seeks a Serb: Ethnic Cleansing Alleged as Trial Begins in the Hague*, Boston Globe, Nov. 9, 1994, at 26, *available in* LEXIS, World Library, Allnws File; *Yugo War Crimes Court Asks Germany to Extradite Bosnian Serb*, Agence France Presse, Nov. 8, 1994, *available in* LEXIS, World Library, Allnws File; *see also* Melinda Crane-Engel, *Germany vs. Genocide*, N.Y. Times, Oct. 30, 1994, § 6, at 56, *available in* LEXIS, World Library, Allnws File. Germany amended its law soon afterward to permit the extradition of foreign residents (like the accused) to the Tribunal and expects to amend the Constitution to permit the extradition of citizens as well. *Bonn Changes Law to Hand Over War Criminals*, Reuters, Dec. 16, 1994, *available in* LEXIS, World Library, Allnws File.

[151] See *supra* note 12.

[152] See *supra* notes 42–43 and accompanying text.

[153] Statute, *supra* note 20, art. 9, requires national courts upon "formal request" to defer to the International Tribunal in the exercise of concurrent jurisdiction. *Id.* art. 29 requires cooperation and assistance in such areas as identification and location of persons; taking of testimony and production of evidence; service of documents; arrest and detention of persons; and surrender and transfer of accused persons to the International Tribunal.

[154] "One lever for persuasion is sanctions. . . . A more extreme option would be punitive measures like those imposed on Libya for its failure to produce for trial the suspects in the bombing of Pan Am 103." Lewis, *supra* note 105. Others have

One thing is clear. The new legal regime is an enormous advance for the world community. It constitutes an objective and fair system of criminal justice to be applied in all instances falling within its jurisdiction. This court is clearly a prototype for other such tribunals and it carries with it the moral and political force of the world community.

But has the creation of the International Tribunal for the Former Yugoslavia moved the world community closer to establishing a permanent international criminal court? In all probability, it has. In the past, the major barrier to this goal has been the conflict between state sovereignty and the jurisdiction of such a tribunal. States are generally reluctant to expose their citizens (especially politicians and senior military commanders) to potential criminal prosecutions for conduct undertaken in the name of the state.[155] If the International Tribunal is largely successful in carrying out its mandate, its record will dispel many of the more principled concerns of states. It is suggested that the Tribunal's accomplishments and the international revulsion toward gross human rights violations in the dark pockets of the world will persuade enough states to put aside their traditional jurisdictional jealousy over crimes and subscribe to a treaty-based permanent international criminal court in the not too distant future.

---

advocated a more active role for the CSCE. Dennis DeConcini & Steny H. Hoyer, *Bosnia War-Crimes Tribunal Could Be Boosted by CSCE*, Christian Sci. Monitor, July 14, 1994, at 18, *available in* LEXIS, World Library, Allnws File. At its December 1994 summit, however, the CSCE failed to reach a consensus regarding the situation in Bosnia, "although a number of member states were pressing for at least a statement condemning the most recent Bosnian Serb aggression." *CSCE Conference Ends amid Dissent over Bosnia — Kohl "Deeply Depressing,"* Week in Germany, Dec. 9, 1994, *available in* LEXIS, World Library, Allnws File.

[155] Many national armed forces maintain a war crimes investigation section, but they are usually concerned with crimes perpetrated against their own citizens or troops. *E.g.*, Alfred de Zayas, *The Wermacht War Crimes Bureau, 1939–1945* (1989). It is also common knowledge that the U.S. Judge Advocate General's Office conducted a series of investigations subsequent to Operation Desert Storm that focused on possible war crimes committed by Iraqi personnel. *See Analysis: Dual Containment — Clinton's New Policy on the Middle East Region*, Moneyclips, May 29, 1993, *available in* LEXIS, World Library, Allnws File.

5
An Ad Hoc International Tribunal for the Prosecution of Serious Violations of International Humanitarian Law in the Former Yugoslavia[*]

Roman A. Kolodkin[**]

INTRODUCTION

Security Council Resolutions 808 and 827, establishing the ad hoc International Tribunal for the Prosecution of Persons Responsible for Serious Violations of International Humanitarian Law Committed in the Territory of the Former Yugoslavia since 1991,[1] usher in a new era in

---

[*] © 1995 Roman A. Kolodkin.
 Editor's note: research for this article was updated through December 31, 1994. However, the text was prepared prior to the establishment on November 8, 1994, of the International Tribunal for Rwanda and does not consider the implications of this development. The Tribunal for Rwanda has institutional ties to the International Tribunal for the Former Yugoslavia, sharing the chief prosecutor and the appeals chamber. S.C. Res. 955, U.N. SCOR, 49th Year, 3453d mtg. at 1, U.N. Doc. S/RES/955 (1994), *reprinted in* appendix D of this issue of *Criminal Law Forum* and *available in* U.N. Gopher\Documents\Security Council Resolutions.

[**] Deputy Director, Legal Department, Ministry of Foreign Affairs, Russian Federation; J.D., Moscow State University 1982; S.J.D., Moscow State University 1986. This article reflects the personal views of the author.

[1] S.C. Res. 808, U.N. SCOR, 48th Year, 3175th mtg. at 1, U.N. Doc. S/RES/808 (1993), *reprinted in* appendix A of this issue of *Criminal Law Forum* and *available in* U.N. Gopher\Documents\Security Council Resolutions; S.C. Res. 827, U.N.

the development of international law and international relations. For the first time, beyond the framework of state responsibility, beyond victors' justice, the whole international community, not just a group of states, is using international law to assume state functions of criminal justice to prosecute perpetrators of serious crimes committed in the territory of several states. Analysis of the legal aspects of this phenomenon is important from the prospect, first of all, of creating a permanent international criminal court and, possibly, other ad hoc tribunals and, second of all, of forming thereby an international criminal justice regime.

The first attempt to put into practice the idea of ascribing international criminal responsibility to persons guilty of actions "against the whole world" was made by the victors in World War I. The Treaty of Versailles provided for organizing an ad hoc tribunal to try Kaiser Wilhelm II "for a supreme offence against international morality and the sanctity of treaties."[2] In fact, however, the tribunal was never set up — nor a permanent court, which should have been established pursuant to the 1937 Convention for the Prevention and Punishment of Terrorism and its companion instrument, the Convention for the Creation of an International Criminal Court, neither of which ever entered into force.[3]

The creation of the first effective international criminal tribunals, at Nuremberg and Tokyo, appeared possible as a result of the victory of the Allies in World War II. The trials of war criminals, and their individual responsibility for the crimes alleged, derived from the state responsibility of the Axis powers. It is not by accident that in the

---

SCOR, 48th Year, 3217th mtg. at 1, U.N. Doc. S/RES/827 (1993), *reprinted in* appendix A of this issue of *Criminal Law Forum* and *in* 32 I.L.M. 1203.

[2] Treaty of Versailles, June 28, 1919, art. 227, 2 Bevans 43. The treaty also contemplated trials by national or international military tribunals of other persons "accused of having committed acts in violation of the laws and customs of war." *Id.* arts. 228–230.

[3] Convention for the Prevention and Punishment of Terrorism, *opened for signature* Nov. 16, 1937, *reprinted in* 7 *International Legislation* 862 (Manley O. Hudson ed., 1941) (which received a single ratification from India); Convention for the Creation of an International Criminal Court, *opened for signature* Nov. 16, 1937, *reprinted in* 7 *International Legislation, supra,* at 878 (which received no ratifications).

statutes of both tribunals, the first crime over which they were given jurisdiction was labeled "*[c]rimes against peace:* namely, planning, preparation, initiation or waging a war of aggression, or a war in violation of international treaties, agreements or assurances, or participation in a common plan or conspiracy for the accomplishment of any of the foregoing."[4]

Although the possibility of an international criminal jurisdiction is contemplated by two universal international treaties in force,[5] attempts to adopt a statute for, let alone set up, an international criminal court, within the UN framework,[6] have been uniformly unsuccessful. Until the

---

[4] Charter of the International Military Tribunal, Aug. 8, 1945, art. 6(a), 82 U.N.T.S. 284. The Nuremberg tribunal was established pursuant to Agreement for the Prosecution and Punishment of the Major War Criminals of the European Axis, Aug. 8, 1945, 82 U.N.T.S. 279.

To similar effect is Charter of the International Military Tribunal for the Far East, Jan. 19, 1946 *(as amended* Apr. 26, 1946), art. 5(a), 4 Bevans 21, *reprinted in* 1 Benjamin Ferencz, *Defining International Aggression* 523 (1975). The International Military Tribunal for the Far East was established in Tokyo pursuant to Special Proclamation by the Supreme Commander for the Allied Powers, Establishment of an International Military Tribunal for the Far East, Jan. 19, 1946, 4 Bevans 20, *reprinted in* 1 Ferencz, *supra,* at 522.

[5] Convention on the Prevention and Punishment of the Crime of Genocide, *adopted* Dec. 9, 1948, art. VI, 78 U.N.T.S. 277; International Convention on the Suppression and Punishment of the Crime of Apartheid, *adopted* Nov. 30, 1973, art. V, 1015 U.N.T.S. 243.

[6] G.A. Res. 489 (V), U.N. GAOR, 5th Sess., Supp. No. 20, at 77, U.N. Doc. A/1775 (1950), created a seventeen-member Committee on International Criminal Jurisdiction. The Committee met in Geneva during August 1951, "and at the end of its deliberations it issued a very comprehensive report to which was attached a draft Statute for an International Criminal Court." 2 Benjamin Ferencz, *An International Criminal Court: A Step toward World Peace* 34–35 (1980); *Report of the Committee on International Criminal Jurisdiction on Its Session Held from 1 to 31 August 1951,* U.N. GAOR, 7th Sess., Supp. No. 11, at 21, U.N. Doc. A/2136 (1952) (including the draft statute), *reprinted in* 2 Ferencz, *supra,* at 337 [hereinafter *1951 Committee Report*]. This draft remained just a draft, although it continued to be a topic of debate in the General Assembly for the next several years. *Report of the 1953 Committee on International Criminal Jurisdiction, 27 July–20 August 1953,* U.N. GAOR, 9th Sess., Supp. No. 12, at 23, U.N. Doc. A/2645 (1954) (including a revised draft statute), *reprinted in* 2 Ferencz, *supra,* at 429.

late 1980s the outcome could not have been different: the cold war—competing attitudes on the part of the main actors of the international system toward the values on which such a court should be built, lack of agreement on the general principles of law, mutual distrust, and so forth—doomed any effort in this direction to failure from the very beginning. The necessary legal conditions also were lacking—such as shared recognition of the fact that human rights is no longer an exclusively internal affair of the state; recognition of the fact that obligations in this sphere are *erga omnes;* acknowledgment of the right of the international community to become involved in the face of human rights violations; and, finally, recognition of the fact that massive and grave violations of human rights may be determined to be a threat to international peace or a breach of the peace. In light of these considerations, criticism that prior to the crisis in the former Yugoslavia, ad hoc tribunals have never been set up—not for the conflicts in Korea, Vietnam, Afghanistan, Iran, or elsewhere—becomes meaningless.

It was only in the late 1980s to early 1990s that a paradigm of international relations began to form in which the international community, not in the context of victors and vanquished, could make a decision on intervening in such a sensitive and traditionally exclusive area of state competence as criminal justice. The occurrence of "widespread violations of international humanitarian law" within the territory of the former Yugoslavia[7] coincided with the emergence of the objective political and legal preconditions, including the will of the main actors of the international system, necessary for the creation of an international judicial mechanism. Today, the establishment of an ad hoc international criminal tribunal is a reality, and the creation of a permanent international criminal court based on the work of the International Law Commission (ILC) did not seem too far off at the time of writing.[8]

---

[7] *Report of the Secretary-General pursuant to Paragraph 2 of Security Council Resolution 808 (1993),* ¶¶ 6–11, U.N. Doc. S/25704 & Add.1 (1993), *reprinted in* appendix B of this issue of *Criminal Law Forum* and *in* 32 I.L.M. 1163 [hereinafter *Secretary-General's Report*].

[8] At its forty-sixth session, in the summer of 1994, the ILC adopted a Draft Statute for an International Criminal Court, in *Report of the International Law Commission*

THE ESTABLISHMENT OF THE TRIBUNAL

In the discussions regarding the creation of a tribunal for the former Yugoslavia, three main procedures for setting up such a court were considered: international treaty, Security Council resolution, and General Assembly resolution.

The conclusion of an international treaty seemed the most classic, traditional, or, in the words of Alain Pellet, "orthodox" way.[9] Indeed, all previous international tribunals, whether they were created only on paper or actually were put into operation, had been established by treaty.[10] This can be explained by the very nature of traditional international law, the basis of which is the sovereign equality of states. Hence the necessity of securing the express consent of the interested states to the creation of an international criminal court (that is, ceding or transferring the sovereign prerogative of prosecuting crimes committed in each state's territory and/or by its nationals), as well as the assertion of the court's jurisdiction over crimes committed in the territory of the interested states and/or by their nationals.[11]

---

on Its Forty-sixth Session, U.N. GAOR, 49th Sess., Supp. No. 10, at 43, U.N. Doc. A/49/10 (1994) [hereinafter *1994 ILC Report*], which was debated the following fall in the Sixth Committee of the General Assembly, *Report of the Sixth Committee*, U.N. GAOR, 49th Sess., Agenda Item 137, U.N. Doc. A/49/738, at 17 (1994). Unfortunately, the Sixth Committee, *id.* at 17–18, and the General Assembly, G.A. Res. 49/53, U.N. GAOR, 49th Sess., 84th plen. mtg., U.N. Doc. A/49/53 (1994), failed to take decisive action toward implementing the ILC's proposals, and it is now unclear where the Draft Statute stands, Thalif Deen, *United Nations: U.N. Split over International Criminal Court*, Inter Press Serv., Dec. 21, 1994, *available in* LEXIS, World Library, Allnws File.

[9] Alain Pellet, *Le Tribunal criminel international pour l'ex-Yougoslavie: poudre aux yeux ou avancée décisive?*, 98 Revue Générale de Droit International Public 7, 25 (1994).

[10] The International Military Tribunal for the Far East might be viewed to a certain extent as an exception to this rule, but the proclamation by General Douglas MacArthur was based on previous agreements among the Allies, most notably at the Potsdam and Moscow conferences. See sources cited *supra* note 4, and in particular Editor's Note to Special Proclamation, 4 Bevans at 20–21.

[11] The Mexican commentary on the creation of a tribunal, for instance, noted that the establishment of an international criminal court is closely tied to the exercise of

The establishment of an ad hoc tribunal takes place after the fact, when it is already known in principle in what territory and by the nationals of which states the targeted crimes have been committed. In such a situation, a treaty providing for the establishment of a tribunal, with the participation of the implicated states, may simply be impossible. Expedience would therefore dictate that the tribunal be set up by resolution of a competent international organization.

In the context of the former Yugoslavia, the treaty approach, and this approach alone, was put forward by the special rapporteurs on Bosnia, Herzegovina, and Croatia in the framework of the CSCE Moscow Human Dimension Mechanism.[12] However, it should be remembered that this proposal was oriented principally toward the adoption of a convention (the statute of the tribunal) within the Conference on Security and Cooperation in Europe, because as a "political arrangement" the CSCE has no competence to establish a tribunal by means of a resolution.[13]

---

sovereignty on the part of states with territorial and personal jurisdiction. Note verbale from the Permanent Representative of Mexico to the Secretary-General, Mar. 12, 1993, U.N. Doc. S/25417 (1993), transmitting the views of the Mexican government on the establishment of an international tribunal for the former Yugoslavia under S.C. Res. 808 [hereinafter Mexican Proposal]. See *id.* ¶ 3.

The French Committee of Jurists similarly stressed that the institution of an international jurisdiction directly affects the sovereignty of states. Letter from the Permanent Representative of France to the Secretary-General, Feb. 10, 1993, U.N. Doc. S/25266 (1993), transmitting a report on the establishment of an international criminal tribunal for the former Yugoslavia prepared by a national Committee of Jurists [hereinafter French Proposal]. In particular, see *id.* ¶ 27.

[12] CSCE Rapporteurs (Corell–Turk–Thune), Moscow Human Dimension Mechanism to Bosnia, Herzegovina, and Croatia, *Proposal for an International War Crimes Tribunal for the Former Yugoslavia* (1993) [hereinafter CSCE Proposal]; *see also* Letter from the Permanent Representative of Sweden to the Secretary-General, Feb. 18, 1993, U.N. Doc. S/25307 (1993), annexing a summary of CSCE Proposal, *supra*, and the text of a decision by CSCE participating states on this proposal.

[13] It should be noted that the draft reflects the option that the CSCE participating States or some of these States take the initiative to establish the Tribunal. But the text could be used also in a United Nations context, although some modifications would be necessary. The possibility of the Security Council deciding under Chapter VII of the Charter of the United Nations to establish

The advantage of a treaty approach lies in the possibility for all states with competence *ratione loci* and *ratione personae* over the crimes within the tribunal's jurisdiction both to become parties to the treaty, expressing thereby a willing consent to the establishment of an international jurisdiction, and to take part in the process of elaborating the statute of the tribunal and setting up the court. As mentioned in the *Report of the Secretary-General pursuant to Paragraph 2 of Security Council Resolution 808 (1993)*, a treaty approach "would allow the States participating in the negotiation and conclusion of the treaty fully to exercise their sovereign will, in particular whether they wish to become parties to the treaty or not."[14]

However, this advantage becomes a disadvantage if the interested states reject participation in the treaty. In that event, the treaty, as well as the tribunal, is rendered meaningless.[15] As Pellet has noted, if an ad hoc tribunal is to be created by treaty, then it must be ratified by all interested states; otherwise the creation of the court would have no point since it would lack the means to exercise its jurisdiction.[16]

Yet, even if some states ratified such a treaty, problems would remain. For instance, how many ratifications would be required for the treaty to enter into force? How many to ensure the authority and legitimacy of the tribunal?[17] A further question is whether it would be more expedient to establish a court on a regional or subregional basis,

---

an international jurisdiction has been mentioned in the discussion. Even if such a decision should prove possible, legally and politically, the issues dealt with in the present report still have to be resolved.

CSCE Proposal, *supra* note 12, at 142.

[14] *Secretary-General's Report, supra* note 7, ¶ 19.

[15] It is truly incomprehensible that the convention prepared by the CSCE rapporteurs did not base its entry into force on ratification by the concerned states (art. 61), even though the convention depends on the principle of "ceded jurisdiction." CSCE Proposal, *supra* note 12, at 41–49, 219. It is unclear what "ceded jurisdiction" might mean in the case of nonparticipation in the convention by the states with primary territorial and personal jurisdiction!

[16] Pellet, *supra* note 9, at 26–27.

[17] French Proposal, *supra* note 11, at 12.

with the participation only of interested, neighboring states, and whether such a court would be as fully legitimate as a world court.[18]

Finally, it is obvious as a practical matter that it would take too long to set up by treaty an ad hoc tribunal in a situation where grave crimes have already been committed and are continuing to be committed and where, furthermore, the situation poses a threat to, or even constitutes a breach of, the peace.[19]

The second approach suggested for creating a tribunal for the former Yugoslavia was approval of its statute by a resolution of the UN General Assembly.

In the 1950s, the Committee on International Criminal Jurisdiction was constituted by the General Assembly to examine the possibility of establishing a permanent court.[20] The Committee considered several mechanisms, including a General Assembly resolution, but this option was effectively rejected. As the Committee explained: "Under the Charter, the court could only be established as a subsidiary organ," with the Assembly as the principal organ. "[B]ut a subsidiary body could not have a competence falling outside the competence of its principal, and it [is] questionable whether the General Assembly [is] competent to administer justice."[21]

Correct in relation to the establishment of a permanent court, this argument should apply also to the suggested role of the Assembly in the establishment of an ad hoc tribunal, even if, as proposed by the Organization of the Islamic Conference (OIC) for the former Yugoslavia, the Assembly's role were carefully limited. The OIC suggested that the Assembly approve the statute of the tribunal within thirty days of the

---

[18] The late Professor G. Tunkin (whose student I had the honor to be) firmly objected, during the discussions on the Russian draft statute, see *infra* note 32, to the treaty approach, stressing, in particular, the fact that it could become a precedent for the future creation of local tribunals by treaty.

[19] "As has been pointed out in many of the comments received, the treaty approach incurs the disadvantage of requiring considerable time to establish an instrument and then to achieve the required number of ratifications for entry into force." *Secretary-General's Report*, supra note 7, ¶ 20.

[20] See *supra* note 6.

[21] *1951 Committee Report*, supra note 6, ¶ 21.

adoption of a Security Council resolution providing for the creation of the tribunal in accordance with chapter VII.[22] That is, responsibility would be shared between the Security Council and the General Assembly, with the Council establishing the tribunal and the Assembly determining the basis of its functioning.

Pellet is a strong advocate of the competence of the General Assembly to create an international criminal court (on either a permanent or an ad hoc basis). He reasons as follows from the UN Charter:

> by virtue of articles 10 and 11, the General Assembly has general competence regarding any questions or matters appearing within the scope of the Charter;

> although the Assembly may in principle make only recommendations, it nonetheless "may establish such subsidiary organs as it deems necessary for the performance of its functions" (article 22); it follows that nothing prevents the General Assembly from creating an international criminal court so long as it merely recommends, but does not require, that states submit to this court;

> the establishment of such a court would be fully consistent with the mission of the General Assembly, for one of the purposes of the United Nations is to encourage "respect for human rights and for fundamental freedoms for all" (article 1(3), as well as article 55's preamble), and the creation of an international criminal court would undoubtedly assist in the attainment of this goal.[23]

This analysis is hardly correct. The UN Charter, even given its broadest, most legally expansive interpretation, does not confer on the General

---

[22] Letter from the Permanent Representatives of Egypt, Iran, Malaysia, Pakistan, Saudi Arabia, Senegal, and Turkey, on behalf of the Organization of the Islamic Conference, to the Secretary-General, Mar. 31, 1993, U.N. Doc. S/25512, transmitting the recommendations of the OIC on the establishment of an ad hoc tribunal for the former Yugoslavia. See *id.* ¶ 2.

[23] Pellet, *supra* note 9, at 25–26.

Assembly the competence necessary to create either a permanent court or an ad hoc tribunal.

If the Assembly were to create a tribunal as a subsidiary organ, the argument advanced by the Committee on International Criminal Jurisdiction would come into play: one cannot transfer to another those powers that one does not possess, and the General Assembly clearly does not have judicial powers.

Here it is important to consider the difference between an international criminal court and, let's say, the UN Administrative Tribunal. The latter scrutinizes disputes relating to intraorganizational matters. For this reason, the Assembly could, in accordance with the UN Charter, make a binding decision on the establishment of this body and the adoption of its Statute. In contrast, the establishment and the sphere of activity of an international criminal court (both permanent and ad hoc) do not relate in any respect to intraorganizational matters.

If we consider the establishment of a tribunal by the General Assembly from another angle—as a measure to effect the peaceful settlement of a threat to, or a breach of, the peace in the event that the Security Council fails to perform its functions as provided by the UN Charter—another obstacle arises. The Charter does not give the Assembly the right to make any binding decisions on issues of this nature.[24] Articles 10, 11, 13, and 14, in particular, empower the General Assembly to make only recommendations.[25] Because of this limitation, the OIC proposal is unsound: the General Assembly is not authorized to adopt a statute for an ad hoc tribunal, to make it mandatory for states to cooperate with this tribunal, and, further, to make orders and decisions of the tribunal binding on states.[26]

---

[24] U.N. Charter arts. 10–11, 13–14; *see also id.* arts. 12(1) ("While the Security Council is exercising in respect of any . . . situation the functions assigned to it in the present Charter, the General Assembly shall not make any recommendation with regard to that . . . situation unless the Security Council so requests."), 18 ("recommendations with respect to the maintenance of international peace and security" qualify as "important questions" and require a two-thirds majority vote of members present and voting).

[25] French Proposal, *supra* note 11, ¶¶ 33, 43.

[26] The ILC Working Group on a Draft Statute for an International Criminal Court also "concluded that it would be extremely difficult to establish the Court by

In light of all the foregoing concerns, the establishment of a tribunal and the adoption of its statute by means of a Security Council resolution appeared to the majority of analysts to be the sole option that answered both the legal and the practical demands of the situation. Nonetheless, there were objections to this approach as well. According to a senior official from Yugoslavia, "under the Charter of the United Nations, the Security Council has no mandate to set up such a tribunal or to adopt its statute," chapter VII of the UN Charter does not provide for the establishment of such an organ, and the invocation of article 29 of the UN Charter is legally unfounded and arbitrary. He went on to state: "It is obvious that such a tribunal is not a subsidiary organ of the Security Council. No independent tribunal, particularly an International Tribunal, can be a subsidiary organ of any body."[27]

Nonetheless, the following arguments can be made in favor of setting up the International Tribunal for the Former Yugoslavia by Security Council resolution. Article 24(1) of the UN Charter provides:

> In order to ensure prompt and effective action by the United Nations, its Members confer on the Security Council primary responsibility for the maintenance of international peace and security, and agree that in carrying out its duties under this responsibility the Security Council acts on their behalf.

Article 25 obliges all member states "to accept and carry out the decisions of the Security Council."

---

resolution of a United Nations body, without the support of a treaty. General Assembly resolutions do not impose binding, legal obligations on States in relation to conduct external to the functioning of the United Nations itself." *1994 ILC Report, supra* note 8, at 46.

[27]   Letter from the Permanent Mission of Yugoslavia to the Secretary-General, May 19, 1993, U.N. Doc. S/25801 (1993), transmitting Letter of May 17 from the Deputy Prime Minister and Minister for Foreign Affairs of the Federal Republic of Yugoslavia on the establishment of an international tribunal for the former Yugoslavia under S.C. Res. 808. See Letter of May 17, *supra*, at 3. According to Mexican Proposal, *supra* note 11, ¶ 4, the Charter "does not contain any concrete provision that could be used as a basis for the competence of the Security Council or the General Assembly to make an obligatory decision on the establishment of an ad hoc criminal court."

Acting in accordance with chapter VII of the Charter—headed "Action with Respect to Threats to the Peace, Breaches of the Peace, and Acts of Aggression"—the Security Council, pursuant to article 39, "shall determine the existence of any threat to the peace, breach of the peace, or act of aggression and shall make recommendations, or decide what measures shall be taken in accordance with Articles 41 and 42, to maintain or restore international peace and security."

Finally, article 41 of the Charter provides that the Security Council "may decide what measures not involving the use of armed force are to be employed to give effect to its decisions, and it may call upon the Members of the United Nations to apply such measures." This article sets out a nonexhaustive list of such measures (for example, interruption of economic relations and severance of diplomatic relations).[28]

Having "determined" in the preamble to Resolution 808 that the situation of "widespread violations of international humanitarian law occurring within the territory of the former Yugoslavia, including reports of mass killings and the continuance of the practice of 'ethnic cleansing,'" constituted "a threat to international peace and security" (article 39 of the Charter), the Security Council gave the green light for starting a mechanism, encompassed by the above-mentioned articles of the Charter, including article 41, without express reference to charter VII. Following that, the Council could, in the same resolution, having announced its determination "to put an end to such crimes and to take effective measures to bring to justice the persons who are responsible for them" and having expressed its conviction "that in the particular circumstances of the former Yugoslavia the establishment of an international tribunal would enable this aim to be achieved and would contribute to the restoration and maintenance of peace," *legitimately* decree that such an ad hoc tribunal should be set up.[29]

Security Council Resolution 827 completed the process, formally establishing the International Tribunal for the Former Yugoslavia and

---

[28] In this connection, see French Proposal, *supra* note 11, ¶¶ 34–40; Pellet, *supra* note 9, at 28.

[29] S.C. Res. 808, *supra* note 1. It is important to note that this resolution was adopted unanimously.

adopting its Statute.[30] It should be noted that the most comprehensive draft statutes submitted to the Secretary-General regarding the establishment of the Tribunal—those prepared by Italy,[31] Russia,[32] the United States,[33] and France[34]—assumed the legitimacy and expedience of this approach.

Still, the view that the Tribunal may not legally be established as a subsidiary organ of the Security Council must be considered. Under article 29 of the Charter, the Security Council "may establish such subsidiary organs as it deems necessary for the performance of its functions." The Charter does not, however, assign any judicial functions to the Security Council itself, and it would seem to follow that the Council cannot then establish a subsidiary organ to perform judicial functions. This would be *ultra vires* its authority. Given that the Charter appears by its terms to allow the Security Council to set up the Tribunal as a chapter VII measure, the Secretary-General should not have looked to article 29 as a legal basis for creating the Tribunal and characterized it as a subsidiary organ under that provision.[35]

---

[30] S.C. Res. 827, *supra* note 1. The Statute of the International Tribunal is set out as an annex to *Secretary-General's Report, supra* note 7, and is *reprinted in* appendix B of this issue of *Criminal Law Forum* and *in* 32 I.L.M. 1192.

[31] Letter from the Permanent Representative of Italy to the Secretary-General, Feb. 16, 1993, U.N. Doc. S/25300 (1993), transmitting a draft statute for an international criminal tribunal for the former Yugoslavia prepared by a national Commission of Jurists [hereinafter Italian Proposal].

[32] Letter from the Permanent Representative of the Russian Federation to the Secretary-General, Apr. 5, 1993, U.N. Doc. S/25537 (1993), transmitting a draft statute for an international criminal tribunal for the former Yugoslavia [hereinafter Russian Proposal].

[33] Letter from the Permanent Representative of the United States of America to the Secretary-General, Apr. 5, 1993, U.N. Doc. S/25575 (1993), transmitting views and proposals on establishing an international criminal tribunal for the former Yugoslavia.

[34] French Proposal, *supra* note 11.

[35] In this particular case, the Security Council would be establishing, as an enforcement measure under Chapter VII, a subsidiary organ within the terms of Article 29 of the Charter, but one of a judicial nature. This organ would, of course, have to perform its functions independently of political consider-

The Secretary-General's characterization of the Security Council's decision to set up the Tribunal as an "enforcement measure" under charter VII[36] also seems hardly to be correct. This creates the impression that the establishment of Tribunal is directed against certain states or parties to a conflict, jeopardizing the authority of the Tribunal and calling its impartiality into question, especially given that one of the former Yugoslavian states objects to the establishment of the Tribunal by the Security Council.[37]

While I believe that the Security Council acted within its authority in creating the Tribunal, a permanent international criminal court could not be similarly constituted and Resolutions 808 and 827 should not be considered as setting a precedent in this regard. The establishment of a permanent criminal court needs to be prospective. It cannot be undertaken retrospectively, when the targeted crimes have already been or are being committed, particularly in a situation where the Security Council has identified a threat to, or a breach of, the peace. A permanent court is an institution intended to deal with future contingencies. For this reason, chapter VII cannot be invoked and, consequently,

---

ations; it would not be subject to the authority or control of the Security Council with regard to the performance of its judicial functions. As an enforcement measure under Chapter VII, however, the life span of the international tribunal would be linked to the restoration and maintenance of international peace and security in the territory of the former Yugoslavia, and Security Council decisions related thereto.

Secretary-General's Report, supra note 7, ¶ 28.

[36]   *Id.* ¶¶ 23, 28.

[37]   The Russian draft statute recommended the participation of the former Yugoslavian states in the process of elaborating a statute for an ad hoc tribunal and of deciding upon its organization. This proposal also contemplated giving these states the opportunity to express their approval or disapproval of such a statute before the Security Council voted to approve it, although their disapproval would not have blocked the statute's adoption. Russian Proposal, *supra* note 32, at 15. On the position of the Federal Republic of Yugoslavia toward the Tribunal, see Mark Fuller, *Yugoslavia: Croatia, Bosnia Set to Surrender War Crimes Suspects*, Inter Press Serv., Oct. 11, 1994, *available in* LEXIS, World Library, Allnws File; *Federal Affairs: War Crimes Prosecutor Holds Talks with Federal Officials*, BBC Summary of World Broadcasts (Yugo. Telegraph Serv.), Oct. 10, 1994, *available in* LEXIS, World Library, Allnws File.

there is no legal basis for setting up such a court by Security Council resolution. For this purpose, an international treaty seems to be the most appropriate method.

THE APPLICABLE LAW

Along with the question of how to set up an international criminal tribunal comes the question of what law it should apply. This is a core problem whether the institution is permanent or ad hoc. There are two requirements here—the first is observance of the fundamental principle of criminal law—*nullum crimen, nulla poena sine lege*. The second is that there needs to be an international consensus on what conduct should be defined and punishable as criminal according to generally recognized rules of international law and what particular offenses are of sufficient gravity that they affect the entire community of nations and may appropriately be prosecuted in an international forum.

In recommending what substantive law an ad hoc tribunal for the former Yugoslavia should apply—international or national—the CSCE rapporteurs decided in favor of the latter.[38] They thought this approach would correspond most closely with the principle of legality: the criminal laws of the new states in the region are modeled largely on the penal legislation of the former Socialist Federal Republic of Yugoslavia, which body of law had been fully in conformity with international law in that it provided for individual criminal responsibility in the case of genocide, war crimes, crimes against the humanity, and so forth.[39]

In contrast, all the draft statutes and commentaries submitted to the Secretary-General on the subject of a tribunal for the former Yugosla-

---

[38]   CSCE Proposal, *supra* note 12, at 50–57, 177–79.

[39]   For example, Penal Code art. 125 (Yugo.) went beyond the Fourth Geneva Convention, Geneva Convention Relative to the Protection of Civilian Persons in Time of War, *adopted* Aug. 12, 1949, arts. 146–147, 75 U.N.T.S. 287, in criminalizing offenses in fulfillment of the obligation to enact domestic legislation to punish grave breaches, 4 *The Geneva Conventions of 12 August 1949: Commentary* 590 n.1, 594 (Jean S. Pictet gen. ed., 1958).

via took the position that international law should be the primary source of law. This approach is categorically embraced by the French draft:

> [T]he essential starting-point would seem to be the international character both of the crimes themselves and [of] the institution which will be entrusted with the task of judging them. Accordingly, . . . it is unthinkable that the Tribunal should apply, both as regards procedure and as regards law, national rules that are specific to a given State or States.
>
> . . . .
>
> [With regard to] the question of the applicable law . . . an international judicial body cannot render a judgement on the basis of domestic law, even though that law may recapitulate the rule of general international law.[40]

At the same time, there were some suggestions that national legislation should constitute a subsidiary, or secondary, source of law. For example, the Russian and Italian draft statutes proposed that punishment should be determined pursuant to the legislation of the state in which the crime took place.[41] The position of the French jurists seems to be the most consistent and the most forward-looking for both the establishment of another ad hoc criminal tribunal and the creation of a permanent court.[42]

While it so happens that in the region of the former Yugoslavia, domestic legislation criminalizes the offenses set out in articles 2–5 of the Statute of the Tribunal, it is submitted that the Security Council could have set up a court with competence over these crimes even if this had not been the case. The *nullum crimen* principle is embodied in the

---

[40] French Proposal, *supra* note 11, ¶¶ 52 (citation omitted), 57.

[41] Russian Proposal, *supra* note 32, art. 22(1); Italian Proposal, *supra* note 31, art. 7. Canada also acknowledged the subsidiary role of national legislation. Letter from the Permanent Representative of Canada to the Secretary-General, Apr. 13, 1993, U.N. Doc. S/25549 (1993), transmitting comments on the establishment of an international tribunal for the former Yugoslavia under S.C. Res. 808. See *id.* ¶ 11.

[42] French Proposal, *supra* note 11.

International Covenant on Civil and Political Rights.[43] According to article 15(1), "[n]o one shall be held guilty of any criminal offence on account of any act or omission which did not constitute a criminal offence, under national or international law, at the time when it was committed." By its terms, this formulation of the principle of legality embraces both national and international law. Article 15(2) further provides: "Nothing in this article shall prejudice the trial and punishment of any person for any act or omission which, at the time when it was committed, was criminal according to the general principles of law recognized by the community of nations." Similar provisions are incorporated into the European Convention for the Protection of Human Rights and Fundamental Freedoms.[44] Therefore, the absence of domestic legislation qualifying particular conduct as criminal, and providing sanctions, in the state in which it took place does not preclude prosecution and punishment by an international tribunal where the

---

[43] International Covenant on Civil and Political Rights, *adopted* Dec. 19, 1966, art. 15, 999 U.N.T.S. 171.

[44] European Convention for the Protection of Human Rights and Fundamental Freedoms, *opened for signature* Nov. 4, 1950, art. 7, Europ. T.S. 5. Similarly, the Draft Code of Crimes against the Peace and Security of Mankind provides that the "characterization of an act or omission as a crime against the peace and security of mankind is independent of internal law. The fact that an act or omission is or is not punishable under internal law does not affect this characterization." Draft Code of Crimes against the Peace and Security of Mankind art. 2, in *Report of the International Law Commission on Its Forty-third Session,* U.N. GAOR, 46th Sess., Supp. No. 10, at 238, U.N. Doc. A/46/10 (1991). It is important to note further that the 1994 Draft Statute for an International Criminal Court relies on international law alone to satisfy the principle of legality:

> Article 39: Principle of Legality *(Nullum Crimen Sine Lege)*
>
> An accused shall not be held guilty:
>
>> (a) [with respect to the crime of genocide, the crime of aggression, serious violations of the laws and customs applicable in armed conflict, or crimes against humanity] unless the act or omission in question constituted a crime under international law.

1994 ILC Report, supra note 8, at 112.

conduct constitutes a crime, and particularly a crime against mankind, under general principles of law "recognized by the community of nations."

The Statute of the International Court of Justice identifies the "general principles of law recognized by civilized nations" as one of the main sources of international law, thus making them part of international law.[45] What is important here is the idea that the community of nations not only recognizes the existence of general principles of law but also shares an understanding of what falls within the scope of this term. Now, it can be said that the general principles of law are the substantive and procedural rules of different legal systems that are deemed to constitute rules of general international law and are so recognized by the community of nations.[46] Thus, the administration of international criminal justice on the basis of general principles of law means the application of the principles and rules of general international law.

The juridical construction of an international court that is constituted to decide cases of crimes against mankind or, in other words, offenses against the rules of international law, and that applies, for this purpose, international law—and primarily general principles of law—appears legitimate and logically consistent. This scheme is extremely important for a permanent court because it makes possible the application of similar, universal standards in all cases, regardless of the state in which the crime is committed and the municipal legislation that would apply in a domestic prosecution. In contrast, the application of national law (even taking into account the similarity among states in domestic legislation relating to particular conduct) would necessarily involve substantive differences in the definition of the offense and differences in the applicable procedural rules depending, for example, on

---

[45] I.C.J. Statute art. 38(1)(c).

[46] The Soviet doctrine of international law, which was based upon the class nature of law and upon the idea that national legal systems embody different class structures and interests, did not recognize the possibility of the existence of general principles of substantive law spanning different national legal systems. Rather, such technical and procedural concepts as *lex posterior derogat priori* and *res judicata* were recognized as the general principles of law. *See* 1 *International Law Course* 208–10 (R. Mullerson & G. Tunkin eds., 1989).

where the crime was committed or the nationality of the perpetrator.

The preceding does not mean that the application of national legislation by an international criminal court is completely foreclosed. It may, and obviously should, be invoked by the court, but only as a subsidiary means for determining precisely what are the general principles of law that should be applied. Should the statute of a permanent international criminal court expressly specify the applicable law, it would be expedient to identify national legislation as a subsidiary source, just as the Statute of the International Court of Justice identifies "judicial decisions and the teachings of the most highly qualified publicists of the various nations, as subsidiary means for the determination of rules of law."[47]

The creation of the ad hoc International Tribunal for the Former Yugoslavia is a significant event in and of itself and certainly represents a considerable step toward the establishment of an international criminal justice regime. It is quite possible, however, that as a practical matter the Tribunal will encounter serious problems — most notable among them, access to persons suspected in the commitment of crimes falling under its jurisdiction. For this reason in particular, it is hardly expedient to tie up the establishment of a permanent international criminal court with the question of the effectiveness of the International Tribunal for the Former Yugoslavia. What is important is to analyze the process of resolving the legal problems that surfaced in connection with the creation of the ad hoc Tribunal and to redouble our efforts toward the establishment of a permanent organ of international criminal justice, the more so since all the necessary legal and political conditions are now in place for such an undertaking.

---

[47] I.C.J. Statute art. 38(1)(d).

6
Politics and the International Tribunal for the Former Yugoslavia*

*David P. Forsythe***

> *Of course, this is all the result of a political process.*[1]
>
> *Jurisdiction without political will is an ineffectual weapon.*[2]

Those who would draw a clear distinction between law and politics are to be found more in ivory towers than in corridors of power. If politics refers to the struggle to exercise power in the making of policy, and if law refers to formalized policy, then it can easily be seen that law and politics substantially overlap. Werner Levi has the relationship right, certainly about basic principles in public international law: "[P]olitics decides who the lawmaker and what the formulation of the law shall be;

---

* *Editor's note:* research for this article was updated through January 6, 1995.

** Professor and Chair, Political Science Department, University of Nebraska at Lincoln, Lincoln, Nebraska, United States; B.A., Wake Forest University 1964; M.A., Princeton University 1966; Ph.D., Princeton University 1968.

[1] Herman von Hebel, *An International Tribunal for the Former Yugoslavia,* 11(4) Neth. Q. Hum. Rts. 437, 455 (1993).

[2] Sadruddin Aga Khan, *War Crimes without Punishment,* N.Y. Times, Feb. 8, 1994, at A23, *available in* LEXIS, World Library, Allnws File.

law formalizes these decisions and makes them binding."[3]

The International Tribunal for the Prosecution of Persons Responsible for Serious Violations of International Humanitarian Law Committed in the Territory of the Former Yugoslavia since 1991 was the result of a political decision. Key states decided, for reasons examined below, to create such a court. This policy decision was then legalized by subjecting the policy to a certain procedure: voting in the UN Security Council with reference to chapter VII of the UN Charter, pertaining to threats to international peace and security. This procedure had the effect of making the rulings by the Tribunal legally binding, obviating the necessity of a separate treaty, which some states might have rejected. As H.L.A. Hart has explained, it is the "secondary rule of recognition" that makes the primary rule legally binding.[4] The "secondary" rule of legal procedure transforms a pure policy choice into a substantive legal rule.

The tripartite thesis of this essay, which focuses on the politics behind the Tribunal (and antecedent fact-finding Commission of Experts), and not at all on the application of legal rules by the Tribunal, is as follows:

> Key states decided on the policy of creating a court for reasons that were (beyond covert maneuvering) morally cogent but never politically compelling.

> Obstacles to the Tribunal's successful functioning always were, and still are, profound, leading to the depressing conclusion that such endeavors cannot basically succeed in contemporary international relations.

> While there are pluses and minuses in either creating or not creating such a court, perhaps in another half-century a similar endeavor might basically succeed—in which case this disappointing exercise will have become of more positive value.

---

[3] Werner Levi, *Law and Politics in the International Society* 31 (1976).

[4] *See generally* H.L.A. Hart, *The Concept of Law* (1961).

COVERT AND COGENT POLICIES

Like most enterprises, the Tribunal came into existence because of mixed motives. One set of motives must be inferred from circumstantial evidence, documentary evidence being lacking for the moment. But those motives are reasonably plain nevertheless.

A number of European states, most clearly the United Kingdom, felt the need to give the appearance of doing something about violations of humanitarian law in the former Yugoslavia. Lacking the political will to act decisively to curtail abuses of prisoners and civilians, they endorsed or went along with the creation of the Tribunal. They were also concerned that the Tribunal, seeking punitive judgments, would interfere with diplomatic efforts to terminate the fighting, efforts that depend on the cooperation of suspected war criminals. Since these states have never supported the Tribunal with significant personnel and financial contributions or important documentary evidence, it is clear that they do not regard the Tribunal as a serious venture. Their real political motives have remained covert: to placate opinion by formally supporting the court, but to give free reign to diplomacy.

Agreement that the Commission of Experts and the Tribunal have been underfunded, understaffed, and otherwise lacking in support indicates that many states do not regard this exercise of international criminal justice as a top priority. The very creation of the Commission showed a lack of seriousness about war crimes trials. If one wanted to act vigorously and expeditiously, one would have proceeded directly to the appointment of an international prosecutor, with adequate staff. Creating first the Commission, then later an office of prosecutor as part of the Tribunal,[5] with only a small staff, reflected widespread state

---

[5] The Commission was set up pursuant to S.C. Res. 780, U.N. SCOR, 47th Year, 1992 S.C. Res. & Dec. at 36, U.N. Doc. S/INF/48 (1992), *reprinted in* appendix A of this issue of *Criminal Law Forum*. The Tribunal was set up pursuant to S.C. Res. 808, U.N. SCOR, 48th Year, 3175th mtg. at 1, U.N. Doc. S/RES/808 (1993), *reprinted in* appendix A of this issue of *Criminal Law Forum* and *available in* U.N. Gopher\Documents\Security Council Resolutions; S.C. Res. 827, U.N. SCOR, 48th Year, 3217th mtg. at 1, U.N. Doc. S/RES/827 (1993), *reprinted in* appendix A of this issue of *Criminal Law Forum* and *in* 32 I.L.M. 1203; *Report of the Secretary-General pursuant*

hesitancy about the entire venture. Indeed, the Security Council tiptoed toward the Tribunal, rather than endorse this judicial exercise quickly and firmly.

The British record is quite evident in this regard. In public, Britain went on record several times in support of war crimes proceedings. Behind the scenes, the British were a brake on various proposals. They provided little money, scant personnel, and few documents to the Commission and Tribunal. British officials made known to the press that they had strong misgivings about the practicality of what they saw as a U.S. push for criminal proceedings. Several circles of British opinion knew well that their government did not really favor judicial proceedings.[6]

As a historical digression, it is worth recalling that during World War II, the initial British position was that top German leaders did not deserve what eventually became the Nuremberg proceedings, but rather should be dealt with "by a political decision of the Allied powers," presumably execution without trial. In fairness, Franklin D. Roosevelt also endorsed this plan for a time, until Josef Stalin, of all people, opposed it.[7]

The contemporary French and Italian record is somewhat more ambivalent, as is the German. Both France and Italy participated actively in drafting the Tribunal's Statute.[8] In other ways, France spoke

---

to Paragraph 2 of *Security Council Resolution 808 (1993)*, U.N. Doc. S/25704 & Add.1 (1993), *reprinted in* appendix B of this issue of *Criminal Law Forum* and *in* 32 I.L.M. 1163 (including the Statute of the Tribunal and commentary) [hereinafter *Secretary-General's Report*].

[6] Robert Block & Stephen Castle, *MPs Unite in Condemning Britain's Record on War Crime Prosecutions*, The Independent, Aug. 8, 1993, at 14, *available in* LEXIS, World Library, Allnws File; Simon Tisdall & Chris Stephen, *U.S. Is Set On Prosecuting Yugoslav War Criminals*, The Guardian (Manchester), Jan. 28, 1993, at 8, *available in* LEXIS, World Library, Allnws File; Ian Traynor, *War-Crimes Court Takes First Faltering Steps, But Hague Tribunal Is Under-funded, Under-staffed, and Confronted by Opposition in the West*, Montreal Gazette, Nov. 19, 1993, at D15, *available in* LEXIS, World Library, Allnws File.

[7] Telford Taylor, *The Anatomy of the Nuremberg Trials* 29, 30–31 (1992).

[8] Letter from the Permanent Representative of France to the Secretary-General, Feb. 10, 1993, U.N. Doc. S/25266 (1993), transmitting a report on the establishment

out strongly against war crimes, particularly when the Socialist party controlled the government, and provided some evidentiary documents. But neither France nor Italy offered much financial support to the Commission and Tribunal. Press reports periodically linked France with Britain in believing that the Tribunal complicated peacemaking in the Balkans,[9] especially after the conservatives replaced the Socialists in office. France is also reported to have joined Britain and China in watering down various U.S. initiatives about the Commission and Tribunal.[10]

Germany, while not providing much support to the Commission and Tribunal, arrested approximately fifty suspected war criminals among refugees in its territory and appeared to be proceeding either toward holding national trials or turning the suspects over to the United Nations.[11] Denmark and Switzerland also have arrested suspected war

---

of an international criminal tribunal for the former Yugoslavia prepared by a national Committee of Jurists; Letter from the Permanent Representative of Italy to the Secretary-General, Feb. 16, 1993, U.N. Doc. S/25300 (1993), transmitting a draft statute for an international criminal tribunal for the former Yugoslavia prepared by a national Commission of Jurists. The Statute of the International Tribunal is set out as an annex to *Secretary-General's Report, supra* note 5, and is *reprinted in* appendix B of this issue of *Criminal Law Forum* and *in* 32 I.L.M. 1192.

[9] Paul Lewis, *U.S. Official Visits Graves in Croatia,* N.Y. Times, Jan. 7, 1994, at A3, *available in* LEXIS, World Library, Allnws File; John Pomfret, *War Crimes' Punishment Seen Distant: Balkan Probe Lacks Funding and Backing,* Wash. Post, Nov. 12, 1993, at A39, *available in* LEXIS, World Library, Allnws File.

[10] Mark Tran & Hella Pick, *U.N. to Set Up Commission to Investigate Atrocities in Former Yugoslavia: Europeans Dilute U.S. Call for War Crimes Tribunal,* The Guardian (Manchester), Oct. 7, 1992, at 8, *available in* LEXIS, World Library, Allnws File; *U.N. Creates Panel to Examine Atrocities in Yugoslavia,* Montreal Gazette, Oct. 7, 1992, at B5, *available in* LEXIS, World Library, Allnws File.

[11] *U.N. War Crimes Tribunal Off to Difficult Start at the Hague,* U.S. CSCE Digest, Mar. 1994, at 6; Melinda Crane-Engel, *Germany vs. Genocide,* N.Y. Times, Oct. 30, 1994, § 6, at 56, *available in* LEXIS, World Library, Allnws File. The International Tribunal formally requested Germany to transfer to its jurisdiction a Bosnian Serb (Dusan Tadic) currently in custody and suspected of being a "key figure in 'ethnic cleansing' campaigns against Moslems" in the Prijedor region. *Yugo War Crimes Court Asks Germany to Extradite Bosnian Serb,* Agence France Presse, Nov. 8, 1994, *available in* LEXIS, World Library, Allnws File. In response, the German Bundesrat approved amendments proposed by the government to permit the extradition of foreigners to the

criminals.[12]

Some UN officials were also less than enthusiastic about the Tribunal, although here the record is rather unclear. The first head of the Commission of Experts, the Dutch national Frits Kalshoven, was quoted as saying that an international criminal court could not effectively function in an ongoing armed conflict without a clear loser.[13] There was general agreement that the Kalshoven Commission was in no hurry to compile specifics or move quickly toward trials. During his tenure, Commission reports were described off the record as "vague," "inconclusive," "academic," or "full of legal jargon." Kalshoven, however, was also quoted as laying the blame for the Commission's early dismal performance on certain western European states that failed to provide the necessary financial and personnel support. He specifically mentioned Britain, France, Germany, and Italy.[14] The Commission had to rely on

---

Tribunal, and constitutional changes to permit the extradition of citizens are anticipated. *Bonn Changes Law to Hand Over War Criminals,* Reuters, Dec. 16, 1994, *available in* LEXIS, World Library, Allnws File.

[12] *Moslem Refugee Goes on Trial for War Crimes,* Agence France Presse, Nov. 7, 1994, *available in* LEXIS, World Library, Allnws File (discussing Danish prosecution); *20 Cases Sent by Denmark to War Crimes Tribunal on ex-Yugoslavia,* Agence France Presse, Jan. 31, 1994, *available in* LEXIS, World Library, Allnws File; *Swiss Military Court May Court-martial Ex-Yugoslav,* Reuters, Apr. 13, 1994, *available in* LEXIS, World Library, Allnws File; *see also Austria's War Crime Trial of Serb Adjourned,* Reuters, Oct. 20, 1994, *available in* LEXIS, World Library, Allnws File (citing proceedings in Austria, Denmark, and Switzerland). There has now been a conviction in Denmark, with the court imposing an 8-year prison sentence on a Bosnian Muslim who savagely beat and in several cases killed fellow prisoners in a Croat-run camp in cooperation with the camp authorities. *War Crimes Panel Convicts Bosnian,* Chi. Tribune, Nov. 23, 1994, at 3, *available in* LEXIS, World Library, Allnws File. The Austrian proceedings ended in a mistrial and the Supreme Court must assign a new panel of judges to rehear the case. *Serb War Crimes Trial Referred to Supreme Court,* Agence France Presse, Dec. 12, 1994, *available in* LEXIS, World Library, Allnws File.

[13] Roy Gutman, *War Crime Unit Hasn't a Clue: U.N. Setup Seems Designed to Fail,* Newsday, Mar. 4, 1993, at 8, *available in* LEXIS, News Library, Curnws File.

[14] *Exasperation Drives War Crimes Commission Chief to Resign,* Agence France Presse, Oct. 1, 1993, *available in* LEXIS, World Library, Allnws File; Stanley Meisler, *Jury Still Out on Bosnian War Crimes Tribunal Created by U.N.: Balkans—Slow Start,*

nongovernmental organizations (such as Physicians for Human Rights) for some of its field research, along with pro bono efforts on the part of university officials and law students in the United States. Some of the Commission's bills were paid by the private financier George Soros.

Kalshoven, a retired professor of humanitarian law, claimed he was told by high but unnamed UN officials not to go after top Serbian leaders.[15] Deputy UN Legal Counsel Ralph Zacklin was also quoted as having reservations about the wisdom of a court,[16] although Zacklin denied that he was a brake on the Commission or was in the pocket of the British government.[17] It was a fact, however, that the United Nations itself, meaning officials who answered to the Secretary-General, provided only a small number of nonspecialized staff to the Commission. Whether the foot-dragging came from Zacklin, the UN Legal Office, or elsewhere is disputed. Sources in the Legal Office, who refused to speak for the record, argued that their rapid preparation of the Tribunal's Statute indicated genuine support for judicial proceedings.

The Secretary-General appointed one of the Commission's most active members, Cherif Bassiouni, to replace Kalshoven after the latter resigned.[18] Under Bassiouni, the Commission, or more accurately Bassiouni's university in the United States (DePaul), compiled a computerized database pertaining to war crimes. The Commission's final report in the spring of 1994 did not "name names" of suspected war criminals, but it did summarize evidence implicating thousands of suspects.[19] Bassiouni himself, in numerous interviews, made clear his

---

Politics, and Lack of Finances Imperil Attempt to Bring Perpetrators of Atrocities to Justice, L.A. Times, Dec. 25, 1993, at A5, *available in* LEXIS, News Library, Curnws File.

[15] Gutman, *supra* note 13.

[16] Meisler, *supra* note 14.

[17] Gutman, *supra* note 13.

[18] Andrew Kelly, *Head of U.N. War Crimes Panel Resigns*, Reuters, Oct. 1, 1993, *available in* LEXIS, World Library, Allnws File; *Security Council Appoints Prosecutor for Balkans War Crimes*, UPI, Oct. 21, 1993, *available in* LEXIS, World Library, Allnws File.

[19] Letter from the Secretary-General to the President of the Security Council, May 24, 1994, U.N. Doc. S/1994/674 (1994), transmitting *Final Report of the Commission of Experts Established pursuant to Security Council Resolution 780 (1992), available in* U.N.

passionate devotion to juridical justice for war criminals.[20]

The Secretary-General also nominated Bassiouni, Egyptian born but a U.S. national, to be chief prosecutor for the Tribunal. But he was blocked by the same Western powers, plus Russia, who were wary about what they regarded as his excessive enthusiasm for rapid action on war crimes, especially those committed by Serbs. Bassiouni also lacked practical experience in criminal proceedings.[21] (The British candidate for prosecutor had been blocked by Bosnia and its supporters, in retaliation for British lack of real interest in war crimes committed against Bosnian Muslims. So Britain had few qualms about blocking Bassiouni, who was perceived as somewhat sympathetic to Bosnia. State bickering behind the scenes about the prosecutor did little to inspire confidence in the international community's commitment to war crimes as a priority matter.)[22] A prosecutor from Venezuela, Ramón Escovar-Salom, was eventually chosen, only to resign shortly thereafter to join the new government just formed in Caracas.[23] After five months of further delay,

---

Gopher\Current Information\Secretary-General's Reports. For a discussion of the Commission's work, see M. Cherif Bassiouni, *The Commission of Experts Established pursuant to Security Council Resolution 780: Investigating Violations of International Humanitarian Law in the Former Yugoslavia*, in this issue of *Criminal Law Forum*.

[20] *E.g.*, R.C. Longworth, *Peace vs. Justice: DePaul Professor Fears U.N. Sabotaged His Inquiry into Yugoslav War Crimes*, Chi. Tribune, Sept. 2, 1994, at 1, *available in* LEXIS, World Library, Allnws File; Philippe Naughton, *Yugoslav War Crimes Investigator Assails U.N.*, Reuters, Mar. 18, 1994, *available in* LEXIS, World Library, Allnws File.

[21] Paul Lewis, *Disputes Hamper U.N. Drive for a War Crimes Tribunal*, N.Y. Times, Sept. 9, 1993, at A10, *available in* LEXIS, World Library, Allnws File; Stanley Meisler, *U.N. Is Deadlocked on War-Crimes Prosecutor*, Montreal Gazette, Sept. 12, 1993, at B1, *available in* LEXIS, World Library, Allnws File; Ian Williams, *Bosnia Let Down at U.N.*, New Statesman & Soc'y, Sept. 17, 1993, at 10, *available in* LEXIS, News Library, Curnws File.

[22] Anthony Goodman, *No Agreement on Nominee for War Crimes Prosecutor*, Reuters, Sept. 29, 1993, *available in* LEXIS, World Library, Allnws File; Williams, *supra* note 21.

[23] S.C. Res. 877, U.N. SCOR, 48th Sess., 3296th mtg. at 1, U.N. Doc. S/RES/877 (1993), *available in* U.N. Gopher\Documents\Security Council Resolutions

a South African judge was finally appointed in his stead.²⁴ Richard Goldstone has been a vigorous prosecutor thus far, breathing considerable life into the office. But even his integrity is up against formidable forces.²⁵

While the Commission was clearly underfunded, the budget for the Tribunal turned out to be equally controversial. The Secretariat, working closely with major Western governments in a largely secretive process, finally introduced into the General Assembly's Fifth Committee a two-year budget proposal of over $32 million. The Assembly ultimately approved a one-year budget for 1994 of $11 million.²⁶ The

---

(appointing Escovar-Salom); *Venezuelan on War Crimes Panel: Tribunal Will Probe Atrocities in Former Yugoslavia,* Chi. Tribune, Oct. 22, 1993, at 10, *available in* LEXIS, World Library, Allnws File; *Bosnia–Venezuela: Boutros-Ghali Accepts Prosecutor's Resignation,* Inter Press Serv., Feb. 8, 1994, *available in* LEXIS, World Library, Allnws File; *Secretary-General Appoints Graham Blewitt as Acting Deputy Prosecutor, War Crimes Tribunal, for Humanitarian Law Violations in Former Yugoslavia,* U.N. Press Release, U.N. Doc. SG/SM/5221 (Feb. 8, 1994), *available in* U.N. Gopher\Current Information\Press Releases. As acting deputy prosecutor, Graham Blewitt got the process under way. *See* Andrew Kelly, *Charges over War Crimes in Ex-Yugoslavia Due Soon,* Reuters, June 12, 1994, *available in* LEXIS, World Library, Allnws File.

²⁴ S.C. Res. 936, U.N. SCOR, 49th Year, 3401st mtg. at 1, U.N. Doc. S/RES/936 (1994), *available in* U.N. Gopher\Documents\Security Council Resolutions; Paul Lewis, *South African Is to Prosecute Balkan War Crimes,* N.Y. Times, July 9, 1994, at A2, *available in* LEXIS, World Library, Allnws File. On the controversy over finding a replacement for Escovar-Salom, see Stephen Eagleburger, *Balkan War-Crimes Prosecution Bogs Down,* N.Y. Times, July 7, 1994, at A5, *available in* LEXIS, World Library, Allnws File; Anthony Lewis, *At Home Abroad: The Civilized World,* N.Y. Times, July 1, 1994, at A25, *available in* LEXIS, World Library, Allnws File [hereinafter *At Home Abroad*].

²⁵ Editorial, New Yorker, Sept. 19, 1994, at 7 [hereinafter *New Yorker* Editorial].

²⁶ G.A. Res. 48/251, U.N. GAOR, 48th Sess., Agenda Item 159, U.N. Doc. A/RES/48/251 (1994). For more detailed information on the financing of the Tribunal, see Julian J.E. Schutte, *Legal and Practical Implications, from the Perspective of the Host Country, Relating to the Establishment of the International Tribunal for the Former Yugoslavia,* in this issue of *Criminal Law Forum.* For the first quarter of 1995, the Fifth Committee of the General Assembly proposed a budget of $7 million. *Fifth Committee Approves $352.5 Million for UNDOF, UNIFIL, UNOSOM II, International Criminal Tribunal and Human Rights Programmes,* U.N. Press Release, U.N. Doc. GA/AB/2981 (Dec. 21, 1994), *available in* U.N. Gopher\Current Information\Press Releases.

original budget request contemplated almost 70 percent for judges' salaries (each was to make over $100,000 a year, even when no trials were scheduled), administration, and overhead. Another 25 percent was for salaries in the prosecutor's office. This left very little for evidence gathering, translation, counsel fees for indigent defendants, and so on, hardly a serious budget for the active collection of evidence and an ongoing process of fair adjudication.[27]

There were press reports that mediators David Owen (from the United Kingdom, on behalf of the European Union) and Cyrus Vance (from the United States, on behalf of the United Nations) saw the Tribunal as complicating their peacemaking mission, since it would be difficult to get leaders of fighting parties to make peace if after the peace they were to be made to stand trial for war crimes. Both Owen and Vance denied taking this position and went on record in support of war crimes trials. In July 1994 Owen was quoted as saying, "There can be no amnesty for war criminals. I believe the moral order of this world is marred if those who are guilty of war crimes are not brought to justice."[28] Whether this statement was anything more than cosmetic cover may eventually be known.

One or two states clearly did not like the idea of a court but were not prepared to block its creation. Most notable in this regard was China, which of course possessed the veto in the UN Security Council. Others, like Brazil, were closely aligned with Beijing. They wanted to elevate state sovereignty over international action to protect human rights. (While international lawyers debate technicalities, it remains clear that international humanitarian law is mostly a subdivision of international human rights law. The former can be generally and fairly referred to as mostly covering human rights in armed conflict.)[29] China and

---

[27] Thomas S. Warrick, *Crime against Humanity: International Effort to Hold Individuals Accountable for Genocide in Jeopardy*, Ottawa Citizen, Dec. 27, 1994, at A13, *available in* LEXIS, World Library, Allnws File (citing $562,300 of $32.6 million); Editorial, *Prosecute Bosnia's War Criminals*, N.Y. Times, Jan. 4, 1995, at A18 [hereinafter *N.Y. Times* Editorial] (citing less than 2 percent of $28 million).

[28] *At Home Abroad, supra* note 24.

[29] See the exchange between Hans-Peter Gasser, Legal Advisor to the International Committee of the Red Cross, and myself in Int'l Rev. Red Cross, Jan.–Feb. 1994, at 81.

Brazil, among other states, nevertheless felt it unwise to come out openly and determinedly against the Tribunal's creation.[30]

In sum to this point, the Yugoslav tribunal came into existence with considerable, if mostly covert, caution. Sadruddin Aga Khan, a former UN High Commissioner for Refugees who understands the UN system well and who is close to several governments, lambasted "international leaders" who pretended to support trials for war criminals while actually making those trials remote.[31] About six months earlier, the *New York Times* had editorialized that "foot-dragging on war crimes" should stop.[32]

More enthusiastic about the Commission and Tribunal was another group of states led by the United States and including the Netherlands, Canada, Norway, New Zealand, Pakistan, and a few others. The Netherlands, for example, provided a military unit to protect those doing field examinations of alleged atrocities, as well as forensic and other experts. Canada offered a team of military investigators to the Commission. The United States provided more supplemental funding for the Commission and Tribunal, beyond the assessed budget, than any other state (some $13 million to date).[33] The United States also

---

[30] See the discussions in the Security Council on the creation of ad hoc tribunals for the former Yugoslavia, U.N. SCOR, 48th Year, 3217th mtg. at 33, 36, U.N. Doc. S/PV.3217 (1993), and Rwanda, U.N. SCOR, 49th Year, 3453d mtg. at 9–12, U.N. Doc. S/PV.3453 (1994).

[31] Aga Khan, *supra* note 2.

[32] Editorial, *Foot-dragging on War Crimes*, N.Y. Times, Aug. 5, 1993, at A20, *available in* LEXIS, World Library, Allnws File.

[33] Thomas W. Lippman, *U.S. Accuses the Serbs of More Atrocities*, Int'l Herald Tribune, Dec. 30, 1994, *available in* LEXIS, World Library, Allnws File (reporting contribution of $13 million in cash and services to the Tribunal); *N.Y. Times* Editorial, *supra* note 27 (reporting $13 million for investigative work, including two dozen officials). Lack of UN funding for, and contributions of various governments to, the Commission are discussed in detail in Bassiouni, *supra* note 19; on the contribution of the Netherlands as host country to the Tribunal, see Schutte, *supra* note 26; official contributions to the Tribunal are noted in *Annual Report of the International Tribunal for the Prosecution of Persons Responsible for Serious Violations of International Humanitarian Law Committed in the Territory of the Former Yugoslavia since 1991*, ¶¶ 183–188, U.N. SCOR, 49th Year, Agenda Item 152, U.N. Doc. S/1994/1007 (1994). Of course, the

submitted almost five hundred documents indicating probable crimes, although there was some controversy behind the scenes about the withholding of supposedly classified information; it seconded almost two dozen officials to help with preparation of prosecutions; and it lobbied other states to vote for and otherwise support this effort in international criminal justice.[34] The U.S. National Security Council appointed a group charged with collecting information for possible indictments.[35]

Some of these states may not have acted totally free from the political calculation that one should give the impression of doing something decisive about violations, while avoiding direct and costly intervention in the fighting. Nevertheless, their concrete support for the Commission and Tribunal indicated a relatively serious effort to make the process successful. The United States, perhaps reflecting a legal strain in its diplomatic history, was a clear leader in the matter of the Tribunal. A UN official commented in an off-the-record interview in early fall 1994 that the United States stood virtually alone in viewing the war crimes proceedings as a serious venture. And it was the United States and New Zealand that took the lead in seeking to expand the existing tribunal to cover war crimes in Rwanda after the massacres in

---

United States, by being in arrears on its assessed UN payments, has also hampered the Tribunal, and it has not yet contributed to a voluntary UN trust fund for this body.

For further information, see *General Assembly Authorizes $90 Million for UNPROFOR, MINURSO, International War Crimes Tribunal*, U.N. Press Release, U.N. Doc. GA/8661 (Apr. 14, 1994), *available in* U.N. Gopher\Current Information\Press Releases (noting voluntary contributions from the United States, Pakistan, and the Netherlands); *Pakistan Gives $1 Million to Bosnian War Crimes Tribunal*, UPI, Feb. 1, 1994, *available in* LEXIS, World Library, Allnws File; Maryann Stenberg, *United Nations: Australians Help in Bosnia War Crime Prosecution*, The Age (Melbourne), June 21, 1994, *available in* LEXIS, World Library, Allnws File (discussing Australian personnel working for the International Tribunal); Carol J. Williams, *No Amnesty for Perpetrators of Balkans Atrocities, U.S. Says*, N.Y. Times, Jan. 7, 1994, at A6, *available in* LEXIS, World Library, Allnws File (noting U.S. promises of support). *But see* Eagleburger, *supra* note 24 (speaking about promises of staff from Britain and Canada, then Acting Deputy Prosecutor Graham Blewitt said, "They're not materializing, and I have some doubts that they will materialize.").

[34] Bruce Zagaris, *Clinton Administration Supports War Crimes Tribunal*, Am. Soc'y Int'l L. Newsl., Mar.–May 1994, at 17.

[35] *Id.*

the spring of 1994.[36]

These supportive states appealed to cogent reasons for criminal prosecution, reasons at least partially noted by several commentators.[37] First, since international humanitarian law existed on the books, it would undermine that law not to provide for criminal proceedings. Avoiding prosecution now would make legal protection more difficult in the future. Second, there was a need to build on the precedent of the Nuremberg and Tokyo war crimes trials. Not to do so would be a step backward. It was important not to engage simply in victors' justice; the International Tribunal for the Former Yugoslavia should function even while the conflict was in progress, and not just against the losing party.

---

[36] By S.C. Res. 935, U.N. SCOR, 49th Year, 3400th mtg. at 1, ¶ 2, U.N. Doc. S/RES/935 (1994), *reprinted in* appendix D of this issue of *Criminal Law Forum* and *available in* U.N. Gopher\Documents\Security Council Resolutions, the Security Council requested the Secretary-General to establish an impartial Commission of Experts to investigate reports of "grave violations of international humanitarian law committed in the territory of Rwanda," including evidence of possible acts of genocide. This body submitted both a preliminary and a final report. Letter from the Secretary-General to the President of the Security Council, Oct. 1, 1994, U.N. Doc. S/1994/1125 (1994), transmitting *Preliminary Report of the Independent Commission of Experts Established in Accordance with Security Council Resolution 935 (1994), available in* U.N. Gopher\Current Information\Secretary-General's Reports; Letter from the Secretary-General to the President of the Security Council, Dec. 9, 1994, U.N. Doc. S/1994/1405 (1994), transmitting *Final Report of the Commission of Experts Established pursuant to Security Council Resolution 935 (1994), available in* U.N. Gopher\Current Information\Secretary-General's Reports. The Security Council voted in November 1994 to establish the International Tribunal for Rwanda, with institutional ties to the International Tribunal for the Former Yugoslavia. The relevant resolution adopts and annexes the Tribunal's Statute. S.C. Res. 955, U.N. SCOR, 49th Year, 3453d mtg. at 1, U.N. Doc. S/RES/955 (1994), *reprinted in* appendix D of this issue of *Criminal Law Forum* and *available in* U.N. Gopher\Documents\Security Council Resolutions.

For background, see James Bone, *U.S. Urges Separate Genocide Court for Rwanda*, The Times (London), Oct. 5, 1994, *available in* LEXIS, World Library, Allnws File; Raymond Bonner, *U.N. Commission Recommends Rwanda "Genocide" Tribunal*, N.Y. Times, Sept. 29, 1994, at A13, *available in* LEXIS, World Library, Allnws File; Andrew Kelly, *Goldstone Willing to Prosecute Rwanda War Crimes*, Reuters, Oct. 11, 1994, *available in* LEXIS, World Library, Allnws File.

[37] Theodor Meron, *The Case for War Crimes Trials in Yugoslavia*, Foreign Aff., Summer 1993, at 122; Aryeh Neier, *War Crimes Tribunal Is an Imperative*, Hum. Rts. Brief, Spring 1994, at 6.

Third, there was a need to promote healing among the combatants. Not to do so would leave group hostilities to fester and erupt again. Only by seeking individual justice through a criminal court could one get neighbors in the Balkans to put the past, with its group antagonisms, behind them.

These are indeed morally cogent reasons, especially to supporters of a legal approach to problem-solving.

COMPELLING PROBLEMS

What is morally cogent may not prove politically compelling. If in domestic court one presents a creative argument for the protection of human rights, but the timing is premature in terms of what the court will accept as controlling legal interpretation, one has actually set back the cause of human rights at least temporarily. A new and potentially promising theory of controlling law is discredited. Timing is a critical calculation.[38]

Likewise in international law, if one creates a criminal court that basically fails in its efforts, one has set back the cause of human rights at least for a time. As Professor Diane F. Orentlicher was quoted as saying, if the Tribunal fails "its establishment will have done far more harm to fundamental principles of international law than if criminal accountability had never been attempted."[39] According to international law expert Edith Brown Weiss: "The situation is dangerous. If governments let the process falter or stop . . . we will have undermined the process of accountability introduced many decades ago by the Nuremberg and Tokyo Tribunals."[40] The obstacles to the success of an

---

[38] Howard Tolley, Jr., *Interest Group Litigation to Enforce Human Rights*, Pol. Sci. Q., Winter 1990, at 617.

[39] Lois Tuttle & Ayesha Qayyum, *International War Crimes Tribunal for the Former Yugoslavia*, Hum. Rts. Brief, Spring 1994, at 5; *see also* Diane F. Orentlicher, Am. Soc'y Int'l L. Newsl., Mar.–May 1993, at 1.

[40] Edith Brown Weiss, *Message from the President*, Am. Soc'y Int'l L. Newsl., June–Aug. 1994, at 1, 4.

international criminal court for the former Yugoslavia are profound.[41]

Almost every combatant in this theater of armed conflict is a war criminal. What armed partisan has not shot at civilians or attacked civilian areas or abused prisoners? It is generally agreed that serious violations of humanitarian law have widely occurred among Serbs, Croats, and Bosnians, even if Serbian partisans have committed a disproportionate share.

If the Tutsi government in Rwanda spoke of holding war crimes trials for thirty-two thousand persons involved in murders totaling somewhere between half a million and one million after the internal war and genocide there, how many persons should be tried in the Balkans? Contemplation of such a process calls to mind a cartoon about South Africa under apartheid. Two white officials stand on a balcony, overlooking a sea of black demonstrators that stretches to the horizon. One official turns to the other and says, "Arrest them." It is indeed comical. Some problems are simply too large for a judicial solution. Bassiouni has been quoted as saying, "We have enough material to keep a hundred lawyers busy for years."[42] This attitude reflects a lawyer's enthusiasm for legal process, rather than a more practical understanding of what the political will finds supportable and sustainable.

The leaders of the various fighting parties—those who ordered or allowed the systematic rapes, the torture and summary execution of prisoners, the policy of intentionally targeting civilians and nonfortified cities and towns and objects essential to the survival of the civilian population—are unlikely ever to be prosecuted and convicted. Their cooperation is needed to end the fighting. Ending the fighting would eliminate the major cause of affronts to human dignity in the region, and these leaders are unlikely to cooperate fully with peacemakers without assurances of immunity or amnesty.

The dilemma was concisely summarized by Morris Abram, a U.S. lawyer long active in human rights. Abram has represented the U.S. government at different times in different ways:

---

[41] Herman Schwartz, *War Crimes Trials—Not a Good Idea*, Hum. Rts. Brief, Spring 1994, at 7.

[42] Meisler, *supra* note 14.

It is a very tough call whether to point the finger or try to negotiate with people. As a lawyer, of course, I would like to prosecute everybody who is guilty of these heinous things. As a diplomat or as a politician or as a statesman, I also would like to stop the slaughter, bring it to a halt. You have two things that are in real conflict here . . . I don't know the proper mix.[43]

Would leaders of states turn over their subordinates, those who actually ran the prison camps and were locally in charge of ethnic cleansing and other atrocities? Could trials be held of intermediate or field commanders? That is doubtful. Someone like Slobodan Milosevic in Belgrade might turn in his political opponents who openly boast of war crimes,[44] but this is hardly systematic or equitable cooperation.

It is said that sanctions could be applied to states failing to hand over suspected war criminals. But it is not easy to get UN-mandated sanctions applied to states. It was only with great difficulty that UN sanctions were applied to pariah Libya for failure to extradite two suspected terrorists in the bombing of a Pan American jet over Lockerbie, Scotland, and even then an oil embargo was not instituted.[45] If fighting in the Balkans were to cease, outside interest in sanctions on states for not extraditing war criminals—sanctions that hurt the sanctioning states as well—would decline markedly.

The UN protection force (UNPROFOR) in the Balkans has no mandate to arrest persons for war crimes. The International Committee of the Red Cross refuses to divulge relevant information, citing its need to have the cooperation of fighting parties in order to try to protect and assist persons in a practical way. Without the cooperation of national leaders in the area, it will be extremely difficult to compile evidence of violations that will stand up in court, especially concerning the identity of those who gave illegal commands.

---

[43] Gutman, *supra* note 13.

[44] *New Yorker* Editorial, *supra* note 25.

[45] S.C. Res. 748, U.N. SCOR, 47th Year, 1992 S.C. Res. & Dec. at 52, U.N. Doc. S/INF/48 (1992), *reprinted in* 31 I.L.M. 750.

A judicial process in which a few lower ranking persons who fled the area as refugees are put on trial, while their commanders are not, recalls the dissatisfaction with the trial of Lt. William Calley in the wake of the My Lai massacre in Vietnam. When U.S. soldiers killed not less than three hundred unresisting Vietnamese civilians, including infants and senior citizens, no captains, colonels, majors, or generals were ever convicted. Under the *Yamashita* precedent from the Far Eastern war crimes trials after World War II, commanders are responsible for war crimes occurring in their zone of responsibility if they knew or should have known of the violations.[46] But the U.S. military chain of command sought to conceal events at My Lai until journalists and others outside the chain of command broke the story. From that atrocity one lieutenant was convicted of war crimes, but paroled after minimal time in incarceration.[47] Such a history does no great credit to humanitarian law. Similarly, trials of small fish from the Balkans, while arguably better than no trials at all, leave a similar distaste for this type of criminal justice. It is profoundly unjust.

Given these difficulties and others (such as which laws apply to which persons, using what legal conception), it would have been preferable in the Balkans to deal with war crimes by an international truth commission along the lines of the model in El Salvador, combined with national criminal proceedings. Such an approach would not have overextended further the already overextended United Nations, which exists perpetually on the edge of financial ruin and which does not need a controversial judicial effort to complicate further its record in the Balkans. Truth commissions have made a positive contribution to national reconciliation in El Salvador and elsewhere. The latter were not international, and in some

---

[46] United States v. Yamashita (1945), 4 UN War Crimes Comm'n, *Law Reports of Trials of War Criminals* 1 (1947), aff'd, 327 U.S. 1 (1946); Richard L. Lael, *The Yamashita Precedent: War Crimes and Command Responsibility* (1982).

[47] United States v. Calley, 46 C.M.R. 1131 (U.S. C.M.R.), aff'd, 48 C.M.R. 19 (U.S. C.M.A. 1973); Richard Hammer, *The Court-martial of Lt. Calley* (1971); Jeffrey F. Addicott & William A. Hudson, Jr., *The Twenty-fifth Anniversary of My Lai: A Time to Inculcate the Lessons,* 139 Mil. L. Rev. 153, 161 n.35 (1993) (discussing Calley's incarceration and parole).

cases not even authorized by the government.⁴⁸ Nevertheless, they did play a constructive role. Even private truth commissions have established facts, allowed various parties to look to the future, led to reform legislation, and perhaps somewhat deterred future violations of human rights. As of the time of writing, South Africa was planning to institute a truth commission, combined with an amnesty for violators of human rights who openly admitted their crimes.⁴⁹ Pretoria had obviously concluded that criminal proceedings were not the only or even the best path to reconciliation and deterrence.

National prosecutions, while subject to some political calculations, could still have the effect of convicting notorious criminals and keeping other criminals bottled up in their state. Since there is universal jurisdiction over grave breaches of the Geneva Conventions of 1949, violations of the laws or customs of war, genocide, crimes against humanity,⁵⁰ and (for some states like the United States) torture,⁵¹ states have adequate jurisdictional grounds for moving against criminals who come into their jurisdiction.

---

⁴⁸ Lawrence Weschler, *A Miracle, a Universe: Settling Accounts with Torturers* (1990); Priscilla B. Hayner, *Fifteen Truth Commissions, 1974–1994: A Comparative Study*, Hum. Rts. Q., Nov. 1994, at 597.

⁴⁹ Aryeh Neier, Letter to the Editor, *South Africa's Lesson for Haiti*, N.Y. Times, Oct. 8, 1994, § 1, at 17, *available in* LEXIS, News Library, Curnws File.

⁵⁰ The question of universal jurisdiction over these crimes is discussed at length in C.P.M. Cleiren & M.E.M. Tijssen, *Rape and Other Forms of Sexual Assault in the Armed Conflict in the Former Yugoslavia: Legal, Procedural, and Evidentiary Issues*, in this issue of *Criminal Law Forum*.

⁵¹ Act of Apr. 30, 1994, Pub. L. No. 103-236, § 506, 108 Stat. 463, 506 (1994) (adding 18 U.S.C. §§ 2340–2340B). There is also the possibility of a civil action under U.S. law. Filartiga v. Pena-Irala, 630 F.2d 876 (2d Cir. 1980) (construing Alien Tort Claim Act, 28 U.S.C. § 1350, to hold that official torture constitutes an actionable claim as a violation of the law of nations). However, 28 U.S.C. § 1350 arguably has a requirement of government involvement in the torts alleged, and this element may be construed very narrowly. *E.g.*, Sanchez-Espinoza v. Reagan, 770 F.2d 202 (D.C. Cir. 1985) (Alien Tort Claim Act inapplicable to acts allegedly committed by Nicaraguan *contras);* Doe v. Karadzic, 866 F. Supp. 734 (S.D.N.Y. 1994) (on appeal) (neither Alien Tort Claim Act nor Torture Victim Protection Act applicable to acts allegedly carried out by Bosnian Serb military forces).

THE FUTURE

Since the Tribunal has been created, and evidence compiled on war crimes, the best that can be hoped for is that some convictions will be obtained in a process that is widely regarded as procedurally correct. The equivalents of Goering and Eichmann, much less Hitler,[52] will not be tried, but neither will they be free to visit Disneyland on vacation.[53]

This process will lay another stone in the foundation for better international criminal proceedings in the future. It is not true that failure to prosecute spells the end of humanitarian law. Failure to prosecute leading Iraqi war criminals after Desert Storm in 1991[54] has not erased attention to humanitarian law violations in the territory of the former Yugoslavia, although failure to put Saddam Hussein in the dock (if there had been a practical way to do that) may have encouraged the Milosevics (of the new Yugoslavia) and Karadzics (of the Bosnian Serbs) of the world to adopt illegal means and methods in armed conflict. Still, perhaps in an armed conflict around 2050, there might be an international war crimes tribunal that functioned better than this one.

The sine qua non for such a court is solid, serious international support for international humanitarian law. This does not exist in sufficient degree in the 1990s to allow the International Tribunal for the Former Yugoslavia to be a great success. This lack of solidarity is precisely why a permanent, standing criminal court for all armed conflicts, or all international crimes, has not been created. While such

---

[52] The first person indicted by the International Tribunal for the Former Yugoslavia (Dragan Nikolic) is alleged to have been the commander of a concentration camp operated by the Bosnian Serbs. Roger Cohen, *Tribunal Charges Serbian Camp Commander with War Crimes*, N.Y. Times, Nov. 8, 1994, at A5, *available in* LEXIS, World Library, Allnws File.

[53] In *Filartiga*, 630 F.2d at 878–79, the accused was found in the United States when he overstayed a visitor's visa.

[54] Note the quick change of mood in mid-April 1991. *U.N. Experts to Study EC Call for Saddam Hussein Trial*, Reuters, Apr. 16, 1991, *available in* LEXIS, World Library, Allnws File; *U.S. and EC Moving Apart on Saddam Hussein Crimes Trial*, Reuters, Apr. 18, 1991, *available in* LEXIS, World Library, Allnws File.

a court was discussed in the International Law Commission[55] and in the Sixth Committee of the UN General Assembly in the fall of 1994, this proposal ran into stiff opposition from the United States and has basically been put on hold.[56]

Efforts to organize international war crimes trials for events in Rwanda during 1994 were highly problematic. Early UN factfinding efforts were laughable because of lack of personnel and resources. Most outside states were even less interested in, and supportive of, war crimes trials in Africa than in Europe. Within Rwanda, despite brave talk of numerous trials by the incoming (Tutsi-controlled) government, there was no functioning court system. The fact that a UN investigative commission concluded that genocide had been orchestrated by certain Hutus, or that the Security Council voted to create a new war crimes tribunal, with prosecutor and appeals chamber shared with the Yugoslav court, does not guarantee practical progress toward fair and effective proceedings.[57]

In evaluating the International Tribunal for the Former Yugoslavia, one might recall that when the Commission and Tribunal were created, various international organizations had tried to mitigate the

---

[55] Draft Statute for an International Criminal Court, in *Report of the International Law Commission on Its Forty-sixth Session*, U.N. GAOR, 49th Sess., Supp. No. 10, at 43, U.N. Doc. A/49/10 (1994). For a discussion of the Commission's work in this area, see Peter Burns, *An International Criminal Tribunal: The Difficult Union of Principle and Politics*, in this issue of *Criminal Law Forum*.

[56] *Report of the Sixth Committee*, U.N. GAOR, 49th Sess., Agenda Item 137, U.N. Doc. A/49/738, at 17 (1994); G.A. Res. 49/53, U.N. GAOR, 49th Sess., 84th plen. mtg., U.N. Doc. A/49/53 (1994); Thalif Deen, *United Nations: U.N. Split over International Criminal Court*, Inter Press Serv., Dec. 21, 1994, *available in* LEXIS, World Library, Allnws File.

[57] Raymond Bonner, *In Sea of Aid, Rwandans Lack Basics*, N.Y. Times, Nov. 2, 1994, at A10, *available in* LEXIS, World Library, Allnws File; Andrew Jay Cohen, *On the Trail of Genocide*, N.Y. Times, Sept. 7, 1994, at A23, *available in* LEXIS, World Library, Allnws File; Martin Garbus, *Jurists without Borders*, N.Y. Times, Nov. 17, 1994, at A25, *available in* LEXIS, World Library, Allnws File; *Rwanda's Mass of Murderers*, The Economist, Oct. 29, 1994, at 43. *See generally supra* note 36 and accompanying text. On possible French involvement in the Rwandan genocide, see Howard W. French, *Tense Times for France–Africa Tie*, N.Y. Times, Nov. 9, 1994, at A12, *available in* LEXIS, World Library, Allnws File.

suffering in the Balkans without great success. Not only the United Nations but also the Conference on Security and Cooperation in Europe (CSCE) and the European Union had tried and largely failed.[58] NATO had been ineffectual in dealing with violence. The International Committee of the Red Cross and other private organizations were also active but failed to achieve decisive results. The Tribunal was therefore born out of weakness—the weakness that comes from lack of political solidarity and will.

It is also well to recall that, as Alexander Hamilton argued in *The Federalist* No. 78, courts are the weakest branch of government—depending upon voluntary cooperation from the executive branch and the public for successful implementation of their judgments. If this is true for national courts, it is certainly true for international tribunals, whose judgments depend for enforcement on the voluntary cooperation of states vastly more powerful than such bodies. Thus, when the International Court of Justice ruled against the United States in its dispute with Nicaragua,[59] the United States effectively ignored the judgment. Similarly, when the Court issued an interim order about genocide in proceedings brought by Bosnia against Yugoslavia,[60] there was no discernible effect on the parties. One should not always look for a judicial remedy to international problems, especially on issues so highly contentious that an armed conflict is already under way.

It seems likely that for the foreseeable future international humanitarian law will continue to be applied (or not) as soft law by soldiers and diplomats, with a helping hand from other actors like the International Committee of the Red Cross.[61] The unfortunate reality is

---

[58] James C. O'Brien, Current Developments, *The International Tribunal for Violations of International Humanitarian Law in the Former Yugoslavia*, 87 Am. J. Int'l L. 639 (1993).

[59] Military and Paramilitary Activities (Nicar. v. U.S.), 1986 I.C.J. 4 (June 27).

[60] Application of the Convention on the Prevention and Punishment of the Crime of Genocide (Bosnia & Herz. v. Yugo.), 1993 I.C.J. 3 (Apr. 8) (request for provisional measures), *reprinted in* 32 I.L.M. 888; later proceedings, 1993 I.C.J. 325 (Sept. 13) (order on further request for provisional measures), *reprinted in* 32 I.L.M. 1599.

[61] One form of soft law is genuine law that is not, or is only rarely, adjudicated in court. Another form of soft law is an international instrument that is not yet accorded

that the conditions of international relations, or for that matter domestic politics, are not yet conducive to much success for a judicial approach treating humanitarian and related law as hard law to be adjudicated by an international court.

Even national adjudication is problematic. Just as the United States did not move vigorously against its own military personnel for extensive civilian damage in Iraq and Panama,[62] much less My Lai, so the Israeli government has not moved vigorously against its military personnel for violations of law in Israeli-occupied territory.[63] Punishments have frequently been disproportionately light. This forced reliance on soft, rather than hard, law seems ironic, given the considerable attention that lawyers pay to the fine print of humanitarian law.

In the last analysis, it is better to have soft law than no law at all. A premature attempt to convert it into hard law, however, is highly likely to be deeply disappointing, if not a "tragic farce,"[64] at least in the short run.

---

the name of law, but which is generally treated as an authoritative guideline for behavior. It is never adjudicated.

[62] *See, e.g., Hidden Casualties: Environmental, Health, and Political Consequences of the Persian Gulf War* pt. 6 (Saul Bloom et al. eds., 1994); Human Rights Watch, *Needless Deaths in the Gulf War* (1991).

[63] Norman G. Finkelstein, *Israel and Iraq: A Double Standard in the Application of International Law*, Monthly Rev., July 1991, at 25; *The West Bank: Black-flag Order*, The Economist, June 23, 1990, at 37; *see also* John Bierman, *A Call to Arms*, Maclean's, July 9, 1990, at 30.

[64] Schwartz, *supra* note 41, at 8.

7
Legal and Practical Implications, from the Perspective of the Host Country, Relating to the Establishment of the International Tribunal for the Former Yugoslavia*

Julian J.E. Schutte**

INTRODUCTION

Security Council Resolution 808, adopted February 22, 1993, provided for the establishment of an international tribunal for the prosecution of persons responsible for serious violations of international humanitarian law committed in the territory of the former Yugoslavia since 1991.[1] In this resolution, the Security Council requested the Secretary-General to submit within sixty days a report on all aspects of

---

*   © 1995 Julian J.E. Schutte.
    Editor's note: research for this article was updated through December 31, 1994.

** Director, Legal Service, Council of the European Union, Brussels, Belgium; Professor Extraordinary in the Law of European Cooperation in Criminal Matters, University of Amsterdam, Amsterdam, Netherlands; LL.M., University of Leiden 1969. At the time of writing, the author was a Senior Legal Advisor in the Netherlands Ministry of Justice and Chairman of the European Committee on Crime Problems of the Council of Europe.

1   S.C. Res. 808, U.N. SCOR, 48th Year, 3175th mtg. at 1, U.N. Doc. S/RES/808 (1993), *reprinted in* appendix A of this issue of *Criminal Law Forum* and *available in* U.N. Gopher\Documents\Security Council Resolutions.

the matter, including specific proposals and options for effective and expeditious implementation, taking into account suggestions put forward by member states. It was immediately apparent that one important issue to be addressed by the Secretary-General was finding a seat for the International Tribunal.

Some of the member states that forwarded comments to the Secretary-General suggested the Hague as a possible site, given that the International Court of Justice has its seat there.[2] Although the government of the Netherlands, in its submission to the Secretary-General, had not expressed any preference, it was of course aware that other states had proposed the Hague. Nonetheless, the government felt it was inappropriate to suggest locating the Tribunal in the Netherlands or to seek the support of any other government on this question.

In Resolution 827, adopted May 25, 1993,[3] the Security Council approved the *Report of the Secretary-General pursuant to Paragraph 2 of Security Council Resolution 808 (1993).*[4] This report sets out a draft Statute for the Tribunal, commentary and background, and a preliminary budget. The proposal in article 31 of the Statute to locate the Tribunal at the Hague caught the government of the Netherlands unprepared, but it responded immediately by stating that it felt honored and that it was looking forward to working out appropriate arrangements with the United Nations in compliance with Resolution 827. The Security Council made the final "determination of the seat of the International Tribunal . . . subject to the conclusion of appropriate arrangements between the United Nations and the Netherlands acceptable to the

---

[2] Statute of the International Court of Justice art. 22.

[3] S.C. Res. 827, U.N. SCOR, 48th Year, 3217th mtg. at 1, U.N. Doc. S/RES/827 (1993), *reprinted in* appendix A of this issue of *Criminal Law Forum* and *in* 32 I.L.M. 1203.

[4] *Report of the Secretary-General pursuant to Paragraph 2 of Security Council Resolution 808 (1993),* U.N. Doc. S/25704 & Add.1 (1993), *reprinted in* appendix B of this issue of *Criminal Law Forum* and *in* 32 I.L.M. 1163 [hereinafter *Secretary-General's Report*]. The Statute of the International Tribunal is set out as an annex to *Secretary-General's Report, supra,* and is *reprinted in* appendix B of this issue of *Criminal Law Forum* and *in* 32 I.L.M. 1192 [hereinafter Statute].

Council."[5]

On May 26, 1993, the government of the Netherlands set up a number of task forces to assess the possible implications of establishing the Tribunal at the Hague and to lay the groundwork for accomplishing all the steps that would have to be taken to realize this goal. From the outset, it was recognized that decisions would have to be made concerning such matters as identifying suitable premises where the Tribunal might be housed, planning and carrying out renovations necessary to accommodate all the requirements of a courthouse where criminal trials would be conducted, making pretrial detention facilities available to the Tribunal, putting into place security measures in respect of both the premises to be used by the Tribunal and the personnel working for or in conjunction with the Tribunal, estimating and meeting the financial responsibilities of the host country, preparing legislative measures, and negotiating a headquarters agreement with the United Nations.

A year later, most of these decisions had been taken and had been or were being implemented. This is a small miracle, given that there was great uncertainty until mid-April 1994 whether the United Nations would be willing and able to accept the financial implications of the Security Council's decision to set up the Tribunal. The provision in article 32 of the Tribunal's Statute, as approved by the Security Council—that the "expenses of the International Tribunal shall be borne by the regular budget of the United Nations in accordance with Article 17 of the Charter of the United Nations"—has created serious difficulties in that the General Assembly felt that this infringed its budgetary prerogatives. The arrangement contemplated by article 32 prompted severe criticism from the UN Advisory Committee on Administrative and Budgetary Questions (ACABQ) of the Secretariat's proposals for staffing and financing the Tribunal.[6] Initial requests for an institution of about

---

[5] S.C. Res. 827, *supra* note 3, ¶ 6.

[6] Advisory Comm. on Administrative & Budgetary Questions, *Report on the Establishment of the International Tribunal*, U.N. GAOR, 47th Sess., Agenda Item 155, U.N. Doc. A/47/980 (1993); *Report of the Advisory Comm. on Administrative and Budgetary Questions*, U.N. GAOR, 48th Sess., Agenda Item 159, U.N. Doc. A/48/765 (1993); *Report of the Advisory Comm. on Administrative and Budgetary Questions*, U.N.

four hundred persons, to be deployed in premises offering three courtrooms, were cut down to about a hundred persons, excluding the judges, and a single courtroom. In monetary terms, this means that in December 1993 the General Assembly refused to approve the Secretary-General's proposal for a $33.2 million budget for the biennium 1994–1995, on the advice of the ACABQ, and reduced to $5.6 million the allocation for the first half of 1994.[7] In April 1994, the General Assembly approved a total of only $11 million for the whole of 1994, but at the same time it authorized the Secretary-General to enter into long-term leases for the premises of the Tribunal, thus providing some guarantee that adequate financial resources would be allocated for the following years.[8]

Not until the budget question was resolved in the spring of 1994 could the Netherlands implement decisions that involved large expenditures, such as the reconstruction of the premises housing the Tribunal and the construction of a prison unit to be used exclusively by the Tribunal. These facilities were expected to be ready for use in the fall of 1994.

GAOR, 48th Sess., Agenda Item 159, U.N. Doc. A/48/915 (1994). In G.A. Res. 47/235, U.N. GAOR, 47th Sess., Supp. No. 49 (vol. II), at 36, ¶ 3, U.N. Doc. A/47/49 (1993), the General Assembly adopted without vote a resolution expressing concern that advice given by the Secretariat to the Security Council regarding the financing of the Tribunal did not respect the role of the General Assembly as set out in U.N. Charter art. 17.

[7]   *Report of the Secretary-General as Requested by the General Assembly in Resolution 47/235*, U.N. GAOR 5th Comm., 48th Sess., Agenda Item 159, U.N. Doc. A/C.5/48/44 (1993); G.A. Dec. 48/461, U.N. GAOR, 48th Sess., Supp. No. 49, at 368, U.N. Doc. A/48/49 (1993). In this article, all monetary amounts are in U.S. dollars.

[8]   G.A. Res. 48/251, U.N. GAOR, 48th Sess., Agenda Item 159, U.N. Doc. A/RES/48/251 (1994). The Secretary-General had submitted a revised budget in *Report of the Secretary-General as Requested by the General Assembly in Resolution 47/235: Revised Estimates*, U.N. GAOR 5th Comm., 48th Sess., Agenda Item 159, U.N. Doc. A/C.5/48/44/Add.1 (1994). In late December 1994, the Fifth Committee proposed a budget of $7 million to carry the Tribunal through the first quarter of 1995. *Fifth Committee Approves $352.5 Million for UNDOF, UNIFIL, UNOSOM II, International Criminal Tribunal and Human Rights Programmes*, U.N. Press Release, U.N. Doc. GA/AB/2981 (Dec. 21, 1994), *available in* U.N. Gopher\Current Information\Press Releases.

OVERVIEW OF LEGAL INSTRUMENTS RELATING TO THE ESTABLISHMENT OF THE TRIBUNAL

Statute of the Tribunal

When preparations for hosting the International Tribunal at the Hague were begun, the only applicable instrument was the Statute of the Tribunal as adopted by the Security Council in Resolution 827.[9] The Statute gives some indication as to the size and number of chambers; the distribution of functions among the judges, the prosecutor, and the registrar; the need for pretrial detention facilities; the reliance on states for legal assistance and enforcement of prison sentences; and the UN's assumption of financial responsibility for the Tribunal.

With regard to allocating expenses, the United Nations and the government of the Netherlands agreed as follows. The United Nations would pay the salaries of people working for the Tribunal, including defense counsel; the per diem and travel costs of witnesses; and the cost of keeping accused persons detained. All expenses involved in providing security and protection in the Netherlands for persons working for the Tribunal, as well as in securing the premises of the Tribunal, would be incumbent on the host country.

It was also quickly agreed that the matter of pretrial detention would be wholly the responsibility of the Tribunal and that the Tribunal would have to have facilities of its own, completely separate from the prison system of the Netherlands and governed exclusively by UN rules. Initially, however, the financial implications of this understanding were not fully appreciated by the United Nations. It was realized only after some time that the Dutch government had no spare prison facilities and, although prepared to arrange for construction, was not inclined to bear the total cost of such an undertaking. Since it is UN policy not to invest in real property for an uncertain but probably rather short period, the parties agreed on the conclusion of a lease of a new detention unit, some details of which will be described later in this article.

---

[9] Statute, *supra* note 4; S.C. Res. 827, *supra* note 3, ¶ 2 (whereby the Security Council "adopt[ed] the Statute of the International Tribunal annexed to the [Secretary-General's] report").

The most serious difficulty arose in connection with finding premises for the Tribunal. Much to the regret of the UN Secretariat, there was no brand-new, fully equipped, but otherwise empty courthouse available in the Hague that the government was willing to offer at a token rent of a dollar per year. Since the decision to locate the Tribunal in the Hague had not been actively solicited by the Dutch government, but was rather a determination in which the government was willing to acquiesce, it was not prepared to provide a building for free or for a symbolic sum to the United Nations, as is the case with certain UN offices in some other countries, and take charge of all the attendant costs, such as construction of a courtroom with gallery, detention cells to hold defendants during the days of trial, and internal security facilities. In support of its position, the government relied on the express language of article 32 of the Statute of the Tribunal: "The expenses of the International Tribunal shall be borne by the regular budget of the United Nations in accordance with Article 17 of the Charter of the United Nations." The UN Secretariat, for its part, took the position that article 32 applied only to the extent that there would be any expenses to the United Nations and that it was hoped that these could be kept minimal as a result of generous offers by the host country.

It soon turned out that the most suitable location available for a short term was not government property but a building owned by an insurance company (the Aegon Building). This company was willing to host the judges and the limited staff of the Tribunal rent-free during the first half of 1994, with the understanding that before the end of that period a long-term lease would be concluded with the United Nations. The same company indicated that it was willing to offer a loan to the United Nations, to be amortized in the lease, through which the United Nations would be able to finance the necessary renovations of the building. On this basis, a lease was concluded between the United Nations and the insurance company in July 1994. These arrangements are discussed later in the article.

Headquarters Agreement

Among the matters to be negotiated between the United Nations and the Netherlands was a headquarters agreement. An agreement of this nature was worked out, and in principle assented to, by the UN Secretariat and the government of the Netherlands in the fall of 1993. However, the parties deferred signing until the necessary steps concerning the financing of the Tribunal had been taken by the General Assembly. Negotiations were finally completed in June 1994, the parties signed in July, and the Headquarters Agreement entered into force.[10] This instrument follows to a large extent the traditional pattern of headquarters agreements, setting out the juridical personality of the Tribunal, as well as the privileges and immunities of the Tribunal and its personnel, in accordance with the Convention on the Privileges and Immunities of the United Nations[11] and the Vienna Convention on Diplomatic Relations.[12]

Among other things, the Headquarters Agreement provides in article I(b) that the prison facilities for carrying out detention on the authority of the Tribunal are part of "the premises of the Tribunal" and thus subject to the same protections as the courthouse. Under the relevant provisions, the "premises of the Tribunal shall be inviolable" (article V) and the "competent authorities shall exercise due diligence to ensure the security and protection of the Tribunal" (article VII). There are also provisions relating to witnesses and experts appearing before the Tribunal (article XVIII), counsel (article XIX), accused persons (article XX), and cooperation with the competent authorities of the host country (articles XXI and XXII). Article XVIII provides for safe-conduct guarantees for witnesses and experts appearing from outside the host country pursuant to a summons or request from the Tribunal. Such persons shall not be prosecuted, detained, or subjected to any other restriction of their liberty by the authorities of the host country in respect of acts or convictions prior to their entry into the territory of the Netherlands. Nor shall they be subjected by the host country to any measure that may affect the free and independent exercise of their functions for the Tribunal. Immunity for witnesses and experts ceases after a period of

---

[10] Agreement concerning the Headquarters of the International Tribunal for the Prosecution of Persons Responsible for Serious Violations of International Humanitarian Law Committed in the Territory of the Former Yugoslavia since 1991, July 29, 1994, Neth.–United Nations, 1994 Tractatenblad van het Koninkrijk der Nederlanden (Neth. Treaty Ser.) No. 189.

[11] *Adopted* Feb. 13, 1946, 1 U.N.T.S. 15.

[12] *Done* Apr. 18, 1961, 500 U.N.T.S. 95.

fifteen days from the date their presence is no longer required by the Tribunal and they have not left the country or, having left, have returned otherwise than in response to another summons or request from the Tribunal.

Under article XIX, counsel who appear before the Tribunal shall not be subjected by the host country to any measure that may affect the free and independent exercise of their functions under the Statute. Some rights and immunities are specifically listed, in particular, immunity from criminal and civil process in respect of words spoken or written or acts performed in their official capacity as counsel. However, article XIX explicitly states that it shall be without prejudice to the applicability of professional disciplinary rules.[13]

Article XX includes a safe-conduct provision for suspects and accused persons similar to the one that applies to witnesses and experts.

Finally, article XXI of the Headquarters Agreement stipulates that the Tribunal shall comply with all security directives in place between it and the host country or issued, in coordination with the UN Security Service, by the authorities responsible for security within the "penitentiary institution of the host country where the Tribunal area of detention is located." This provision has led to the elaboration of a special arrangement, as explained subsequently.

---

[13] According to the Tribunal's Rules of Procedure and Evidence, defense counsel may in appropriate cases be referred to the disciplinary authorities of the country in which they are admitted to practice. International Tribunal for the Prosecution of Persons Responsible for Serious Violations of International Humanitarian Law Committed in the Territory of the Former Yugoslavia since 1991, Rules of Procedure and Evidence R. 46(b), U.N. Doc. IT/32 (1994), *amended by* U.N. Doc. IT/32/Rev.1 (1994), *reprinted in* appendix C of this issue of *Criminal Law Forum* [hereinafter I.T. R. Proc. & Evid.]. The preceding rule provides further that existing international associations of lawyers are not precluded from setting up an ad hoc disciplinary board to whose authority defense counsel appearing before the International Tribunal shall have to submit.

Editor's note: the Rules of Procedure and Evidence were amended Oct. 4, 1994, U.N. Doc. IT/32/Rev.2 (1994), and Jan. 30, 1995, U.N. Doc. IT/32/Rev.3 (1995). This article is based on U.N. Doc. IT/Rev.1. Appendix C prints the most recent text of the rules, U.N. Doc. IT/Rev.3, indicating all deletions from, and additions to, U.N. Doc. IT/32/Rev.1, so that the reader can reconstruct the full text of this earlier version.

Rules of Procedure and Evidence of the Tribunal

The judges of the Tribunal were elected by the General Assembly in September 1993.[14] They held their inaugural session in November 1993[15] and subsequently elaborated and adopted Rules of Procedure and Evidence,[16] pursuant to article 15 of the Statute of the Tribunal. Some of these rules have a direct bearing on the relationship between the Tribunal and the host country.

Thus, rule 34 provides, in accordance with article 22 of the Statute, for setting up a victim and witness unit, under the authority of the registrar of the Tribunal, to recommend protective measures for victims and witnesses and to provide them with counseling and support. Under article XXVI of the Headquarters Agreement, the competent authorities of the Netherlands are required to take such action as may be necessary to insure the safety of persons referred to in the agreement, including witnesses and persons accompanying them. Apparently, we have here an issue of divided, or shared, responsibility between host country and Tribunal, which has to be elaborated in common arrangements. Such arrangements may provide for the involvement or assistance of nongovernmental organizations, subject of course to acceptable security guarantees and to a clear understanding of the allocation of the costs involved (which may not be negligible).

Rules 44–46, relating to the admission and assignment of defense counsel, affect the host country in that lawyers from other countries admitted thereunder by the Tribunal and notified to the Dutch govern-

---

[14] G.A. Dec. 47/328, U.N. GAOR, 47th Sess., Supp. No. 49 (vol. II), at 45, U.N. Doc. A/47/49 (1993); *Despite Truce, Muslims and Croats Fight,* N.Y. Times, Sept. 19, 1993, § 1, at 18, *available in* LEXIS, News Library, Curnws File; *U.N. Names 11 to War Crimes Panel: Serbian Leader Says Peace Plan Is Near,* Hous. Chronicle, Sept. 18, 1993, at A24, *available in* LEXIS, News Library, Curnws File.

[15] *Report on First Session of International Tribunal for War Crimes in Former Yugoslavia,* U.N. Press Release, U.N. Doc. SC/5767 (Dec. 23, 1993), *available in* U.N. Gopher\Current Information\Press Releases; *International War Crimes Tribunal for Former Yugoslavia Elects Its President, Members of Appeals and Trial Chambers,* Fed. News Serv., Nov. 19, 1993, *available in* LEXIS, World Library, Allnws File.

[16] See *supra* note 13.

ment shall have free access to the Netherlands and be exempted from all immigration restrictions.

Rule 57 recognizes specifically that the host country has a role to play in the transfer of arrested persons to the Tribunal. Under this rule, the Dutch authorities are responsible for arranging the transport of such persons through the territory of the Netherlands under the escort of Dutch police personnel. Thus, any arrangement for a transfer between a third country and the Netherlands has to be made through the competent Dutch authorities, which are to assist the Tribunal in providing for the transport of arrested persons from the borders of the Netherlands or its airports to the detention facility of the Tribunal, as provided in rule 64. The reference in that rule to the possibility of detention facilities provided by another country seems to be relevant only in cases where the Tribunal would be sitting elsewhere than in the Hague, "when it considers it necessary for the efficient exercise of its functions."[17]

Rule 65 takes account of the possibility of provisional release. Under rule 65(C), "[t]he Trial Chamber may impose such conditions upon the release of the accused as it may determine appropriate, including . . . such conditions as are necessary to ensure his presence for trial . . . ." This rule is to be understood as permitting the imposition of conditions on the accused only, and not on the host country or any other country. An order by the Tribunal not to allow a person who has been conditionally released by the Tribunal to leave the (host) country might impose an unacceptable security risk on that jurisdiction, which it may have good reason not to accept.

Particularly sensitive are the rules on contempt of court (rule 77) and perjury (rule 91). The Statute of the Tribunal is completely silent about these issues. It confers jurisdiction on the Tribunal only for designated offenses[18] and imposes express obligations on states to cooperate with the Tribunal in the investigation and prosecution of these

---

[17] S.C. Res. 827, *supra* note 3, ¶ 6.

[18] Statute, *supra* note 4, arts. 2–5 (conferring jurisdiction over grave breaches of the Geneva Conventions of 1949, violations of the laws or customs of war, genocide, and crimes against humanity, respectively).

offenses alone.[19] The Tribunal itself is empowered under article 23 to pronounce judgments and impose sentences and penalties only on persons convicted of serious violations of international humanitarian law, and only terms of imprisonment imposed by virtue of this article are subject to the enforcement powers of article 27. In short, none of these provisions explicitly confers competence on the Tribunal to enforce any of its own sentences.

The oversight of contempt and perjury may be considered a serious lacuna in the Statute, and the judges in drafting their Rules of Procedure and Evidence have rightfully addressed the matter and assumed an implied jurisdiction in both cases. In principle, this decision is entirely appropriate: a tribunal that does not have the power to deal with contempt or perjury committed in the course of proceedings before it, lacks credibility. The judges' initiative and courage in drafting specific rules in this area must be commended. However, the rules leave open a number of questions that are relevant from the perspective of the host country. Thus, rule 77(a) states that "a witness who refuses or fails contumaciously to answer a question relevant to the issue before a Chamber may be found in contempt of the Tribunal. The Chamber may impose a fine not exceeding US$10,000 or a term of imprisonment not exceeding six months." Unfortunately, the rules are silent on the procedures to be followed for finding a witness in contempt—can he be taken into custody, will there be a separate trial on the basis of a written charge, has the witness the right to be assisted by defense counsel and, if so, on what terms, is there a right of appeal both for the witness and for the prosecutor—and, perhaps even more serious, the rules fail to deal with the issue of enforcement—how is a fine to be enforced, what happens when a fine remains unpaid in whole or in part, and where is a term of imprisonment to be served?

The latter issues in particular are of direct interest to the Netherlands since it may be assumed that that is the country to be approached first to assist in enforcement of citations for contempt or perjury. Apparently, the Tribunal takes the view that imprisonment imposed under rule 77 (or rule 91, for that matter) might be carried out in its own detention facilities. This is, however, very much open to challenge.

---

[19] *Id.* art. 29.

Having implied powers to deal with contempt and perjury is one thing, but claiming the right to enforce a sentence of imprisonment imposed in such a case is quite another, particularly where the Statute of the Tribunal does not confer any power of enforcement on the Tribunal. Imprisonment in instances of contempt or perjury would have to be enforced in the detention unit leased by the United Nations, which would make it difficult to comply with the principle contained in rule 8(b) of the UN Standard Minimum Rules for the Treatment of Prisoners that untried prisoners shall be kept separate from convicted prisoners.[20] Any request to the host country to provide for separate prison units to be leased by the United Nations for enforcement purposes might be countered by the argument that there is nothing in the Statute that obliges the Netherlands to comply with such a request. The same sort of argument could be advanced by other states requested to assist the Tribunal by accepting convicted witnesses to serve out sentences for contempt or perjury.

This is even more serious in the case of perjury (rule 91) than in the case of contempt. In contrast to rule 77, rule 91 addresses some procedural matters, although no explicit provision is made for taking into custody an alleged perjurious witness or obliging states to transfer such persons to the Tribunal. Maximum penalties provided for acts of perjury committed before the Tribunal are a fine of $10,000 (the same maximum as for contempt) and/or imprisonment of twelve months (rule 91(e)). With all respect to the judges and fully understanding their hesitation to overstretch their inherent or implied powers, I find these maximum penalties disproportionately low to constitute an adequate deterrent. Compared to maximum penalties for perjury in criminal cases provided in the domestic legislation of most states — typically five or more, but up to fifteen, years of imprisonment[21] — the penalties provided in rule 91 are so inconsequential as to jeopardize the credibility and

---

[20] E.S.C. Res. 663 (XXIV) C, U.N. ESCOR, 24th Sess., Supp. No. 1, at 11, U.N. Doc. E/3048 (1957), *amended by* E.S.C. 2076 (LXII), U.N. ESCOR, 62d Sess., Supp. No. 1, at 35, U.N. Doc. E/5988 (1977).

[21] *E.g.*, Belg. Crim. Code art. 216 (15 years); Fr. Crim. Code art. 361 (5–10 years); Ger. Crim. Code arts. 153–154 (1–5 years); Ital. Crim. Code art. 372 (6 years); Neth. Crim. Code art. 207 (6 years); U.K. Perjury Act § 1(1) (7 years).

authority of the Tribunal. Particularly in the kind of criminal cases subject to the jurisdiction of the Tribunal, the chance of perjury is far from remote and has to be taken extremely seriously. Therefore, problems like perjury and contempt should not be resolved through the exercise of implied powers but should be addressed in a straightforward manner in the Statute itself.

In my view, the Security Council should incorporate supplemental provisions into the Statute explicitly conferring competence on the Tribunal to deal with cases of contempt of court and perjury, setting maximum penalties (say, imprisonment of six months for contempt and of at least six years for perjury), requiring the Tribunal to adopt specific rules of procedure and evidence for such cases (including rules on provisional arrest), extending the obligations on states to cooperate with the Tribunal under article 29 to such offenses (including the surrender of suspects), and making article 27 on the enforcement of sentences explicitly applicable to the enforcement of prison sentences imposed for contempt and perjury. Thus, the most serious lacuna in the Statute would be filled in a way consistent with the principles of the rule of law and legal certainty.

Finally, the Rules of Procedure and Evidence may create some practical problems with regard to the enforcement of prison sentences. Because rule 102 provides that the sentence shall begin to run from the day it is pronounced, as long as no agreement has been reached on the date and terms of a transfer for purposes of enforcement with the state designated under article 29 of the Statute to carry out the sentence, the Tribunal may have to start enforcement in its own detention facilities. Again, strictly speaking, the Tribunal has no enforcement powers of its own and any time spent in the Tribunal's detention unit pursuant to a sentencing order may arguably be considered illegal. To forestall this possibility, the Tribunal may feel obliged to turn to the host country in order to help it bridge the gap between the moment the sentence begins to run and the date on which the convicted person is transferred to another state.[22] It would, in my view, have been legally more sound to

---

[22] The Netherlands has already indicated its willingness to assist the Tribunal in enforcing sentences, in accordance with Statute, *supra* note 4, art. 27. See *infra* note 24 and accompanying text.

allow the Tribunal to retain custody over convicted defendants until such time as transfer can be effected to the state(s) selected to administer prison sentences, with any time spent in custody in the Tribunal's detention unit after pronouncement of the sentence deducted from the term to be served in the administering state(s). Such a scheme would also have avoided the need for the complicated provisions set out in rules 102 and 118.[23]

Domestic Legislation

All UN member states undoubtedly have to take steps under their domestic legal systems to enable them to comply with their obligations under Security Council Resolution 827 and the Statute of the Tribunal. The Netherlands has adopted such an act, containing provisions in connection with the establishment of the International Tribunal for the Prosecution of Persons Responsible for Serious Violations of International Humanitarian Law Committed in the Territory of the Former

---

[23] I.T. R. Proc. & Evid., *supra* note 13, R. 102, deals with the status of the convicted person and provides in relevant part:

> (A) The sentence shall begin to run from the day it is pronounced . . . . However, as soon as notice of appeal is given, the enforcement of the judgement shall thereupon be stayed until the decision on the appeal has been delivered, the convicted person meanwhile remaining in detention . . . .
>
> (B) If . . . the convicted person has been released, or is for any other reason at liberty, and he is not present when the judgement is pronounced, the Trial Chamber shall issue a warrant for his arrest. . . .

Id. R. 118 deals with the status of the accused following appeal and provides in relevant part:

> (A) A sentence pronounced by the Appeals Chamber shall be enforced immediately.
>
> (B) Where the accused is not present when the judgement is due to be delivered . . . [for any reason], the Appeals Chamber may deliver its judgement in the absence of the accused and shall, unless it pronounces his acquittal, order his arrest or surrender to the Tribunal.

Yugoslavia since 1991.[24] The act, consisting of eighteen articles, sets out a number of definitions (article 1) and special procedures for the surrender to the Tribunal of suspected persons who are found in the Netherlands (articles 2–5). The latter measures are in fact simplified extradition procedures, under the exclusive jurisdiction of the District Court of the Hague. Only two possible grounds for refusal are recognized (article 4):

> the failure to establish that the person concerned actually is the person wanted by the Tribunal; or

> a finding that the offenses for which the surrender is requested are obviously outside the subject matter jurisdiction of the Tribunal.

Article 6 deals with compelling persons who are found in the Netherlands to comply with orders of the Tribunal to appear as witnesses or experts.

Article 7 is specific in relation to the position of the Netherlands as the host country and deals with the escort over Dutch territory of persons who are being surrendered by third states to the Tribunal. This article applies also to persons who have been summoned to appear from abroad and have refused to comply voluntarily. Under this article, the Netherlands also takes responsibility for transporting persons between the different premises of the Tribunal (detention unit and courthouse).

Articles 8–10 deal with the rendering of judicial and police assistance to the Tribunal by providing information *sua sponte* from police records, hearing witnesses, seizing items of evidence, performing special investigations, and so on. Article 10 contains the same sort of safe-conduct provision for witnesses and experts appearing from abroad as is set out in article XVIII of the Headquarters Agreement. When complying with a request or summons from the Tribunal to appear or even when brought compulsorily before the Tribunal, witnesses and experts shall not be prosecuted, arrested, or otherwise restricted in their

---

[24] Act of Apr. 21, 1994, 1994 Official Bull. Acts & Royal Decrees 308 (entered into force May 4, 1994) (Neth.).

liberty by Dutch authorities for acts or omissions or convictions prior to their arrival in the Netherlands. Such immunity lapses if the witness or expert has not left the territory of the Netherlands within fifteen days from the date his or her presence is no longer necessary to the Tribunal, or if the person has returned unbidden to the Netherlands after having left Dutch territory.

Articles 11–14 deal with the enforcement in the Netherlands of prison sentences imposed by the Tribunal, indicating that the Netherlands will be among the states prepared to accept convicted persons under article 27 of the Statute. Under article 12 of the act, existing legislative provisions in the Netherlands on the enforcement of foreign criminal sentences are to be applied in a simplified manner. The District Court of the Hague is exclusively competent to grant exequatur in respect of the Tribunal's sentences; the only ground for refusal is where "on balance of all relevant interests a decision to enforce the Tribunal's sentence in the Netherlands cannot be taken."

Article 13 relates to the exercise of the host country's penal enforcement functions. This article makes it possible to commence in the Netherlands a term of imprisonment imposed by the Tribunal but to transfer further enforcement to a third state, subject to the Tribunal's consent. Article 14 contains a derogation from article 122(1) of the Constitution of the Netherlands in that it confers the power to grant pardons, in the case of sentences enforced in the Netherlands, on the president of the Tribunal rather than the head of state.

Article 15 gives the necessary authority to Dutch law enforcement officials to escort convicted persons through the territory of the Netherlands on their way to a third state to be handed over for purposes of enforcement.

Articles 16 and 17 address immunity: persons who cannot claim immunity in respect of the jurisdiction of the Tribunal cannot claim the same in respect of the jurisdiction of Dutch courts and the enforcement of their decisions. At the same time, article 17 explicitly states that Dutch law does not apply to a deprivation of liberty to be served on the authority of the Tribunal within the detention facilities of the Tribunal in the Netherlands. Entry into force is the subject of article 18.

In order to give full effect to the implementing legislation, measures have been taken to establish permanent contacts between the registrar of the Tribunal and the public prosecutor associated with the

District Court of the Hague. Moreover, the Ministry of Justice of the Netherlands has been designated to serve as intermediary in contacts between the Tribunal and third states with regard to the surrender of persons to the Tribunal; the receiving of witnesses, and persons accompanying them, within the territory of the host country; and the provision of the necessary visa and other travel documents to persons working for, or appearing before, the Tribunal.

Lease of Detention Facilities

The provision of detention units to the Tribunal has been formalized through a lease between the Netherlands and the United Nations.[25] Through this contract, the state has let a complex of cell units on the premises of an existing Dutch penal institution (the Scheveningen Penitentiary Complex), including specified furnishings and facilities. These units have been newly constructed by the government on behalf of the United Nations, in accordance with UN requirements. The investment costs are to be partially amortized in the lease. The lease agreement specifies that the leased premises shall be regarded as Tribunal premises, governed by the rules on protection, privileges, and immunities contained in the Headquarters Agreement, and that the United Nations shall be responsible for all aspects of detention, including the security and welfare of the detainees. The contract has the usual clauses on use, maintenance, defects, liability, inspection, amendment, and termination. The initial term of the contract is four years, after which the lease may be renewed, subject to an eventual adjustment of the lease payment. Payment is based on a fee per cell per year, plus a sum for facilities for every person actually detained. Facilities include food, laundry, heating, electricity, water, cleaning, and medical and spiritual services. The United Nations is to provide prison personnel, who may to a large extent be recruited locally.

Agreement Relating to Security in the UN Detention Unit

In connection with the lease, which is an agreement governed by private law, a separate agreement under public law has been drawn up between

---

[25] Lease of Detention Units, Neth.–United Nations, July 14, 1994.

the Ministry of Justice of the Netherlands and the Tribunal to deal with matters relating to security and order within the Scheveningen Penitentiary Complex.[26] The UN detention unit is located within the premises of this Dutch facility and can be reached only by gaining access to the Dutch portion of the complex first. This implies that checks on persons and property have to be performed by Dutch authorities before anyone or anything can enter the UN unit. Moreover, the governor of the complex has responsibility generally for security and order within the prison facility as a whole. He has to insure, for example, that there shall be no mixing up of Tribunal detainees (and their visitors) and detainees held under Dutch judicial authority (and their visitors). UN personnel present in the penitentiary complex have to observe the rules and regulations applicable to the complex as a whole. Of course, the agreement fully respects the responsibility of the UN officer in charge of security and order within the UN unit. Within the UN unit, the commanding officer and his staff are bound by the Rules of Detention adopted by the Tribunal.[27] The agreement also details procedures to be followed in cases of emergency or differences of view between the competent authorities of the host country and those of the United Nations.

Rules of Detention of the Tribunal

In May 1994, at the end of their third session, the judges of the International Tribunal adopted a set of about ninety rules governing the detention of persons awaiting trial before the Tribunal.[28] The Rules of Detention take into account the relevant UN norms and standards on

---

[26] Agreement on Matters relating to Security and Order of the Leased Premises within the Penitentiary Complex Scheveningen, July 14, 1994, Neth.–International Tribunal for the Former Yugoslavia.

[27] See *infra* note 28.

[28] International Tribunal for the Prosecution of Persons Responsible for Serious Violations of International Humanitarian Law Committed in the Territory of the Former Yugoslavia since 1991, Rules Governing the Detention of Persons Awaiting Trial or Appeal before the Tribunal or Otherwise Detained on the Authority of the Tribunal, U.N. Doc. IT/38/Rev.3 (1994).

the treatment of prisoners,[29] the European Prison Rules, as adopted by the Committee of Ministers of the Council of Europe in 1987,[30] as well as the relevant laws and regulations of the host country. Apart from a set of definitions (following the preamble), a set of basic principles (rules 1–8), and a provision on amendment (rule 92), the rules are divided essentially into two parts: rules on the management of the prison unit (rules 9–59) and rules on the rights of detainees (rules 60–88). There are also some rules on the transport and removal of detainees (rules 89–91).

The rules on management address such issues as the reception of detainees, accommodations, personal hygiene, clothing, food, physical exercise, medical care, discipline, segregation and isolation, and the use of force and instruments of restraint. The rules on the rights of detainees deal with such matters as communications and visits, legal assistance, spiritual welfare, work and recreation, personal possessions, and complaint procedures.

The Rules of Detention were drafted in close consultation with the authorities of the Netherlands, in accordance with the spirit of article VI of the Headquarters Agreement. Without entering into details here, it is obvious that many of the provisions set out in the rules are of direct relevance to the host country, particularly given the location of the UN prison unit within the Scheveningen Penitentiary Complex.

Lease of the Aegon Building

Another legal document of paramount importance for the establishment of the International Tribunal is the lease between the United Nations and the Aegon Insurance Company, in whose building the offices of the judges, the registrar, and the prosecutor, as well as the courtroom and all

---

[29] *E.g.*, Standard Minimum Rules, *supra* note 20; Recommendations on the Treatment of Foreign Prisoners, in *Seventh United Nations Congress on the Prevention of Crime and the Treatment of Offenders, Milan, 26 August–6 September 1985: Report Prepared by the Secretariat* 53, U.N. Doc. A/CONF.121/22/Rev.1, U.N. Sales No. E.86.IV.1 (1986); Basic Principles for the Treatment of Prisoners, G.A. Res. 45/111, U.N. GAOR, 45th Sess., Supp. No. 49A, at 199, U.N. Doc. A/45/49 (1990).

[30] Council of Europe, Recommendation R (87) 3 (Feb. 12, 1987).

associated facilities — offices for the defense, separate rooms for accommodating witnesses for the defense and for the prosecution, access for the public to a gallery, press rooms, detention cells — are to be located. Since this is a contract between the United Nations and a private party, I am not at liberty to reveal any of its details.[31] Part of the contract, however, consists of a loan to be granted by the insurance company to the United Nations, to finance the reconstruction needed to make the building suitable for its new tasks. This loan is to be amortized through the rent to be paid by the United Nations to the Aegon Company for use of the building.

These renovations, as well as the renovations financed by the host government to secure the exterior of the building, were put under the supervision of a project team, acting under the assignment of both the United Nations (registrar of the Tribunal) and the host government (Ministry of Foreign Affairs), and representing the Tribunal, the insurance company, the Netherlands Government Service for Public Buildings, and the Ministries of Foreign Affairs, Justice, and Interior. Executive responsibility was assigned to the Service for Public Buildings of the Netherlands Ministry of Housing and Town and Country Planning.

EXCLUSIVE RESPONSIBILITIES OF THE NETHERLANDS

According to article XXVI of the Headquarters Agreement, the competent authorities of the Netherlands "shall take effective and adequate action which may be required to ensure the appropriate security, safety and protection of persons" designated in the agreement, "indispensable for the proper functioning of the Tribunal, free from interference of any kind." Article VII of the same agreement stipulates that the competent authorities of the Netherlands

> shall exercise due diligence to ensure the security and protection of the Tribunal and to ensure that the tranquility of the

---

[31] Nor is the contract (signed July 13, 1994) likely to be made public down the road.

Tribunal is not disturbed by the intrusion of persons or groups of persons from outside the premises of the Tribunal or by disturbances in their immediate vicinity and shall provide to the premises of the Tribunal the appropriate protection as may be required.

Article VII goes on to state that the competent authorities shall, if "requested by the President or the Registrar of the Tribunal, . . . provide adequate police force necessary for the preservation of law and order on the premises of the Tribunal or in the immediate vicinity thereof, and for the removal of persons therefrom." These articles focus on responsibilities that are also incumbent on the host country under generally accepted principles of public international law.

Measures to insure the physical security of the courthouse building include constructing a fence, with an entry booth where all checks on visitors and their luggage will take place; protecting the windows; and installing electronic detection systems.

Measures to protect persons with diplomatic status include security installations at their private homes and, depending on the assessed level of danger, their transportation and escort in armored cars, personal guards, and static or semistatic surveillance. As far as other persons working for the Tribunal are concerned, no particular measures are envisaged, although of course in particular cases protection may need to be provided.

Security for accused persons will be rather complex. Special protective measures have to be taken in respect of their transport, for which, as stated earlier, the host country bears full responsibility. Their detention inside the boundaries of the Scheveningen Penitentiary Complex also entails the design and operation of specific security measures.

The category of witnesses is probably the most difficult in terms of developing appropriate protective measures: it is unpredictable how large this group will turn out to be, under what conditions witnesses will reach the country, what their actual needs will be, and how their stay in the host country will be organized. Moreover, as provided in the Statute of the Tribunal (article 22) and its Rules of Procedure and Evidence (rule 34), the United Nations has responsibility for the protection of victims and witnesses, and it will therefore be necessary to coordinate the

UN's exercise of this responsibility and the Dutch government's implementation of protective measures.

Witness protection should in the first place be oriented toward the provision of security from harassment, intimidation, or revenge. Second, assistance should be available for those who need medical, psychological, or spiritual help. Most witnesses are likely to have gone through traumatic experiences, the effect of which may be worsened through appearance in court and in particular through cross-examination. Some nongovernmental organizations may be willing to offer assistance of this nature, but having these organizations involved could produce further security risks, both for victims/witnesses and for persons providing assistance to them, which the Dutch government and the United Nations would have to face. Third, whereas witnesses who testify before the Tribunal are in principle free to move throughout the territory of the host country, their right to stay in the Netherlands is not unlimited but is linked rather to their being required by the Tribunal. Once their presence is no longer needed, they shall have to return to their country of origin—unless of course they apply for asylum in the host country, a possibility that cannot be ruled out and for which the host country shall have to be prepared. Once returned to their country of origin, these persons may need continued attention in terms of protection against intimidation or worse, as well as social and psychological treatment. The latter is obviously not a responsibility of the host country, although the Netherlands may nonetheless come in for criticism if needed aftercare is not provided.

Given the nature of the cases subject to the jurisdiction of the Tribunal, as well as the nature of the conflict in the former Yugoslavia, attempts to commit acts of violence against the Tribunal must be anticipated. Such violence may well be of a terroristic nature, involving the use of explosives or firearms. The Netherlands has a rather large population of immigrants from the former Yugoslavia (some 18,800 persons), and it is well known that within this group the level of illegal possession of firearms and other weapons is relatively high. There are far higher numbers of former Yugoslavs living in Germany and in other parts of western Europe. As it is fairly easy to travel throughout Europe, with or without valid travel documents, retaliatory activity poses a real threat to the Tribunal.

Once the Tribunal is hearing its first cases, with all the accompanying publicity, the security risks are likely to become considerable. The host country has to be prepared to counter serious threats with appropriate security measures, including measures to forestall various forms of violence, for an extended period of time. This may entail the deployment of manpower and the dedication of materiel to a much greater extent than the Dutch government has ever been called upon to do. Indeed, the annual costs to the host country are, in the worst case scenario, likely to turn out to be substantially higher than the costs the United Nations will bear for operating the Tribunal.

The presence of a UN military force in the territory of the former Yugoslavia (UNPROFOR) may further complicate the proper functioning of the Tribunal and its relations with the host country. The Netherlands is one of the states that contribute military units to UNPROFOR. It is quite likely that UNPROFOR will be called upon to protect staff from the prosecutor's office who are conducting investigations in the territory of the former Yugoslavia if they meet with local interference. This role may make UNPROFOR personnel vulnerable to actions by people who have an interest in preventing the prosecutor from collecting evidence or initiating cases. Such risks may also occur if UNPROFOR is called upon to assist the Tribunal in transporting people either from one place in the former Yugoslavia to another or abroad.

The responsibility of the states participating in UNPROFOR for upholding strict neutrality in the execution of UNPROFOR's mandate, as well as for insuring the security of their nationals in the field, may outweigh their readiness openly to assist, or to allow UNPROFOR to assist, the Tribunal in carrying out its tasks. Here again, the concerns of the Netherlands may be particularly acute, since as host country, the Netherlands may—rightly or wrongly—be considered to be in the best position to impede the functioning of the Tribunal, and its government may therefore be identified as the most suitable target for blackmail.

This threat is compounded because the Netherlands has exclusive responsibility for escorting over Dutch territory persons who have been arrested elsewhere at the request of the Tribunal and are to be surrendered to it. As noted earlier, this responsibility extends to receiving arrested persons at the land borders or at international airports in the Netherlands, transporting such persons to the detention facility of the Tribunal, and transporting detainees between the prison unit of the

Tribunal and the courthouse. This means, in practical terms, that states surrendering persons to the Tribunal shall have not only to inform the Tribunal but also to contact the competent Dutch authorities[32] in order to agree on a date and place of surrender. In cases where a Dutch commercial carrier is used for transporting persons from abroad to the Netherlands, Dutch law enforcement officials will assume responsibility once the accused person is on board and will serve as escorts to the Netherlands.

The same obligations and procedures apply mutatis mutandis in cases where persons sentenced by the Tribunal are to be transported to other countries in order to serve their sentences there, as contemplated by article 27 of the Statute of the Tribunal.

SOME LESSONS TO BE LEARNED WITH A VIEW TOWARD SETTING UP A PERMANENT COURT

The International Law Commission (ILC) has been requested by the General Assembly of the United Nations to draft a statute for a permanent international criminal court. This is not the place to describe the history of this mandate and the results that have been achieved so far by the ILC. Even if the ILC has made substantial progress over the last few years in this area, it is still too early to say whether any of its proposals will ultimately receive sufficient support in the international community.[33]

---

[32] Neth. Ministry of Justice, Int'l Judicial Assistance Section, the Hague; or Public Prosecutor, District Court, the Hague.

[33] G.A. Res. 47/33, U.N. GAOR, 47th Sess., Supp. No. 49, at 287, ¶ 6, U.N. Doc. A/47/49 (1992) (requesting the ILC to "continue its work on the question [of an international criminal jurisdiction] by undertaking the project for the elaboration of a draft statute for an international criminal court as a matter of priority"); *Report of the Working Group on a Draft Statute for an International Criminal Court*, in *Report of the International Law Commission on Its Forty-fifth Session*, U.N. GAOR, 48th Sess., Supp. No. 10, at 255, U.N. Doc. A/48/10 (1993); G.A. Res. 48/31, U.N. GAOR, 48th Sess., Supp. No. 49, at 328, ¶ 6, U.N. Doc. A/48/49 (1993) (requesting the ILC "to continue its work as a matter of priority on this question with a view to elaborating a draft statute,

One thing is clear though: a permanent court cannot be created by a binding Security Council resolution under chapter VII of the UN Charter, as was the ad hoc Tribunal for the Former Yugoslavia, but has to find its authority in an international convention, to be approved and adopted by states in accordance with their constitutional procedures. This indispensable requirement of constitutionalism, legal certainty, and justice may at the same time cause a tremendous amount of uncertainty, arbitrariness, inequality, and indeed unfairness, if for understandable practical reasons the creation and functioning of such a permanent court is not made dependent on acceptance by all or virtually all the states in the world—uncertainty as to the number of states that eventually will participate in the operation of the court, the number and nature of cases to be administered by it, and the availability of financial and human resources; arbitrariness in the legal systems represented and the types of cases prosecuted; inequality in the distribution of financial contributions and the appointment of officials; and so on.

Such a court must be created as an institution of the United Nations—managed, financed, and controlled pursuant to existing UN procedures and practices, with the United Nations as a whole taking responsibility for the court, even if not all member states were prepared to accept its jurisdiction. It is simply impossible to envisage hosting a permanent international criminal court if the host country did not have

---

if possible at its forty-sixth session in 1994"); U.N. Press Release, U.N. Doc. DH/1640 4 (May 9, 1994), *available in* U.N. Gopher\Current Information\Daily Highlights (noting that at the request of the General Assembly, the ILC at its forty-sixth session, May 2–July 22, 1994, is attempting to complete its work on the "establishment of an international criminal court, or another international trial mechanism, dealing with crimes against the peace and security of mankind"); U.N. Press Release, U.N. Doc. DH/1691 (July 21 1994), *available in* U.N. Gopher\Current Information\Daily Highlights (reporting that the ILC has completed its revision of a Draft Statute for an International Criminal Court). The ILC submitted its draft to the General Assembly's Sixth (Legal) Committee in the fall of 1994. Draft Statute for an International Criminal Court, in *Report of the International Law Commission on Its Forty-sixth Session*, U.N. GAOR, 49th Sess., Supp. No. 10, at 43, U.N. Doc. A/49/10 (1994). With strong opposition from the United States, the ILC proposal has now essentially been put on hold. G.A. Res. 49/53, U.N. GAOR, 49th Sess., 84th plen. mtg., U.N. Doc. A/49/53 (1994); Thalif Deen, *United Nations: U.N. Split over International Criminal Court*, Inter Press Serv., Dec. 21, 1994, *available in* LEXIS, World Library, Allnws File.

a stable, responsible counterpart with which to work. Such a counterpart can only be the United Nations and certainly not an arbitrary and varying group of states parties to a founding convention.

Creating a new UN institution would require amendment of the UN Charter or, if the court were to be integrated into the International Court of Justice (ICJ), amendment of the ICJ's Statute.[34] Amendments to the UN Charter and their entry into force require a qualified majority: adoption by a two-thirds majority of the members of the General Assembly and ratification by two-thirds of the member states, including all permanent members of the Security Council.[35] Moreover, the establishment of a permanent court is one thing; such a court cannot function in a legal vacuum, presupposing the creation of legally binding obligations on UN member states to cooperate with the court in respect of offenses subject to its jurisdiction through waiver of the exercise of national jurisdiction, arrest and surrender of suspects, legal assistance, intelligence sharing, enforcement of sentences, granting of transit permits, and so forth.

Assuming that these legal obstacles could be overcome, a potential host country would need to evaluate and make an informed decision about its willingness and competence to handle the practical implications of the establishment of such a permanent court in terms of security risks, long-term financial commitments by the United Nations, required premises (including detention facilities), enforcement responsibilities, employment, government assistance, and related issues. Such projections would depend on specific information about the scope of the court's jurisdiction, the procedures for triggering the exercise of its jurisdiction, and the likelihood that such procedures would be invoked.

Both the security risks and the financial implications—for the United Nations and the host country—may be massive, particularly if one wanted to create a permanent court that dealt with more than just a couple of cases each year. A very rough calculation, based on the first assessments made for the International Tribunal for the Former Yugoslavia when the United Nations suggested the creation of an organization of about four hundred employees, working in a courthouse

---

[34] U.N. Charter art. 108; Statute of the International Court of Justice art. 69.

[35] U.N. Charter art. 108.

containing three secured courtrooms and running a few dozen cases a year, would suggest an annual budget for the United Nations of about $90 million and for the host country of about $20 million, including the cost of renovations and other construction programs but excluding set-asides for future investments and renovations. The financial burden on the host country might increase substantially in the face of lengthy periods involving high security risks, requiring permanent or semipermanent personal protection for individuals and their relatives who are in danger. These figures, it seems to me, constitute an insuperable obstacle to the realization of the whole project.

Of course, these costs might be reduced if the court were kept small—at about the size of the ad hoc Tribunal for the Former Yugoslavia—and if there were mechanisms put in place for keeping the court's workload commensurate with its resources. But this option raises the question of whether it is worthwhile amending the UN Charter for such a limited purpose.

The preferable route would seem to be to let the International Tribunal pursue its experimental course and see whether an example is set, to be followed if ever again the madness of an armed conflict, in which policies of deliberate and systematic violation of the most elementary principles of international humanitarian law are carried out, moves the international community to create a similar institution under chapter VII of the UN Charter. There have already been calls for a tribunal with jurisdiction over the massive violations of human rights that have been perpetrated in Rwanda's civil war.[36] Any future action by

---

[36] Since these words were written, the Security Council requested the Secretary-General to establish an impartial Commission of Experts to investigate reports of "grave violations of international humanitarian law committed in the territory of Rwanda, including the evidence of possible acts of genocide." S.C. Res. 935, U.N. SCOR, 49th Year, 3400th mtg. at 1, ¶ 2, U.N. Doc. S/RES/935 (1994), *reprinted in* appendix D of this issue of *Criminal Law Forum* and *available in* U.N. Gopher\Documents\Security Council Resolutions. For background, see Anthony Goodman, *Spain Urges Rwanda War Crimes Commission*, Reuters, June 14, 1994, *available in* LEXIS, World Library, Allnws File; *U.N. Should Extend Mandate of Crimes Tribunal to Rwanda*, Agence France Presse, July 2, 1994, *available in* LEXIS, World Library, Allnws File. The Commission was set up and it reported back to the Security Council in due course. Letter from the Secretary-General to the President of the Security Council, Oct. 1, 1994, U.N. Doc. S/1994/1125 (1994), transmitting *Preliminary Report of the Independent Commission of Experts*

the Security Council to set up an ad hoc tribunal under chapter VII must be well coordinated with the General Assembly and with the host government. But if the United Nations is disposed to spend huge amounts of money on the administration of criminal justice in the world, the better alternative to a series of ad hoc courts or even a permanent court might be generously to finance technical assistance programs in states with underdeveloped or poorly functioning criminal justice systems, in order to help them tackle their own problems, rather than let them indulge in phantasms.

Established in Accordance with Security Council Resolution 935 (1994); Letter from the Secretary-General to the President of the Security Council, Dec. 9, 1994, U.N. Doc. S/1994/1405 (1994), transmitting *Final Report of the Commission of Experts Established pursuant to Security Council Resolution 935 (1994), available in* U.N. Gopher\Current Information\Secretary-General Reports. S.C. Res. 955, U.N. SCOR, 49th Year, 3453d mtg. at 1, U.N. Doc. S/RES/955 (1994), *reprinted in* appendix D of this issue of *Criminal Law Forum* and *available in* U.N. Gopher\Documents\Security Council Resolutions, establishes the International Tribunal for Rwanda, with institutional ties to the International Tribunal for the Former Yugoslavia, and sets out the Rwandan Tribunal's Statute.

IV
Substantive and Procedural Issues

8
A Slovenian Perspective on the Statute and Rules of the International Tribunal for the Former Yugoslavia[*]

Pavel Dolenc[**]

INTRODUCTION

Security Council Resolution 827 (1993), on the establishment of the International Tribunal for the Prosecution of Persons Responsible for Serious Violations of International Humanitarian Law Committed in the Territory of the Former Yugoslavia since 1991, and the Statute of the International Tribunal, directly impinge on the sovereignty and domestic law of UN member states. These instruments require member states to

---

[*]   *Editor's note:* research for this article was updated through December 31, 1994. The Criminal Code and the Code of Criminal Procedure of the Republic of Slovenia went into effect January 1, 1995. This article discusses the codes of the former Yugoslavia, which were in force in Slovenia until that date. The constitutional provisions that are cited are those of the new Constitution of the Republic of Slovenia, which went into effect in 1992.

   Criminal Law Forum would like to thank Ljubo Bavcon, Professor of Law, and Ivanka Sket, Information Specialist, at the Institute of Criminology, Faculty of Law, University of Ljubljana, for their generous assistance in preparing this article for publication.

[**]   Public Prosecutor, Public Prosecutor's Office of the Republic of Slovenia, Ljubljana, Slovenia; LL.B., University of Ljubljana. This article was translated by Ivanka Sket, Information Specialist, Institute of Criminology, Faculty of Law, University of Ljubljana, Ljubljana, Slovenia; B.A., University of Ljubljana.

cooperate fully with the work of the Tribunal. Paragraph 4 of Resolution 827 provides specifically that

> all States shall cooperate fully with the International Tribunal and its organs in accordance with the present resolution and the Statute of the International Tribunal and that consequently all States shall take any measures necessary under their domestic law to implement the provisions of the present resolution and the Statute, including the obligation of States to comply with requests for assistance or orders issued by a Trial Chamber under Article 29 of the Statute.

Article 29 of the Statute elaborates:

> 1. States shall cooperate with the International Tribunal in the investigation and prosecution of persons accused of committing serious violations of international humanitarian law.
>
> 2. States shall comply without undue delay with any request for assistance or an order issued by a Trial Chamber, including, but not limited to:
>
>> (a) the identification and location of persons;
>> (b) the taking of testimony and the production of evidence;
>> (c) the service of documents;
>> (d) the arrest or detention of persons;
>> (e) the surrender or the transfer of the accused to the International Tribunal.

Under article 29, all states established in the territory of the former Yugoslavia are required to submit to the jurisdiction of the Tribunal in regard to criminal offenses within its competence, as well as in regard to the investigation and apprehension of persons alleged to have committed such offenses.

The legal basis for these obligations is explained in paragraphs 125–126 of the *Report of the Secretary-General pursuant to Paragraph 2 of*

Security Council Resolution 808 (1993), which sets out the text of the Tribunal's Statute:

> 125. [T]he establishment of the International Tribunal on the basis of a Chapter VII decision creates a binding obligation on all States to take whatever steps are required to implement the decision. In practical terms, this means that all States would be under an obligation to cooperate with the International Tribunal and to assist it in all stages of the proceedings to ensure compliance with requests for assistance in the gathering of evidence, hearing of witnesses, suspects and experts, identification and location of persons and the service of documents. Effect shall also be given to orders issued by the Trial Chambers, such as warrants of arrest, search warrants, warrants for surrender or transfer of persons, and any other orders necessary for the conduct of the trial.
>
> 126. [A]n order by a Trial Chamber for the surrender or transfer of persons to the custody of the International Tribunal shall be considered to be the application of an enforcement measure under Chapter VII of the Charter of the United Nations.

Since the Tribunal's Statute addresses both substantive and procedural matters that are likely to be approached differently in different jurisdictions, member states will have to take measures to eliminate potential conflicts between the Tribunal's Statute and Rules of Procedure and Evidence, on the one hand, and their domestic law, on the other. Moreover, while the Statute provides for concurrent jurisdiction between national courts and the International Tribunal (article 9(1)), it also gives the Tribunal authority to require national courts to defer to its competence (article 9(2)). This provision will also undoubtedly necessitate appropriate action at the national level.

It is not expected that many Slovenians will be indicted or even investigated by the office of the prosecutor of the International Tribunal, nor are any serious conflicts of jurisdiction between the Tribunal and the courts of Slovenia anticipated. Armed conflict in the context of the breakup of Yugoslavia was of relatively short duration in Slovenia, and the number of casualties was low. (In connection with these events, criminal proceedings against some members of the armed forces of the former Yugoslavia have been instituted in the Slovenian courts, but final judgments have not yet been rendered.) However, it is possible that some citizens of Slovenia may be indicted or that foreigners may be apprehended in Slovenia or transported through its territory who did participate in criminal offenses that fall under the jurisdiction of the International Tribunal. For this reason, it is useful to survey differences between the rules that will be applied by the Tribunal and the legal order of Slovenia and examine potential difficulties that will have to be resolved.

LEGAL EFFECT OF SECURITY RESOLUTION 827 AND OTHER APPLICABLE INSTRUMENTS

The Republic of Slovenia became a member of the United Nations in May 1992 and is therefore bound by the principles set out in article 2 of the UN Charter. Among other obligations, it has to "give the United Nations every assistance in any action it takes in accordance with" the Charter (article 2(5)). Under article 25 and chapter VII generally, member states must accept and carry out the decisions of the Security Council. Member states also have an obligation under article 49 mutually to assist one another in carrying out measures adopted by the Security Council.

Security Council Resolution 827 and the Statute of the International Tribunal were unilateral acts on the part of the Council exercising its chapter VII powers. This maneuver avoided a long drawn out process to create a court and, more important, the possibility that a tribunal would not be set up at all. While establishing such an ad hoc court seems well within the Security Council's mandate under chapter VII to maintain or restore international peace and security, a question arises whether the provisions of Resolution 827 and the Statute are directly binding on Slovenia's legal institutions, or whether it is necessary to take affirmative steps to give them legal effect. This question could have been resolved more easily, both under international law and under Slovenian law, if the Tribunal had been established by treaty, notwithstanding that the Tribunal can certainly make a valuable contribution to restoring peace in the region.

Under articles 8 and 153 of the Constitution of Slovenia, all domestic laws and regulations must be harmonized with generally recognized principles of international law and with international treaties that have been ratified by Parliament and published in the *Official Gazette*. In this way, the Constitution acknowledges that generally recognized principles of international law and duly ratified treaties take precedence over domestic legislation. The way in which the Tribunal was established is relevant here since the Constitution does not address the question of the force and authority of unilateral acts by international organs like the Security Council. While Slovenia, as a member of the United Nations, is bound to cooperate with the International Tribunal, it will have to adopt appropriate regulations to carry out its obligations under the Statute and the Tribunal's rules, given this gap in domestic law.

A further question arises whether Slovenia is to render judicial assistance and other forms of cooperation—in particular, extradition—through its criminal justice agencies or through its administrative organs. There is no doubt that judicial proceedings are preferable from the point of view of protecting the rights of the accused. Recourse to administrative organs would, however, be more efficient and more economical. Inasmuch as Slovenia would be acting to comply with its obligations under international law to cooperate with the Tribunal, and not taking some sort of arbitrary, *ultra vires* action, it appears that the legislature could assign this function to the competent administrative bodies in conformity with the domestic legal order and the relevant international instruments (the European Convention on Human Rights, especially articles 5 and 6, and the International Covenant on Civil and Political Rights, especially articles 9 and 14).

DIFFICULTIES RELATING TO EXTRADITION

The most problematic aspect of cooperation with the Tribunal undoubtedly concerns extradition. The Constitution expressly forbids the extradition of Slovenian citizens to a foreign state (article 47). With regard to foreigners present in Slovenia, extradition is permitted under the Constitution only "in those cases that are covered by international agreements binding on Slovenia" (article 47). Articles 524–540 of the Code of Criminal Procedure set out the legal conditions that must be met in order to grant an extradition request of a person who "is not a citizen" (article 525). By their terms these provisions address the question of extradition to another *state*. The Constitution is silent on the question of extradition at the request of a nonstate entity such as the Tribunal, and it is silent in general about how to reconcile conflicts between constitutional provisions and international legal requirements.

There is an additional complication because the Statute of the Tribunal and its Rules of Procedure and Evidence refer to the "surrender" of accused persons, whereas the Slovenian Constitution and the Code refer to "extradition." While there does not seem to be any substantive difference between the two mechanisms, it may pose some difficulty in interpreting the constitutional provision governing extradition and the relevant provisions of the Code of Criminal Procedure. Further questions, discussed below, arise with respect to the nexus between extradition and domestic legal protections against double jeopardy and other procedural constraints.

OFFENSES COMMITTED BY YUGOSLAVIAN ARMED FORCES PRIOR TO SLOVENIA'S RECOGNITION AS A SOVEREIGN STATE

Immediately after Slovenia's declaration of independence but before its recognition by the international community as a sovereign state, the armed forces of the former Yugoslavia attempted, under orders from the presidency, to seize control of all strategic points (borders, airports, major traffic routes, and so on). As a result, armed confrontations occurred between Yugoslavian and Slovenian military forces. At the same time, the Yugoslav army used airpower, armored units, and heavy artillery against civilians and civil targets. The question is whether the International Tribunal will consider these acts on the part of the Yugoslav army to have occurred in a situation that comes within the scope of common articles 2 or 3 of the Geneva Conventions. This determination is relevant with respect to the applicability of Additional Protocols I and II to the Conventions, assuming that they are ultimately read into the Statute, as some international law experts have proposed. These instruments confer a different set of protections on the victims of international and noninternational armed conflicts, respectively.

CRIMINAL LAW ISSUES

Under article 15 of the Statute, the Tribunal has authority to promulgate rules of procedure and evidence but not substantive rules of criminal law. The Tribunal's Rules of Procedure and Evidence apparently contemplate that generally recognized principles of substantive criminal law will apply: rule 67, for instance, describes the procedure to be followed where the defense intends to interpose an alibi or "any special defence, including . . . diminished or lack of mental responsibility"; rule 73 discusses preliminary motions raising such claims as lack of jurisdiction, defects in the form of the indictment, and inadmissibility of evidence. The Statute itself addresses preparation and attempt, instigation and complicity, lack of official immunity, respondeat superior, and lack of a defense based on following orders (article 7), as well as certain sentencing questions (article 24). Nonetheless, considerable uncertainty remains about such issues as intent, defenses like self-defense, necessity, and mistake of fact or law, inchoate crimes, minimum and maximum sentences, liability of juveniles, rehabilitation, and amnesty.

In this connection, it is important to point out that the principle of legality, *nullum crimen sine lege,* is a requirement of the Constitution of Slovenia. According to this principle, no punishment may be imposed for conduct that was not prohibited by positive law at the time of its commission and for which a penalty was not prescribed. The Security Council has attempted to respect this universally recognized principle in defining the subject-matter jurisdiction of the Tribunal in its Statute. As the *Report of the Secretary-General pursuant to Paragraph 2 of Security Council Resolution 808 (1993)* explains:

> 34. [T]he application of the principle *nullum crimen sine lege* requires that the international tribunal should apply rules of

international humanitarian law which are beyond any doubt part of customary law so that the problem of adherence of some but not all States to specific conventions does not arise. This would appear to be particularly important in the context of an international tribunal prosecuting persons responsible for serious violations of international humanitarian law.

35. The part of conventional international humanitarian law which has beyond doubt become part of international customary law is the law applicable in armed conflict as embodied in: the Geneva Conventions of 12 August 1949 for the Protection of War Victims; the Hague Convention (IV) Respecting the Laws and Customs of War on Land and the Regulations annexed thereto of 18 October 1907; the Convention on the Prevention and Punishment of the Crime of Genocide of 9 December 1948; and the Charter of the International Military Tribunal of 8 August 1945.

In domestic legal systems, criminal proscriptions and penalties typically are embodied in a code. In international law, one looks instead to treaties, generally recognized principles of law, and customary law. These sources must precisely define the targeted offense or offenses *(lex certa)*, with no analogy admissible, and set out minimum and maximum sentences. The Statute falls short in this regard.

In particular, articles 3 and 5 are not an exhaustive listing of prohibited and punishable conduct. Article 3 enumerates specific violations of the laws or customs of war but expressly states that such "violations shall include, but not be limited to" the enumerated acts. Article 5 includes a list of crimes against humanity but also provides for the prosecution of "other inhumane acts." While analogy *inter legem* is not forbidden outright in criminal law and cannot be entirely avoided, it is nevertheless undesirable because it "softens" the principle of *lex certa*, whereby no conduct constitutes an offense unless precisely defined by law.

The Statute also appears to violate the principle of *nullum crimen sine lege* because it fails to specify penalty ranges. Instead, "[i]n determining the terms of imprisonment, the Trial Chambers shall have recourse to the general practice regarding prison sentences in the courts of the former Yugoslavia" (article 24). Unfortunately, the reference to "the general practice regarding prison sentences in the courts of the former Yugoslavia" is not unambiguous: does this direct the Tribunal exclusively to consult judgments by the courts in similar cases, or is the Tribunal also to take account of articles 38, 41, 42, 43, and 48 of the Criminal Code of the former Yugoslavia, which deal generally with sentencing issues (minimum and maximum prison terms, aggravating and extenuating circumstances, and so on). The Rules of Procedure and Evidence provide for a maximum penalty of life imprisonment (rule 101) but otherwise retain the wide discretion in sentencing embodied in article 24 of the Statute of the Tribunal.

Other problems remain. For example, the Statute fails to address the special situation of persons who commit crimes as juveniles, although many domestic legal systems prosecute and punish juvenile offenders separately from adults. Another question arises with respect to illegally obtained property. Article 24(3) of the Statute provides that "[i]n addition to imprisonment, the Trial Chambers may order the return of any property and proceeds acquired by criminal conduct, including by means of duress, to their rightful owners." In contemplating only restitution to the owners of property, this provision fails to go far enough in vindicating victims' property rights, and it fails completely to address the question of forfeiture if the property and/or proceeds cannot be returned to the victim.

PROCEDURAL ISSUES

Article 15 of the Statute provides that "[t]he judges of the International Tribunal shall adopt rules of procedure and evidence for the conduct of the pre-trial phase of the proceedings, trials and appeals, the admission of evidence, the protection of victims and witnesses and other appropriate matters." A question of principle may be raised here as to whether it is appropriate to delegate rulemaking authority to the same body, namely, the judicial organ of the Tribunal, that must apply these rules. Although this sort of delegation may be typical in common law countries, it is not generally practiced in continental legal systems.

Personal jurisdiction of the International Tribunal is closely related to the principle of *non bis in idem*, raising yet another concern for Slovenia. Article 31 of the Constitution of Slovenia includes protection from double jeopardy:

> No person shall be sentenced or punished, or face sentence or punishment, twice for the same criminal act where the first proceeding was legally halted or where the charge or charges arising from such criminal act against the person was or were dismissed in the first proceedings, or where the person was acquitted or was convicted in the first proceedings.

Criminal legislation in Slovenia grounds jurisdiction over persons primarily in the principle of territoriality, giving domestic courts competence in respect of crimes committed by anyone in the territory of Slovenia. In such cases prosecuted by domestic courts, the principle of *non bis in idem* clearly applies. Moreover, the Code of Criminal Procedure prohibits extradition of foreigners in cases where the accused has already been tried by a domestic court or criminal proceedings are pending against him or her (article 525). However, if an offender has been tried and convicted abroad for an offense committed in Slovenian territory, criminal proceedings can be instituted in Slovenia provided the conditions set out in article 108 of the Criminal Code are satisfied. In such cases, the constitutional protection against double jeopardy does not seem to apply. These aspects of Slovenian law pose some difficulties in light of the Tribunal's Statute and will have to be addressed by appropriate domestic measures.

Article 10(1) of the Statute provides that "[n]o person shall be tried before a national court for acts constituting serious violations of international humanitarian law under the present Statute, for which he or she has already been tried by the International Tribunal." Assuming that trial by the Tribunal is treated as equivalent to trial by a foreign court, this provision seems to run up against the availability of domestic criminal proceedings for crimes committed in Slovenia but prosecuted abroad as contemplated by the Criminal Code.

Article 10(2) of the Statute goes on to permit

> [a] person who has been tried by a national court for acts constituting serious violations of international humanitarian law [to] be subsequently tried by the International Tribunal . . . if:
>
>> (a) the act for which he or she was tried was characterized as an ordinary crime; or
>> (b) the national court proceedings were not impartial or independent, were designed to shield the accused from international criminal responsibility, or the case was not diligently prosecuted.

Although article 10(2) in principle provides reasonable limits on retrial by the Tribunal, it conflicts with Slovenia's constitutional protection from double jeopardy and the restriction on extradition in the Code of Criminal Procedure that were noted above. Moreover, it may be difficult as a practical matter to determine whether the conditions identified in article 10(2)(b) have been satisfied. Slovenia will therefore have to adopt a special regulation on implementation of the Statute that permits extradition of an accused for retrial before the International Tribunal.

Another difficulty arises in the case of citizens of Slovenia who commit crimes abroad (which would include the territory of other former Yugoslav republics) and of foreigners who commit crimes abroad against Slovenian citizens. Under the Criminal Code, a domestic prosecution can be undertaken if the accused has not served the full sentence imposed by a foreign court for such crimes. Proceedings cannot be instituted in Slovenia, however, if a foreign court has pronounced a judgment of acquittal in this type of case. These provisions of the Criminal Code of the former Yugoslavia would seem to conflict with the protection against double jeopardy in the new Slovenian Constitution and with article 10(1) of the Statute if the International Tribunal is treated like a foreign court.

There is also no current provision in Slovenia under which domestic courts may defer to the Tribunal as provided in article 9(2) of the Statute. It will be necessary, therefore, to adopt appropriate measures to implement this provision as well.

The role of the prosecutor as set out in articles 16 and 18 of the

Statute raises further concerns. Under both the Statute and the relevant Rules of Procedure and Evidence (most important in this regard are rules 37, 39–40, and 47–51), the prosecutor has full authority over investigations and pretrial proceedings. According to article 18(2), the prosecutor "shall have the power to question suspects, victims and witnesses, to collect evidence and to conduct on-site investigations." Under article 18(4), "[u]pon a determination that a *prima facie* case exists, the Prosecutor shall prepare an indictment containing a concise statement of the facts and the crime or crimes with which the accused is charged under the Statute. The indictment shall be transmitted to a judge of the Trial Chamber." Such powers in the prosecutor are not in accordance with Slovenian criminal procedure. Under article 158 of the Code of Criminal Procedure, the prosecutor orders investigations while the investigating magistrate carries them out. That is, the public prosecutor can only propose questioning and other forms of investigation, suggest what evidence to collect, and what measures to take in order to secure the presence of suspects (including pretrial detention) and other persons. It appears, then, that a special regulation on the implementation of the Statute will have to be adopted to permit the Tribunal's prosecutor to carry out functions normally carried out by an investigating magistrate in Slovenia.

In connection with the prosecutor's broad investigatory powers under the Statute and the rules, questions arise about the admissibility of certain types of evidence where Slovenian law may limit search and seizure; examples include bank accounts, dwellings and persons, documents and other physical objects that are not in a suspect's possession, exhumation, and autopsy. The Rules of Procedure and Evidence provide expressly that the Tribunal "shall not be bound by national rules of evidence" (rule 89(A)), but leave open the door, in cases not specifically addressed, to applying "rules of evidence which will best favour a fair determination of the matter" and "are consonant with the spirit of the Statute and the general principles of law" (rule 89(B)). It is not clear how the Tribunal is to decide whether Slovenian restrictions relating to ephemeral evidence or evidence protected by confidentiality, privacy, and so forth may come into play under the criteria laid out in rule 89(B).

Nor is it clear under the Statute that the accused can make preliminary motions to challenge the admissibility of evidence, jurisdiction, or the indictment. While rule 73 (providing for preliminary motions by the accused to object to jurisdiction, the form of the indictment, the admissibility of evidence, the joinder of counts or of trials, or the denial of a request for assignment of counsel) appears now largely to have filled this gap, in conformity with article 9 of the International Covenant on Civil and Political Rights, it is by no means evident that accused persons will be able, as also contemplated by article 9 of the covenant, to seek compensation from the Tribunal for unlawful arrest and imprisonment.

With respect to the rights of the accused, as embodied in the Statute (article 21) and in the Tribunal's Rules of Procedure and Evidence (parts 5–6), there is no conflict with domestic guarantees of a fair trial. At the same time, however, Slovenian law makes no provision for the conduct of in camera proceedings or the protection of victims' and witnesses' identity, as provided in article 22 of the Statute and in rules 75 and 79.

Another problem concerns the availability of review proceedings to the prosecutor under article 26 of the Statute (rule 119 elaborates upon but does essentially alter the right of review):

> Where a new fact has been discovered which was not known at the time of the proceedings before the Trial Chambers or the Appeals Chamber and which could have been a decisive factor in reaching the decision, the convicted person or the Prosecutor may submit to the International Tribunal an application for review of the judgement.

The prosecutor's ability to request review appears to conflict with the prohibition on double jeopardy set out in both the Constitution and the draft Slovenian Code of Criminal Procedure (later codified in article 372(3)). Thus, measures regarding implementation of the Statute will have to provide expressly for Slovenia's cooperation in such proceedings.

RENDERING ASSISTANCE

Security Council Resolution 827 and the Statute of the Tribunal enjoin states to cooperate in the investigation, arrest, and surrender of suspects and to provide other forms of judicial assistance (article 29). Article 18(2) authorizes the prosecutor to "seek the assistance of the State authorities concerned" with regard to questioning suspects, victims, and witnesses; collecting evidence; and carrying out on-site investigations. Rule 39(iii) is to similar effect. Rule 40 provides that in cases of urgency, the prosecutor may "request any State (i) to arrest a suspect provisionally; (ii) to seize physical evidence; and (iii) to take all necessary measures to prevent the escape of a suspect or an accused, injury to or intimidation of a victim or witness, or the destruction of evidence." Other rules deal with the execution of arrest warrants (rules 55–57, 59), extradition (rule 58), restitution of illegally obtained property (rules 105–106), and related matters, but the way in which cooperation is to be effected between local authorities and the Tribunal remains unclear. As a general matter, the cognate provisions of the Code of Criminal Procedure of the Republic of Slovenia, *de lege lata* and *de lege ferenda*, would appear to permit cooperation with the International Tribunal because they do not refer to a foreign state and its organs but rather to foreign organs in general, which can be understood to encompass the International Tribunal and its components. Nonetheless, the medium of cooperation could range from diplomatic channels, to direct communication between the Tribunal and domestic criminal justice or administrative agencies, to reliance on Interpol as an intermediary.

In domestic criminal proceedings in Slovenia, arrest and pretrial detention are available only for suspects. In exceptional circumstances, an eyewitness at the scene of crime may be detained until the arrival of the investigating magistrate but only for a maximum of six hours. Other than suspects, persons may not be taken into custody—even if upon being duly summoned they fail to appear in court without a valid justification. In such cases, the person may be forcibly brought before the court but the sole remedy is a fine. These provisions, then, do not permit the detention of victims or witnesses who might be needed to testify before the International Tribunal.

With respect to the extradition of suspects, there are constitutional problems in the case of citizens, noted earlier, as well as procedural difficulties in the case of noncitizens. In regard to the latter, the Code of Criminal Procedure (article 526) provides that the extradition of an accused may be initiated exclusively upon the request of a foreign state; that is, there is no provision for handling requests from a foreign organ like the Tribunal. Therefore, domestic law will need to be brought into conformity with Slovenia's extradition obligations under both the Statute and the Rules of Procedure and Evidence.

Arrest as an incident to the extradition of a foreigner who has committed a crime is permitted in Slovenia in accordance with article 528 of the Code of Criminal Procedure. Under this provision, the police are authorized in urgent cases where there is a danger that the foreigner will flee, and upon the request of a competent foreign organ, to make an arrest and bring the suspect before an investigating magistrate, who can order pretrial detention. While normally the investigating magistrate has additional measures at his disposal for securing the defendant's presence, it is uncertain whether a domestic court could authorize such other measures if the Tribunal had already issued a warrant for arrest and an accompanying extradition request. Moreover, although the Code of Criminal Procedure (article 525) specifies a series of prerequisites to the extradition of a foreigner, since it does not set out a procedure for responding to an extradition request from an international organ like the Tribunal, it is unclear that a domestic court would have jurisdiction to determine whether the necessary prerequisites had been satisfied or to hear a claim that a decision to permit extradition had been improvidently granted. To the extent that national legislation or extradition treaties pose a "legal impediment to the surrender or transfer of the accused to the Tribunal," to quote rule 58 of the Tribunal's Rules of Procedure and Evidence, such obstacles should be removed by a special regulation on implementation of the Statute.

ENFORCEMENT OF SENTENCES

Article 27 of the Statute provides that

> [i]mprisonment shall be served in a State designated by the International Tribunal from a list of States which have indicated to the Security Council their willingness to accept convicted persons. Such imprisonment shall be in accordance with the applicable law of the State concerned, subject to the supervision of the International Tribunal.

Slovenia's draft Code of Criminal Procedure permits enforcement of criminal sentences imposed by a foreign court in accordance with the relevant bilateral or multilateral prisoner transfer treaty provided the local court conforms the sanction to domestic penalties. Although, as noted earlier, sentencing by the Tribunal is not regulated by international treaty but by the Statute and the Rules of Procedure and Evidence, the obligation on Slovenia under the UN Charter (especially articles 25 and 48) to cooperate with the Tribunal; the unavailability of the death penalty under the Statute (article 24(1)), as under Slovenian law; and the conformity of sentences under article 24 of the Statute generally to sentencing under the law of the former Yugoslavia should permit Slovenia, if it offers to enforce judgments handed down by the Tribunal, to carry them out without conflict with domestic law. This issue is largely theoretical, however, since the *Report of the Secretary-General* (paragraph 121) appears to rule out the enforcement of sentences in states located in the territory of the former Yugoslavia "given the nature of the crimes in question and the international character of the tribunal."

BIBLIOGRAPHY

Affirmation of the Principles of International Law Recognized by the Charter of the Nuremberg Tribunal, G.A. Res. 95 (I), U.N. Doc. A/64/Add.1, at 188 (1946)

Agreement for the Prosecution and Punishment of the Major War Criminals of the European Axis, Aug. 8, 1945, 82 U.N.T.S. 279

Bassiouni, M. Cherif. *Draft Statute—International Tribunal.* Association Internationale de Droit Pénal, Nouvelles Études Penales No. 10, 2d ed. 1993

————, ed. *Commentaries on the International Law Commission's 1991 Draft Code of Crimes against the Peace and Security of Mankind.* Association Internationale de Droit Pénal, Nouvelles Études Penales No. 11, 1993

Bavcon, Ljubo et al. *Kazenski zakon SFR Jugoslavije s pojasnili, sodno prakso in literaturo [Criminal Code of the Socialist Federal Republic of Yugoslavia, with commentary, judicial practice, and literature*]. Ljubljana, CZ Uradni list SR Slovenije, 1984

Charter of the International Military Tribunal at Nuremberg, Aug. 8, 1945, 82 U.N.T.S. 284

Convention on the Prevention and Punishment of the Crime of Genocide, *adopted* Dec. 9, 1948, 78 U.N.T.S. 277

European Convention for the Protection of Human Rights and Fundamental Freedoms, *opened for signature* Nov. 4, 1950, Europ. T.S. 5

Geneva Convention for the Amelioration of the Condition of the Wounded and Sick in Armed Forces in the Field (Geneva Convention I), *adopted* Aug. 12, 1949, 75 U.N.T.S. 31

Geneva Convention for the Amelioration of the Condition of Wounded, Sick, and Shipwrecked Members of Armed Forces at Sea (Geneva Convention II), *adopted* Aug. 12, 1949, 75 U.N.T.S. 85

Geneva Convention Relative to the Treatment of Prisoners of War (Geneva Convention III), *adopted* Aug. 12, 1949, 75 U.N.T.S. 135

Geneva Convention Relative to the Protection of Civilian Persons in Time of War (Geneva Convention IV), *adopted* Aug. 12, 1949, 75 U.N.T.S. 287

Hague Convention (IV) Respecting the Laws and Customs of War on Land, and Annex to the Convention (Regulations Respecting the Laws and Customs of War on Land), Oct. 18, 1907, 205 Consol. T.S. 227, *reprinted in Documents on the Laws of War* 44 (Adam Roberts & Richard Guelff eds., 2d ed. 1989)

International Covenant on Civil and Political Rights, *adopted* Dec. 19, 1966, 999 U.N.T.S. 171

International Tribunal for the Prosecution of Persons Responsible for Serious Violations of International Humanitarian Law Committed in the Territory of the Former Yugoslavia since 1991. Rules of Procedure and Evidence, U.N. Doc. IT/32 (1994), *amended by* U.N. Doc. IT/32/Rev.1 (1994), U.N.

Doc. IT/32/Rev.2 (1994), U.N. Doc. IT/32/Rev.3 (1995), *reprinted in* appendix C of this issue of *Criminal Law Forum*. *(Editor's note:* this article is based on U.N. Doc. IT/Rev.1.)

Kazenski zakon SFR Jugoslavija in kazenski zakon SR Slovenije [Criminal Code of the Socialist Federal Republic of Yugoslavia and Criminal Code of the Socialist Republic of Slovenia]. Ljubljana, CZ Uradni list SR Slovenije, 1989

Predlog kazenskega zakonika Republike Slovenije—EPA 290—druga obravnava [Draft Criminal Code of the Republic of Slovenia—Second Reading]. Porocevalec 20/1994/8, §§ 2–57

Predlog zakona o kazenskem postopku—EPA 287—druga obravnava [Draft Code of Criminal Procedure—Second Reading]. Porocevalec 20/1994/8, §§ 73–141

Protocol Additional to the Geneva Conventions of 12 August 1949, and Relating to the Protection of Victims of International Armed Conflicts (Additional Protocol I), *adopted* June 8, 1977, 1125 U.N.T.S. 3 (entered into force Dec. 7, 1978)

Protocol Additional to the Geneva Conventions of 12 August 1949, and Relating to the Protection of Victims of Non-international Armed Conflicts (Additional Protocol II), *adopted* June 8, 1977, 1125 U.N.T.S. 609 (entered into force Dec. 7, 1978)

Report of the Secretary-General pursuant to Paragraph 2 of Security Council Resolution 808 (1993), U.N. Doc. S/25704 & Add.1 (1993), *reprinted in* appendix B of this issue of *Criminal Law Forum* and *in* 32 I.L.M. 1163

S.C. Res. 827, U.N. SCOR, 48th Year, 3217th mtg. at 1, U.N. Doc. S/RES/827 (1993), *reprinted in* appendix A of this issue of *Criminal Law Forum* and *in* 32 I.L.M. 1203

Statute of the International Tribunal (set out as an annex to *Report of the Secretary-General, supra), reprinted in* appendix B of this issue of *Criminal Law Forum* and *in* 32 I.L.M. 1192

United Nations Charter, June 26, 1945; *amended* Dec. 17, 1963; Dec. 20, 1965; Dec. 20, 1971

Ustava Republike Slovenije [Constitution of the Republic of Slovenia]. Ljubljana, CZ Uradni list Republike Slovenije, 1992

Zakon o kazenskem postopku [Code of Criminal Procedure]. Ljubljana, CZ Uradni list SR Slovenije, 1991

9
Rape and Other Forms of Sexual Assault in the Armed Conflict in the Former Yugoslavia: Legal, Procedural, and Evidentiary Issues[*]

C.P.M. Cleiren[**] *and*
M.E.M. Tijssen[***]

INTRODUCTION

Rape and other forms of sexual assault have always been a part of warfare,[1] but never before has such attention been given to these crimes as at present, especially with regard to the atrocities alleged to

---

[*] *Editor's note:* research for this article was updated through December 31, 1994. As this article went to press, revisions reflecting a few of the amendments made in January 1995 to the Tribunal's Rules of Procedure and Evidence were added.

[**] Professor of Criminal Law and Criminal Procedure, and Head, Department of Criminal Law and Criminology, Erasmus University of Rotterdam; Ad Hoc Judge, Court of Appeal, Rotterdam, Netherlands; J.D., University of Nijmegen 1978; Ph.D., University of Leiden 1989. The author was a member of the Commission of Experts Established pursuant to Security Council Resolution 780 (1992).

[***] Staff member, Bureau HALT (government diversion program for juvenile delinquents), the Hague; Assistant to Menno Kamminga, Professor of Public International Law, Erasmus University of Rotterdam, Rotterdam, Netherlands; J.D., Erasmus University of Rotterdam 1990.

[1] For general information on rape and other forms of sexual assault in times of armed conflict, see Susan Brownmiller, *Against Our Will: Men, Women, and Rape* (1975); Theodor Meron, *Henry's Wars and Shakespeare's Laws: Perspectives on the Law of War in the Later Middle Ages* (1993).

have been committed in the war in the former Yugoslavia. A multitude of rape and sexual assault cases have been reported in this conflict. Several sources have published detailed information with regard to alleged atrocities and their estimated number.[2] The *Final Report of the Commission of Experts Established pursuant to Security Council Resolution 708 (1992)*[3] also provides extensive factual documentation of rape and sexual assault cases and the circumstances under which such crimes have allegedly been committed.[4]

This study is concerned with the question of whether, and under what circumstances, it will be possible successfully to prosecute and convict perpetrators of rape and other types of sexual assault. It is emphasized that this effort should take place in full compliance with due process requirements. For purposes of this study, we have chosen to focus on the jurisdiction of the International Tribunal for the Prosecution of Persons Responsible for Serious Violations of International Humanitarian Law Committed in the Territory of the Former Yugoslavia since 1991, established by the Security Council in 1993.[5]

---

[2]   *E.g.,* CSCE Rapporteurs (Corell–Turk–Thune), Moscow Human Dimension Mechanism to Bosnia, Herzegovina, and Croatia, *Proposal for an International War Crimes Tribunal for the Former Yugoslavia* (1993); Letter from the Permanent Representative of Sweden to the Secretary-General, Feb. 18, 1993, U.N. Doc. S/25307 (1993), annexing a summary of this report and the text of a decision by CSCE participating states on the report; Amnesty International, *Bosnia–Herzegovina: Rape and Sexual Abuse by Armed Forces* (1993); Helsinki Watch, *War Crimes in Bosnia–Herzegovina* (1992); Theodor Meron, Editorial Comment, *Rape as a Crime under International Humanitarian Law*, 87 Am. J. Int'l L. 425 & n.6 (1993).

[3]   Letter from the Secretary-General to the President of the Security Council, May 24, 1994, U.N. Doc. S/1994/674 (1994), transmitting *Final Report of the Commission of Experts Established pursuant to Security Council Resolution 780 (1992)*, available in U.N. Gopher\Current Information\Secretary-General's Reports [hereinafter *Final Report*].

[4]   The Commission of Experts was set up by S.C. Res. 780, U.N. SCOR, 47th Year, 1992 S.C. Res. & Dec. at 36, U.N. Doc. S/INF/48 (1992), *reprinted in* appendix A of this issue of *Criminal Law Forum*.

[5]   The Security Council set up the International Tribunal through S.C. Res. 808, U.N. SCOR, 48th Year, 3175th mtg. at 1, U.N. Doc. S/RES/808 (1993), *reprinted in* appendix A of this issue of *Criminal Law Forum* and *available in* U.N. Gopher\Documents\Security Council Resolutions; S.C. Res. 827, U.N. SCOR, 48th Year, 3217th mtg. at 1, U.N. Doc. S/RES/827 (1993), *reprinted in* appendix A of this issue

Both the Statute of the International Tribunal and the accompanying commentary by the UN Secretary-General, set out in the *Report of the Secretary-General pursuant to Paragraph 2 of Security Council Resolution 808 (1993)*,[6] contemplate jurisdiction over rape and other sex crimes.

Article 5 of the Tribunal's Statute, in important respects following the Charter of the International Military Tribunal at Nuremberg, expressly confers jurisdiction over rape under the heading of "crimes against humanity."[7] Jurisdiction, at least over cases of rape (if not also other forms of sexual assault), may be grounded as well in article 2 of the Statute as "grave breaches of the Geneva Conventions of 1949";[8] article 3 as "violations of the laws or customs of war";[9] and article 4 as "genocide."[10] The Tribunal's jurisdiction under the Statute derives both from "international customary law which is not laid down in conventions" and from the "part of conventional international humanitarian law which has beyond doubt become part of international customary law."[11]

---

of *Criminal Law Forum* and *in* 32 I.L.M. 1203. In this connection, see *Report of the Secretary-General pursuant to Paragraph 2 of Security Council Resolution 808 (1993)*, U.N. Doc. S/25704 & Add.1 (1993), *reprinted in* appendix B of this issue of *Criminal Law Forum* and *in* 32 I.L.M. 1163 [hereinafter *Secretary-General's Report*]. The Statute of the International Tribunal is set out as an annex to *Secretary-General's Report, supra*, and is *reprinted in* appendix B of this issue of *Criminal Law Forum* and *in* 32 I.L.M. 1192 [hereinafter Statute]. For background, see Peter Burns, *The International Criminal Tribunal: The Difficult Union of Principle and Politics*, in this issue of *Criminal Law Forum*.

[6]   *Secretary-General's Report, supra* note 5, ¶¶ 11, 48; Statute, *supra* note 5, art. 5.

[7]   On the Tribunal's jurisdiction over such crimes, see *infra* section entitled "Crimes against Humanity." On the relevant provision of the Nuremberg Charter, see *infra* text accompanying note 20.

[8]   On the Tribunal's jurisdiction over such crimes, see *infra* section entitled "Grave Breaches of the Geneva Conventions of 1949."

[9]   On the Tribunal's jurisdiction over such crimes, see *infra* section entitled "Violations of the Laws or Customs of War."

[10]   On the Tribunal's jurisdiction over such crimes, see *infra* section entitled "Genocide."

[11]   *Secretary-General's Report, supra* note 5, ¶¶ 33, 35. See section *infra* entitled "Violations of the Laws or Customs of War."

The proceedings before the International Tribunal for the Former Yugoslavia offer a historic opportunity to set a precedent for the international prosecution of perpetrators of rape and other types of sexual assault in times of armed conflict—an opportunity that, in turn, may encourage bringing more resources to bear on violence of a sexual nature in everyday life. Such a breakthrough will not easily be realized. Moreover, in order to receive the support of the international community, this opportunity must be pursued with exemplary attention to due process. From this perspective, we survey a series of issues raised by the prosecution of sex crimes within the scope of the Statute of the Tribunal.[12] It should be kept in mind that, for purposes of this study, we are talking about civilian victims,[13] who fall under the protection of the Fourth Geneva Convention.[14] We also want to point out that this study is written from the continental perspective of a civil law–based culture.

SCOPE OF PROTECTION

Crimes of Violence of a Sexual Nature

We start our analysis from the legal point of view that rape and other types of sexual assault should not be regarded as specifically gender-based offenses but as crimes of violence of a sexual nature, although gender should not be disregarded when such crimes are committed against women. If violence is considered to be the determining element, then there is no ground to distinguish between male and female victims, or between adult and child victims. Until now, however, international law

---

[12] For a more technical discussion, see *Final Report*, *supra* note 3, annex II.

[13] While victims of rape and other forms of sexual assault can, of course, be prisoners of war or belligerents, we have chosen to focus on the law concerning civilians, as this category embraces the majority of sexual assault victims in the region of the former Yugoslavia.

[14] Geneva Convention Relative to the Protection of Civilian Persons in Time of War, *adopted* Aug. 12, 1949, 75 U.N.T.S. 287 [hereinafter Geneva Convention IV].

has not paid much attention to sexual assaults on men. This is hardly surprising since homosexuality is a topic not freely talked about in many cultures. But sexual assaults on men both of a homosexual nature and not of a homosexual nature (such as mutilation of genitals) have been reported in the war in the former Yugoslavia. In general, it can be said that customary international humanitarian law does not discriminate on the ground of sex and that, therefore, the law relevant to sexual assaults on women should apply with equal force to men.[15]

Although we endorse the view that violence is the common and signal feature of these crimes, and in that regard they should be treated like other offenses within the competence of the Tribunal (such as murder or torture), the sexual element does distinguish them from other crimes of violence because, besides infringing upon the victim's corporal integrity, sexual assaults of any type also violate the victim's sexual integrity.[16]

Rape versus Other Forms of Sexual Assault

Contrary to the trend in domestic penal codes, the offense of "rape" is not precisely defined in international humanitarian law. We believe that this term may be broadly interpreted to encompass other forms of sexual assault. The Secretary-General's reference in his commentary on the Statute to "rape and other forms of sexual assault, including enforced prostitution,"[17] lends support to this argument. Distinctions with regard to the severity of the crime committed can be reflected in sentencing.

---

[15] See R.J. Cook, *Accountability in International Law for Violations of Women's Rights by Non-state Actors*, in *Reconceiving Reality: Women and International Law* 93, 104–05 (American Society of International Law Studies in Transnational Legal Policy No. 25, Dorinda G. Dallmeyer ed., 1993).

[16] See Vikki Bell, *Beyond the "Thorny Question": Feminism, Foucault, and the Desexualisation of Rape*, 19 Int'l J. Soc. L. 83 (1991); Hannecke Acker & Marijke Rawie, *Seksueel geweld tegen vrouwen en meisjes* 16 (Neth. Ministerie van Sociale Zaken en Werkgelegenheid 1982); *Seksueel geweld: iedere vrouw en ieder meisje kan er mee te maken krijgen* 7 (Heleen de Boer et al. eds., 1988).

[17] *Secretary-General's Report, supra* note 5, ¶ 48.

VIOLENCE AGAINST WOMEN FROM A CHANGING SOCIAL AND LEGAL PERSPECTIVE

Developments in international law that relate to the problem of violence against women reflect a slow but gradual improvement in the position of women in societies worldwide. At the same time, the evolution of international law, and for our purposes humanitarian law, has had a corresponding liberalizing effect on social attitudes. A quick historical look shows a parallel evolution in humanitarian law toward greater concern for the honor and safety of women, and in society away from the view—widespread until the second half of the eighteenth century—that sexual assaults on women were merely contraventions of family honor or even of the property interests of the relevant males! Since that time, rape and other forms of sexual assault against women have tended increasingly to be treated as crimes prohibited per se. For example, nineteenth-century humanitarian law proscribed "[a]ll wanton violence ... against persons in the invaded country ... all rape" (Lieber's Code of 1863) and demanded that "[f]amily honour and rights, the lives of individuals, as well as their religious convictions and practice, must be respected" (Oxford Manual of 1880).[18]

---

[18] Lieber's Code, a comprehensive set of principles governing the conduct of belligerents in enemy territory, was drafted for the Union forces in the U.S. Civil War. This was the first attempt to codify the customary law of warfare, and Lieber's Code became the basis for later efforts at codification on the international level. Francis Lieber, Instructions for the Government of Armies of the United States in the Field, *promulgated* Apr. 24, 1863, art. 44, *reprinted in The Laws of Armed Conflicts* 3 (Dietrich Schindler & Jiri Toman eds., 1988). The Oxford Manual was drafted by Gustave Moynier under the auspices of the Institute of International Law as a model for domestic legislation on the laws and customs of war. Laws of War on Land (Oxford Manual), *adopted* Sept. 9, 1880, art. 49, *reprinted in The Laws of Armed Conflicts, supra*, at 35. A similar provision appears in the Declaration of Brussels, an early draft codification of the laws of war at the international level. Final Protocol and Project of an International Declaration Concerning the Laws and Customs of War, Aug. 27, 1874, art. 38, *reprinted in The Laws of Armed Conflicts, supra*, at 25 (demanding respect for "[f]amily honour and rights, and the lives and property of persons, as well as their religious convictions and their practice").

All these documents were influential in the preparation of both Hague Convention (II) with Respect to the Laws and Customs of War on Land, with Annexed Regu-

This century witnessed the first step in a process leading to the identification of rape as a crime under international law, and specifically as a "crime against humanity":

> Crimes against humanity were first recognized in the Charter and Judgement of the Nurnberg Tribunal, as well as in Law No. 10 of the Control Council for Germany. Crimes against humanity are aimed at any civilian population and are prohibited regardless of whether they are committed in an armed conflict, international or internal in character.[19]

Article 6(c) of the Nuremberg Charter proscribed:

> *Crimes against humanity:* namely, murder, extermination, enslavement, deportation, and other inhumane acts committed against any civilian population, before or during the war, or persecutions on political, racial or religious grounds in execution of or in connection with any crime within the jurisdiction of the Tribunal, whether or not in violation of the domestic law of the country where perpetrated.[20]

---

lations, July 29, 1899, and Hague Convention (IV) Respecting the Laws and Customs of War on Land, with Annexed Regulations, Oct. 18, 1907 [hereinafter Hague Convention IV], *reprinted in parallel columns in The Laws of Armed Conflicts, supra,* at 63.

[19] *Secretary-General's Report, supra* note 5, ¶ 47 (citations omitted).

[20] The International Military Tribunal at Nuremberg was established pursuant to Agreement for the Prosecution and Punishment of the Major War Criminals of the European Axis, Aug. 8, 1945, 82 U.N.T.S. 279. The Charter of the International Military Tribunal at Nuremberg is set out in *id.* at 284 [hereinafter Nuremberg Charter]. The proceedings are reported in the multivolume *Trial of the Major War Criminals before the International Military Tribunal, Nuremberg, 14 October 1945–1 October 1946* (1947–1949). For the judgment, see 22 *id.* at 411 [hereinafter Nuremberg Judgment].

The International Military Tribunal for the Far East was established in Tokyo pursuant to Special Proclamation by the Supreme Commander for the Allied Powers, Establishment of an International Tribunal for the Far East, Jan. 19, 1946, 4 Bevans 20, *reprinted in* 1 Benjamin Ferencz, *Defining International Aggression* 522 (1975). It operated pursuant to Charter of the International Military Tribunal for the Far East, Jan. 19, 1946 *(as amended* Apr. 26, 1946), 4 Bevans 21, *reprinted in* 1 Ferencz, *supra,* at 523.

The enumeration of crimes in article 6(c) of the Nuremberg Charter should be considered exhaustive in form only, not in substance, since this provision incorporates the catchall phrase "and other inhumane acts."[21] Law No. 10 of the Control Council for Germany, which governed proceedings against less senior Axis war criminals who were tried in Germany (1946–1949) by national tribunals established by agreement among the four Allied powers (France, Britain, the United States, and the Soviet Union), expressly defined rape as a crime against humanity:

> *Crimes against Humanity.* Atrocities and offences, including but not limited to murder, extermination, enslavement, deportation, imprisonment, torture, rape, or other inhumane acts committed against any civilian population, or persecutions on political, racial or religious grounds whether or not in violation of the domestic laws of the country where perpetrated.[22]

The proceedings are available on microfilm. *Record of the Proceedings of the International Military Tribunal for the Far East, Tokyo, Japan* (1946–1948) [hereinafter *IMTFE Record of Proceedings*]. Majority and dissenting opinions have been collected in *The Tokyo Judgment: The International Military Tribunal for the Far East, 29 April 1946–12 November 1948* (Bert V.A. Röling & Christiaan Frederik Rüter eds., 1977) [hereinafter *Tokyo Judgment*]. For additional sources, see *infra* note 27.

[21] See Egon Schwelb, *Crimes against Humanity*, 23 Brit. Y.B. Int'l L. 178, 191 (1946).

[22] Allied Control Council Law No. 10, Dec. 20, 1945, art. II(1)(c), in Control Council for Germany, Official Gazette, Jan. 31, 1946, at 50, *reprinted in Documents on Prisoners of War* 304 (Naval War College International Law Studies Vol. 60, Howard S. Levie ed., 1979) (including "rape" under the heading of crimes against humanity as one of the "atrocities and offences"). On the nexus between this law and the Nuremberg Charter, see Frank C. Newman, *United Nations Human Rights Covenants and the United States Government: Diluted Promises, Foreseeable Futures*, 42 DePaul L. Rev. 1241, 1250–51 (1993); Diane F. Orentlicher, *Settling Accounts: The Duty to Prosecute Human Rights Violations of a Prior Regime*, 100 Yale L.J. 2537, 2587–90 (1991).

The proceedings under Control Council Law No. 10 are reported in the multivolume *Trials of War Criminals before the Nuernberg Military Tribunals under Control Council Law No. 10, Nuernberg, October 1946–April 1949* (1949–1953) [hereinafter *Trials of War Criminals*]. As with Control Council Law No. 10, the International Military Tribunal for the Far East considered rape a war crime. 2 *Tokyo Judgment*,

Moreover, unlike the Nuremberg Charter, Control Council Law No. 10 did *not* limit the category of crimes against humanity to offenses committed "in execution of or in connection with any [other] crime within the jurisdiction" of the tribunal. While it may be debated whether Control Council Law No. 10 itself constitutes customary international law, it surely may be read in conjunction with the Nuremberg Charter in support of a liberal construction of article 6(c). The express inclusion of rape as a crime against humanity (and its delinkage from other crimes) in article 5 of the Statute of the International Tribunal for the Former Yugoslavia may be viewed as the culmination of this progressive tendency in international humanitarian law.

The social conditions behind the evolution of international humanitarian law in the latter part of this century have been generated in large part by the emergence of feminism and by the growing awareness among physicians, psychiatrists, and psychologists that sexual assault is a very serious crime of violence of a sexual nature, which causes a wide range of harmful effects for the victim, her family, and her community.[23] The Vienna Declaration and Programme of Action, issued at the end of the 1993 UN World Conference on Human Rights, identified violence against women generally, and the specific abuses of sexual harassment and sexual exploitation, as practices incompatible with human dignity. Recommendation 38 asserted that violations of the human rights of women in situations of armed conflict, including murder, systematic rape, sexual slavery, and forced pregnancy, are "violations of the fundamental principles of international human rights and humanitarian law" and require a "particularly effective response."[24] In endorsing the view that gender-based violence is a human rights violation, not an incident of war, the conference delegates took into account

---

supra note 20, at 965, 971–72, 988–89; 1 *id.* at 385. For a discussion, see Meron, *supra* note 2, at 425–26. *See generally infra* section entitled "Aspects of Prosecution."

[23] *See, e.g.,* Ann Wolbert Burgess & Lynda Lytle Holmstrom, *Rape: Victims of Crisis* (1974); Anne E. Goldfeld et al., *The Physical and Psychological Sequelae of Torture: Symptomatology and Diagnosis,* 259 JAMA 2725 (1988); Shana Swiss & Joan E. Giller, *Rape as a Crime of War: A Medical Perspective,* 270 JAMA 612 (1993).

[24] Vienna Declaration and Programme of Action, U.N. Doc. A/CONF.157/24 (pt. I), at 20 (1993), *reprinted in* 32 I.L.M. 1661.

reports of the atrocities allegedly being committed in the former Yugoslavia.[25] This position reflects the growing tendency in international law to treat crimes against humanity as violations of fundamental human rights from which no derogation is allowed[26] and might therefore influence the Tribunal in its interpretation and application of the Statute.

---

[25] *See* Donna J. Sullivan, Current Developments, *Women's Human Rights and the 1993 World Conference on Human Rights,* 88 Am. J. Int'l L. 152, 155–56 (1994).

[26] Rape and other forms of sexual assault can be caught by both conventional and customary law prohibitions on torture or other cruel, inhuman, or degrading treatment and on forced labor or enslavement — offenses that come within Nuremberg Charter, *supra* note 20, art. 6(c); Draft Code of Crimes against the Peace and Security of Mankind art. 21, in *Report of the International Law Commission on Its Forty-third Session,* U.N. GAOR, 46th Sess., Supp. No. 10, at 238, U.N. Doc. A/46/10 (1991) [hereinafter Draft Code]. A selective set of references follows.

With regard to torture, see Universal Declaration of Human Rights art. 5, G.A. Res. 217A (III), U.N. Doc. A/810, at 71 (1948); Geneva Convention IV, *supra* note 14, arts. 3, 27, 32; International Covenant on Civil and Political Rights, *adopted* Dec. 19, 1966, art. 7, 999 U.N.T.S. 171; Convention against Torture and Other Cruel, Inhuman, or Degrading Treatment or Punishment, G.A. Res. 39/46, U.N. GAOR, 39th Sess., Supp. No. 51, at 197, U.N. Doc. A/39/51 (1984) [hereinafter Torture Convention]; *see also* European Convention for the Protection of Human Rights and Fundamental Freedoms, *opened for signature* Nov. 4, 1950, art. 3, Europ. T.S. 5; European Convention for the Prevention of Torture and Inhuman or Degrading Treatment or Punishment, *done* Nov. 26, 1987, Europ. T.S. 126.

With regard to forced labor, see ILO Convention (No. 29) Concerning Forced or Compulsory Labour, *adopted* June 28, 1930, 39 U.N.T.S. 55 *(as amended* 1946); ILO Convention (No. 105) Concerning the Abolition of Forced Labour, *adopted* June 25, 1956, 320 U.N.T.S. 291; International Covenant on Civil and Political Rights, *supra,* art. 8.

With regard to slavery, see Slavery Convention, Sept. 25, 1926, 60 L.N.T.S. 253; Protocol Amending the Slavery Convention of September 25, 1926, *opened for signature* Dec. 7, 1953, 212 U.N.T.S. 17; Supplementary Convention on the Abolition of Slavery, the Slave Trade, and Institutions and Practices Similar to Slavery, *adopted* Sept. 7, 1956, 266 U.N.T.S. 3; Universal Declaration of Human Rights, *supra,* art. 4; International Covenant on Civil and Political Rights, *supra,* art. 8.

For background, see Theodor Meron, *Human Rights and Humanitarian Norms as Customary Law* (1989) [hereinafter Meron, *Human Rights*]; Theodor Meron, Editorial Comment, *War Crimes in Yugoslavia and the Development of International Law,* 88 Am. J. Int'l L. 78 (1994) [hereinafter Meron, *War Crimes in Yugoslavia*]; Sydney L. Goldenberg, *Crimes against Humanity, 1945–1970: A Study in the Making and Unmaking of International Criminal Law,* 10 W. Ont. L. Rev. 1 (1971).

ASPECTS OF PROSECUTION

The history of warfare reveals some rare examples of individuals charged with responsibility for the crime of rape perpetrated by soldiers under their command. One such instance is the Tokyo trials following World War II, which included the "Rape of Nanking" trial and the trial of Admiral Toyoda. The latter was charged, among other things, with "[w]illfully and unlawfully disregarding and failing to discharge his duties by ordering, directing, inciting, causing, permitting, ratifying and failing to prevent Japanese Naval personnel of units and organizations under his command, control and supervision to abuse, mistreat, torture, rape, kill and commit other atrocities."[27]

In general, however, international lawyers have paid scant attention to rape and other types of sexual assault committed in armed conflict, leaving arrest and prosecution to the criminal justice system of the country in which such offenses allegedly have been committed. As a result, very few prosecutions have been undertaken—because the legal systems of states engaged in armed conflict generally function erratically, at best, or because the victorious party often grants amnesty to agents of the defeated state, either due generally to a lack of political will or due specifically to a belief that sexual offenses should be concealed from the public. This creates a bizarre situation: in most countries, drivers are routinely fined for parking cars in the wrong place, whilst perpetrators of violent crimes like rape committed in armed conflict escape sanctions of any sort.[28] The International Tribunal has the potential to begin to correct the traditional neglect of acts of violence of a sexual nature within the framework of international humanitarian law.

---

[27] William H. Parks, *Command Responsibility for War Crimes*, 62 Mil. L. Rev. 1, 69–70 (1973); *see also* Brownmiller, *supra* note 1, at 56–62. For the official transcript of the proceedings in United States v. Soema Toyoda, see *IMTFE Record of Proceedings*, *supra* note 20. The Rape of Nanking trial is reported in 4 UN War Crimes Comm'n, *Law Reports of Trials of War Criminals* 87 (1947). On the International Military Tribunal for the Far East, see Richard H. Minear, *Victors' Justice: The Tokyo War Crimes Trial* (1971); Bert V.A. Röling & Antonio Cassese, *The Tokyo Trial and Beyond* (1993); *see also* sources cited *supra* note 20.

[28] *See* Brownmiller, *supra* note 1, ch. 3.

Nullum Crimen, Nulla Poena sine Lege

While the field of humanitarian law is still in the process of development, the principle of *nullum crimen, nulla poena sine lege* has traditionally been considered an inviolable requirement of international law.[29] It was on the basis of the *nullum crimen* principle that the Statute of the Tribunal was limited to customary law (including conventional law that is "beyond doubt" part of customary law).[30] This raises the question whether the Statute correctly identifies the core humanitarian conventions that have passed unequivocally into customary law: "the Geneva Conventions of 12 August 1949 for the Protection of War Victims; the Hague Convention (IV) Respecting the Laws and Customs of War on Land and the Regulations annexed thereto of 18 October 1907; the Convention on the Prevention and Punishment of the Crime of Genocide of 9 December 1948; and the Charter of the International Military Tribunal of 8 August 1945."[31]

While some of the basic rights codified in the four Geneva Conventions[32] have clearly attained the status of *jus cogens*, Theodor Meron suggests that the conventions *as a whole* should not be regarded as customary international law. He argues that while all "contain a core of principles . . . that express customary law," the "identification of the various provisions as customary or conventional law presents the greatest difficulties," particularly for the Fourth Geneva Convention (which is the most pertinent to this discussion). This means that the customary law status of each provision must be considered separately, although writing more recently Meron has conceded that "[f]or the most part . . . the

---

[29] *Secretary-General's Report, supra* note 5, ¶ 34.

[30] *Id.* ¶¶ 34–35.

[31] *Id.* ¶ 35; these are codified in Statute, *supra* note 5, arts. 2–5.

[32] Geneva Convention IV, *supra* note 14; Geneva Convention for the Amelioration of the Condition of the Wounded and Sick in Armed Forces in the Field, *adopted* Aug. 12, 1949, 75 U.N.T.S. 31 [hereinafter Geneva Convention I]; Geneva Convention for the Amelioration of the Condition of Wounded, Sick, and Shipwrecked Members of Armed Forces at Sea, *adopted* Aug. 12, 1949, 75 U.N.T.S. 85 [hereinafter Geneva Convention II]; Geneva Convention Relative to the Treatment of Prisoners of War, *adopted* Aug. 12, 1949, 75 U.N.T.S. 135 [hereinafter Geneva Convention III].

Fourth Geneva Convention concerns customary law, and . . . even peremptory norms."[33] There appears to be no such doubt about the Genocide Convention. In its landmark advisory opinion on the convention, the International Court of Justice recognized that the principles underlying the convention are declaratory of customary law.[34] Nor is there any question about the customary law status of the Hague Convention (IV)[35] or the Nuremberg Charter.[36]

Additional Protocols I and II to the Geneva Conventions, which date to 1977,[37] have not been applied very often since their ratification.[38] While they are not yet deemed unequivocally to form part of customary

---

[33] *Compare* Meron, *Human Rights, supra* note 26, at 46, *with* Theodor Meron, *The Case for War Crimes Trials in Yugoslavia,* Foreign Aff., Summer 1993, at 122, 129 [hereinafter Meron, *War Crimes Trials*], *and* Jordan J. Paust, *Applicability of International Criminal Laws to Events in the Former Yugoslavia,* 9 Am. U. J. Int'l L. & Pol'y 449, 512 n.43 (1994) ("The nature of most portions of the Geneva Conventions are now viewed as customary law."). *See generally* Meron, *Human Rights, supra,* at 41–62; Theodor Meron, *The Geneva Conventions as Customary Law,* 81 Am. J. Int'l L. 348 (1987).

[34] Reservations to the Convention on the Prevention and Punishment of the Crime of Genocide, 1951 I.C.J. 15, 23 (May 28) (considering Convention on the Prevention and Punishment of the Crime of Genocide, *adopted* Dec. 9, 1948, 78 U.N.T.S. 277 [hereinafter Genocide Convention]). Meron, *Human Rights, supra* note 26, at 20, agrees that Genocide Convention, *supra,* embodies customary law.

[35] Hague Convention IV, *supra* note 18; Nuremberg Judgment, *supra* note 20, at 414; *Secretary-General's Report, supra* note 5, ¶ 42.

[36] *See* Affirmation of the Principles of International Law Recognized by the Charter of the Nuremberg Tribunal, G.A. Res. 95 (I), U.N. Doc. A/64/Add.1, at 188 (1946) [hereinafter Affirmation of Nuremberg Principles].

[37] Protocol Additional to the Geneva Conventions of 12 August 1949, and Relating to the Protection of Victims of International Armed Conflicts, *adopted* June 8, 1977, 1125 U.N.T.S. 3 (entered into force Dec. 7, 1978) [hereinafter Additional Protocol I]; Protocol Additional to the Geneva Conventions of 12 August 1949, and Relating to the Protection of Victims of Non-international Armed Conflicts, *adopted* June 8, 1977, 1125 U.N.T.S. 609 (entered into force Dec. 7, 1978) [hereinafter Additional Protocol II].

[38] According to Meron, *Human Rights, supra* note 26, at 76 & nn.209–210, in the Iran–Iraq conflict both the International Committee of the Red Cross and the parties invoked Additional Protocol I, *supra* note 37.

international law,[39] some provisions nonetheless do codify customary international law and there seems to be growing support for the treatment of many of the remaining provisions as such.[40] Therefore, we will discuss the application of these instruments (insofar as they appear to be declaratory of customary law) to the prosecution of rape and sexual assault.

An additional question may be raised here: must alleged perpetrators of the crime of rape, or other forms of sexual assault, in the former Yugoslavia (or similar armed conflicts) have been aware that they were committing a crime of a universal character, for which they could be prosecuted? We think not. These offenses are prohibited not only by international humanitarian law but also by the penal law of all civilized nations. The former Socialist Federal Republic of Yugoslavia was a party to the Geneva Conventions and actually went beyond these instruments in expressly criminalizing rape in domestic legislation enacted in fulfillment of its obligation under the conventions to sanction grave breaches.[41] This state was also a party to the Genocide Convention and to Additional Protocols I and II to the Geneva Conventions.[42] It is at

---

[39] "While the conventions are now unquestionably part of customary international law and therefore binding on nonparties . . . the status of the protocols is less secure and it is likely that only states that have affirmatively agreed to be bound by them are in fact so bound." Timothy L.H. McCormack & Gerry J. Simpson, *The International Law Commission's Draft Code of Crimes against the Peace and Security of Mankind: An Appraisal of the Substantive Provisions*, 5 Crim. L.F. 1, 37 (1994).

[40] *See* Nico Keijzer, *Internationale berechting van oorlogsmisdrijven in het voormalige Joegoslavië*, Militair Rechterlijk Tijdschrift, Nov.–Dec. 1993, at 62, 66; Meron, *Human Rights*, *supra* note 26, at 62–78; Howard S. Levie, *The 1977 Protocol I and the United States*, 38 St. Louis Univ. L.J. 469 (1994).

[41] 4 *The Geneva Conventions of 12 August 1949: Commentary* 590 n.1, 594 (Jean S. Pictet gen. ed., 1958) (citing Yugoslav Penal Code art. 125, which went beyond Geneva Convention IV, *supra* note 14, art. 147, in criminalizing the following offenses in fulfillment of the obligation under *id.* art. 146 to enact domestic legislation to punish grave breaches: forced change of nationality, forced conversion to another religion, forced prostitution, intimidation and terrorization, collective punishments, illegal detention in a concentration camp, and starving of the population) [hereinafter *Geneva Conventions: Commentary*]. See *infra* note 66 and accompanying text.

[42] Office of Public Information, United Nations, *The Crime of Genocide: A United Nations Convention Aimed at Preventing Destruction of Groups and at Punishing*

least arguable that the new republics arising out of the former Yugoslavia are bound by these international obligations.[43]

Universal Jurisdiction

The International Tribunal was established by the Security Council as an exercise of its authority, under chapter VII of the UN Charter, to maintain or restore international peace and security, and member states are required, in particular by articles 25 and 48 of the Charter, to cooperate with the Tribunal.[44] This duty is elaborated upon in Security Council Resolution 827 and the Statute of the Tribunal, which enjoin member states to cooperate in the investigation, arrest, and surrender of suspects and to render other forms of assistance.[45] Except for Serbia and

---

Those Responsible 4 (1973) [hereinafter *Crime of Genocide*]; Jiri Toman, *Index of the Geneva Conventions for the Protection of War Victims of 12 August 1949*, at 194 (1973).

[43] *See* Vienna Convention on Succession of States in Respect of Treaties, *opened for signature* Aug. 23, 1978, arts. 34–35, U.N. Doc. A/CONF.80/31/Corr.2 (1978), *reprinted in* 17 I.L.M. 1488. Paust, *supra* note 33, at 499–504, concludes that the new states in the region are bound by Yugoslavia's treaty obligations under the UN Charter, the Geneva Conventions, Additional Protocols I and II, the Genocide Convention, the Torture Convention, and other international humanitarian law instruments. To similar effect, see Meron, *War Crimes Trials, supra* note 33, at 129 ("The case for applying the grave breaches provisions to the Yugoslav conflict is strengthened by the fact that all states involved have agreed to honor the obligations of the former Yugoslavia under the Geneva conventions. All [these] states have also accepted the 'Statement of Principles' approved by the London Conference on Yugoslavia [in 1992], concerning compliance with international humanitarian law . . . .").

[44] *See Secretary-General's Report, supra* note 5, ¶¶ 125–126.

[45] In S.C. Res. 827, *supra* note 5, ¶ 4, the Security Council

> *[d]ecide[d]* that all States shall cooperate fully with the International Tribunal and its organs in accordance with the present resolution and the Statute of the International Tribunal and that consequently all States shall take any measures necessary under their domestic law to implement the provisions of the present resolution and the Statute, including the obligation of States to comply with requests for assistance or orders issued by a Trial Chamber under Article 29 of the Statute[.]

Montenegro, the new republics of the former Yugoslavia have been admitted to membership in the United Nations and therefore are bound to comply with these obligations. It is nonetheless instructive to inquire whether the sources of humanitarian law that are incorporated into articles 2–5 of the Statute give independent grounds—namely, universal jurisdiction—to detain and surrender persons alleged to have committed the crimes over which the Tribunal has subject matter jurisdiction. A brief review generally suggests that this is so.

In the context of international armed conflict, universal jurisdiction undoubtedly attaches to grave breaches of the Geneva Conventions, and for our particular purpose the Fourth Geneva Convention,[46] grave breaches of Additional Protocol I,[47] acts in violation

---

Statute, *supra* note 5, art. 29, reiterates the obligation on states to cooperate and sets out a nonexhaustive list of areas in which assistance must be rendered:

1. States shall cooperate with the International Tribunal in the investigation and prosecution of persons accused of committing serious violations of international humanitarian law.

2. States shall comply without undue delay with any request for assistance or an order issued by a Trial Chamber, including, but not limited to:

(a) the identification and location of persons;
(b) the taking of testimony and the production of evidence;
(c) the service of documents;
(d) the arrest or detention of persons;
(e) the surrender or the transfer of the accused to the International Tribunal.

[46] Grave breaches are listed in Geneva Convention I, *supra* note 32, art. 50; Geneva Convention II, *supra* note 32, art. 51; Geneva Convention III, *supra* note 32, art. 130; Geneva Convention IV, *supra* note 14, art. 147. The obligations on states with respect to punishing grave breaches are set out in Geneva Convention I, *supra*, art. 49; Geneva Convention II, *supra*, art. 50; Geneva Convention III, *supra*, art. 129; Geneva Convention IV, *supra*, art. 146.

On the universality of jurisdiction over grave breaches of the Geneva Conventions, see 4 *Geneva Conventions: Commentary, supra* note 41, at 587; Claude Pilloud et al., International Comm. of the Red Cross, *Commentary on the Additional Protocols of 8 June 1977 to the Geneva Conventions of 12 August 1949*, at 975 (Yves Sandoz et al. eds., 1987). For a detailed discussion asserting universal jurisdiction over grave breaches of the Geneva Conventions, war crimes and crimes against humanity,

of the Genocide Convention,[48] and crimes against humanity.[49] The serious nature of these crimes obliges governments to prevent their commission and to prosecute alleged perpetrators thereof.[50] Failing

---

genocide, and certain other infractions of international law, see Kenneth C. Randall, *Universal Jurisdiction under International Law*, 66 Tex. L. Rev. 785, 800–37 (1988).

[47] Additional Protocol I, *supra* note 37, art. 85. Pilloud et al., *supra* note 46, at 973, notes that Additional Protocol I, *supra*, arts. 85–91, "supplements the articles of the Convention relating to the repression of breaches, while extending the application of that system of repression to breaches of the Protocol." In particular, Additional Protocol I supplements the list of grave breaches set out in the Geneva Conventions, and "acts described as grave breaches in the Conventions are grave breaches of the Protocol if they are committed against new categories of persons and objects protected under the Protocol." Pilloud et al., *supra*, at 977. Moreover, "grave breaches of the Conventions and the Protocol are qualified as war crimes." *Id.*

[48] Genocide Convention, *supra* note 34, art. 6 (contemplating the possibility of trial by "such international penal tribunal as may have jurisdiction with respect to those Contracting Parties which shall have accepted its jurisdiction" or by "a competent Tribunal of the State in the territory of which the act was committed"); *Crime of Genocide*, *supra* 42, at 4. Noting that the convention contemplates the possibility of an international tribunal but does not actually set up such a body, Roger S. Clark, *The Influence of the Nuremberg Trial on the Development of International Law*, in *The Nuremberg Trial and International Law* 249, 255–56 (George Ginsburgs & V.N. Kudriavtsev eds., 1990), suggests, to the contrary, that the convention seems to "point in the direction of a denial of universality to be exercised by individual states."

[49] Nuremberg Charter, *supra* note 20, art. 6(c); Draft Code, *supra* note 26, art. 21. The recognition of crimes against humanity as an international crime "signifies that specific mass violations of human rights do not belong any longer to the sphere of domestic jurisdiction. The international community is now legally entitled to intervene in such cases." Röling & Cassese, *supra* note 27, at 56.

[50] In practical terms, this means, for example, that if rape and other sexual offenses constitute a grave breach under the Geneva Conventions, states are required to enact legislation providing for effective penal sanctions and to search out and punish (or extradite) suspected perpetrators. See *supra* note 46; Bert V.A. Röling, *Aspects of the Criminal Responsibility for Violations of the Laws of War*, in *The New Humanitarian Law of Armed Conflict* 199, 211 (Antonio Cassese ed., 1979). With regard to infractions of the Geneva Conventions and Protocols that are not grave breaches, states are required to take measures for their suppression but no duty arises to provide for punishment. Geneva Convention IV, *supra* note 14, art. 146; Additional Protocol I, *supra* note 37, art. 86(1).

appropriate domestic action, the international community may step in to prosecute offenders, notwithstanding considerations of state sovereignty.[51] Moreover, assuming that the offenses of rape and other forms of sexual assault fell outside the scope of these conventional sources but nonetheless could be characterized as war crimes under customary law, universal jurisdiction would arise under the customary law applicable to international armed conflict.[52]

The law relative to noninternational, or internal, armed conflict,[53] however, does not use the term "war crime" and perhaps would not support prosecution as a matter of customary international law under the principle of universal jurisdiction.[54] The states that drafted and adopted Additional Protocol II to the Geneva Conventions were reluctant to recognize the existence of rules of customary international law that govern noninternational conflicts. States still consider such conflicts generally to be governed by national, rather than international, law. It may be that for the prosecution of alleged perpetrators of rape and other sexual assaults, committed in areas where the conflict is considered to be of an internal character, "unless the parties to [the] conflict agree otherwise, the only offences . . . for which universal jurisdiction [would] exist[ ] are 'crimes against humanity' and genocide, which apply irrespective of the conflicts' classification."[55] A similar exception arises where the internal armed conflict is deemed to have the status of a true civil war, or a "belligerency." That is, "common Article 2 of the Geneva Conventions along with all of the general proscriptions and Protocol I thereto . . . in addition to the more general customary law of war" apply to an internal armed conflict if the combatant group

---

[51] *See, e.g.*, 4 *Geneva Conventions: Commentary*, *supra* note 41, at 593 (discussing Geneva Convention IV, *supra* note 14, art. 146(2)).

[52] *See* Röling, *supra* note 50, at 212. For a discussion of Hague Convention IV, *supra* note 18, see *infra* section entitled "Violations of the Laws or Customs of War."

[53] Geneva Conventions I–IV, *supra* notes 14, 32, common art. 3; Additional Protocol II, *supra* note 37.

[54] *See generally* Howard S. Levie, *The Law of Non-international Armed Conflict: Protocol II to the 1949 Geneva Conventions* (1987).

[55] *Final Report*, *supra* note 3, ¶ 42.

meets accepted criteria for insurgent status. These include "(1) sustained use of force; (2) an armed force with a responsible command structure; (3) general control of significant territory; and (4) the semblance of a governmental structure, especially one negotiating at the international level."[56] In general, however, in an internal, rather than international, armed conflict, the legal bases to undertake an international prosecution may be narrower, though this area of law remains unsettled.[57]

Criminal Responsibility

The Statute of the International Tribunal for the Former Yugoslavia is predicated on individual criminal responsibility for both the perpetrators of crimes within the Tribunal's competence and their superiors. Article 7(1) assigns individual criminal responsibility to persons who "planned, instigated, ordered, committed or otherwise aided and abetted in the planning, preparation or execution" of crimes within the competence of the Tribunal. Where "acts referred to in articles 2 to 5 of the present Statute [were] committed by a subordinate," the perpetrator's superior will be personally criminally responsible "if he knew or had reason to know that the subordinate was about to commit such acts or had done so and the superior failed to take the necessary and reasonable measures to prevent such acts or to punish the perpetrators thereof."[58] These provisions, which permit liability to extend up the political and military command structure both for setting policy and for acts of omission, have their legal and historical antecedents in the trials of Axis leaders at Nuremberg and Tokyo following the second world war.[59] This approach

---

[56] Paust, *supra* note 33, at 507, 506 (citations omitted). See *infra* notes 96–98 and accompanying text.

[57] *See* Meron, *War Crimes Trials, supra* note 33, at 128; Theodor Meron, *Draft Model Declaration on Internal Strife*, Int'l Rev. Red Cross, Jan.–Feb. 1988, at 59; Denise Plattner, *The Penal Repression of Violations of International Humanitarian Law Applicable in Non-international Armed Conflicts*, Int'l Rev. Red Cross, Sept.–Oct. 1990, at 409, 414. For further discussion, see *infra* section entitled "Noninternational Conflict."

[58] Statute, *supra* note 5, art. 7(3).

[59] Liability for acts of omission figured, for example, in the following World War II war crimes prosecutions. United States v. Pohl, in 5 *Trials of War Criminals, supra*

to criminal responsibility was subsequently reiterated and approved in a number of important multilateral initiatives.[60]

In the war in the former Yugoslavia, paramilitary activity is very common and very complex. Although under the Third Geneva Convention a resistance force or a guerilla organization cannot be considered an independent party to a conflict, participants in such groups are bound by the Geneva Conventions if their organization can be shown to be related to the state.[61] Given the recognition in international law of the responsibility of government, including political leaders, public officials, and even heads of state, for the prevention and punishment of grave breaches of the Geneva Conventions and Protocols, of war crimes under customary law, and of the offenses prosecuted at Nuremberg and Tokyo,[62] the Statute's express rejection of official immunity as a defense may make it possible (as at Nuremberg and Tokyo) to tie the criminal activities of paramilitary and irregular units to the top levels of government. Under article 7(2) of the Statute, "The official position of any accused person, whether as Head of State or

---

note 22, Case No. 4; United States v. Ohlendorf (Einsatzgruppen Case), in 4 *Trials of War Criminals*, *supra*, Case No. 9; United States v. Soema Toyoda, *discussed in* Parks, *supra* note 27, at 69–73; United States v. Yamashita (1945), in 4 UN War Crimes Comm'n, *supra* note 27, at 1, 34, *aff'd*, 327 U.S. 1 (1946); *see also* Richard L. Lael, *The Yamashita Precedent: War Crimes and Command Responsibility* (1982).

[60]   Affirmation of Nuremberg Principles, *supra* note 36; Genocide Convention, *supra* note 34, art. 4; Convention on the Non-applicability of Statutory Limitations to War Crimes and Crimes against Humanity art. 2, G.A. Res. 2391 (XXIII), U.N. GAOR, 23d Sess., Supp. No. 18, at 40, U.N. Doc. A/7218 (1968); Additional Protocol I, *supra* note 37, art. 86(2); Frits Kalshoven, International Comm. of the Red Cross, *Constraints on the Waging of War* 18–19 (1991); I.A. Lediakh, *The Application of the Nuremberg Principles by Other Military Tribunals and National Courts*, in *The Nuremberg Trial and International Law*, *supra* note 48, at 263, 266–67.

[61]   Geneva Convention III, *supra* note 32, art. 4(A)(2); *see also* Additional Protocol I, *supra* note 37, arts. 43, 50; Pilloud et al., *supra* note 46, at 517.

[62]   *E.g.*, Geneva Convention IV, *supra* note 14, art. 146; Genocide Convention, *supra* note 34, art. 4; Additional Protocol I, *supra* note 37, art. 86(2); Draft Code, *supra* note 26, arts. 21–22. For a discussion, see 4 *Geneva Conventions: Commentary*, *supra* note 41, at 589–96; Cook, *supra* note 15, at 98–99; Kalshoven, *supra* note 60, at 18–19; Röling, *supra* note 50, at 220–27.

Government or as a responsible Government official, shall not relieve such person of criminal responsibility nor mitigate punishment." This provision is particularly important with regard to prosecuting sexual assault in the former Yugoslavia. The systematic manner in which rape and other crimes with a sexual component are alleged to have been committed tends to show that they were a means of implementing the policy of "ethnic cleansing."[63]

SOURCES OF LAW

Grave Breaches of the Geneva Conventions of 1949

Article 2 of the Statute gives the Tribunal "the power to prosecute persons committing or ordering to be committed grave breaches of the Geneva Conventions of 12 August 1949."[64] The grave breaches enumerated in article 2 that are relevant here are the following: "(b) torture or inhuman treatment, including biological experiments; (c) wilfully causing great suffering or serious injury to body or health."

Rape and other forms of sexual assault can be considered to fall into these categories. The International Committee of the Red Cross (ICRC) commentary to articles 146 and 147 of the Fourth Geneva Convention states that inhuman treatment is treatment contrary to article 27 of the Fourth Geneva Convention, which expressly prohibits rape; that inhuman treatment should not be confined to physical injury or injury to health but includes measures that cause "grave injury" to human dignity; and that "[o]ther grave breaches of the same character as

---

[63] Defined as "rendering an area ethnically homogeneous by using force or intimidation to remove persons of given groups from the area." *Final Report*, *supra* note 3, ¶ 129 (quoting *Interim Report*, *infra*, ¶ 55); *see also id.* ¶¶ 128, 237. Letter from the Secretary-General to the President of the Security Council, Feb. 9, 1993, U.N. Doc. S/25274 (1993), transmitting *Interim Report of the Commission of Experts Established pursuant to Security Council Resolution 780 (1992)*.

[64] Each of the conventions identifies a set of "particularly serious violations that qualify as 'grave breaches' or war crimes." *Secretary-General's Report*, *supra* note 5, ¶ 38. See *supra* note 46.

those listed in Article 147 can be easily imagined."[65] The commentary goes on to note that "[t]his was well understood when the Yugoslav Penal Code (Article 125) was adopted": by a law dated February 27, 1951, Yugoslavia provided sanctions against not only all the grave breaches set out in the 1949 Geneva Conventions but also, in the provision relating to war crimes against civilian populations, a "considerably larger" list of punishable offenses that included forced prostitution.[66]

Specifically under article 2(b) of the Tribunal's Statute, the categorization of sexual assault as a grave breach is supported by the 1984 United Nations Convention against Torture and Other Cruel, Inhuman, or Degrading Treatment or Punishment.[67] The convention defines torture, in relevant part, as

> any act by which severe pain or suffering, whether physical or mental, is inflicted on a person for such purposes as . . . punishing him for an act that he or a third person has committed or is suspected of having committed, or intimidating or coercing him or a third person, or for any reason based on discrimination of any kind.[68]

Support for prosecuting rape under article 2(c) of the Statute comes from an ICRC Aide-Mémoire of December 3, 1992, which asserts that the grave breach of "wilfully causing great suffering or serious injury to body or health" (article 147 of the Fourth Geneva Convention) covers rape.[69] In a recent report on Bosnia–Herzegovina, Amnesty International also considers "rape and sexual abuse . . . forms of torture or cruel, inhuman or degrading treatment."[70]

Assuming that sexual assault constitutes a grave breach and thus

---

[65] 4 *Geneva Conventions: Commentary, supra* note 41, at 598, 594.

[66] *Id.* at 594, 590 n.1. See *supra* note 41.

[67] Torture Convention, *supra* note 26.

[68] *Id.* art. 1.

[69] Meron, *supra* note 2, at 426 (citing ICRC Aide-Mémoire).

[70] Amnesty International, *supra* note 2, at 2.

a war crime, it is sufficient for the prosecution to prove a single act, rather than a pattern of conduct.[71] At the same time, it also must be proven that the alleged perpetrator is linked to one side of the armed conflict, acting against neutral citizens or citizens of a belligerent state. This burden may not be particularly significant: in the post–World War II Axis trials, it was established that the alleged perpetrator "need not necessarily be a soldier."[72] However, the situation in the former Yugoslavia is less clear than in World War II, so it remains to be seen whether this requirement will be as readily fulfilled here. Moreover, in general with respect to prosecuting grave breaches, it is necessary to establish that the offenses in question have occurred in the context of an *international* armed conflict.[73] The Tribunal will therefore have to determine on a case-by-case basis whether the context in which the offenses allegedly occurred was international or internal in nature.[74]

Violations of the Law or Customs of War

Article 3 of the Statute gives the Tribunal "the power to prosecute persons violating the laws or customs of war" as set out in the 1907

---

[71] Rhonda Copelon, *Surfacing Gender: Reconceptualizing Crimes against Women in Time of War,* in *Mass Rape: The War against Women in Bosnia–Herzegovina* 4 (Alexandra Stiglmayer ed., 1994). As noted *supra* notes 46–47, grave breaches are identified, inter alia, in Geneva Convention IV, *supra* note 14, art. 147, and Additional Protocol I, *supra* note 37, art. 85. The sole criterion that makes an offense a grave breach is that it must be "committed against persons or property protected by the Conventions." Pilloud et al., *supra* note 46, at 976. Meron, *War Crimes Trials, supra* note 33, at 131 (emphasis added), lists a number of offenses and states that they "would all be covered by war crimes under customary international law and by the grave breaches provisions of the Geneva Conventions. *When committed on a mass scale, such violations would also give rise to charges of crimes against humanity and of genocide* . . . ." The italicized statement implies that crimes do not need to be committed on a mass scale to constitute grave breaches and other war crimes.

[72] *See* Meron, *supra* note 2, at 426 n.19.

[73] "The Geneva Conventions constitute rules of international humanitarian law and provide the core of the customary law applicable in *international armed conflicts.* These Conventions regulate the conduct of war from the humanitarian perspective . . . ." *Secretary-General's Report, supra* note 5, ¶ 37 (emphasis added).

[74] *Final Report, supra* note 3, ¶¶ 42–44.

Hague Convention (IV) Respecting the Laws and Customs of War on Land, and annexed regulations, and as "interpreted and applied" by the Nuremberg Tribunal.[75] For the most part, the offenses listed in the Statute relate to methods of waging war that are not directly relevant here, such as use of "weapons calculated to cause unnecessary suffering" or attacks on undefended buildings or settlements. However, the enumeration in article 3 of such offenses is not exhaustive.[76] We believe that with regard to the crimes of rape and other forms of sexual assault, article 46 of the 1907 Hague Convention (IV), providing protection for "family honour and rights [and] the lives of persons," is one set of protections that can be read into article 3 of the Statute of the International Tribunal for the Former Yugoslavia.[77] But we would suggest more broadly that article 3 of the Statute encompasses any violations of customary international law that can be considered war crimes. We believe that certain provisions of the Fourth Geneva Convention and of Additional Protocol I are declaratory of customary international law relating to war crimes and would permit the Tribunal to prosecute rape and other forms of sexual assault as such within the scope of article 3 of the Statute. With regard to sexual offenses, the relevant provisions include article 27 of the Fourth Geneva Convention, which is derived from article 46 of the Hague Convention (IV). Article 27 is widely held to codify customary international law.[78] It expressly prohibits rape, enforced prostitution, and any form of indecent assault in the context of an international armed conflict. Similarly, article 76(1) of Additional Protocol I expressly prohibits "rape, forced prostitution and any other form of indecent assault."[79] This provision (like article 75 of Additional

---

[75] *Secretary-General's Report, supra* note 5, ¶ 44.

[76] "Such violations shall include, *but not be limited to:* . . . ." Statute, *supra* note 5, art. 3 (emphasis added).

[77] Hague Convention IV, *supra* note 18, art. 46 (annex); Meron, *supra* note 2, at 425. See *supra* section entitled "Violence against Women from a Changing Social and Legal Perspective."

[78] *See, e.g.,* 4 *Geneva Conventions: Commentary, supra* note 41, at 199–201; Meron, *Human Rights, supra* note 26, at 47.

[79] Additional Protocol I, *supra* note 37, art. 76(1) (singling out women as the "object of special respect").

Protocol I) offers a catchall protection for persons not protected by any other provisions of the Geneva Conventions or Additional Protocol I.[80]

Additional Protocol I also identifies as grave breaches "inhuman and degrading practices involving outrages upon personal dignity, based on racial discrimination" that are "committed wilfully and in violation of the Conventions or the Protocol."[81] Even if Additional Protocol I cannot in its entirety be considered to be part of customary international law, it is to be expected that this provision, article 85(4)(c), can in any event be applied with regard to violations of the 1949 Geneva Conventions and those parts of Protocol I that can be considered customary international law, including rape and other sexual assaults.[82] While the prosecution would have to prove the element of racial discrimination here, this provision, unlike the Genocide Convention,[83] does not require a showing that the crime was committed with the discriminatory intent of destroying a group of persons. The prosecution must, however, establish that the crimes were committed wilfully in violation of the Geneva Conventions or Additional Protocol I.[84] At the moment, it remains unclear as an evidentiary matter how to prove these elements.

Another rule of customary international law set out in Additional Protocol I concerns the necessity of distinguishing between civilians and

---

[80] Pilloud et al., *supra* note 46, at 892–93. The United States takes the position that Additional Protocol I, *supra* note 37, art. 75, embodies customary international law, although it has not ratified this instrument. For a detailed discussion of the U.S. position, see Levie, *supra* note 40; Meron, *Human Rights, supra* note 26, at 62–70. Levie, *supra*, at 470 n.4, lists all the articles the United States believes are declaratory of customary law.

[81] Additional Protocol I, *supra* note 37, art. 85(4)(c).

[82] *See* Meron, *supra* note 2; Meron, *War Crimes Trials, supra* note 33, at 129; Meron, *War Crimes in Yugoslavia, supra* note 26, at 84. According to Paust, *supra* note 33, at 518, rape used as a tactic for purposes of ethnic cleansing "is covered by customary laws of war" (citing, *e.g.*, Geneva Convention IV, *supra* note 32, arts. 3, 16, 27, 31–33, 147; Additional Protocol I, *supra* note 37, arts. 51, 75, 76; Additional Protocol II, *supra* note 37, arts. 4, 13). *See generally supra* section entitled "Crimes of Violence of a Sexual Nature"; *supra* text accompanying notes 32–33, 37–40, 65–70.

[83] Genocide Convention, *supra* note 34, art. 2.

[84] Pilloud et al., *supra* note 46, at 1001–02; Kalshoven, *supra* note 60, at 22.

combatants in armed conflict and of justifying attacks on the basis of military necessity.[85] This rule can surely be considered part of customary international law: it was first articulated in the Declaration of St. Petersburg of 1868 and has since been reaffirmed in many multilateral instruments, such as Resolution XXVIII, adopted at the Twentieth International Conference of the Red Cross, held in 1965 in Vienna, and General Assembly Resolution 2444 (XXIII).[86]

REPRISALS

Additional Protocol I to the Geneva Conventions prohibits rape and other forms of sexual assault as reprisals against civilians.[87] Even if this instrument is not considered applicable under the Tribunal's Statute, reprisals are prohibited against protected persons under the Fourth Geneva Convention.[88] The application of these rules is subject to the customary international law of armed conflict.[89]

---

[85] In particular, see Additional Protocol I, *supra* note 37, arts. 48, 51, 85(3)(a)–(b). Violation of this rule is a grave breach. *Id.* art. 85(3).

[86] St. Petersburg Declaration Renouncing the Use, in Time of War, of Explosive Projectiles under 400 Grammes' Weight, Dec. 11, 1868, 138 Consol. T.S. 297, *reprinted in Documents on the Laws of War* 30 (Adam Roberts & Richard Guelff eds., 2d ed. 1989); Protection of Civilian Populations against the Dangers of Indiscriminate Warfare, ICRC Res. XXVIII, in *The Laws of Armed Conflicts, supra* note 18, at 259; G.A. Res. 2444 (XXIII), U.N. GAOR, 23d Sess., Supp. No. 18, at 50, U.N. Doc. A/7218 (1968) (affirming ICRC Res. XXVIII). The United States takes the position that this General Assembly resolution embodies customary international law. *See* Meron, *Human Rights, supra* note 26, at 69–70.

[87] Additional Protocol I, *supra* note 37, arts. 51(6), 76(1).

[88] Geneva Convention IV, *supra* note 14, art. 33 ("No protected person may be punished for an offence he or she has not personally committed."). *Id.* art. 4 defines protected persons as follows: "Persons protected by the Convention are those who, at a given moment and in any manner whatsoever, find themselves, in case of a conflict or occupation, in the hands of a Party to the conflict or Occupying Power of which they are not nationals."

[89] *Final Report, supra* note 3, ¶¶ 63–66; Meron, *Human Rights, supra* note 26, at 47, identifies the prohibition on collective punishment and reprisal set out in Geneva Convention IV, *supra* note 14, art. 33, as embodying customary law.

NONINTERNATIONAL CONFLICT

To the extent that rape or other forms of sexual assault allegedly perpetrated in the region of the former Yugoslavia have been committed in circumstances that are not regarded as international armed conflict,[90] it is uncertain whether the Tribunal would have jurisdiction under the laws or customs of war as embodied in the Statute (if the crimes can be considered crimes against humanity or genocide, jurisdiction would attach even if the conflict were internal). Nonetheless, we believe there is great normative force behind the customary law applicable in noninternational armed conflict and offer a brief discussion.

Common article 3 of the Geneva Conventions of 1949 provides a list of fundamental protections applicable in armed conflict. Relevant here is the prohibition on "violence to life and person, in particular murder of all kinds, mutilation, cruel treatment and torture" and "outrages upon personal dignity, in particular humiliating and degrading treatment."[91] Although common article 3 states that it is applicable specifically to noninternational armed conflict, the International Court of Justice ruled in the *Nicaragua* case that these principles constitute "elementary considerations of humanity" and they cannot be breached in an armed conflict, *regardless* of whether it is international or national in character.[92] The *Secretary-General's Report* cites this opinion with approval (although in a discussion of crimes against humanity).[93] The *Final Report* of the Commission of Experts takes a much more limited view: "[V]iolations of the laws or customs of war referred to in article 3 of the statute of the International Tribunal are offences when committed in international, but not in internal armed conflicts."[94]

Another possibility in cases of sexual assault committed in noninternational armed conflict is to look to Additional Protocol II.

---

[90] See *supra* text accompanying notes 53–57.

[91] Geneva Conventions I–IV, *supra* notes 14, 32, common art. 3(1)(a), (c).

[92] Military and Paramilitary Activities (Nicar. v. U.S.), 1986 I.C.J. 4, 114 (June 27) (citation omitted).

[93] See *Secretary-General's Report, supra* note 5, ¶ 47 n.9.

[94] *Final Report, supra* note 3, ¶ 54. *But see infra* note 98.

Article 4 identifies "fundamental guarantees" and contains a prohibition on rape, enforced prostitution, and other forms of sexual assault. By its terms, Additional Protocol II applies only where the armed conflict takes "place in the territory of a High Contracting Party between its armed forces and dissident armed forces or other organized groups which, under responsible command, exercise such control over a part of its territory as to enable them to carry out sustained and concerted military operations and to implement this Protocol."[95] According to the ICRC commentary on Additional Protocol II, this threshold for application "seems fairly high" but realistic since the insurgents must be in a position to implement the protocol.[96]

Meron, however, criticizes "the proposition that beyond the express provisions of Protocol II, regulation of internal armed conflict is relegated to the domestic law of states":

> Protocol II also contains a basic core of human rights. Some of these rights have already been recognized as customary in human rights instruments and should also be considered as such when stated in instruments of humanitarian law. This is confirmed by the recent ICRC commentary [cited above].[97]

The ICRC commentary supports Meron's argument:

> Protocol II contains virtually all the irreducible rights of the Covenant on Civil and Political Rights . . . . These rights are based on rules of universal validity to which States can be held, *even in the absence of any treaty obligation or any explicit commitment on their part.*
>
> . . . [Even if the combatants are not parties to the protocol] this does not mean that anything is permitted. "The human person remains under the protection of the principles of

---

[95] Additional Protocol II, *supra* note 37, art. 1(1).

[96] Pilloud et al., *supra* note 46, at 1353–54 (discussing Additional Protocol II, *supra* note 37, art. 1).

[97] Meron, *Human Rights, supra* note 26, at 73 (citing Pilloud et al., *supra* note 46, at 1340).

humanity and the dictates of the public conscience": . . . Since they reflect public conscience, the principles of humanity actually constitute a universal reference point and apply independently of the Protocol.

. . . [Moreover,] *the existence of customary norms in internal armed conflicts should not be totally denied.* An example that might be given is the respect for and protection of the wounded. Irrespective of the qualification of the conflict as an internal or international conflict, the codes of conduct are not fundamentally different.[98]

Genocide

Article 4 of the Statute is modeled closely on the 1948 Convention on the Prevention and Punishment of the Crime of Genocide. The Statute defines the offense as follows: "Genocide means any of the following acts committed with intent to destroy, in whole or in part, a national, ethnical, racial or religious group, as such."[99] In enumerating the acts that constitute genocide (where the requisite intent is present), the Statute also conforms to the Genocide Convention:

(a)   killing members of the group;
(b)   causing serious bodily or mental harm to members of the group;
(c)   deliberately inflicting on the group conditions of life calculated to bring about its physical destruction in whole or in part;

---

[98] *Id.* at 1340–42 (citations omitted) (emphasis added); *see also* Remarks by Madeleine Albright, Representative of the United States, U.N. SCOR, 48th Year, 3217th mtg. at 15, U.N. Doc. S/PV.3217 (1993) ("it is understood that the 'laws or customs of war' referred to in Article 3 [of the Tribunal's Statute] include all obligations under humanitarian law agreements in force in the territory of the former Yugoslavia at the time the acts were committed, including common article 3 of the 1949 Geneva Conventions, and the 1977 Additional Protocols to these Conventions").

[99] Statute, *supra* note 5, art. 4(2) (following Genocide Convention, *supra* note 34, art. 2).

(d)   imposing measures intended to prevent births within the group;
(e)   forcibly transferring children of the group to another group.[100]

For our purposes, the relevant acts are enumerated in article 4(2)(b)–(d).

In alleging genocide, the prosecution has an advantage in that a conviction may be had not only for any of the above acts but also for "conspiracy to commit genocide; direct and public incitement to commit genocide; attempt to commit genocide; and complicity in genocide."[101] Furthermore, genocide is not restricted to situations involving armed conflict (international or internal) but may be committed in times of peace. On the other hand, it is not yet clear what level of proof will satisfy the intent requirement. This will depend in part on whether ethnic cleansing can be proven as the aim, or at least an aspect, of the war in the former Yugoslavia. Moreover, although a single act from the above list (for example, castration) performed by a private individual apparently can constitute genocide,[102] it remains to be seen under what conditions such an individual deed will be considered genocide by the International Tribunal.

Crimes against Humanity

Article 5 of the Statute creates jurisdiction over crimes against humanity. As noted earlier, the Statute expressly includes rape in this provision, and we construe this reference to "rape" to include other forms of sexual assault.[103]

Specifically, article 5 confers on the Tribunal "the power to prosecute persons responsible for the following crimes when committed in armed conflict, whether international or internal in character, and

---

[100]   *Id.* (following Genocide Convention, *supra* note 34, art. 2).

[101]   *Id.* art. 4(3).

[102]   Meron, *War Crimes Trials, supra* note 33, at 130.

[103]   *Id.* art. 5(g). See *supra* notes 19–22 and accompanying text.

directed against any civilian population." This provision lists the following acts as crimes against humanity:

(a) murder;
(b) extermination;
(c) enslavement;
(d) deportation;
(e) imprisonment;
(f) torture;
(g) rape;
(h) persecutions on political, racial and religious grounds;
(i) other inhumane acts.

The *Secretary-General's Report* offers this definition of crimes against humanity:

> inhumane acts of a very serious nature, such as wilful killing, torture or rape, committed as part of a widespread or systematic attack against any civilian population on national, political, ethnic, racial or religious grounds. In the conflict in the territory of the former Yugoslavia, such inhumane acts have taken the form of so-called "ethnic cleansing" and widespread and systematic rape and other forms of sexual assault, including enforced prostitution.[104]

In his commentary to the Statute, the Secretary-General takes the position that this category of offense is applicable only to armed conflict.[105] We disagree. We would suggest that since Nuremberg the law of crimes against humanity has evolved to the point that it is immaterial whether they are committed in armed conflict or not. This is the position taken by the Draft Code of Crimes against the Peace and Security of Mankind in the provision modeled on article 6(c) of the

---

[104] *Secretary-General's Report, supra* note 5, ¶ 48.

[105] *Id.* ¶ 47 ("Crimes against humanity are aimed at any civilian population and are prohibited regardless of whether they are committed *in an armed conflict*, international or internal in character.") (citation omitted) (emphasis added); *see also id.* n.9.

Nuremberg Charter and also by many international law experts.[106]

As quoted above, the *Secretary-General's Report* specifies that such crimes must be perpetrated as part of a "widespread or systematic attack" against a *civilian population*. The reference to civilian "population" indicates that the category of crimes against humanity excludes isolated incidents. Similarly, "widespread" refers to the commission of such crimes on a large scale or to a pattern of abuse. Reports and other available information relating to the former Yugoslavia point to a pattern in which an area is conquered, the women are taken away and raped while in detention, or rapes are committed on the spot in the presence of the victim's family. "Systematic" refers to a pattern of abuse of which rape is one element; in other words, rape is used as a tool of war, given its potential to cause great distress to the victim, her family, and her community. Reports also tend to point to such a systematic use of rape. It has been alleged that when an area is conquered, the inhabitants are subjected both to rape and other types of sexual assault and to murder, particularly in and around detention camps. This review suggests that article 5 does not contemplate jurisdiction for inhumane acts that do not appear to form part of a larger attack.[107]

As elaborated in the *Secretary-General's Report*, article 5 also incorporates an intent element: the commentary refers to inhumane acts committed on "national, political, ethnic, racial or religious" grounds. This element should be easier to prove than the intent requirement in the crime of genocide (under article 4) because it is necessary only to show that the alleged perpetrator knew or should have known that his conduct could contribute to the destruction of the group in question.[108]

---

[106] Draft Code, *supra* note 26, art. 21; McCormack & Simpson, *supra* note 39, at 15. *See generally* M. Cherif Bassiouni, *Crimes against Humanity in International Criminal Law* 248 (1992); Yougindra Khushalani, *Dignity and Honour of Women as Basic and Fundamental Human Rights* 32 (1982); Christiaan Frederik Rüter, *Enkele aspecten van de strafrechtelijke reactie op oorlogsmisdrijven en misdrijven tegen de menselijkheid* 37–38 (1973). *See supra* note 26 and accompanying text.

[107] For further discussion, see *Final Report*, *supra* note 3, ¶ 77; Copelon, *supra* note 71, at 7; Goldenberg, *supra* note 26, at 48–49; Schwelb, *supra* note 21, at 191.

[108] *Secretary-General's Report*, *supra* note 5, ¶ 48; *see* 2 Pieter Nicolaas Drost, *The Crime of State: Penal Protection for Fundamental Freedoms of Persons and Peoples* 33, 81–84 (1959).

Finally, the prosecution will have to prove state involvement to make out a case of crimes against humanity. This element may not be too difficult to satisfy because it will suffice to show that the government, which is responsible for prevention and suppression, instigated or at least tolerated such crimes.[109]

In sum, the distinguishing features of crimes against humanity are their serious nature and the context in which they take place. Such crimes can be committed by anybody: it is not necessary to establish that the perpetrator was a belligerent.[110]

PRACTICAL APPLICATION OF THE LAW

The possible sources of law upon which the prosecution might rely in cases of rape and other types of sexual assault are described above. We have tried to stress that, on the one hand, the Tribunal's prosecution of such crimes in the former Yugoslavia fits within the natural development of international humanitarian law; on the other hand, it will be difficult for the prosecution to prove that a specific offense falls under one or more of the articles that set out the subject-matter jurisdiction of the Tribunal. As in a domestic prosecution, each element of the alleged crime will have to be proven and this will require a great deal of case preparation. Here we focus on some evidentiary issues.

Every developed legal system has rules of evidence that guide the

---

[109] The most recent amendments of the Tribunal's Rules of Procedure and Evidence in January 1995 added a provision that will support a finding of state involvement where the government in question has not been recognized by the international community: *"State:* A State Member or non-Member of the United Nations or a self-proclaimed entity *de facto* exercising governmental functions, whether recognised as a State or not." International Tribunal for the Prosecution of Persons Responsible for Serious Violations of International Humanitarian Law Committed in the Territory of the Former Yugoslavia since 1991, Rules of Procedure and Evidence R. 2(A), U.N. Doc. IT/32 (1994), *amended by* U.N. Doc. IT/32/Rev.1 (1994), U.N. Doc. IT/32/Rev.2 (1994), U.N. Doc. IT/Rev.3 (1995), *reprinted in* appendix C of this issue of *Criminal Law Forum.*

[110] *See* Rüter, *supra* note 106, at 37–38; Goldenberg, *supra* note 26, at 19, 48–49.

process of gathering and assessing data to support a factually and legally sound result. The Commission of Experts established under Security Council Resolution 780 was directed by the Council to conduct an inquiry with a view to providing the Secretary-General with its conclusions on evidence of grave breaches of the Geneva Conventions and other violations of international humanitarian law in the territory of the former Yugoslavia. However, when the Commission started work in 1992, there were no rules of procedure and evidence related to possible future trials to guide it. In addition, the Commission had no authority to develop policy with regard to future prosecutions. Until the Tribunal itself was constituted and later adopted evidentiary rules,[111] the Commission remained uncertain about the importance and status of any evidence it collected and on the manner in which the anticipated rules of procedure and evidence could or should influence its investigations. Due to this lack of guidance, the Commission had to chart its own course with respect to seeking out and evaluating data. Especially in relation to the investigation of rape and sexual assault, the nature of the Commission's mandate, combined with lack of direction on evidentiary matters (not to mention the practical constraints on fact-finding while an armed conflict is in progress), complicated its task.

As an initial point, it should be noted that questions of evidence relate very directly both to the law of evidence and to the applicable substantive law. We have already seen that rape and sexual assault might be prosecuted under several articles of the Tribunal's Statute, each with its own evidentiary requirements. Given the variety among domestic legal systems in the proof of rape cases—whether, for example, proof of force and penetration is required, whether prior sexual history is admissible, whether corroboration is required, and so forth—it was very difficult to determine what evidence to collect. For example, from a prosecutorial perspective in a legal system that requires corroboration (as most legal systems do), it hardly seems to make sense to collect statements of victims of rape if no corroborative evidence can be found.

---

[111] *See generally* M. Cherif Bassiouni, *The Commission of Experts Established pursuant to Security Council Resolution 780 (1992): Investigating Violations of International Humanitarian Law in the Former Yugoslavia*, in this issue of *Criminal Law Forum;* Burns, *supra* note 5.

While this concern calls into question the prosecutorial value of examining statements by individual rape victims, the Commission's mandate was not focused on prosecution, and it could therefore rely on such statements as part of the process of compiling evidence of violations of international humanitarian law. In particular, given the possibility of prosecuting rape as a crime against humanity, lack of corroboration was not an insurmountable obstacle—more important was to collect evidence that such crimes were being committed in a systematic way or were encouraged by policy.

Rule 96 of the Tribunal's Rules of Procedure and Evidence sets out the following requirements in "cases of sexual assault":

(i) no corroboration of the victim's testimony shall be required;

(ii) consent shall not be allowed as a defence if the victim

(a) has been subjected to or threatened with or has had reason to fear violence, duress, detention or psychological oppression, or
(b) reasonably believed that if she did not submit, another might be so subjected, threatened or put in fear;

(iii) before evidence of the victim's consent is admitted, the accused shall satisfy the Trial Chamber *in camera* that the evidence is relevant and credible;

(iv) prior sexual conduct of the victim shall not be admitted in evidence.[112]

Rule 96(i) resolves the problem of corroboration noted above, easing the prosecution's burden. However, the due process function that corroboration is claimed to serve must be met by other procedural protections, in

---

[112] The Tribunal finalized Rules of Procedure and Evidence in early 1994 but amended them several times since then. See *supra* note 109. Rule 96(iii) was added in January 1995 in U.N. Doc. IT/Rev.3 (1995), *supra* note 109.

particular, cross-examination, and it is not clear whether rule 96(ii) as written poses an unacceptable risk of harassment of victims who testify. Rule 96(iii), which was added in January 1995,[113] as well as the establishment of the victim and witness unit at the International Tribunal, may decrease this risk.

A final concern relates to lack of familiarity on the part of defendants and witnesses from a civil law tradition with the largely common law–oriented proceedings before the Tribunal. The potential for misunderstanding, errors, and other problems must not be underestimated even with representation provided by counsel. In the future, this problem might be alleviated by the establishment of a permanent tribunal with a well-developed and broadly disseminated set of rules of procedure and evidence.

The situation in the former Yugoslavia cried out for a response from the international community. The United Nations took up this challenge by giving the crimes of rape and sexual assault a place in the Statute of the International Tribunal. The enumeration of rape as one of the modes of committing a crime against humanity in article 5 represents a watershed in the history of international law: this is the first time that rape has been so characterized in an instrument of this stature. If the Tribunal succeeds in prosecuting the planners and perpetrators of these crimes, we may anticipate a deterrent effect in future armed conflicts and, possibly, more serious attention to sexual assault in domestic legal systems.

---

[113] See *supra* notes 109, 112.

10
Rules of Procedure and Evidence of the International Tribunal for the Former Yugoslavia*

*Daniel D. Ntanda Nsereko***

INTRODUCTION

The International Tribunal for the Prosecution of Persons Responsible for Serious Violations of International Humanitarian Law Committed in the Territory of the Former Yugoslavia since 1991 adopted its Rules of Procedure and Evidence on February 11, 1994. The rules came into force on March 14, 1994.[1] The Tribunal acted

---

*   *Editor's note:* research for this article was updated through December 31, 1994. As this article went to press, revisions reflecting a few of the amendments made in January 1995 to the Tribunal's Rules of Procedure and Evidence were added.

**   Associate Professor and former Head, Department of Law, University of Botswana, Gaborone, Botswana; LL.B., University of East Africa 1968; M.C.J., Howard University 1970; LL.M., New York University 1971; J.S.D., New York University 1975. At the time of writing, the author was Walter S. Owen Visiting Professor of Law, University of British Columbia, Vancouver, British Columbia, Canada.

[1]   International Tribunal for the Prosecution of Persons Responsible for Serious Violations of International Humanitarian Law Committed in the Territory of the Former Yugoslavia since 1991, Rules of Procedure and Evidence, U.N. Doc. IT/32 (1994), *amended by* U.N. Doc. IT/32/Rev.1 (1994), U.N. Doc. IT/32/Rev.2 (1994), U.N. Doc. IT/Rev.3 (1995), *reprinted in* appendix C of this issue of *Criminal Law Forum*. This article was written on the basis of U.N. Doc. IT/32/Rev.1 (1994) [hereinafter I.T. R. Proc. & Evid.], but it addresses some key changes effected by U.N. Doc. IT/32/Rev.3 (1995).

under a provision of its Statute mandating it to adopt "rules of procedure and evidence for the conduct of the pre-trial phase of the proceedings, trials and appeals, the admission of evidence, the protection of victims and witnesses, and other appropriate matters."[2]

The only precedent before the Tribunal were the rules of the International Military Tribunal at Nuremberg, Germany, promulgated under article 13 of the Nuremberg Charter.[3] In keeping with the letter and spirit of the Charter, which enjoined the tribunal to "adopt and apply to the greatest possible extent expeditious and non-technical procedure,"[4] that tribunal's rules were indeed thin, comprising only eleven brief articles.[5] Their precedential value to the International Tribunal on Yugoslavia was, therefore, minimal. As it were, then, the Tribunal started from a clean slate. It relied heavily on proposals from the U.S. government and from nongovernmental organizations such as the U.S.-based Lawyers Committee for Human Rights. It also took into account the rules of procedure and evidence prevailing in the major legal systems of the world. Viewed as a whole, however, the rules tend to lean more toward the common law adversarial system than toward the civil law inquisitorial system, in keeping with the Statute's preference for a modified adversarial model.

The Rules of Procedure and Evidence, along with the Statute, cater for simple, expeditious, but fair trials, balancing the rights of the

---

[2] *Report of the Secretary-General pursuant to Paragraph 2 of Security Council Resolution 808 (1993)*, U.N. Doc. S/25704 & Add.1 (1993), *reprinted in* appendix B of this issue of *Criminal Law Forum* and *in* 32 I.L.M. 1163 [hereinafter *Secretary-General's Report*]. The Statute of the International Tribunal is set out as an annex to *Secretary-General's Report, supra,* and is *reprinted in* appendix B of this issue of *Criminal Law Forum* and *in* 32 I.L.M. 1192 [hereinafter Statute]. See Statute, *supra,* art. 15.

[3] The International Military Tribunal at Nuremberg was established pursuant to Agreement for the Prosecution and Punishment of the Major War Criminals of the European Axis, Aug. 8, 1945, 82 U.N.T.S. 279. The Charter of the International Military Tribunal at Nuremberg is set out in *id.* at 284 [hereinafter Nuremberg Charter].

[4] Nuremberg Charter, *supra* note 3, art. 19.

[5] International Military Tribunal, Rules of Procedure, *adopted* Oct. 29, 1945, in 1 *Trial of the Major War Criminals before the International Military Tribunal, Nuremberg, 14 November 1945–1 October 1946,* at 19 (1947) [hereinafter Nuremberg Rules].

accused and the interests of the international public. They incorporate most of the applicable standards relating to criminal justice that the United Nations has advocated all along, including the provisions of the International Covenant on Civil and Political Rights relating to a fair trial,[6] which among other things preclude trials in absentia.[7] The Tribunal's rules also ban the death penalty—in keeping with UN pronouncements on this matter.[8] Likewise, the rules declare inadmissible any evidence obtained as a result of torture, in keeping with the relevant UN convention.[9] The Tribunal also has adopted rules governing the detention of persons awaiting trial or appeal, which conform to UN standards.[10] In doing all this, the Tribunal, which is a "subsidiary organ [of

---

[6] Statute, *supra* note 2, art. 21, reproduces International Covenant on Civil and Political Rights, *adopted* Dec. 19, 1966, art. 14, 999 U.N.T.S. 171 [hereinafter International Covenant].

[7] International Covenant, *supra* note 6, art. 14(3)(d).

[8] Statute, *supra* note 2, art. 24(1), goes further than International Covenant, *supra* note 6, art. 6. In this connection, see G.A. Res. 2857 (XXVI), U.N. GAOR, 26th Sess., Supp. No. 29, at 94, U.N. Doc. A/8429 (1972) (calling for the progressive restriction of the number of offenses for which the death penalty may be imposed).

[9] I.T. R. Proc. & Evid., *supra* note 1, R. 95 ("Evidence obtained directly or indirectly by means which constitute a serious violation of internationally protected human rights shall not be admissible."), reflects Convention against Torture and Other Cruel, Inhuman, or Degrading Treatment or Punishment art. 15, G.A. Res. 39/46, U.N. GAOR, 39th Sess., Supp. No. 51, at 197, U.N. Doc. A/39/51 (1984) [hereinafter Torture Convention].

[10] International Tribunal for the Prosecution of Persons Responsible for Serious Violations of International Humanitarian Law Committed in the Territory of the Former Yugoslavia since 1991, Rules Governing the Detention of Persons Awaiting Trial or Appeal before the Tribunal or Otherwise Detained on the Authority of the Tribunal, U.N. Doc. IT/38/Rev.3 (1994). These rules rely on various sets of principles and standards, including Basic Principles for the Treatment of Prisoners, G.A. Res. 45/111, U.N. GAOR, 45th Sess., Supp. No. 49A, at 199, U.N. Doc. A/45/49 (1990); Model Agreement on the Transfer of Foreign Prisoners and Recommendations on the Treatment of Foreign Prisoners, in *Seventh United Nations Congress on the Prevention of Crime and the Treatment of Offenders: Report Prepared by the Secretariat* 53, U.N. Doc. A/CONF.121/22/Rev.1, U.N. Sales No. E.86.IV.1 (1986); Standard Minimum Rules for the Treatment of Prisoners, E.S.C. Res. 663 (XXIV) C, U.N. ESCOR, 24th Sess., Supp. No. 1, at 11, U.N. Doc. E/3048 (1957), *amended by* E.S.C. 2076 (LXII), U.N. ESCOR, 62d Sess., Supp. No. 1, at 35, U.N. Doc. E/5988 (1977).

the Security Council] within the terms of Article 29 of the Charter,"[11] is attempting to practice what the United Nations preaches and thereby to create a model of fair criminal proceedings that may be emulated by member states and at the same time may help to dispel any accusations of victors' justice by its detractors.

This article discusses and analyzes the Tribunal's Rules of Procedure and Evidence as they relate to jurisdiction, initiation of proceedings, trial, and presentation of evidence. It also briefly deals with other salient points, particularly in relation to appellate and review procedures and the treatment of victims. Where there are lacunae in the rules, the article posits suggestions for filling those lacunae.

JURISDICTION

According to article 8 of the Statute, the Tribunal has jurisdiction to try crimes, as defined in articles 2–5, committed in the territory of the former Socialist Federal Republic of Yugoslavia, including its land surface, airspace, and territorial waters. This jurisdiction is not affected by the new boundaries that sprang up following the disintegration of the former republic. However, the Statute is conspicuously silent on crimes committed partly within and partly outside the territory of the former Yugoslavia. It is also silent on crimes commenced outside the territory that have an impact within it. An example of the latter are letter bombs posted abroad to addresses within the territory, where they detonate and cause injury. Rule 2.3 of the U.S. proposal would have specified that a "crime is considered to have been committed in the territory of the former Yugoslavia if any part of the planning, instigation, ordering, execution, or completion of the crime took place" within the territory.[12]

---

[11] *Secretary-General's Report*, supra note 2, ¶ 28. For a discussion of the characterization of the Tribunal as a subsidiary organ, see Roman A. Kolodkin, *An Ad Hoc International Tribunal for the Prosecution of Serious Violations of International Humanitarian Law in the Former Yugoslavia*, in this issue of *Criminal Law Forum*.

[12] Letter from the Permanent Representative of the United States of America to the Secretary-General, Apr. 5, 1993, U.N. Doc. S/25575 (1993), transmitting views and proposals on establishing an international criminal tribunal for the former Yugoslavia.

Despite the failure to adopt this language, the Tribunal, it is submitted, does have jurisdiction to try persons who commit crimes in the manner described above. This jurisdiction is based on the well-established principle that a state has jurisdiction over acts committed elsewhere that nonetheless have an effect within that state.[13] To deny jurisdiction under these particular circumstances would let perpetrators escape from international justice.

Article 8 of the Statute further provides that only crimes committed on or after January 1, 1991, are within the Tribunal's competence. According to the Secretary-General's commentary on the Statute, this date was chosen because it is "a neutral date which is not tied to any specific event and is clearly intended to convey the notion that no judgment as to the international or internal character of the conflict [in Yugoslavia] is being exercised."[14] The Statute does not, however, indicate whether there is a limitation period after which charges for the crimes within the Tribunal's competence shall become time-barred. Some jurisdictions impose limitation periods after which prosecutions are not allowed, although notorious offenses such as murder are usually excepted from such limitations.[15] Other jurisdictions do not impose limitation periods at all save for minor or summary offenses.[16] The rationale for limitation periods is that failure to charge a suspected offender within a set period offends against the principle of justice within a reasonable time. As is often said, "justice delayed is justice denied" and "justice is sweetest when it is freshest." Additionally, inordinate delay in framing charges does not conduce to a fair trial. For example, witnesses on both sides may disappear or, because of the long lapse of time, may forget what transpired. Material evidence may also disappear or be rendered worthless due to exposure to the elements. The public—whose

---

[13] S.S. "Lotus" (Fr. v. Turk.), 1927 P.C.I.J. (ser. A) No. 10.

[14] *Secretary-General's Report, supra* note 2, ¶ 62.

[15] *E.g.*, Criminal Procedure and Evidence Act § 26, Laws of Bots. ch. 08:02 (excluding murder from a general limitation period of 20 years from the commission of the offense); to similar effect, Criminal Procedure Act of 1977, § 18 (S. Afr.), *analyzed in* Etienne Du Toit, *Commentary on the Criminal Procedure Act* 1-12 (1987).

[16] Celia Hampton, *Criminal Procedure* 15 (3d ed. 1982).

support for criminal proceedings is vital—may also lose interest. As far as the International Tribunal is concerned, it may be argued that limitation periods are inappropriate, since the offenses it was created to try are so grave. Furthermore, most, if not all, of the offenses within the Tribunal's competence *ratione materiae* are covered by the Convention on the Non-applicability of Statutory Limitations to War Crimes and Crimes against Humanity, which exempts them from statutory limitations irrespective of the date of their commission.[17]

Both the Statute and the Rules of Procedure and Evidence provide that the Tribunal and national courts have concurrent jurisdiction over persons who commit crimes within the mandate of the Tribunal. Nevertheless, as an organ of a superior legal order, "[t]he International Tribunal shall have primacy over national courts. At any stage of the procedure, the International Tribunal may formally request national courts to defer to the competence of the International Tribunal . . . ."[18] Part 2 of the rules governs the procedure for deferral.

When it appears to the prosecutor that acts within the competence of the International Tribunal have been or are still subject to investigation or court proceedings in any country, he may request the country concerned to furnish him with information in respect of such investigations or proceedings.[19] Article 29 of the Statute obliges the country so requested to comply promptly with the request. On receiving the information, the prosecutor may "propose to the Trial Chamber designated by the President that a formal request be made that the national court defer to the competence of the Tribunal."[20] Rule 9 identifies the following grounds for requesting a deferral:

(i) the act being investigated or which is the subject of those proceedings is characterized as an ordinary crime;

---

[17] Convention on the Non-applicability of Statutory Limitations to War Crimes and Crimes against Humanity art. 1, G.A. Res. 2391 (XXIII), U.N. GAOR, 23d Sess., Supp. No. 18, at 40, U.N. Doc. A/7218 (1968).

[18] Statute, *supra* note 2, art. 9(2).

[19] I.T. R. Proc. & Evid., *supra* note 1, R. 8.

[20] *Id.* R. 9.

(ii) there is a lack of impartiality or independence, or the investigations or proceedings are designed to shield the accused from international criminal responsibility, or the case is not diligently prosecuted; or

(iii) what is in issue is closely related to, or otherwise involves, significant factual or legal questions which may have implications for investigations or prosecutions before the Tribunal[.]

If the trial chamber is satisfied that any of the grounds for deferral is established, it issues a formal request, pursuant to rule 10(A), to the state concerned that its national court defer to the competence of the Tribunal. Rule 10(B) states that the "request for deferral shall include a request that the results of the investigation and a copy of the court's records and the judgement, if already delivered, be forwarded to the Tribunal." This information is doubtless useful to the prosecutor in his further investigations in the case and in planning his strategy for the prosecution. The rules are silent, however, on the mode of communicating the request. It can only be assumed that it will be made through normal diplomatic channels or through other efficient and expeditious means that the registrar of the Tribunal may deem appropriate.[21] Under rule 11, failure by the requested state to respond or to give a response that satisfies the trial chamber seized with the matter within sixty days entitles the president of the Tribunal to report the matter to the Security

---

[21] In November 1994 the International Tribunal formally requested Germany to transfer to its jurisdiction a Bosnian Serb then in custody who was suspected of being a key figure in ethnic cleansing campaigns against Moslems in the Prijedor region. Peter S. Canellos, *U.N. Tribunal Seeks a Serb: Ethnic Cleansing Alleged as Trial Begins in the Hague,* Boston Globe, Nov. 9, 1994, at 26, *available in* LEXIS, World Library, Allnws File; *Yugo War Crimes Court Asks Germany to Extradite Bosnian Serb,* Agence France Presse, Nov. 8, 1994, *available in* LEXIS, World Library, Allnws File. To make the transfer of this prisoner possible, the German Bundesrat approved amendments proposed by the government to permit the extradition of foreigners to the Tribunal, and constitutional changes to permit the extradition of German citizens are anticipated. *Bonn Changes Law to Hand Over War Criminals,* Reuters, Dec. 16, 1994, *available in* LEXIS, World Library, Allnws File.

Council. Presumably, if the Security Council chooses to take up the matter and persuasion fails, more drastic measures may be used, such as trade sanctions or diplomatic isolation, as in the case of Libya following the downing of a Pan American passenger plane over Lockerbie, Scotland.[22]

In accord with the principle of *non bis in idem*, or the rule against double jeopardy, article 10(1) of the Statute forbids national courts from trying any person for "acts constituting serious violations of international humanitarian law" for which this individual has already been tried by the International Tribunal. It apparently does not matter whether the Tribunal acquitted or convicted the accused, or even whether the acquittal was based on a technicality. In defending this rule in the context of English law in respect of a person who has already been convicted, Professor Fitzgerald said: "English criminal law is based on the idea that once a person has been convicted and sentenced and has undergone the punishment imposed upon him, he has paid the penalty. To allow the authorities to prosecute him again in order to seek the imposition of some further punishment would be unduly oppressive."[23] In the event of acquittal, Fitzgerald contended:

> The prosecution may subsequently obtain fresh evidence conclusive of his guilt, or they may be able to demonstrate that the defence succeeded by perjury and conspiracy to defeat the ends of justice. In such a case, there would be something to say, in the interests of truth and justice, in favour of allowing the defendant to be tried again. . . . [Nonetheless, once] a man has been acquitted, it is felt that it would be too harsh to allow the prosecution further bites at the cherry. The defendant must be allowed to order his affairs with some certainty. This means of course that occasionally the guilty slip through the net, and nothing can be done about it. This disadvantage is outweighed, however, by the gain in freedom from oppression, which the

---

[22] S.C. Res. 748, U.N. SCOR, 47th Year, 1992 S.C. Res. & Dec. at 52, U.N. Doc. S/INF/48 (1992).

[23] Patrick John Fitzgerald, *Criminal Law and Punishment* 172 (1962).

possibility of perpetual exposure to prosecution would entail. Moreover, if the practice were allowed, not only those wrongly acquitted but those who were actually innocent would be at the mercy of the potential tyranny of a prosecutor.[24]

In the event a national court violates the injunction on double jeopardy, rule 13 requires the appropriate trial chamber to "issue a reasoned order requesting the national court permanently to discontinue its proceedings. If the national court fails to do so, the President [of the Tribunal] may report the matter to the Security Council."

It is submitted that the arguments for barring national courts from exposing a defendant to double jeopardy should apply with equal force to the International Tribunal itself. The Tribunal should not entertain prosecutions of persons who have already been before it and have been either convicted or acquitted in respect of the same acts. The only exception to this rule should be in cases where the prosecutor, with the permission of the Tribunal, withdraws the charges before judgment without prejudice to the possibility of reinstituting them.[25] A retrial ordered by the appeals chamber on a successful appeal by the prosecutor is also not constrained by the principle of *non bis in idem*.

The case of a person who has already been tried by national courts is different. The Statute contemplates that such a person may be tried by the International Tribunal on the following grounds:

> (i) the act for which he or she was tried was characterized as an ordinary crime; or
>
> (ii) the national court proceedings were not impartial or independent, were designed to shield the accused from international criminal responsibility, or the case was not diligently prosecuted.[26]

---

[24] *Id.*

[25] *See* I.T. R. Proc. & Evid., *supra* note 1, R. 51.

[26] Statute, *supra* note 2, art. 10(2); *see also* I.T. R. Proc. & Evid., *supra* note 1, R. 12.

These grounds cannot be gainsaid. The atrocities that have been and continue to be committed in the territory of the former Yugoslavia seem, to a large extent, to be along ethnic or religious lines. They may also be part of the official policy of the new national entities that have replaced Yugoslavia. It is conceivable that the courts in the new national entities may go through a facade of trials that result in acquittals, just for the sake of shielding the culprits from international criminal responsibility. It is well, therefore, for rule 12 to declare that "determinations of national courts are not binding on the Tribunal" and for the Tribunal to reserve to itself the right to reopen any defendant's case in order to satisfy the demands of international justice.

For sentencing purposes, however, the Tribunal is required to take into account the sentence already served by a person it convicts of the same acts as those that were the subject of proceedings before a national court.[27]

INITIATION OF PROCEEDINGS

The Prosecutor

The office of prosecutor is an extremely important organ within the International Tribunal. Inasmuch as the prosecutor initiates the proceedings before the Tribunal, he is probably the most visible and most active of all its functionaries. According to the Statute, the prosecutor must be a person of "high moral character" and must possess "the highest level of competence and experience in the conduct of investigations and prosecutions of criminal cases."[28] Like the judges, he is appointed for a four-year, renewable term by the Security Council on the recommendation of the Secretary-General.[29] So, in addition to meeting the stated qualifications, the candidate for the office of

---

[27] Statute, *supra* note 2, art. 10(3); I.T. R. Proc. & Evid., *supra* note 1, R. 101(B)(v).

[28] Statute, *supra* note 2, art. 16(4).

[29] *Id.*

prosecutor must be politically acceptable to the Council.[30]

The prosecutor is responsible for "the investigation and prosecution of persons responsible for serious violations of international humanitarian law committed in the territory of the former Yugoslavia since 1 January 1991."[31] In the performance of his duties he "shall act independently as a separate organ of the International Tribunal. He shall not seek or receive instructions from any Government or from any other source."[32] What are these "other sources"? Clearly, they must include private individuals, and governmental and nongovernmental organizations (NGOs). By forbidding the prosecutor to seek or receive instructions from any quarter, the Statute clearly underscores the functional independence of this office. "[A]ny other source" must also include the Tribunal and the Security Council. The judges cannot, for example, purport to instruct the prosecutor on matters that fall squarely

---

[30] That the Security Council would insist on political acceptability became evident when it turned down the Secretary-General's first nominee, the highly regarded DePaul University law professor Cherif Bassiouni (member, and later chairman, of the Commission of Experts appointed to investigate serious violations of international humanitarian law in the former Yugoslavia). In the fall of 1993, the Council elected Ramón Escovar-Salom of Venezuela, S.C. Res. 877, U.N. SCOR, 48th Sess., 3296th mtg. at 1, U.N. Doc. S/RES/877 (1993), *available in* U.N. Gopher\Documents\Security Council Resolutions, who resigned in early 1994, before taking up his duties, to accept an appointment in the newly formed Venezuelan government. The vacancy was not filled until July 1994, when Judge Richard Goldstone of South Africa was appointed to the post. S.C. Res. 936, U.N. SCOR, 49th Year, 3401st mtg. at 1, U.N. Doc. S/RES/936 (1994), *available in* U.N. Gopher\Documents\Security Council Resolutions.

On the controversy over initially selecting a prosecutor, see Paul Lewis, *Disputes Hamper U.N. Drive for a War Crimes Tribunal*, N.Y. Times, Sept. 9, 1993, at A10, *available in* LEXIS, World Library, Allnws File; Stanley Meisler, *U.N. Is Deadlocked on War-Crimes Prosecutor*, Montreal Gazette, Sept. 12, 1993, at B1, *available in* LEXIS, World Library, Allnws File; *Venezuelan on War Crimes Panel: Tribunal Will Probe Atrocities in Former Yugoslavia*, Chi. Tribune, Oct. 22, 1993, at 10, *available in* LEXIS, World Library, Allnws File. On the controversy over replacing Escovar-Salom, see Stephen Eagleburger, *Balkan War-Crimes Prosecution Bogs Down*, N.Y. Times, July 7, 1994, at A5, *available in* LEXIS, World Library, Allnws File; Anthony Lewis, *At Home Abroad: The Civilized World*, N.Y. Times, July 1, 1994, at A25, *available in* LEXIS, World Library, Allnws File.

[31] Statute, *supra* note 2, art. 16(1).

[32] *Id.* art. 16(2).

within his discretion. They cannot order him to prosecute a particular individual or prevent him from discontinuing proceedings at any stage before judgment, for he is *dominus litis*.[33] Likewise, although the prosecutor is ultimately accountable to the Security Council for the discharge of his mandate, he is not subject to its authority in the day-to-day fulfillment of his duties. If he were, his work would not accord with fundamental principles of fairness.

The prosecutor is the sole arbiter of whether to prosecute or not. That suggests that he has discretion in this matter. There are actually varying perceptions on the scope of prosecutorial discretion. Anglo-American law gives the public prosecutor discretion not to prosecute even when there is abundant evidence against a suspect. The rationale is that public interest may sometimes be better served by nonprosecution than by prosecution. The discretion not to prosecute must, of course, be exercised with the utmost circumspection, especially in the case of serious offenses. Continental European jurisdictions, such as Germany, do not vest the public prosecutor with similar latitude. According to the principle of legality, *Legalitätsprinzip,* the German prosecutor must prosecute in all cases (except petty offenses) where there is sufficient evidence.[34] Failure to prosecute is itself an offense. The rationale for *Legalitätsprinzip* is apparently the need to insulate the prosecutor from political interference, especially from the minister of justice.[35]

Neither the Statute nor the rules gives any indication whether the prosecutor enjoys the discretion of nonprosecution: can he decline to prosecute even where there appears to be sufficient evidence, or must he prosecute at all costs, according to *Legalitätsprinzip?* It is submitted that where there is sufficient evidence to warrant prosecution, the prosecutor should have no discretion but to prosecute. Availability of sufficient evidence should be the sole criterion in making the decision of whether to prosecute, and this determination must, of course, lie

---

[33] On this issue, see Gouriet v. Union of Post Office Workers, 1978 App. Cas. 435 (1977); R. v. Sikumba, [1955] 3 S. Afr. L. Rep. 125 (E. Dist. Local Div.).

[34] StPO (Criminal Procedure Statute) § 152(II) (Ger.) (requiring public prosecutor to take action against all prosecutable offenses if there is sufficient factual basis).

[35] *See* John H. Langbein, *Comparative Criminal Procedure: Germany* 91 (1977).

exclusively with the prosecutor. This view is based on two premises: the exceptionally grave nature of the offenses that the prosecutor is mandated to prosecute and the fact that a special tribunal has been established at great cost to try such offenses. The mandatory terms of article 18(4) of the Statute and of rule 47(A) support this conclusion.[36] Given the widespread media coverage of the atrocities committed in the territory of the former Yugoslavia it would be an outrage to the international public were the prosecutor to decline to go forward with a case for reasons other than insufficiency of evidence.

Investigation

Article 18 of the Statute provides as follows:

> 1. The Prosecutor shall initiate investigations *ex officio* or on the basis of information obtained from any source, particularly from Governments, United Nations organs, intergovernmental and non-governmental organizations. The Prosecutor shall assess the information received or obtained and decide whether there is sufficient basis to proceed.
>
> 2. The Prosecutor shall have the power to question suspects, victims and witnesses, to collect evidence and to conduct on-site investigations. In carrying out these tasks the Prosecutor may, as appropriate, seek the assistance of the State authorities concerned.

Rule 39 elaborates on the prosecutor's powers. It provides that in the conduct of investigations, he may

> (i) summon and question suspects, victims and witnesses

---

[36] Statute, *supra* note 2, art. 18(4), provides that "[u]pon a determination that a *prima facie* case exists, the Prosecutor *shall* prepare an indictment" (emphasis added); I.T. R. Proc. & Evid., *supra* note 1, R. 47(A), similarly provides that "[i]f in the course of an investigation the Prosecutor is satisfied that there is sufficient evidence to provide reasonable grounds for believing that a suspect has committed a crime within the jurisdiction of the Tribunal, he *shall* prepare . . . an indictment" (emphasis added).

and record their statements, collect evidence and conduct on-site investigations;

(ii) undertake such other matters as may appear necessary for completing the investigation and the preparation and conduct of the prosecution at the trial;

(iii) seek, to that end, the assistance of any State authority concerned, as well as of any relevant international body including the International Criminal Police Organization (INTERPOL); and

(iv) request such orders as may be necessary from a Trial Chamber or a Judge.

There are salient points raised by these provisions that merit some comment.

The first point is that the prosecutor may initiate investigations himself. Alternatively, he may do so on the basis of information obtained from other sources that the Statute lists. Conspicuously absent from this list, however, are individuals, especially victims or relatives of victims. Under national systems, law enforcement agencies invariably, though not exclusively, initiate proceedings on the basis of reports or complaints of victims, their relatives, or their friends. Nothing in the Statute or the rules precludes the prosecutor from acting on the basis of information from such individuals. That said, however, there is no gainsaying that the prosecutor will rely more heavily on information from NGOs, both national and international. The Lawyers Committee for Human Rights has underscored the significant contribution that NGOs can make to the prosecutor's investigatory efforts:

> The Prosecutor's Office will be limited by a number of factors, including staffing and budgetary constraints, remoteness from the scene of the alleged crimes, a limited access in the theatre of war, and a lack of intimate familiarity with the cultural and social context in which the alleged crimes took place and in which the victims and perpetrators live. The initiatives already undertaken by various NGOs to collect information about the events in the territory of the former Yugoslavia make it inevitable that NGOs already possess [such] important facts and information . . . as the names and statements of victims,

witnesses, and suspects, personal observations, including video taped evidence, and other pieces of physical evidence, including medical records.[37]

While the prosecutor will doubtless carefully scrutinize reports submitted to him by NGOs and other outside sources for accuracy, he will have to be doubly cautious in relying on information supplied by local NGOs or by individuals, who might be acting out of partisan motives. He must make sure that all such information was obtained by methods that conform to internationally accepted standards. Storage and preservation of evidence must also be such as to be above all reasonable suspicion of tampering. To guide NGOs and individuals in collecting and preserving, storing, and transmitting information, the prosecutor should prepare and distribute guidelines. Adherence to these guidelines will ensure that the information supplied, if credible, will be admissible before the Tribunal.

The second point is that the prosecutor has power under rule 39(i) to "summon and question suspects, victims and witnesses and record their statements." Both the Statute and the rules have a lot to say about the interrogation of suspects. They are, however, silent on victims and witnesses. In particular, they do not indicate what should follow where the interrogatee, particularly the witness, does not cooperate with the investigator. What if a witness, for example, does not answer the summons or, if she does, refuses to talk or to answer questions truthfully? In common law countries, investigators generally get information from prospective witnesses on a cooperative basis. They cannot compel them to talk.[38] Rule 39(iii) authorizes the prosecutor to seek the assis-

---

[37] Lawyers Comm. for Human Rights, Preliminary Observations on the Role of Non-governmental Organizations 5 (memorandum submitted to the Round Table on the International War Crimes Tribunal, organized by the Centre for Anti-war Action—Belgrade, Brussels, Belgium, Mar. 3–4, 1994). The contribution of NGOs is discussed at some length in M. Cherif Bassiouni, *The Commission of Experts Established pursuant to Security Council Resolution 780: Investigating Violations of International Humanitarian Law in the Former Yugoslavia*, in this issue of *Criminal Law Forum*.

[38] *E.g.*, Criminal Procedure and Evidence Act § 30(1), Laws of Bots. ch. 08:02, permits a police officer to ask any person who may, in his opinion, be able to give evidence in regard to the commission or suspected commission of an offense to furnish "his full name and address." This is all the officer is authorized to elicit out of a witness.

tance of the state authorities concerned. Although such authorities may be able to secure the attendance of witnesses for questioning, it is doubtful that they can force them to talk, particularly where domestic law does not so permit. Additionally, were a prospective witness to fail to answer a subpoena for questioning, would he be guilty of an offense? States will no doubt have to enact mutual assistance laws under which individuals within their borders will be obliged to honor, under the threat of punishment, process and orders issued by a trial chamber under rule 39(iv).[39]

Rule 39 also authorizes the prosecutor to conduct on-site investigations. Generally speaking, what kind of information should an investigator look for? According to the Lawyers Committee for Human Rights:

> The primary task of the war crimes investigator is the collection and preservation of physical evidence, identification of witnesses, the collection of testimony that can be presented at trial and the identification of alleged perpetrators for indictment. Statements from witnesses, victims and persons involved in war crimes are particularly useful. . . . Investigators should look for actual victims or eyewitnesses as well as secondhand sources. Information they should obtain includes the names of witnesses to the events and other victims, whether living or not; the names of perpetrators, if known, and any distinguishing features; physical descriptions or exact locations of places where violations occurred; the names of people in charge of the camps or in command of forces if known; and descriptions of uniforms or which particular unit was involved. It is also important to

---

[39] In this regard, see Statute, *supra* note 2, art. 29; *Annual Report of the International Tribunal for the Prosecution of Persons Responsible for Serious Violations of International Humanitarian Law Committed in the Territory of the Former Yugoslavia since 1991,* ¶¶ 84–94, 172–182, U.N. SCOR, 49th Year, Agenda Item 152, U.N. Doc. S/1994/1007 (1994). States usually assist each other in these matters under treaties of mutual assistance in criminal matters and the national legislation implementing them. For further discussion, see David McClean, *International Judicial Assistance* (1992); William A. Schabas, *International Judicial Assistance,* 5 Crim. L.F. 137 (1994) (reviewing McClean's treatise).

collect any information that may be evidence of crimes being organized. Finally, it is critical to get addresses of victims and witnesses and the names and addresses of friends and relatives who will be able to locate the victim or witness if that person moves. Ultimately, there will have to be live testimony of war crimes.

Documentary evidence of war crimes also should be collected. Even if some evidence is not admissible, it may be likely to lead to the discovery of admissible evidence or useful for impeachment or to refresh recollection. The following is some, but not all, of the evidence that may be available and useful: photographs, including photographs of the sites of crimes and of injuries; hospitalization records or documentation of physical examinations; photographs, videotapes and audio tapes. Local war crimes commissions also may be an excellent source for information.[40]

Rule 40 also authorizes the prosecutor to request any state concerned, as a matter of urgency,

(i) to arrest a suspect provisionally;

(ii) to seize physical evidence;

(iii) to take all necessary measures to prevent the escape of a suspect or an accused, injury to or intimidation of a victim or witness, or the destruction of evidence.

Rule 41 places on the prosecutor responsibility for the retention, storage, and security of information and physical evidence obtained in the course of investigations. Such evidence may be needed in future proceedings. Where a piece of evidence is unlikely to be used again in

---

[40] Lawyers Comm. for Human Rights, International Tribunal on War Crimes in the Former Yugoslavia: Establishment, Proceedings to Date, and Jurisdiction 29 (memorandum submitted to the Round Table on the International War Crimes Tribunal, organized by the Centre for Anti-war Action—Belgrade, Brussels, Belgium, Mar. 3–4, 1994).

other cases, it would be proper and advisable for the prosecutor to return it to its rightful owner (if known). It should not, however, be returned if it was used to perpetrate a crime and the owner either knew about, or acquiesced in, such use. In that case, it is suggested that the prosecutor should seek an order for its forfeiture to the Tribunal or the competent national authorities or for its destruction.[41]

Questioning of Suspects

From the language of both the Statute and the rules it seems to be a fait accompli that the suspect must submit to the questioning process by the prosecutor. However, before questioning, the suspect must be informed in a language he speaks and understands that he is entitled to have counsel of his own choice present during questioning or to have free legal assistance assigned to him if he does not have sufficient means to pay for representation and that he is entitled to have the free assistance of an interpreter if he does not understand or speak the language to be used for questioning.[42]

The rules do not explicitly state that a suspect, as opposed to an accused person, has a right to remain silent or to refuse to answer certain questions put to him. It is submitted that the suspect does have such a right. This right is implicit from article 21(4)(g) of the Statute, which guarantees to the accused the right "not to be compelled to testify against himself or to confess guilt." The *Secretary-General's Report* explains that "the International Tribunal must fully respect internationally recognized standards regarding the rights of the accused at all stages of its proceedings," citing in particular article 14 of the International Covenant on Civil and Political Rights.[43] Unless this right is recognized to operate at this stage, it would have little significance to the accused later on, because the fate of a criminal case is usually determined by what goes on at the pretrial interrogation sessions.

It is hoped that the right to remain silent will not be nullified,

---

[41] *See* I.T. R. Proc. & Evid., *supra* note 1, RR. 88(B), 105.

[42] *Id.* R. 42(A).

[43] *Secretary-General's Report, supra* note 2, ¶ 106. *See supra* note 6.

as is the case in some civil law jurisdictions where an accused person's election to remain silent during custodial interrogation is taken into account by the court when it is determining the issue of guilt.[44]

It is also noteworthy that questioning must be conducted in the presence of defense counsel, unless the suspect has voluntarily waived that right and has not changed her mind.[45] Counsel must be one of the suspect's own choice. However, if the suspect is indigent and does not have sufficient means to hire counsel, the registrar may assign one at the expense of the Tribunal.[46] Indigence is to be determined by the registrar according to the criteria he establishes with the approval of the judges.[47] Where the suspect fails either to obtain counsel or to request assignment of counsel under rule 45(C), the registrar must assign him one unless he has waived this right in writing.[48]

Right to counsel at pretrial interrogations is vital. It ensures that such interrogations are conducted fairly. In particular, it ensures that the suspect's right to remain silent is not nullified by improper interrogation tactics. It reduces the likelihood of coercion by the interrogator, and if coercion has been exerted counsel will be able to testify about it before the court. It also ensures that when the suspect elects to make a statement, the statement is accurately recorded and reported by the interrogator. Where that statement amounts to a confession, counsel's

---

[44] The latest revision of the rules corrected this deficiency. U.N. Doc. IT/32/Rev.3 (1995), *supra* note 1, R. 42(A)(iii), expressly confers on the suspect during investigation "the right to remain silent, and to be cautioned that any statement he makes shall be recorded and may be used in evidence." On civil law practice, see Manfred Pieck, *The Accused's Privilege against Self-incrimination in the Civil Law*, 11 Am. J. Comp. L. 585 (1962). On the recent, highly controversial change in England regarding the drawing of an adverse inference from the accused's silence, see *infra* note 128.

[45] Statute, *supra* note 2, art. 18(3); I.T. R. Proc. & Evid., *supra* note 1, R. 42(B).

[46] Statute, *supra* note 2, art. 18(3); I.T. R. Proc. & Evid., *supra* note 1, R. 42(A)(i). Counsel is picked from a list kept by the registrar. The list contains names of lawyers who speak one or both of the working languages of the Tribunal, are admitted to practice law in any state or are university professors of law, and have indicated their willingness to be assigned to indigent suspects or accused. *Id.* RR. 44–45.

[47] I.T. R. Proc. & Evid., *supra* note 1, R. 45(B).

[48] *Id.* R. 45(E).

presence ensures that it is freely and voluntarily made.[49]

Also important is the requirement that questioning be either tape-recorded or video-recorded.[50] The suspect must be informed in a language she speaks and understands that the interrogation is being recorded.[51] In the event of a break in the questioning, the fact and the time of the break must be recorded before the tape-recording or video-recording ends; the time of resumption of questioning must also be recorded.[52] This is no doubt intended to explain to the audience of the recording the reason for the break and to ensure a smooth flow in the narrative. It also guards against tampering. At the conclusion of questioning, the suspect must be allowed to clarify anything she said or to add anything she wants.[53] The recording must then be transcribed and a copy of both the recording and the transcript supplied to the suspect.[54] Thereafter, the original audiotape or videotape is sealed in the presence of the suspect, under the signature of the prosecutor and the suspect.[55]

While the recording of questioning may be costly, it is nonetheless a vital element in the proper administration of criminal justice. The fact that the recording is being made should tend to restrain the interrogator from coercing the suspect, at least during the formal interview, and to reduce the frequency of allegations of coerced confessions. The recordings will enable the Tribunal to assess the demeanor of the participants and the fairness of the proceedings.

---

[49] *See generally* Daniel D. Ntanda Nsereko, *The Poisoned Tree: Responses to Involuntary Confessions in Criminal Proceedings in Botswana, Uganda, and Zambia*, 5 Afr. J. Int'l & Comp. L. 609 (1993) [hereinafter Nsereko, *The Poisoned Tree*]; Daniel D. Ntanda Nsereko, *The Right to Legal Representation in Botswana*, 18 Isr. Y.B. Hum. Rts. 211 (1988).

[50] I.T. R. Proc. & Evid., *supra* note 1, R. 43.

[51] *Id.* R. 43(i).

[52] *Id.* R. 43(ii).

[53] *Id.* R. 43(iii).

[54] *Id.* R. 43(iv).

[55] *Id.* R. 43(v).

The rules do not provide the interrogator with any guidelines on how to question the suspect. In the absence of such guidelines, it is suggested that the rule of thumb be fairness. Such fairness can be achieved only where the environment within which the questioning is conducted is free from coercion or oppression. The suspect should be free to talk or not to talk. When he decides to talk, he should be allowed to do so in his own words, without prompting by the interrogator. The interrogator may, of course, ask questions that help to keep the narrative clear and to ensure that what the suspect means is what is recorded. However, she must not, under the guise of clarifying, cross-examine the suspect. As noted previously, the suspect must be provided with an interpreter if he does not speak or understand the language used in questioning.[56] The rules do not provide for written statements by the interrogatee, but there is no reason why he should not elect to write his statement instead of answering questions by the interrogator. Where he does, the interrogator should not question him, save to clarify points in the written statement.

Indictment and Pretrial Proceedings

If the prosecutor is satisfied that there is sufficient evidence to support a reasonable belief that a suspect committed an offense within the Tribunal's mandate, he must prepare an indictment.[57] Under rule 47(b), "The indictment shall set forth the name and particulars of the suspect, and a concise statement of the facts of the case and of the crime with which the suspect is charged." An indictment may join two or more persons charged with the same crime or with different crimes committed in the course of the same transaction.[58] It may likewise charge an accused person (or persons) with two or more crimes, if those crimes form part of a series of crimes that constitute one transaction and were

---

[56]   *Id.* R. 42(A)(ii).

[57]   Statute, *supra* note 2, art. 18(4); I.T. R. Proc. & Evid., *supra* note 1, R. 47(A); *see Secretary-General's Report, supra* note 2, ¶ 95.

[58]   I.T. R. Proc. & Evid., *supra* note 1, R. 48.

committed by the same accused person (or persons).[59] Each crime must, however, be described in a separate count.

Rule 47 requires the prosecutor to file the indictment with the registrar, who, in turn, places it before a judge of a trial chamber for review. On the appointed day, the prosecutor formally presents the indictment before the reviewing judge. He may at this stage also present to the judge any additional material in support of any of the counts in the indictment. The purpose of the review is to sift meritorious from nonmeritorious cases. A meritorious case is one that establishes a prima facie case.[60] The dismissal of an indictment or a count does not preclude the prosecutor from subsequently bringing a new indictment or count based on the acts underlying that indictment or count provided that there is additional evidence to support it.[61] This rule is in accord with the practice obtaining in common law jurisdictions that precludes courts from treating the dismissal of a charge at the preliminary inquiry stage as an acquittal and thus bringing into play the plea of *autrefois acquit*.[62]

An indictment may be amended without leave at any time before its confirmation; thereafter, amendment must be by leave of the trial chamber.[63] Similarly, an indictment may be withdrawn without leave at any time before its confirmation; thereafter, it can be withdrawn only with the leave of the judge who confirmed it or, if at trial, with leave of the trial chamber.[64]

At the time of confirmation, the confirming judge may, in consultation with the prosecutor, order that there be no disclosure of the indictment until it has been served on the accused or all the accused.[65]

---

[59] *Id.* R. 49.

[60] Statute, *supra* note 2, art. 19(1); *see* I.T. R. Proc. & Evid., *supra* note 1, R. 47(D).

[61] I.T. R. Proc. & Evid., *supra* note 1, R. 47(E).

[62] This plea is essentially the same as *non bis in idem*. See *supra* note 23–24 and accompanying text.

[63] I.T. R. Proc. & Evid., *supra* note 1, R. 50.

[64] *Id.* R. 51.

[65] *Id.* R. 53(A).

Nondisclosure at this stage is intended to ensure that the accused does not, on hearing of the indictment, disappear so as to avoid arrest and trial. For the same reason, the judge may also ban disclosure of part of an indictment or any particular document or information that is filed in support of the indictment.[66]

Upon confirmation of an indictment, the judge may, at the request of the prosecutor, issue a warrant for the arrest of the accused. The warrant must be accompanied by a copy of the indictment and a statement of the accused's rights. These rights include the right to remain silent and the right "to be cautioned that any statement he makes shall be recorded and may be used in evidence."[67] The registrar transmits the warrant to the national authorities of the state in whose territory or under whose jurisdiction and control the accused resides or was last known to be, along with the request that they execute it. The request must include instructions to the effect that at the time of arrest the rights of the accused must be read to him in a language he understands.[68] When the arrest is being made, a member of the prosecutor's office may be present.[69] This provision is probably intended to ensure compliance with all the rules relating to arrest, to advisement of rights, and to (subsequent) questioning. The state authorities to which the warrant is transmitted must execute it promptly and diligently.[70] "Upon the arrest of the accused, the State concerned shall detain him, and shall promptly notify the Registrar. The transfer of the accused to the seat of the Tribunal shall be arranged between the State authorities concerned and the Registrar."[71] The local authorities cannot set up their national laws or existing treaty obligations as an excuse for not surrendering the accused, since the obligations they assume under article 29 of the Statute

---

[66] *Id.* R. 53(B).

[67] *Id.* R. 55(A).

[68] *Id.* R. 55(B).

[69] *Id.* R. 55(C).

[70] *Id.* R. 56.

[71] *Id.* R. 57.

override such laws or treaty obligations.[72]

Where the national authorities are unable to execute an arrest warrant, they must so report to the registrar, giving the reasons for their inability.[73] If, after the lapse of a reasonable time, no report is made, "this shall be deemed a failure to execute the warrant of arrest and the Tribunal, through the President, may notify the Security Council accordingly."[74] At this point, the prosecutor has several other options. One is to place a notice in the newspapers in the country where the accused may be found, "intimating to the accused that service of an indictment against him is sought."[75] Another is to have an international arrest warrant issued and transmitted to all states.[76] However, the rules clearly preclude trial in absentia. Article 21(4)(d) of the Statute specifically recognizes as fundamental the accused's right "to be tried in his presence." The only exception is where the accused has "persisted in disruptive conduct following a warning that he may be removed." In that case, the accused may be removed from the courtroom and the proceedings will continue in his absence.[77]

Upon arrest and transfer to the seat of the Tribunal, the accused must be brought for arraignment before a trial chamber "without delay."[78] Under rule 62(i), the trial chamber must satisfy itself that the accused's right to counsel has been respected. The court then reads, or causes to be read, to the accused the indictment in a language that she speaks and understands. After that, the court is to "call upon the accused to enter a plea of guilty or not guilty; should the accused fail to

---

[72] *Id.* R. 58. For a detailed discussion of this topic, see Kenneth S. Gallant, *Securing the Presence of Defendants before the International Tribunal for the Former Yugoslavia: Breaking with Extradition,* in this issue of *Criminal Law Forum.*

[73] I.T. R. Proc. & Evid., *supra* note 1, R. 59(A).

[74] *Id.* R. 59(B).

[75] *Id.* R. 60.

[76] *Id.* R. 61(D).

[77] *Id.* R. 80(B).

[78] *Id.* R. 62.

do so, [the trial chamber shall] enter a plea of not guilty on his behalf."[79] It is suggested that in a case where the accused pleads guilty, the trial chamber should, before recording the plea, ensure that the plea is freely and voluntarily made and that it is unequivocal. To satisfy itself that the plea is unequivocal, the trial chamber should review the elements of the crime charged and require the accused to say whether she agrees with them or not. Where the accused disagrees with any fact that is essential to the charge, then her plea is equivocal. The trial chamber must in this event enter a plea of not guilty.

It is the general practice in common law jurisdictions that once an accused person has been arraigned, the prosecutor is not allowed to question him. The contest is already set. In contrast, the rules of the Tribunal permit questioning at this point. However, the prosecutor must satisfy the following conditions: defense counsel must be present, the questioning must be recorded pursuant to rule 43, and the "[p]rosecutor shall at the beginning of the questioning caution the accused that he is not obliged to say anything unless he wishes to do so but that whatever he says may be given in evidence."[80] In spite of these safeguards, it is submitted that this provision gives the prosecution an unfair advantage since the defense has no similar right to question prosecution witnesses.[81] It is therefore hoped that the prosecutor will resort to postarraignment questioning only in exceptional cases.

After being transferred to the seat of the Tribunal, the accused must be detained at the Tribunal's detention unit, leased from the host country, pending arraignment and trial.[82] Once detained, the accused can be released only on the order of a trial chamber in exceptional

---

[79]   *Id.* R. 62(iii).

[80]   *Id.* R. 63.

[81]   The accused is entitled to inspect "books, documents, photographs and tangible objects in his custody or control, which are material to the preparation of the defence, or are intended for use by the Prosecutor as evidence at trial or were obtained from or belonged to the accused." *Id.* R. 66(B).

[82]   *Id.* R. 64. For a discussion of these arrangements, see Julian J.E. Schutte, *Legal and Practical Implications, from the Perspective of the Host Country, Relating to the Establishment of the International Tribunal for the Former Yugoslavia*, in this issue of *Criminal Law Forum*.

circumstances.[83] Unfortunately, the rules provide no clue as to what these exceptional circumstances are, although ill health is probably one. Even then, the trial chamber must be satisfied that the accused will appear for trial and will not pose a danger to any victim, witness, or any other person.[84] The trial chamber "may [also] impose such conditions upon the release of the accused as it may determine appropriate, including the execution of a bail bond and the observance of such conditions as are necessary to ensure his presence for trial and the protection of others."[85] These conditions are not indicated in the rules, but they would include restrictions on the accused's movements, confiscation of her travel documents, and a requirement that she periodically report to designated authorities. They might also include execution of a bail bond. Considering that the rules subscribe to the presumption of innocence, the provisional release restrictions are quite stringent. The only justification for this stringency that comes to mind is the gravity of the offenses over which the Tribunal has jurisdiction and the desire to avoid a public outcry over allowing accused persons to be at large. Offsetting the stringency of the provisional release rule is the provision that "the period, if any, during which the convicted person was detained in custody pending his surrender to the Tribunal or pending trial" may be taken into account for sentencing purposes.[86]

FAIR TRIAL

The Statute and the Rules of Procedure and Evidence rely upon the principles of a fair trial that are already well established under international human rights law. One of these principles is the right to trial in

---

[83] I.T. R. Proc. & Evid., *supra* note 1, R. 65(B).

[84] *Id.*

[85] *Id.* R. 65(C).

[86] *Id.* R. 101(B)(iv).

public.[87] It is a cardinal principle of law that justice not only must be done but also must manifestly appear to be done. As one English judge has stated:

> If the way that courts behave cannot be hidden from the public ear and eye this provides a safeguard against judicial arbitrariness or idiosyncrasy and maintains the public confidence in the administration of justice.[88]

In accord with this principle, both the Statute and the rules endeavor to have proceedings before the Tribunal be as public and as transparent as possible. The indictment itself is of a public character, save where the interests of justice demand otherwise.[89] Apart from deliberations, proceedings before the trial chamber, including the pronouncement of the judgment, must be public: the court must be open to members of the public and particularly to the press.[90] The public and the press may be excluded only for reasons of public order or morality; the safety, security, or nondisclosure of the identity of a victim or witness; or the protection of the interests of justice.[91] Also important is the fact that the trial chambers have discretion to permit "[p]hotography, video-recording or audio-recording of the trial, otherwise than by the Registry" (presumably, the media).[92] This provision will help to keep the public around the world abreast of developments in any case before the Tribunal.

The presence on the Tribunal of competent and impartial judges is another indicium of a fair trial. According to the Statute,

---

[87] *See* Statute, *supra* note 2, art. 21(2); I.T. R. Proc. & Evid., *supra* note 1, R. 78.

[88] Attorney-General v. Leveller Magazine, 1979 App. Cas. 440, 450 (Lord Diplock).

[89] I.T. R. Proc. & Evid., *supra* note 1, RR. 52–53.

[90] *Id.* RR. 78–79, 88; Statute, *supra* note 2, arts. 21(2), 23(2).

[91] I.T. R. Proc. & Evid., *supra* note 1, R. 79(A). The reasons for ordering a closed session must be made public. *Id.* R. 79(B).

[92] *Id.* R. 81(D).

> [t]he judges shall be persons of high moral character, impartiality and integrity who possess the qualifications required in their respective countries for appointment to the highest judicial offices. In the overall composition of the Chambers due account shall be taken of the experience of the judges in criminal law, international law, including international humanitarian law[,] and human rights law.[93]

Additionally, before taking up their duties, the judges must make a "solemn declaration" to perform their duties and exercise their powers "honourably, faithfully, impartially, and conscientiously."[94] In keeping with this oath, the rules take meticulous care to ensure that no judge will sit on a case where, given the particular circumstances, he or she might not be, or appear to be, impartial. For this reason, a trial chamber that issues a request for deferral to the Tribunal is not allowed to handle subsequent proceedings in the case.[95] A judge of a trial chamber who reviews and confirms an indictment against an accused person is also forbidden to sit as a member of the chamber that tries that person.[96] A member of the appeals chamber is similarly forbidden to sit on any appeal in a case in which he or she sat as a member of the trial chamber.[97] Most important, a judge of either chamber who has a "personal interest" in a case or "concerning which he has or has had any association which might affect his impartiality" must voluntarily recuse himself or herself.[98] For the same reasons, the accused or the prosecutor may also apply to the presiding judge of a trial chamber for the recusal of a member of that chamber.[99] It is suggested that such an application

---

[93] Statute, *supra* note 2, art. 13(1).

[94] I.T. R. Proc. & Evid., *supra* note 1, R. 14(A).

[95] *Id.* R. 10(C).

[96] *Id.* R. 15(C).

[97] *Id.* R. 15(D).

[98] *Id.* R. 15(A).

[99] *Id.* R. 15(B).

should not be honored save on well-attested grounds that point to a likelihood of bias on the part of the judge.

Another important right is the right of the accused to defend himself. As noted earlier, article 21(4)(a) of the Statute provides that the accused must be informed "promptly and in detail in a language which he understands of the nature and cause of the charge against him." The arrest warrant itself, also discussed earlier, must be accompanied by a "statement of the rights of the accused."[100] Additionally, the accused must be given "adequate time and facilities for the preparation of his defence and to communicate with counsel of his own choosing."[101] In practice, this would mean granting reasonable adjournments to enable the accused person to prepare his or her case. As for facilities, the rules require the prosecutor to give the accused copies of transcripts of interrogation proceedings, along with the tapes thereof.[102] Where he amends the indictment, the prosecutor must furnish the accused with a copy of the amended indictment, together with all supporting documents.[103] In this event, the rules specifically require that, where necessary, the trial date must be postponed to ensure adequate time for the preparation of the defense.[104] Furthermore, "as soon as practicable after the initial appearance of the accused," the prosecutor must make available to the defense copies of the supporting material that accompanied the indictment at the time of its confirmation.[105] Again, the prosecutor "shall on request permit the defence to inspect any books, documents, photographs and tangible objects in his custody or control, which are material to the preparation of the defence, or are intended for use by the Prosecutor as evidence at trial or were obtained from or belonged to the accused."[106] The prosecutor must also notify the defense

---

[100] *Id.* R. 55(A).

[101] Statute, *supra* note 2, art. 21(4)(b).

[102] I.T. R. Proc. & Evid., *supra* note 1, R. 43(iv).

[103] Reading *id.* R. 50 together with RR. 47(A), 62(ii), 66(A).

[104] *Id.* R. 50.

[105] *Id.* R. 66(A).

[106] *Id.* R. 66(B).

of the witnesses he intends to call to prove the accused's guilt or to rebut the accused's defense of alibi or any special defense if the accused has notified the prosecution of his or her intention to offer any such defense.[107]

Where the accused asks, pursuant to rule 66(B), to inspect material evidence in the prosecutor's custody, this triggers the prosecutor's right to inspect "any books, documents, photographs and tangible objects, which are within the custody or control of the defence and which it intends to use as evidence at the trial."[108] This reciprocal disclosure of evidence by the prosecution and the defense is unusual, at least in many common law jurisdictions. Because the prosecution is considered to be the stronger of the two parties and bears the burden of proof, it is often obliged to disclose, whereas the defense is usually not required to disclose anything in advance. The procedure under the rule is commendable in that it conduces to an even combat and reduces the possibility of surprise at trial. Nevertheless, inasmuch as the prosecutor has an absolute obligation under rule 68 to disclose any evidence that tends to exculpate the accused, with no parallel obligation on the accused to disclose incriminating evidence, the rules overall appear to tilt the scales in favor of the accused.[109]

Regarding the right to counsel, a suspect must be informed of this right before questioning by the prosecutor,[110] at the time of arrest,[111] and at her initial appearance before a trial chamber.[112] Where a suspect or an accused has not waived the right to counsel, counsel must be

---

[107]   *Id.* RR. 67(A)(i), 69(B).

[108]   *Id.* R. 67(C).

[109]   *Id.* R. 68 does not discuss the consequences of nondisclosure. In some common law jurisdictions, nondisclosure may be fatal to the prosecution's case because it results in a failure of justice. *E.g.,* Mahadeo v. R., [1936] 2 All E.R 813 (P.C.) (appeal taken from Fiji); R. v. Stinchcombe, [1991] 3 S.C.R. 326, 332 (Can.) (Sopinka, J.); R. v. Fere, [1956–57] 8 Uganda L. Rep. 126 (High Ct. 1957).

[110]   I.T. R. Proc. & Evid., *supra* note 1, R. 42(A)(i).

[111]   *Id.* R. 55(A).

[112]   *Id.* R. 62(i).

present at all stages of the proceedings: pretrial interrogation,[113] taking depositions,[114] questioning the accused,[115] the trial proper,[116] and the hearing of the appeal, if any.[117] As noted earlier, the Tribunal may assign counsel *pro deo* to an indigent defendant.[118] This counsel will not necessarily be counsel of the accused's own choice.[119]

The rules also embody the right to confront prosecution witnesses[120] and to call and examine one's own witnesses.[121] According to article 21(4)(e) of the Statute, the accused is entitled "to examine, or have examined, the witnesses against him and to obtain the attendance and examination of witnesses on his behalf under the same conditions as witnesses against him." All of these elements are reflected in rule 85, regulating the presentation of evidence at trial. A few observations are in order.

First, the rules are silent over a procedure well known to the common law whereby the court may acquit the accused at the conclusion of the prosecution's case if the prosecution fails to establish a prima facie case.[122] A prima facie case is not established if (1) there is no evidence connecting the accused to the alleged offense, (2) the prosecution fails to

---

[113]   *Id.* R. 42(B).

[114]   *See id.* R. 71(C).

[115]   *Id.* R. 63.

[116]   *Id.* R. 62(i); Statute, *supra* note 2, art. 21(4)(d).

[117]   See sources cited *supra* note 116.

[118]   See *supra* notes 46–48 and accompanying text.

[119]   Under the rules of the International Military Tribunal, defendants were entitled to be assisted by counsel of their own choice at the expense of the tribunal, provided they applied for that "particular counsel" and he were available. Nuremberg Rules, *supra* note 5, R. 2(d).

[120]   I.T. R. Proc. & Evid., *supra* note 1, R. 85(B).

[121]   *Id.* R. 85.

[122]   A prima facie case is established if there is "such evidence that, if it be uncontradicted at the trial, a reasonable minded jury may convict upon it." *Ex parte* Bidwell, [1937] 1 K.B. 305, 314 (1936).

prove all the essential elements of the offense charged, (3) the prosecution witnesses have been too discredited during cross-examination to be credible, or (4) the prosecution evidence is so fragmentary as to be unsafe of belief. Termination of the proceedings at this stage is in accord with the principle that the party who alleges must prove, that the prosecution bears the initial evidentiary burden of proof, and that the prosecution must not expect to rely on the defense (through its witnesses) to establish its case. The Tribunal seems to have adopted the civil law practice, which does not require the prosecution to establish a prima facie case before the accused can be called upon to answer it. Under civil law rules of procedure, it is apparently common to begin the evidence-taking process by the judge questioning the accused before the prosecution has called its witnesses.[123]

Second, it is noteworthy that rule 85(B) specifically allows the judge "at any stage [to] put any question to the witness." It is hoped that this provision will not be interpreted as a license for judges to descend pell-mell into the arena of trial combat and conduct the questioning of witnesses unrestrained. It is submitted that the questioning of witnesses should, as a general rule, be left to the parties through their counsel on the ground that a "judge who observes the demeanour of the witnesses while they are being examined by counsel has from his detached position a much more favourable opportunity of forming a just appreciation than a judge who himself conducts the examination."[124] A judge should be free to ask questions, but only for the sake of resolving ambiguities and clarifying certain points that might have been overlooked by counsel. She must, however, do so with restraint, especially where both parties are represented. The following judicial guidelines may be of use to the judges of the International Tribunal:

> (a)   [A judge] should refrain from asking questions of witnesses or the accused in such a way as to create the impres-

---

[123] Mirjan Damaska, *Evidentiary Barriers to Conviction and Two Models of Criminal Procedure: A Comparative Study*, 121 U. Pa. L. Rev. 506 (1973); Pieck, *supra* note 44.

[124] Yuill v. Yuill, [1945] 1 All E.R. 183, 189 (Eng. C.A. 1944) (Lord Greene), *cited with approval in* Lemme v. State, 1985 Bots. L. Rep. 576; *accord* R. v. Roopsing, [1956] 4 S. Afr. L. Rep. 509 (App. Div.).

sion that he is not conducting the trial in an open-minded or impartial manner. This may arise from the frequency, length, timing, form, tone or contents of the questions.

(b)   He should also refrain from questioning witnesses or the accused in such a way or to such an extent that it may preclude him from detachedly or objectively appreciating and adjudicating upon the issues being fought out before him.

(c)   He should also refrain from questioning a witness or an accused person in a way that may intimidate or disconcert him or unduly influence the quality or nature of his replies and thus affect his demeanor or impair his credibility.[125]

The third observation relates to the right against self-incrimination. Article 21(4)(g) of the Statute provides that the accused has the right "not to be compelled to testify against himself or to confess guilt." This means not only refusing to answer particular questions but also refusing to take the witness stand and be subjected to any form of questioning. While the rules clearly contemplate that the witness can elect not to talk,[126] the issue arises whether the Tribunal will draw adverse inferences from the exercise of this right either at the pretrial stage or at trial. In the United States, the court may not, consistently with the Constitution, draw an adverse inference from the accused's decision to remain silent.[127] But courts in other common law[128] and civil

---

[125]   *Lemme*, 1985 Bots. L. Rep. at 580 (Aguda, J.).

[126]   I.T. R. Proc. & Evid., *supra* note 1, R. 85(C), provides that "[t]he accused may, *if he so desires*, appear as a witness in his own defence" (emphasis added). *Id.* RR. 55(A), 63 provide for the right to remain silent.

[127]   U.S. Const. amend. V; Griffin v. California, 380 U.S. 609 (1965).

[128]   *E.g.*, Waugh v. R., 1950 App. Cas. 203 (P.C.) (appeal taken from Jam.); Attorney-General v. Moagi, 1981 Bots. L. Rep. 1; Vezeau v. R., [1977] 2 S.C.R. 277 (Can. 1976); S. v. Mehlape, [1963] 2 S. Afr. L. Rep. 29, 34 (App. Div. 1962). In *Waugh*, 1950 App. Cas. at 211, the Privy Council noted that in England, as in Jamaica, "it is a matter for the judge's discretion whether he shall comment on the fact that a prisoner has not given evidence; but the very fact that the prosecution are not permitted

law[129] jurisdictions often make such inferences within certain parameters. Drawing an adverse inference, it is submitted, renders nugatory the accused's right to remain silent. Once again, the Tribunal's rules do not address this point. It is hoped that the judges will decide to uphold the right to remain silent by not penalizing defendants who invoke it.

RULES OF EVIDENCE

Rules of evidence provide the means by which a court ascertains the truth. They ensure, as much as is humanly possible, that the innocent are not convicted and that the guilty are not let off the hook. Unfortunately, rules of evidence tend to be complex, technical, and incapable of complete codification. They are, for the most part, developed by the courts in response to the need of arriving at the truth in particular situations. Part VI, section 3, of the Rules of Procedure and Evidence deals with evidence in proceedings before the trial chambers. This section comprises only ten of the Tribunal's one hundred twenty-five rules. While rule 89(A) provides that these rules "shall govern the proceedings" and that the trial chambers "shall not be bound by national rules of evidence," this section contains few substantive provisions. Only such matters as confessions, similar acts, judicial notice, evidence in sex-

---

to comment on that fact shows how careful a judge should be in making such comment." Under *Waugh* and later cases, the judge may not, however, comment that the defendant's failure to testify is evidence of guilt. R. v. Sparrow, 57 Crim. App. 352 (Eng. C.A. 1973) (citing *Waugh*).

The law in England changed recently. The Criminal Justice and Public Order Act, 1994, §§ 34–39 (Eng. & Wales), now permits the fact-finder (jury or judge) to draw an adverse inference from the accused's silence. This provision and others curtailing the right to silence during questioning, as well as the right to peaceful assembly, have provoked a public uproar. For some background, see Fred Barbash, *British Law Draws New Line on Crime: Classic Rights Suffer a Setback as Police Powers Get Big Boost*, Int'l Herald Trib., Nov. 12, 1994, *available in* LEXIS, World Library, Allnws File; Charles Glass, *A Modern Enactment of the Star Chamber*, The Independent, Nov. 9, 1994, at 18, *available in* LEXIS, UK Library, Ukpaper File.

[129] Damaska, *supra* note 123; Pieck, *supra* note 44.

related cases, and lawyer–client privilege are specifically covered. It would have been a gargantuan task to draw up a comprehensive code covering all evidentiary issues. Thus, the Tribunal has left it to each trial chamber to apply, in cases not otherwise provided for, "rules of evidence which will best favour a fair determination of the matter before it and [which] are consonant with the spirit of the Statute and the general principles of law."[130] This provision would appear to permit the judges to be guided by national rules of evidence in filling lacunae. The "spirit of the Statute" is best captured by article 20(1), which requires that trials be "fair and expeditious" and pay "full respect for the rights of the accused and due regard for the protection of victims and witnesses." The "general principles of law" would seem to bear the same meaning as under article 38(1)(c) of the Statute of the International Court of Justice, that is, "the general principles of law recognized by civilized nations."

Admissible Evidence

According to rule 89(C), "[a] Chamber may admit any relevant evidence which it deems to have probative value." In this context, "relevant evidence" means evidence that conduces to prove or disprove any fact or matter in issue before the court. Evidence with "probative value" is evidence that has persuasive value or tends to prove or disprove the fact or matter in issue. Probity is thus the qualitative value of evidence, making it persuasive or giving it weight or cogency. It is the duty of the court to evaluate any piece of evidence and determine what its probative value is, if any. In doing so, the court takes into account a multitude of factors, including the credibility of witnesses.

Evidence may be relevant and have some probative value. Yet, for overriding policy considerations, it may be inadmissible. Thus, according to rule 89(D), "[a] Chamber may exclude evidence if its probative value is substantially outweighed by the need to ensure a fair

---

[130] I.T. R. Proc. & Evid., *supra* note 1, R. 89(B), compares well with Nuremberg Charter, *supra* note 3, art. 19 ("The Tribunal shall not be bound by technical rules of evidence. It shall adopt and apply to the greatest possible extent expeditious and non-technical procedure, and shall admit any evidence which it deems to have probative value.").

trial." It remains to be seen in what circumstances the trial chambers will deem it necessary to exclude relevant and probative evidence. One such category of evidence is likely to be hearsay. Evidence is hearsay when the person who is attempting to testify to it in court is not the one who actually perceived it with her own senses but is only reporting or repeating what someone else who is not before the court said. Subject to certain exceptions, hearsay evidence is inadmissible, particularly in common law jurisdictions, because its probity cannot be tested by cross-examination. It may be inaccurate or distorted through repetition, or it may be a downright fabrication the authenticity of which cannot be verified. Another category of evidence that may be deemed inadmissible is a mere opinion by a person who is not an expert, in a matter that does not call for particular expertise. To admit such evidence would be to usurp the judges' function of making inferences or formulating opinions or conclusions on the basis of the evidence before them.

Confessions obtained as a result of improper interrogation procedures constitute yet another category of relevant evidence that may be excluded for reasons of fairness. For example, if certain information were elicited from the accused before she was advised of her right to counsel or her right to remain silent, contrary to rule 63, it would not be fair to admit this evidence. Testimonial evidence should also be inadmissible if the way in which it was recorded did not conform to the mandatory procedures set out in rule 43. Such evidence would be suspect and unreliable. A confession must also be excluded if it was not freely and voluntarily made by the accused, because in that event it may be untrue. Regarding confessions made in the course of questioning by the prosecutor, rule 92 creates a presumption: if "the requirements of Rule 63 were strictly complied with," the confession shall be deemed "to have been free and voluntary unless the contrary is proved." This rule, unlike the position under the common law, casts the burden of proving involuntariness on the accused. This is not easy, particularly in cases where the accused alleges physical torture by methods that leave no detectable traces, such as denial of sleep, immersion in freezing water, or partial suffocation.

While it is unlikely that the prosecutor will use such illegal means at interrogation sessions that are tape-recorded or video-recorded, the accused may be able to show that the atmosphere during interrogations, the duration of questioning, and the manner of questioning were sufficiently oppressive, in effect, to force a confession.[131] The accused may also be able to show that at the time of questioning he was already laboring under threats or pressure or promises and that these influences had not dissipated when he "confessed."[132]

Considering the difficulties that a defendant may face in attempting to prove involuntariness, it is suggested that the standard or quantum of proof should be on a balance of probabilities or a preponderance of evidence, and not beyond a reasonable doubt.

Rule 95 also expressly excludes evidence "obtained directly or indirectly by means which constitute a serious violation of internationally protected human rights." One such right is "human dignity." Torture has been condemned as an "offence to human dignity."[133] As one way of combatting the use of torture in the administration of criminal justice, the Convention against Torture and Other Cruel, Inhuman, or Degrading Treatment or Punishment requires each state party to "ensure that any statement which is established to have been made as a result of torture shall not be invoked as evidence in any proceedings, except against a person accused of torture as evidence that the statement was made."[134] It is interesting to note that the convention talks of "any statement" rather than "any confession." "Confession" is a technical term with limited meaning: it means a statement by the accused amounting to an admission of guilt; it is the equivalent of a plea of guilty. Such a statement must be unequivocal and must admit all the ingredients of the offense.[135] A statement that admits some but not all

---

[131] *See* State v. Bagwasi, 1968–70 Bots. L. Rep. 129 (High Ct. 1969) (Dendy Young, C.J.) (discussing "physiological methods not involving physical pain [that] can result in breaking down the resistance of an individual and inducing him to confess").

[132] *See* Nsereko, *The Poisoned Tree, supra* note 49.

[133] Declaration on the Protection of All Persons from Being Subjected to Torture and Other Cruel, Inhuman, or Degrading Treatment or Punishment art. 2, G.A. Res. 3452 (XXX), U.N. GAOR, 30th Sess., Supp. No. 34, at 91, U.N. Doc. A/10034 (1975) [hereinafter Torture Declaration].

[134] Torture Convention, *supra* note 9, art. 15; *see also* Torture Declaration, *supra* note 133, art. 12.

[135] *E.g.,* Pakala Narayana Swami v. King-Emperor, [1939] 1 All E.R. 396, 405 (P.C.) (appeal taken from India) (Lord Atkin) (defining confession as a statement that

the elements of the offense is not a confession but is nevertheless useful. In some jurisdictions, such statements, called "admissions," may be introduced into evidence even when they have been improperly elicited from the accused as long as they do not amount to a confession.[136] "Statement," in contrast, is a wider term and includes everything said, including confessions and admissions. Therefore, any statement, be it a confession or an admission and by whomsoever made, induced by torture will be inadmissible under both the Torture Convention and the Tribunal's rules.

A related concept is what, in some jurisdictions, is referred to as "pointing-out evidence." This is evidence obtained by law enforcement agents when an accused person in custody points out something, say, an instrument used to commit a crime or the proceeds of crime. The agents recover the thing and subsequently use it in evidence against the accused. The accused often "agrees" to point out the evidence as a result of prolonged interrogation, psychological pressure, and even torture. Some jurisdictions admit objects discovered as a result of the pointing out even though the pointing out forms part of an inadmissible confession.[137] Those who argue in favor of admitting pointing-out evidence say that it is truthful, because the thing pointed out has actually been found. They also say that to deny the prosecution the use of this evidence would be to prejudice the public interest and impede the due administration of justice. It would also frustrate law enforcement agents

---

"admit[s] in terms either the offence or, at any rate, substantially all the facts which constitute the offence"); R. v. Becker, [1929] 2 S. Afr. L. Rep. 167, 171 (App. Div. 1928) (DeVilliers, A.C.J.) (defining confession as "an unequivocal acknowledgment of . . . guilt, the equivalent of a plea of guilty before a court of law"); *accord* Mohalenyane v. State, 1984 Bots. L. Rep. 291 (High Ct.); *accord* State v. Haban, [1971] 2 Bots. L. Rep. 66 (High Ct.).

[136] *E.g., Mohalenyane,* 1984 Bots. L. Rep. at 291.

[137] *E.g.,* Criminal Procedure and Evidence Act § 229, Laws of Bots. ch. 08:02; Evidence Act § 29(A) *(as amended* by Decree No. 25 of 1971), Laws of Uganda ch. 43. Pointing-out evidence that formed part of an inadmissible confession was held to be admissible by the Uganda Supreme Court, the Court saying that it would have been "negligent" on the part of the police officer if he had not acted on the otherwise inadmissible information given to him by the accused. Sserunkuma v. Uganda, S. Ct. Crim. App. No. 8 of 1989 (Uganda Nov. 2, 1990).

in their zeal to fight crime and to bring criminals to book. The flip side of these arguments is that to admit evidence obtained as a result of improper or illegal methods would be to place a judicial imprimatur on such methods and to encourage law enforcement agents in lawless conduct. Admission of such evidence brings the administration of justice into disrepute. It also ignores the human rights of the accused—the protection of which should be an aim of the criminal justice system. As far as the International Tribunal is concerned, such evidence, if it forms part of a confession obtained as a result of torture, would be inadmissible as having been "obtained *directly or indirectly* by means which constitute a serious violation of internationally protected human rights."[138]

Could evidence obtained as a result of illegal searches and seizures or by trickery or as a result of crime also be excluded on this basis? The answer will turn on whether the means employed constituted "a serious violation" of "internationally protected human rights." In many common law jurisdictions, excepting Canada and the United States, illegally obtained evidence is admissible provided that it is relevant.[139] The courts in these jurisdictions do, however, retain some discretion to exclude such evidence if its admission would work an injustice to the accused. There is no doubt that evidence obtained as a result of an unauthorized search violates the accused's right to privacy, personal integrity, and quiet enjoyment of property, which are without doubt internationally protected.[140] Whether evidence thus obtained will be excluded depends on whether the International Tribunal will consider the violations "serious." Since it is implicit in the wording of the rules that the Tribunal has power to overlook some of these violations and admit evidence obtained as a result, it will have to determine issues of seriousness on a case-by-case basis, not in a blanket manner.

---

[138] I.T. R. Proc. & Evid., *supra* note 1, R. 95 (emphasis added).

[139] *E.g.*, Kuruma Son of Kaniu v. R., 1955 App. Cas. 197 (P.C.) (appeal taken from Kenya); Bercove v. Hermes, 49 A.L.R. 156 (Austl. Fed. Ct. W. Austl. 1983); Police v. Machirus, [1977] 1 N.Z.L.R. 288 (1976); Nile Petro Station v. R., [1956–57] 8 Uganda L. Rep. 68 (High Ct. 1956).

[140] Universal Declaration of Human Rights arts. 3, 12, 17, G.A. Res. 217A (III), U.N. Doc. A/810, at 71 (1948) [hereinafter Universal Declaration]; International Covenant, *supra* note 6, arts. 9(1), 17.

Privileged Evidence

Rule 97 forbids the disclosure of *all* lawyer–client communications unless the client consents to the disclosure or has voluntarily disclosed the content of the communication to a third party, who then gives evidence of that disclosure. The privilege is essential for enabling the client to talk freely with counsel without fear that what she tells the lawyer may be used against her. Candor and full and uninhibited disclosure of information enables lawyers effectively to represent clients.

In spite of the wording of rule 97, it must be assumed that certain communications—notably, those made for the purpose of violating the law—are not, in fact, privileged. Casual conversations made for purposes other than the obtaining or dispensing of legal services would also not be privileged. It is submitted that rule 97 is limited only to such communications as are made to the lawyer in her professional capacity and for the purpose of obtaining legal services. Communications made for other purposes should be subject to disclosure without the consent of the client. As noted earlier, rule 97 itself permits a third party to whom a lawyer–client communication has been disclosed by the client to give evidence of that disclosure.[141] The rationale here seems to be that by disclosing the contents of the communication to a third party, the client violates its confidential nature and does so, it is assumed, for purposes other than obtaining legal advice.[142]

The rules are silent about communications between spouses. Are they to be privileged, as they are under the laws of most common law jurisdictions? What of information in the possession of governments? Will governments be under an obligation to disclose such information if subpoenaed by one of the parties?[143] These are issues that the Tribunal may have to answer.

---

[141] I.T. R. Proc. & Evid., *supra* note 1, R. 97(ii).

[142] Apropos the discussion of privilege is *id.* R. 70, which provides in relevant part that "reports, memoranda, or other internal documents prepared by a party, its assistants or representatives in connection with the investigation or preparation of the case, are not subject to disclosure or notification."

[143] Bassiouni, *supra* note 37, discusses the difficulties that lack of access to government documents posed to the Commission of Experts.

Evidence in Cases of Sexual Assault

A feature of the law of evidence in common law jurisdictions that is not shared by their civil law counterparts is the requirement, in some cases, of corroboration before a fact in issue is said to be proved. Corroborative evidence is evidence independent of the principal witness that confirms in some material particular not only that the crime has been committed but also that the accused committed it. In such cases as treason and perjury, corroborative evidence is mandatory. In other cases, such as those involving child victims and sexual offenses, corroboration is not mandatory, but the courts do, as a matter of practice amounting to a rule of law, caution juries (and where there is no jury, judges caution themselves) about the danger inherent in basing a conviction on the uncorroborated evidence of one witness—the complainant. Courts will typically caution in a sexual assault case, for example, "that it is not safe to convict upon the uncorroborated testimony of the prosecutrix, but that the jury, if they are satisfied of the truth of her evidence, may, after paying attention to that warning, nevertheless convict."[144] The rationale for the cautionary rule in sex-related offenses is the alleged need to guard against false accusations, especially by women who consent to a sexual act but later deny consent. This view, championed most notably by Professor Glanville Williams,[145] assumes that women are more vengeful and more prone to tell lies or to fantasize than men.

The cautionary rule has been severely criticized as being misogynistic,[146] as offering an insult to women,[147] as perpetuating women's

---

[144] R. v. Jones, 19 Crim. App. 40, 41 (Eng. Crim. App. 1925) (Lord Hewart). England recently abolished the caution in rape cases. Criminal Justice and Public Order Act of 1994, § 32 (Eng. & Wales). For a brief account, see Marcel Berlins, *Writ Large*, The Guardian (Manchester), Nov. 9, 1994, at T15, *available in* LEXIS, World Library, Allnws File.

[145] Glanville Williams, *Textbook of Criminal Law* 238 (2d ed. 1983).

[146] Alice Armstrong, *Evidence in Rape Cases in Four Southern African Countries*, 33 J. Afr. L. 172 (1989).

[147] Armand Arabian, *The Cautionary Instruction in Sex Cases: A Lingering Insult*, 10 Sw. U. L. Rev. 585 (1978).

subordination,[148] and as treating the victim of a sexual attack as an accomplice to the crime.[149]

While a few jurisdictions have abolished this practice, many more still insist on it. For its part, the International Tribunal does not require any corroboration, let alone cautioning by the judges. Indeed, the Rules of Procedure and Evidence specifically dispense with corroboration in cases of sexual assault.[150] This position is in accord with UN aims and principles, particularly the promotion of equality between men and women.[151]

In the same vein, the rules impose strictures on the defense of consent and make it difficult to invoke with success. They endeavor to ensure that consent to a sexual act has been free and voluntary. Consent is not allowed as a defense if the victim "has been subjected to or threatened with or has had reason to fear violence, duress, detention or psychological oppression, or reasonably believed that if she did not submit, another might be so subjected, threatened or put in fear."[152]

The rules also declare as inadmissible evidence of prior sexual conduct of the victim.[153] Such evidence, if it is intended to show the victim as promiscuous, is not only unfair but also irrelevant. Prior consensual sexual relations between the accused and the victim might be

---

[148] Kathy Mack, *Continuing Barriers to Women's Credibility: A Feminist Perspective on the Proof Process*, 4 Crim. L.F. 327 (1993).

[149] Armstrong, *supra* note 146.

[150] I.T. R. Proc. & Evid., *supra* note 1, R. 96(i).

[151] *E.g.*, Universal Declaration, *supra* note 140, arts. 1, 2; International Covenant, *supra* note 6, arts. 2, 3; Declaration on the Elimination of Discrimination against Women, G.A. Res. 2263 (XXII), U.N. GAOR, 22d Sess., Supp. No. 16, at 35, U.N. Doc. A/6716 (1967); Convention on the Elimination of All Forms of Discrimination against Women, G.A. Res. 34/180, U.N. GAOR, 34th Sess., Supp. No. 46, at 193, U.N. Doc. A/34/46 (1979).

[152] I.T. R. Proc. & Evid., *supra* note 1, R. 96(ii). The latest revision of the rules added a requirement, R. 96 (iii), that "before evidence of the victim's consent is admitted, the accused shall satisfy the Trial Chamber *in camera* that the evidence is relevant and credible." U.N. Doc. IT/32/Rev.3 (1995), *supra* note 1.

[153] I.T. R. Proc. & Evid., *supra* note 1, R. 96(iii) (now R. 96(iv)).

relevant to the issue of consent to the act in question, and some jurisdictions admit it in evidence.[154] The rules, however, exclude all evidence of prior sexual conduct, presumably on the ground that it is prejudicial to the victim.

Evidence of a Consistent Pattern of Conduct

Character evidence relates to past criminal conduct, propensity or disposition to do certain things, and general reputation in the accused's community. Evidence of character in these three senses should not be admissible to prove that the accused committed the offense in question. It is highly prejudicial: it may lead the court to the conclusion that the accused is a bad person who because of past conduct is likely to be guilty of the offense charged. The court may also be deflected from determining guilt and punishment on the basis of the pending charge to examining past conduct instead. Evidence of character is also irrelevant. The fact that the accused committed similar acts in the past, or that he has a propensity to do so, does not ipso facto mean that he did so again on the occasion in question. Proof of guilt must be based on the proven facts, uninfluenced by prior conduct that does not form part of the charge.[155]

One instance in which bad character may be introduced in evidence is when, in the course of cross-examining a prosecution witness or giving evidence herself, the accused puts her good character in issue. Here the prosecution will be allowed to show the accused's bad character on the theory that character is indivisible: the accused cannot show only the good aspects of her character without opening the whole of it to scrutiny by the court. The prosecution also may be allowed to introduce evidence of bad character where the accused's line of defense is such as to cast aspersions on the character of the prosecutor or any prosecution

---

[154] *E.g.,* R. v. Riley, 18 Q.B. 481 (Cr. Cas. Res. 1887); R. v. Bashir, 54 Crim. App. 1 (Eng. Leeds Assizes 1969); *see* R. v. Hopkins, 15 Crim. App. (Sent.) 373 (Eng. C.A. 1993).

[155] *See generally* Sara Sun Beale, *Prior Similar Acts in Prosecutions for Rape and Child Sex Abuse,* 4 Crim. L.F. 307 (1993).

witnesses.[156]

Another instance where bad character evidence may be admissible is where the accused has in the past committed acts of a nature and in a manner similar to the acts in issue before the court. Such past acts may be relevant to identify their perpetrator. For example, in *R. v. Straffen*, where the accused was charged with murder by strangling, evidence of two previous murders was admitted, not to show propensity to commit murder, but because the manner in which all the murders had been committed was so similar that it provided positive evidence of identity.[157]

Though, as *Straffen* demonstrates, prior similar acts evidence may be admitted in any type of case, it may be most useful in prosecuting sexual crimes. These offenses usually take place in private, with no corroborative evidence.[158] Decisions in such cases turn, therefore, on the credibility of the complainant and the accused. Properly admitted evidence of prior similar acts can be highly probative.[159] It is thus not without reason that rule 93 provides that "[e]vidence of a consistent pattern of conduct may be admissible in the interests of justice." However, considering the danger inherent in such evidence, it is suggested that the trial chambers should admit it only exceptionally and only provided its probative value in relation to the issue the court is trying to resolve is so high that it outweighs the prejudicial effect of such evidence on the accused.

---

[156] Stirland v. Director of Public Prosecutions, 1944 App. Cas. 315; R. v. Watts, 77 Crim. App. 126 (Eng. C.A. 1983); *Cross on Evidence* 404 (7th ed. 1990).

[157] [1952] 2 Q.B. 911 (Crim. App.); *accord* Director of Public Prosecutions v. Boardman, 1975 App. Cas. 421 (1974).

[158] This is particularly so in cases where adult women are the victims. Because of the shame involved, victims may not call for help and may not report the crime soon enough to preserve crucial physical evidence (saliva, semen). No physical injury may occur to them either because they are already sexually active or because they do not physically resist the attacker for fear of further hurt.

[159] For an excellent discussion of the justification for this species of evidence see Beale, *supra* note 155.

Mode of Taking Evidence

According to rule 90, evidence before the trial chambers must be given viva voce by witnesses. This mode of taking evidence enables the judges to hear the evidence directly from the witnesses, to observe their demeanor, and thereby to assess their veracity. Based on the so-called principle of immediacy, the direct taking of evidence avoids the pitfalls of distortion that were inherent in the inquisitorial system. Under that system, judges seldom came in contact with the defendant or his witnesses. They acted solely on the evidence contained in the *acta inquisitionis*, which was prepared by the prosecution.

Desirable though the physical presence of witnesses in court may be, there are occasions where live testimony may not be practicable. For that reason, rule 90(A) permits "the witness [to] be heard by means of a deposition as provided for in rule 71." Needless to say, the party seeking to take a deposition must obtain leave and must satisfy the court of the exceptional circumstances justifying it.[160]

Regarding the actual taking of evidence before the trial chambers, the rules require every witness to make a solemn declaration before testifying.[161] Though obliged to answer truthfully all questions put to her, a witness is entitled to refuse to answer questions or to make any statement that "might tend" to incriminate her.[162] A witness who knowingly and wilfully gives false testimony is liable to prosecution and, if convicted, to a fine not exceeding $10,000, or a term of imprisonment of twelve months, or both.[163]

The rules are silent as to whether the defendant, if he elects to give evidence on his behalf, is also obliged to make a solemn declaration pursuant to rule 90(B). Would he be allowed to make an unsworn statement from the dock? If so, will he be liable to cross-examination? Under the common law he *cannot* be cross-examined. Under the civil

---

[160] I.T. R. Proc. & Evid., *supra* note 1, R. 71(A)–(B).

[161] *Id.* R. 90(B).

[162] *Id.* R. 90(D).

[163] *Id.* R. 91(E).

law he *can be* cross-examined. Which way will the Tribunal go?

We have noted the judges' role in the examination of witnesses. They also have power, *proprio motu* or on the application of a party, to summon new witnesses or to recall those who have already appeared to give additional evidence.[164] They may also dispense with proof of "facts of common knowledge" by taking judicial notice of them.[165] Last, before making a finding of guilt, the majority of judges in the chamber must be satisfied that guilt on each count in the indictment has been proven beyond a reasonable doubt.[166]

CONCLUDING REMARKS

This article has examined the International Tribunal's Rules of Procedure and Evidence. Regarding procedure, the major focus has been on those rules that regulate the proceedings at the pretrial and trial stages. These are the most critical phases of the proceedings. Space has not permitted a discussion of sentencing, which of course is equally critical. Fortunately, the rules on sentencing are uncontroversial. They allow both the prosecution and the defense to submit information that may assist the trial chamber in determining an appropriate sentence.[167] From the defense standpoint, this is the occasion to make a plea in mitigation: raising all matters that tend to lessen the moral blameworthiness of the offense and to justify the imposition of a lenient sentence. The prosecutor, too, will be able to bring to the attention of the trial chamber all the aggravating factors that may justify a severe sentence. Regarding the sentence itself, it should be noted that the Statute prescribes imprisonment as the only form of punishment that the trial

---

[164] *Id.* R. 98.

[165] *Id.* R. 94.

[166] *Id.* R. 87. The judges must vote separately on each count in the indictment. According to *id.* R. 88(C), the trial judges may append a separate or dissenting opinion to the judgment.

[167] *Id.* R. 100.

chambers may impose,[168] although the court may also order "the return of any property and proceeds acquired by criminal conduct, including by means of duress, to their rightful owners."[169] In determining the appropriate term of imprisonment to impose, the court is directed to take into account "the general practice regarding prison sentences in the courts of the former Yugoslavia" and "the gravity of the offence and the individual circumstances of the convicted person."[170] The rules flesh out this general mandate with a comprehensive but nonexhaustive list of additional factors to weigh.[171]

While the Statute and the rules strive to ensure that the accused gets a fair trial, they do not ignore victims, as is often the case under national criminal justice systems. Not only do they create a victim and witness unit within the registrar's office to address the special needs of victims,[172] but also they provide for the possibility of compensation. The rules state that for purposes of lodging claims for compensation the judgment of the Tribunal "shall be final and binding as to the criminal responsibility of the convicted person."[173] However, instead of setting up an international compensation scheme, the rules contemplate "an action in a national court or other competent body to obtain compensation."[174] This assumes, incorrectly in many cases, that appropriate claims mecha-

---

[168] Statute, *supra* note 2, art. 24(1); *see also* I.T. R. Proc. & Evid., *supra* note 1, R. 101(A) (providing that a "convicted person may be sentenced to imprisonment for a term up to and including the remainder of his life").

[169] Statute, *supra* note 2, art. 24(3); *see also* I.T. R. Proc. & Evid., *supra* note 1, R. 105.

[170] Statute, *supra* note 2, art. 24(1)–(2); *see also* I.T. R. Proc. & Evid., *supra* note 1, R. 101(B). These provisions are criticized in Pavel Dolenc, *A Slovenian Perspective on the Statute and Rules of the International Tribunal for the Former Yugoslavia*, in this issue of *Criminal Law Forum*.

[171] I.T. R. Proc. & Evid., *supra* note 1, R. 101(B).

[172] *Id.* R. 34; *see* Statute, *supra* note 2, art. 22. The unit's primary function is to recommend protective measures during trial and to provide counseling and support for victims, in particular in cases of rape and sexual assault.

[173] I.T. R. Proc. & Evid., *supra* note 1, R. 106(C).

[174] *Id.* R. 106(B).

nisms exist at the national level and that convicted persons will be able to satisfy judgments for compensation, a promise on the part of the international community that is likely to remain unfulfilled.

The Tribunal's appeals system is a veritable improvement on the Nuremberg system. It gives parties an opportunity to test the correctness of the trial chambers' decisions by the appeals chamber, which, being detached from the trial contest, can bring its sober assessment of the settled facts and the applicable law to bear on the case. Remarkable, too, is the fact that both sides to the proceedings are treated equally. The prosecution, contrary to the practice under some national systems, is permitted to appeal (like the defendant) against an "error on a question of law invalidating the decision; or an error of fact which has occasioned a miscarriage of justice."[175] Equally remarkable are the provisions for review "[w]here a new fact has been discovered which was not known to the moving party at the time of the proceedings before a Trial Chamber or the Appeals Chamber, and could not have been discovered through the exercise of due diligence."[176]

Nonetheless, lawyers with trial experience will be left with a sense of frustration from the rules. They will find many lacunae, especially in the provisions relating to evidence (for example, competence of witnesses, the kinds of questions that may or may not be asked during examination-in-chief, cross-examination, and reexamination, the extent to which hearsay and opinion evidence may be admitted). Fortunately, rule 89(B), which allows the trial chambers to apply rules of evidence that will best favor a fair determination of the issues, offers to the Tribunal and the lawyers who appear before it a golden opportunity to craft a workable and just procedural and evidentiary regime that will foster the interests of international justice. Admittedly, this will require imagination, open-mindedness, and patience.

At the conclusion of the Nuremberg trials, Otto Pannenbecker,

---

[175] Statute, *supra* note 2, art. 25(1). For the rules on appeal, see I.T. R. Proc. & Evid., *supra* note 1, RR. 107–118.

[176] I.T. R. Proc. & Evid., *supra* note 1, R. 119. For the rules on review, see Statute, *supra* note 2, art. 26; I.T. R. Proc. & Evid., *supra*, RR. 119–122. The prosecutor has a right to request review only "within one year after the final judgement has been pronounced." *Id.* R. 119.

who represented one of the defendants, expressed satisfaction that the proceedings had been fair. He said this although his client was convicted and executed.[177] The Statute and the Rules of Procedure and Evidence of the International Tribunal for the Former Yugoslavia aim at ensuring that at the conclusion of its proceedings, all fair-minded observers will come to the same firm conclusion as did Pannenbecker after Nuremberg. Only a fair trial can serve as a valuable precedent for the future and draw the support of the international community in the nascent international criminal justice system.

---

[177] Steven Fogelson, Note, *The Nuremberg Legacy: An Unfulfilled Promise,* 63 S. Cal. L. Rev. 833, 860 (1990).

11
Securing the Presence of Defendants before the International Tribunal for the Former Yugoslavia: Breaking with Extradition[*]

Kenneth S. Gallant[**]

Unlike the victors' war crimes tribunals at Nuremberg and Tokyo, the International Tribunal for the Prosecution of Persons Responsible for Serious Violations of International Humanitarian Law Committed in the Territory of the Former Yugoslavia since 1991 will probably not find most of its defendants already captured and ready to be tried. As the Tribunal prepares for prosecutions even before the end of war in the region, the persons who are responsible for war crimes and other violations of international humanitarian law are, in many cases, still combatants or commanders. Thus, the Tribunal's ability to obtain the presence of defendants will in a pivotal way determine its success or

---

[*] © 1995 Kenneth S. Gallant.
Editor's note: research for this article was updated through December 31, 1994. As this article went to press, revisions reflecting a few of the amendments made in January 1995 to the Tribunal's Rules of Procedure and Evidence were added.

[**] Professor of Law and Fellow, Martin Institute for Peace Studies and Conflict Resolution, University of Idaho, Moscow, Idaho, United States; A.B., Harvard College 1973; J.D., University of Pennsylvania 1977. Some of the ideas in this article will be presented to the International Law Association project on extradition and human rights. I would like to thank the Martin Institute for financial support for this article. Very useful comments and criticisms were provided by Alfred P. Rubin, Joan Fitzpatrick, Christopher Pyle, and M. Cherif Bassiouni.

failure in bringing criminals to justice. Moreover, the way in which the Tribunal goes about obtaining the presence of defendants will determine how far it advances the cause of human rights in international criminal procedure.

"Extradition" is the term usually used to describe the process "whereby one sovereign surrenders to another sovereign a person sought after as an accused criminal or a fugitive offender."[1] Extradition has a long history in international law and has developed a complex set of procedures and exceptions.[2] The word "extradition" does not, however, appear either in the constitutive documents of the International Tribunal for the Former Yugoslavia—Security Council Resolution 827 and the Statute of the Tribunal—or in the *Report of the Secretary-General pursuant to Paragraph 2 of Security Council Resolution 808 (1993)*, by which the Secretariat presented the Statute to the Security Council.[3] Instead, the Statute, its implementing Rules of Procedure and Evidence,[4]

---

[1] M. Cherif Bassiouni, *International Extradition and World Public Order* 1 (1974).

[2] *See generally id.;* 2 *International Criminal Law: Procedure* ch. 7 (M. Cherif Bassiouni ed., 1986); Satya Deva Bedi, *Extradition in International Law and Practice* (1968).

[3] S.C. Res. 827, U.N. SCOR, 48th Year, 3217th mtg. at 1, U.N. Doc. S/RES/827 (1993), *reprinted in* appendix A of this issue of *Criminal Law Forum* and *in* 32 I.L.M. 1203; *Report of the Secretary-General pursuant to Paragraph 2 of Security Council Resolution 808 (1993)*, U.N. Doc. S/25704 & Add.1 (1993), *reprinted in* appendix B of this issue of *Criminal Law Forum* and *in* 32 I.L.M. 1163 [hereinafter *Secretary-General's Report*]. The Statute of the Tribunal is set out as an annex to *Secretary-General's Report, supra*, along with commentary, and is *reprinted in* appendix B of this issue of *Criminal Law Forum* and *in* 32 I.L.M. 1192 [hereinafter Statute]. S.C. Res. 827, *supra*, ¶ 1, "approve[d]" *Secretary-General's Report, supra*, making it as authoritative an interpretive tool as any "legislative history" can be under international law. *Cf.* Vienna Convention on the Law of Treaties, *done* May 23, 1969, art. 32, 1155 U.N.T.S. 331 (consulting the "preparatory work of the treaty and the circumstances of its conclusion" may be a supplementary means of interpretation).

[4] International Tribunal for the Prosecution of Persons Responsible for Serious Violations of International Humanitarian Law Committed in the Territory of the Former Yugoslavia since 1991, Rules of Procedure and Evidence, U.N. Doc. IT/32 (1994), *amended by* U.N. Doc. IT/32/Rev.1 (1994), U.N. Doc. IT/32/Rev.2 (1994), U.N. Doc. IT/Rev.3 (1995), *reprinted in* appendix C of this issue of *Criminal Law Forum*. This article was written on the basis of U.N. Doc. IT/32/Rev.1 (1994) [hereinafter I.T. R.

and the *Secretary-General's Report* make reference to the process by which defendants[5] will be brought before the Tribunal, from the states in which

---

Proc. & Evid.], but it addresses some key changes effected by U.N. Doc. IT/32/Rev.3 (1995) [hereinafter I.T. R. Proc. & Evid. (Rev.3)].

[5] The term "accused" is used for the criminal defendant in both the Statute and the Rules of Procedure and Evidence. "Defendant" will be used in the first portion of this article, discussing the basis of the Tribunal's jurisdiction, because it is the word most frequently used by English-speaking lawyers to describe someone accused of a crime. "Accused" and "accused person" will be used interchangeably with "defendant" in the second portion, which deals with the rules related to securing the presence of persons accused of serious violations of humanitarian law in the former Yugoslavia. "Suspect" is used in the rules to describe a person who is under investigation but not yet indicted, and will be so used in this article. In this connection, see *infra* text accompanying notes 29–30.

The Tribunal is limited to the prosecution of defendants who are "natural persons"; the Statute does not, however, purport to limit its jurisdiction to nationals of UN member states. Statute, *supra* note 3, art. 6; *see Secretary-General's Report, supra* note 3, ¶¶ 50–51. I.T. R. Proc. & Evid. (Rev.3), *supra* note 4, R. 2(A), introduced a broad definition of "state" as a "State Member or non-Member of the United Nations or a self-proclaimed entity *de facto* exercising governmental functions, whether recognised as a State or not," which will make it possible to show state involvement in international crimes that include this element where the accused is a partisan of an entity that has not been recognized as a state by the international community. There is no provision for jurisdiction over crimes alleged against public or private corporate bodies or associations. This is contrary to the modern trend in many nations, which is to extend criminal liability to corporations.

The territorial and temporal limits of the Tribunal's jurisdiction are the territory of the former Socialist Federal Republic of Yugoslavia, and the period starting on January 1, 1991, respectively. Statute, *supra*, arts. 1, 8.

One uncertainty in the jurisdictional sections is whether the Tribunal has jurisdiction over persons who conspired to commit crimes in the territory of the former Yugoslavia but acted wholly outside that territory—such as a person who supplied arms with the knowledge or intent that they would be used to commit genocide in the former Yugoslavia. Under general international law, a state may exercise jurisdiction over a criminal act the ill effects of which are felt in that state's territory. *Cf.* S.S. "Lotus" (Fr. v. Turk.), 1927 P.C.I.J. (ser. A) No. 10. This principle would suggest that the jurisdiction of a court claiming authority over the territory of the former Yugoslavia would include jurisdiction over persons such as our hypothetical arms supplier.

Although reasonable, and in accord with the purpose for the establishment of the Tribunal, this argument does not emerge directly from the *Lotus* case or the text of the Statute. Instead, it is an extension of the *Lotus* principle to international tribunals.

they are found, as "transfer" or "surrender."[6]

This change in terminology reflects important conceptual and operative differences between transfer or surrender under the Statute and under traditional extradition. The establishment of the Tribunal represents a great theoretical advance in the international enforcement of human rights. Unfortunately, a few of the Tribunal's Rules of Procedure and Evidence fail to capitalize on this advance, and some rules pose dangers to the human rights of potential defendants.

THE CONCEPTUAL BREAKTHROUGH: PERSONAL JURISDICTION GROUNDED IN CHAPTER VII OF THE UN CHARTER

International Obligation to Surrender Defendants to the Tribunal

The Security Council and the Secretary-General claim authority to establish and provide for the operation of the Tribunal under chapter

---

Moreover, it would not provide for the prosecution of persons whose acts, though intended to have effects in the former Yugoslavia, were committed entirely outside that territory, and never actually affected it — such as an arms supplier whose shipments failed to reach their destination.

[6] Statute, *supra* note 3, arts. 19(2) ("surrender or transfer"), 20(2) ("transfer[ ]"), 29(2)(e) ("the surrender or the transfer"); I.T. R. Proc. & Evid., *supra* note 4, RR. 57 ("transfer"), 58 ("surrender or transfer"); *Secretary-General's Report, supra* note 3, ¶ 126 ("surrender or transfer"). See sections *infra* entitled "The Change from Extradition Law" and "Arrest or Failure to Arrest the Accused."

In early November 1994, the Tribunal handed down its first indictment, of a suspect at large presumably in Bosnia. Sara Henley, *U.N. War Crimes Tribunal Charges First Suspect,* Reuters, Nov. 8, 1994, *available in* LEXIS, World Library, Allnws File. At the same time, the Tribunal requested Germany to transfer to its jurisdiction a Bosnian Serb in custody there. Peter S. Canellos, *U.N. Tribunal Seeks a Serb: Ethnic Cleansing Alleged as Trial Begins in the Hague,* Boston Globe, Nov. 9, 1994, at 26, *available in* LEXIS, World Library, Allnws File; *Yugo War Crimes Court Asks Germany to Extradite Bosnian Serb,* Agence France Presse, Nov. 8, 1994, *available in* LEXIS, World Library, Allnws File. Germany promptly amended its law to permit such a transfer. *Bonn Changes Law to Hand Over War Criminals,* Reuters, Dec. 16, 1994, *available in* LEXIS, World Library, Allnws File.

VII of the UN Charter. This chapter gives the Security Council authority to take a wide range of military and nonmilitary measures to restore and maintain international peace and security. The Council made a determination, under the authority of articles 39 and 41 of the Charter, that the situation in the former Yugoslavia constituted a threat to international peace and security and that an international tribunal would contribute to ending widespread violations of international humanitarian law in the region, as well as to the restoration and maintenance of peace.[7] Member states are bound under articles 48 and 49 of the Charter to assist in carrying out this decision. Specifically, the Security Council

> *[d]ecide[d]* that all States shall cooperate fully with the International Tribunal and its organs in accordance with the present resolution [827] and the Statute of the International Tribunal and that consequently all States shall take any measures necessary under their domestic law to implement the provisions of the present resolution and the Statute, including the obligation of States to comply with requests for assistance or orders issued by a Trial Chamber under Article 29 of the Statute[.][8]

---

[7] S.C. Res. 827, *supra* note 3; S.C. Res. 808, U.N. SCOR, 48th Year, 3175th mtg. at 1, U.N. Doc. S/RES/808 (1993), *reprinted in* appendix A of this issue of *Criminal Law Forum* and *available in* U.N. Gopher\Documents\Security Council Resolutions; Statute, *supra* note 3, preamble; *Secretary-General's Report, supra* note 3, ¶¶ 22–28, 125–126.

This article will evaluate the consequences of this argument for securing jurisdiction over defendants by the Tribunal, and for human rights and international criminal procedure. Elaboration of the argument supporting the lawfulness of the Security Council's establishment of the Tribunal is found in Roman A. Kolodkin, *An Ad Hoc International Tribunal for the Prosecution of Serious Violations of International Humanitarian Law in the Former Yugoslavia,* in this issue of *Criminal Law Forum;* Monroe Leigh et al., American Bar Ass'n Sec. Int'l Law and Practice, *Report on the International Tribunal to Adjudicate War Crimes Committed in the Former Yugoslavia* 9–11 (1993); *see also* Theodor Meron, *War Crimes in Yugoslavia and the Development of International Law,* 88 Am. J. Int'l L. 78 (1994). For criticism of the Statute based on infringement of the sovereign equality of states, see Alfred P. Rubin, *An International Criminal Tribunal for Former Yugoslavia?,* 6 Pace Int'l L. Rev. 7 (1994).

[8] S.C. Res. 827, *supra* note 3, ¶ 4.

Article 29(1) of the Tribunal's Statute elaborates: "States shall cooperate with the International Tribunal in the investigation and prosecution of persons accused of committing serious violations of international humanitarian law." Article 29(2) specifies that such assistance requires compliance with orders of the Tribunal's trial chambers, including, but not limited to, the identification and location of persons, the arrest or detention of persons, and the surrender or transfer of defendants to the Tribunal. The *Secretary-General's Report* states that the "obligation to cooperate" extends to "all stages of the proceedings."[9] In particular, an order of the Tribunal for the surrender or transfer of persons "shall be considered to be the application of an enforcement measure under Chapter VII of the Charter of the United Nations."[10]

Cooperation in surrendering or transferring defendants to the Tribunal is thus an international obligation of all states. This obligation is superior to any domestic law that might prevent surrender or transfer either generally or in individual cases.[11] The Rules of Procedure and Evidence reiterate that the obligations of article 29 of the Statute prevail over any national legal impediment, including a state's extradition treaties, to the surrender or transfer of a defendant to the Tribunal.[12] The rules also provide for reference to the Security Council of cases where a state fails or refuses to execute an arrest warrant of the Tribunal.[13] These provisions effectuate the theory of the Tribunal's powers described in Resolution 827, the Statute, and the *Secretary-General's Report*.

The obligations on states in regard to arresting and rendering

---

[9] *Secretary-General's Report, supra* note 3, ¶ 125.

[10] *Id.* ¶ 126; *see also id.* ¶ 125; S.C. Res. 827, *supra* note 3, ¶ 4; Statute, *supra* note 3, art. 29.

[11] *See Secretary-General's Report, supra* note 3, ¶ 125; I.T. R. Proc. & Evid., *supra* note 4, R. 58. On the broad definition of state introduced in I.T. R. Proc. & Evid. (Rev.3), *supra* note 4, R. 2(A), see *supra* note 5.

[12] The only reference to extradition in the rules appears in I.T. R. Proc. & Evid., *supra* note 4, R. 58.

[13] *Id.* RR. 59(B), 61(E).

defendants to the International Tribunal go beyond the theoretical model of the Nuremberg and Tokyo war crimes trials. In all three cases—Nuremberg, Tokyo, and the former Yugoslavia—the tribunals claimed or claim jurisdiction over individual defendants for war crimes, crimes against humanity, and related grave offenses. However, in the postwar trials, the basis of personal jurisdiction was the law of war itself. After World War II, the victorious Allies had power as occupying forces over potential defendants, and among themselves the Allies established courts to try Axis leaders and partisans.[14] Beyond the application of international criminal law to individuals,[15] the Nuremberg Charter broke new theoretical ground in delegating to a multinational court the power of each victorious nation to try those persons it had captured.[16]

But both the Nuremberg and the Tokyo tribunal gained their authority directly from the states that had created them, as extensions of

---

[14] The International Military Tribunal at Nuremberg was established pursuant to an agreement concluded by the United Kingdom, the United States, France, and the Soviet Union. Agreement for the Prosecution and Punishment of the Major War Criminals of the European Axis, Aug. 8, 1945, 82 U.N.T.S. 279 [hereinafter London Agreement]. The Charter of the International Military Tribunal at Nuremberg is set out in *id.* at 284 [hereinafter Nuremberg Charter].

The International Military Tribunal for the Far East (IMTFE) was set up in Tokyo pursuant to Special Proclamation by the Supreme Commander for the Allied Powers, Establishment of an International Tribunal for the Far East, Jan. 19, 1946, 4 Bevans 20, *reprinted in* 1 Benjamin Ferencz, *Defining International Aggression* 522 (1975) [hereinafter IMTFE Proclamation]. It operated pursuant to Charter of the International Military Tribunal for the Far East, Jan. 19, 1946 *(as amended* Apr. 26, 1946), 4 Bevans 21, *reprinted in* 1 Ferencz, *supra*, at 523. The IMTFE was even more explicitly military in origin than the Nuremberg tribunal. Its Charter was amended in response to a determination by the committee on war criminality of the Allies' Far Eastern Commission that all members of the Commission, including India and the Philippines, should have a judge on the court. Arnold C. Brackman, *The Other Nuremberg* 69 (1987). The U.S. Supreme Court stated that the IMTFE was not a court of the United States but the creation of an "agent of the Allied Powers." Hirota v. MacArthur, 338 U.S. 197 (1948).

[15] It is sometimes forgotten that "offenses against the law of nations," such as piracy, were criminalized by individual states long before World War II. *E.g.*, U.S. Const. art. I, § 8, cl. 10 (giving Congress power to provide for punishment of such crimes).

[16] See *supra* note 14 and accompanying text.

the states' own sovereign powers.[17] The International Tribunal for the Former Yugoslavia, in contrast, takes its authority directly from the constitutional powers of an international organization, the United Nations, and specifically from the mandate of the Security Council to maintain peace and security. The basis of the Tribunal's personal jurisdiction is not that individual states that capture defendants have yielded jurisdiction to a multinational court. Instead, the Security Council asserts that it may establish a tribunal with authority to compel cooperation from national courts and governments in obtaining the presence of defendants, in support of its efforts to restore and maintain peace and security.[18] Whether the Security Council's claim of an enforceable right to obtain the presence of defendants before the Tribunal can be enforced in practice against, for example, the new Yugoslavia (Serbia and Montenegro) remains to be seen. However, without this claim of paramount jurisdiction over individuals, it would be virtually impossible to bring human rights violators to justice against the wishes of states with a competing interest in shielding them.[19]

---

[17] *E.g.,* London Agreement, *supra* note 14, preamble, arts. 3 (requiring signatories to make available for investigation and prosecution the "major war criminals detained by them"), 7 (permitting signatories to terminate the agreement); Nuremberg Charter, *supra* note 14, arts. 1 (creation of the tribunal by the four powers), 2–3 (each of the powers to appoint a member of the court, who could not be challenged by either prosecution or defense), 14–15 (prosecutors appointed by the four powers); IMTFE Proclamation, *supra* note 14 (the U.S., British, Russian—not Soviet—and Chinese governments agreed to give power to the Supreme Allied Commander to issue all orders to implement terms of surrender, including stern justice to war criminals).

The reference to the "United Nations" in London Agreement, *supra,* art. 5, is to the predecessor of the current body and does not mean to suggest that this court was the creation of an international organization. Like the Nuremberg tribunal, the Tokyo war crimes tribunal was based upon the power of the military victors who had captured the defendants. *See* Brackman, *supra* note 14, at 59–61, 69.

[18] S.C. Res. 827, *supra* note 3; S.C. Res. 808, *supra* note 3; *see also Secretary-General's Report, supra* note 3, ¶¶ 22–28.

[19] *Cf.* S.C. Res. 748, U.N. SCOR, 47th Year, 1992 S.C. Res. & Dec. at 52, U.N. Doc. S/INF/48 (1992) (imposing sanctions on Libya for failure to extradite two of its nationals wanted for the bombing of Pan Am flight 103). This resolution may be seen as a precedent for S.C. Res. 827, *supra* note 3, to the extent that it asserted the principle that the Security Council may demand the production of individual defendants accused

Nonetheless, the assertion in the *Secretary-General's Report* that an order of the Tribunal to surrender or transfer persons to its custody "shall be considered to be the application of an enforcement measure" under chapter VII[20] is extraordinary and problematic. It can be read to mean that such an order is the legal and moral equivalent of a Security Council resolution. It is questionable whether the Security Council can or should delegate its authority in this respect. Fortunately, a more moderate reading is possible and will serve the purpose of the Tribunal. As the *Secretary-General's Report* notes, the Security Council may create a subsidiary organ as a chapter VII enforcement measure.[21] For such an organ to be useful within the scheme of chapter VII, it may need to be given authority to make binding decisions, which can be treated as applications of the enforcement measures set forth by the Security Council in Resolution 827 and other resolutions relevant to the situation in the former Yugoslavia. The Tribunal's Rules of Procedure and Evidence interpret the Statute in this way. Rule 59(B) provides that "[i]f, within a reasonable time after the warrant of arrest has been transmitted to the State, no report is made on action taken, this shall be deemed a failure to execute the warrant of arrest and the Tribunal, through the President, may notify the Security Council accordingly."[22]

---

of violations of international law, even in the face of contrary extradition law. *See also* Interpretation and Application of the 1971 Montreal Convention Arising from the Aerial Incident at Lockerbie (Libya v. U.S.), 1992 I.C.J. 114, 217 (Apr. 14) (dissenting opinion of Judge El-Kosheri) (indicating that Libyan courts were an inappropriate forum to try Libyan government employees accused of the bombing of flight 103) [hereinafter *Lockerbie* case].

Of course, national courts may in many instances be appropriate for trying human rights violators. For example, domestic armed forces are required under international law to conform their conduct to the laws and customs of war. *See Secretary-General's Report, supra* note 3, ¶ 35. To the extent that a sovereign state enforces this body of law against its own soldiers, an international tribunal is unnecessary.

[20]   *Secretary-General's Report, supra* note 3, ¶ 126.

[21]   *Id.* ¶¶ 27–28.

[22]   *See also* I.T. R. Proc. & Evid., *supra* note 4, RR. 61(E) ("If the Prosecutor satisfies the Trial Chamber that the failure to effect personal service was due in whole or in part to a failure or refusal of a State to cooperate with the Tribunal in accordance with Article 29 of the Statute, the Trial Chamber shall so certify, in which event the President

The *Secretary-General's Report* also recognizes the limitations of a tribunal established as a chapter VII measure to restore and maintain peace. The life span of the Tribunal is expressly "linked to the restoration and maintenance of international peace in the territory of the former Yugoslavia, and Security Council decisions related thereto."[23]

Nor does the claim of primacy for the Tribunal extend to the creation of substantive humanitarian law. Primacy is limited strictly to matters of jurisdiction, investigation, securing the presence of defendants and evidence, and ensuring that punishment occurs in accordance with the judgments of the court.[24]

Change from Extradition Law

As noted earlier, the general means for transferring criminal defendants from the jurisdiction of one sovereign state to another sovereign state is

---

shall notify the Security Council."), 11 (states may be referred to the Security Council for failure to defer to the competence of the Tribunal). This is the reading of the Tribunal's authority given by President Judge Antonio Cassese. *The International Tribunal on War Crimes,* CNN's Diplomatic License, Nov. 20, 1994, *available in* LEXIS, World Library, Allnws File.

[23] *Secretary-General's Report, supra* note 3, ¶ 28.

[24] Statute, *supra* note 3, arts. 9(2) (primacy of the Tribunal over national courts for purposes of jurisdiction), 27 (imprisonment pursuant to sentence under supervision of the Tribunal), 29 (requirement of state cooperation in investigation and securing presence of defendants); *Secretary-General's Report, supra* note 3, ¶¶ 29, 65, 121–123, 125–126.

Neither the Statute nor the *Secretary-General's Report* addresses the question whether the Security Council has authority to "legislate" such standards under U.N. Charter ch. VII. Of course, if the Security Council purported to create new humanitarian law and then to apply it to individual criminal cases arising before the enactment thereof, this would violate the principle of *nullum crimen sine lege* (an act is not criminal in the absence of law). *See* International Covenant on Civil and Political Rights, *adopted* Dec. 19, 1966, art. 15, 999 U.N.T.S. 171 [hereinafter International Covenant]; Leigh et al., *supra* note 7, at 11–13. According to *Secretary-General's Report, supra,* ¶ 34, "the application of the principle *nullum crimen sine lege* requires that the international tribunal should apply rules of international humanitarian law which are beyond any doubt part of customary law so that the problem of adherence of some but not all States to specific conventions does not arise."

extradition. Equality and reciprocity among states are the hallmarks of extradition, and it is an instrument of national policy. Although imperfect, extradition has been useful both for promoting criminal law enforcement and for protecting the rights of criminal defendants.

In modern practice, states are under no general international law obligation to extradite accused criminals: extradition occurs pursuant to a bilateral or multilateral treaty or other international agreement, or on the basis of reciprocity or comity between the states concerned.[25] Extradition is generally subject to those human rights protections against arbitrary arrest and detention that are contained in the constitution, the relevant extradition treaty, or the national legislation of the state in which the defendant is found.[26] This procedure is also subject to exceptions based upon national policy (such as the common but not universal rule against extraditing nationals).

M. Cherif Bassiouni, probably the most frequently cited English-

---

[25] For a discussion and citations, see 1 M. Cherif Bassiouni, *International Extradition: United States Law and Practice* 10–12, 25–33 (2d rev. ed. 1987). A similar position is expressed in *Lockerbie* case, *supra* note 19, at 136–37 (concurring opinion of Judges Evensen, Tarassov, Guillaume & Aguilar Mawdsley). Bassiouni, *supra*, at 10 & nn.14–15, notes that two major early theorists, Grotius and de Vattel, held contrary views.

[26] *See* 1 Bassiouni, *supra* note 25, at 31–33. A controversial decision of the European Court of Human Rights, Soering v. United Kingdom, 161 Eur. Ct. H.R. (ser. A) (1989), indicates that under European Convention for the Protection of Human Rights and Fundamental Freedoms, *opened for signature* Nov. 4, 1950, Europ. T.S. 5, a requested state is responsible also for determining that the person to be extradited will not be subject to torture or inhuman or degrading punishment or to an unfair trial. For some criticisms of this decision, see Stephan Breitenmoser & Gunter E. Wilms, *Human Rights v. Extradition: The Soering Case*, 11 Mich. J. Int'l L. 845 (1990); Richard B. Lillich, Note, *The Soering Case*, 85 Am. J. Int'l L. 128 (1991); Donald K. Piragoff & Marcia V.J. Kran, *The Impact of Human Rights Principles on Extradition from Canada and the United States: The Role of National Courts*, 3 Crim. L.F. 225, 231–36 (1992); Bernard Robertson, *Extradition, Inhumane Treatment, and the Death Penalty*, 154 Just. Peace 231 (1990); Michael P. Shea, *Expanding Judicial Scrutiny of Human Rights in Extradition Cases after Soering*, 17 Yale J. Int'l L. 85 (1992). Everything that is said in this article about the need to prevent arbitrary arrest and detention can of course be said about the need to ensure fair trials and humane conditions of punishment following conviction by the International Tribunal.

language scholar of extradition, argues that a *jus cogens* norm has arisen requiring that states either extradite or prosecute *(aut dedere aut judicare)* those persons that another state accuses of a crime defined under international law.[27] This argument has been accepted by at least one judge of the International Court of Justice.[28] Nothing in this argument suggests, however, that the same national protections against arbitrary arrest and detention that apply traditionally to extradition would not apply in the case of an obligatory extradition or prosecution under the rule of *aut dedere aut judicare.*

The absence of the word "extradition" from Resolution 827, the Tribunal's Statute, and the *Secretary-General's Report* is not unprecedented. The obligation to prosecute accused persons or to make them available to another contracting state for prosecution, without the use of the word "extradition," appears, for example, in the Geneva Conventions of 1949.[29] This suggests that the rendering of defendants to another state under the rubric of *aut dedere aut judicare* may be done through nonextradition procedures, such as deportation of an undesirable alien. However, under the Geneva Conventions, while a state has the option

---

[27] 1 Bassiouni, *supra* note 25, at 10, 13–24, bases this argument on a plethora of multilateral conventions creating or recognizing crimes under international law, ranging from genocide and war crimes through airline hijacking, counterfeiting, and international commercial bribery. These conventions generally contain requirements that signatories criminalize certain acts, cooperate in their suppression, prosecute alleged offenders, and/or extradite alleged offenders.

[28] *Lockerbie* case, *supra* note 19, at 179 (dissenting opinion of Judge Weeramantry) (relying upon Bassiouni, *supra* note 25). *But see id.* at 136–37 (concurring opinion of Judges Evensen, Tarassov, Guillaume & Aguilar Mawdsley).

[29] Geneva Convention for the Amelioration of the Condition of the Wounded and Sick in Armed Forces in the Field (Geneva Convention I), *adopted* Aug. 12, 1949, art. 49, 75 U.N.T.S. 31; Geneva Convention for the Amelioration of the Condition of Wounded, Sick, and Shipwrecked Members of Armed Forces at Sea (Geneva Convention II), *adopted* Aug. 12, 1949, art. 50, 75 U.N.T.S. 85; Geneva Convention Relative to the Treatment of Prisoners of War (Geneva Convention III), *adopted* Aug. 12, 1949, art. 129, 75 U.N.T.S. 135; Geneva Convention Relative to the Protection of Civilian Persons in Time of War (Geneva Convention IV), *adopted* Aug. 12, 1949, art. 146, 75 U.N.T.S. 287.

of prosecuting or handing over a defendant for prosecution, the transfer is to be done "in accordance with . . . its own legislation" and only when the requesting state "has made out a *prima facie* case."[30] Thus, the Geneva Conventions recognize the right of states to prosecute, rather than turn over defendants, and to do either in accordance with their own legal protections for defendants. Security Resolution 827 and the Statute, along with the Tribunal's Rules of Procedure and Evidence, do not recognize these traditional rights of sovereignty.

In fact, these instruments expressly reject national limits on the transfer of defendants to the Tribunal. Once the Tribunal confirms an indictment and issues an arrest warrant and an order for surrender to the Tribunal based thereon,[31] any state concerned is under a binding obligation to arrest the accused and transfer him or her to the seat of the Tribunal.[32] As discussed above, the *Secretary-General's Report* treats an order of the Tribunal to surrender or transfer a defendant as an application of an obligatory Security Council enforcement measure. Although the Statute provides that national courts retain concurrent jurisdiction over violations of humanitarian law in the former Yugoslavia, the Tribunal has primacy.[33] The formula *aut dedere aut judicare* is replaced by a mandatory requirement of transfer to the Tribunal at its order.

The Security Council and the Tribunal have rejected traditional extradition law, as well as the *aut dedere aut judicare* formula, for good

---

[30] See sources cited *supra* note 29. For a discussion of a recent prosecution and conviction in Israel of an Israeli national who could not as a citizen be extradited under the Offences Committed Abroad (Amendment of Enactments) Law of 1978, notwithstanding the existence of an extradition treaty between Israel and the United States, but who could be prosecuted locally, see Mark D. Cohen, Developments in Criminal Law and Criminal Justice, *New York v. Kirman/Israel v. Kirman: A Prosecution in Tel Aviv under Israeli Law for a Narcotics Offense Committed in New York*, 4 Crim. L.F. 597 (1993).

[31] Statute, *supra* note 3, art. 19; I.T. R. Proc. & Evid. (Rev.3), *supra* note 4, RR. 47(D), 55(B).

[32] Statute, *supra* note 3, art. 29; I.T. R. Proc. & Evid., *supra* note 4, RR. 56–57.

[33] Statute, *supra* note 3, art. 9(2); *see also Secretary-General's Report, supra* note 3, ¶ 65.

reason. The model of sovereign equality and reciprocity is inadequate to deal with the offenses within the Tribunal's subject-matter jurisdiction. In many instances, these crimes have been committed by persons working on behalf of state policy, or in the name of state policy, or in the name of a group aspiring to state or government status. The requirement that a state prosecute if it does not extradite is insufficient where there is reason to suspect that such a prosecution will not be conducted in good faith. Without the support of a legal obligation to transfer defendants and without the muscle of the Security Council, neither the Tribunal nor the concerned states are likely to try many defendants charged with humanitarian crimes in the former Yugoslavia[34] and thereby to vindicate the fundamental human rights of the victims of that region's vicious, uncivil war.

The consequence for defendants' human rights of the supremacy of the Tribunal's personal jurisdiction is that the procedural protections for criminal defendants normally provided in the transnational context by extradition law become completely the responsibility of the Tribunal. Local human rights protections, such as constitutional and statutory guarantees against arbitrary arrest or search and seizure, are superseded by an international obligation to provide defendants and evidence to the Tribunal.[35] The Security Council and the Tribunal must therefore ensure that the latter's procedures adequately protect the rights of suspects and defendants: the extent to which current procedures do so is discussed subsequently.

---

[34] Rubin, *supra* note 7, doubts that some states will cooperate with the Tribunal even with Security Council backing, and for this, among other reasons, has severe reservations about the Tribunal. The public position of some former Yugoslavian states is discussed in Pavel Dolenc, *A Slovenian Perspective on the Statute and Rules of the International Tribunal for the Former Yugoslavia*, in this issue of *Criminal Law Forum*; Mark Fuller, *Yugoslavia: Croatia, Bosnia Set to Surrender War Crimes Suspects*, Inter Press Serv., Oct. 11, 1994, *available in* LEXIS, World Library, Allnws File; *Federal Affairs: War Crimes Prosecutor Holds Talks with Federal Officials*, BBC Summary of World Broadcasts (Yugo. Telegraph Serv.), Oct. 10, 1994, *available in* LEXIS, World Library, Allnws File.

[35] See section *supra* entitled "The International Obligation to Surrender Defendants to the Tribunal."

Limits of the Tribunal's Model of Personal Jurisdiction as a Standard for a Proposed Permanent Court

It may prove difficult to generalize the Tribunal's model to a permanent international criminal court.[36] A permanent court might assert mandatory jurisdiction over individuals by treaty or by other mechanisms that adhere more closely to considerations of national sovereignty.[37] To be effective as a standing judicial organ, such a court would need to be able to obtain the presence of defendants in situations in which the Security Council had not made the partly judicial, partly political determination that there was a threat to peace.[38] In cases of state-sponsored or state-condoned human rights violations, a permanent international criminal court would also need an enforcement mechanism, a function now fulfilled by the Security Council with regard to the ad hoc Tribunal.[39] Whatever form such a mechanism ultimately takes, unless the UN Charter were amended along these lines, the Security Council would not

---

[36] In this regard, see *Report of the Working Group on a Draft Statute for an International Criminal Court,* in *Report of the International Law Commission on Its Forty-fifth Session,* U.N. GAOR, 48th Sess., Supp. No. 10, at 255, U.N. Doc. A/48/10 (1993) [hereinafter ILC 1993 Draft Statute]. A substantially revised Draft Statute for an International Criminal Court appears in *Report of the International Law Commission on Its Forty-sixth Session,* U.N. GAOR, 49th Sess., Supp. No. 10, at 43, U.N. Doc. A/49/10 (1994) [hereinafter ILC 1994 Draft Statute].

[37] *See, e.g.,* ILC 1993 Draft Statute, *supra* note 36, arts. 1, 4 (proposing that a permanent international criminal tribunal could be established by states' becoming "parties" to its constitutive instrument, similar to the process of adopting a treaty), 23–24, 26 (suggesting that states should be able to refuse to recognize the court's jurisdiction over certain classes of crime), 33 (proposing different levels of obligation upon states to surrender defendants to the court depending on whether the state in question is party to the statute and has accepted the court's jurisdiction over the particular crime(s) charged).

[38] *Cf. Secretary-General's Report, supra* note 3, ¶ 28 (linking the duration of the Tribunal to its role in restoring and maintaining peace in the region).

[39] While ILC 1993 Draft Statute, *supra* note 36, art. 25, and ILC 1994 Draft Statute, *supra* note 36, art. 23, suggest that the Security Council could refer certain cases to the proposed permanent court, other aspects of the relationship between the two organs are unclear, including whether the Security Council would have the power to take enforcement action where a state refused to arrest or surrender a defendant.

be the appropriate body to be enforcing orders of a permanent criminal court absent a threat to, or a breach of, international peace and security.

THE OPERATIVE EFFECT: SECURING THE PRESENCE OF DEFENDANTS WHILE PROTECTING THEIR RIGHTS

The process of bringing an accused person[40] before the Tribunal consists of several stages, encompassing investigation, arrest, transfer, and pretrial detention. This section discusses in detail and makes recommendations concerning only those provisions that directly affect the ability of the Tribunal to protect the human rights of victims and defendants in the process of securing the presence of the latter.[41]

The procedures of the Tribunal are subject to the same dangers and opportunities as criminal procedure in any jurisdiction. All systems of criminal procedure are designed to protect society and its members. And all of them present dangers to the privacy and freedom of individuals, whether guilty or innocent.

The theme that runs through the relevant provisions of the Statute and the Rules of Procedure and Evidence is the primacy of the Tribunal over national authorities and law in the process of charging and securing the presence of accused persons. Thus, if the human rights of an accused are to be protected, they must be protected by the Tribunal in a principled way. Ad hoc reliance upon the good faith of prosecutorial and judicial officers is not enough. The binding law of the Tribunal, both its constitutive documents and its Rules of Procedure and Evidence, ought to evince a strong regard for the human rights of all persons. Similarly, protection of the most important rights should be written into

---

[40] See *supra* note 5.

[41] Among the many human rights issues connected with criminal procedure outside the scope of this article are the rights of suspects and nonsuspects to be free from unreasonable search and seizure, the right to remain silent both before and after arrest, and the right to humane conditions of imprisonment.

the constituent document of any future international criminal court, rather than left to its implementing rules of procedure.

Investigation

The prosecutor constitutes an independent organ of the Tribunal, with authority to investigate suspected crimes.[42] Investigations may be initiated on the basis of information received from "any source."[43] In carrying out investigations, the prosecutor may seek the assistance of state and international authorities when necessary.[44] The Rules of Procedure and Evidence interpret the Statute, Security Council Resolution 827, and the *Secretary-General's Report* to allow the Tribunal to issue orders obligating states to grant investigative assistance to the prosecutor.[45]

---

[42] On the powers and functions of the prosecutor, see Statute, *supra* note 3, arts. 16, 18; I.T. R. Proc. & Evid. (Rev.3), *supra* note 4, R. 37, pts. 4–8. The prosecutor "shall not seek or receive instruction from any Government or from any other source." Statute, *supra*, art. 16(2).

[43] Statute, *supra* note 3, art. 18(1); *Secretary-General's Report, supra* note 3, ¶ 93. These provisions identify nongovernmental organizations as potential sources of information, as well as governments, UN organs, and intergovernmental organizations.

[44] Statute, *supra* note 3, art. 18(2) (state authorities); I.T. R. Proc. & Evid., *supra* note 4, R. 39(iii) (state and international authorities, including INTERPOL).

[45] U.N. Charter ch. VII is the theoretical basis for this authority, as it is for the obligation on states to surrender defendants to the Tribunal. Under Statute, *supra* note 3, art. 29(1), states are required to cooperate with the Tribunal in the investigation and prosecution of cases within the Tribunal's jurisdiction. Under *id.* art. 29(2), this assistance includes compliance with orders of the trial chambers, such as (but not limited to) the identification and location of persons, the taking of testimony and the production of evidence, and the service of documents. As noted earlier, *Secretary-General's Report, supra* note 3, ¶ 125, provides that the "obligation to cooperate" extends to "all stages of the proceedings" and specifically mentions "search warrants," as well as the obligations set forth in Statute, *supra,* art. 29, and noted above. S.C. Res. 827, *supra* note 3, ¶ 4, imposes similar obligations on states to "cooperate fully with the International Tribunal" and to "take any measures necessary under their domestic law to implement the provisions of the present resolution and the Statute." I.T. R. Proc. & Evid., *supra* note 4, R. 39(iv), authorizes the prosecutor to seek "such orders as may be necessary" from a trial chamber or judge, leaving the unmistakable impression that an order of the Tribunal in aid of an investigation is binding on states.

An argument that requests for investigative assistance are binding on states even without an order of the Tribunal can be made out. The Statute provides that states "shall cooperate with the International Tribunal in the investigation and prosecution of persons accused of committing serious violations of international humanitarian law" and "shall comply without undue delay with any request for assistance or an order issued by a Trial Chamber."[46] The *Secretary-General's Report* similarly provides that

> the establishment of the International Tribunal on the basis of a Chapter VII decision . . . . means that all States would be under an obligation to cooperate with the International Tribunal and to assist it in all stages of the proceedings to ensure compliance with requests for assistance in the gathering of evidence, hearing of witnesses, suspects and experts, identification and location of persons and the service of documents. Effect shall also be given to orders issued by the Trial Chambers, such as warrants of arrest, search warrants, warrants for surrender or transfer of persons, and any other orders necessary for the conduct of the trial.[47]

The human rights concern here can be illustrated by the rights of privacy and personal security. Neither the Statute nor the Rules of Procedure and Evidence set any standard (for example, probable cause to believe that material evidence is at a specific place) for the issuance of search warrants. This conflicts with guarantees in Universal Declaration of Human Rights art. 12, G.A. Res. 217A (III), U.N. Doc. A/810, at 71 (1948) (protecting privacy, family, home, correspondence, honor, and reputation); International Covenant, *supra* note 24, art. 17 (protecting privacy, family, home, correspondence, honor, and reputation). Indeed, the only constraint upon the investigative reach of the prosecutor is found in I.T. R. Proc. & Evid. (Rev.3), *supra* note 4, R. 95, which introduces a less precise standard than the rules formerly embodied: "No evidence shall be admissible if obtained by methods which cast substantial doubt on its reliability or if its admission is antithetical to, and would seriously damage, the integrity of the proceedings," replaces "Evidence obtained directly or indirectly by means which constitute a serious violation of internationally protected human rights shall not be admissible."

[46] Statute, *supra* note 3, art. 29.

[47] *Secretary-General's Report, supra* note 3, ¶ 125.

Additionally, by Resolution 827 the Security Council "decided" that states shall take the measures necessary under their domestic law to implement the obligation to cooperate with requests for assistance or orders issued by a trial chamber.[48] These provisions can support an inference that states must cooperate with requests for assistance from the prosecutor. The rules, by contrast, protect against prosecutorial overzealousness by providing for judicial orders of the Tribunal during an investigation, implying that the prosecutor should seek to make requests for assistance to states binding by obtaining appropriate orders, but the most recent version of the rules now makes it explicit that states must comply with requests of the prosecutor in "cases of urgency."[49]

An investigatory body with the authority to require state cooperation is necessary to enforce international humanitarian and human rights law where states cannot be trusted to do their own enforcement. International investigative authority is the indispensable prerequisite to the bringing of charges against those who may be protected by their own or friendly governments. Otherwise, the only persons prosecuted will likely be those who, like the Nuremberg and Tokyo defendants, have already been captured and investigated by parties with an interest in vigorous prosecution. The creation of an independent prosecutor on an adversarial model does, however, create a need for judicial oversight, which is absent from the Statute and incomplete in the rules. How the rules on securing the presence of defendants before the Tribunal address this problem is discussed in detail below.[50]

Indictment

BRINGING THE INDICTMENT

Under the Statute, if the prosecutor determines that a prima facie case exists, he or she "shall prepare an indictment containing a concise

---

[48] S.C. Res. 827, *supra* note 3, ¶ 4.

[49] I.T. R. Proc. & Evid. (Rev.3), *supra* note 4, RR. 39(iv), 40. See *supra* note 45 and accompanying text.

[50] For a brief discussion of how the Statute and Rules of Procedure and Evidence create potential problems for the protection of privacy, see *supra* note 45.

statement of the facts and the crime or crimes with which the suspect is charged."[51] Under the Rules of Procedure and Evidence, the prosecutor "shall" prepare an indictment if "satisfied that there is sufficient evidence to provide reasonable grounds for believing that a suspect has committed a crime."[52]

Because there is no basis for the rules to change the mandate of the Tribunal set forth in the Statute, "reasonable grounds" must include at least a prima facie case against the suspect.[53] "Reasonable grounds for believing that a suspect has committed a crime" could also be interpreted as the standard of proof that the evidence of the prima facie case must meet before the prosecutor draws up an indictment. That is, the prosecutor would need to be satisfied not only that there is evidence supporting a prima facie case against the defendant, but also that the evidence is strong enough to provide reasonable grounds to believe the defendant has committed the crime.

The prosecutor shall forward to the registrar of the Tribunal the indictment, "together with supporting material."[54] The rules concerning indictments do not state what supporting material can or should be forwarded, but a later rule suggests that it should consist of some or all of the evidence on which the prosecutor has made the decision to seek

---

[51] Statute, *supra* note 3, art. 18(4); *cf. Secretary-General's Report*, *supra* note 3, ¶ 95 (upon the determination of a prima facie case, the prosecutor "would," rather than "shall," prepare an indictment).

[52] I.T. R. Proc. & Evid., *supra* note 4, R. 47(A).

[53] It is surprising that the grant of rulemaking authority to the Tribunal, Statute, *supra* note 3, art. 15; *Secretary-General's Report*, *supra* note 3, ¶ 83, does not explicitly provide that the Rules of Procedure and Evidence may not conflict with the Statute or with general international human rights law. Nonetheless, there is no warrant to assume that the Tribunal intended (or had the authority) to weaken the requirement of a prima facie case before indictment by adopting I.T. R. Proc. & Evid., *supra* note 4, R. 47(A).

[54] I.T. R. Proc. & Evid., *supra* note 4, R. 47(A). The registrar essentially serves as the clerk of the Tribunal. One of the registrar's specific duties is to act as the Tribunal's "channel of communication." *Id.* R. 33. The registry has been criticized because it serves both the judges and the prosecutor's office but not defense counsel. Leigh et al., *supra* note 7, at 18–21 (discussing Statute, *supra* note 3, art. 11(c)).

an indictment.[55] The registrar sends the indictment and other material to a judge[56] who has been assigned to review indictments.[57]

The judge reviews the indictment and confirms or dismisses each count therein.[58] Confirmation of an indictment is the legal act that charges a defendant and initiates a case in the Tribunal. Under the Statute, the judge "shall" confirm the indictment "[i]f satisfied that a *prima facie* case has been established by the Prosecutor."[59] The rules contain no elaboration of this standard. The prosecutor has the opportunity to present to the judge "additional material in support of any count,"[60] but once again the content of the material is left unspecified.[61] A count or indictment that is dismissed may be resubmitted on the basis of additional supporting evidence.[62]

These provisions can be rationalized in the following manner. Each count of an indictment must allege sufficient facts against the defendant to make out a prima facie case of the crime charged. The prosecutor must present supporting evidence, in the form of affidavits, exhibits, or otherwise, to convince the judge that there is reasonable ground to believe that the defendant has committed the crime alleged.

---

[55] I.T. R. Proc. & Evid., *supra* note 4, R. 61(B)–(C).

[56] Some readers may be interested to note that "Prosecutor," "Registrar," and "State" are capitalized in the Statute, but not "judge" (capitalized in the Rules of Procedure and Evidence) or "accused" (lowercased in both instruments).

[57] I.T. R. Proc. & Evid. (Rev.3), *supra* note 4, R. 47(C) (implementing Statute, *supra* note 3, art. 18(4)). Under *id.* R. 28, judges are rotated through this assignment monthly.

[58] I.T. R. Proc. & Evid., *supra* note 4, R. 47(D) (implementing Statute, *supra* note 3, art. 19(1)). Under the rules, different persons, as well as different counts against one person, may be charged in a single indictment if all charges arise from the same transaction. *Id.* RR. 48–49.

[59] Statute, *supra* note 3, art. 19(1).

[60] I.T. R. Proc. & Evid., *supra* note 4, R. 47(D).

[61] *See also* I.T. R. Proc. & Evid. (Rev.3), *supra* note 4, R. 61(B).

[62] I.T. R. Proc. & Evid., *supra* note 4, R. 47(E).

The prosecutor is not limited to the evidence sent up with the indictment but may present additional evidence when the matter is heard by the judge.

Nonetheless, the failure of the Statute and rules as written to set forth an explicit evidentiary standard for confirming an indictment is a substantial weakness. The rules should be revised to require the judge to find reasonable cause (or probable cause) from the evidence to believe that the accused has committed a crime before confirming a count in an indictment. This will prevent accused persons from being arrested, detained,[63] and subjected to trial essentially upon the unsupported word of a prosecutorial official. It cannot have been the intent of the Security Council to authorize arrest and detention in violation of universal minimum human rights standards forbidding arbitrary deprivations of freedom,[64] especially in light of the Statute's inclusion of many other internationally recognized procedural protections.[65]

Requiring an evidentiary standard of reasonable cause (or even probable cause) to believe an accused has committed the crime charged before confirming an indictment should not interfere with prosecution. If the prosecutor cannot make such a showing by the time the indictment is submitted, it is unlikely that a conviction beyond a reasonable doubt[66] can be obtained.

---

[63] See sections *infra* entitled "Detention and Advice of Rights of the Accused" and "Surrender or Transfer of the Accused to the Seat of the Tribunal."

[64] Universal Declaration of Human Rights, *supra* note 45, art. 9 (right against "arbitrary arrest, detention or exile"); International Covenant, *supra* note 24, art. 9(1) (right to liberty and security of person; protection against arbitrary arrest or detention; deprivation of liberty only "on such grounds and in accordance with such procedure *[sic]* as are established by law"); *see* M. Cherif Bassiouni, *Human Rights in the Context of Criminal Justice: Identifying International Procedural Protections and Equivalent Protections in National Constitutions*, 3 Duke J. Comp. & Int'l L. 235, 259–62 (1993).

[65] Statute, *supra* note 3, art. 21 (following International Covenant, *supra* note 24, art. 14); *see also Secretary-General's Report*, *supra* note 3, ¶ 106.

[66] I.T. R. Proc. & Evid., *supra* note 4, R. 87(A). A matter as fundamental as the standard of proof of guilt should be included in the constitutive documents of any future international criminal court, rather than left to the court's rules of procedure.

PUBLIC NATURE OF THE INDICTMENT

Upon confirmation, the indictment is generally a public document.[67] However, the judge may "in consultation with the Prosecutor, order that there be no public disclosure of the indictment" until served on all persons accused therein.[68] This is to prevent the flight of the accused. The judge or trial chamber may,

> in consultation with the Prosecutor, also order that there be no disclosure of an indictment, or part thereof, or of all or any part of any particular document or information, if satisfied that the making of such an order is required to give effect to a provision of the Rules, to protect confidential information obtained by the Prosecutor, or is otherwise in the interests of justice.[69]

No standard for the making of such an order more specific than the interests of justice is given. The indictment must, however, be read to the accused.[70]

Issuance of a Warrant or Summons

The judge "may" issue an arrest warrant, bearing the seal of the Tribunal, at the request of the prosecutor on the basis of the confirmed indictment.[71] The warrant is to be accompanied by a copy of the indictment and a statement of the rights of the defendant.[72]

---

[67] *Id.* R. 52.

[68] *Id.* R. 53(A).

[69] I.T. R. Proc. & Evid. (Rev.3), *supra* note 4, R. 53(B).

[70] I.T. R. Proc. & Evid., *supra* note 4, RR. 55(B), 62(ii), are similar to International Covenant, *supra* note 24, art. 14(3)(a).

[71] Statute, *supra* note 3, art. 19(2); *see* I.T. R. Proc. & Evid., *supra* note 4, R. 55(A). Under *id.* R. 54, warrants "may" be issued by the judge or trial chamber *proprio motu*, as well as at the prosecutor's request.

[72] I.T. R. Proc. & Evid., *supra* note 4, R. 55(A). The protections of which the accused is to be informed are set forth in Statute, *supra* note 3, art. 21; I.T. R. Proc. &

While no standard for the issuance of an arrest warrant is set forth in either the Statute or the Rules of Procedure and Evidence, the *Secretary-General's Report* suggests that issuance is a ministerial duty of the judge confirming the indictment.[73] The rules provide for the possibility of summonses,[74] as well as warrants, without setting out a standard to determine when each should be employed. Perhaps surprisingly, there is no provision in the rules for issuance of a preindictment arrest warrant where a suspect is likely to go into hiding before the completion of an investigation. The Statute appears to allow such a warrant,[75] but the rules provide only for a prosecutorial request for assistance in such a case.[76]

While summonses for court appearances are useful in preventing pretrial incarceration or humiliating arrests for misdemeanors, they are inappropriate for persons charged with serious violations of international humanitarian law. The issuance of warrants for the arrest of indicted

---

Evid. (Rev.3), *supra* note 4, RR. 42–43. Interestingly, *id.* RR. 42(A)(iii), 55(A) also set forth a right "to remain silent" and to be warned that statements may be used in evidence. These provisions go beyond Statute, *supra*, art. 21(g), which states that an accused cannot be "compelled to testify against himself or to confess guilt."

[73] *Secretary-General's Report, supra* note 3, ¶ 97 ("Upon confirmation of the indictment, the judge would, at the request of the Prosecutor, issue . . . orders and warrants for the arrest . . . of persons . . . ."). *But see* Statute, *supra* note 3, art. 19(2) ("Upon confirmation of an indictment, the judge may . . . issue such orders and warrants . . . as may be required . . . ."); I.T. R. Proc. & Evid., *supra* note 4, R. 54 (the judge "may" issue warrants). The use of the permissive "may" is puzzling in light of the use of the stronger "shall" in Statute, *supra,* arts. 18(4), 19(1) (providing that the prosecutor "shall" prepare an indictment and the judge "shall" confirm it, if both are convinced a prima facie case exists).

[74] A summons is an order to appear in court, and a defendant who has been summonsed usually is not taken into custody except upon failure to appear. The only references in the rules to summonses appear in I.T. R. Proc. & Evid., *supra* note 4, RR. 54, 105.

[75] *See* Statute, *supra* note 3, art. 29(2)(a), (d); *see also* ILC 1994 Draft Statute, *supra* note 36, art. 28 (proposing a scheme of provisional arrest warrants for preindictment arrests).

[76] See section *supra* entitled "Investigation" (on whether states must comply with such requests) and section *infra* entitled "Provisional Arrest before Indictment" (on dangers of warrantless provisional arrests).

persons should be explicitly made a ministerial duty of the judge confirming the indictment. The summons provision should be replaced with a procedure for the voluntary surrender of an accused either directly to agents of the Tribunal or to a state for transfer to the Tribunal; at the very least, a summons should not be issued unless the prosecutor agrees that a warrant is not necessary to secure the presence of the accused.

Arrest or Failure to Arrest the Accused

PROCEDURE ON WARRANT

The warrant and an order for surrender of the accused to the Tribunal are transmitted by the registrar of the Tribunal to the national authorities of the state in which the accused resides or was last known to be,[77] along with "instructions that at the time of arrest the indictment and the statement of the rights of the accused be read to him in a language he understands and that he be cautioned in that language."[78] In general, the task of locating and arresting the accused is left to these national authorities,[79] though a member of the prosecutor's office may be present from the time of the arrest.[80]

Arrest of an accused on a warrant is an international legal obligation of states. States "shall comply without undue delay" with an order of a trial chamber, including an order for "the arrest or detention of persons."[81]

If the arrest warrant is not executed, the rules provide for a series of escalating steps to try to apprehend the accused. First, the state to which the warrant was transmitted must report to the registrar of the Tribunal the reasons for its inability to execute the warrant. If such a report is not forthcoming, the Tribunal may notify the Security

---

[77] I.T. R. Proc. & Evid. (Rev.3), *supra* note 4, R. 55(B).

[78] *Id.*

[79] I.T. R. Proc. & Evid., *supra* note 4, R. 56.

[80] *Id.* R. 55(C).

[81] Statute, *supra* note 3, art. 29(2)(d); *see also* I.T. R. Proc. & Evid., *supra* note 4, R. 56.

Council.[82] Upon failure of the state to make an arrest, the prosecutor may then have the registrar ask states to advertise the indictment in newspapers of wide circulation in any territory where there is reason to believe the accused might be found.[83]

If these measures fail to result in an arrest, the prosecutor may ask a judge to lay the indictment before the entire trial chamber to which the judge is assigned. The judge shall do so if satisfied that the prosecutor has taken all reasonable steps to serve the accused pursuant to the procedures described above.[84] The indictment shall be presented in open court, "together with all the evidence that was before the Judge who initially confirmed the indictment"; the prosecutor may also call and examine "any witness whose statement has been submitted to the confirming Judge" and present additional evidence.[85] If the trial chamber "is satisfied . . . that there are reasonable grounds for believing that the accused has committed all or any of the crimes charged in the indictment, it shall so determine" and have the relevant portions of the indictment read out.[86] The chamber "shall also issue an international arrest warrant . . . which shall be transmitted to all States."[87]

If a state fails or refuses to cooperate with the Tribunal in arresting an accused, the president of the Tribunal may refer the matter to the Security Council. This may occur after the original transmission of the arrest warrant to a state and the failure of that state to report to the Tribunal on action taken,[88] or after the prosecutor satisfies the trial chamber that "the failure to effect personal service was due in whole or in part to a failure or refusal of a State to cooperate with the Tribunal in accordance with Article 29 of the Statute."[89]

---

[82] I.T. R. Proc. & Evid., *supra* note 4, R. 59.

[83] *Id.* R. 60.

[84] *Id.* R. 61(A)–(B).

[85] I.T. R. Proc. & Evid. (Rev.3), *supra* note 4, R. 61(B)–(C).

[86] *Id.* R. 61(C).

[87] I.T. R. Proc. & Evid., *supra* note 4, R. 61(D).

[88] *Id.* R. 59(B).

[89] *Id.* R. 61(E).

The reliance upon national authorities to effect arrest is necessary because it is not yet politically feasible to establish an international police force with arrest powers. This means, however, that arrest of persons in the territory of a state, government, or military force unfriendly to the Tribunal will likely depend upon the willingness and ability of the Security Council to use its enforcement powers to secure compliance.

The procedures for issuance of an international arrest warrant are unduly complex. Because of their public nature (surprising in light of other provisions in the rules for secrecy of indictments and for provisional arrest), they may provide some criminals with the opportunity to disappear. No legitimate interest of defendants is served by delaying the issuance of a warrant valid in all states. Therefore, the rules should be amended to require the registrar, at the prosecutor's request, to transmit the arrest warrant signed by a judge, along with the indictment and supporting material, to any state within whose jurisdiction the prosecutor believes the accused might be found or, at the prosecutor's request, to all states.

The process of presenting the indictment and evidence to the trial chamber in public should be reserved for cases in which all reasonable means for apprehending the accused have failed. In such a case, this procedure serves as a public memorial of the crimes within the Tribunal's jurisdiction.

PROVISIONAL ARREST BEFORE INDICTMENT

The Rules of Procedure and Evidence also permit preindictment arrest. During an investigation, the prosecutor may "[i]n case of urgency" request a state to arrest a suspect[90] provisionally or otherwise prevent the suspect's flight.[91] No standard for the strength of the case against the suspect is set forth. This authority is presumably derived from the prosecutor's ability under the Statute to seek appropriate assistance from the relevant state authorities.[92] Whether a request for a provisional arrest is

---

[90] See *supra* note 5 on the use of "suspect" rather than "accused."

[91] I.T. R. Proc. & Evid., *supra* note 4, R. 40(i), (iii).

[92] Statute, *supra* note 3, art. 18(2); *see also id.* art. 29.

obligatory is not clear in the Statute, but the revised rules state that it is.[93]

The provisional arrest rule[94] contains obvious dangers for human rights. Being standardless, it allows the prosecutor, unfettered by judicial review, arbitrarily to request a state to arrest a suspect. Given that prosecutorial requests for assistance are now clearly binding on states,[95] then the prosecutor appears to have the ability to supersede national human rights protections concerning arrest and detention without substituting the protections of judicial review by the Tribunal. Even if the rules had not been so amended, a prosecutorial request for a preindictment arrest would put great pressure on a state to make an arrest in violation of national or international standards prohibiting arbitrary arrest and detention.

The rules should be further amended to permit preindictment arrest warrants to be issued only upon a showing by affidavit of reasonable or probable cause to believe that the suspect has committed a crime within the Tribunal's jurisdiction and might flee or commit further crimes if not immediately taken into custody. This would strengthen the ability of the Tribunal to obtain the presence of defendants because such warrants would unquestionably be orders of the Tribunal binding upon states.[96] It would also protect persons from unreasonable seizure by guaranteeing judicial review of all decisions to arrest.[97] Protection from

---

[93] See section *supra* entitled "Investigation" (discussing mandatory investigative assistance pursuant to orders of the trial chambers under Statute, *supra* note 3, art. 29); I.T. R. Proc. & Evid. (Rev.3), *supra* note 4, R. 40.

[94] I.T. R. Proc. & Evid. (Rev.3), *supra* note 4, R. 40(i).

[95] *Id.* R. 40. See section *supra* entitled "Investigation."

[96] Statute, *supra* note 3, art. 29(2); *see also* ILC 1994 Draft Statute, *supra* note 36, art. 28.

[97] At the Conference on International Criminal Justice: Historic and Contemporary Perspectives, Instituto Superiore Internazionale di Scienze Criminali, Siracusa, Italy, Dec. 6, 1994, the Hon. Richard Goldstone, Prosecutor of the International Tribunal for the Former Yugoslavia, speaking informally, proposed that provisional arrest without a warrant should be permitted, but review of the grounds for arrest should be available from the Tribunal within 48 hours.

prolonged detention could be guaranteed by requiring release within a brief period of time, perhaps thirty days, if no indictment were confirmed by the Tribunal. Such a revised rule should also clarify whether a person who has been provisionally arrested will be incarcerated under the jurisdiction of the arresting state or transferred to the jurisdiction of the Tribunal.

Detention and Advice of Rights of the Accused

The rules provide that the accused be detained pending transfer to the seat of the Tribunal.[98] "Once detained, an accused may not be released except upon an order of a Trial Chamber,"[99] which suggests that the arresting state has no authority to release the defendant pursuant to its own law. The accused is to be read the indictment and advised of his or her rights under the Statute and rules "in a language that he understands."[100] Among the rights to be communicated is the right "to remain silent,"[101] which was recently added to the list of rights accorded suspects during investigation.[102]

Because of the danger that the arresting state may not be wholly friendly to the purposes of the Tribunal, and thus may improperly grant pretrial release to an accused, the rules should be made explicit that only the Tribunal, and not the arresting state, can grant pretrial release. At the same time, in order to prevent unjustifiable pretrial detention, the rules should require that the prosecutor seek prompt transfer of the accused from the custody of the arresting state to the Tribunal; if such transfer is not sought, power to grant pretrial release should revert to the arresting state.

---

[98]   I.T. R. Proc. & Evid., *supra* note 4, R. 57.

[99]   *Id.* R. 65(A).

[100]   *Id.* R. 55(A)–(B).

[101]   *Id.* R. 55(A).

[102]   I.T. R. Proc. & Evid. (Rev.3), *supra* note 4, R. 42(A)(iii).

Surrender or Transfer of the Accused to the Seat of the Tribunal

The subject of giving an accused over to the Tribunal is treated briefly in both the Statute and the Rules of Procedure and Evidence. An arrested person is to be "transferred to the International Tribunal,"[103] and states are enjoined "to comply without undue delay" with an order for "the surrender or the transfer of the accused to the International Tribunal."[104] The rules state that the arresting state shall promptly notify the registrar of the arrest, and "transfer of the accused to the seat of the Tribunal shall be arranged between the State authorities concerned and the Registrar."[105] As discussed above, the obligation to transfer an accused to the Tribunal prevails over any national law or extradition treaty that might impede transfer.[106]

The Statute and rules do not provide for the transmission to the arresting state of a statement of the evidence against the accused. Therefore, the courts of that state will not be in a position to determine the sufficiency of the evidence against the accused under either national or international law. At best, the warrant and confirmed indictment will be proof that a judge of the Tribunal has determined that a prima facie case exists.

Thus, the state in which the accused is arrested has no authority to protect his or her rights, except to provide humane conditions of detention pending transfer or surrender. All other protections of the accused's human rights must occur, if at all, under the jurisdiction of the Tribunal.

This is the reason that review of the evidence by a judge of the Tribunal before indictment is so critical. Given the Security Council's assertion of authority for the Tribunal, the state in which the accused is found may not challenge the propriety of arrest and transfer, other than to determine that the arrest warrant and indictment are genuine and that

---

[103] Statute, *supra* note 3, art. 20(2).

[104] *Id.* art. 29(2)(e).

[105] I.T. R. Proc. & Evid., *supra* note 4, R. 57.

[106] *Id.* R. 58. See *supra* notes 8–13, 19–22, 31–33 and accompanying text.

the arrested person is indeed the accused named in the warrant. Arbitrariness of arrest and detention is unlikely to be remedied by the Tribunal before trial.[107]

After transfer, the rules provide that pretrial release is exceptional, to be ordered only by the trial chamber (rather than a single judge) if the chamber is "satisfied that the accused will appear for trial and, if released, will not pose a danger to any victim, witness or other person."[108] While such a rule would be harsh in a court with jurisdiction over ordinary crimes, it is reasonable given that the only crimes over which the Tribunal has jurisdiction are serious violations of international humanitarian law. The harshness of this rule, however, emphasizes the need to ensure that persons are not arrested and detained except upon reasonable (or probable) cause.

Rearrest may occur if "necessary . . . to secure the presence of an accused"[109] without any requirement that the conditions of release have been violated. This rule should be clarified to require an articulable reason to believe that the accused has violated or will not comply with the conditions of release before an order revoking pretrial release is entered. The rule should also be modified to permit revocation of pretrial release if there is an articulable reason to believe the accused has harmed, threatened, or intimidated any victim or witness or is preparing or attempting to do so.

CONCLUSION

The Tribunal's Rules of Procedure and Evidence as currently written should be amended to ensure that, in the process of obtaining the

---

[107] The only permitted pretrial motions challenging the validity of detention are objections based on lack of jurisdiction and on defects in the form of the indictment. I.T. R. Proc. & Evid., *supra* note 4, R. 73(A)(i)–(ii).

[108] *Id.* R. 65(B). The trial chamber may require a bail bond and the observance of other conditions to ensure the defendant's presence for trial and the protection of others. *Id.* R. 65(C).

[109] *Id.* R. 65(D).

presence of persons accused of serious violations of international humanitarian law, the rights of individuals are not violated. In a few instances, the rules need strengthening to guard against the possibility that guilty persons may escape. On the whole, however, the creation of the International Tribunal represents a significant advance for the United Nations and for international law in using criminal prosecutions to enforce international humanitarian law within a framework of procedural safeguards.

V
Appendixes

Appendix A

Security Council Resolutions on the Establishment of the International Tribunal for the Former Yugoslavia

RESOLUTION 780 (1992)[*]

Adopted unanimously by the Security Council at its 3119th meeting, October 6, 1992. S.C. Res. 780, U.N. SCOR, 47th Year, 1992 S.C. Res. & Dec. at 36, U.N. Doc. S/INF/48 (1992). Footnotes have been omitted.

The Security Council,

Reaffirming its resolution 713 (1991) of 25 September 1991 and all subsequent relevant resolutions,

Recalling paragraph 10 of its resolution 764 (1992) of 13 July 1992, in which it reaffirmed that all parties are bound to comply with the obligations under international humanitarian law and in particular the Geneva Conventions of 12 August 1949, and that persons who

---

[*] *Editor's note:* The Commission of Experts established under S.C. Res. 780 prepared three reports, which are cited here in reverse chronological order. Letter from the Secretary-General to the President of the Security Council, May 24, 1994, U.N. Doc. S/1994/674 (1994), transmitting *Final Report of the Commission of Experts Established pursuant to Security Council Resolution 780 (1992), available in* U.N. Gopher\Current Information\Secretary-General's Reports\June 1994; Letter from the Secretary-General to the President of the Security Council, Oct. 5, 1993, U.N. Doc. S/26545 (1993), transmitting *Second Interim Report of the Commission of Experts Established pursuant to Security Council Resolution 780 (1992);* Letter from the Secretary-General to the President of the Security Council, Feb. 9, 1993, U.N. Doc. S/25274 (1993), transmitting *Interim Report of the Commission of Experts Established pursuant to Security Council Resolution 780 (1992).*

commit or order the commission of grave breaches of the Conventions are individually responsible in respect of such breaches,

Recalling also its resolution 771 (1992) of 13 August 1992, in which, *inter alia*, it demanded that all parties and others concerned in the former Yugoslavia, and all military forces in Bosnia and Herzegovina, immediately cease and desist from all breaches of international humanitarian law,

Expressing once again its grave alarm at continuing reports of widespread violations of international humanitarian law occurring within the territory of the former Yugoslavia and especially in Bosnia and Herzegovina, including reports of mass killings and the continuance of the practice of "ethnic cleansing",

1. *Reaffirms* its call, in paragraph 5 of resolution 771 (1992), upon States and, as appropriate, international humanitarian organizations to collate substantiated information in their possession or submitted to them relating to the violations of humanitarian law, including grave breaches of the Geneva Conventions being committed in the territory of the former Yugoslavia, and requests States, relevant United Nations bodies, and relevant organizations to make this information available within thirty days of the adoption of the present resolution and as appropriate thereafter, and to provide other appropriate assistance to the Commission of Experts referred to in paragraph 2 below;

2. *Requests* the Secretary-General to establish, as a matter of urgency, an impartial Commission of Experts to examine and analyse the information submitted pursuant to resolution 771 (1992) and the present resolution, together with such further information as the Commission of Experts may obtain through its own investigations or efforts, of other persons or bodies pursuant to resolution 771 (1992), with a view to providing the Secretary-General with its conclusions on the evidence of grave breaches of the Geneva Conventions and other violations of international humanitarian law committed in the territory of the former Yugoslavia;

3. *Also requests* the Secretary-General to report to the Council on the establishment of the Commission of Experts;

4. *Further requests* the Secretary-General to report to the Council on the conclusions of the Commission of Experts and to take account of these conclusions in any recommendations for further appropriate steps called for by resolution 771 (1992);

5. *Decides* to remain actively seized of the matter.

RESOLUTION 808 (1993)**

Adopted unanimously by the Security Council at its 3175th meeting, February 22, 1993. S.C. Res. 808, U.N. SCOR, 48th Year, 1993 S.C. Res. & Dec. at 28, U.N. Doc. S/INF/49 (1993). Footnotes have been omitted.

The Security Council,

Reaffirming its resolution 713 (1991) of 25 September 1991 and all subsequent relevant resolutions,

Recalling paragraph 10 of its resolution 764 (1992) of 13 July 1992, in which it reaffirmed that all parties are bound to comply with the obligations under international humanitarian law, in particular the Geneva Conventions of 12 August 1949, and that persons who commit or order the commission of grave breaches of the Conventions are individually responsible in respect of such breaches,

Recalling also its resolution 771 (1992) of 13 August 1992, in which, *inter alia*, it demanded that all parties and others concerned in the former Yugoslavia, and all military forces in Bosnia and Herzegovina, immediately cease and desist from all breaches of international humanitarian law,

---

** *Editor's note:* the official text of this resolution, set out here, differs slightly from the text released as S.C. Res. 808, U.N. Doc. S/RES/808 (1993), at the time the resolution was adopted. The official text became available only as this issue of *Criminal Law Forum* went to press, and the contributors refer to the version initially made public.

Recalling further its resolution 780 (1992) of 6 October 1992, in which it requested the Secretary-General to establish, as a matter of urgency, an impartial commission of experts to examine and analyse the information submitted pursuant to resolutions 771 (1992) and 780 (1992), together with such further information as the commission may obtain, with a view to providing the Secretary-General with its conclusions on the evidence of grave breaches of the Geneva Conventions and other violations of international humanitarian law committed in the territory of the former Yugoslavia,

Having considered the interim report of the Commission of Experts established by resolution 780 (1992) [S/25274], in which the Commission observed that a decision to establish an ad hoc international tribunal in relation to events in the territory of the former Yugoslavia would be consistent with the direction of its work,

Expressing once again its grave alarm at continuing reports of widespread violations of international humanitarian law occurring within the territory of the former Yugoslavia, including reports of mass killings and the continuance of the practice of "ethnic cleansing",

Determining that this situation constitutes a threat to international peace and security,

Determined to put an end to such crimes and to take effective measures to bring to justice the persons who are responsible for them,

Convinced that in the particular circumstances of the former Yugoslavia the establishment of an international tribunal would enable this aim to be achieved and would contribute to the restoration and maintenance of peace,

Noting in this regard the recommendation by the Co-Chairmen of the Steering Committee of the International Conference on the Former Yugoslavia for the establishment of such a tribunal [S/25221],

Taking note with grave concern of the report of the European Community investigative mission into the treatment of Muslim women in the former Yugoslavia [S/25240],

Taking note of the report of the committee of jurists submitted by France [S/25266], the report of the commission of jurists submitted by Italy [S/25300], and the report transmitted by the Permanent Representative of Sweden on behalf of the Chairman-in-Office of the Conference on Security and Cooperation in Europe [S/25307],

1. *Decides* that an international tribunal shall be established for the prosecution of persons responsible for serious violations of international humanitarian law committed in the territory of the former Yugoslavia since 1991;

2. *Requests* the Secretary-General to submit for consideration by the Council at the earliest possible date, and if possible no later than sixty days after the adoption of the present resolution, a report on all aspects of this matter, including specific proposals and where appropriate options for the effective and expeditious implementation of the decision contained in paragraph 1 above, taking into account suggestions put forward in this regard by Member States;

3. *Decides* to remain actively seized of the matter.

RESOLUTION 827 (1993)[***]

Adopted unanimously by the Security Council at its 3217th meeting, May 25, 1993. S.C. Res. 827, U.N. SCOR, 48th Year, 1993 S.C. Res. & Dec. at 29, U.N. Doc. S/INF/49 (1993). Footnotes have been omitted.

The Security Council,

Reaffirming its resolution 713 (1991) of 25 September 1991 and all subsequent relevant resolutions,

---

[***] *Editor's note:* as with S.C. Res. 808, the official text of S.C. Res. 827, set out here, differs slightly from the version initially made public and cited by the contributors.

Having considered the report of the Secretary-General of 3 and 17 May 1993 pursuant to paragraph 2 of resolution 808 (1993) [S/25704 & Add.1],

Expressing once again its grave alarm at continuing reports of widespread and flagrant violations of international humanitarian law occurring within the territory of the former Yugoslavia, and especially in the Republic of Bosnia and Herzegovina, including reports of mass killings, massive, organized and systematic detention and rape of women and the continuance of the practice of "ethnic cleansing", including for the acquisition and the holding of territory,

Determining that this situation continues to constitute a threat to international peace and security,

Determined to put an end to such crimes and to take effective measures to bring to justice the persons who are responsible for them,

Convinced that in the particular circumstances of the former Yugoslavia the establishment as an ad hoc measure by the Council of an international tribunal and the prosecution of persons responsible for serious violations of international humanitarian law would enable this aim to be achieved and would contribute to the restoration and maintenance of peace,

Believing that the establishment of an international tribunal and the prosecution of persons responsible for the above-mentioned violations of international humanitarian law will contribute to ensuring that such violations are halted and effectively redressed,

Noting in this regard the recommendation by the Co-Chairmen of the Steering Committee of the International Conference on the Former Yugoslavia for the establishment of such a tribunal [S/25221],

Reaffirming in this regard its decision in resolution 808 (1993) of 22 February 1993 that an international tribunal shall be established for the prosecution of persons responsible for serious violations of international humanitarian law committed in the territory of the former Yugoslavia since 1991,

Considering that, pending the appointment of the prosecutor of the international tribunal, the Commission of Experts established pursuant to resolution 780 (1992) should continue on an urgent basis the collection of information relating to evidence of grave breaches of the Geneva Conventions and other violations of international humanitarian law as proposed in its interim report [S/25274],

Acting under Chapter VII of the Charter of the United Nations,

1. *Approves* the report of the Secretary-General [S/25704 & Add.1];

2. *Decides* hereby to establish an international tribunal for the sole purpose of prosecuting persons responsible for serious violations of international humanitarian law committed in the territory of the former Yugoslavia between 1 January 1991 and a date to be determined by the Security Council upon the restoration of peace and to this end to adopt the statute of the International Tribunal annexed to the report of the Secretary-General;

3. *Requests* the Secretary-General to submit to the judges of the International Tribunal, upon their election, any suggestions received from States for the rules of procedure and evidence called for in article 15 of the statute of the International Tribunal;

4. *Decides* that all States shall cooperate fully with the International Tribunal and its organs in accordance with the present resolution and the statute of the Tribunal and that consequently all States shall take any measures necessary under their domestic law to implement the provisions of the present resolution and the statute, including the obligation of States to comply with requests for assistance or orders issued by a trial chamber under article 29 of the statute;

5. *Urges* States and intergovernmental and non-governmental organizations to contribute funds, equipment and services to the International Tribunal, including the offer of expert personnel;

6. *Decides* that the determination of the seat of the International Tribunal is subject to the conclusion of appropriate arrangements between the United Nations and the Netherlands acceptable to the Council, and that the Tribunal may sit elsewhere when it considers it necessary for the efficient exercise of its functions;

7. *Decides* also that the work of the International Tribunal shall be carried out without prejudice to the right of the victims to seek, through appropriate means, compensation for damages incurred as a result of violations of international humanitarian law;

8. *Requests* the Secretary-General to implement urgently the present resolution and in particular to make practical arrangements for the effective functioning of the International Tribunal at the earliest time and to report periodically to the Council;

9. *Decides* to remain actively seized of the matter.

Appendix B

*Report of the Secretary-General pursuant to Paragraph 2 of Security Council Resolution 808 (1993), including the Statute of the Tribunal**

INTRODUCTION

1.　By paragraph 1 of resolution 808 (1993) of 22 February 1993, the Security Council decided "that an international tribunal shall be established for the prosecution of persons responsible for serious violations of international humanitarian law committed in the territory of the former Yugoslavia since 1991".

2.　By paragraph 2 of the resolution, the Secretary-General was requested "to submit for consideration by the Council at the earliest possible date, and if possible no later than 60 days after the adoption of the present resolution, a report on all aspects of this matter, including specific proposals and where appropriate options for the effective and expeditious implementation of the decision [to establish an international tribunal], taking into account suggestions put forward in this regard by Member States."

3.　The present report is presented pursuant to that request.[1]

A

4.　Resolution 808 (1993) represents a further step taken by the Security Council in a series of resolutions concerning serious violations of

---

*　*Editor's note:* U.N. Doc. No. S/25704 & Add.1 (1993). Inconsistencies in style in this document have not been corrected.

[1]　On 19 April 1993, the Secretary-General addressed a letter to the President of the Security Council informing him that the report would be made available to the Security Council no later than 6 May 1993.

international humanitarian law occurring in the territory of the former Yugoslavia.

5. In resolution 764 (1992) of 13 July 1992, the Security Council reaffirmed that all parties to the conflict are bound to comply with their obligations under international humanitarian law and in particular the Geneva Conventions of 12 August 1949, and that persons who commit or order the commission of grave breaches of the Conventions are individually responsible in respect of such breaches.

6. In resolution 771 (1992) of 13 August 1992, the Security Council expressed grave alarm at continuing reports of widespread violations of international humanitarian law occurring within the territory of the former Yugoslavia and especially in Bosnia and Herzegovina, including reports of mass forcible expulsion and deportation of civilians, imprisonment and abuse of civilians in detention centres, deliberate attacks on non-combatants, hospitals and ambulances, impeding the delivery of food and medical supplies to the civilian population, and wanton devastation and destruction of property. The Council strongly condemned any violations of international humanitarian law, including those involved in the practice of "ethnic cleansing", and demanded that all parties to the conflict in the former Yugoslavia cease and desist from all breaches of international humanitarian law. It called upon States and international humanitarian organizations to collate substantiated information relating to the violations of humanitarian law, including grave breaches of the Geneva Conventions, being committed in the territory of the former Yugoslavia and to make this information available to the Council. Furthermore, the Council decided, acting under Chapter VII of the Charter of the United Nations, that all parties and others concerned in the former Yugoslavia, and all military forces in Bosnia and Herzegovina, should comply with the provisions of that resolution, failing which the Council would need to take further measures under the Charter.

7. In resolution 780 (1992) of 6 October 1992, the Security Council requested the Secretary-General to establish an impartial Commission of Experts to examine and analyse the information as requested by resolution 771 (1992), together with such further information as the Commission may obtain through its own investigations or efforts, of other persons or bodies pursuant to resolution 771 (1992), with a view to providing the Secretary-

General with its conclusions on the evidence of grave breaches of the Geneva Conventions and other violations of international humanitarian law committed in the territory of the former Yugoslavia.

8.   On 14 October 1992 the Secretary-General submitted a report to the Security Council pursuant to paragraph 3 of resolution 780 (1992) in which he outlined his decision to establish a five-member Commission of Experts (S/24657). On 26 October 1992, the Secretary-General announced the appointment of the Chairman and members of the Commission of Experts.

9.   By a letter dated 9 February 1993, the Secretary-General submitted to the President of the Security Council an interim report of the Commission of Experts (S/25274), which concluded that grave breaches and other violations of international humanitarian law had been committed in the territory of the former Yugoslavia, including wilful killing, "ethnic cleansing", mass killings, torture, rape, pillage and destruction of civilian property, destruction of cultural and religious property and arbitrary arrests. In its report, the Commission noted that should the Security Council or another competent organ of the United Nations decide to establish an ad hoc international tribunal, such a decision would be consistent with the direction of its work.

10.   It was against this background that the Security Council considered and adopted resolution 808 (1993). After recalling the provisions of resolutions 764 (1992), 771 (1992) and 780 (1992) and, taking into consideration the interim report of the Commission of Experts, the Security Council expressed once again its grave alarm at continuing reports of widespread violations of international humanitarian law occurring within the territory of the former Yugoslavia, including reports of mass killings and the continuation of the practice of "ethnic cleansing". The Council determined that this situation constituted a threat to international peace and security, and stated that it was determined to put an end to such crimes and to take effective measures to bring to justice the persons who are responsible for them. The Security Council stated its conviction that in the particular circumstances of the former Yugoslavia the establishment of an international tribunal would enable this aim to be achieved and would contribute to the restoration and maintenance of peace.

11.   The Secretary-General wishes to recall that in resolution 820 (1993) of 17 April 1993, the Security Council condemned once again all violations of international humanitarian law, including in particular, the practice of "ethnic cleansing" and the massive, organized and systematic detention and rape of women, and reaffirmed that those who commit or have committed or order or have ordered the commission of such acts will be held individually responsible in respect of such acts.

B

12.   The Security Council's decision in resolution 808 (1993) to establish an international tribunal is circumscribed in scope and purpose: the prosecution of persons responsible for serious violations of international humanitarian law committed in the territory of the former Yugoslavia since 1991. The decision does not relate to the establishment of an international criminal jurisdiction in general nor to the creation of an international criminal court of a permanent nature, issues which are and remain under active consideration by the International Law Commission and the General Assembly.

C

13.   In accordance with the request of the Security Council, the Secretary-General has taken into account in the preparation of the present report the suggestions put forward by Member States, in particular those reflected in the following Security Council documents submitted by Member States and noted by the Council in its resolution 808 (1993): the report of the committee of jurists submitted by France (S/25266), the report of the commission of jurists submitted by Italy (S/25300), and the report submitted by the Permanent Representative of Sweden on behalf of the Chairman-in-Office of the Conference on Security and Cooperation in Europe (CSCE) (S/25307). The Secretary-General has also sought the views of the Commission of Experts established pursuant to Security Council resolution 780 (1992) and has made use of the information gathered by that Commission. In addition, the Secretary-General has taken into account suggestions or comments put forward formally or informally by the following Member States since the adoption of resolution 808 (1993): Australia, Austria, Belgium, Brazil, Canada, Chile, China, Denmark, Egypt,* Germany, Iran (Islamic Republic of),* Ireland, Italy, Malaysia,* Mexico,

Netherlands, New Zealand, Pakistan,* Portugal, Russian Federation, Saudi Arabia,* Senegal,* Slovenia, Spain, Sweden, Turkey,* United Kingdom of Great Britain and Northern Ireland, United States of America and Yugoslavia. He has also received suggestions or comments from a non-member State (Switzerland). [*On behalf of the members of the Organization of the Islamic Conference (OIC) and as members of the Contact Group of OIC on Bosnia and Herzegovina.]

14. The Secretary-General has also received comments from the International Committee of the Red Cross (ICRC) and from the following non-governmental organizations: Amnesty International, Association Internationale des Jeunes Avocats, Ethnic Minorities Barristers' Association, Fédération Internationale des Femmes des Carrières Juridiques, International Criminal Police Organization, Jacob Blaustein Institution for the Advancement of Human Rights, Lawyers Committee for Human Rights, National Alliance of Women's Organisations (NAWO), and Parliamentarians for Global Action. Observations have also been received from international meetings and individual experts in relevant fields.

15. The Secretary-General wishes to place on record his appreciation for the interest shown by all the Governments, organizations and individuals who have offered valuable suggestions and comments.

D

16. In the main body of the report which follows, the Secretary-General first examines the legal basis for the establishment of the International Tribunal foreseen in resolution 808 (1993). The Secretary-General then sets out in detail the competence of the International Tribunal as regards the law it will apply, the persons to whom the law will be applied, including considerations as to the principle of individual criminal responsibility, its territorial and temporal reach and the relation of its work to that of national courts. In succeeding chapters, the Secretary-General sets out detailed views on the organization of the international tribunal, the investigation and pre-trial proceedings, trial and post-trial proceedings, and cooperation and judicial assistance. A concluding chapter deals with a number of general and organizational issues such as privileges and immunities, the seat of the international tribunal, working languages and financial arrangements.

17. In response to the Security Council's request to include in the report specific proposals, the Secretary-General has decided to incorporate into the report specific language for inclusion in a statute of the International Tribunal. The formulations are based upon provisions found in existing international instruments, particularly with regard to competence *ratione materiae* of the International Tribunal. Suggestions and comments, including suggested draft articles, received from States, organizations and individuals as noted in paragraphs 13 and 14 above, also formed the basis upon which the Secretary-General prepared the statute. Texts prepared in the past by United Nations or other bodies for the establishment of international criminal courts were consulted by the Secretary-General, including texts prepared by the United Nations Committee on International Criminal Jurisdiction,[2] the International Law Commission, and the International Law Association. Proposals regarding individual articles are, therefore, made throughout the body of the report; the full text of the statute of the International Tribunal is contained in the annex to the present report.

I. *The Legal Basis for the Establishment of the International Tribunal*

18. Security Council resolution 808 (1993) states that an international tribunal shall be established for the prosecution of persons responsible for serious violations of international humanitarian law committed in the territory of the former Yugoslavia since 1991. It does not, however, indicate how such an international tribunal is to be established or on what legal basis.

19. The approach which, in the normal course of events, would be followed in establishing an international tribunal would be the conclusion of a treaty by which the States parties would establish a tribunal and approve its statute. This treaty would be drawn up and adopted by an appropriate international body (e.g., the General Assembly or a specially convened conference), following which it would be opened for signature and ratification. Such an approach would have the advantage of allowing for a

---

[2] The 1953 Committee on International Criminal Jurisdiction was established by General Assembly resolution 687 (VII) of 5 December 1952.

detailed examination and elaboration of all the issues pertaining to the establishment of the international tribunal. It also would allow the States participating in the negotiation and conclusion of the treaty fully to exercise their sovereign will, in particular whether they wish to become parties to the treaty or not.

20. As has been pointed out in many of the comments received, the treaty approach incurs the disadvantage of requiring considerable time to establish an instrument and then to achieve the required number of ratifications for entry into force. Even then, there could be no guarantee that ratifications will be received from those States which should be parties to the treaty if it is to be truly effective.

21. A number of suggestions have been put forward to the effect that the General Assembly, as the most representative organ of the United Nations, should have a role in the establishment of the international tribunal in addition to its role in the administrative and budgetary aspects of the question. The involvement of the General Assembly in the drafting or the review of the statute of the International Tribunal would not be reconcilable with the urgency expressed by the Security Council in resolution 808 (1993). The Secretary-General believes that there are other ways of involving the authority and prestige of the General Assembly in the establishment of the International Tribunal.

22. In the light of the disadvantages of the treaty approach in this particular case and of the need indicated in resolution 808 (1993) for an effective and expeditious implementation of the decision to establish an international tribunal, the Secretary-General believes that the International Tribunal should be established by a decision of the Security Council on the basis of Chapter VII of the Charter of the United Nations. Such a decision would constitute a measure to maintain or restore international peace and security, following the requisite determination of the existence of a threat to the peace, breach of the peace or act of aggression.

23. This approach would have the advantage of being expeditious and of being immediately effective as all States would be under a binding obligation to take whatever action is required to carry out a decision taken as an enforcement measure under Chapter VII.

24. In the particular case of the former Yugoslavia, the Secretary-General believes that the establishment of the International Tribunal by means of a Chapter VII decision would be legally justified, both in terms of the object and purpose of the decision, as indicated in the preceding paragraphs, and of past Security Council practice.

25. As indicated in paragraph 10 above, the Security Council has already determined that the situation posed by continuing reports of widespread violations of international humanitarian law occurring in the former Yugoslavia constitutes a threat to international peace and security. The Council has also decided under Chapter VII of the Charter that all parties and others concerned in the former Yugoslavia, and all military forces in Bosnia and Herzegovina, shall comply with the provisions of resolution 771 (1992), failing which it would need to take further measures under the Charter. Furthermore, the Council has repeatedly reaffirmed that all parties in the former Yugoslavia are bound to comply with the obligations under international humanitarian law and in particular the Geneva Conventions of 12 August 1949, and that persons who commit or order the commission of grave breaches of the Conventions are individually responsible in respect of such breaches.

26. Finally, the Security Council stated in resolution 808 (1993) that it was convinced that in the particular circumstances of the former Yugoslavia, the establishment of an international tribunal would bring about the achievement of the aim of putting an end to such crimes and of taking effective measures to bring to justice the persons responsible for them, and would contribute to the restoration and maintenance of peace.

27. The Security Council has on various occasions adopted decisions under Chapter VII aimed at restoring and maintaining international peace and security, which have involved the establishment of subsidiary organs for a variety of purposes. Reference may be made in this regard to Security Council resolution 687 (1991) and subsequent resolutions relating to the situation between Iraq and Kuwait.

28. In this particular case, the Security Council would be establishing, as an enforcement measure under Chapter VII, a subsidiary organ within the terms of Article 29 of the Charter, but one of a judicial nature. This organ would, of course, have to perform its functions independently of political

considerations; it would not be subject to the authority or control of the Security Council with regard to the performance of its judicial functions. As an enforcement measure under Chapter VII, however, the life span of the international tribunal would be linked to the restoration and maintenance of international peace and security in the territory of the former Yugoslavia, and Security Council decisions related thereto.

29. It should be pointed out that, in assigning to the International Tribunal the task of prosecuting persons responsible for serious violations of international humanitarian law, the Security Council would not be creating or purporting to "legislate" that law. Rather, the International Tribunal would have the task of applying existing international humanitarian law.

30. On the basis of the foregoing considerations, the Secretary-General proposes that the Security Council, acting under Chapter VII of the Charter, establish the International Tribunal. The resolution so adopted would have annexed to it a statute the opening passage of which would read as follows:

Having been established by the Security Council acting under Chapter VII of the Charter of the United Nations, the International Tribunal for the Prosecution of Persons Responsible for Serious Violations of International Humanitarian Law Committed in the Territory of the Former Yugoslavia since 1991 (hereinafter referred to as "the International Tribunal") shall function in accordance with the provisions of the present Statute.

II.   *Competence of the International Tribunal*

31. The competence of the International Tribunal derives from the mandate set out in paragraph 1 of resolution 808 (1993). This part of the report will examine and make proposals regarding these fundamental elements of its competence: *ratione materiae* (subject-matter jurisdiction), *ratione personae* (personal jurisdiction), *ratione loci* (territorial jurisdiction) and *ratione temporis* (temporal jurisdiction), as well as the question of the concurrent jurisdiction of the International Tribunal and national courts.

32. The statute should begin with a general article on the competence of the International Tribunal which would read as follows:

Article 1 — Competence of the International Tribunal

The International Tribunal shall have the power to prosecute persons responsible for serious violations of international humanitarian law committed in the territory of the former Yugoslavia since 1991 in accordance with the provisions of the present Statute.

A. COMPETENCE *RATIONE MATERIAE* (SUBJECT-MATTER JURISDICTION)

33. According to paragraph 1 of resolution 808 (1993), the international tribunal shall prosecute persons responsible for serious violations of international humanitarian law committed in the territory of the former Yugoslavia since 1991. This body of law exists in the form of both conventional law and customary law. While there is international customary law which is not laid down in conventions, some of the major conventional humanitarian law has become part of customary international law.

34. In the view of the Secretary-General, the application of the principle *nullum crimen sine lege* requires that the international tribunal should apply rules of international humanitarian law which are beyond any doubt part of customary law so that the problem of adherence of some but not all States to specific conventions does not arise. This would appear to be particularly important in the context of an international tribunal prosecuting persons responsible for serious violations of international humanitarian law.

35. The part of conventional international humanitarian law which has beyond doubt become part of international customary law is the law applicable in armed conflict as embodied in: the Geneva Conventions of 12 August 1949 for the Protection of War Victims;[3] the Hague Convention (IV) Respecting the Laws and Customs of War on Land and the Regulations annexed thereto of 18 October 1907;[4] the Convention on the Prevention

---

[3] Convention for the Amelioration of the Condition of the Wounded and Sick in Armed Forces in the Field of 12 August 1949, Convention for the Amelioration of the Condition of the Wounded, Sick and Shipwrecked Members of Armed Forces at Sea of 12 August 1949, Convention relative to the Treatment of Prisoners of War of 12 August 1949, Convention relative to the Protection of Civilian Persons in Time of War of 12 August 1949 (United Nations, Treaty Series, vol. 75, Nos. 970–973).

[4] Carnegie Endowment for International Peace, *The Hague Conventions and Declarations of 1899 and 1907* (New York, Oxford University Press, 1915), p. 100.

and Punishment of the Crime of Genocide of 9 December 1948;[5] and the Charter of the International Military Tribunal of 8 August 1945.[6]

36. Suggestions have been made that the international tribunal should apply domestic law in so far as it incorporates customary international humanitarian law. While international humanitarian law as outlined above provides a sufficient basis for subject-matter jurisdiction, there is one related issue which would require reference to domestic practice, namely, penalties (see para. 111 below).

Grave breaches of the 1949 Geneva Conventions

37. The Geneva Conventions constitute rules of international humanitarian law and provide the core of the customary law applicable in international armed conflicts. These Conventions regulate the conduct of war from the humanitarian perspective by protecting certain categories of persons: namely, wounded and sick members of armed forces in the field; wounded, sick and shipwrecked members of armed forces at sea; prisoners of war; and civilians in time of war.

38. Each Convention contains a provision listing the particularly serious violations that qualify as "grave breaches" or war crimes. Persons committing or ordering grave breaches are subject to trial and punishment. The lists of grave breaches contained in the Geneva Conventions are reproduced in the article which follows.

39. The Security Council has reaffirmed on several occasions that persons who commit or order the commission of grave breaches of the 1949

---

[5] United Nations, Treaty Series, vol. 78, No. 1021.

[6] The Agreement for the Prosecution and Punishment of the Major War Criminals of the European Axis, signed at London on 8 August 1945 (United Nations, Treaty Series, vol. 82, No. 251); *see also* Judgement of the International Military Tribunal for the Prosecution and Punishment of the Major War Criminals of the European Axis (United States Government Printing Office, Nazi Conspiracy and Aggression, Opinion and Judgement) and General Assembly resolution 95 (I) of 11 December 1946 on the Affirmation of the Principles of International Law Recognized by the Charter of the Nurnberg Tribunal.

Geneva Conventions in the territory of the former Yugoslavia are individually responsible for such breaches as serious violations of international humanitarian law.

40. The corresponding article of the statute would read:

Article 2—Grave breaches of the Geneva Conventions of 1949

The International Tribunal shall have the power to prosecute persons committing or ordering to be committed grave breaches of the Geneva Conventions of 12 August 1949, namely the following acts against persons or property protected under the provisions of the relevant Geneva Convention:

(a) wilful killing;
(b) torture or inhuman treatment, including biological experiments;
(c) wilfully causing great suffering or serious injury to body or health;
(d) extensive destruction and appropriation of property, not justified by military necessity and carried out unlawfully and wantonly;
(e) compelling a prisoner of war or a civilian to serve in the forces of a hostile power;
(f) wilfully depriving a prisoner of war or a civilian of the rights of fair and regular trial;
(g) unlawful deportation or transfer or unlawful confinement of a civilian;
(h) taking civilians as hostages.

Violations of the laws or customs of war

41. The 1907 Hague Convention (IV) Respecting the Laws and Customs of War on Land and the Regulations annexed thereto comprise a second important area of conventional humanitarian international law which has become part of the body of international customary law.

42. The Nurnberg Tribunal recognized that many of the provisions contained in the Hague Regulations, although innovative at the time of their adoption were, by 1939, recognized by all civilized nations and were regarded as being declaratory of the laws and customs of war. The Nurnberg Tribunal also recognized that war crimes defined in article 6(b)

of the Nurnberg Charter were already recognized as war crimes under international law, and covered in the Hague Regulations, for which guilty individuals were punishable.

43. The Hague Regulations cover aspects of international humanitarian law which are also covered by the 1949 Geneva Conventions. However, the Hague Regulations also recognize that the right of belligerents to conduct warfare is not unlimited and that resort to certain methods of waging war is prohibited under the rules of land warfare.

44. These rules of customary law, as interpreted and applied by the Nurnberg Tribunal, provide the basis for the corresponding article of the statute which would read as follows:

Article 3 — Violations of the laws or customs of war

The International Tribunal shall have the power to prosecute persons violating the laws or customs of war. Such violations shall include, but not be limited to:

(a) employment of poisonous weapons or other weapons calculated to cause unnecessary suffering;
(b) wanton destruction of cities, towns or villages, or devastation not justified by military necessity;
(c) attack, or bombardment, by whatever means, of undefended towns, villages, dwellings, or buildings;
(d) seizure of, destruction or wilful damage done to institutions dedicated to religion, charity and education, the arts and sciences, historic monuments and works of art and science;
(e) plunder of public or private property.

Genocide

45. The 1948 Convention on the Prevention and Punishment of the Crime of Genocide confirms that genocide, whether committed in time of peace or in time of war, is a crime under international law for which individuals shall be tried and punished. The Convention is today considered part of international customary law as evidenced by the International Court

of Justice in its Advisory Opinion on Reservations to the Convention on the Prevention and Punishment of the Crime of Genocide, 1951.[7]

46.   The relevant provisions of the Genocide Convention are reproduced in the corresponding article of the statute, which would read as follows:

Article 4 — Genocide

1.   The International Tribunal shall have the power to prosecute persons committing genocide as defined in paragraph 2 of this article or of committing any of the other acts enumerated in paragraph 3 of this article.

2.   Genocide means any of the following acts committed with intent to destroy, in whole or in part, a national, ethnical, racial or religious group, as such:

(a)   killing members of the group;
(b)   causing serious bodily or mental harm to members of the group;
(c)   deliberately inflicting on the group conditions of life calculated to bring about its physical destruction in whole or in part;
(d)   imposing measures intended to prevent births within the group;
(e)   forcibly transferring children of the group to another group.

3.   The following acts shall be punishable:

(a)   genocide;
(b)   conspiracy to commit genocide;
(c)   direct and public incitement to commit genocide;
(d)   attempt to commit genocide;
(e)   complicity in genocide.

Crimes against humanity

47.   Crimes against humanity were first recognized in the Charter and Judgement of the Nurnberg Tribunal, as well as in Law No. 10 of the

---

[7] Reservations to the Convention on the Prevention and Punishment of the Crime of Genocide: Advisory Opinion of 28 May 1951, International Court of Justice Reports, 1951, p. 23.

Control Council for Germany.[8] Crimes against humanity are aimed at any civilian population and are prohibited regardless of whether they are committed in an armed conflict, international or internal in character.[9]

48. Crimes against humanity refer to inhumane acts of a very serious nature, such as wilful killing, torture or rape, committed as part of a widespread or systematic attack against any civilian population on national, political, ethnic, racial or religious grounds. In the conflict in the territory of the former Yugoslavia, such inhumane acts have taken the form of so-called "ethnic cleansing" and widespread and systematic rape and other forms of sexual assault, including enforced prostitution.

49. The corresponding article of the statute would read as follows:

Article 5 — Crimes against humanity

The International Tribunal shall have the power to prosecute persons responsible for the following crimes when committed in armed conflict, whether international or internal in character, and directed against any civilian population:

(a) murder;
(b) extermination;
(c) enslavement;
(d) deportation;
(e) imprisonment;
(f) torture;
(g) rape;

---

[8] Official Gazette of the Control Council for Germany, No. 3, p. 22, Military Government Gazette, Germany, British Zone of Control, No. 5, p. 46, Journal Officiel du Commandement en Chef Français en Allemagne, No. 12 of 11 January 1946.

[9] In this context, it is to be noted that the International Court of Justice has recognized that the prohibitions contained in common article 3 of the 1949 Geneva Conventions are based on "elementary considerations of humanity" and cannot be breached in an armed conflict, regardless of whether it is international or internal in character. Case concerning Military and Paramilitary Activities in and against Nicaragua (Nicaragua v. United States of America), Judgement of 27 June 1986: I.C.J. Reports, 1986, p. 114.

(h) persecutions on political, racial and religious grounds;
(i) other inhumane acts.

B. Competence *Ratione Personae* (Personal Jurisdiction) and Individual Criminal Responsibility

50. By paragraph 1 of resolution 808 (1993), the Security Council decided that the International Tribunal shall be established for the prosecution of persons responsible for serious violations of international humanitarian law committed in the territory of the former Yugoslavia since 1991. In the light of the complex of resolutions leading up to resolution 808 (1993) (see paras. 5–7 above), the ordinary meaning of the term "persons responsible for serious violations of international humanitarian law" would be natural persons to the exclusion of juridical persons.

51. The question arises, however, whether a juridical person, such as an association or organization, may be considered criminal as such and thus its members, for that reason alone, be made subject to the jurisdiction of the International Tribunal. The Secretary-General believes that this concept should not be retained in regard to the International Tribunal. The criminal acts set out in this statute are carried out by natural persons; such persons would be subject to the jurisdiction of the International Tribunal irrespective of membership in groups.

52. The corresponding article of the statute would read:

Article 6 — Personal jurisdiction

The International Tribunal shall have jurisdiction over natural persons pursuant to the provisions of the present Statute.

Individual criminal responsibility

53. An important element in relation to the competence *ratione personae* (personal jurisdiction) of the International Tribunal is the principle of individual criminal responsibility. As noted above, the Security Council has reaffirmed in a number of resolutions that persons committing serious violations of international humanitarian law in the former Yugoslavia are individually responsible for such violations.

54. The Secretary-General believes that all persons who participate in the planning, preparation or execution of serious violations of international humanitarian law in the former Yugoslavia contribute to the commission of the violation and are, therefore, individually responsible.

55. Virtually all of the written comments received by the Secretary-General have suggested that the statute of the International Tribunal should contain provisions with regard to the individual criminal responsibility of heads of State, government officials and persons acting in an official capacity. These suggestions draw upon the precedents following the Second World War. The Statute should, therefore, contain provisions which specify that a plea of head of State immunity or that an act was committed in the official capacity of the accused will not constitute a defence, nor will it mitigate punishment.

56. A person in a position of superior authority should, therefore, be held individually responsible for giving the unlawful order to commit a crime under the present statute. But he should also be held responsible for failure to prevent a crime or to deter the unlawful behaviour of his subordinates. This imputed responsibility or criminal negligence is engaged if the person in superior authority knew or had reason to know that his subordinates were about to commit or had committed crimes and yet failed to take the necessary and reasonable steps to prevent or repress the commission of such crimes or to punish those who had committed them.

57. Acting upon an order of a Government or a superior cannot relieve the perpetrator of the crime of his criminal responsibility and should not be a defence. Obedience to superior orders may, however, be considered a mitigating factor, should the International Tribunal determine that justice so requires. For example, the International Tribunal may consider the factor of superior orders in connection with other defences such as coercion or lack of moral choice.

58. The International Tribunal itself will have to decide on various personal defences which may relieve a person of individual criminal responsibility, such as minimum age or mental incapacity, drawing upon general principles of law recognized by all nations.

59. The corresponding article of the statute would read:

Article 7 — Individual criminal responsibility

1. A person who planned, instigated, ordered, committed or otherwise aided and abetted in the planning, preparation or execution of a crime referred to in articles 2 to 5 of the present Statute, shall be individually responsible for the crime.

2. The official position of any accused person, whether as Head of State or Government or as a responsible Government official, shall not relieve such person of criminal responsibility nor mitigate punishment.

3. The fact that any of the acts referred to in articles 2 to 5 of the present Statute was committed by a subordinate does not relieve his superior of criminal responsibility if he knew or had reason to know that the subordinate was about to commit such acts or had done so and the superior failed to take the necessary and reasonable measures to prevent such acts or to punish the perpetrators thereof.

4. The fact that an accused person acted pursuant to an order of a Government or of a superior shall not relieve him of criminal responsibility, but may be considered in mitigation of punishment if the International Tribunal determines that justice so requires.

C. COMPETENCE *RATIONE LOCI* (TERRITORIAL JURISDICTION) AND *RATIONE TEMPORIS* (TEMPORAL JURISDICTION)

60. Pursuant to paragraph 1 of resolution 808 (1993), the territorial and temporal jurisdiction of the International Tribunal extends to serious violations of international humanitarian law to the extent that they have been "committed in the territory of the former Yugoslavia since 1991".

61. As far as the territorial jurisdiction of the International Tribunal is concerned, the territory of the former Yugoslavia means the territory of the former Socialist Federal Republic of Yugoslavia, including its land surface, airspace and territorial waters.

62. With regard to temporal jurisdiction, Security Council resolution 808 (1993) extends the jurisdiction of the International Tribunal to violations committed "since 1991". The Secretary-General understands this to mean anytime on or after 1 January 1991. This is a neutral date which

is not tied to any specific event and is clearly intended to convey the notion that no judgement as to the international or internal character of the conflict is being exercised.

63. The corresponding article of the statute would read:

Article 8— Territorial and temporal jurisdiction

The territorial jurisdiction of the International Tribunal shall extend to the territory of the former Socialist Federal Republic of Yugoslavia, including its land surface, airspace and territorial waters. The temporal jurisdiction of the International Tribunal shall extend to a period beginning on 1 January 1991.

D. CONCURRENT JURISDICTION AND THE PRINCIPLE OF *NON-BIS-IN-IDEM*

64. In establishing an international tribunal for the prosecution of persons responsible for serious violations committed in the territory of the former Yugoslavia since 1991, it was not the intention of the Security Council to preclude or prevent the exercise of jurisdiction by national courts with respect to such acts. Indeed national courts should be encouraged to exercise their jurisdiction in accordance with their relevant national laws and procedures.

65. It follows therefore that there is concurrent jurisdiction of the International Tribunal and national courts. This concurrent jurisdiction, however, should be subject to the primacy of the International Tribunal. At any stage of the procedure, the International Tribunal may formally request the national courts to defer to the competence of the International Tribunal. The details of how the primacy will be asserted shall be set out in the rules of procedure and evidence of the International Tribunal.

66. According to the principle of *non-bis-in-idem,* a person shall not be tried twice for the same crime. In the present context, given the primacy of the International Tribunal, the principle of *non-bis-in-idem* would preclude subsequent trial before a national court. However, the principle of *non-bis-in-idem* should not preclude a subsequent trial before the International Tribunal in the following two circumstances:

    (a) The characterization of the act by the national court did not correspond to its characterization under the statute; or

(b) Conditions of impartiality, independence or effective means of adjudication were not guaranteed in the proceedings before the national courts.

67. Should the International Tribunal decide to assume jurisdiction over a person who has already been convicted by a national court, it should take into consideration the extent to which any penalty imposed by the national court has already been served.

68. The corresponding articles of the statute would read:

Article 9 — Concurrent jurisdiction

1. The International Tribunal and national courts shall have concurrent jurisdiction to prosecute persons for serious violations of international humanitarian law committed in the territory of the former Yugoslavia since 1 January 1991.

2. The International Tribunal shall have primacy over national courts. At any stage of the procedure, the International Tribunal may formally request national courts to defer to the competence of the International Tribunal in accordance with the present Statute and the Rules of Procedure and Evidence of the International Tribunal.

Article 10 — Non-bis-in-idem

1. No person shall be tried before a national court for acts constituting serious violations of international humanitarian law under the present Statute, for which he or she has already been tried by the International Tribunal.

2. A person who has been tried by a national court for acts constituting serious violations of international humanitarian law may be subsequently tried by the International Tribunal only if:

(a) the act for which he or she was tried was characterized as an ordinary crime; or
(b) the national court proceedings were not impartial or independent, were designed to shield the accused from international criminal responsibility, or the case was not diligently prosecuted.

Appendix B: Secretary-General's Report and Statute 405

3. In considering the penalty to be imposed on a person convicted of a crime under the present Statute, the International Tribunal shall take into account the extent to which any penalty imposed by a national court on the same person for the same act has already been served.

III. The Organization of the International Tribunal

69. The organization of the International Tribunal should reflect the functions to be performed by it. Since the International Tribunal is established for the prosecution of persons responsible for serious violations of international humanitarian law committed in the territory of the former Yugoslavia, this presupposes an international tribunal composed of a judicial organ, a prosecutorial organ and a secretariat. It would be the function of the prosecutorial organ to investigate cases, prepare indictments and prosecute persons responsible for committing the violations referred to above. The judicial organ would hear the cases presented to its Trial Chambers, and consider appeals from the Trial Chambers in its Appeals Chamber. A secretariat or Registry would be required to service both the prosecutorial and judicial organs.

70. The International Tribunal should therefore consist of the following organs: the Chambers, comprising two Trial Chambers and one Appeals Chamber; a Prosecutor; and a Registry.

71. The corresponding article of the statute would read as follows:

Article 11 — Organization of the International Tribunal

The International Tribunal shall consist of the following organs:

(a) The Chambers, comprising two Trial Chambers and an Appeals Chamber;
(b) The Prosecutor; and
(c) A Registry, servicing both the Chambers and the Prosecutor.

A. THE CHAMBERS

1. Composition of the Chambers

72. The Chambers should be composed of 11 independent judges, no 2 of whom may be nationals of the same State. Three judges would serve

in each of the two Trial Chambers and five judges would serve in the Appeals Chamber.

73. The corresponding article of the statute would read as follows:

Article 12 — Composition of the Chambers

The Chambers shall be composed of eleven independent judges, no two of whom may be nationals of the same State, who shall serve as follows:

(a) Three judges shall serve in each of the Trial Chambers;
(b) Five judges shall serve in the Appeals Chamber.

2. Qualifications and election of judges

74. The judges of the International Tribunal should be persons of high moral character, impartiality and integrity who possess the qualifications required in their respective countries for appointment to the highest judicial offices. Impartiality in this context includes impartiality with respect to the acts falling within the competence of the International Tribunal. In the overall composition of the Chambers, due account should be taken of the experience of the judges in criminal law, international law, including international humanitarian law and human rights law.

75. The judges should be elected by the General Assembly from a list submitted by the Security Council. The Secretary-General would invite nominations for judges from States Members of the United Nations as well as non-member States maintaining permanent observer missions at United Nations Headquarters. Within 60 days of the date of the invitation of the Secretary-General, each State would nominate up to two candidates meeting the qualifications mentioned in paragraph 74 above, who must not be of the same nationality. The Secretary-General would forward the nominations received to the Security Council. The Security Council would, as speedily as possible, establish from the nominations transmitted by the Secretary-General, a list of not less than 22 and not more than 33 candidates, taking due account of the adequate representation of the principal legal systems of the world. The President of the Security Council would then transmit the list to the General Assembly. From that list, the General Assembly would proceed as speedily as possible to elect the 11 judges of the International

Tribunal. The candidates declared elected shall be those who have received an absolute majority of the votes of the States Members of the United Nations and of the States maintaining permanent observer missions at United Nations Headquarters. Should two candidates of the same nationality obtain the required majority vote, the one who received the higher number of votes shall be considered elected.

76. The judges shall be elected for a term of four years. The terms and conditions of service shall be those of the Judges of the International Court of Justice. They shall be eligible for re-election.

77. In the event of a vacancy occurring in the Chambers, the Secretary-General, after consultation with the Presidents of the Security Council and the General Assembly, would appoint a person meeting the qualifications of paragraph 74 above, for the remainder of the term of office concerned.

78. The corresponding article of the statute would read as follows:

Article 13 — Qualifications and election of judges

1. The judges shall be persons of high moral character, impartiality and integrity who possess the qualifications required in their respective countries for appointment to the highest judicial offices. In the overall composition of the Chambers due account shall be taken of the experience of the judges in criminal law, international law, including international humanitarian law and human rights law.

2. The judges of the International Tribunal shall be elected by the General Assembly from a list submitted by the Security Council, in the following manner:

(a) The Secretary-General shall invite nominations for judges of the International Tribunal from States Members of the United Nations and non-member States maintaining permanent observer missions at United Nations Headquarters;

(b) Within sixty days of the date of the invitation of the Secretary-General, each State may nominate up to two candidates meeting the qualifications set out in paragraph 1 above, no two of whom shall be of the same nationality;

(c) The Secretary-General shall forward the nominations received to the Security Council. From the nominations received the Security

Council shall establish a list of not less than twenty-two and not more than thirty-three candidates, taking due account of the adequate representation of the principal legal systems of the world;

(d) The President of the Security Council shall transmit the list of candidates to the President of the General Assembly. From that list the General Assembly shall elect the eleven judges of the International Tribunal. The candidates who receive an absolute majority of the votes of States Members of the United Nations and of the non-member States maintaining permanent observer missions at United Nations Headquarters, shall be declared elected. Should two candidates of the same nationality obtain the required majority vote, the one who received the higher number of votes shall be considered elected.

3. In the event of a vacancy in the Chambers, after consultation with the Presidents of the Security Council and of the General Assembly, the Secretary-General shall appoint a person meeting the qualifications of paragraph 1 above, for the remainder of the term of office concerned.

4. The judges shall be elected for a term of four years. The terms and conditions of service shall be those of the Judges of the International Court of Justice. They shall be eligible for re-election.

3. *Officers and members of the Chambers*

79. The judges would elect a President of the International Tribunal from among their members who would be a member of the Appeals Chamber and would preside over the appellate proceedings.

80. Following consultation with the members of the Chambers, the President would assign the judges to the Appeals Chamber and to the Trial Chambers. Each judge would serve only in the chamber to which he or she was assigned.

81. The members of each Trial Chamber should elect a presiding judge who would conduct all of the proceedings before the Trial Chamber as a whole.

82. The corresponding article of the statute would read as follows:

Article 14 — Officers and members of the Chambers

1. The judges of the International Tribunal shall elect a President.

2. The President of the International Tribunal shall be a member of the Appeals Chamber and shall preside over its proceedings.

3. After consultation with the judges of the International Tribunal, the President shall assign the judges to the Appeals Chamber and to the Trial Chambers. A judge shall serve only in the Chamber to which he or she was assigned.

4. The judges of each Trial Chamber shall elect a Presiding Judge, who shall conduct all of the proceedings of the Trial Chamber as a whole.

4. *Rules of procedure and evidence*

83. The judges of the International Tribunal as a whole should draft and adopt the rules of procedure and evidence of the International Tribunal governing the pre-trial phase of the proceedings, the conduct of trials and appeals, the admission of evidence, the protection of victims and witnesses and other appropriate matters.

84. The corresponding article of the statute would read as follows:

Article 15 — Rules of procedure and evidence

The judges of the International Tribunal shall adopt rules of procedure and evidence for the conduct of the pre-trial phase of the proceedings, trials and appeals, the admission of evidence, the protection of victims and witnesses and other appropriate matters.

B. THE PROSECUTOR

85. Responsibility for the conduct of all investigations and prosecutions of persons responsible for serious violations of international humanitarian law committed in the territory of the former Yugoslavia since 1 January 1991 should be entrusted to an independent Prosecutor. The Prosecutor

should act independently as a separate organ of the International Tribunal. He or she shall not seek or receive instructions from any Government or from any other source.

86. The Prosecutor should be appointed by the Security Council, upon nomination by the Secretary-General. He or she should possess the highest level of professional competence and have extensive experience in the conduct of investigations and prosecutions of criminal cases. The Prosecutor should be appointed for a four-year term of office and be eligible for reappointment. The terms and conditions of service of the Prosecutor shall be those of an Under-Secretary-General of the United Nations.

87. The Prosecutor would be assisted by such other staff as may be required to perform effectively and efficiently the functions entrusted to him or her. Such staff would be appointed by the Secretary-General on the recommendation of the Prosecutor. The Office of the Prosecutor should be composed of an investigation unit and a prosecution unit.

88. Staff appointed to the Office of the Prosecutor should meet rigorous criteria of professional experience and competence in their field. Persons should be sought who have had relevant experience in their own countries as investigators, prosecutors, criminal lawyers, law enforcement personnel or medical experts. Given the nature of the crimes committed and the sensitivities of victims of rape and sexual assault, due consideration should be given in the appointment of staff to the employment of qualified women.

89. The corresponding article of the statute would read as follows:

Article 16 — The Prosecutor

1. The Prosecutor shall be responsible for the investigation and prosecution of persons responsible for serious violations of international humanitarian law committed in the territory of the former Yugoslavia since 1 January 1991.

2. The Prosecutor shall act independently as a separate organ of the International Tribunal. He or she shall not seek or receive instructions from any Government or from any other source.

3. The Office of the Prosecutor shall be composed of a Prosecutor and such other qualified staff as may be required.

4. The Prosecutor shall be appointed by the Security Council on nomination by the Secretary-General. He or she shall be of high moral character and possess the highest level of competence and experience in the conduct of investigations and prosecutions of criminal cases. The Prosecutor shall serve for a four-year term and be eligible for reappointment. The terms and conditions of service of the Prosecutor shall be those of an Under-Secretary-General of the United Nations.

5. The staff of the Office of the Prosecutor shall be appointed by the Secretary-General on the recommendation of the Prosecutor.

C. THE REGISTRY

90. As indicated in paragraph 69 above, a Registry would be responsible for the servicing of the International Tribunal. The Registry would be headed by a Registrar, whose responsibilities shall include but should not be limited to the following:

(a) Public information and external relations;
(b) Preparation of minutes of meetings;
(c) Conference-service facilities;
(d) Printing and publication of all documents;
(e) All administrative work, budgetary and personnel matters; and
(f) Serving as the channel of communications to and from the International Tribunal.

91. The Registrar should be appointed by the Secretary-General after consultation with the President of the International Tribunal. He or she would be appointed to serve for a four-year term and be eligible for reappointment. The terms and conditions of service of the Registrar shall be those of an Assistant Secretary-General of the United Nations.

92. The corresponding article of the statute would read as follows:

Article 17—The Registry

1. The Registry shall be responsible for the administration and servicing of the International Tribunal.

2. The Registry shall consist of a Registrar and such other staff as may be required.

3. The Registrar shall be appointed by the Secretary-General after consultation with the President of the International Tribunal. He or she shall serve for a four-year term and be eligible for reappointment. The terms and conditions of service of the Registrar shall be those of an Assistant Secretary-General of the United Nations.

4. The staff of the Registry shall be appointed by the Secretary-General on the recommendation of the Registrar.

IV. Investigation and Pre-trial Proceedings

93. The Prosecutor would initiate investigations *ex officio*, or on the basis of information obtained from any source, particularly from Governments or United Nations organs, intergovernmental and non-governmental organizations. The Prosecutor would assess the information received or obtained and decide whether there is a sufficient basis to proceed.

94. In conducting his investigations, the Prosecutor should have the power to question suspects, victims and witnesses, to collect evidence and to conduct on-site investigations. In carrying out these tasks, the Prosecutor may, as appropriate, seek the assistance of the State authorities concerned.

95. Upon the completion of the investigation, if the Prosecutor has determined that a *prima facie* case exists for prosecution, he would prepare an indictment containing a concise statement of the facts and the crimes with which the accused is charged under the statute. The indictment would be transmitted to a judge of a Trial Chamber, who would review it and decide whether to confirm or to dismiss the indictment.

96. If the investigation includes questioning of the suspect, then he should have the right to be assisted by counsel of his own choice, including the right to have legal assistance assigned to him without payment by him in any such case if he does not have sufficient means to pay for it. He shall also be entitled to the necessary translation into and from a language he speaks and understands.

97. Upon confirmation of the indictment, the judge would, at the request of the Prosecutor, issue such orders and warrants for the arrest, detention, surrender and transfer of persons, or any other orders as may be necessary for the conduct of the trial.

98. The corresponding articles of the statute would read as follows:

Article 18—Investigation and preparation of indictment

1. The Prosecutor shall initiate investigations *ex officio* or on the basis of information obtained from any source, particularly from Governments, United Nations organs, intergovernmental and non-governmental organizations. The Prosecutor shall assess the information received or obtained and decide whether there is sufficient basis to proceed.

2. The Prosecutor shall have the power to question suspects, victims and witnesses, to collect evidence and to conduct on-site investigations. In carrying out these tasks the Prosecutor may, as appropriate, seek the assistance of the State authorities concerned.

3. If questioned, the suspect shall be entitled to be assisted by counsel of his own choice, including the right to have legal assistance assigned to him without payment by him in any such case if he does not have sufficient means to pay for it, as well as to necessary translation into and from a language he speaks and understands.

4. Upon a determination that a *prima facie* case exists, the Prosecutor shall prepare an indictment containing a concise statement of the facts and the crime or crimes with which the accused is charged under the Statute. The indictment shall be transmitted to a judge of the Trial Chamber.

Article 19—Review of the indictment

1. The judge of the Trial Chamber to whom the indictment has been transmitted shall review it. If satisfied that a *prima facie* case has been established by the Prosecutor, he shall confirm the indictment. If not so satisfied, the indictment shall be dismissed.

2. Upon confirmation of an indictment, the judge may, at the request of the Prosecutor, issue such orders and warrants for the arrest,

V. Trial and Post-trial Proceedings

A. COMMENCEMENT AND CONDUCT OF TRIAL PROCEEDINGS

99. The Trial Chambers should ensure that a trial is fair and expeditious and that proceedings are conducted in accordance with the rules of procedure and evidence and with full respect for the rights of the accused. The Trial Chamber should also provide appropriate protection for victims and witnesses during the proceedings.

100. A person against whom an indictment has been confirmed would, pursuant to an order or a warrant of the International Tribunal, be informed of the contents of the indictment and taken into custody.

101. A trial should not commence until the accused is physically present before the International Tribunal. There is a widespread perception that trials *in absentia* should not be provided for in the statute as this would not be consistent with article 14 of the International Covenant on Civil and Political Rights,[10] which provides that the accused shall be entitled to be tried in his presence.

102. The person against whom an indictment has been confirmed would be transferred to the seat of the International Tribunal and brought before a Trial Chamber without undue delay and formally charged. The Trial Chamber would read the indictment, satisfy itself that the rights of the accused are respected, confirm that the accused understands the indictment, and instruct the accused to enter a plea. After the plea has been entered, the Trial Chamber would set the date for trial.

103. The hearings should be held in public unless the Trial Chamber decides otherwise in accordance with its rules of procedure and evidence.

104. After hearing the submissions of the parties and examining the

---

[10] United Nations, Treaty Series, vol. 999, No. 14668, p. 171, and vol. 1057, p. 407 *(procès-verbal* of rectification of authentic Spanish test).

witnesses and evidence presented to it, the Trial Chamber would close the hearing and retire for private deliberations.

105. The corresponding article of the statute would read:

Article 20—Commencement and conduct of trial proceedings

1. The Trial Chambers shall ensure that a trial is fair and expeditious and that proceedings are conducted in accordance with the rules of procedure and evidence, with full respect for the rights of the accused and due regard for the protection of victims and witnesses.

2. A person against whom an indictment has been confirmed shall, pursuant to an order or an arrest warrant of the International Tribunal, be taken into custody, immediately informed of the charges against him and transferred to the International Tribunal.

3. The Trial Chamber shall read the indictment, satisfy itself that the rights of the accused are respected, confirm that the accused understands the indictment, and instruct the accused to enter a plea. The Trial Chamber shall then set the date for trial.

4. The hearings shall be public unless the Trial Chamber decides to close the proceedings in accordance with its rules of procedure and evidence.

B. RIGHTS OF THE ACCUSED

106. It is axiomatic that the International Tribunal must fully respect internationally recognized standards regarding the rights of the accused at all stages of its proceedings. In the view of the Secretary-General, such internationally recognized standards are, in particular, contained in article 14 of the International Covenant on Civil and Political Rights.[10]

107. The corresponding article of the statute would read as follows:

---

[10] *Editor's note:* this note is intended to refer the reader to the preceding note of the same number, which contains a citation to the International Covenant on Civil and Political Rights. This note as such has no text.

Article 21 — Rights of the accused

1. All persons shall be equal before the International Tribunal.

2. In the determination of charges against him, the accused shall be entitled to a fair and public hearing, subject to article 22 of the Statute.

3. The accused shall be presumed innocent until proved guilty according to the provisions of the present Statute.

4. In the determination of any charge against the accused pursuant to the present Statute, the accused shall be entitled to the following minimum guarantees, in full equality:

(a) to be informed promptly and in detail in a language which he understands of the nature and cause of the charge against him;
(b) to have adequate time and facilities for the preparation of his defence and to communicate with counsel of his own choosing;
(c) to be tried without undue delay;
(d) to be tried in his presence, and to defend himself in person or through legal assistance of his own choosing; to be informed, if he does not have legal assistance, of this right; and to have legal assistance assigned to him, in any case where the interests of justice so require, and without payment by him in any such case if he does not have sufficient means to pay for it;
(e) to examine, or have examined, the witnesses against him and to obtain the attendance and examination of witnesses on his behalf under the same conditions as witnesses against him;
(f) to have the free assistance of an interpreter if he cannot understand or speak the language used in the International Tribunal;
(g) not to be compelled to testify against himself or to confess guilt.

C. Protection of Victims and Witnesses

108. In the light of the particular nature of the crimes committed in the former Yugoslavia, it will be necessary for the International Tribunal to ensure the protection of victims and witnesses. Necessary protection measures should therefore be provided in the rules of procedure and evidence for victims and witnesses, especially in cases of rape or sexual

assault. Such measures should include, but should not be limited to the conduct of *in camera* proceedings, and the protection of the victim's identity.

109. The corresponding article of the statute would read as follows:

Article 22—Protection of victims and witnesses

The International Tribunal shall provide in its rules of procedure and evidence for the protection of victims and witnesses. Such protection measures shall include, but shall not be limited to, the conduct of *in camera* proceedings and the protection of the victim's identity.

D. JUDGEMENT AND PENALTIES

110. The Trial Chambers would have the power to pronounce judgements and impose sentences and penalties on persons convicted of serious violations of international humanitarian law. A judgement would be rendered by a majority of the judges of the Chamber and delivered in public. It should be written and accompanied by a reasoned opinion. Separate or dissenting opinions should be permitted.

111. The penalty to be imposed on a convicted person would be limited to imprisonment. In determining the term of imprisonment, the Trial Chambers should have recourse to the general practice of prison sentences applicable in the courts of the former Yugoslavia.

112. The International Tribunal should not be empowered to impose the death penalty.

113. In imposing sentences, the Trial Chambers should take into account such factors as the gravity of the offence and the individual circumstances of the convicted person.

114. In addition to imprisonment, property and proceeds acquired by criminal conduct should be confiscated and returned to their rightful owners. This would include the return of property wrongfully acquired by means of duress. In this connection the Secretary-General recalls that in resolution 779 (1992) of 6 October 1992, the Security Council endorsed the

principle that all statements or commitments made under duress, particularly those relating to land and property, are wholly null and void.

115. The corresponding articles of the statute would read as follows:

Article 23 — Judgement

1. The Trial Chambers shall pronounce judgements and impose sentences and penalties on persons convicted of serious violations of international humanitarian law.

2. The judgement shall be rendered by a majority of the judges of the Trial Chamber, and shall be delivered by the Trial Chamber in public. It shall be accompanied by a reasoned opinion in writing, to which separate or dissenting opinions may be appended.

Article 24 — Penalties

1. The penalty imposed by the Trial Chamber shall be limited to imprisonment. In determining the terms of imprisonment, the Trial Chambers shall have recourse to the general practice regarding prison sentences in the courts of the former Yugoslavia.

2. In imposing the sentences, the Trial Chambers should take into account such factors as the gravity of the offence and the individual circumstances of the convicted person.

3. In addition to imprisonment, the Trial Chambers may order the return of any property and proceeds acquired by criminal conduct, including by means of duress, to their rightful owners.

E. APPELLATE AND REVIEW PROCEEDINGS

116. The Secretary-General is of the view that the right of appeal should be provided for under the Statute. Such a right is a fundamental element of individual civil and political rights and has, *inter alia,* been incorporated in the International Covenant on Civil and Political Rights. For this reason, the Secretary-General has proposed that there should be an Appeals Chamber.

117. The right of appeal should be exercisable on two grounds: an error on a question of law invalidating the decision or, an error of fact which has occasioned a miscarriage of justice. The Prosecutor should also be entitled to initiate appeal proceedings on the same grounds.

118. The judgement of the Appeals Chamber affirming, reversing or revising the judgement of the Trial Chamber would be final. It would be delivered by the Appeals Chamber in public and be accompanied by a reasoned opinion to which separate or dissenting opinions may be appended.

119. Where a new fact has come to light which was not known at the time of the proceedings before the Trial Chambers or the Appeals Chamber, and which could have been a decisive factor in reaching the decision, the convicted person or the Prosecutor should be authorized to submit to the International Tribunal an application for review of the judgement.

120. The corresponding articles of the statute would read as follows:

Article 25—Appellate proceedings

1. The Appeals Chamber shall hear appeals from persons convicted by the Trial Chambers or from the Prosecutor on the following grounds:

   (a) an error on a question of law invalidating the decision; or
   (b) an error of fact which has occasioned a miscarriage of justice.

2. The Appeals Chamber may affirm, reverse or revise the decisions taken by the Trial Chambers.

Article 26—Review proceedings

Where a new fact has been discovered which was not known at the time of the proceedings before the Trial Chambers or the Appeals Chamber and which could have been a decisive factor in reaching the decision, the convicted person or the Prosecutor may submit to the International Tribunal an application for review of the judgement.

F. ENFORCEMENT OF SENTENCES

121. The Secretary-General is of the view that, given the nature of the crimes in question and the international character of the tribunal, the

enforcement of sentences should take place outside the territory of the former Yugoslavia. States should be encouraged to declare their readiness to carry out the enforcement of prison sentences in accordance with their domestic laws and procedures, under the supervision of the International Tribunal.

122. The Security Council would make appropriate arrangements to obtain from States an indication of their willingness to accept convicted persons. This information would be communicated to the Registrar, who would prepare a list of States in which the enforcement of sentences would be carried out.

123. The accused would be eligible for pardon or commutation of sentence in accordance with the laws of the State in which sentence is served. In such an event, the State concerned would notify the International Tribunal, which would decide the matter in accordance with the interests of justice and the general principles of law.

124. The corresponding articles of the statute would read as follows:

Article 27—Enforcement of sentences

Imprisonment shall be served in a State designated by the International Tribunal from a list of States which have indicated to the Security Council their willingness to accept convicted persons. Such imprisonment shall be in accordance with the applicable law of the State concerned, subject to the supervision of the International Tribunal.

Article 28—Pardon or commutation of sentences

If, pursuant to the applicable law of the State in which the convicted person is imprisoned, he or she is eligible for pardon or commutation of sentence, the State concerned shall notify the International Tribunal accordingly. The President of the International Tribunal, in consultation with the judges, shall decide the matter on the basis of the interests of justice and the general principles of law.

VI. Cooperation and Judicial Assistance

125. As pointed out in paragraph 23 above, the establishment of the International Tribunal on the basis of a Chapter VII decision creates a

binding obligation on all States to take whatever steps are required to implement the decision. In practical terms, this means that all States would be under an obligation to cooperate with the International Tribunal and to assist it in all stages of the proceedings to ensure compliance with requests for assistance in the gathering of evidence, hearing of witnesses, suspects and experts, identification and location of persons and the service of documents. Effect shall also be given to orders issued by the Trial Chambers, such as warrants of arrest, search warrants, warrants for surrender or transfer of persons, and any other orders necessary for the conduct of the trial.

126. In this connection, an order by a Trial Chamber for the surrender or transfer of persons to the custody of the International Tribunal shall be considered to be the application of an enforcement measure under Chapter VII of the Charter of the United Nations.

127. The corresponding article of the statute would read as follows:

Article 29 — Cooperation and judicial assistance

1. States shall cooperate with the International Tribunal in the investigation and prosecution of persons accused of committing serious violations of international humanitarian law.

2. States shall comply without undue delay with any request for assistance or an order issued by a Trial Chamber, including, but not limited to:

(a) the identification and location of persons;
(b) the taking of testimony and the production of evidence;
(c) the service of documents;
(d) the arrest or detention of persons;
(e) the surrender or the transfer of the accused to the International Tribunal.

VII. General Provisions

A. THE STATUS, PRIVILEGES AND IMMUNITIES OF THE INTERNATIONAL TRIBUNAL

128. The Convention on the Privileges and Immunities of the United Nations of 13 February 1946 would apply to the International Tribunal, the

judges, the Prosecutor and his staff, and the Registrar and his staff. The judges, the Prosecutor, and the Registrar would be granted the privileges and immunities, exemptions and facilities accorded to diplomatic envoys in accordance with international law. The staff of the Prosecutor and the Registrar would enjoy the privileges and immunities of officials of the United Nations within the meaning of articles V and VII of the Convention.

129.   Other persons, including the accused, required at the seat of the International Tribunal would be accorded such treatment as is necessary for the proper functioning of the International Tribunal.

130.   The corresponding article of the statute would read:

Article 30 — The status, privileges and immunities of the International Tribunal

      1.   The Convention on the Privileges and Immunities of the United Nations of 13 February 1946 shall apply to the International Tribunal, the judges, the Prosecutor and his staff, and the Registrar and his staff.

      2.   The judges, the Prosecutor and the Registrar shall enjoy the privileges and immunities, exemptions and facilities accorded to diplomatic envoys, in accordance with international law.

      3.   The staff of the Prosecutor and of the Registrar shall enjoy the privileges and immunities accorded to officials of the United Nations under articles V and VII of the Convention referred to in paragraph 1 of this article.

      4.   Other persons, including the accused, required at the seat of the International Tribunal shall be accorded such treatment as is necessary for the proper functioning of the International Tribunal.

B.   SEAT OF THE INTERNATIONAL TRIBUNAL

131.   While it will be for the Security Council to determine the location of the seat of the International Tribunal, in the view of the Secretary-General, there are a number of elementary considerations of justice and fairness, as well as administrative efficiency and economy which should be taken into account. As a matter of justice and fairness, it would not be appropriate for the International Tribunal to have its seat in the territory of

the former Yugoslavia or in any State neighbouring upon the former Yugoslavia. For reasons of administrative efficiency and economy, it would be desirable to establish the seat of the International Tribunal at a European location in which the United Nations already has an important presence. The two locations which fulfil these requirements are Geneva and The Hague. Provided that the necessary arrangements can be made with the host country, the Secretary-General believes that the seat of the International Tribunal should be at The Hague.

132. The corresponding article of the statute would read:

Article 31 — Seat of the International Tribunal

The International Tribunal shall have its seat at The Hague.

C. Financial Arrangements

133. The expenses of the International Tribunal should be borne by the regular budget of the United Nations in accordance with Article 17 of the Charter of the United Nations.

134. The corresponding article of the statute would read:

Article 32 — Expenses of the International Tribunal

The expenses of the International Tribunal shall be borne by the regular budget of the United Nations in accordance with Article 17 of the Charter of the United Nations.

D. Working Languages

135. The working languages of the Tribunal should be English and French.

136. The corresponding article of the statute would read as follows:

Article 33 — Working languages

The working languages of the International Tribunal shall be English and French.

E. ANNUAL REPORT

137. The International Tribunal should submit an annual report on its activities to the Security Council and the General Assembly.

138. The corresponding article of the statute would read:

Article 34—Annual report

The President of the International Tribunal shall submit an annual report of the International Tribunal to the Security Council and to the General Assembly.

ANNEX

Statute of the International Tribunal

Having been established by the Security Council acting under Chapter VII of the Charter of the United Nations, the International Tribunal for the Prosecution of Persons Responsible for Serious Violations of International Humanitarian Law Committed in the Territory of the Former Yugoslavia since 1991 (hereinafter referred to as "the International Tribunal") shall function in accordance with the provisions of the present Statute.

Article 1—Competence of the International Tribunal

The International Tribunal shall have the power to prosecute persons responsible for serious violations of international humanitarian law committed in the territory of the former Yugoslavia since 1991 in accordance with the provisions of the present Statute.

Article 2—Grave breaches of the Geneva Conventions of 1949

The International Tribunal shall have the power to prosecute persons committing or ordering to be committed grave breaches of the Geneva Conventions of 12 August 1949, namely the following acts against persons or property protected under the provisions of the relevant Geneva Convention:

(a) wilful killing;
(b) torture or inhuman treatment, including biological experiments;
(c) wilfully causing great suffering or serious injury to body or health;
(d) extensive destruction and appropriation of property, not justified by military necessity and carried out unlawfully and wantonly;
(e) compelling a prisoner of war or a civilian to serve in the forces of a hostile power;
(f) wilfully depriving a prisoner of war or a civilian of the rights of fair and regular trial;
(g) unlawful deportation or transfer or unlawful confinement of a civilian;
(h) taking civilians as hostages.

Article 3 — Violations of the laws or customs of war

The International Tribunal shall have the power to prosecute persons violating the laws or customs of war. Such violations shall include, but not be limited to:

(a) employment of poisonous weapons or other weapons calculated to cause unnecessary suffering;
(b) wanton destruction of cities, towns or villages, or devastation not justified by military necessity;
(c) attack, or bombardment, by whatever means, of undefended towns, villages, dwellings, or buildings;
(d) seizure of, destruction or wilful damage done to institutions dedicated to religion, charity and education, the arts and sciences, historic monuments and works of art and science;
(e) plunder of public or private property.

Article 4 — Genocide

1. The International Tribunal shall have the power to prosecute persons committing genocide as defined in paragraph 2 of this article or of committing any of the other acts enumerated in paragraph 3 of this article.

2. Genocide means any of the following acts committed with intent to destroy, in whole or in part, a national, ethnical, racial or religious group, as such:

(a) killing members of the group;
(b) causing serious bodily or mental harm to members of the group;
(c) deliberately inflicting on the group conditions of life calculated to bring about its physical destruction in whole or in part;
(d) imposing measures intended to prevent births within the group;
(e) forcibly transferring children of the group to another group.

3. The following acts shall be punishable:

(a) genocide;
(b) conspiracy to commit genocide;
(c) direct and public incitement to commit genocide;
(d) attempt to commit genocide;
(e) complicity in genocide.

Article 5 — Crimes against humanity

The International Tribunal shall have the power to prosecute persons responsible for the following crimes when committed in armed conflict, whether international or internal in character, and directed against any civilian population:

(a) murder;
(b) extermination;
(c) enslavement;
(d) deportation;
(e) imprisonment;
(f) torture;
(g) rape;
(h) persecutions on political, racial and religious grounds;
(i) other inhumane acts.

Article 6—Personal jurisdiction

The International Tribunal shall have jurisdiction over natural persons pursuant to the provisions of the present Statute.

Article 7—Individual criminal responsibility

1. A person who planned, instigated, ordered, committed or otherwise aided and abetted in the planning, preparation or execution of a crime referred to in articles 2 to 5 of the present Statute, shall be individually responsible for the crime.

2. The official position of any accused person, whether as Head of State or Government or as a responsible Government official, shall not relieve such person of criminal responsibility nor mitigate punishment.

3. The fact that any of the acts referred to in articles 2 to 5 of the present Statute was committed by a subordinate does not relieve his superior of criminal responsibility if he knew or had reason to know that the subordinate was about to commit such acts or had done so and the superior failed to take the necessary and reasonable measures to prevent such acts or to punish the perpetrators thereof.

4. The fact that an accused person acted pursuant to an order of a Government or of a superior shall not relieve him of criminal responsibility, but may be considered in mitigation of punishment if the International Tribunal determines that justice so requires.

Article 8—Territorial and temporal jurisdiction

The territorial jurisdiction of the International Tribunal shall extend to the territory of the former Socialist Federal Republic of Yugoslavia, including its land surface, airspace and territorial waters. The temporal jurisdiction of the International Tribunal shall extend to a period beginning on 1 January 1991.

Article 9—Concurrent jurisdiction

1. The International Tribunal and national courts shall have concurrent jurisdiction to prosecute persons for serious violations of

international humanitarian law committed in the territory of the former Yugoslavia since 1 January 1991.

2.   The International Tribunal shall have primacy over national courts. At any stage of the procedure, the International Tribunal may formally request national courts to defer to the competence of the International Tribunal in accordance with the present Statute and the Rules of Procedure and Evidence of the International Tribunal.

Article 10—Non-bis-in-idem

1.   No person shall be tried before a national court for acts constituting serious violations of international humanitarian law under the present Statute, for which he or she has already been tried by the International Tribunal.

2.   A person who has been tried by a national court for acts constituting serious violations of international humanitarian law may be subsequently tried by the International Tribunal only if:

(a)   the act for which he or she was tried was characterized as an ordinary crime; or
(b)   the national court proceedings were not impartial or independent, were designed to shield the accused from international criminal responsibility, or the case was not diligently prosecuted.

3.   In considering the penalty to be imposed on a person convicted of a crime under the present Statute, the International Tribunal shall take into account the extent to which any penalty imposed by a national court on the same person for the same act has already been served.

Article 11—Organization of the International Tribunal

The International Tribunal shall consist of the following organs:

(a)   The Chambers, comprising two Trial Chambers and an Appeals Chamber;
(b)   The Prosecutor; and
(c)   A Registry, servicing both the Chambers and the Prosecutor.

Article 12 — Composition of the Chambers

The Chambers shall be composed of eleven independent judges, no two of whom may be nationals of the same State, who shall serve as follows:

(a)   Three judges shall serve in each of the Trial Chambers;
(b)   Five judges shall serve in the Appeals Chamber.

Article 13 — Qualifications and election of judges

1.   The judges shall be persons of high moral character, impartiality and integrity who possess the qualifications required in their respective countries for appointment to the highest judicial offices. In the overall composition of the Chambers due account shall be taken of the experience of the judges in criminal law, international law, including international humanitarian law and human rights law.

2.   The judges of the International Tribunal shall be elected by the General Assembly from a list submitted by the Security Council, in the following manner:

(a)   The Secretary-General shall invite nominations for judges of the International Tribunal from States Members of the United Nations and non-member States maintaining permanent observer missions at United Nations Headquarters;
(b)   Within sixty days of the date of the invitation of the Secretary-General, each State may nominate up to two candidates meeting the qualifications set out in paragraph 1 above, no two of whom shall be of the same nationality;
(c)   The Secretary-General shall forward the nominations received to the Security Council. From the nominations received the Security Council shall establish a list of not less than twenty-two and not more than thirty-three candidates, taking due account of the adequate representation of the principal legal systems of the world;
(d)   The President of the Security Council shall transmit the list of candidates to the President of the General Assembly. From that list the General Assembly shall elect the eleven judges of the International Tribunal. The candidates who receive an absolute

majority of the votes of the States Members of the United Nations and of the non-Member States maintaining permanent observer missions at United Nations Headquarters, shall be declared elected. Should two candidates of the same nationality obtain the required majority vote, the one who received the higher number of votes shall be considered elected.

3. In the event of a vacancy in the Chambers, after consultation with the Presidents of the Security Council and of the General Assembly, the Secretary-General shall appoint a person meeting the qualifications of paragraph 1 above, for the remainder of the term of office concerned.

4. The judges shall be elected for a term of four years. The terms and conditions of service shall be those of the judges of the International Court of Justice. They shall be eligible for re-election.

Article 14 — Officers and members of the Chambers

1. The judges of the International Tribunal shall elect a President.

2. The President of the International Tribunal shall be a member of the Appeals Chamber and shall preside over its proceedings.

3. After consultation with the judges of the International Tribunal, the President shall assign the judges to the Appeals Chamber and to the Trial Chambers. A judge shall serve only in the Chamber to which he or she was assigned.

4. The judges of each Trial Chamber shall elect a Presiding Judge, who shall conduct all of the proceedings of the Trial Chamber as a whole.

Article 15 — Rules of procedure and evidence

The judges of the International Tribunal shall adopt rules of procedure and evidence for the conduct of the pre-trial phase of the proceedings, trials and appeals, the admission of evidence, the protection of victims and witnesses and other appropriate matters.

Article 16 — The Prosecutor

1. The Prosecutor shall be responsible for the investigation and prosecution of persons responsible for serious violations of international humanitarian law committed in the territory of the former Yugoslavia since 1 January 1991.

2. The Prosecutor shall act independently as a separate organ of the International Tribunal. He or she shall not seek or receive instructions from any Government or from any other source.

3. The Office of the Prosecutor shall be composed of a Prosecutor and such other qualified staff as may be required.

4. The Prosecutor shall be appointed by the Security Council on nomination by the Secretary-General. He or she shall be of high moral character and possess the highest level of competence and experience in the conduct of investigations and prosecutions of criminal cases. The Prosecutor shall serve for a four-year term and be eligible for reappointment. The terms and conditions of service of the Prosecutor shall be those of an Under-Secretary-General of the United Nations.

5. The staff of the Office of the Prosecutor shall be appointed by the Secretary-General on the recommendation of the Prosecutor.

Article 17 — The Registry

1. The Registry shall be responsible for the administration and servicing of the International Tribunal.

2. The Registry shall consist of a Registrar and such other staff as may be required.

3. The Registrar shall be appointed by the Secretary-General after consultation with the President of the International Tribunal. He or she shall serve for a four-year term and be eligible for reappointment. The terms and conditions of service of the Registrar shall be those of an Assistant Secretary-General of the United Nations.

4. The staff of the Registry shall be appointed by the Secretary-General on the recommendation of the Registrar.

Article 18—Investigation and preparation of indictment

1. The Prosecutor shall initiate investigations *ex officio* or on the basis of information obtained from any source, particularly from Governments, United Nations organs, intergovernmental and non-governmental organizations. The Prosecutor shall assess the information received or obtained and decide whether there is sufficient basis to proceed.

2. The Prosecutor shall have the power to question suspects, victims and witnesses, to collect evidence and to conduct on-site investigations. In carrying out these tasks, the Prosecutor may, as appropriate, seek the assistance of the State authorities concerned.

3. If questioned, the suspect shall be entitled to be assisted by counsel of his own choice, including the right to have legal assistance assigned to him without payment by him in any such case if he does not have sufficient means to pay for it, as well as to necessary translation into and from a language he speaks and understands.

4. Upon a determination that a *prima facie* case exists, the Prosecutor shall prepare an indictment containing a concise statement of the facts and the crime or crimes with which the accused is charged under the Statute. The indictment shall be transmitted to a judge of the Trial Chamber.

Article 19—Review of the indictment

1. The judge of the Trial Chamber to whom the indictment has been transmitted shall review it. If satisfied that a *prima facie* case has been established by the Prosecutor, he shall confirm the indictment. If not so satisfied, the indictment shall be dismissed.

2. Upon confirmation of an indictment, the judge may, at the request of the Prosecutor, issue such orders and warrants for the arrest, detention, surrender or transfer of persons, and any other orders as may be required for the conduct of the trial.

Article 20 — Commencement and conduct of trial proceedings

1. The Trial Chambers shall ensure that a trial is fair and expeditious and that proceedings are conducted in accordance with the rules of procedure and evidence, with full respect for the rights of the accused and due regard for the protection of victims and witnesses.

2. A person against whom an indictment has been confirmed shall, pursuant to an order or an arrest warrant of the International Tribunal, be taken into custody, immediately informed of the charges against him and transferred to the International Tribunal.

3. The Trial Chamber shall read the indictment, satisfy itself that the rights of the accused are respected, confirm that the accused understands the indictment, and instruct the accused to enter a plea. The Trial Chamber shall then set the date for trial.

4. The hearings shall be public unless the Trial Chamber decides to close the proceedings in accordance with its rules of procedure and evidence.

Article 21 — Rights of the accused

1. All persons shall be equal before the International Tribunal.

2. In the determination of charges against him, the accused shall be entitled to a fair and public hearing, subject to article 22 of the Statute.

3. The accused shall be presumed innocent until proved guilty according to the provisions of the present Statute.

4. In the determination of any charge against the accused pursuant to the present Statute, the accused shall be entitled to the following minimum guarantees, in full equality:

    (a) to be informed promptly and in detail in a language which he understands of the nature and cause of the charge against him;
    (b) to have adequate time and facilities for the preparation of his defence and to communicate with counsel of his own choosing;

(c) to be tried without undue delay;
(d) to be tried in his presence, and to defend himself in person or through legal assistance of his own choosing; to be informed, if he does not have legal assistance, of this right; and to have legal assistance assigned to him, in any case where the interests of justice so require, and without payment by him in any such case if he does not have sufficient means to pay for it;
(e) to examine, or have examined, the witnesses against him and to obtain the attendance and examination of witnesses on his behalf under the same conditions as witnesses against him;
(f) to have the free assistance of an interpreter if he cannot understand or speak the language used in the International Tribunal;
(g) not to be compelled to testify against himself or to confess guilt.

Article 22—Protection of victims and witnesses

The International Tribunal shall provide in its rules of procedure and evidence for the protection of victims and witnesses. Such protection measures shall include, but shall not be limited to, the conduct of *in camera* proceedings and the protection of the victim's identity.

Article 23—Judgement

1. The Trial Chambers shall pronounce judgements and impose sentences and penalties on persons convicted of serious violations of international humanitarian law.

2. The judgement shall be rendered by a majority of the judges of the Trial Chamber, and shall be delivered by the Trial Chamber in public. It shall be accompanied by a reasoned opinion in writing, to which separate or dissenting opinions may be appended.

Article 24—Penalties

1. The penalty imposed by the Trial Chamber shall be limited to imprisonment. In determining the terms of imprisonment, the Trial Chambers shall have recourse to the general practice regarding prison sentences in the courts of the former Yugoslavia.

2. In imposing the sentences, the Trial Chambers should take into account such factors as the gravity of the offence and the individual circumstances of the convicted person.

3. In addition to imprisonment, the Trial Chambers may order the return of any property and proceeds acquired by criminal conduct, including by means of duress, to their rightful owners.

Article 25 — Appellate proceedings

1. The Appeals Chamber shall hear appeals from persons convicted by the Trial Chambers or from the Prosecutor on the following grounds:

(a) an error on a question of law invalidating the decision; or
(b) an error of fact which has occasioned a miscarriage of justice.

2. The Appeals Chamber may affirm, reverse or revise the decisions taken by the Trial Chambers.

Article 26 — Review proceedings

Where a new fact has been discovered which was not known at the time of the proceedings before the Trial Chambers or the Appeals Chamber and which could have been a decisive factor in reaching the decision, the convicted person or the Prosecutor may submit to the International Tribunal an application for review of the judgement.

Article 27 — Enforcement of sentences

Imprisonment shall be served in a State designated by the International Tribunal from a list of States which have indicated to the Security Council their willingness to accept convicted persons. Such imprisonment shall be in accordance with the applicable law of the State concerned, subject to the supervision of the International Tribunal.

Article 28 — Pardon or commutation of sentences

If, pursuant to the applicable law of the State in which the convicted person is imprisoned, he or she is eligible for pardon or commutation of sentence, the State concerned shall notify the International Tribunal accordingly. The President of the International Tribunal, in consultation with the judges, shall decide the matter on the basis of the interests of justice and the general principles of law.

Article 29—Cooperation and judicial assistance

1. States shall cooperate with the International Tribunal in the investigation and prosecution of persons accused of committing serious violations of international humanitarian law.

2. States shall comply without undue delay with any request for assistance or an order issued by a Trial Chamber, including, but not limited to:

(a) the identification and location of persons;
(b) the taking of testimony and the production of evidence;
(c) the service of documents;
(d) the arrest or detention of persons;
(e) the surrender or the transfer of the accused to the International Tribunal.

*Article 30—The status, privileges and immunities
of the International Tribunal*

1. The Convention on the Privileges and Immunities of the United Nations of 13 February 1946 shall apply to the International Tribunal, the judges, the Prosecutor and his staff, and the Registrar and his staff.

2. The judges, the Prosecutor and the Registrar shall enjoy the privileges and immunities, exemptions and facilities accorded to diplomatic envoys, in accordance with international law.

3. The staff of the Prosecutor and of the Registrar shall enjoy the privileges and immunities accorded to officials of the United Nations under articles V and VII of the Convention referred to in paragraph 1 of this article.

4. Other persons, including the accused, required at the seat of the International Tribunal shall be accorded such treatment as is necessary for the proper functioning of the International Tribunal.

Article 31 — Seat of the International Tribunal

The International Tribunal shall have its seat at The Hague.

Article 32 — Expenses of the International Tribunal

The expenses of the International Tribunal shall be borne by the regular budget of the United Nations in accordance with Article 17 of the Charter of the United Nations.

Article 33 — Working languages

The working languages of the International Tribunal shall be English and French.

Article 34 — Annual report

The President of the International Tribunal shall submit an annual report of the International Tribunal to the Security Council and to the General Assembly.

ADDENDUM

1. In my letter dated 3 May 1993 to the President of the Security Council by which I informed him of the submission of the report on the establishment of an international tribunal for the prosecution of persons responsible for serious violations of international humanitarian law committed in the territory of the former Yugoslavia since 1991, I also indicated that an addendum containing cost estimates relating to the implementation of the report would also be submitted.

2. Should the Security Council establish the international tribunal on the basis set out in the main part of the report, it is estimated that the operating costs of the Tribunal for the first full year of operation would be approximately $ 31.2 million. It should be stressed that these are preliminary

estimates and further review and revision of basic assumptions would be necessary.

3. A breakdown of the estimated operating costs for the first full year of operation of the tribunal, by main categories of expenditure, is provided for information purposes in the annex to the present addendum. These estimates cover staff of 373, plus 11 judges and related operating costs, including language and verbatim records services, but do not include a significant number of costs for which no accurate estimates can be ascertained at this time. Not included are, among others, possible rental of premises, detention facilities before and during the trial, imprisonment and other costs which may arise in the course of establishing the Tribunal.

Annex

Cost estimate (thousands of United States dollars)

FIRST FULL YEAR OF OPERATION

Objects of expenditure

1.	The Chambers	3600
2.	The Prosecutor	5300
3.	The Registry (including conference services)	19900
4.	Programme support (including external printing, equipment, communications and supplies)	2400
TOTAL		31200

Appendix C

International Tribunal for the Prosecution of Persons Responsible for Serious Violations of International Humanitarian Law Committed in the Territory of the Former Yugoslavia since 1991 Rules of Procedure and Evidence[*]

PART ONE—GENERAL PROVISIONS

Rule 1—Entry into Force

These Rules of Procedure and Evidence, adopted pursuant to Article 15 of the Statute of the Tribunal, shall come into force on 14 March 1994.

Rule 2—Definitions

(A)   In the Rules, unless the context otherwise requires, the following terms shall mean:

---

[*]   *Editor's note:* U.N. Doc. IT/32 (1994), *amended by* U.N. Doc. IT/32/Rev.1 (1994), U.N. Doc. IT/32/Rev.2 (1994), U.N. Doc. IT/32/Rev.3 (1995). Unless otherwise noted, the articles in this issue of *Criminal Law Forum* are based on U.N. Doc. IT/32/Rev.1 (1994). This appendix prints the most recent text of the rules, set out in U.N. Doc. IT/32/Rev.3 (1995), indicating in {braces} all deletions from U.N. Doc. IT/32/Rev.1 (1994), and indicating in **boldface** type all additions to that document, so that the reader can compare the current text of the rules with the version the contributors are discussing. (Part and section titles are set in boldface type as a matter of style but none of these has changed.) Where the numerical or letter designation of a provision has changed, the new designation is indicated in boldface type but the former designation is not shown. It can be determined by examining the other changes in the rule. In Rule 77, for example, the addition of sub-rules 77(C) and 77(D) necessitated the redesignation of the provision that was previously sub-rule 77(C) as sub-rule 77(E).

Rules:	The Rules referred to in Rule 1;
Statute:	The Statute of the Tribunal adopted by Security Council resolution 827 of 25 May 1993;
Tribunal:	The International Tribunal for the Prosecution of Persons Responsible for Serious Violations of International Humanitarian Law Committed in the Territory of the Former Yugoslavia since 1991, established by Security Council resolution 827 of 25 May 1993;
Accused:	A person against whom an indictment has been submitted in accordance with Rule 47;
Arrest:	The act of taking a suspect or an accused into custody by a national authority;
Bureau:	A body composed of the President, the Vice-President and the Presiding Judges of the Trial Chambers;
Investigation:	All activities undertaken by the Prosecutor under the Statute and the Rules for the collection of information and evidence;
Party:	The Prosecutor or the accused;
President:	The President of the Tribunal;
Prosecutor:	The Prosecutor appointed pursuant to Article 16 of the Statute;
Regulations:	**The provisions framed by the Prosecutor pursuant to Sub-rule 37(A) for the purpose of directing the functions of his office;**
State:	**A State Member or non-Member of the United Nations or a self-proclaimed entity *de facto* exercising governmental functions, whether recognised as a State or not;**
Suspect:	A person concerning whom the Prosecutor possesses **reliable** information which tends to show that he may have committed a crime over which the Tribunal has jurisdiction;
Transaction:	**A number of acts or omissions whether occurring as one event or a number of events, at the same or different locations and being part of a common scheme, strategy or plan;**
Victim:	A person against whom a crime over which the Tribunal has jurisdiction has allegedly been committed.

(B)   In the Rules, the masculine shall include the feminine and the singular the plural, and vice-versa.

Appendix C: Rules of Procedure and Evidence

Rule 3—Languages

(A)   The working languages of the Tribunal shall be English and French.

(B)   An accused shall have the right to use his own language.

(C)   Any other person appearing before the Tribunal {may, subject to Sub-rule (D), use his own language if he}, **other than as counsel, who** does not have sufficient knowledge of either of the two working languages, **may use his own language.**

(D)   Counsel for an accused may apply to the Presiding Judge of a Chamber for leave to use a language other than the two working ones or the language of the accused. If such leave is granted, the expenses of interpretation and translation shall be borne by the Tribunal to the extent, if any, determined by the President, taking into account the rights of the defence and the interests of justice.

(E)   The Registrar shall make any necessary arrangements for interpretation and translation into and from the working languages.

Rule 4—Meetings away from the Seat of the Tribunal

A Chamber may exercise its functions at a place other than the seat of the Tribunal, if so authorised by the President in the interests of justice.

Rule 5—Non-compliance with Rules

Any objection by a party to an act of another party on the ground of non-compliance with the Rules **or Regulations** shall be raised at the earliest opportunity; it shall be upheld, and the act declared null, only if the act was inconsistent with the fundamental principles of fairness and has occasioned a miscarriage of justice.

Rule 6—Amendment of the Rules

(A)   Proposals for amendment of the Rules may be made by a Judge, the Prosecutor or the Registrar and shall be adopted if agreed to by not less than seven Judges at a plenary meeting of the Tribunal convened with notice of the proposal addressed to all Judges.

(B)   An amendment to the Rules may be otherwise adopted, provided it is unanimously approved by the Judges.

(C)   An amendment shall enter into force immediately, but shall not operate to prejudice the rights of the accused in any pending case.

Rule 7—Authentic Texts

The English and French texts of the Rules shall be equally authentic. In case of discrepancy, the version which is more consonant with the spirit of the Statute and the Rules shall prevail.

PART TWO—PRIMACY OF THE TRIBUNAL

Rule 8—Request for Information

Where it appears to the Prosecutor that a crime within the jurisdiction of the Tribunal is or has been the subject of investigations or criminal proceedings instituted in the {national} courts **of any State,** he may request the State to forward to him all relevant information in that respect, and the State shall transmit to him such information forthwith in accordance with {Article 29(1)} **Article 29** of the Statute.

Rule 9—Prosecutor's Request for Deferral

Where it appears to the Prosecutor that in any such investigations or criminal proceedings instituted in the {national} courts of any State:

>   (i)   the act being investigated or which is the subject of those proceedings is characterized as an ordinary crime;
>   (ii)   there is a lack of impartiality or independence, or the investigations or proceedings are designed to shield the accused from international criminal responsibility, or the case is not diligently prosecuted; or
>   (iii) what is in issue is closely related to, or otherwise involves,

significant factual or legal questions which may have implications for investigations or prosecutions before the Tribunal,

the Prosecutor may propose to the Trial Chamber designated by the President that a formal request be made that {the national} **such** court defer to the competence of the Tribunal.

Rule 10 — Formal Request for Deferral

(A)   If it appears to the Trial Chamber seised of a proposal for deferral that, on any of the grounds specified in Rule 9, deferral is appropriate, the Trial Chamber may issue a formal request to the State concerned that its {national} court defer to the competence of the Tribunal.

(B)   A request for deferral shall include a request that the results of the investigation and a copy of the court's records and the judgement, if already delivered, be forwarded to the Tribunal.

(C)   Where deferral to the Tribunal has been requested by a Trial Chamber, any subsequent proceedings shall be held before the other Trial Chamber.

Rule 11 — Non-compliance with a Request for Deferral

If, within sixty days after a request for deferral has been notified by the Registrar to the State under whose jurisdiction the investigations or criminal proceedings have been instituted, the State fails to file a response which satisfies the Trial Chamber that the State has taken or is taking adequate steps to comply with the order, the Trial Chamber may request the President to report the matter to the Security Council.

*Rule 12 — Determinations of {National} Courts **of Any State***

Subject to Article 10(2) of the Statute, determinations of {national} courts **of any State** are not binding on the Tribunal.

Rule 13 — Non Bis in Idem

When the President receives reliable information to show that criminal proceedings have been instituted against a person before a {national} court of any State for a crime for which that person has already been tried by the Tribunal, a Trial Chamber shall, following *mutatis mutandis* the procedure provided in Rule 10, issue a reasoned order requesting {the national} **that** court permanently to discontinue its proceedings. If {the national} **that** court fails to do so, the President may report the matter to the Security Council.

PART THREE—ORGANIZATION OF THE TRIBUNAL

Section 1 — The Judges

Rule 14—Solemn Declaration

(A) Before taking up his duties each Judge shall make the following solemn declaration:

> I solemnly declare that I will perform my duties and exercise my powers as a Judge of the International Tribunal for the Prosecution of Persons Responsible for Serious Violations of International Humanitarian Law Committed in the Territory of the Former Yugoslavia since 1991 honourably, faithfully, impartially and conscientiously.

(B) The declaration, signed by the Judge and witnessed by the Secretary-General of the United Nations or his representative, shall be kept in the records of the Tribunal.

Rule 15—Disqualification of Judges

(A) A Judge may not sit on a trial or appeal in any case in which he has a personal interest or concerning which he has or has had any association which might affect his impartiality. He shall in any such circumstance withdraw, and the President shall assign another Judge to sit in his place.

(B) Any party may apply to the Presiding Judge of a Chamber for the disqualification and withdrawal of a Judge of that Chamber from a trial upon the above grounds. The Presiding Judge shall confer with the Judge in question, and if necessary the Bureau shall determine the matter. If the Bureau upholds the application, the President shall assign another Judge to sit in place of the disqualified Judge.

(C) The Judge of the Trial Chamber who reviews an indictment against an accused, pursuant to Article 19 of the Statute and Rule 47, shall not sit as a member of the Trial Chamber for the trial of that accused.

(D) No member of the Appeals Chamber shall sit on any appeal in a case in which he sat as a member of the Trial Chamber.

(E) If a Judge is, for any reason, unable to continue sitting in a part-heard case, the Presiding Judge may, if that inability seems likely to be of short duration, adjourn the proceedings; otherwise he shall report to the President who may assign another Judge to the case and order either a rehearing or, with the consent of the accused, continuation of the proceedings from that point.

Rule 16—Resignation

A Judge who decides to resign shall communicate his resignation in writing to the President who shall transmit it to the Secretary-General of the United Nations.

Rule 17—Precedence

(A) All Judges are equal in the exercise of their judicial functions, regardless of dates of election, appointment, age or period of service.

(B) The Presiding Judges of the Trial Chambers shall take precedence according to age after the President and the Vice-President.

(C) Judges elected or appointed on different dates shall take precedence according to the dates of their election or appointment; Judges elected or appointed on the same date shall take precedence according to age.

(D) In case of re-election, the total period of service as a Judge of the Tribunal shall be taken into account.

Section 2—The Presidency

Rule 18—Election of the President

(A) The President shall be elected for a term of two years, or such shorter term as shall coincide with the duration of his term of office as a Judge. He may be re-elected once.

(B) If the President ceases to be a member of the Tribunal or resigns his office before the expiration of his term, the Judges shall elect from among their number a successor for the remainder of the term.

(C) The President shall be elected by a majority of the votes of the Judges composing the Tribunal. If no Judge obtains such a majority, the second ballot shall be limited to the two Judges who obtained the greatest number of votes on the first ballot. In the case of equality of votes on the second ballot, the Judge who takes precedence in accordance with Rule 17 shall be declared elected.

Rule 19—Functions of the President

The President shall preside at all plenary meetings of the Tribunal; he shall coordinate the work of the Chambers and supervise the activities of the Registry as well as exercise all the other functions conferred on him by the Statute and the Rules.

Rule 20—The Vice-President

(A) The Vice-President shall be elected for a term of two years, or such shorter term as shall coincide with the duration of his term of office as a Judge. He may be re-elected once.

(B) The Vice-President may sit as a member of a Trial Chamber or of the Appeals Chamber.

(C) Sub-rules 18(B) and (C) shall apply *mutatis mutandis* to the Vice-President.

Rule 21—Functions of the Vice-President

Subject to Sub-rule 22(B), the Vice-President shall exercise the functions of the President in case of his absence or inability to act.

Rule 22—Replacements

(A)   If neither the President nor the Vice-President can carry out the functions of the President, these shall be assumed by the senior Judge, determined in accordance with Rule 17.

(B)   If the President is unable to exercise his functions as Presiding Judge of the Appeals Chamber, that Chamber shall elect a Presiding Judge from among its number.

Section 3—Internal Functioning of the Tribunal

Rule 23— The Bureau

(A)   The Bureau shall be composed of the President, the Vice-President and the Presiding Judges of the Trial Chambers.

(B)   The President shall consult the other members of the Bureau on all major questions relating to the functioning of the Tribunal.

(C)   A Judge may draw the attention of any member of the Bureau to issues that in his opinion ought to be discussed by the Bureau or submitted to a plenary meeting of the Tribunal.

Rule 24—Plenary Meetings of the Tribunal

The Judges shall meet in plenary to:

(i)   elect the President and Vice-President;
(ii)   adopt and amend the Rules;
(iii)   adopt the Annual Report provided for in Article 34 of the Statute;
(iv)   decide upon matters relating to the internal functioning of the Chambers and the Tribunal;
(v)   determine or supervise the conditions of detention;
(vi)   exercise any other functions provided for in the Statute or in the Rules.

Rule 25 — Dates of Plenary Sessions

(A) The dates of the plenary sessions of the Tribunal shall normally be agreed upon in July of each year for the following calendar year.

(B) Other plenary meetings shall be convened by the President if so requested by at least six Judges, and may be convened whenever the exercise of his functions under the Statute or the Rules so requires.

Rule 26 — Quorum and Vote

(A) The quorum for each plenary meeting of the Tribunal shall be seven Judges.

(B) Subject to Sub-rules 6(A) and (B) and Sub-rule 18(C), the decisions of the plenary meetings of the Tribunal shall be taken by the majority of the Judges present. In the event of an equality of votes, the President or the Judge who acts in his place shall have a casting vote.

Section 4 — The Chambers

Rule 27 — Rotation

(A) Judges shall rotate on a regular basis between the Trial Chambers and the Appeals Chamber. Rotation shall take into account the efficient disposal of cases.

(B) The Judges shall take their places in their new Chamber as soon as the President thinks it convenient, having regard to the disposal of part-heard cases.

(C) The President may at any time temporarily assign a member of a Trial Chamber or of the Appeals Chamber to another Chamber.

Rule 28 — Assignment to Review Indictments

The President shall, in July of each year and after consultation with the Judges, assign for each month of the next calendar year {a} **one** Judge {of a} **from each** Trial Chamber as the {Judge} **Judges** to whom indictments shall be transmitted for review under Rule 47, and shall publish the list of assignments.

Rule 29 — Deliberations

The deliberations of the Chambers shall take place in private and remain secret.

Section 5 — The Registry

Rule 30 — Appointment of the Registrar

The President shall seek the opinion of the Judges on the candidates for the post of Registrar, before consulting with the Secretary-General of the United Nations pursuant to Article 17(3) of the Statute.

Rule 31 — Appointment of the Deputy Registrar and Registry Staff

The Registrar, after consultation with the Bureau, shall make his recommendations to the Secretary-General of the United Nations for the appointment of the Deputy Registrar and other Registry staff.

Rule 32 — Solemn Declaration

(A)   Before taking up his duties, the Registrar shall make the following declaration before the President:

> I solemnly declare that I will perform the duties incumbent upon me as Registrar of the International Tribunal for the Prosecution of Persons Responsible for Serious Violations of International Humanitarian Law Committed in the Territory of the Former Yugoslavia since 1991 in all loyalty, discretion and good conscience and that I will faithfully observe all the provisions of the Statute and the Rules of Procedure and Evidence of the Tribunal.

(B)   Before taking up his duties, the Deputy Registrar shall make a similar declaration before the President.

(C)   Every staff member of the Registry shall make a similar declaration before the Registrar.

Rule 33—Functions of the Registrar

The Registrar shall assist the Chambers, the plenary meetings of the Tribunal, the Judges and the Prosecutor in the performance of their functions. Under the authority of the President, he shall be responsible for the administration and servicing of the Tribunal and shall serve as its channel of communication.

Rule 34—Victims and Witnesses Unit

(A)   There shall be set up under the authority of the Registrar a Victims and Witnesses Unit consisting of qualified staff to:

> (i)   recommend protective measures for victims and witnesses in accordance with Article 22 of the Statute; and
> (ii)   provide counselling and support for them, in particular in cases of rape and sexual assault.

(B)   Due consideration shall be given, in the appointment of staff, to the employment of qualified women.

Rule 35—Minutes

Except where a full record is made under Rule 81, the Registrar, or Registry staff designated by him, shall take minutes of the plenary meetings of the Tribunal and of the sittings of the Chambers, other than private deliberations.

Rule 36—Record Book

The Registrar shall keep a Record Book which shall list, **subject to Rule 53,** all the particulars of each case brought before the Tribunal. The Record Book shall be open to the public.

Section 6—The Prosecutor

Rule 37—Functions of the Prosecutor

(A)   The Prosecutor shall {exercise} **perform** all the functions provided by the Statute in accordance with the Rules and such Regulations, consistent with the Statute and the Rules, as may be framed by him. Any alleged inconsistency in the Regulations shall be brought to the attention of the Bureau to whose opinion the Prosecutor shall defer.

(B)   His powers under Parts Four to Eight of the Rules may be exercised by staff members of the Office of the Prosecutor authorised by him, or by any person acting under his direction.

Rule 38 — Deputy Prosecutor

(A)   The Prosecutor shall make his recommendations to the Secretary-General of the United Nations for the appointment of a Deputy Prosecutor.

(B)   The Deputy Prosecutor shall exercise the functions of the Prosecutor in the event of his absence or inability to act or upon the Prosecutor's express instructions.

PART FOUR — INVESTIGATIONS AND RIGHTS OF SUSPECTS

Section 1 — Investigations

Rule 39 — Conduct of Investigations

In the conduct of an investigation, the Prosecutor may:

> (i)   summon and question suspects, victims and witnesses and record their statements, collect evidence and conduct on-site investigations;
> (ii)   undertake such other matters as may appear necessary for completing the investigation and the preparation and conduct of the prosecution at the trial, **including the taking of special measures to provide for the safety of potential witnesses and informants;**
> (iii) seek, to that end, the assistance of any State authority concerned, as well as of any relevant international body including the International Criminal Police Organization (INTERPOL); and
> (iv)   request such orders as may be necessary from a Trial Chamber or a Judge.

Rule 40—Provisional Measures

In case of urgency, the Prosecutor may request any State:

    (i)   to arrest a suspect provisionally;
    (ii)   to seize physical evidence;
    (iii)   to take all necessary measures to prevent the escape of a suspect or an accused, injury to or intimidation of a victim or witness, or the destruction of evidence.

The State concerned shall comply forthwith, in accordance with Article 29 of the Statute.

Rule 41—Retention of Information

The Prosecutor shall be responsible for the retention, storage and security of information and physical evidence obtained in the course of his investigations.

Rule 42—Rights of Suspects during Investigation

(A) A suspect who is to be questioned by the Prosecutor shall have the following rights, of which he shall be informed by the Prosecutor prior to questioning, in a language he speaks and understands:

    (i)   the right to be assisted by counsel of his choice or to have legal assistance assigned to him without payment if he does not have sufficient means to pay for it; {and}
    (ii)   the right to have the free assistance of an interpreter if he cannot understand or speak the language to be used for questioning; **and**
    (iii)   **the right to remain silent, and to be cautioned that any statement he makes shall be recorded and may be used in evidence.**

(B) Questioning of a suspect shall not proceed without the presence of counsel unless the suspect has voluntarily waived his right to counsel. In case of waiver, if the suspect subsequently expresses a desire to have counsel, questioning shall thereupon cease, and shall only resume when the suspect has obtained or has been assigned counsel.

Appendix C: Rules of Procedure and Evidence

Rule 43 — Recording Questioning of Suspects

Whenever the Prosecutor questions a suspect, the questioning shall be tape-recorded or video-recorded, in accordance with the following procedure:

(i) the suspect shall be informed in a language he speaks and understands that the questioning is being tape-recorded or video-recorded;

(ii) in the event of a break in the course of the questioning, the fact and the time of the break shall be recorded before tape-recording or video-recording ends and the time of resumption of the questioning shall also be recorded;

(iii) at the conclusion of the questioning the suspect shall be offered the opportunity to clarify anything he has said, and to add anything he may wish, and the time of conclusion shall be recorded;

(iv) the tape shall then be transcribed **as soon as practicable after the conclusion of questioning** and a copy of the transcript supplied to the suspect, together with a copy of the recorded tape or, if multiple recording apparatus was used, one of the original recorded tapes; and

(v) after a copy has been made, if necessary, of the recorded tape for purposes of transcription, the original recorded tape or one of the original tapes shall be sealed in the presence of the suspect under the signature of the Prosecutor and the suspect.

Section 2 — Of Counsel

Rule 44 — Appointment and Qualifications of Counsel

Counsel engaged by a suspect or an accused shall file his power of attorney with the Registrar at the earliest opportunity. A counsel shall be considered qualified to represent a suspect or accused if he satisfies the Registrar that he is admitted to the practice of law in a State, or is a University professor of law.

Rule 45 — Assignment of Counsel

(A) A list of counsel who speak one or both of the working languages of the Tribunal, meet the requirements of Rule 44 and have indicated their willingness to be assigned by the Tribunal to indigent suspects or accused, shall be kept by the Registrar.

(B)   The criteria for determination of indigency shall be established by the Registrar and approved by the Judges.

(C)   In assigning counsel to an indigent suspect or accused, the following procedure shall be observed:

> (i)   a request for assignment of counsel shall be made to the Registrar;
> (ii)   the Registrar shall enquire into the means of the suspect or accused and determine whether the criteria of indigency are met;
> (iii)   if he decides that the criteria are met, he shall assign counsel from the list; if he decides to the contrary, he shall inform the suspect or accused that the request is refused.

(D)   If a request is refused, a further request may be made by a suspect or an accused to the Registrar upon showing a change in circumstances.

{(E)   The Registrar shall assign counsel to a suspect or an accused who fails to obtain counsel or to request assignment of counsel, unless the suspect or the accused elects in writing to conduct his own defence.} *[Editor's note: see Rule 45(F).]*

(E)   The Registrar shall, in consultation with the Judges, establish the criteria for the payment of fees to assigned counsel.

(F)   If a suspect or an accused elects to conduct his own defence, he shall so notify the Registrar in writing at the first opportunity.

(G)   Where an alleged indigent person is subsequently found not to be indigent, the Chamber may make an order of contribution to recover the cost of providing counsel.

Rule 46 — Misconduct of Counsel

(A)   A Chamber may, after a warning, refuse audience to counsel if, in its opinion, his conduct is offensive, abusive or otherwise obstructs the proper conduct of the proceedings.

(B)   A Judge or a Chamber may also, with the approval of the President, communicate any misconduct of counsel to the professional body regulating the conduct of counsel in his State of admission or, if a professor and not otherwise admitted to the profession, to the governing body of his University.

PART FIVE—PRE-TRIAL PROCEEDINGS

Section 1—Indictments

Rule 47—Submission of Indictment by the Prosecutor

(A)   If in the course of an investigation the Prosecutor is satisfied that there is sufficient evidence to provide reasonable grounds for believing that a suspect has committed a crime within the jurisdiction of the Tribunal, he shall prepare and forward to the Registrar an indictment for confirmation by a Judge, together with supporting material.

(B)   The indictment shall set forth the name and particulars of the suspect, and a concise statement of the facts of the case and of the crime with which the suspect is charged.

(C)   The Registrar shall forward the indictment and accompanying material to {the Judge} **one of the Judges** currently assigned under Rule 28, who will inform the Prosecutor of the date fixed for review of the indictment.

(D)   On reviewing the indictment, the Judge shall hear the Prosecutor, who may present additional material in support of any count. The Judge may confirm or dismiss each count or may adjourn the review.

(E)   The dismissal of a count in an indictment shall not preclude the Prosecutor from subsequently bringing a new indictment based on the acts underlying that count if supported by additional evidence.

Rule 48—Joinder of Accused

Persons accused of the same or different crimes committed in the course of the same transaction may be jointly charged and tried.

Rule 49—Joinder of Crimes

Two or more crimes may be joined in one indictment if the series of acts committed together form the same transaction, and the said crimes were committed by the same accused.

Rule 50—Amendment of Indictment

The Prosecutor may amend an indictment, without leave, at any time before its confirmation, but thereafter only with leave of the Judge who confirmed it or, if at trial, with leave of the Trial Chamber. If leave to amend is granted, the amended indictment shall be transmitted to the accused and to his counsel and where necessary the date for trial shall be postponed to ensure adequate time for the preparation of the defence.

Rule 51—Withdrawal of Indictment

(A) The Prosecutor may withdraw an indictment, without leave, at any time before its confirmation, but thereafter only with leave of the Judge who confirmed it or, if at trial, only with leave of the Trial Chamber.

(B) The withdrawal of the indictment shall be promptly notified to the suspect or the accused and to his counsel.

Rule 52—Public Character of Indictment

Subject to Rule 53, upon confirmation by a Judge of a Trial Chamber, the indictment shall be made public.

Rule 53—Non-disclosure of Indictment

(A) When confirming an indictment the Judge may, in consultation with the Prosecutor, order that there be no public disclosure of the indictment until it is served on the accused, or, in the case of joint accused, on all the accused.

(B) A Judge or Trial Chamber may, in consultation with the Prosecutor, also order that there be no {public} disclosure of an indictment, or part thereof, or **of all or any part** of any particular document or information *[sic]*, if satisfied that the making of such an order is **required to give effect to a provision of the Rules, to protect confidential information obtained by the Prosecutor, or is otherwise** in the interests of justice.

Section 2—*Orders and Warrants*

Rule 54—General Rule

At the request of either party or *proprio motu*, a Judge or a Trial Chamber may issue such orders, summonses, **subpoenas** and warrants as may be necessary for the purposes of an investigation or for the preparation or conduct of the trial.

Rule 55—Execution of Arrest Warrants

(A)   A warrant of arrest shall be signed by a Judge and shall bear the seal of the Tribunal. It shall be accompanied by a copy of the indictment, and a statement of the rights of the accused. These rights include those set forth in Article 21 of the Statute, and in Rules 42 and 43 *mutatis mutandis*, together with the right of the accused to remain silent, and to be cautioned that any statement he makes shall be recorded and may be used in evidence.

(B)   A warrant for the arrest of the accused and **an order for** his surrender to the Tribunal shall be transmitted by the Registrar to the national authorities of the State in whose territory or under whose jurisdiction or control the accused resides, or was last known to be, together with instructions that at the time of arrest the indictment and the statement of the rights of the accused be read to him in a language he understands and that he be cautioned in that language.

(C)   When an arrest warrant issued by the Tribunal is executed, a member of the Prosecutor's Office may be present as from the time of arrest.

Rule 56—Cooperation of States

The State to which a warrant of arrest is transmitted shall act promptly and with all due diligence to ensure proper and effective execution thereof, in accordance with Article 29 of the Statute.

Rule 57—Procedure after Arrest

Upon the arrest of the accused, the State concerned shall detain him, and shall promptly notify the Registrar. The transfer of the accused to the seat of the Tribunal shall be arranged between the State authorities concerned, **the authorities of the host country** and the Registrar.

Rule 58—National Extradition Provisions

The obligations laid down in Article 29 of the Statute shall prevail over any legal impediment to the surrender or transfer of the accused to the Tribunal which may exist under the national law or extradition treaties of the State concerned.

Rule 59—Failure to Execute a Warrant

(A)   Where the State to which a warrant of arrest has been transmitted has been unable to execute the warrant, it shall report forthwith its inability to the Registrar, and the reasons therefor.

(B)   If, within a reasonable time after the warrant of arrest has been transmitted to the State, no report is made on action taken, this shall be deemed a failure to execute the warrant of arrest and the Tribunal, through the President, may notify the Security Council accordingly.

Rule 60—Advertisement of Indictment

At the request of the Prosecutor, a form of advertisement shall be transmitted by the Registrar to the national authorities of any State or States in whose territory the Prosecutor has reason to believe that the accused may be found, for publication in newspapers having wide circulation in that territory, intimating to the accused that service of an indictment against him is sought.

Rule 61—Procedure in Case of Failure to Execute a Warrant

(A)   If a warrant of arrest has not been executed, and personal service of the indictment has consequently not been effected, and the Prosecutor satisfies a Judge of a Trial Chamber that:

(i) he has taken all reasonable steps to effect personal service, including recourse to the appropriate authorities of the State in whose territory or under whose jurisdiction and control the person to be served resides or was last known to him to be; and

(ii) he has otherwise tried to inform the accused of the existence of the indictment by seeking publication of newspaper advertisements pursuant to Rule 60,

the Judge shall order that the indictment be submitted by the Prosecutor to the Trial Chamber.

(B) Upon obtaining such an order the Prosecutor shall submit the indictment to the Trial Chamber in open court, together with all the evidence that was before the Judge who initially confirmed the indictment. **The Prosecutor may also call before the Trial Chamber and examine any witness whose statement has been submitted to the confirming Judge.**

(C) If the Trial Chamber is satisfied on that evidence, together with such additional evidence as the Prosecutor may tender, that there are reasonable grounds for believing that the accused has committed all or any of the crimes charged in the indictment, it shall so determine. The Trial Chamber shall have the relevant parts of the indictment read out by the Prosecutor together with an account of the efforts to effect service referred to in Sub-rule (A) above.

(D) The Trial Chamber shall also issue an international arrest warrant in respect of the accused which shall be transmitted to all States.

(E) If the Prosecutor satisfies the Trial Chamber that the failure to effect personal service was due in whole or in part to a failure or refusal of a State to cooperate with the Tribunal in accordance with Article 29 of the Statute, the Trial Chamber shall so certify, in which event the President shall notify the Security Council.

Rule 62 — Initial Appearance of Accused

Upon his transfer to the seat of the Tribunal, the accused shall be brought before a Trial Chamber without delay, and shall be formally charged. The Trial Chamber shall:

(i) satisfy itself that the right of the accused to counsel is respected;
(ii) read or have the indictment read to the accused in a language he speaks and understands, and satisfy itself that the accused understands the indictment;
(iii) call upon the accused to enter a plea of guilty or not guilty; should the accused fail to do so, enter a plea of not guilty on his behalf;
(iv) in case of a plea of not guilty, instruct the Registrar to set a date for trial;
(v) in case of a plea of guilty, instruct the Registrar to set a date for the pre-sentence hearing;
(vi) instruct the Registrar to set {a date for trial} such other dates as appropriate.

Rule 63 — Questioning of Accused

After the initial appearance of the accused the Prosecutor shall not question him unless his counsel is present and the questioning is tape-recorded or video-recorded in accordance with the procedure provided for in Rule 43. The Prosecutor shall at the beginning of the questioning caution the accused that he is not obliged to say anything unless he wishes to do so but that whatever he says may be given in evidence.

Rule 64 — Detention on Remand

Upon his transfer to the seat of the Tribunal, the accused shall be detained in facilities provided by the host country, or by another country. The President may, on the application of a party, request modification of the conditions of detention of an accused.

Rule 65 — Provisional Release

(A) Once detained, an accused may not be released except upon an order of a Trial Chamber.

(B) Release may be ordered by a Trial Chamber only in exceptional circumstances, **after hearing the host country** and only if it is satisfied that the accused will appear for trial and, if released, will not pose a danger to any victim, witness or other person.

(C) The Trial Chamber may impose such conditions upon the release of the accused as it may determine appropriate, including the execution of a bail bond and the observance of such conditions as are necessary to ensure his presence for trial and the protection of others.

(D) If necessary, the Trial Chamber may issue a warrant of arrest to secure the presence of an accused who has been released or is for any other reason at liberty.

Section 3 — Production of Evidence

Rule 66 — Disclosure by the Prosecutor

(A) The Prosecutor shall make available to the defence, as soon as practicable after the initial appearance of the accused, copies of the supporting material which accompanied the indictment when confirmation was sought **as well as all prior statements obtained by the Prosecutor from the accused or from prosecution witnesses.**

(B) The Prosecutor shall on request, **subject to Sub-rule (C),** permit the defence to inspect any books, documents, photographs and tangible objects in his custody or control, which are material to the preparation of the defence, or are intended for use by the Prosecutor as evidence at trial or were obtained from or belonged to the accused.

(C) **Where information is in the possession of the Prosecutor, the disclosure of which may prejudice further or ongoing investigations, or for any other reasons may be contrary to the public interest or affect the security interests of any State, the Prosecutor may apply to the Trial Chamber sitting *in camera* to be relieved from the obligation to disclose pursuant to Sub-rule (B). When making such application the Prosecutor shall provide the Trial Chamber (but only the Trial Chamber) with the information that is sought to be kept confidential.**

Rule 67 — Reciprocal Disclosure

(A) As early as reasonably practicable and in any event prior to the commencement of the trial:

(i) the Prosecutor shall notify the defence of the names of the witnesses that he intends to call in proof of the guilt of the accused and in rebuttal of any defence plea of which the Prosecutor has received notice in accordance with Sub-rule (ii) below;

(ii) the defence shall notify the Prosecutor of its intent to offer:

(a) the defence of alibi; in which case the notification shall specify the place or places at which the accused claims to have been present at the time of the alleged crime and the names and addresses of witnesses and any other evidence upon which the accused intends to rely to establish the alibi;

(b) any special defence, including that of diminished or lack of mental responsibility; in which case the notification shall specify the names and addresses of witnesses and any other evidence upon which the accused intends to rely to establish the special defence.

(B) Failure of the defence to provide notice under this Rule shall not limit the right of the accused to testify on the above defences.

(C) If the defence makes a request pursuant to Sub-rule 66(B), the Prosecutor shall be entitled to inspect any books, documents, photographs and tangible objects, which are within the custody or control of the defence and which it intends to use as evidence at the trial.

(D) If either party discovers additional evidence or material which should have been produced earlier pursuant to the Rules, that party shall promptly notify the other party and the Trial Chamber of the existence of the additional evidence or material.

Rule 68 — Disclosure of Exculpatory Evidence

The Prosecutor shall, as soon as practicable, disclose to the defence the existence of evidence known to the Prosecutor which in any way tends to suggest the innocence or mitigate the guilt of the accused {of a crime charged in the indictment} **or may affect the credibility of prosecution evidence.**

Rule 69—Protection of Victims and Witnesses

(A) In exceptional circumstances, the Prosecutor may apply to a Trial Chamber to order the non-disclosure of the identity of a victim or witness who may be in danger or at risk until such person is brought under the protection of the Tribunal.

(B) Subject to Rule 75, the identity of the victim or witness shall be disclosed in sufficient time prior to the trial to allow adequate time for preparation of the defence.

Rule 70—Matters not Subject to Disclosure

(A) Notwithstanding the provisions of Rules 66 and 67, reports, memoranda, or other internal documents prepared by a party, its assistants or representatives in connection with the investigation or preparation of the case, are not subject to disclosure or notification under those Rules.

(B) If the Prosecutor is in possession of information which has been provided to him on a confidential basis and which has been used solely for the purpose of generating new evidence, that initial information and its origin shall not be disclosed by the Prosecutor without the consent of the person or entity providing the initial information and shall in any event not be given in evidence without prior disclosure to the accused.

Section 4—Depositions

Rule 71—Depositions

(A) At the request of either party, a Trial Chamber may, in exceptional circumstances and in the interests of justice, order that a deposition be taken for use at trial, and appoint, for that purpose, a Presiding Officer.

(B) The motion for the taking of a deposition shall be in writing and shall indicate the name and whereabouts of the person whose deposition is sought, the date and place at which the deposition is to be taken, a statement of the matters on which the person is to be examined, and of the exceptional circumstances justifying the taking of the deposition.

(C) If the motion is granted, the party at whose request the deposition is to be taken shall give reasonable notice to the other party, who shall have the right to attend the taking of the deposition and cross-examine the person whose deposition is being taken.

(D) Deposition evidence may also be given by means of a video-conference.

(E) The Presiding Officer shall ensure that the deposition is taken in accordance with the Rules and that a record is made of the deposition, including cross-examination and objections raised by either party for decision by the Trial Chamber. He shall transmit the record to the Trial Chamber.

Section 5—Preliminary Motions

Rule 72—General Provisions

(A) After the initial appearance of the accused, either party may move before a Trial Chamber for appropriate relief or ruling. Such motions may be written or oral, at the discretion of the Trial Chamber.

(B) The Trial Chamber shall dispose of preliminary motions *in limine litis* **and without interlocutory appeal, save in the case of dismissal of an objection based on lack of jurisdiction.**

Rule 73—Preliminary Motions by Accused

(A) Preliminary motions by the accused shall include:

   (i) objections based on lack of jurisdiction;
   (ii) objections based on defects in the form of the indictment;
   (iii) applications for the exclusion of evidence obtained from the accused or having belonged to him;
   (iv) applications for severance of crimes joined in one indictment under Rule 49, or for separate trials under Sub-rule 82(B);
   (v) objections based on the denial of request for assignment of counsel.

(B) Any of the motions by the accused referred to in Sub-rule (A) shall be brought within sixty days after his initial appearance, and in any case before the hearing on the merits.

(C)   Failure to apply within the time-limit prescribed shall constitute a waiver of the right. Upon a showing of good cause, the Trial Chamber may grant relief from the waiver.

PART SIX—PROCEEDINGS BEFORE TRIAL CHAMBERS

Section 1 — General Provisions

Rule 74—Amicus Curiae

A Chamber may, if it considers it desirable for the proper determination of the case, invite or grant leave to a State, organization or person to appear before it and make submissions on any issue specified by the Chamber.

*Rule 75—**Measures for the** Protection of Victims and Witnesses*

(A)   A Judge or a Chamber may, *proprio motu* or at the request of either party, or of the victim or witness concerned, order appropriate measures for the privacy and protection of victims and witnesses, provided that the measures are consistent with the rights of the accused.

(B)   A Chamber may hold an *{ex parte (non-contradictoire)}* **in camera** proceeding to determine whether to order:

> (i)   measures to prevent disclosure to the public or the media of the identity or whereabouts of a victim or a witness, or of persons related to or associated with him by such means as:
>
>> (a)   expunging names and identifying information from the Chamber's public records;
>> (b)   non-disclosure to the public of any records identifying the victim;
>> (c)   giving of testimony through image- or voice-altering devices or closed circuit television; and
>> (d)   assignment of a pseudonym;

(ii) closed sessions, in accordance with Rule 79;

(iii) appropriate measures to facilitate the testimony of vulnerable victims and witnesses, such as one-way closed circuit television.

(C) A Chamber shall, whenever necessary, control the manner of questioning to avoid any harassment or intimidation.

Rule 76—Solemn Declaration by Interpreters and Translators

Before performing any duties, an interpreter or a translator shall solemnly declare to do so faithfully, independently, impartially and with full respect for the duty of confidentiality.

Rule 77—Contempt of {Court} **the Tribunal**

(A) Subject to the provisions of {Sub-rule 90(D)} **Sub-rule 90(E)**, a witness who refuses or fails contumaciously to answer a question relevant to the issue before a Chamber may be found in contempt of the Tribunal. The Chamber may impose a fine not exceeding US$10,000 or a term of imprisonment not exceeding six months.

(B) The Chamber may, however, relieve the witness of the duty to answer, for reasons which it deems appropriate.

(C) **Any person who attempts to interfere with or intimidate a witness may be found guilty of contempt and sentenced in accordance with Sub-rule (A).**

(D) **Any judgement rendered under this Rule shall be subject to appeal.**

(E) Payment of a fine shall be made to the Registrar to be held in a separate account.

Rule 78—Open Sessions

All proceedings before a Trial Chamber, other than deliberations of the Chamber, shall be held in public, unless otherwise provided.

Rule 79—Closed Sessions

(A) The Trial Chamber may order that the press and the public be excluded from all or part of the proceedings for reasons of:

>   (i)   public order or morality;
>   (ii) safety, security or non-disclosure of the identity of a victim or witness as provided in Rule 75; or
>   (iii) the protection of the interests of justice.

(B) The Trial Chamber shall make public the reasons for its order.

Rule 80—Control of Proceedings

(A) The Trial Chamber may exclude a person from the courtroom in order to protect the right of the accused to a fair and public trial, or to maintain the dignity and decorum of the proceedings.

(B) The Trial Chamber may order the removal of an accused from the courtroom and continue the proceedings in his absence if he has persisted in disruptive conduct following a warning that he may be removed.

Rule 81—Records of Proceedings and Evidence

(A) The Registrar shall cause to be made and preserve a full and accurate record of all proceedings, including audio-recordings, transcripts and, when deemed necessary by the Trial Chamber, video-recordings.

(B) The Trial Chamber may order the disclosure of all or part of the record of closed proceedings when the reasons for ordering its non-disclosure no longer exist.

(C) The Registrar shall retain and preserve all physical evidence offered during the proceedings.

(D) Photography, video-recording or audio-recording of the trial, otherwise than by the Registry, may be authorised at the discretion of the Trial Chamber.

Section 2—Case Presentation

Rule 82—Joint and Separate Trials

(A)   In joint trials, each accused shall be accorded the same rights as if he were being tried separately.

(B)   The Trial Chamber may order that persons accused jointly under Rule 48 be tried separately if it considers it necessary in order to avoid a conflict of interests that might cause serious prejudice to an accused, or to protect the interests of justice.

Rule 83—Instruments of Restraint

Instruments of restraint, such as handcuffs, shall not be used except as a precaution against escape during transfer or for security reasons, and shall be removed when the accused appears before a Chamber.

Rule 84—Opening Statements

Before presentation of evidence by the Prosecutor, each party may make an opening statement. The defence may however elect to make its statement after the Prosecutor has concluded his presentation of evidence and before the presentation of evidence for the defence.

Rule 85—Presentation of Evidence

(A)   Each party is entitled to call witnesses and present evidence. Unless otherwise directed by the Trial Chamber in the interests of justice, evidence at the trial shall be presented in the following sequence:

        (i)   evidence for the prosecution;
        (ii)   evidence for the defence;
        (iii)   prosecution evidence in rebuttal;
        (iv)   defence evidence in rejoinder;
        (v)   evidence ordered by the Trial Chamber pursuant to Rule 98.

(B)   Examination-in-chief, cross-examination and re-examination shall be

Appendix C: Rules of Procedure and Evidence 469

allowed in each case. It shall be for the party calling a witness to examine him in chief, but a Judge may at any stage put any question to the witness.

(C) The accused may, if he so desires, appear as a witness in his own defence.

Rule 86—Closing Arguments

After the presentation of all the evidence, the Prosecutor may present an initial argument, to which the defence may reply. The Prosecutor may, if he wishes, present a rebuttal argument, to which the defence may present a rejoinder.

Rule 87—Deliberations

(A) When both parties have completed their presentation of the case, the Presiding Judge shall declare the hearing closed, and the Trial Chamber shall deliberate in private. A finding of guilt may be reached only when a majority of the Trial Chamber is satisfied that guilt has been proved beyond reasonable doubt.

(B) The Trial Chamber shall vote separately on each charge contained in the indictment. If two or more accused are tried together under Rule 48, separate findings shall be made as to each accused.

Rule 88—Judgement

(A) The judgement shall be pronounced in public {and in the presence of the accused}, on a date of which notice shall have been given to the parties and counsel **and at which they shall be entitled to be present.**

(B) If the Trial Chamber finds the accused guilty of a crime and concludes from the evidence that unlawful taking of property by the accused was associated with it, it shall make a specific finding to that effect in its judgement. The Trial Chamber may order restitution as provided in Rule 105.

(C) {A Judge of the Trial Chamber may append a separate or dissenting opinion to the judgement.} **The judgement shall be rendered by a** majority of the Judges. It shall be accompanied or followed as soon as possible by a reasoned opinion in writing, to which separate or dissenting opinions may be appended.

Section 3—Rules of Evidence

Rule 89—General Provisions

(A) The rules of evidence set forth in this Section shall govern the proceedings before the Chambers. The Chambers shall not be bound by national rules of evidence.

(B) In cases not otherwise provided for in this Section, a Chamber shall apply rules of evidence which will best favour a fair determination of the matter before it and are consonant with the spirit of the Statute and the general principles of law.

(C) A Chamber may admit any relevant evidence which it deems to have probative value.

(D) A Chamber may exclude evidence if its probative value is substantially outweighed by the need to ensure a fair trial.

(E) A Chamber may request verification of the authenticity of evidence obtained out of court.

Rule 90—Testimony of Witnesses

(A) Witnesses shall, in principle, be heard directly by the Chambers {.} {In cases, however, where it is not possible to secure the presence of a witness, a Chamber may order} **unless a Chamber has ordered** that the witness be heard by means of a deposition as provided for in Rule 71.

(B) Every witness shall, before giving evidence, make the following solemn declaration:

> I solemnly declare that I will speak the truth, the whole truth and nothing but the truth.

(C)   A child who, in the opinion of the Chamber, does not understand the nature of a solemn declaration, may be permitted to testify without that formality, if the Chamber is of the opinion that he is sufficiently mature to be able to report the facts of which he had knowledge and that he understands the duty to tell the truth. A judgement, however, cannot be based on such testimony alone.

(D)   A witness, other than an expert, who has not yet testified shall not be present when the testimony of another witness is given. However, a witness who has heard the testimony of another witness shall not for that reason alone be disqualified from testifying.

(E)   A witness may {decline to make} **object to making** any statement which might tend to incriminate him. **The Chamber may, however, compel the witness to answer the question. Testimony compelled in this way shall not be used as evidence in a subsequent prosecution against the witness for any offence other than perjury.**

Rule 91 — False Testimony under Solemn Declaration

(A)   A Chamber, on its own initiative or at the request of a party, may warn a witness of the duty to tell the truth and the consequences that may result from a failure to do so.

(B)   If a Chamber has strong grounds for believing that a witness has knowingly and wilfully given false testimony, it may direct the Prosecutor to investigate the matter with a view to the preparation and submission of an indictment for false testimony.

(C)   The rules of procedure and evidence in Parts Four to Eight shall apply *mutatis mutandis* to proceedings under this Rule.

(D)   No Judge who sat as a member of the Trial Chamber before which the witness appeared shall sit for the trial of the witness for false testimony.

(E)   The maximum penalty for false testimony under solemn declaration shall be a fine of US$10,000 or a term of imprisonment of twelve months, or both. The payment of any fine imposed shall be made to the Registrar to be held in the account referred to in {Sub-rule 77(C)} **Sub-rule 77(E).**

Rule 92 — Confessions

A confession by the accused given during questioning by the Prosecutor shall, provided the requirements of Rule 63 were strictly complied with, be presumed to have been free and voluntary unless the contrary is proved.

Rule 93 — Evidence of Consistent Pattern of Conduct

(A) Evidence of a consistent pattern of conduct may be admissible in the interests of justice.

(B) **Acts tending to show such a pattern of conduct shall be disclosed by the Prosecutor to the defence pursuant to Rule 66.**

Rule 94 — Judicial Notice

A Trial Chamber shall not require proof of facts of common knowledge but shall take judicial notice thereof.

Rule 95 — Evidence Obtained by Means Contrary to Internationally Protected Human Rights

{Evidence obtained directly or indirectly by means which constitute a serious violation of internationally protected human rights shall not be admissible.} **No evidence shall be admissible if obtained by methods which cast substantial doubt on its reliability or if its admission is antithetical to, and would seriously damage, the integrity of the proceedings.**

Rule 96 — Evidence in Cases of Sexual Assault

In cases of sexual assault:

    (i)   no corroboration of the victim's testimony shall be required;
    (ii)   consent shall not be allowed as a defence if the victim

        (a)   has been subjected to or threatened with or has had reason to fear violence, duress, detention or psychological oppression; or

(b)   reasonably believed that if {she} **the victim** did not submit, another might be so subjected, threatened or put in fear;

(iii)   before evidence of the victim's consent is admitted, the accused shall satisfy the Trial Chamber *in camera* that the evidence is relevant and credible;
(iv)   prior sexual conduct of the victim shall not be admitted in evidence.

Rule 97 — Lawyer-Client Privilege

All communications between lawyer and client shall be regarded as privileged, and consequently not subject to disclosure at trial, unless:

(i)   the client consents to such disclosure; or
(ii)   the client has voluntarily disclosed the content of the communication to a third party, and that third party then gives evidence of that disclosure.

Rule 98 — Power of Chambers to Order Production of Additional Evidence

A Trial Chamber may order either party to produce additional evidence. It may itself summon witnesses and order their attendance.

Section 4 — Sentencing Procedure

Rule 99 — Status of the Acquitted Person

(A)   In case of acquittal, the accused shall be released immediately.

(B)   If, at the time the judgement is pronounced, the Prosecutor advises the Trial Chamber in open court of his intention to file notice of appeal pursuant to Rule 108, the Trial Chamber may, at the request of the Prosecutor, issue a warrant for the arrest of the accused to take effect immediately.

Rule 100 — Pre-sentencing Procedure

If a Trial Chamber finds the accused guilty of a crime, the Prosecutor and the defence may submit any relevant information that may assist the Trial Chamber in determining an appropriate sentence.

Rule 101 — Penalties

(A)   A convicted person may be sentenced to imprisonment for a term up to and including the remainder of his life.

(B)   In determining the sentence, the Trial Chamber shall take into account the factors mentioned in Article 24(2) of the Statute, as well as such factors as:

>   (i)   any aggravating circumstances;
>   (ii)   any mitigating circumstances including the substantial cooperation with the Prosecutor by the convicted person before or after conviction;
>   (iii)   the general practice regarding prison sentences in the courts of the former Yugoslavia;
>   {(iv)   the period, if any, during which the convicted person was detained in custody pending his surrender to the Tribunal or pending trial;} *[Editor's note:* see Rule 101(E).]
>   **(iv)**   the extent to which any penalty imposed by a {national} court **of any State** on the convicted person for the same act has already been served, as referred to in Article 10(3) of the Statute.

(C)   The Trial Chamber shall indicate whether multiple sentences shall be served consecutively or concurrently.

(D)   The sentence shall be pronounced in public and in the presence of the convicted person, subject to Sub-rule 102(B).

(E)   Credit shall be given to the convicted person for the period, if any, during which the convicted person was detained in custody pending his surrender to the Tribunal or pending trial or appeal.

Rule 102 — Status of the Convicted Person

(A)   The sentence shall begin to run from the day it is pronounced under Sub-rule 101(D). However, as soon as notice of appeal is given, the enforcement of the judgement shall thereupon be stayed until the decision on the appeal has been delivered, the convicted person meanwhile remaining in detention, as provided in Rule 64.

(B) If, by a previous decision of the Trial Chamber, the convicted person has been released, or is for any other reason at liberty, and he is not present when the judgement is pronounced, the Trial Chamber shall issue a warrant for his arrest. On arrest, he shall be notified of the conviction and sentence, and the procedure provided in Rule 103 shall be followed.

Rule 103—Place of Imprisonment

(A) Imprisonment shall be served in a State designated by the Tribunal from a list of States which have indicated their willingness to accept convicted persons.

(B) Transfer of the convicted person to that State shall be effected as soon as possible after the time-limit for appeal has elapsed.

Rule 104—Supervision of Imprisonment

All sentences of imprisonment shall be supervised by the Tribunal or a body designated by it.

Rule 105—Restitution of Property

(A) After a judgement of conviction containing a specific finding as provided in Sub-rule 88(B), the Trial Chamber shall, at the request of the Prosecutor, or may, at its own initiative, hold a special hearing to determine the matter of the restitution of the property or the proceeds thereof, and may in the meantime order such provisional measures for the preservation and protection of the property or proceeds as it considers appropriate.

(B) The determination may extend to such property or its proceeds, even in the hands of third parties not otherwise connected with the crime of which the convicted person has been found guilty.

(C) Such third parties shall be summoned before the Trial Chamber and be given an opportunity to justify their claim to the property or its proceeds.

(D) Should the Trial Chamber be able to determine the rightful owner on the balance of probabilities, it shall order the restitution either of the property or the proceeds {as} **or make such other order as it may deem** appropriate.

(E) Should the Trial Chamber not be able to determine ownership, it shall notify the competent national authorities and request them so to determine.

(F) Upon notice from the national authorities that an affirmative determination has been made, the Trial Chamber shall order the restitution either of the property or the proceeds or make such other order as it may deem appropriate.

(G) The Registrar shall transmit to the competent national authorities any summonses, orders and requests issued by a Trial Chamber pursuant to {Sub-rules (C), (D) and (E)} **Sub-rules (C), (D), (E) and (F).**

Rule 106—Compensation to Victims

(A) The Registrar shall transmit to the competent authorities of the States concerned the judgement finding the accused guilty of a crime which has caused injury to a victim.

(B) Pursuant to the relevant national legislation, a victim or persons claiming through him may bring an action in a national court or other competent body to obtain compensation.

(C) For the purposes of a claim made under Sub-rule (B) the judgement of the Tribunal shall be final and binding as to the criminal responsibility of the convicted person for such injury.

PART SEVEN—APPELLATE PROCEEDINGS

Rule 107—General Provision

The rules of procedure and evidence that govern proceedings in the Trial Chambers shall apply *mutatis mutandis* to proceedings in the Appeals Chamber.

Rule 108—Notice of Appeal

(A)   **Subject to Sub-rule (B),** a party seeking to appeal a judgement **or sentence** shall, not more than thirty days from the date on which the judgement **or sentence** was pronounced, file with the Registrar and serve upon the other {party} **parties** a written notice of appeal, setting forth the grounds.

(B)   **Such delay shall be fixed at fifteen days in case of an appeal from a judgement dismissing an objection based on lack of jurisdiction or a decision rendered under Rule 77 or Rule 91.**

Rule 109—Record on Appeal

(A)   The record on appeal shall consist of the parts of the trial record, as certified by the Registrar, designated by the parties.

(B)   The parties, within thirty days of the certification of the trial record by the Registrar, may by agreement designate the parts of that record which, in their opinion, are necessary for the decision on the appeal.

(C)   Should the parties fail so to agree within that time, the Appellant and the Respondent shall each designate to the Registrar, within sixty days of the certification, the parts of the trial record which he considers necessary for the decision on the appeal.

(D)   The Appeals Chamber shall remain free to call for the whole of the trial record.

Rule 110—Copies of Record

The Registrar shall make a sufficient number of copies of the record on appeal for the use of the Judges of the Appeals Chamber and of the parties.

Rule 111—Appellant's Brief

An Appellant's brief of argument and authorities shall be served on the other party and filed with the Registrar within ninety days of the certification of the record.

Rule 112 — Respondent's Brief

A Respondent's brief of argument and authorities shall be served on the other party and filed with the Registrar within thirty days of the filing of the Appellant's brief.

Rule 113 — Brief in Reply

An Appellant may file a brief in reply within fifteen days after the filing of the Respondent's brief.

Rule 114 — Date of Hearing

After the expiry of the time-limits for filing the briefs provided for in Rules 111, 112 and 113, the Appeals Chamber shall set the date for the hearing and the Registrar shall notify the parties.

Rule 115 — Additional Evidence

(A)   A party may apply by motion to present before the Appeals Chamber additional evidence which was not available to it at the trial. Such motion must be served on the other party and filed with the Registrar not less than fifteen days before the date of the hearing.

(B)   The Appeals Chamber shall authorise the presentation of such evidence if it considers that the interests of justice so require.

Rule 116 — Extension of Time-limits

The Appeals Chamber may grant a motion to extend a time-limit upon a showing of good cause.

Rule 116 bis — Expedited Appeals Procedure

(A)   An appeal under Sub-rule 108(B) shall be heard expeditiously on the basis of the original record of the Trial Chamber and without the necessity of any written brief.

(B)   All delays and other procedural requirements shall be fixed by an order of the President issued on an application by one of the parties,

or *proprio motu* should no such application have been made within fifteen days after the filing of the notice of appeal.

(C)   Rules 109 to 114 shall not apply to such appeals.

Rule 117—Judgement on Appeal

(A)   The Appeals Chamber shall pronounce judgement on the basis of the record on appeal together with such additional evidence as has been presented to it.

(B)   The judgement shall be rendered by a majority of the Judges. It shall be accompanied or followed as soon as possible by a reasoned opinion in writing, to which separate or dissenting opinions may be appended.

(C)   In appropriate circumstances the Appeals Chamber may order that the accused be re-tried according to law.

(D)   The judgement shall be pronounced in public, {and in the presence of the accused} on a date of which notice shall have been given to the parties and counsel **and at which they shall be entitled to be present.**

Rule 118—Status of the Accused Following Appeal

(A)   A sentence pronounced by the Appeals Chamber shall be enforced immediately.

(B)   Where the accused is not present when the judgement is due to be delivered, either as having been acquitted on all charges or as a result of an order issued pursuant to Rule 65, or for any other reason, the Appeals Chamber may deliver its judgement in the absence of the accused and shall, unless it pronounces his acquittal, order his arrest or surrender to the Tribunal.

PART EIGHT — REVIEW PROCEEDINGS

Rule 119—Request for Review

Where a new fact has been discovered which was not known to the moving party at the time of the proceedings before a Trial Chamber or the Appeals

Chamber, and could not have been discovered through the exercise of due diligence, the defence or, within one year after the final judgement has been pronounced, the Prosecutor, may make a motion to that Chamber for review of the judgement.

Rule 120 — Preliminary Examination

If a majority of Judges of the Chamber that pronounced the judgement agree that the new fact, if proved, could have been a decisive factor in reaching a decision, the Chamber shall review the judgement, and pronounce a further judgement after hearing the parties.

Rule 121 — Appeals

The judgement of a Trial Chamber on review may be appealed in accordance with the provisions of Part Seven.

Rule 122 — Return of Case to Trial Chamber

If the judgement to be reviewed is under appeal at the time the motion for review is filed, the Appeals Chamber may return the case to the Trial Chamber for disposition of the motion.

PART NINE — PARDON AND COMMUTATION OF SENTENCE

Rule 123 — Notification by States

If, according to the law of the State in which a convicted person is imprisoned, he is eligible for pardon or commutation of sentence, the State shall, in accordance with Article 28 of the Statute, notify the Tribunal of such eligibility.

Rule 124 — Determination by the President

The President shall, upon such notice, determine, in consultation with the Judges, whether pardon or commutation is appropriate.

Rule 125 — General Standards for Granting Pardon or Commutation

In determining whether pardon or commutation is appropriate, the President shall take into account, *inter alia*, the gravity of the crime or crimes for which the prisoner was convicted, the treatment of similarly-situated prisoners, the prisoner's demonstration of rehabilitation, as well as any substantial cooperation of the prisoner with the Prosecutor.

Appendix D

Security Council Resolutions on the Establishment of the International Tribunal for Rwanda, including the Statute of the Tribunal

RESOLUTION 935 (1994)[*]

Adopted unanimously by the Security Council at its 3400th meeting, July 1, 1994. S.C. Res. 935, U.N. SCOR, 49th Year, 3400th mtg. at 1, U.N. Doc. S/RES/935 (1994).

The Security Council,

Reaffirming all its previous resolutions on the situation in Rwanda,

Reaffirming, in particular, resolutions 918 (1994) and 925 (1994), which expanded the United Nations Assistance Mission for Rwanda (UNAMIR), and *stressing* in this connection the need for early deployment of the expanded UNAMIR to enable it to carry out its mandate,

---

[*] *Editor's note:* The Commission of Experts established under S.C. Res. 935 prepared two reports, which are cited here in reverse chronological order. Letter from the Secretary-General to the President of the Security Council, Dec. 9, 1994, U.N. Doc. S/1994/1405 (1994), transmitting *Final Report of the Commission of Experts Established pursuant to Security Council Resolution 935 (1994), available in* U.N. Gopher\Current Information\Secretary-General's Reports\Dec. 1994; Letter from the Secretary-General to the President of the Security Council, Oct. 1, 1994, U.N. Doc. S/1994/1125 (1994), transmitting *Preliminary Report of the Independent Commission of Experts Established in Accordance with Security Council Resolution 935 (1994), available in* U.N. Gopher\Current Information\Secretary-General's Reports\Oct. 1994.

Recalling the statement by the President of the Security Council of 30 April 1994 (S/PRST/1994/21) in which the Security Council, *inter alia*, condemned all breaches of international humanitarian law in Rwanda, particularly those perpetrated against the civilian population, and recalled that persons who instigate or participate in such acts are individually responsible,

Recalling also the requests it addressed to the Secretary-General in the statement by the President of the Security Council of 30 April 1994 and in resolution 918 (1994), concerning the investigation of serious violations of international humanitarian law committed in Rwanda during the conflict,

Having considered the report of the Secretary-General of 31 May 1994 (S/1994/640), in which he noted that massacres and killings have continued in a systematic manner throughout Rwanda and also noted that only a proper investigation can establish the facts in order to enable the determination of responsibility,

Welcoming the visit to Rwanda and to the region by the United Nations High Commissioner for Human Rights and *noting* the appointment, pursuant to resolution S-3/1 of 25 May 1994 adopted by the United Nations Commission on Human Rights, of a Special Rapporteur for Rwanda,

Expressing once again its grave concern at the continuing reports indicating that systematic, widespread and flagrant violations of international humanitarian law, including acts of genocide, have been committed in Rwanda,

Recalling that all persons who commit or authorize the commission of serious violations of international humanitarian law are individually responsible for those violations and should be brought to justice,

1. *Requests* the Secretary-General to establish, as a matter of urgency, an impartial Commission of Experts to examine and analyse

information submitted pursuant to the present resolution, together with such further information as the Commission of Experts may obtain through its own investigations or the efforts of other persons or bodies, including the information made available by the Special Rapporteur for Rwanda, with a view to providing the Secretary-General with its conclusions on the evidence of grave violations of international humanitarian law committed in the territory of Rwanda, including the evidence of possible acts of genocide;

2. *Calls upon* States and, as appropriate, international humanitarian organizations to collate substantiated information in their possession or submitted to them relating to grave violations of international humanitarian law, including breaches of the Convention on the Prevention and Punishment of the Crime of Genocide, committed in Rwanda during the conflict, and *requests* States, relevant United Nations bodies, and relevant organizations to make this information available within thirty days of the adoption of the present resolution and as appropriate thereafter, and to provide appropriate assistance to the Commission of Experts referred to in paragraph 1;

3. *Requests* the Secretary-General to report to the Council on the establishment of the Commission of Experts, and *further requests* the Secretary-General, within four months from the establishment of the Commission of Experts, to report to the Council, on the conclusions of the Commission and to take account of these conclusions in any recommendations for further appropriate steps;

4. *Also requests* the Secretary-General and as appropriate the High Commissioner for Human Rights through the Secretary-General to make the information submitted to the Special Rapporteur for Rwanda available to the Commission of Experts and to facilitate adequate coordination and cooperation between the work of the Commission of Experts and the Special Rapporteur in the performance of their respective tasks;

5. *Urges* all concerned fully to cooperate with the Commission of Experts in the accomplishment of its mandate, including

responding positively to requests from the Commission for assistance and access in pursuing investigations;

6. *Decides* to remain actively seized of the matter.

RESOLUTION 955 (1994)

Adopted by a vote of 13–1–1 by the Security Council at its 3453d meeting, November 8, 1994. S.C. Res. 955, U.N. SCOR, 49th Year, 3453d mtg. at 1, U.N. Doc. S/RES/955 (1994).

The Security Council,

Reaffirming all its previous resolutions on the situation in Rwanda,

Having considered the reports of the Secretary-General pursuant to paragraph 3 of resolution 935 (1994) of 1 July 1994 (S/1994/879 and S/1994/906), and *having taken note* of the reports of the Special Rapporteur for Rwanda of the United Nations Commission on Human Rights (S/1994/1157, annex I and annex II),

Expressing appreciation for the work of the Commission of Experts established pursuant to resolution 935 (1994), in particular its preliminary report on violations of international humanitarian law in Rwanda transmitted by the Secretary-General's letter of 1 October 1994 (S/1994/1125),

Expressing once again its grave concern at the reports indicating that genocide and other systematic, widespread and flagrant violations of international humanitarian law have been committed in Rwanda,

Determining that this situation continues to constitute a threat to international peace and security,

Determined to put an end to such crimes and to take effective measures to bring to justice the persons who are responsible for them,

Convinced that in the particular circumstances of Rwanda, the prosecution of persons responsible for serious violations of international humanitarian law would enable this aim to be achieved and would contribute to the process of national reconciliation and to the restoration and maintenance of peace,

Believing that the establishment of an international tribunal for the prosecution of persons responsible for genocide and the other above-mentioned violations of international humanitarian law will contribute to ensuring that such violations are halted and effectively redressed,

Stressing also the need for international cooperation to strengthen the courts and judicial system of Rwanda, having regard in particular to the necessity for those courts to deal with large numbers of suspects,

Considering that the Commission of Experts established pursuant to resolution 935 (1994) should continue on an urgent basis the collection of information relating to evidence of grave violations of international humanitarian law committed in the territory of Rwanda and should submit its final report to the Secretary-General by 30 November 1994,

Acting under Chapter VII of the Charter of the United Nations,

1. *Decides* hereby, having received the request of the Government of Rwanda (S/1994/1115), to establish an international tribunal for the sole purpose of prosecuting persons responsible for genocide and other serious violations of international humanitarian law committed in the territory of Rwanda and Rwandan citizens responsible for genocide and other such violations committed in the territory of neighbouring States, between 1 January 1994 and 31 December 1994 and to this end to adopt the Statute of the International Criminal Tribunal for Rwanda annexed hereto;

2. *Decides* that all States shall cooperate fully with the International Tribunal and its organs in accordance with the present resolution and the Statute of the International Tribunal and that

consequently all States shall take any measures necessary under their domestic law to implement the provisions of the present resolution and the Statute, including the obligation of States to comply with requests for assistance or orders issued by a Trial Chamber under Article 28 of the Statute, and *requests* States to keep the Secretary-General informed of such measures;

      3.   *Considers* that the Government of Rwanda should be notified prior to the taking of decisions under articles 26 and 27 of the Statute;

      4.   *Urges* States and intergovernmental and non-governmental organizations to contribute funds, equipment and services to the International Tribunal, including the offer of expert personnel;

      5.   *Requests* the Secretary-General to implement this resolution urgently and in particular to make practical arrangements for the effective functioning of the International Tribunal, including recommendations to the Council as to possible locations for the seat of the International Tribunal at the earliest time and to report periodically to the Council;

      6.   *Decides* that the seat of the International Tribunal shall be determined by the Council having regard to considerations of justice and fairness as well as administrative efficiency, including access to witnesses, and economy, and subject to the conclusion of appropriate arrangements between the United Nations and the State of the seat, acceptable to the Council, having regard to the fact that the International Tribunal may meet away from its seat when it considers it necessary for the efficient exercise of its functions; and *decides* that an office will be established and proceedings will be conducted in Rwanda, where feasible and appropriate, subject to the conclusion of similar appropriate arrangements;

      7.   *Decides* to consider increasing the number of judges and Trial Chambers of the International Tribunal if it becomes necessary;

      8.   *Decides* to remain actively seized of the matter.

Annex

Statute of the International Tribunal for Rwanda

Having been established by the Security Council acting under Chapter VII of the Charter of the United Nations, the International Criminal Tribunal for the Prosecution of Persons Responsible for Genocide and Other Serious Violations of International Humanitarian Law Committed in the Territory of Rwanda and Rwandan citizens responsible for genocide and other such violations committed in the territory of neighbouring States, between 1 January 1994 and 31 December 1994 (hereinafter referred to as "the International Tribunal for Rwanda") shall function in accordance with the provisions of the present Statute.

Article 1 — Competence of the International Tribunal for Rwanda

The International Tribunal for Rwanda shall have the power to prosecute persons responsible for serious violations of international humanitarian law committed in the territory of Rwanda and Rwandan citizens responsible for such violations committed in the territory of neighbouring States, between 1 January 1994 and 31 December 1994, in accordance with the provisions of the present Statute.

Article 2 — Genocide

1. The International Tribunal for Rwanda shall have the power to prosecute persons committing genocide as defined in paragraph 2 of this article or of committing any of the other acts enumerated in paragraph 3 of this article.

2. Genocide means any of the following acts committed with intent to destroy, in whole or in part, a national, ethnical, racial or religious group, as such:

   (a) Killing members of the group;
   (b) Causing serious bodily or mental harm to members of the group;

(c) Deliberately inflicting on the group conditions of life calculated to bring about its physical destruction in whole or in part;
(d) Imposing measures intended to prevent births within the group;
(e) Forcibly transferring children of the group to another group.

3. The following acts shall be punishable:

(a) Genocide;
(b) Conspiracy to commit genocide;
(c) Direct and public incitement to commit genocide;
(d) Attempt to commit genocide;
(e) Complicity in genocide.

Article 3—Crimes against humanity

The International Tribunal for Rwanda shall have the power to prosecute persons responsible for the following crimes when committed as part of a widespread or systematic attack against any civilian population on national, political, ethnic, racial or religious grounds:

(a) Murder;
(b) Extermination;
(c) Enslavement;
(d) Deportation;
(e) Imprisonment;
(f) Torture;
(g) Rape;
(h) Persecutions on political, racial and religious grounds;
(i) Other inhumane acts.

Article 4—Violations of Article 3 common to the Geneva Conventions and of Additional Protocol II

The International Tribunal for Rwanda shall have the power to prosecute persons committing or ordering to be committed serious violations of Article 3 common to the Geneva Conventions of 12 August 1949 for the

Protection of War Victims, and of Additional Protocol II thereto of 8 June 1977. These violations shall include, but shall not be limited to:

(a) Violence to life, health and physical or mental well-being of persons, in particular murder as well as cruel treatment such as torture, mutilation or any form of corporal punishment;
(b) Collective punishments;
(c) Taking of hostages;
(d) Acts of terrorism;
(e) Outrages upon personal dignity, in particular humiliating and degrading treatment, rape, enforced prostitution and any form of indecent assault;
(f) Pillage;
(g) The passing of sentences and the carrying out of executions without previous judgement pronounced by a regularly constituted court, affording all the judicial guarantees which are recognized as indispensable by civilized peoples;
(h) Threats to commit any of the foregoing acts.

Article 5—Personal jurisdiction

The International Tribunal for Rwanda shall have jurisdiction over natural persons pursuant to the provisions of the present Statute.

Article 6—Individual criminal responsibility

1. A person who planned, instigated, ordered, committed or otherwise aided and abetted in the planning, preparation or execution of a crime referred to in articles 2 to 4 of the present Statute, shall be individually responsible for the crime.

2. The official position of any accused person, whether as Head of State or Government or as a responsible Government official, shall not relieve such person of criminal responsibility nor mitigate punishment.

3. The fact that any of the acts referred to in articles 2 to 4 of the present Statute was committed by a subordinate does not relieve his or her superior of criminal responsibility if he or she knew or had reason to know that the subordinate was about to commit such acts or had done so

and the superior failed to take the necessary and reasonable measures to prevent such acts or to punish the perpetrators thereof.

4. The fact that an accused person acted pursuant to an order of a Government or of a superior shall not relieve him or her of criminal responsibility, but may be considered in mitigation of punishment if the International Tribunal for Rwanda determines that justice so requires.

Article 7 — Territorial and temporal jurisdiction

The territorial jurisdiction of the International Tribunal for Rwanda shall extend to the territory of Rwanda including its land surface and airspace as well as to the territory of neighbouring States in respect of serious violations of international humanitarian law committed by Rwandan citizens. The temporal jurisdiction of the International Tribunal for Rwanda shall extend to a period beginning on 1 January 1994 and ending on 31 December 1994.

Article 8 — Concurrent jurisdiction

1. The International Tribunal for Rwanda and national courts shall have concurrent jurisdiction to prosecute persons for serious violations of international humanitarian law committed in the territory of Rwanda and Rwandan citizens for such violations committed in the territory of neighbouring States, between 1 January 1994 and 31 December 1994.

2. The International Tribunal for Rwanda shall have primacy over the national courts of all States. At any stage of the procedure, the International Tribunal for Rwanda may formally request national courts to defer to its competence in accordance with the present Statute and the Rules of Procedure and Evidence of the International Tribunal for Rwanda.

Article 9 — Non bis in idem

1. No person shall be tried before a national court for acts constituting serious violations of international humanitarian law under the present Statute, for which he or she has already been tried by the International Tribunal for Rwanda.

2. A person who has been tried by a national court for acts constituting serious violations of international humanitarian law may be subsequently tried by the International Tribunal for Rwanda only if:

(a) The act for which he or she was tried was characterized as an ordinary crime; or
(b) The national court proceedings were not impartial or independent, were designed to shield the accused from international criminal responsibility, or the case was not diligently prosecuted.

3. In considering the penalty to be imposed on a person convicted of a crime under the present Statute, the International Tribunal for Rwanda shall take into account the extent to which any penalty imposed by a national court on the same person for the same act has already been served.

Article 10 — Organization of the International Tribunal for Rwanda

The International Tribunal for Rwanda shall consist of the following organs:

(a) The Chambers, comprising two Trial Chambers and an Appeals Chamber;
(b) The Prosecutor; and
(c) A Registry.

Article 11 — Composition of the Chambers

The Chambers shall be composed of eleven independent judges, no two of whom may be nationals of the same State, who shall serve as follows:

(a) Three judges shall serve in each of the Trial Chambers;
(b) Five judges shall serve in the Appeals Chamber.

Article 12 — Qualification and election of judges

1. The judges shall be persons of high moral character, impartiality and integrity who possess the qualifications required in their respective countries for appointment to the highest judicial offices. In the

overall composition of the Chambers due account shall be taken of the experience of the judges in criminal law, international law, including international humanitarian law and human rights law.

2. The members of the Appeals Chamber of the International Tribunal for the Prosecution of Persons Responsible for Serious Violations of International Law Committed in the Territory of the Former Yugoslavia since 1991 (hereinafter referred to as "the International Tribunal for the Former Yugoslavia") shall also serve as the members of the Appeals Chamber of the International Tribunal for Rwanda.

3. The judges of the Trial Chambers of the International Tribunal for Rwanda shall be elected by the General Assembly from a list submitted by the Security Council, in the following manner:

(a) The Secretary-General shall invite nominations for judges of the Trial Chambers from States Members of the United Nations and non-member States maintaining permanent observer missions at United Nations Headquarters;
(b) Within thirty days of the date of the invitation of the Secretary-General, each State may nominate up to two candidates meeting the qualifications set out in paragraph 1 above, no two of whom shall be of the same nationality and neither of whom shall be of the same nationality as any judge on the Appeals Chamber;
(c) The Secretary-General shall forward the nominations received to the Security Council. From the nominations received the Security Council shall establish a list of not less than twelve and not more than eighteen candidates, taking due account of adequate representation on the International Tribunal for Rwanda of the principal legal systems of the world;
(d) The President of the Security Council shall transmit the list of candidates to the President of the General Assembly. From that list the General Assembly shall elect the six judges of the Trial Chambers. The candidates who receive an absolute majority of the votes of the States Members of the United Nations and of the non-Member States maintaining permanent observer missions at United Nations Headquarters, shall be declared elected. Should two candidates of the same nationality obtain the required majority vote, the one who received the higher number of votes shall be considered elected.

4. In the event of a vacancy in the Trial Chambers, after consultation with the Presidents of the Security Council and of the General Assembly, the Secretary-General shall appoint a person meeting the qualifications of paragraph 1 above, for the remainder of the term of office concerned.

5. The judges of the Trial Chambers shall be elected for a term of four years. The terms and conditions of service shall be those of the judges of the International Tribunal for the Former Yugoslavia. They shall be eligible for re-election.

Article 13—Officers and members of the Chambers

1. The judges of the International Tribunal for Rwanda shall elect a President.

2. After consultation with the judges of the International Tribunal for Rwanda, the President shall assign the judges to the Trial Chambers. A judge shall serve only in the Chamber to which he or she was assigned.

3. The judges of each Trial Chamber shall elect a Presiding Judge, who shall conduct all of the proceedings of that Trial Chamber as a whole.

Article 14—Rules of procedure and evidence

The judges of the International Tribunal for Rwanda shall adopt, for the purpose of proceedings before the International Tribunal for Rwanda, the rules of procedure and evidence for the conduct of the pre-trial phase of the proceedings, trials and appeals, the admission of evidence, the protection of victims and witnesses and other appropriate matters of the International Tribunal for the Former Yugoslavia with such changes as they deem necessary.

Article 15—The Prosecutor

1. The Prosecutor shall be responsible for the investigation and prosecution of persons responsible for serious violations of international

humanitarian law committed in the territory of Rwanda and Rwandan citizens responsible for such violations committed in the territory of neighbouring States, between 1 January 1994 and 31 December 1994.

2. The Prosecutor shall act independently as a separate organ of the International Tribunal for Rwanda. He or she shall not seek or receive instructions from any Government or from any other source.

3. The Prosecutor of the International Tribunal for the Former Yugoslavia shall also serve as the Prosecutor of the International Tribunal for Rwanda. He or she shall have additional staff, including an additional Deputy Prosecutor, to assist with prosecutions before the International Tribunal for Rwanda. Such staff shall be appointed by the Secretary-General on the recommendation of the Prosecutor.

Article 16—The Registry

1. The Registry shall be responsible for the administration and servicing of the International Tribunal for Rwanda.

2. The Registry shall consist of a Registrar and such other staff as may be required.

3. The Registrar shall be appointed by the Secretary-General after consultation with the President of the International Tribunal for Rwanda. He or she shall serve for a four-year term and be eligible for reappointment. The terms and conditions of service of the Registrar shall be those of an Assistant Secretary-General of the United Nations.

4. The staff of the Registry shall be appointed by the Secretary-General on the recommendation of the Registrar.

Article 17—Investigation and preparation of indictment

1. The Prosecutor shall initiate investigations *ex officio* or on the basis of information obtained from any source, particularly from Governments, United Nations organs, intergovernmental and non-governmental organizations. The Prosecutor shall assess the information received or obtained and decide whether there is sufficient basis to proceed.

2. The Prosecutor shall have the power to question suspects, victims and witnesses, to collect evidence and to conduct on-site investigations. In carrying out these tasks, the Prosecutor may, as appropriate, seek the assistance of the State authorities concerned.

3. If questioned, the suspect shall be entitled to be assisted by counsel of his or her own choice, including the right to have legal assistance assigned to the suspect without payment by him or her in any such case if he or she does not have sufficient means to pay for it, as well as to necessary translation into and from a language he or she speaks and understands.

4. Upon a determination that a *prima facie* case exists, the Prosecutor shall prepare an indictment containing a concise statement of the facts and the crime or crimes with which the accused is charged under the Statute. The indictment shall be transmitted to a judge of the Trial Chamber.

Article 18 — Review of the indictment

1. The judge of the Trial Chamber to whom the indictment has been transmitted shall review it. If satisfied that a *prima facie* case has been established by the Prosecutor, he or she shall confirm the indictment. If not so satisfied, the indictment shall be dismissed.

2. Upon confirmation of an indictment, the judge may, at the request of the Prosecutor, issue such orders and warrants for the arrest, detention, surrender or transfer of persons, and any other orders as may be required for the conduct of the trial.

Article 19 — Commencement and conduct of trial proceedings

1. The Trial Chambers shall ensure that a trial is fair and expeditious and that proceedings are conducted in accordance with the rules of procedure and evidence, with full respect for the rights of the accused and due regard for the protection of victims and witnesses.

2. A person against whom an indictment has been confirmed shall, pursuant to an order or an arrest warrant of the International Tribunal for Rwanda, be taken into custody, immediately informed of the charges against him or her and transferred to the International Tribunal for Rwanda.

3. The Trial Chamber shall read the indictment, satisfy itself that the rights of the accused are respected, confirm that the accused understands the indictment, and instruct the accused to enter a plea. The Trial Chamber shall then set the date for trial.

4. The hearings shall be public unless the Trial Chamber decides to close the proceedings in accordance with its rules of procedure and evidence.

Article 20—Rights of the accused

1. All persons shall be equal before the International Tribunal for Rwanda.

2. In the determination of charges against him or her, the accused shall be entitled to a fair and public hearing, subject to article 21 of the Statute.

3. The accused shall be presumed innocent until proved guilty according to the provisions of the present Statute.

4. In the determination of any charge against the accused pursuant to the present Statute, the accused shall be entitled to the following minimum guarantees, in full equality:

(a) To be informed promptly and in detail in a language which he or she understands of the nature and cause of the charge against him or her;
(b) To have adequate time and facilities for the preparation of his or her defence and to communicate with counsel of his or her own choosing;
(c) To be tried without undue delay;
(d) To be tried in his or her presence, and to defend himself or herself in person or through legal assistance of his or her own choosing; to be informed, if he or she does not have legal assistance, of this right; and to have legal assistance assigned to him or her, in any case where the interests of justice so require, and without payment by him or her in any such case if he or she does not have sufficient means to pay for it;

(e) To examine, or have examined, the witnesses against him or her and to obtain the attendance and examination of witnesses on his or her behalf under the same conditions as witnesses against him or her;

(f) To have the free assistance of an interpreter if he or she cannot understand or speak the language used in the International Tribunal for Rwanda;

(g) Not to be compelled to testify against himself or herself or to confess guilt.

Article 21 — Protection of victims and witnesses

The International Tribunal for Rwanda shall provide in its rules of procedure and evidence for the protection of victims and witnesses. Such protection measures shall include, but shall not be limited to, the conduct of *in camera* proceedings and the protection of the victim's identity.

Article 22 — Judgement

1. The Trial Chambers shall pronounce judgements and impose sentences and penalties on persons convicted of serious violations of international humanitarian law.

2. The judgement shall be rendered by a majority of the judges of the Trial Chamber, and shall be delivered by the Trial Chamber in public. It shall be accompanied by a reasoned opinion in writing, to which separate or dissenting opinions may be appended.

Article 23 — Penalties

1. The penalty imposed by the Trial Chamber shall be limited to imprisonment. In determining the terms of imprisonment, the Trial Chambers shall have recourse to the general practice regarding prison sentences in the courts of Rwanda.

2. In imposing the sentences, the Trial Chambers should take into account such factors as the gravity of the offence and the individual circumstances of the convicted person.

3. In addition to imprisonment, the Trial Chambers may order the return of any property and proceeds acquired by criminal conduct, including by means of duress, to their rightful owners.

Article 24—Appellate proceedings

1. The Appeals Chamber shall hear appeals from persons convicted by the Trial Chambers or from the Prosecutor on the following grounds:

(a) An error on a question of law invalidating the decision; or
(b) An error of fact which has occasioned a miscarriage of justice.

2. The Appeals Chamber may affirm, reverse or revise the decisions taken by the Trial Chambers.

Article 25—Review proceedings

Where a new fact has been discovered which was not known at the time of the proceedings before the Trial Chambers or the Appeals Chamber and which could have been a decisive factor in reaching the decision, the convicted person or the Prosecutor may submit to the International Tribunal for Rwanda an application for review of the judgement.

Article 26—Enforcement of sentences

Imprisonment shall be served in Rwanda or any of the States on a list of States which have indicated to the Security Council their willingness to accept convicted persons, as designated by the International Tribunal for Rwanda. Such imprisonment shall be in accordance with the applicable law of the State concerned, subject to the supervision of the International Tribunal for Rwanda.

Article 27—Pardon or commutation of sentences

If, pursuant to the applicable law of the State in which the convicted person is imprisoned, he or she is eligible for pardon or commutation of sentence, the State concerned shall notify the International Tribunal for Rwanda accordingly. There shall only be pardon or commutation of sentence if the President of the International Tribunal for Rwanda, in consultation with the judges, so decides on the basis of the interests of justice and the general principles of law.

Article 28 — Cooperation and judicial assistance

1. States shall cooperate with the International Tribunal for Rwanda in the investigation and prosecution of persons accused of committing serious violations of international humanitarian law.

2. States shall comply without undue delay with any request for assistance or an order issued by a Trial Chamber, including, but not limited to:

(a) The identification and location of persons;
(b) The taking of testimony and the production of evidence;
(c) The service of documents;
(d) The arrest or detention of persons;
(e) The surrender or the transfer of the accused to the International Tribunal for Rwanda.

Article 29 — The status, privileges and immunities of the International Tribunal for Rwanda

1. The Convention on the Privileges and Immunities of the United Nations of 13 February 1946 shall apply to the International Tribunal for Rwanda, the judges, the Prosecutor and his or her staff, and the Registrar and his or her staff.

2. The judges, the Prosecutor and the Registrar shall enjoy the privileges and immunities, exemptions and facilities accorded to diplomatic envoys, in accordance with international law.

3. The staff of the Prosecutor and of the Registrar shall enjoy the privileges and immunities accorded to officials of the United Nations under articles V and VII of the Convention referred to in paragraph 1 of this article.

4. Other persons, including the accused, required at the seat or meeting place of the International Tribunal for Rwanda shall be accorded such treatment as is necessary for the proper functioning of the International Tribunal for Rwanda.

Article 30—Expenses of the International Tribunal for Rwanda

The expenses of the International Tribunal for Rwanda shall be expenses of the Organization in accordance with Article 17 of the Charter of the United Nations.

Article 31—Working languages

The working languages of the International Tribunal shall be English and French.

Article 32—Annual report

The President of the International Tribunal for Rwanda shall submit an annual report of the International Tribunal for Rwanda to the Security Council and to the General Assembly.

For Product Safety Concerns and Information please contact our EU
representative GPSR@taylorandfrancis.com
Taylor & Francis Verlag GmbH, Kaufingerstraße 24, 80331 München, Germany